BRITISH ECONOMIC AND SOCIAL HISTORY
1700–1977

To F.J.R. of Liverpool University,
Teacher and Friend

BRITISH ECONOMIC AND SOCIAL HISTORY
1700–1977

J. WALKER, M.A., Ph.D.
*(Sometime Ramsay Muir Fellow of Liverpool University
and formerly Head of the Department of Humanities,
Huddersfield College of Technology)*

revised by

C. W. MUNN, B.A., Ph.D.
*(Department of Economic History
University of Glasgow)*

SECOND EDITION

MACDONALD AND EVANS

MACDONALD AND EVANS LTD
Estover, Plymouth PL6 7PZ

First published 1968
Reprinted (with amendments) 1973
Second edition 1979

© MACDONALD & EVANS LTD 1979

This book is copyright and may not be reproduced in whole or *in part* (except for purposes of review) without the express permission of the publishers in writing.

ISBN: 0 7121 0266 3

Printed in Great Britain by Fletcher & Son Ltd, Norwich

PREFACE TO THE FIRST EDITION

This book describes some of the more important social and economic changes that have arisen from the industrialisation of British society from the eighteenth century to the present day. But as surveys of social and economic trends cannot be confined within set periods, pre-1700 material has been included. The number of topics that have a claim for inclusion is very large; I have, therefore, been obliged to make a selection, choosing those which in my judgment will prove most helpful to Sixth Forms, and to students reading for the certificates and diplomas of the Department of Education and Science Joint Committee for National Awards in Business Studies. The book also, it is hoped, will be read by those members of the general public interested in the main currents of social and economic change. In order to assist readers towards some understanding of current social and economic issues I have written four chapters on post-1939 Britain. But in attempting to bring our island story up to date, I have, as will be readily understood, been in danger of being overtaken by events.

The book is the fruits of a lifetime of teaching and examining, and the reading of innumerable books and articles in the publications of learned societies and in newspapers. It is impossible, therefore, to acknowledge my heavy indebtedness to all the authors from whose writings I have culled facts and opinions, but for some of the statistical material I have made use of the translation by Dr W. O. Henderson and Dr W. H. Chaloner of Werner Schlote's *British Overseas Trade*. My best thanks are also due to my former colleagues Mrs C. Dangerfield and Dr H. Robinson of Huddersfield College of Technology, to Mr G. E. Wilson, Principal of Oastler College of Education, Mr S. H. Grattan-Guinness, Deputy Education Officer, Huddersfield, and to my brother Mr Alan Walker, Headmaster of the County Grammar School, Gosport, who read some of the chapters as first drafted, pointed out errors and suggested improvements. In particular I owe a deep debt of gratitude to my former colleague, Mr J. O'Connell, who painstakingly read all the chapters and made innumerable helpful criticisms and suggestions. For any shortcomings, however, which may still remain, the responsibility is wholly my own. I also owe a debt to my wife, without whose help and encouragement the writing of the book would have been almost impossible.

J. W.

September 1968

PREFACE TO THE SECOND EDITION

In revising and updating Dr Walker's book my concern has been to detail the main social and economic changes which have taken place since 1967 when the first edition was published and to integrate the new chapter with the rest of the text. Like Dr Walker, indeed as with any book dealing with current affairs, I am in danger of being overtaken by events.

The changes which have taken place since the Second World War have occurred at a pace far greater than anything ever experienced before. The rate of growth of the economy has been faster than that achieved during the Industrial Revolution yet politicians and businessmen view it with alarm as being too slow. Growth has been exceptionally rapid in some sectors such as transport and communications while other sectors such as shipbuilding and heavy engineering have continued to decline. Membership of the European Economic Community is likely to give further acceleration to the speed of change and to the growing conflict of interests between the developed countries and the Third World.

Economic changes and the associated problems have given rise to greater government involvement in the economy and the attendant social problems have necessitated the extension of the Welfare State. Despite rising living standards for all sectors of society, inequalities of opportunity and achievement persist to a very marked extent.

The extension of welfare and education since 1945 has made people more aware of these inequalities and more determined to do something about them. For this reason the period since the war has seen the growth of a more participative democracy as people have become sensitised to social problems and have sought to have more control over their own destinies. This has been evidenced by the growth of such things as civil rights movements, community councils and consumer protection. Doubtless this trend will continue into the future.

September 1978 C.W.M.

CONTENTS

PART I
Agrarian and Industrial Changes, 1700–1850

I.	The Nature and Causes of Industrialisation	1
II.	Industry and Agriculture before the Machine Age	15
III.	The Agrarian Revolution	30
IV.	Industrial Changes—Iron, Coal and Steam Power	43
V.	Industrial Changes—The Textile Industries	55

PART II
Means of Communication in the Pre-Railway Age

VI.	Roads	64
VII.	Canals	75

PART III
Overseas Commerce and Fiscal Policies, 1700–1850

VIII.	The Commercial Revolution	86
IX.	British Overseas Trade, 1780–1850	103
X.	The State and Economic Policy	108
XI.	The Genesis of the Free Trade Movement	118
XII.	The Achievement of Free Trade	125

PART IV
The Nineteenth-Century Revolution in Means of Communication

XIII.	Railways	136
XIV.	Shipping	150

PART V
Finance

XV.	Banking and Finance	164

PART VI
Social Reform

XVI.	The Poor Law	179
XVII.	Factory and Mining Legislation	190
XVIII.	Public Health and Housing	204
XIX.	Education	217

CONTENTS

PART VII
WORKING CLASS MOVEMENTS

XX.	The Chartist and Co-operative Movements	234
XXI.	Trade Unionism to 1876	248

PART VIII
GREAT BRITAIN IN THE ERA OF FREE TRADE, 1850–1919

XXII.	Science and Technological Changes	259
XXIII.	Industry and Trade	271
XXIV.	Agriculture	281
XXV.	The Tariff Reform Movement	291
XXVI.	Trade Unionism after 1876 and the Rise of the Labour Party	302

PART IX
GREAT BRITAIN DURING THE INTER-WAR YEARS, 1919–39

XXVII.	The British Economy after The First World War	315
XXVIII.	The State and Economic Affairs, 1919–29	328
XXIX.	The State and Economic Affairs, 1929–39	335
XXX.	The Genesis of the Welfare State	352

PART X
GREAT BRITAIN AFTER THE OUTBREAK OF THE SECOND WORLD WAR, 1939–77

XXXI.	The War Years, 1939–45	366
XXXII.	Great Britain and the Post-War World 1945–67	372
XXXIII.	Economic Problems	383
XXXIV.	Social Problems	396
XXXV.	British Economy and Society 1967–77	409
	INDEX OF ACTS	435
	GENERAL INDEX	438

PART I

AGRARIAN AND INDUSTRIAL CHANGES, 1700–1850

Chapter I

THE NATURE AND CAUSES OF INDUSTRIALISATION

Human beings, in order to survive, need food, clothing, warmth and shelter. The satisfaction of these physical wants is as compelling to twentieth-century man as it was to his Old Stone Age ancestors. But twentieth-century man lives less precariously than his predecessors because he has a greater command over the forces of nature. Throughout the greater part of his existence man has earned a livelihood using simple tools, operated by hand, supplemented to a limited extent by animal, wind and water power. Hence living standards, for all but a privileged few, were very low and uncertain. Man lived in an age of scarcity, with famine a constant threat, obtaining at the best of times little more than a bare subsistence. Under such circumstances the safe gathering in of the harvest was a cause for rejoicing. Failure to do so was a major catastrophe. Millions of men and women in Latin America, Africa and in the densely peopled monsoon lands of Asia are still living in the age of scarcity. But for the aid of charitable societies, such as for example, Oxfam, countless thousands would starve to death. In contrast much higher standards of living are enjoyed by people living in Western Europe, North America, Australia and New Zealand. In these favoured lands the age of plenty has succeeded the age of scarcity. This development, a relatively recent one, may be said to have begun with the use of steam power in eighteenth-century Britain.

Before the age of steam power man earned a precarious living by hard toil. Yet despite the inadequacies of their capital equipment our forefathers performed amazing feats. Modern tourists can do no other than contemplate with awe the astonishingly large stones at Stonehenge and Avebury, wondering how the pre-historic inhabitants of Wessex with levers and muscular power shaped, transported and erected them. Nearby at Silbury Hill is the largest artificial mound in Europe. Equally impressive are the stupendous hill fortifications at Maiden Castle near Dorchester and the pre-historic flint mines at Grime's Graves in Norfolk, dug by miners using deer horn picks and shovels made from animal shoulder blades in the dim, smoky light given off by chalk lamps filled with animal fat and moss wicks. Such massive earth-moving feats inevitably invite comparison with those of Irish navvies who, with iron picks and shovels, constructed the massive embankments and tunnels designed by nineteenth-century railway engineers.

There is much that we would like to know, but do not, about the peoples who inhabited our island in the remote past, but we do know with certainty that their economy was primarily a rural one. The growing of cereals and the care of domestic animals were the customary occupation of the majority of the early inhabitants of Great Britain. This continued to be the case until the eighteenth century. Since then significant changes have taken place in the British economy. Power-driven machinery has superseded handicraft industry, multiplying enormously the rate at which commodities can be produced. At the same time means of transport were revolutionised and the techniques of cultivating the soil and rearing domestic animals fundamentally improved. The substitution of mechanical for muscular power has brought about a decrease in the proportion of people employed on the land, and an increase in the proportion of producers of manufactured articles and of workers employed in commercial and service occupations. The rise and expansion of industrialisation, pioneered in Great Britain, later became a feature of the economic development of many other countries.

To this change in world economy the name "Industrial Revolution" has been given. The change is one that has profoundly affected the whole of human society, with considerable effects on the ways people live and think. Knowledge of this revolutionary upheaval in human affairs is essential for an understanding of current social and economic problems. Besides, the society we live in did not come into existence in a single moment of time. Rather it has evolved gradually, nearly all that we see around us being an inheritance from the past. Hence the unique importance of historical studies.

The changes taking place in the social and economic environment were not accepted readily. People's habits do not easily alter. Only gradually and with reluctance does the custom of the past yield to that of the present. New ways of doing things tend to be bitterly opposed by those whose traditional way of life is threatened. This is as characteristic of ourselves as of our forefathers. The Luddites and machine breakers of the early nineteenth century have their modern counterparts in trade unionists taking part in demarcation disputes, and in members of craft trades who impose restrictive conditions on recruitment long after industrial changes have outdated ancient skills. This understandable human reaction to change helps to explain why industrial changes in the eighteenth and nineteenth centuries were less sudden than the term "Industrial Revolution" would seem to imply. Popular acceptance of the term dates from 1884 when Arnold Toynbee's *Lectures on the Industrial Revolution of the Eighteenth Century in England* were published.

Toynbee's view that an industrial revolution took place between 1760 and 1830 still has currency. The year 1760, memorable as the one in which George III came to the throne, has no significance whatever as the starting point of a process of quickening economic development in Great Britain. Rather, to quote from Prof. John U. Nef's *War and Human Progress* (1950):

"An unprecedented acceleration of industrial progress began, not in 1750 or 1760, but in the 1780s. It was then also that the movement of industrial labour from domestic to factory manufacture became unprecedently rapid.... After 1785 the powerful steam-driven machinery and the new methods of making iron with the help of coal came into extensive use for the first time. In Great Britain the critical turning point which differentiates British from continental progress ... was in the middle eighties. For example, the island was producing little more than a third as much iron as France in 1780. Between 1785 and 1797 the output in Great Britain approximately doubled. During the next eight years, it approximately doubled again, reaching about 250,000 tons in 1805."

Actually, however, one cannot truthfully assign specific dates to economic and social change. The basic factors of modern industrialisation, capitalism, the aggregation of workers on one site, the use of power, wind and water to drive machinery, were known long before 1760. Even steam power, familiar to Hero of Alexandria in the century preceding the birth of Christ, had been used since the end of the seventeenth century to pump water from mines.

Neither can we assign a specific date to the completion of a movement which is still proceeding at an ever quickening pace. Certainly not 1830. No British industry can be described as fully technologically transformed by 1830. Industrial capitalism had made considerable progress in some branches of the iron and textile industries by 1830, but their modernisation was far from complete. In the weaving sections of the cotton and woollen textile industries there were in 1830 more hand-loom workers than factory operatives. Only gradually did power-driven machinery displace handworkers, much more quickly in the cotton than in the woollen industries. In other contemporary industries the use of mechanical steam power had not even commenced. Most consumable commodities long continued to be produced in domestic workshops. This was the case for instance in the various metal manufactures such as nail manufactures in Staffordshire and in the Sheffield cutlery trades. The persistence well into the twentieth century of a domestic system of industry was well illustrated by Dr J. R. Harris in a useful television "Industrial Archaeology" lecture. In it Dr Harris drew attention to the watch industry at Prescot and elsewhere in Lancashire, the separate parts such as cases, hands and balance wheels being made by individual craftsmen and sold to merchant factors for assembly elsewhere.

As the introduction of the new industrial techniques was a slow process modern historians have been reluctant to describe it as a "revolution." Nevertheless although it has become generally accepted that the change was evolutionary rather than revolutionary in character, it still remains true that the extended use of steam power in late eighteenth- and early nineteenth-century Britain brought into existence an industrial society very different in character from that known in earlier centuries. But why, we may ask, did this expansion of industrialisation take place, and why was it pioneered in Great Britain? No wholly convincing answers can be given to these questions. Great Britain of course possessed natural resources and advantages that made industrial expansion possible. She had possessed since 1689 a stable political system. Cut off from Europe by the sea, she was not, unlike her continental neighbours, exposed to the hazards of foreign invasion. An ample rainfall and many fast-flowing Pennine streams endowed her with water-power resources put to good use before the steam-power era. The geographical discoveries of the late fifteenth and sixteenth centuries had placed her astride the leading world trade routes. She had considerable coal and iron resources, located in some areas in close proximity to one another, and near the sea, making the export of manufactured goods relatively easy through the estuaries of the Thames, Severn, Trent, Mersey and Clyde which providentially penetrated far inland. In contrast the coal and iron resources of European countries and the U.S.A., being geographically separated and located far from the sea, could not be fully exploited until the railway age.

A catalogue of the natural resources of Great Britain cannot by itself provide a complete explanation of that acceleration of technology that has been described as the Industrial Revolution. The eighteenth century is memorable because, during it, ingenious men devised machines which increased industrial production many times. It would be naïve, however, to imagine that a steam engine, for example, could not have been invented earlier because James Watt was not born until 1736. Such a theory pre-supposes that genius is the only element in scientific and technological discoveries, and ignores the truth that in general inventors are men concerned to find solutions to contemporary problems. Leonardo da Vinci (1452–1519), one of the most versatile geniuses of all time, and his contemporary Leon Battista Alberti (1404–72) were exceptionally gifted men in the realm of applied science. But their ingenuity did not trigger off an industrial revolution in fifteenth-century Florence. In eighteenth-century Britain in contrast, where an efficient means of pumping water out of mines was urgently needed, James Watt and his contemporaries invented the steam engine, one of the principal factors in the subsequent transformation of industrial processes. It is not too fanciful to imagine that if fifteenth-century Florentines had prospected for minerals in deep mines da Vinci and Alberti would have sought a solution to the problem of underground drainage. Italians in their day, however, were faced with the problems of controlling spring floods of rivers, hence da Vinci designed machines for excavating earth and suggested brushwood matting to protect dykes. It is also worth noting that in fifteenth-century Italy, where, as in our day, war stimulated inventive activity in weapons of destruction, da Vinci attempted to design a steam-propelled gun and submarine weapons.

Inventors search for means of improving existing practices, but their creative minds can only operate within the limitations imposed by the knowledge, technology and intellectual concepts of their day and age. For instance da Vinci had no steel plates for his submarines. Inventors in the early eighteenth century could not have given to mankind efficient dynamos and electric motors, or have solved the problems of transmitting electric signals and power over long distances, because the scientific discoveries which have enabled electricity to become a common form of energy had not then been made. They were capable, however, of inventing the steam engine, which made waterwheels and windmills obsolete, because advances had been made in the scientific study of heat and mechanics. In the seventeenth century the researches of Galileo, Huygens and Newton had made mechanics the leading natural science. In the eighteenth century, experiments in utilising the expansive force of steam were successful, following scientific research into the essential nature of heat. The Scottish universities, Edinburgh and Glasgow, were in the forefront of this scientific progress. Not the least important of those to whom Watt was indebted for his subsequent fame as a pioneer in the evolution of the steam engine was Professor Joseph Black (1728–99) who made many important discoveries in physics and chemistry during his tenure of Chairs at Glasgow and Edinburgh Universities.

We are not concerned to explain the change in the seventeenth century from a medieval, religious and teleological outlook to a modern, scientific and mechanistic one, and the widespread use of the experimental method, but merely to note that from that time onwards there was considerable interest in scientific and technological studies. Francis Bacon (1561–1626) suggested that scientific study should be encouraged because new knowledge meant new opportunities for invention. Members of the Royal Society in the seventeenth century did not consider that scientific research should be carried on merely to satisfy human curiosity about the laws of nature. By the Charter given to them by Charles II in 1662 they were directed not only to study "all things mathematical, philosophical and mechanical" but also to direct their minds to the "improvement of all useful arts, manufactures, mechanical practices, engines and inventions." In the eighteenth century collaboration between scientists and technologists was continued in national and local learned societies whose members included scientists, business men, engineers and inventors, and by the publication of technical journals and dictionaries of arts and sciences. Among the societies founded to promote investigation in both science and industrial problems were the Society of Arts (1754), the Lunar Society in Birmingham whose members attended monthly dinners at the time of the full moon, the Royal Society of Edinburgh and the Literary and Philosophical Society in Manchester. Watt, Boulton, Wedgwood and Priestley were members of the Lunar Society. John Dalton (1766–1844), whose Atomic Theory (1808) was one of the many scientific contributions which made possible the development of modern industrial chemistry, was introduced in 1794 to the Manchester Literary and Philosophical Society by Robert Owen, becoming its Secretary in 1800. The latter part of the eighteenth century is memorable as the period in which the foundations of modern chemistry were laid by Antione Laurent Lavoisier (1743–94) in France, and in England by the Unitarian clergyman Joseph Priestley (1733–1894) and the aristocratic Henry Cavendish (1731–1810).

The advancements achieved during the seventeenth and eighteenth centuries in scientific and technological knowledge were not confined to Great Britain. It was a Western European achievement. In contemporary France, Holland, Germany and Italy much progress was made in the pursuit of scientific knowledge and in its application to trade and industry. Members of the French "Academie des Sciences," founded in the reign of Louis XIV, were required by the monarch to carry out scientific and technological investigations in order to find solutions to industrial problems. Between these scientific societies in Britain and Europe there was considerable correspondence and exchange of ideas. The development of a form of society in Western Europe in which a scientific and technological attitude of mind was widespread partially accounts for subsequent economic trends in Europe, but not why they were pioneered in Great Britain. That industrial expansion took place earlier in Great Britain than elsewhere suggests that in the eighteenth century only in Great Britain were present all the conditions necessary for rapid technological change.

Considerable increases in the production of commodities can only take place where the market, capital, transport and labour needs of producers are adequate. In eighteenth-century Britain there were ample opportunities to make increased and cheaper production worth while. Since Tudor times the enterprise of chartered trading companies and the foundation of overseas colonies had created markets the demands of which could not be satisfied by traditional methods of production. Hence ingenious men were stimulated to devise machines powered first by water and later by steam. Such a technological advance, however, could not have taken place unless capital had been available at low rates of interest to finance the new and still untried methods of production. Britain was in this respect fortunate: wealthy merchants, who had accumulated capital from the profits of overseas trade, and large landowners, were willing to take the considerable risks of investing money in the new enterprise. Much of this capital was accumulated by business men, reared in Puritan, Methodist and Quaker traditions of frugality and thrift to whom "Heaven is not the dumping ground for the failures of Earth." Further, during the eighteenth century banking facilities became more readily available. Far different was the situation in such countries as Russia and Prussia, where in the absence of an enterprising well-to-do middle class, industrial development had to be stimulated by such monarchs as Peter the Great and Frederick the Great.

The transport needs of an expanding industry were met by improved means of inland communication, roads and canals, and to overseas markets by the provision of better dock facilities and state encouragement by navigation laws for merchant shipping. The contemporary exodus from rural to urban areas following the enclosures of open fields and commons increased the industrial labour force. In addition, an increasing population, both a partial cause and effect of industrialisation, not only made more labour available but also increased the number of purchasers of the commodities produced.

The eighteenth-century population expansion was a major factor in contemporary economic growth. Of all the problems facing mankind nowadays the most serious is the rate at which world population is expanding. Can the resources of our planet, it is being anxiously asked, be extended indefinitely to meet the increasing demand for food? Rapid population growth in Britain led to the same question being asked by the Rev. Thomas Robert Malthus in his *Essay on Population*, the first edition of which was published in 1798. We have only vague and imperfect knowledge of the number of people inhabiting Great Britain before the first official census in 1801. From the seventeenth century, when the value of such knowledge began to be realised, attempts were made to estimate the size of the population. The data used, however, was unreliable. The eighteenth-century philosopher and theologian, Dr Richard Price, basing his estimates on the window tax returns, actually concluded that the population had declined between 1690 and 1777. Such evidence as we possess today indicates that before the eighteenth century population increased slowly, expansion being temporarily halted by outbursts of disease, notably by the Black Death in the mid-fourteenth century. It has been estimated that the population of England and Wales, about 2 million in 1066, had risen to 5·8 million by 1700. During this period, although there was a high birth rate, there was also a high death rate due to scanty medical knowledge, bad social conditions, precarious harvests and relatively low yields of food per acre. From about the mid-eighteenth century, however, an unprecedented demographic change took place. The population of England and Wales began to expand from approximately 6 million in 1740 to 8,890,000 in 1801. The rate of population growth continued to be considerable after 1801, the population of England and Wales being 17,928,000 in 1851 and 32,528,000 in 1901.

The commencement of rapid population growth in Great Britain during the second half of the eighteenth century cannot be attributed to one primary cause. Historians at one time considered that it was due to the fall in the death rate, particularly in the infant mortality rate, following advances in medical knowledge and scientific discoveries such as vaccination. Nowadays we understand that the motivating forces of the population expansion were complex. A notable feature of the British and European demographic revolution was that it was associated with a marked rise in living standards. In this respect it differed from the population expansion which simultaneously took place in Ireland and is today taking place in Asiatic, African and Latin American countries inhabited by rural populations living in a state of chronic malnutrition. In contrast population expansion in Britain and Europe occurred at a time when there was, firstly, a great increase in resources available for the maintenance of life and, secondly, when scientific and technological progress permitted improvements in the social environment. Before the eighteenth century economic conditions were such that rapid population growth was impossible. People being dependent upon locally grown food were exposed to the hazards of starvation in the event of the failure of the harvest. Means of communication were too primitive to permit movement of such bulky and perishable commodities as foodstuffs. Therefore shortages in one area could not be relieved by regular supplies from areas possessing a surplus.

An improvement in the dietary standards of the people of Great Britain was made possible by the availability of greater supplies of home-grown food. This was due to a series of good harvests from 1730 and to the changes in agricultural practices known as the Agrarian Revolution. The more widespread introduction of the turnip into crop rotation led to more meat and milk being produced. Crop yields increased. Grain prices were low while improvements in internal means of communication ended the dependence of consumers upon local producers and the distressing circumstances that had hitherto followed harvest failures. This increased food production was achieved by the labour of fewer workers. Great Britain therefore had to solve the problems of finding a means of subsistence for ever increasing numbers of her people for whom there was no work available on the land. The solution was the redeployment of surplus land workers in industries, localised in new industrial towns, in which by the use of power-driven machines productivity was dramatically increased. With the passage of time, increasingly, capital resources were diverted into the development of large-scale industries producing commodities for sale in the home and in overseas markets.

Once started the upward movement of population accelerated as it was paralleled by an increase in market demand for the commodities produced by power-driven machinery. One of the most powerful stimulants to population increase in Britain and Europe was the existence of vast, unoccupied areas overseas. Their settlement and exploitation had important consequences. When population threatens to outgrow native food supplies two remedies can be tried: firstly, exporting manufactures in exchange for food, and secondly, exporting people to areas where virgin soils are awaiting the plough. Countries like Britain and Germany were able to provide work for a large proportion, but not all, of their people, by investing capital in manufacturing industries. Countries like Ireland and Italy exported men as they lacked the resources needed for large-scale industrialisation. The fecundity of European peoples was responsible for a global population redistribution during the nineteenth century.

Before 1800 migration was on a very small scale. Migration on a really big scale can only take place when there is peaceful intercourse between the peoples of the world, and when cheap and efficient transport is readily available. Further, there must be widely diffused knowledge of opportunities available in distant lands. Not until comparatively recent times have world conditions permitted mass migration. Mass migration began in the 1840s. The United States was the country at first to which most European emigrants went. Later, Canada, the British Dominions in the southern hemisphere, the Argentine and Brazil attracted many. Between 1820 and 1930 some 60 million people left Europe, 40 million of whom went to the U.S.A. Before 1880 emigration to the U.S.A. was mainly from Great Britain and Ireland. After 1880 increasing numbers of Scandinavians, Germans, and Eastern and Southern Europeans flooded through New York harbour, driven to the New World by hunger and ambition, and by religious and racial persecution. Gold discoveries and later the offer of free homesteads persuaded many of the immigrants that a better life was possible in the new lands than that they had experienced in their original homelands. The import needs of the rapidly developing overseas communities, and the additional supplies of raw materials they made available, increased the amount of industrialisation in Britain and Europe, while the foodstuffs they exported powerfully affected the agricultural systems of the Old World.

During the 1880–1914 period there were also mass migration movements from India to Burma, Malaya, Samoa, Fiji, South Africa, British Guiana and the West Indies; from China to Manchuria, the U.S.A. and South-east Asia; from Japan to British Columbia, the U.S.A. and Brazil; from Russia into Siberia and Turkestan; and from the Mediterranean lands of Europe into South America.

A notable feature of economic development in eighteenth- and nineteenth-century Britain was that it was pioneered by private enterprise. Before 1700 the older systems of state regulation and control of economic life were breaking down. Particularly in the industries which had grown up after the passage of the Elizabethan Statute of Artificiers and Apprentices (1563) there was freedom from hampering regulations. The revolt against the opinion that governments should regulate trade and industry received massive support by the publication in 1776 of Adam Smith's *Wealth of Nations*. The investment of capital therefore in new methods and processes was not hindered by legal obstacles. The dominance of *laisser-faire* ideas in the ensuing period of rapid economic and social change has been adversely criticised by some historians. In their view "the horrors that ensued in England," to quote Arnold Toynbee, are attributable to avoidance by governments of their social responsibilities by unduly delaying the taking of legislative and administrative action to provide remedies. Such an estimate of the social consequences of the Industrial Revolution is based on the postulate that the degrading conditions under which the lower classes lived and worked were unknown before the era of dark satanic mills. This is not true. Some modern historians have argued that industrialisation made possible an improvement in the standard of life for large sections of the working class. So far from degrading the working classes it created the conditions which made it possible for them to improve their lot by organised action in trade unions and in the arena of politics.

The Industrial Revolution was a less sudden break with the past than used commonly to be supposed. Capitalist ownership of the means of production and the employment of wage-paid labour was widespread long before 1700. In woollen manufacturing, as early as the fourteenth century, the widening of the market and the need to co-ordinate the activities of combers, carders, spinners, weavers and craftsmen employed in the finishing processes led to control of the industry by middlemen. These middlemen, known as master clothiers, provided the finance and materials and bridged the gap between producers and consumers. In the sixteenth century, industries which needed expensive plant and equipment were necessarily organised on capitalist principles. The shipbuilding, coalmining, iron smelting, glass, ordnance and coppermining industries, which developed considerably in the reign of Queen Elizabeth I, can be cited as examples. There were even industries at this time organised on a joint stock basis. But although capitalist control was well established before 1700 it was mainly in the hands of men concerned with buying and selling. Craftsmen often owned their own tools, their homes being workshops. The employment of workers in establishments housing machinery owned by capitalist employers, although known in the sixteenth century, did not become the dominant form of industrial production until the nineteenth century.

A major factor in stimulating economic growth and change was the increasing tendency for economic life in Britain to be organised on a national rather than a local basis. Local producers in the past had, as might be expected, resisted competition which destroyed their monopoly. The Chester company of cappers, for example, complained to the town authorities in 1520 that they were "in grete decay" because local shopkeepers were retailing caps made in London and elsewhere. Such attempts to prevent the emergence of a nation economy were numerous but proved to be ineffectual. That Britain had a highly organised nation economy before 1700 can be illustrated by the response of productive enterprise in many parts of the country to the pull of the London market. London was not only the administrative capital but also a centre of trade, industry and finance. There was a great deal of regional specialisation in both industry and agriculture, producers marketing their wares far afield, payment often being made by bills drawn on London.

As there were no internal customs barriers the only obstacles to the free interchange of commercial commodities were those imposed by nature. After the passage of the Act of Union in 1707, England, Wales and Scotland formed a free trade unit, the largest in contemporary Europe. In European countries in contrast economic development was impeded by rigid state control, internal tariff barriers, guild restrictive practices and a multiplicity of currencies, weights and measures. Further, by 1700 only in Britain, the Dutch Republic and to a lesser degree in France had a form of society been established based, not on forced labour, but on freedom of contract. Considerable economic growth and change can only take place in a society whose members are legally free to choose their own occupations. Before 1789 a majority of Europeans were serfs, tied to the soil, living in a static form of society, in which the relationships between masters and men were based on tradition and custom. But in Britain serfdom had all but disappeared before 1700. Its economic basis had been undermined in the late Middle Ages by the introduction of a money economy, by the expansion of trade and by the development of urban life. From the fifteenth century onwards the legal barriers to villein freedom had been removed by the intervention of the Court of Chancery in the relations between lords and villeins. Villeins became copyholders possessing the common law rights of freemen. Their tenurial rights were subject to the jurisdiction of the royal not the manorial courts. "Now Copyholders," Chief Justice Coke could say at the beginning of the seventeenth century, "stand upon a sure ground, now they weigh not their lord's displeasure, they shake not at every blast of wind, they eat, drink and sleep securely."

In Britain the establishment of legal, contractual freedom, the basis of modern human relationships, was an unobtrusive process brought about by a series of judicial decisions. The movement towards emancipation in Europe was more sudden and may be said to have commenced with the outbreak of the French Revolution in 1789. In France the legal basis of serfdom was destroyed by a series of measures passed by the National Assembly on the night of 4th–5th August 1789. The example set by France was copied in other parts of the continent. The new order was introduced into the Rhinelands following their invasion by the armies of Napoleon I.

Serfdom was abolished in Scandinavia, by royal decree in Prussia in 1807 and by the issue of the Edict of Emancipation by the Czar Alexander II of Russia in 1861. The abolition of slavery in the British Empire in 1833 was part of the movement of emancipation. As a result of these measures economic life ceased to be based on foundations of forced labour. Men obtained freedom of movement, legal freedom to choose their occupations, freedom to buy and sell and freedom to dispose of their property. These changes made growth possible and expansion inevitable.

European economic development was also grievously retarded by a number of major wars between 1689 and 1815. In the first half of the nineteenth century Europe lagged behind Great Britain in the use of new industrial techniques. The only European country in which modern industrialisation had taken root by 1815 was the southern half of the Congress Kingdom of the Netherlands, the Belgium of 1830. Possessing considerable coal resources, Belgium had been able to develop her manufacturing resources during the wars behind the protective barriers of Napoleon I's continental system. France emerged from the 1792–1815 wars stripped of her colonial empire and as a country which had fallen behind Great Britain in the race for commercial and industrial supremacy.

In the second half of the eighteenth century the population of France was two and a half times larger than that of England. With a well developed urban life, a considerable overseas trade and a flourishing manufacturing industry, France before 1789 was entering on a phase of industrial expansion. A Boulton and Watt steam engine was in use at Le Creuzot in 1782 and grants were made by the French Government to assist the development of a cotton industry using English spinning inventions. Then came the Revolution of 1789. Even if it had not occurred it is unlikely that France would have progressed as rapidly as Great Britain. In some ways the Revolution of 1789 assisted industrial and commercial progress by removing obstacles to free enterprise, unifying weights and measures by the adoption of the metric system and welding the country into an economic unity. Under the Emperor Napoleon I, state assistance was given to industrial development with notable effects on the dyeing and sugar industries. But despite state assistance French industry expanded more slowly than that of Great Britain. The strains and stresses of the long wars no doubt partly account for this, but there are other reasons more deepseated and permanent. It was cheap, good quality coal which explains why Great Britain was able to exploit more successfully her industrial potential. French coal resources are much less extensive and inferior in quality. She has only two large coalfields and some minor ones, the chief coalfield today, that in the north, not being opened up until the second half of the nineteenth century.

A different state of affairs existed in Prussia which by 1815 had expanded to the Rhine. Here there had been a re-birth after the disastrous Jena campaign (1806). Central and local government were remodelled, the land system was reorganised, and by a series of reforms commencing in 1807 serfdom was abolished. The effects of these reforms of Stein and Hardenberg, and Maassen's abolition of internal customs barriers in 1818, were not felt immediately, but their ultimate consequences were profound. Prussia became the pioneer of economic reconstruction in Germany. But in Germany as a whole economic development was hindered by the post-1815 division into thirty-nine states each with its own fiscal arrangements and currency. Until the second half of the nineteenth century industry remained at a very primitive stage of development. Expansion and modernisation came after the achievement of economic unity by the Zollverein and the provisions of transport facilities more efficient than that provided by roads and waterways. "It was railways," the German historian Treitschke wrote, "that first dragged the nation out of its economic stagnation." With the emergence of Germany and the U.S.A., similarly revolutionised by railways, as industrial powers of the first rank, Great Britain in the closing years of the nineteenth century no longer held the position of unquestioned industrial predominance which she held after the Battle of Waterloo (1815).

A student of economic history soon learns that there is no finality in human affairs. Change is a law of life. The merchants of Venice, Genoa and the Germanic Hanseatic League pioneered international trade in the Middle Ages. The Portuguese and the Spaniards played a major part in geographical discoveries in the fifteenth and sixteenth centuries, becoming the centres of world-wide empires. The seventeenth century witnessed Dutch pre-eminence in banking, commerce and agriculture. But Great Britain in the eighteenth and nineteenth centuries was the land in which modern industry based on coal and steam power was born. Nowadays other forms of energy are available, offering opportunities for industrial development to countries not endowed by nature with coal resources. In the twentieth century, therefore, Great Britain is faced with social and economic difficulties markedly different from those of the era in which she was universally recognised as "the Workshop of the World."

Chapter II

INDUSTRY AND AGRICULTURE BEFORE THE MACHINE AGE

Industry

In 1700 Great Britain was primarily an agricultural land, four-fifths of its people living in rural areas. But not all those who inhabited the countryside were engaged in growing crops. Food is only one of the basic needs of man, hence considerable industrial development had taken place before iron and coal transformed the green fields and empty moorlands and valleys of our homeland, covering them with a black pall of soot-laden air. Still to be seen, littering the landscape, are abandoned mines, a visible proof that mining for metals in Britain is centuries old. In Roman times, and much earlier, lead was exported from the Mendips, Flintshire, Derbyshire, Yorkshire and Shropshire. From the Bronze Age, until the twentieth century, Cornwall was the world's leading producer of tin and copper. It is only in modern times, with the opening of mines in the Americas, Australia and Malaya, that Cornwall ceased to export tin and copper, instead sending thousands of her sons overseas to earn a livelihood as miners in foreign lands.

In 1780 the nations of the world purchased not only Cornish tin and copper, but also woollen cloth. "The woollen manufactures of Great Britain," Daniel Defoe wrote in 1728, "are the general wear in all the countries of Europe—go where you will you will find it."

At the end of the seventeenth century Gregory King calculated that woollen manufacture accounted for about one-fifth of the national income. Reasons for the dominant position wool occupied in the British economy are to be found in the peculiar character of British pastures, the fact that in past centuries it was the only great clothing material, while compared with other important sheep rearing regions, Spain, Silesia and Eastern France, Britain was relatively peaceful and secure. Climate and relief ensured ample water supplies, and of importance before the age of steam, water power. The areas in which sheep flourished best were the dry oolitic and chalk uplands of the South East. The wool manufacturing industry was widely distributed, but as early as the fifteenth century it was tending to become localised in the West Country, East Anglia and the Aire, Calder and Colne Valleys of the West Riding of Yorkshire. Kendal cloth was produced in Westmorland, and in South Lancashire, Manchester Cottons, from cotton imported from Cyprus and Smyrna mixed with wool or linen.

The West Country, the counties of Gloucester, Wiltshire, Somerset and Devon, was the home of the long-woolled Cotswold sheep. Each county produced specialised fabrics but the region was particularly noteworthy for the manufacture of broadcloth, cloth of very high quality. The magnificent Perpendicular churches and the substantial houses which still survive in this part of England are eloquent of the affluence and culture of the wealthy citizens who made woollen cloth the foundation of England's commercial greatness. The East Anglian district, the counties of Norfolk, Suffolk and North Essex, was peculiarly favoured in two ways. Firstly by its agricultural wealth and secondly by its geographical position in proximity to the Netherlands, which made it the outlet for wool transported by pack horses from the West Country. In the Middle Ages much English wool was exported through a number of ports between the Wash and the Thames, including Boston, Dunwich, King's Lynn, Ipswich and Colchester. Into the area came streams of immigrants after the Norman Conquest and during the reign of Edward III (1327–77). Skill in the production of woollen cloths was acquired through contact with these aliens. From the fourteenth century, in the many small towns and villages in the area, the worsted industry took root. The industry was saved from decline in the 1560s by the influx of refugees driven from the Netherlands by Spanish persecutions. They introduced the manufacture of high quality cloths know as the "new draperies," marketed under various names—fustians, serges, velours, bays and says. The prosperity of the region was such that Macaulay was able to describe Norwich as being in 1685 "the chief seat of the chief manufacture of the realm."

Much less important in 1700 than that in East Anglia and the West Country was the cloth manufacturing industry in the West Riding. The industry had existed in the Halifax district from at least the early twelfth century, but Yorkshire cloth was poor in quality, coarse woollen kerseys which customers complained were full of holes. By the early eighteenth century, however, the West Riding was manufacturing worsteds and had started on a course of development which ultimately made the valleys of the Aire, Calder and Colne the greatest cloth manufacturing centre in the world. In the middle years of the eighteenth century Samuel Hill of Soyland, near Halifax, was exporting cloth pieces to the Netherlands, Prussia and

Russia, and despatching pattern sheets via St Petersburg and Astrakan to Persia. The men of the West Riding have not bequeathed to us the substantial houses, magnificent churches and monumental brasses that are so eloquent of East Anglian and West Country prosperity. But still to be seen on Pennine moorland hillsides are clusters of houses, built of local millstone grit, in which weavers were living in 1728 when Defoe tells us "every considerable house was a manufactory." Also at Almondbury, Huddersfield, there still exist the homes of woollen hand-workers. The work was carried on in first floor rooms fitted with large window frames, small panes of glass being used as large sheets would have been impossibly expensive.

The industrial system in the West Riding described by Defoe is known as the domestic system. The name "domestic," however, is a very misleading one when used to describe the system of industrial organisation dominant in Britain before the era of power-driven machinery. Industrial organisation was in reality very complex and one of numerous variations. It was certainly not true that the typical industrial worker in the woollen and other industries was a self-employed craftsman producing commodities and selling them direct to consumers. For the most part producers, even though their homes were often workshops, were wage-earners employed by middlemen. In the woollen industry these employers were known as master clothiers. Long before the eighteenth century the industry was organised on capitalist lines, and necessarily so. Bulk purchase of wool from sheep rearers, the need to co-ordinate production in the various specialist crafts of the industry, often geographically remote from one another, and the sale of the cloth pieces either overseas or in the home market, involved the intervention of capitalist middlemen at every stage. These included wool staplers, men of substance, who purchased wool after the annual shearings, yarn merchants who employed spinners and marketed yarn, and clothiers who purchased either wool or yarn, and arranged for their manufacture by wage-paid employees or by themselves. The main function of these middlemen was to organise production and adjust it to meet the needs of a fluctuating market, world-wide in extent. The scale and the point on which they conducted their activities varied considerably. Some were men of considerable wealth, culture and eminence, others barely distinguishable from wage-paid manual workers. The capitalist nature of the industry was so well established that the transference of the productive processes was accomplished with relative ease when the appearance of power-driven machinery made such a change inevitable.

In organisation the woollen industry was not only essentially capitalistic but it was also far from being uniform. In the West Country control tended to be in the hands of wealthy gentlemen clothiers, upon whom the workers were completely dependent for raw materials and employment. Here were to be found many of the evils such as cyclical unemployment and oppression of low paid workers by employers who "heapeth up riches" obtained "by griping and grinding the poor." According to a seventeenth-century ballad, "The Clothier's Delight or the Rich Man's Joy and the Poor Man's Sorrow," clothiers cynically boasted:

> By poor people's labour we fill up our purse
> Although we do get with it many a curse.

There was even the possibility of a factory system becoming dominant in the area. In the first half of the fourteenth century Thomas Blanket of Bristol hired workers to operate hand machines on his own premises. In Henry VIII's reign (1509–47) John Winchcombe (Jack of Newbury) is said to have had a hundred looms in his workshop, and William Stumpe purchased Malmesbury Abbey for use as a factory and negotiated for the sale of Osney Abbey. The Weavers Act of 1555 was passed to stop further developments on these lines, the disappearance of cottage industries being thereby postponed until the use of power-driven machinery. But legislative interference does not fully account for the continued use of homes as workshops. A more likely explanation is that capitalist middlemen did not find the work done on their own premises economically advantageous.

In East Anglia, dependent on wool produced in distant counties, workers suffered the inconvenience of periodical unemployment due to speculative trading and fluctuating market conditions. The organisation of the industry here was very complex. There were wealthy merchants who provided combers with wool, clothiers who distributed yarn to weavers, and finishers and weavers who purchased yarn and, as in Yorkshire, made their own arrangements to sell cloth pieces. In the West Riding there were a few wealthy cloth merchants heavily outnumbered by "working clothiers" who possessed scanty capital resources. Such hardworking, independent producers purchased wool from dealers and sold woven pieces in local markets. Halifax had a Cloth Hall in Elizabeth I's reign and one was erected in 1766 by Sir John Ramsden in Huddersfield. Open once a week on Tuesdays, it was demolished in 1930 and a cinema was built on the site. The cloth market in Leeds, according to Defoe, was "perhaps not to be equalled in the World." Defoe's description of living and working conditions in the Halifax district has been often quoted to support the opinion that nineteenth-century mill hands, having lost their independence, were worse off than their handicraft predecessors. Against this view it ought to be noted, firstly, that conditions in Yorkshire were not typical of those in the country as a whole and, secondly, that not all Yorkshire producers were small masters owning "small enclosures," and in business on their own account. Very considerable numbers of Yorkshire textile workers lived in cottages but worked in "little manufactories" owned by master clothiers. The gulf between master and man existed before the machine age. The use of steam power, necessitating access to greater capital resources, merely widened it, thereby making it more difficult for employees to become employers.

Other textile industries in existence in 1700 were silk weaving, linen and hosiery. Silk weaving owes much to Huguenot refugees who settled in Spitalfields at the end of the seventeenth century. The industry, however, was in a weak position because it was dependent for organzine, that is, thrown silk or yarn, on jealously monopolistic Italian producers. In 1719, however, John and Thomas Lombe built a factory driven by water power, near Derby, for the manufacture of thrown silk. On the expiry of the Lombe patent in 1732 silk factories were erected in Stockport, Manchester and Macclesfield. Silk factories were the forerunners of cotton mills. A generation later centres of silk manufactures became cotton centres, some early cotton mills being converted silk factories. Although silk fabrics were protected by heavy import duties, and were in great demand to clothe the upper classes, the industry never really took firm root. Italian and French workers were more efficient and produced cheaper fabrics. In addition the industry was based on an imported raw material, the export of which was severely restricted by Italian producers.

The linen industry, in contrast, was based on flax, a home produced fibre. The industry was in the main located in Ulster, Fifeshire and Forfarshire. In the eighteenth century hand linen spinning spread into the Highlands of Scotland. The making of hosiery, the general name for knitted goods such as stockings, was located in Yorkshire, Nottingham, Aberdeen and other areas. William Lee's invention of a framework knitting machine in 1589 eventually destroyed hand knitting. Framework workers, known as stockingers, obtained raw materials from an employer from whom they usually rented their machines. Conditions in what was considered to be "a starving trade" were notoriously bad, the small masters who controlled it never being able to provide regular work for their badly paid employees. As was the case with the lace industry, the hosiery trades were not revolutionised by power driven machinery until the second half of the nineteenth century.

When we turn from textiles to iron we find a much more serious state of affairs. Iron, steel and coal, the foundations on which modern civilisation rest, were industries of very limited importance before the industrial revolution. In fact, at the beginning of the eighteenth century, the iron industry was on the verge of disappearance. Iron was produced in Britain before the Roman era but then, and for long afterwards, methods of smelting were expensive, only a small proportion of iron being extracted from the ore. A major reason why costs of production were too great for iron to be in general use was that, before the eighteenth century, charcoal was the only satisfactory fuel used in smelting. The pre-eighteenth-century era can most appropriately be described as "the age of wood." Wood was the principal constructional material, being used in vast quantities by our forefathers for their ships, buildings, vehicles, agricultural implements and for household fuel. The tanning, glass and brewing industries were heavy consumers of wood, as were also the brickmakers, soap boilers and saltpetre and pottery manufacturers. Lastly, wood in the form of charcoal was used at all stages in the manufacture of iron.

We lack accurate knowledge of the timber resources of our island in past centuries, but concern at their unplanned exploitation led to restrictive legislation, in the interests of the navy, in Tudor times. In Charles II's reign the diarist John Evelyn criticised "the devouring iron mills." It would be better, he thought, "to purchase all our iron out of America than to exhaust our woods at home." Not the least of the problems which his friend Samuel Pepys wrestled with at the Admiralty was the provision of suitable timber for naval construction.

It is not easy to locate the centres of iron smelting before 1700. Industrial units were migratory and small in size, and have not left the indelible impressions on the landscape of their huge, modern counterparts. But owing to the dependence of the industry on iron ore, charcoal and water, forges and furnaces had to be located in forested areas, near iron-ore deposits and on sites where water was available to provide power for the bellows and transport for heavy commodities impossible to move by horse power on ill-made trackways. Before 1700 the most important areas of production were the Weald of Kent, Sussex and Surrey and the Forest of Dean. In the Forest of Dean smelters actually made use of refuse material from Roman furnaces as their predecessors had only been capable of extracting a small proportion of the iron the ore contained. From the latter part of the sixteenth century the timber famine had stimulated the expansion of the industry in the Midlands, North and South Wales, the Sheffield area, West Cumberland, Durham and Northumberland.

The Earl of Cork promoted iron smelting in Munster and encouragement was given to the exploitation of the forest wealth of New England. The migration of the iron industry, we learn from a parliamentary report in 1719, spread the evil of deforestation into many English counties. It did not solve the problem of increasing iron production. Contemporary Germany, with more abundant wood resources, produced much more. The total output of English bar iron, less than 20,000 tons in 1720, had fallen to 17,350 tons by 1740. Hence the need for imports from the Baltic countries and the American colonies, mainly from the former. As the search for ample supplies of charcoal had failed, iron masters directed their minds to finding an alternative fuel. The solution was to be found in the use of coal.

The coalmining industry is very old. Coal was used for fuel in Roman Britain but little, if anything, is known about how it was mined or of the way of life of those who produced it. In Durham, coalmining is probably more than a thousand years old. In the Halifax area, where coal outcrops on the hillsides, mining goes back to at least 1308. The sixteenth-century cloth makers of York were envious of the access to "fire, good and cheap," possessed by their Halifax competitors. Early pits were shallow excavations, but before the seventeenth century increasing demand stimulated the sinking of deep shafts. As early as the fourteenth century coal was being mined underground on an extensive scale at Ferryhill between Darlington and Durham. The chief areas of production in the early eighteenth century were on the banks of the Wear and Tyne, Forth and Clyde. Production was small, 2,250,000 tons in 1660, 2,500,000 tons in 1700 and 5,000,000 tons in 1750. The relatively slow rate of expansion indicates that rapid industrial development was not taking place in the first half of the eighteenth century. Coal was used for domestic purposes. Coal burning was banned in London in 1273 but from at least the fourteenth century a considerable export went by sea from Newcastle, hence "the hellish and dismall cloude of Sea Coale" which plagued the inhabitants of Restoration London. Coal had long been used to evaporate salt from sea water and it was also in demand by the brewing, distilling, brickmaking, pottery, sugar refining, soap-boiling, cutlery and nail-making industries.

Before 1700 the industry had become a highly capitalist one, and necessarily so, as pit sinking was a costly and highly speculative venture. In some Durham pits considerable numbers of workers were employed, but any considerable increase in the size and depth of collieries was hampered by technical difficulties. Poisonous gases, fire and water were hazards to be overcome. The keen interest of members of the Royal Society after 1660 in technological problems is shown by their discussions on methods of finding coal, the causes of explosions, the possibility of building canals to reduce coal prices on the London market, underground drainage, and using coal as a substitute for charcoal in smelting iron. The nineteenth century was to see progress in the solution of these problems. But in the eighteenth century the hazards of getting coal became worse, as the use of the steam pumps invented by Savery (1698) and Newcomen (1712) encouraged the sinking of deeper pits. The social problems of the industry were also serious. Women and children were employed. In Scotland colliers lived in a state of bondage, legal emancipation being delayed until 1775 and 1799. In north eastern England, the principal coalmining area, the industry was controlled by an exclusive company, the Hostmen of Newcastle, which regulated prices and output. Despite legislative attempts in the seventeenth century to make combinations in the industry illegal, and the formation in 1760 of combinations by London coal merchants, the Hostmen retained their grip on the London market until the mid-nineteenth century. By that time, however, with the adaptation of the steam engine to drive machinery, and revolutionary changes in means of transport, the coalmining industry was entering on an era of unprecedented expansion.

Agriculture

The post-1700 changes in methods of agriculture and rural life have been described by historians as an agrarian revolution. The Agrarian Revolution was a necessary complement to the Industrial Revolution. Its affects became noticeable during the reign of George III (1760–1820) in an improved rotation of crops, better breeds of animals, new agricultural implements, intensified studies of the possibilities of different types of soil and the enclosure of open fields, commons and wastes. Traditionally cultivation had been organised to provide subsistence, but long before 1700 economic forces had been operating to make land a source of wealth. Bishop Latimer's "farming gentlemen" in the reign of Edward VI (1547–53) invested capital in land in the expectation of good profits. In consequence in some parts of the country traditional farming methods were undermined, production for the market taking the place of production for consumption. Before 1700 only a limited acreage of the countryside had been affected, but during the eighteenth century economic pressures became more acute. In addition to the influence exerted by industrial changes, expansion of urban life and transport improvements, there was the unprecedented increase in the size of the population. In an age when there were no facilities for extensive importation of bulky foodstuffs a change in agricultural practices was imperative. If they had not been introduced, Englishmen would have starved.

The methods of cultivating the soil in general use during the reign of Queen Anne (1702–14) differed in no significant respect from those prevailing when William the Conquerer was crowned, despite the advances made during the sixteenth and seventeenth centuries in knowledge of how to increase production. Eighteenth-century improvements in agricultural practice must be seen in relation to the expansion in biological knowledge and to the agricultural innovations of the preceding two centuries. In agriculture, as in all other fields of human endeavour, men build on knowledge handed down by their forefathers. The microscope made man aware of the world of micro-organisms. In England pioneers in microscopic observations were Robert Hooke (1635–1703) and Nehemiah Crewe (1641–1712), the latter discovering that in the plant world male and female species exist. Contemporary microscopists included the Italian Marcelli Malpighi, and in Holland Jan Swammerdam and Anthony van Leewenhoek. Their discoveries, known to members of the Royal Society, gave to men a knowledge of nature and her ways essential to advances in medicine and to improvements in the practice of agriculture. In the sixteenth century agricultural textbooks were written explaining how low yields could be increased. Fitzherbert's *Boke of Husbandry* (1534) and *Boke of Surveyinge and Improvements* (1539) were published, followed by Thomas Tusser's *Hundreth Good Pointes of Husbandrie* written in verse and re-issued in 1579 as *Five Hundreth Good Pointes of Husbandrie, united to as many Good Pointes of Huswifrey*.

In the seventeenth century several writers suggested improvements which were not generally adopted until the reign of George III, some of them copied from Dutch practices. In many fields of human endeavour, the Dutch in the seventeenth century were the teachers of Europe. In the reign of Charles I, under the direction of the Dutchman, Cornelius Vermuyden, the first considerable drainage scheme was undertaken in the Fens. Worthy of note also is the development of commercial horticulture, which owes much to Dutch example, and the growing practice during the Elizabethan and Stuart periods of cultivating flower and kitchen gardens. Under James I gardeners in the London area were incorporated by Royal Charter as "A Company of the City of London," while later commercial gardening in the home counties was encouraged during the Protectorate of Cromwell. The growing interest in agriculture is reflected in the consideration given to the production of good seed on a commercial basis. By the mid-eighteenth century nurserymen and seed merchants were advertising their wares in printed catalogues.

Outstandingly important among the agricultural pioneers in seventeenth-century England was Sir Robert Weston. Arthur Young considered him to be "a greater benefactor than Newton," a judgment that has some merit in the light of the revolutionary consequences that followed the adoption of Weston's recommendations. A Catholic royalist refugee in Flanders during the Civil War, Weston wrote about 1645 for the instruction of his sons his *Discours of the Husbandrie used in Brabant and Flanders*. Impressed by Flemish agricultural practice, he advocated turnip cultivation for winter fodder and clover sowing for hay. On his return home he practised what he preached on his Surrey estate, but more than a century was to elapse before the rotation of crops he recommended became standard practice in Norfolk.

A pre-condition of farming improvements was that land should be brought into individual ownership. In 1700, however, over large parts of the country agriculture was in the hands of under-capitalised, open field farmers, wedded to customary ways and producing primarily for subsistence. Described by Professor Vinogradoff as "a community of shareholders in husbandry," the open field system prevailed in many parts of Northern Europe from the Bay of Biscay to Russia. Its origins are hidden by the mists which shroud the distant past. Tacitus refers to it in the first century of our era, and Charlemagne in orders issued to his bailiffs. The laws of King Ine make plain that it had long functioned in full working order in his seventh-century kingdom of Wessex, while it has survived to our own time in the Nottinghamshire village of Laxton. The compelling force of custom and human conservatism, potent as they are, cannot alone account for its survival. Excessively complicated and ridiculous as the system may appear to us and to its eighteenth-century critics, its continuance through so many centuries is an indication that it satisfied basic human needs. In periods lacking the tools and equipment of modern men, and the personal security governments nowadays can guarantee, co-operation gave to our forefathers a security that the individual cannot provide for himself against the forces of nature and predatory outsiders. Despite its many disadvantages, the system provided, at least in years of good harvests, a sufficiency for village subsistence, plus a surplus to feed the relatively small urban areas and the non-producing classes.

The essential features of the open field system of cultivation changed little through long centuries. They are usually described as follows. The pattern of life, dating from unquiet times, dictated the needs for the rude dwellings of the inhabitants to be grouped closely together near the manor house and lord's demesne. Outside the village lay the arable land, usually three but sometimes two or even four large fields, fenced in only during the months when crops were growing. The open field cultivators held land in scattered strips, an arrangement which, in modern eyes, appears to be inconvenient. Actually in an age when plough teams were not individually owned, the long, narrow strip was the only satisfactory ploughable unit. In 1700 the holders of the strips were freeholders, owners of the land, or copyholders, descendants of medieval villeins who by the sixteenth century had commuted labour services for fixed monetary payments. The subsequent rise in price levels was advantageous to copyholders, their monetary obligations having by the eighteenth century become a very light burden. The strips were cultivated under a system of rotation, which, when there were three fields, was usually wheat, oats or barley, and fallow. The village area also included the common or waste on which the animals were pastured and the Lammas lands or meadow from which hay was mown. Procedure was rigidly controlled by the Court Leet, strip holders being obliged to conform with "the custom of the manor." That is, they were rigidly restricted by rules handed down from immemorial antiquity.

We must beware, however, of making facile generalisations about pre-1700 village organisation. Few, if any, villages would conform to the pattern of lay-out described in the preceding paragraph. Each village has its own history, the true picture being one of infinite variety, not of standardisation. Not all the villagers cultivated strips in the open fields or possessed rights entitling them to use the commons. In many villages would be found lease-holders cultivating compact farms on long or short leases, some being merely tenants-at-will. Such farms had been carved out of the lord's demesne or from what in past centuries had been uncultivated forest or heath. Sometimes compact farms had come into existence by agreement among open field farms to exchange strips and withdraw them from the area of communal cultivation. At some distance from the village would be found the hovels of the cottagers or squatters. They cut turf and timber from the commons, reared poultry and, more rarely, possessed a cow. The squatters were a useful source from which hired help might be obtained but they lacked written legal rights, possessing only customary rights tacitly sanctioned by long occupation. It is also worth noting that our forefathers could not have sustained life on a purely grain harvest, hence there must have been land on which vegetables such as peas and beans were grown, and after Tudor times, possibly potatoes.

The defects of the open field system were numerous. Land was wasted in innumerable paths, enlarged by careless travellers. Tusser publicised the complaints of open field farmers:

> *In Norfolk behold the dispaire*
> *of tillage too much to be borne*
> *By drovers from faire to faire*
> *and others destroying the corne.*

Occupiers were bound by rigid rules, forced to sow and reap at fixed times and to treat all kinds of soil alike. New crop rotations could not be experimented with unless all agreed. Sir Richard Sutton's Act (1773) permitted changes in land use if the owner, tithe holder and three-quarters of the occupiers approved. Very rarely, however, was advantage taken of the Act to set aside land for the cultivation of such crops as turnips and clover. Further, strips were too narrow to permit of cross ploughing, and adequate drainage was impossible, the arable being full of wet places and overrun with weeds. Time was wasted owing to the scattered layout of strips sited far from the village, hence reaping and carting expenses were unduly high. Vexatious disputes caused bad relationships with litiguous-minded neighbours. The unsheltered, hedgeless open fields afforded no protection to animals whose manure was wasted owing to the immensity of the areas over which they roamed. Promiscuity perpetuated herds of scraggy cattle and flocks of poor quality sheep. It was impossible to prevent disease spreading among animals herded together on the commons, ill-fed half the year and half-starved in winter. Careless strip holders injured the more enterprising, progressive minded farmers being held back by an ignorant, suspicious and prejudiced peasantry. The open field farmers, by and large, were not very progressive, not open to improvements, and lacked capital to manure their strips adequately, to pay for expensive drainage schemes, and to improve their stock by hiring costly bulls and rams. Only men with capital could do these things, and only if they farmed land individually.

The open field system was widespread, but never universal in Great Britain. The area in which it was dominant may be broadly defined as lying between lines from Portland Bill to Bristol and continued along the Welsh border and thence to north of the Tees: along the south coast to Sussex and north to the Wash, excluding the Thames basin. The area thus delimited was Anglo-Saxon. In it the village became the unit of settlement. In Northumberland, Durham, the Lake District, Lancashire, Devon, Cornwall and Scotland, where hill country prevailed, the economy was a pastoral one. The people lived in scattered hamlets and isolated farm houses. The arable was divided into two fields, the infield and the outfield. Continuous cropping, with liberal manuring, was practised on the infield. Part of the outfield was used for crop raising until exhausted and then left fallow, another area being sown. The crops raised were oats, and a coarse variety of barley, called bere. This system of agriculture, perhaps wrongly called "the Celtic System," existed also in parts of the Wolds of the East Riding, in Nottinghamshire and in Norfolk. Its diffusion is most probably explained by geological and climatic factors, as it is found in Europe also in hilly, forested areas of poor soils with heavy rainfall and marshy characteristics.

The open field system was never characteristic of the agricultural pattern in the Thames Valley, where the removal of the forest cover came later, nor in Kent and East Anglia. In Kent, settled by the Jutes, compact holdings were the unit of tenure. In East Anglia Danish settlers introduced a land system in which a higher proportion of the population than elsewhere was "free." From very early times, therefore, in Kent and East Anglia, a money economy, stimulated by the development of trade with Europe and the needs of the London market, led to the appearance of a type of agriculture in which individual producers grew crops for sale.

It was not until the eighteenth and nineteenth centuries that open field methods of cultivation came to an end in the Midland Counties, the area between the Isle of Wight and Yorkshire. The process is a very complex one, hence generalisations are difficult to make. Much more local research is needed before it will be possible to write with certainty on the subject. It is important, however, to realise that the land enclosures of the post-1700 period were the last phase in a process that can be traced back to the thirteenth century. The earliest enclosures were of "the waste" undertaken to meet rising food demands where population was increasing. The Statute of Merton (1236) permitted partial enclosure of the commons by the lord, provided sufficient was left to satisfy the needs of his tenants. But the two periods when enclosing activity was greatest were the sixteenth century and the period of parliamentary enclosures after 1700.

In the Tudor period the desire for wealth became a noticeable mainspring of human action. Land came increasingly to be regarded as a source of profit, greater efficiency being consequently sought in rural affairs. An increased circulation of money, rising prices and considerable development of trade and industry coincided with an increase in the numbers of artisans and merchants, and the development of urban life. The isolation of rural districts therefore begins to break down, production for sale in towns becoming a feature of Tudor agriculture. In the areas affected open fields vanished. The influence of the London food market was particularly important, being felt far afield, and not only in the home counties which supplied corn, fruit, vegetables and dairy produce. In Queen Elizabeth I's reign corn reached London from the distant Trent valley and mutton from the Cotswolds and Northampton. But the sixteenth-century agricultural change which attracted most notice was that for sheep rearing, the contemporary expansion of the woollen industry making wool production extremely profitable.

Sixteenth-century enclosures were of two kinds, by the villagers and by the lords of manors. That undertaken by the villagers was secured by an amicable exchanging of strips and the resultant formation of compact farms cultivated by individuals free from communal controls. Enclosures of this type were recommended by writers like Fitzherbert and Tusser and were productive of improved husbandry. The second type, by the lords of manors, was usually undertaken to profit from the demand for wool. The lord might turn the demesne into sheep pasture, thereby causing unemployment among farm workers, or enclose the arable fields and commons by force or legal chicanery. Contemporary pamphlets, statutes and sermons are eloquent on the resultant decay of tillage and grievous unemployment. One Elizabethan writer complained:

> Sheep have eat up our meadows and our downs
> Our corn, our wood, whole villages and towns.

Sir Thomas More in *Utopia* (1516) and Bishop Latimer, in a sermon preached before Edward VI, were critics of the grievous social consequences of farming for profit in rural England. The decay of tillage and the increase in numbers of wandering beggars and sturdy vagabonds prompted Tudor governments from 1487 onwards to pass a series of Acts against enclosures for sheep farming. Land enclosures were most numerous in the first half of the century and provoked considerable rioting and violent action by workers adversely affected. But before the end of Elizabeth I's reign the movement lost its impetus, due probably not so much to government action and mob violence as to the operation of economic law. Changes in the relative prices of corn and wool made sheep rearing less attractive.

Enclosures for wool production certainly caused acute distress, but they were on a smaller scale than readers of descriptions of contemporary distress might infer. England did not become a vast sheep walk. If it had, Englishmen would have starved for lack of corn. One estimate is that beteen 1455 and 1607 half a million acres were enclosed, the chief areas affected being the Midland counties of Northampton, Leicester, Warwick, Oxford and Buckingham. In the Stuart period it is mixed farming and tillage that attract most attention. There was a certain amount of voluntary enclosure during

AGRARIAN AND INDUSTRIAL CHANGES 29

the seventeenth century, including "intakes" on Pennine moorland and Fenland drainage. Land enclosure on a large scale was postponed until Hanoverian times. It was then that the death blow was delivered to the open field system.

CHAPTER III

THE AGRARIAN REVOLUTION

In the eighteenth century, the introduction of improved agricultural practices became imperative to satisfy the food needs of an expanding population. The necessary agricultural innovations were pioneered by improving gentleman farmers and wealthy landowners, who by their experiments and example exercised a decisive influence in British farming. One of the most notable was Jethro Tull (1674–1741), "the greatest individual improver" British agriculture has ever known. On his farm at Howbery near Crowmarsh in Oxfordshire and from 1709 at Prosperous Farm, Shalbourne in Berkshire, Tull discarded reliance on traditional methods despite opposition from his custom-bound labourers and criticism from sceptical neighbours. The results of his experiments, and the fruits of his observations of the methods used by vine cultivators in South France, were given to the world in *The New Horse Hoeing Husbandry* (1731). "The more the iron is among the roots," Tull wrote, "the better for the crops." He advocated clean farming, deep ploughing and economy in the use of seeds. Instead of sowing broadcast, he invented a device for spacing seeds in regular rows and a horse hoe to uproot the weeds among the growing crops. Although Tull's knowledge of the theory of agricultural science was meagre, much of his practice was beneficial. He claimed to have harvested wheat crops without manuring for thirteen successive years from the same land. This can be criticised as bad farming practice, and cited as evidence of his lack of proper understanding both of the mechanism of plant nutrition, and the part played by manures in increasing the fertility of the soil. Tullian ideas provoked much controversy and gained acceptance very slowly. Nevertheless, his contributions to agricultural advance were considerable, ensuring that a more thorough use was made of the natural resources in the soil than was possible by reliance on traditional methods.

A contemporary of Tull, Viscount Townshend (1674–1738), after disagreeing with his brother-in-law Sir Robert Walpole in 1730, deserted politics for agriculture. On the marshy, sandy soils of his estate at Raynham in West Norfolk, Townshend re-introduced the former Norfolk practice of marling, and used Tull's drilling and hoeing techniques. As his nickname "Turnip" Townshend reminds us, he was famed for the field cultivation of turnips, hitherto garden vegetables, and for popularising the Norfolk four-course rotation, wheat, turnips, barley and clover. This rotation avoided the necessity of leaving land fallow every third year, the clover, which put nitrogen into the soil, keeping the land in good heart. The farmer was provided with cash crops, wheat, and barley for brewing, while the turnips and the clover turned into hay could be fed to the animals. An adequate scientific explanation of Townshend's farming methods had to wait for the researches of nineteenth-century biologists armed with improved microscopes. Meanwhile, the "New Husbandry" proved more profitable than the old methods in the well-drained soils of Norfolk, and gave to that county the lead in English agriculture. In particular, the growing of turnips and clover, by providing winter fodder, made it possible to discontinue the autumn slaughter and to breed better farm stock.

Until the eighteenth century little attention was paid to livestock. The rearing of animals, though it was no doubt one of the most profitable occupations of our ancestors, was also one in which losses were considerable, due to disease and the Michaelmas slaughter. Cows and oxen were reared for milk and draught purposes. Sheep, important for maintaining land fertility and treading the soil, were bred for their wool, skins and manure, ewe's milk being also a source of food and cheese-making. Bred on ill-drained commons and wastes, where mating occurred at random, animals were small in size and weight. The poor quality meat they produced was supplemented by that of pigs, which roamed the woodlands and commons under the care of the village swineherd, and by eggs from domestic poultry. The increasing demand for food, however, made meat production a profitable enterprise. Consequently, attention was directed to securing improved breeds. In an age when modern scientific theories of the mechanism of heredity were unknown, experiments to this end were based upon empirical methods. Impressive improvements nevertheless were obtained, the Smithfield Club (1798) playing a major part in encouraging developments in this field.

The outstanding pioneer in the development of specialised breeds was Robert Bakewell (1725–95) of Dishley Grange near Loughborough in Leicestershire. In his stud book he meticulously recorded the genealogy of his beasts, and carefully selected for breeding purposes animals with the characteristics he wished to perpetuate. His methods produced first the Leicesters and later the New Leicesters, a breed of sheep noted for high grade quality wool. From Dutch stock he bred black carthorses. Less successful were his long-horned cattle, yielding good quality beef, but deficient in milk supply. Possibly Bakewell's comparative lack of success with cattle was due, not to his breeding techniques, but to the poor potential of the Midland breed he used in his experiments. Many farmers visited Dishley Grange and left impressed by what they had seen. Bakewell's importance does not rest wholly upon what he himself accomplished, but also upon the influence he had on others who copied his techniques. George Culley of Northumberland (1753–1813) bred cattle, and John Ellman in Sussex improved the Southdown breed of sheep. Farmers in Durham at the end of the eighteenth century were prominent in developing pasture farming and increasing milk production. Particularly noteworthy were Charles and Robert Colling of Ketton near Darlington (1751–1836). Applying Bakewell's principles, they reared the Durham shorthorns, valuable both for milk and meat. Durham became an exporter of this breed to other parts of the country. By 1820 shorthorns were being marketed for breeding purposes in the United States.

A notable practitioner of the "New Husbandry" techniques was Thomas William Coke, first Earl of Leicester of the second creation (1752–1842). When in 1776 he inherited the Holkham estate near the Norfolk coast, it consisted of thousands of acres of empty wind-swept salt marsh and heather clad commons, over which his wife was warned that two rabbits fought for each blade of grass. Forty years later, the annual rental value of the estate had risen from £2200 to £20,000. Instead of 200 ill-clad, poverty stricken people, there were 1100 inhabitants, well-housed prosperous tenant farmers and their dependants. At a time when, in many counties, agricultural labourers had become paupers, the Workhouse at Holkham had been demolished because it was not needed. These creditable achievements flowed from Coke's intelligent application of the farming techniques pioneered by Tull, Townshend and Bakewell. By practical example on land he farmed himself, and by granting long leases at fair rents to tenants who were given every help and encouragement to discard old ways. Coke turned a desolate waste into a well-tilled estate, stocked with herds of sleek cattle and flocks of well nourished sheep. Between 1778 and 1821 visitors from near and far arrived to see the crops, animals, buildings and implements on the estate. At the last, of what had come to be known as the "Holkham Sheep Shearings," 7000 visitors are said to have been present. Coke planted some 3000 acres with trees, encouraged the use of potatoes as food, taught agricultural methods to his tenants and their children, and pioneered the use of oilcake for fattening Scottish cattle travelling through Norfolk for sale at Smithfield Market.

Like other pioneers, before and since, Coke had difficulty in overcoming the obstinate adherence of his tenants to traditional ways. But before he died, at a very advanced age, he had deservedly earned the deep devotion of a tenantry, whom he had, by precept, example and fair dealing, raised from poverty to prosperity. The example he set in the use of the new techniques was copied by other great landowners. These included the Duke of Bedford, whose annual sheep shearings at Woburn Abbey, like those of Coke, attracted visitors from far and near, Lord Leconfield at Petworth and King George III, who had a model farm at Windsor, and using the pseudonym "Ralph Robinson" contributed to Arthur Young's *Annals of Agriculture*.

The Norfolk system of farming was more suited to the light, well-drained soils of Eastern England than to either the heavier clay lands or the ill-drained, wetter areas of the hilly north and west. But even in areas well suited for the use of the new techniques change came slowly. Many factors explain this, among them shortage of capital, the innate conservatism of working farmers, and the neglect of some landowners to offer terms of tenure sufficiently attractive to overcome innate prejudices against change. Land workers naturally shrank from the considerable alterations involved in the economic and social foundations of village life. In an age of poor transport, the educational and cultural isolation of rural life was not easy to break down. Neither was the problem of finding markets to absorb increased productivity capable of easy solution. Land enclosures, it is worth noting, were speeded up after 1760, when improved transport facilities by road and canal became available, and during the Napoleonic Wars when corn prices were high. Apart, however, from the human and economic factors involved, it should be borne in mind that standardisation of agricultural practice is impossible in a country like our own where, small as it is, there are considerable variations in soils, physical conditions and climate. Methods successful in one area could not be used successfully in others.

The man who more than any other was responsible for publicising the new techniques was Arthur Young (1741–1820), "the greatest of all English writers on agriculture." Although unsuccessful as a practical farmer, Young was a literary artist whose publications gave wide currency to the new knowledge. His books, based on travels in England, France and Ireland, are a mine of information on contemporary farming methods, transport conditions and the way of life of the people. His experiences as a farmer are described in *A Course of Experimental Agriculture* (1770). He wrote down his observations as a traveller in books published between 1768 and 1771, *A Six Weeks Tour through the Southern Counties of England and Wales*,

A Six Months Tour through the North of England and *Farmers' Tour through the East of England*. In 1768 he published *Farmers' Letter to the People of England* and in 1771 the *Farmers' Calendar*. From 1784 onwards Young edited a monthly journal, in 45 volumes, *Annals of Agriculture*. Students of contemporary Ireland and France find of inestimable value his *Tour of Ireland* and *Travels in France*. In 1793 Young was appointed Secretary of the newly formed Board of Agriculture, in essence a society for distributing agricultural knowledge, collecting information and suggesting means of increasing farm productivity. The Board lasted until 1822. Under Young's guidance, until blindness curtailed his activities, a nationwide survey was undertaken, the results of which are of great value to students of the period.

Young noted that, unlike the pre-1789 French aristocracy, the British nobility and gentry were interested in agriculture. Small farmers, on the other hand, except in East Anglia, he castigated for their ignorance and obstinate adherence to old-fashioned ways. Lack of knowledge of the "New Husbandry," outside Norfolk, struck him forcibly. From him we learn that in the early part of the reign of George III enormous areas were uncultivated. Hundreds of thousands of acres in the six northern counties of England and in Devon, Cornwall and Wales consisted of primeval waste land. A large percentage of the rest of Britain was still unused for food production, being undrained swamp, uncleared forest and wild heathland. Such lands, Young considered, were neglected assets that ought to be improved to yield more food. Eighteenth-century travellers braving the hazards of journeying to remote areas like the Lake District were apt to judge such regions like Defoe as "the wildest, most barren and frightful," not as areas of rural charm affording spiritual and mental refreshment.

The remedy for the eighteenth-century need for more food, preached by Young, was land enclosure. This involved, firstly, the productive use of vast areas of forest, fen, moorland and hill country and, secondly, the enclosure of open fields and commons. During the war period (1793–1815), when corn prices rose, considerable areas of waste land were brought under the plough. But the ill-drained wet areas of the North and West, and heavy water-logged clay lands were not suitable for the growth of such crops as turnips and potatoes. To bring them into productive use new underground means of drainage were needed to avoid wastage of manure on water-logged soil. A method of draining sloping land suggested by Joseph Elkington in Warwickshire in 1764 was improved upon by a Perthshire cotton mill manager, James Smith of Deanston, whose treatise *Remarks on Thorough Drainage and Deep Ploughing* was published in 1835, and by the invention in 1843 of porous clay pipes by John Reede.

The aspect of the enclosure movement that has attracted most attention is that which involved the disappearance of open fields and commons. Such enclosures could take place by mutual consent when few landowners were concerned, with interests sufficiently large to ensure that their will prevailed. Land enclosures of this kind took place on an extensive scale, one estimate of their extent in the eighteenth century, that of the historians J. L. and B. Hammond, being eight million acres. Elsewhere it was necessary to promote an Enclosure Bill which was given statutory force by Parliament. The rate of enclosure by this latter procedure, slow in the early eighteenth century, accelerated rapidly after 1760, particularly during the 1770–80 period and during the Napoleonic Wars when the need for home-grown food was very great. Exact knowledge of the acreage affected is hard to ascertain, but the following estimate by the Hammonds in Volume I of their *Village Labourer* may be accepted as probably near the truth.

Years	Common fields and some waste		Waste only	
	Acts	Acreage	Acts	Acreage
1700–60	152	237,845	56	74,518
1761–1801	1,479	2,428,721	521	752,150
1802–44	1,075	1,610,302	808	939,043
TOTAL	2,706	4,276,868	1,385	1,765,711

The area most affected by the enclosures of open fields was the broad belt in the Midlands stretching from the Dorset and Hampshire coasts to Yorkshire. In addition the cultivated area was extended by the enclosure of immense areas of wastes and commons. By the middle of the nineteenth century, almost all open fields had vanished, and the rural landscape had taken on the modern appearance of fields separated by stone walls or hedges.

The initiative in promoting Enclosure Bills was invariably taken by substantial proprietors, others concerned very often not being consulted or informed. In 1774 a Standing Order of the House of Commons laid down that public notices should be affixed to parish church doors on three successive Sundays in August or September. To diminish expense and facilitate procedure it was enacted by the

General Enclosure Act of 1801 "that certain clauses usually contained in such Acts should be compressed in one law." The General Enclosure Act of 1836, permitting enclosure without an Act of Parliament, if two-thirds of those concerned agreed, afforded some measure of protection to the interests of the smaller proprietors. This policy was carried a stage further by the Enclosure Act of 1845. Enclosure Commissioners were appointed to examine enclosure petitions and authorised to implement those they approved. After 1852 the approval of Parliament was necessary for new enclosures and by 1893 that of the Board of Agriculture. This legislation, however, did not effectively prevent common land becoming private property. Between 1845 and 1864, 614,000 acres of common land were fenced off by private landowners. Fortunately, acquisitive landowners were challenged after 1865 when the "Commons Open Spaces and Footpaths Preservation Society" was formed, following a meeting attended by Sir Charles Dilke, John Stuart Mill, Professor T. H. Huxley and others in the chambers of Lord Eversley in the Inner Temple.

To the public-spirited activities of members of this Society and other organisations such as the National Trust and the Council for the Preservation of Rural England, we are indebted for the 1·5 million acres of common land that still remain, comprising about 4 per cent of the land surface of England and Wales. Two-thirds of it consists of moorlands in the northern counties. Other open spaces include the Town Moor in Newcastle upon Tyne, Epping Forest, Wimbledon Common and Hampstead Heath. The preservation of these commons has demanded constant vigilance, the main enemy being not land-grabbing landowners but government departments acting under the provisions of Defence Acts, Highways Acts and Town and Country Planning legislation. But fortunately nowadays, under the Commons Registration Act of 1965, Claims of Rights can be registered. These rights, varying from taking herbage, gorse, underwood, turf or peat, to being allowed to walk across it, once registered with county and county borough councils, will for all time end uncertainties as to how many people enjoy rights of common.

That neither the public interest, nor that of uninfluential occupiers of land was safe-guarded in private Enclosure Bill procedure cannot be disputed. Through Parliaments, which after the Revolution of 1688 were dominated by aristocratic landed interests, well connected landowners were able to secure the passage of Bills, advantageous to themselves and ruinous to the rights and livelihoods of other land occupiers. Arthur Young, strong advocate of enclosures that he was, nevertheless wrote in 1801 that "by nineteen out of twenty Bills the poor are injured." Why was this so? In theory,

Parliamentary Committees had to make sure consideration was given to the opinions of all concerned. In practice, the landed aristocracy was able to ignore all but substantial objectors. Procedure in Parliament was not governed by precise regulations defining the proportion of those concerned in enclosure proposals whose consent should be obtained. Sometimes the consent of three-quarters, sometimes of four-fifths was required. But as these proportions referred to acreage, not to persons, an unfair advantage was given to substantial landowners.

More often than not the consent of the smaller proprietors was assumed in the absence of evidence to the contrary. Promoters of Bills were not required to furnish precise evidence that others agreed. There are numerous reports extant of popular violence against enclosure commissioners, but very few records of poor men presenting evidence to a Parliamentary Committee. Lord Lincoln, in a speech to the House of Commons in 1845, summarised concisely the injustices under which the poor suffered. "This I know," he said, "that in 19 cases out of 20 Committees of this House sitting on Private Bills neglected the rights of the Poor ... they were neglected in consequence of the Committee being permitted to remain in ignorance of the claims of the poor man, because by reason of his very poverty he is unable to come to London for counsel, to produce witnesses and to urge his claims." Further, as enclosure Bills were dealt with in Committees attended only by members interested in making sure promoters got their way, it was inevitable that due consideration would not be given to the cases of the poorer occupiers of land.

The reasons given by land enclosers to justify their actions have an air of plausibility. Public interest, not self interest, was said to be the paramount consideration. Attention was drawn to the technical deficiency of open field agriculture and to the imperative need to satisfy national food requirements. Neither the moral welfare nor the economic interests of the poor themselves, it was said, were served by perpetuating a system which allowed squatters and cottagers to live lives of indolence and intemperance on village commons. The contrary view, held by those enjoying customary rights to use the commons, that their eviction would deprive them of a livelihood and the public of the cheap provisions they produced, received scant support in parliamentary circles. Eviction meant a choice of distasteful alternatives, work in manufacturing towns or pauperisation in their native village.

Any consideration of the consequences of the destruction of the old village community must balance the undoubted greater technical efficiency of the new order of things, against the resultant social evils. Individual farming for profit meant higher yields than was possible under communal husbandry for subsistence. Much uncultivated grassland was ploughed, which sometimes proved to be more productive than the former arable. The use of primitive machines, threshing machines for example, and fertilisers became possible. The application of methods of selection and inbreeding revolutionised livestock and created modern breeds of animals. None of the more than 40 different breeds of British sheep today, for example, existed in 1700. The growing urban centres provided markets for increased production, and improvements in means of communication, first by roads and canals, and later by railways, the means of transporting it. Hence capital was attracted to farming, which became an industry carried on for profit.

The social consequences of land enclosures have been judged more harshly. The crudest judgments picture English villages, supposedly inhabited before 1700 by yeomen farmers, being dispossessed by greedy landlords who amassed large estates, subsequently cultivated by tenant farmers employing landless labourers at near starvation rates of pay. We need not challenge the view that large landowners derived considerable benefits. In an England ruled by an aristocratic landed class it would have been surprising if matters had been arranged otherwise. But to evaluate fairly the results of enclosures other factors must be taken into consideration. Post-1700 enclosures were the culmination of a long and slow process. Not all England was affected by eighteenth-century enclosures. In many areas much enclosure had taken place earlier, betrayed by the still extant pre-1700 farmhouses and cottages scattered over the countryside, not grouped together near church and manor as was customary in medieval open field communities.

The notion that England before 1700 was predominantly a land of small farmers rudely dispossessed after 1700 by land grabbing aristocrats does not square with the facts. Long before 1700 leasehold tenants had become increasingly important, some lessees cultivating large farms on land already enclosed. It was only by leasing land that owners of large estates, whether individual or corporate, could have ensured its productive use. Details of early eighteenth-century farming leases by the Dean and Chapter of Durham Cathedral, for example, are still extant, particularising the farming practice to which tenants were required to adhere. All available evidence points to the conclusion that before the era of parliamentary enclosures capitalist farming was growing in importance. Parliamentary enclosures tended to check rather than to encourage development on these lines. All who could substantiate a legal claim before enclosure commissioners received compact areas in lieu of their open field and common rights. In consequence farms in individual ownership came into existence, farmers and their labourers living in newly constructed dwellings dotted over the countryside. During the war period after 1793, when agriculture was prosperous, a large acreage was enclosed. Farmers cultivating small acreages prospered owing to wartime restrictions on imports and legislative encouragement to corn production to meet the food needs of the home market and the armed forces. Under the Corn Act of 1804 importation was prohibited until the home price was 66*s.* a quarter, a price which gave a good return to the producer. Such a situation encouraged the ploughing up of hitherto unused moor and hill country, it enabled landlords to raise rents, and farm incomes from both large and small farms to increase.

Unfortunately these halcyon times did not endure. The coming of peace in 1815 ended agricultural wartime prosperity. Demobilisation flooded the country with soldiers and sailors for whom there was no work. Government contracts for farm produce ceased. Urban manufacturing centres, where unemployment was high, could not absorb all surplus farm produce. A further blow which befell the rural areas was the accelerating pace of urban industrialisation which deprived agricultural households of by-employments, such as spinning, and struck severe blows at many full-time industrial occupations hitherto rural in location. Despite the Corn Act of 1815, which raised the home price before imports were allowed to 80*s.* a quarter, agriculture became a depressed industry, remaining so until the middle of the nineteenth century. It was the post-1815 depression rather than Enclosure Acts which forced many small farmers to leave the land.

The icy wind of change also had grievous consequences for landlords, who had to accept lower rents, and for large-scale farmers who had speculated during the war and ploughed land more suited to pasture. Many had improvidently spent high wartime incomes on lavish living on the assumption that good times would be permanent. Fine houses, magnificent outbuildings, elegant furniture and wives and daughters who had ceased to assist in the work of the farm, became memories of a way of life that had vanished. Instead, neglected farmsteads, untilled, weedy fields, untrimmed hedges and broken fences were for more than a generation to litter the English rural scene. But the post-1815 depression did not uproot all small farmers. Their numbers declined, but in the mid-nineteenth century they were still a very important element in the English agricultural economy. In 1851 over 60 per cent of English farms were less than 100 acres in size.

The strictures passed on land enclosures as detrimental to the weak have, however, some justification. Enclosure Commissioners in making awards recognised the claims of those who had legal rights, but all too often those with rights based merely on long prescription had their claims disallowed. Before 1640 Tudor and Stuart monarchs had on occasions intervened to disallow enclosures which threatened to depopulate the countryside. Later monarchs, lacking the apparatus of conciliar administration through which their predecessors had ruled, could not protect the lowly deprived of immemorial rights by enclosure procedures sanctified by statutes enacted by an aristocratic oligarchy. But even if compensation was given, in money or small land allotments, the recipients rarely benefited permanently. Money was soon spent, sometimes in the alehouse. Those who were given small holdings, but deprived of the right to use the commons for pasture, were often bought out by wealthier neighbours. Heavy legal charges, and the costs of fencing and clearing land for cultivation, were obligations difficult to honour, hence the sharp rise in the numbers of landless labourers. One such bitterly complained, as Arthur Young has recorded, that "Parliament may be tender of property; all I know is that I had a cow and an Act of Parliament has taken it from me." Misery and squalor were the lot of thousands of dispossessed squatters and cottagers, denied a living wage if working, otherwise left to the tender mercies of overseers who administered the poor law. If they turned poachers, under the savage and inhuman Game Laws passed in the reign of George III, and administered by sporting J.P.s, they risked hanging or transportation. Yet many, like the grossly ill-paid Surrey labourer described by Cobbett, poached, because "it is better to be hanged than to be starved to death."

The tragedy of English agrarian history is that an agricultural proletariat emerged. Yet the course of events elsewhere has shown that open fields and commons could have been enclosed without making landless most of those who cultivated the soil. In Denmark, when land was enclosed in the eighteenth century and improved agricultural techniques were introduced, royal decrees created a nation of peasant proprietors. In Norway and Sweden the open field system was abolished under arrangements which favoured small farmers. In Prussia after 1806 serfdom was abolished and the land system reorganised without uprooting the peasantry from the soil. In France post-1789 revolutionary governments abolished seignorial rights and made peasants owners of the land, achievements which the restored Bourbons after 1815 were powerless to reverse. Lastly, when the Czar Alexander II abolished serfdom in Russia in the 1860s the nightmare of a vast agricultural proletariat was avoided by vesting ownership of land in the village community, known as "the Mir."

There were a few in eighteenth- and nineteenth-century England who urged Parliament to adopt policies giving agricultural workers a stake in land occupation. Writers with an intimate knowledge of prevailing social evils in the countryside recommended this solution. These included Arthur Young, Dr David Davies, a Berkshire Rector who wrote *The Case of Labourers in Husbandry* (1795), Sir F. M. Eden whose three-volumed *The State of the Poor* (1797), is a major source book for the history of the period, and William Cobbett. Cobbett's *Rural Rides* is a blistering comment on early nineteenth-century rural conditions. At the end of the eighteenth century a handful of landowners, including Lord Winchelsea, Lord Carrington, Lord Scarbrough and Lord Egremont, provided allotments for the labourers on their estates. Their example found few imitators. Farmers who preferred labourers to be completely dependent upon them for a livelihood, and shopkeepers who feared loss of custom if labourers grew their own food, were antagonistic to the idea.

A second remedy, to pay agricultural workers a living wage, was likewise rejected. The Elizabethan Statute of Artificiers (1563) had required J.P.s to meet annually to determine wage scales. Although not formally repealed until 1813, the wages clauses of the Act were not operative in the eighteenth century. Samuel Whitbread in 1795 and 1800, with the support of Charles James Fox, proposed the enactment of minimum wage bills. Opposed by the Prime Minister, neither was passed. Instead the Speenhamland system of poor relief was introduced, by which wages below subsistence level were supplemented by a sliding scale of allowances from the poor rate fund. The results were disastrous. Lasting until 1834, the allowance system depressed wage levels, raised poor law costs to fantastic heights, and deprived pauperised labourers of their self respect. Cobbett was angered and sickened by the plight of the half-starved labourers and their ragged wives and children he met on his travels. In *Rural Rides* he wrote, "I never saw human wretchedness equal to this; no, not even among the free negroes of America." The truth of Cobbett's observations is confirmed by those of Arthur Young and by the evidence contained in contemporary novels such as George Eliot's *Middlemarch*.

After the ending of the wars with France in 1815 prosperity eluded all classes of the rural community, landowners, tenant farmers and labourers. The labourers fared much the worst, their misery sparking off serious agrarian disorders in 1830–31. Among the causes of the revolt, which was confined to the southern counties, none was more potent than the tyrannical treatment meted out by parish overseers. Englishmen of the period were thankful that they had escaped the terrors of a revolution similar to that which had destroyed the *ancien régime* in France. The French peasantry, however, on the eve of the revolution of 1830 which brought Louis Philippe to the throne, could reflect that their condition since 1789 had changed for the better. They were free men, cultivating their own small farms. The state of the landless English labourers on the other hand was worse than that of their eighteenth-century forefathers, their standard of living lower and their prospects less hopeful. When they revolted in 1830 they tasted the bitterness of defeat. Nine of the rioters were executed, 400 imprisoned and 457 men and boys were transported to Australia. Unfortunately for them public opinion was not roused to protest, as it did when the Tolpuddle Martyrs were transported for seven years in 1834. The ruthless suppression of agrarian disorder in 1830–31 was the work of members of a governing class, fearful lest the fate of the eighteenth-century French aristocracy should be theirs. At all costs they were determined to prevent their political domination and monopoly of the good things of life being consumed in revolutionary fires.

CHAPTER IV

INDUSTRIAL CHANGES—
IRON, COAL AND STEAM POWER

The "Industrial Revolution" of the eighteenth and nineteenth centuries can be best described as a transition from mankind's centuries-old dependence on wood and water to dependence on coal and iron.

Iron

As already explained, the iron industry at the beginning of the eighteenth century was in a languishing condition owing to the shortage of charcoal. Coal as a possible substitute was suggested before 1700, but its sulphur and phosphorus content made its use, in most people's opinion, impossible. In the early seventeenth century Dud Dudley claimed otherwise. His father, Lord Dudley, took out a patent for him in 1621, but the process, opposed by plantation owners and charcoal burners, has remained a secret. Nowadays it is generally agreed that the Coalbrookdale Quaker, Abraham Darby (1677–1717), in about 1709 was the first to find a substitute for charcoal in the production of cast iron. With Darby's innovation the large scale production of iron may be said to have begun. Using the local "clod coal," which as it happened was suitable for making good burning coke, he successfully pioneered the use of coke as a smelting fuel. Knowledge of the new process remained a close trade secret until the 1730s or 1740s. Obstacles to its widespread adoption were the high sulphur and phosphorous content of the then worked coal measures, and the need for a stronger blast.

The second of the Darby dynasty, Abraham Darby (1711–63), who was using coal about 1750, obtained an improved blast by substituting in 1740 a Newcomen steam engine for a water wheel. Further advances were made at Roebuck's Carron Iron Works in 1768, a four-fold weekly increase in output being secured by the use of John Smeaton's compressed air pump and blowing cylinders. A stronger and steadier blast was obtained by John Wilkinson in 1775, using a steam engine purchased from Boulton and Watt, the ironmasters subsequently becoming good customers of the firm. Fuel consumption was considerably reduced after 1828, when James

Neilson, the manager of the Glasgow Gas Works, suggested heating the air before it reached the furnace. In 1838 a still further reduction was secured when Faber du Faur of Wasseralfugen showed that the waste heat escaping from the top of the furnace could be used to re-heat the blast.

The steam blast made the charcoal furnaces obsolete and led to the migration of the cast-iron furnaces to the coalfields. Until about 1760 coke smelting seems to have been located only in Shropshire, but in the next few years charcoal furnaces rapidly closed down. In 1788 there were only two in the Sussex Weald at Farnhurst and Ashburnham, producing about 300 tons of pig iron annually. In the same year the output of charcoal-smelted pig iron was 11,700 tons, compared with 55,300 tons smelted by coke. Nearly half the coke-smelted pig iron was produced in the Midland counties of Shropshire, Staffordshire and Cheshire. Other areas of production were South Wales and the Sheffield district. In the north-western counties of Lancashire, Cumberland and Westmorland, the charcoal output still exceeded that produced by using coal.

With the increase in output there was a wide extension in the use of cast iron as a constructional material instead of copper, lead, brass and wood in the manufacture of buttons, shoebuckles, agricultural implements, household utensils such as pots and kettles, fire grates, nails, hinges, gun carriages, slave bangles, waterpipes and gas pipes. Before the end of the eighteenth century cast iron was being used in place of timber and masonry in textile mill buildings, and by civil engineers, notably Telford, in the construction of canal aqueducts and bridges. The first iron bridge, that which spans the Severn Gorge at Ironbridge (1779), was constructed from cast iron produced by the third Abraham Darby (1750–91) at Coalbrookdale nearby.

For some time after charcoal had lost the battle with coke in the production of cast iron, it remained the essential fuel in the chief branch of the industry, that of malleable or wrought iron. Coke-smelted iron left the furnace in a liquid state and cooled as cast iron. Being brittle, owing to its high carbon content, the uses of cast iron were very restricted. Wrought iron was made by re-heating "the pigs" at the forge and hammering them to get rid of the excessive carbon content. But as the fuel and iron came in contact, charcoal had to be used; and as the process was an open hearth and lengthy one, output was small.

The growing output of pig iron naturally intensified the search for an alternative fuel for the forges. Experiments were made with varying degrees of success, notably by the German, Blewstone, in the seventeenth century and by Roebuck at the Carron Ironworks (1762).

Roebuck's iron was poor in quality; not so that of the brothers Thomas and George Cranage at Coalbrookdale (1766) whose product found a ready market among the Birmingham nailmakers. Peter Onions at Merthyr Tydfil (1783) patented a puddling process at the same time as the man who has received most acclaim as the possessor of "the grand secret" of making iron, Henry Cort (1740–1823). Born in Lancaster, Cort in 1775 had forges at The Green in Gosport and Fontley in Fareham, Hampshire. In 1783 and 1784 he took out patents for puddling and rolling iron. His method involved the conversion of pig iron into wrought iron in a reverberatory furnace, that is one in which fuel and metal did not come in contact. Such furnaces were known in the seventeenth century and at Coalbrookdale in 1766, but in Cort's process the molten metal was stirred or puddled by "puddlers" using heavy iron rakes. After the metal had cooled it was hammered into rude slabs known as "blooms," subsequently being passed through a series of iron rollers. Using Cort's methods it was possible to obtain 15 tons of bar iron in the same time as one ton by older methods. Those innovations, supplemented later by the use of Nasmyth's steam hammer (1839) and by steam driven puddling sticks (1860), revolutionised the British iron industry. The use of mechanical stirrers, however, coincided in time with the challenge of "the New Steel" to the supremacy of wrought iron.

An undeserved bankruptcy and a small government pension were Cort's rewards for making possible the production of ample supplies of a metal the uses of which are too many to catalogue and too familiar to need description. The very great expansion of iron output is a measure of Cort's achievement, from only 125,000 tons in 1796 to 218,000 tons in 1806, 1,000,000 tons in 1835 and 2,093,736 tons in 1848. Great Britain ceased to depend on imports to satisfy modest needs. She became a major exporter. Between 1806 and 1848 exports of iron rose from 36,925 tons to 619,230 tons, and of hardware from 4629 tons to 18,105 tons. The chief markets were the U.S.A., easily the most important, followed by Asia, Holland, France, Italy and the North American colonies.

Even more important to the British economy than the development of a large export trade were the industrial and social consequences of cheap wrought iron. In the early nineteenth century no British industry was fully mechanised, the most modern, cotton spinning, only partially so. To Abraham Darby and other eighteenth-century pioneers is due the large increase in supplies of cast iron. But cast iron, incapable of withstanding severe strains, had limited uses. It was Cort who pointed the way to the production, on a vast scale, of cheap wrought iron. He enabled mankind to enter "the

Age of Plenty," to consume goods made in factories by steam-powered machines, to travel at unprecedented speeds on iron rails, and to cross the oceans in iron steamships. Cheap wrought iron accounts for the enormous expansion of industry in the nineteenth century, iron and coal becoming the twin pillars on which the new civilisation was erected.

For the iron industry itself the new processes meant changes in location, in size and in organisation. No longer wedded to charcoal, the industry had migrated to the coalfields by the first half of the nineteenth century. Those in the Midlands, South Wales, Clydeside and the Sheffield area were especially important. As the accessible coal and iron beds in Shropshire became worked out, the area lost ground to Staffordshire where forges were built to use the new methods. In South Wales the industry was well endowed with local coal and iron resources, and there were no interests wedded to the use of older methods. On Clydeside also the iron industry was, as in South Wales, a new one, hence the lack of opposition to the adoption of the new techniques. There were ample supplies of "blackband ores," admirably suitable for use in Clydeside furnaces after the invention of Neilson's "hot blast," and cheap water transport facilities for export via the Firth of Forth. The cutlery industry, established in the Sheffield area by the sixteenth century, benefited from Benjamin Huntsman's "crucible steel." The experiments of Huntsman, a Doncaster clock maker, enabled him about 1740 to make steel much superior in quality to any hitherto known. It was first used by French metal workers. Produced in small quantities, at high cost, Huntsman's steel was used in the manufacture of small, expensive articles. The making of steel in large quantities was not possible until the second half of the nineteenth century, commencing with the Bessemer converter (1856) and the Siemens–Martin open hearth process (1866).

The new methods made obsolete traditional skills, necessitating the re-training of workers. Skilled and semi-skilled labour was not at first readily available, a factor which explains why the rate of change was relatively slow. In the newly developing areas, like South Wales and Lanarkshire, labour had to be brought in from outside. In organisation also the iron industry underwent considerable change. In place of the small furnaces and forges of the charcoal age, huge capitalist-controlled iron works came into existence, their owners sometimes controlling also coal-mines, iron-ore-mines and establishments in which hardware commodities were manufactured. The rise to power, both in the political and economic fields, of wealthy iron-masters is a noteworthy feature of the period. The experimental blast furnace of the first Abraham Darby had become a very considerable enterprise in the days of his grandson. Arthur Young, who visited Coalbrookdale in 1776, was very impressed by the beauty of the thickly wooded hills surrounding the glen in which the works were located, contrasting it "with the variety of horrors" in the valley, "the noise of the forges, mills, etc. with all their vast machinery, the flames bursting from the furnaces with the burning of the coal and the smoke of the lime kilns." Coming into existence in 1638, the business was controlled from the reign of Queen Anne by three generations of the Darby family, who also owned coal-mines, iron-mines and forges. The last of the dynasty, Abraham Darby (1750–91), played a major role, in association with "Iron Mad" Wilkinson, in extending the use of cast iron.

"The great Staffordshire iron-master" John Wilkinson (1728–1808) was the son of a Cumberland iron furnace foreman. He and his brother, William, owned ironworks at Bersham near Wrexham, at Broseley near Coalbrookdale and at Bradley near Bilston in South Staffordshire. They possessed coal-mines and iron-mines, extending their interests into South Wales foundries, Cornish tin-mines and Welsh lime kilns and copper-mines. Their activities were even international in scope extending to Germany and Le Creusot in France. For many years Wilkinson issued token copper and silver coins, which had a wide circulation, and printed paper money. In his will he made provision that he should be buried in an iron coffin which according to legend, when the time came to use it, proved to be too small. Wilkinson's importance was not only in the assiduity with which he advocated the use of iron, but also in the contribution he made to solutions of the technical problems of the industry. He was using a Boulton and Watt steam engine to improve the blast at Broseley in 1775, bored cylinders with great precision for the steam engine of James Watt and introduced a new method of boring cannon. For the transportation down the Severn of the ordnance and war materials, made to government order, he built in 1787, the *Trial*, the first iron barge.

"The Iron King" of South Wales, Richard Crawshay, born in Yorkshire, was apprenticed to a London iron-master. Four generations of his family controlled the Cyfarthfa ironworks he founded at Merthyr Tydfil. The chemist, Dr John Roebuck, who founded sulphuric acid works at Birmingham and Prestonpans, was a pioneer in the Scottish iron industry, establishing the Carron Ironworks near Falkirk in 1759. The firm, well known in the twentieth century for the manufacture of household stoves and boilers, was at the end of the eighteenth century, after Roebuck himself had become bankrupt, renowned for the production of ordnance, marketed in many European countries. Also worthy of mention are John Guest, founder of iron works at Dowlais, in Glamorgan, Samuel Walker of Rotherham, who made a large fortune, it is said, by stealing the secrets of Benjamin Huntsman, and Anthony Bacon of Merthyr Tydfil. War needs, between the outbreak of the Seven Years' War in 1756 and the end of the Napoleonic Wars in 1815, played a major part in stimulating expansion in the iron industry. The firms of Walker and Bacon, for example, manufactured cannon for use in the War of American Independence. The Darby family, on the other hand, being Quakers, declined contracts from the Government Department of Ordnance.

Coal

The blighting effects of the rapidly expanding iron industry on the one-time rural landscape are described by Charles Dickens in *The Old Curiosity Shop*. "On every side," he writes of the Black Country about 1840, "and as far as the eye could see into the heavy distance, tall chimneys, crowding on each other, poured out their plague of smoke, obscured the light, and made foul the melancholy air." This quotation reminds us that changes in the iron industry were inextricably linked with expansion in the output of coal. The innovations of the eighteenth and nineteenth centuries gave to coal a new importance. Output was stimulated by increasing industrial demands with the extended use of steam power, by the greater use of coal as household fuel, by the needs of mechanical transport, railways and steamships, by the use of coal gas as an illuminant, and by researches which made possible the utilisation of coal by-products. The use of coal gas for lighting was discussed in 1688 by the Royal Society at the instance of Robert Boyle, and experiments were made in the eighteenth century by British and French scientists. The real credit for making gas-light a practical possibility belongs to an employee of Boulton and Watt, William Murdock. Part of the firm's Soho Works were lit by gas in 1798, and the front of the building illuminated in 1802 to celebrate the Peace of Amiens. In the face of considerable prejudice, no doubt justified, as the gas first used produced sulphurous fumes and an unpleasant amount of moisture, gas became in the early nineteenth century the illuminant of British cities. The streets of Glasgow were lit by gas in 1805, London and Westminster by 1815 and Paris in 1820. Gas works sprung up all over the country, the first being the Gas, Light and Coke Company founded in 1812. Researches were undertaken to increase the illuminating power of gas, culminating in the discoveries of Baron von Welsback in 1885 which trebled the amount of light given out.

Coal output increased from 10 million tons in 1795 to 64 million tons in 1854. This increase was obtained by opening new mines in the Midlands, South Wales and Scotland, and by working deeper seams. But no rapid increase in the size and depth of mines was possible until means were found to drain them effectively, to reduce the hazards of explosions underground, and to solve the problems of underground and surface transport. The need for a pumping device in mines was met by the invention of Savery's fire engine (1698) followed by Newcomen's Atmospheric Engine (1712) and Watt's steam engine (1769). The steam engine proved to be an effective solution to the problem of drainage. Much less satisfactory were the measures taken to safeguard the miner against the hazards of fire and explosions. Light miners must have, but illumination by candle stubs was obviously dangerous. The methods used to get rid of explosive gas, "beating it out" with a coat or the employment of a "fireman" to burn it, were, to say the least, risky. The originator of the miner's safety lamp, Dr William Reid Clanny of Sunderland, exhibited his model to the Royal Society of Arts in 1813. Clanny's lamp was used in Herrington Mill Colliery, County Durham, in 1815. It was in the same year that a significant break through was made in the design of a safety lamp. In 1815 George Stephenson and Sir Humphry Davy both designed safety lamps, based on the same principle and almost identical in design. Stephenson's safety lamp was tested at Killingworth Colliery in the autumn of 1815, a few days before Davy read his paper "On the Fire Damp of Coal Mines" at a meeting of the Royal Society. The Davy safety lamp, an oil burning wick surrounded by a gauze cylinder, was in essence, a scientific instrument for the detection of gas. The safety lamps of Stephenson and Davy did not get rid of the possibility of appalling explosions. In fact because they encouraged the working of deeper seams, their use was a positive menace. As early as the reign of Charles II, Lord Keeper Guildford had pointed out that the sinking of an upcast shaft was the only way to obtain adequate ventilation. On grounds of cost colliery owners often neglected to provide one. It was not until 1862 that a second shaft was made obligatory by Act of Parliament. The electric cap-lamp has in our own day replaced the safety lamp to provide illumination in mines, but the safety lamp or canaries are still the only certain ways of detecting the presence of gases underground.

As pits increased in size the problem of transporting the coal to the bottom of the shaft became more difficult. Originally it was carried by male and female workers. In the middle of the eighteenth century children were employed to lead ponies harnessed to sledges drawn on wooden rails. Iron rails were first used at Coalbrookdale in 1767–71. The report of a Royal Commission in 1842 shocked public opinion with its description of "young females, dressed like boys in trousers, crawling on all fours, with belts round their waists and chains between their legs." In the earlier and shallow pits coal was brought to the surface up sloping shafts or ladders by men and women. Sometimes horse power was used to wind the coal up. The railway pioneer, George Stephenson, when he was a young boy, had charge of a horse gin at a Northumbrian pit. The horse walked round a circular track pulling a rope to which was attached a wicker basket containing coal, the primitive nature of the winding gear making this a hazardous method. The problem was ultimately solved by Andrew Smith's invention of wire rope (1839), and the use of Watt's steam engine to raise and lower metal cages filled with iron tubs. The introduction of machinery for extracting and conveying coal underground came late, as the industry was one in which labour was cheap and plentiful. In 1901 only 1·5 per cent of British coal was machine cut, and as late as 1930 under one-third.

The transport of coal from the pithead to the consumer was made easier by the construction of canals, the first, the Bridgewater Canal, dating from 1761. Really adequate means of making coal available to all parts of the country, however, had to await the railway era. The stranglehold which the Newcastle Vend had over the London market was not ended until railways carried coal from South Wales at a price competitive with that from Tyneside. As late as 1835 2 million tons of London's coal came from the North East and only about 1000 tons from elsewhere. Ten years later the Newcastle Vend had ceased to exist, with no one but Durham and Northumberland coal-owners and the factors of the London coal ring to lament its demise.

Steam Power

Before the eighteenth century, in addition to human muscle and animal power, two other forms of power were in common use, those of wind and water. Windmill sails and water wheels provided power for manufacturing and other purposes until modern times. Windmills, the design of which was improved by Smeaton in the eighteenth century, were used for grinding corn, sawing timber and draining the Fens and Broads. Water power, used in Britain since Roman times, was the most important source of power used by industry. As a source of power, increased reliance was placed on water power from the Tudor period onwards in the metal and coalmining industries, in the manufacture of flour and in the fulling of cloth. Its use was greatly extended in the eighteenth century. Sir Thomas Lombe's five-storied silk mill at Derby (1719) was one of the wonders of the age. Cotton-spinning mills were later erected in Pennine valleys where a water supply of sufficient capacity to turn a water wheel was to be found. These early factories were relatively small in size, restricted in location and dependent upon an unreliable source of power. To increase production, a form of power was required more reliable than streams which were apt to freeze in winter and dry up in summer. The answer was found in the utilisation of the motive power of steam.

The potential of steam was first put to practical use by seventeenth-century inventors searching for a pumping device. These included the Huguenot refugee, Papin, the royalist second Marquis of Worcester, Sir Samuel Morland, at one time Secretary of State to Charles II, and Robert Hooke, the Secretary of the Royal Society.

In 1698 a Devonshire gentleman, Captain Thomas Savery (1610–1715), took out a patent for a steam pump, described as an "Engine to raise Water by Fire!" It was used in Cornish copper-mines, and in 1712 at Camden House, Kensington. Savery's steam pump, however, was slow in operation, expensive to use and of little practical value as it could only raise water fifteen feet. The first practical steam engine was designed by Thomas Newcomen of Dartmouth (1662–1729). He improved on Savery's engine by adding a piston, that is he mechanised the action of a man operating a pump handle. The first of Newcomen's steam beam piston pumping engines was possibly erected near Dudley Castle, Staffordshire, in 1712, and others later were used in Tyneside coal-mines and Cornish copper- and tin-mines. Purchasers of Newcomen's so-called "Atmospheric Engine" included Matthew Boulton, Josiah Wedgwood, the second Abraham Darby and proprietors of urban waterworks. The first to be erected overseas was installed at Königsberg in Hungary (now in Czecho-Slovakia) in 1722, others being erected later in France and the U.S.A. About 1770 the overall thermal efficiency of the engine was improved as a result of experiments made by John Smeaton.

Newcomen has received much less recognition than he deserves. It is to Newcomen, not to James Watt (1736–1819), that the credit belongs for making the first successful practical use of the properties of steam. But his engine had only a limited use, as a pumping device, and was wasteful in fuel consumption. It was James Watt who found the remedy for excessive fuel consumption by inventing in 1765 a separate condenser. Born at Greenock, Watt became a scientific instrument maker at Glasgow University and a protégé of Dr Joseph Black, well known for his research on latent heat. Watt revolutionised the steam engine after ten years of continual and frustrating endeavour. He was financed by Dr Roebuck and, after Roebuck's bankruptcy, by the Birmingham hardware manufacturer, Matthew Boulton (1728–1809). The invention of the steam engine was the least of Watt's difficulties. The real problems were to make steam engines which would be financially and commercially successful. Engineering lagged behind invention. Watt's steam engine was not solely his own creation. He supplied the inventive genius. John Wilkinson and other iron-masters made it a practical possibility by their improvements in the techniques of metal working. Skilled workers employed by Wilkinson made cylinders from which steam leakage did not take place. Roebuck and later Boulton supplied the finance and business ability.

Watt made his first experimental steam pumping engine in 1769. It was not a technical success. In the same year he took out his first patent which included the separate condenser, the steam jacket and the closed top cylinder. Watt's first steam engines, like Newcomen's, were reciprocating engines, that is they were fitted with a movable piston which moved a beam connected to a pump. In 1780 J. Pickard patented a crank for converting the reciprocating or up and down motion of the beam into rotary motion. To get over the difficulty of employing a crank, and thus infringing Pickard's patent, Watt in 1781 devised a system of gear wheels called a sun and planet motion. In 1782 he patented his double acting engine and in 1784 his link parallel motion. In 1788 by fitting a centrifugal governor acting on the steam throttle valve of the Watt rotative beam engine the amount of steam needed was reduced significantly.

Watt's innovations made the steam engine more than a pumping device, steam power ultimately being used to drive machinery in a wide range of industries. Before 1795 Boulton and Watt sub-let the manufacture of components to the firms of Darby, Wilkinson and Roebuck. Watt's workmen supervised the erection of the steam engine on the site, the charge for its use being an annual payment calculated as one-third of the saving in fuel consumption obtained by using it instead of "a fire engine." But Watt's steam engine did not rapidly supersede Newcomen's. In fact, with the improvements made in it by Smeaton, Newcomen's engine was the most popular steam engine before 1800, and in some parts of the country was in use as late as the mid-nineteenth century. Colliery owners, to whom fuel saving was not a matter of real consequence, saw no particular advantage in scrapping it for another make.

Although the extent of the application of steam power to industry during the eighteenth century cannot be accurately determined, its use was more widespread than is still commonly believed. In a paper published in *History* (June 1967) Dr J. R. Harris has suggested "around 1200 steam engines as a realistic production figure for the eighteenth century." Nevertheless the spread of the use of steam power could not have other than a relatively slow progress. Poor transport conditions limited its use to coalfields or to areas which could be reached by water. For instance, engines invoiced for sale to Cornish copper-mine owners were conveyed from the Soho Works of Boulton and Watt in Birmingham by canal and sea transport via Stourport, Gloucester and Bristol. Transhipments made the journey a slow and costly one. An even more serious obstacle to the rapid introduction of steam-powered machinery was the shortage of labour competent to make, operate and service the engines and machines. As the early machines were made by hand there was a lack of uniformity in their individual parts. No two nuts or bolts were identical. Once a machine was made there was no certainty that it would function. The repair or replacement of broken parts presented great difficulty. An incident in the life of George Stephenson will serve to illustrate the point. A Newcomen type of pumping engine, built to the design of John Smeaton, was purchased for use at Killingworth Colliery on Tyneside. When installed it would not function, despite the efforts of Smeaton's expert workers, until Stephenson diagnosed the faults and made the necessary adjustments. Employees, needless to point out, with the mechanical insight of a George Stephenson were not readily available. Even Watt himself advised Boulton against trying to persuade Lancashire cotton spinners to use steam engines instead of water wheels. In any case as Watt realised, steam power could not come into general use "until the illiterate and obstinate people who are entrusted with the care of engines become more intelligent and better acquainted with the machines."

The evolution of a new industry, the machine tool industry, in the first half of the nineteenth century solved this problem. Not until tools were invented to make machines and an adequate number of skilled engineers trained, could there be an industrial revolution. As late as 1835 there were 866 water wheels operating in Lancashire and the West Riding of Yorkshire. The development of a machine tool industry and the emergence of skilled engineering crafts took a long time. The first machines and engines were made by blacksmiths and millwrights working under general instructions as to design, size and shape of the parts required. The modern convenience of standardised parts, mass produced and readily acceptable as the normal order of things, we owe to a group of inventive, skilled engineers. Their tools came into general use from about 1820 onwards. Joseph Bramah (1749–1814), a versatile genius, invented a patent lock (1784) and in 1796 a hydraulic press worked by a high pressure plunger pump. Incidentally it may be mentioned that we owe to Bramah the modern water closet (1778). His pupil, Henry Maudsley (1771–1831) invented the screw cutting lathe (1797) and designed a measuring machine true to one thousandth of an inch. James Nasmyth (1808–90), trained by Maudsley, invented the steam hammer (1839), thereby immeasurably lightening human toil and making possible the manufacture of very large iron bars. In 1848, Richard Roberts, the designer of the self acting spinning mule, invented a machine for punching holes in iron plates. Later Joseph Whitworth (1803–87), one of the greatest of Victorian engineers, whose name is commemorated by the Whitworth Scholarship, Whitworth Street, Manchester, and Whitworth Hall, Manchester University, worked out a series of sizes for screws and machine parts, his sizes becoming in the 1860s the standard generally accepted in Great Britain.

It was in Great Britain that the new industry, engineering, first appeared. Skilled mechanics, called engineers, were at first few in numbers. Their emergence as a distinct group of workmen is marked by the formation in 1851 of the Amalgamated Society of Engineers. These "aristocrats of labour" were responsible for the rapid spread of mechanical devices and the substitution of iron for wood in machine making. Great Britain in 1850 had become "the workshop of the world" because she possessed skilled mechanics, competent to design, operate and service machines. When other countries embarked on the road to industrial transformation, it was British engineers and artisans whom they employed to erect plants and train the personnel to man them.

CHAPTER V

INDUSTRIAL CHANGES—THE TEXTILE INDUSTRIES

The Cotton Industry

The changes that took place in the cotton industry can be cited to support the theory that pressure of market demand stimulated an industrial revolution in Great Britain. The problem of increasing output was solved by mechanisation. Fortunately, the introduction of labour-saving machines was a relatively easy process for two main reasons. Firstly, demand was so great that it was impossible to satisfy it by reliance on traditional methods of production. Secondly, as the industry was a new one, competitive enterprise was not impeded, as it was in the older industries by hampering regulations and strongly entrenched vested interests. The eighteenth-century textile inventions illustrate the truth of the proverb, "Necessity is the mother of invention." They were not the fruits of the application of applied science, but the achievements of ingenious men seeking solutions to practical difficulties. The most urgent was the inability of spinners, usually women, to provide sufficient yarn. In 1759 the Society of Arts offered a prize for a machine capable of spinning more than one thread at a time. In an era of rapidly expanding markets the problem had been made more acute by John Kay's invention in 1733 of the "Flying Shuttle" which doubled the speed of the weaver and enabled him to weave wider cloth. Kay, like many other innovators, earned the praise of posterity but not the gratitude of contemporaries. Rioting by weavers, fearful of unemployment, forced him to take refuge in France where he died forgotten and in poverty.

Many years were to elapse before weavers were rescued from what a contemporary described as "the bondage in which they had lain to the insolence of the spinners." A roller spinning machine was patented by John Wyatt and Lewis Paul in 1738. Shortage of capital and lack of business sense may explain why they did not make it commercially profitable. The "Spinning Jenny" of the Blackburn weaver, James Hargreaves, dates from 1767, the original "Jenny" turning eight spindles. Larger ones were built, with sixteen spindles in 1770, 80 in 1784 and later with as many as 120. The "Jenny," a hand machine, operated in workmen's cottages, made spinning an adult male occupation. Yarn could now be supplied in adequate quantities but for the weft thread only, as like the hand spinning wheel it could not spin a cotton yarn strong enough to be used for the warp.

Richard Arkwright (1732-92) overcame the difficulty in 1769 with his "Water Frame," a machine that spun threads by means of rollers revolving at different speeds. Doubts were cast on the claim that this device was his invention, but there is no disputing that Arkwright was an exceptionally competent business organiser who pioneered cotton spinning into the factory stage. The new yarns were first used by Nottingham hosiers, with one of whom, Jedediah Strutt, Arkwright went into partnership. For Strutt, Arkwright built in 1771 at Cromford near Derby the first large water-wheel driven cotton mill. Other mills powered by water wheels were erected later at Derby, Belper and Manchester. In 1778, Arkwright introduced improvements in the carding and roving processes, but his chief claim to fame, apart from pioneering the transfer of manufacturing from the home to the mill, is that he was the founder of the British cotton industry. The "Water Twist," the yarn spun on his machines, was strong enough to be used for the warp. Henceforth British manufacturers were no longer restricted to the production of mixed fabrics. The production of piece goods made wholly of cotton replaced the former Lancashire mixed cotton and linen fabrics. Although he was deprived of his patents in 1785 he remained the largest cotton spinner in England. With David Dale he founded a cotton mill at New Lanark in Scotland and used steam power in the mill he erected in Nottingham. He was knighted by George III in 1786, dying six years later, leaving a fortune of half a million pounds.

The yarns spun by the "Jennies" and "Water Frames" were rather coarse and therefore not suitable for use in the manufacture of first quality cottons and muslins. Shaw of Bolton was manufacturing muslins in 1763 from imported Indian yarns. Lancashire was rescued from dependence on Indian yarn imports by the invention in 1779 of Samuel Crompton (1753-1827). Crompton's "Muslin Wheel" or "Mule" combined the principles of the "Jenny" and the "Water Frame." It was a hand-operated machine made of wood. Henry Stones of Horwich substituted iron for wood in 1792 and at the same time William Kelly of New Lanark invented a power "Mule" with an increased number of spindles. Later, improvements were made by Wright, one of Arkwright's apprentices. The self-acting "Mule" patented by Richard Roberts in 1825 was still further improved by him in 1830.

As Crompton was too poor to patent his invention others reaped where he had sown. He died in 1827 a poor and embittered man. It was not until 1862 that public recognition of his achievements was given by the erection of a statue in Nelson Square, Bolton; but his son, John, though present at the unveiling ceremony, was not invited to the luncheon which followed it. Crompton's true memorial, however, is not the stone edifice in Nelson Square. It is to be found in the cotton spinning mules of Lancashire and Clydeside, in the wealth of the manufacturers and merchants who profited by his ingenuity, and in the uncounted multitude of operatives to whom his "mule" gave a livelihood. "Mule"-spun yarn, superior in quality to any hitherto known, made Lancashire and Clydeside the centres of an industry which accounted for half the British export trade in the first half of the nineteenth century. It also undermined the centuries-old cotton manufacturing industry of India.

A factory economy necessitated the availability of vastly increased supplies of raw material. Until the end of the eighteenth century cotton was imported from the Levant, the West Indies and Brazil, and to a very limited extent from the U.S.A. By the early nineteenth century, however, following the invention of Eli Whitney's Cotton Gin (1793), huge quantities of cotton, grown in the slave-owning states of the U.S.A., were being unloaded at the docks of Liverpool and Glasgow. Equally important, in making possible a factory economy, was the functioning at the same period in Bolton of a textile machinery industry. A friend of Crompton, Isaac Barlow, left his native Westmorland in 1789 to found the firm of Dobson and Rothwell, known after 1850 as the firm of Messrs Dobson and Barlow. First producing spinning mules, the firm by 1813 had branched out into manufacturing all forms of textile machinery. An indication of the speed with which cotton spinning was becoming a mill-based industry may be obtained from the amount of business done by the firm. Between July 1797 and July 1799 the firm supplied 22 mules to customers, the smallest with 168 spindles and the largest with 408. These were erected in neighbouring villages possessing streams with a sufficient flow of water to drive mill machinery. Later, with the use of steam power, river water was needed for engine and boiler purposes. Mules became larger and mill buildings consequently increased in size.

The factory system first appeared in the spinning side of the cotton industry. For many years after spinners had become mill hands, weaving remained a handicraft occupation, and, as there was no longer a scarcity of yarn, weavers were fully employed. Contemporary writers have recorded that in the early nineteenth century, hand-loom weavers, no longer reluctant to use the "Flying Shuttle," enjoyed a high standard of living. Their high incomes, liberally spent, spread a wave of prosperity throughout the textile areas. It was not to last, although many at the time believed in its permanency, as weaving was considered to be too complicated a process to lend itself to mechanisation. They were proved wrong by a most unlikely man, a clergyman without technical qualifications or knowledge of the industry. In 1785 the Rev. Edmund Cartwright, a Wakefield curate and brother of Major Cartwright the political reform agitator, invented a power loom. Experience enabled him to improve on a clumsy first effort and to open in 1787, at Doncaster, a factory powered by steam. It failed. Power looms were first commercially successful in Clydeside in 1793. Modifications by John Horrocks of Preston, William Radcliffe the master manufacturer of Mellor in Derbyshire, and by Richard Roberts of Manchester, ultimately made possible the successful erection of weaving mills in England.

The period also saw improvements in other branches of the cotton industry. In the closing years of the eighteenth century, Thomas Bell's copper cylinders for calico printing replaced hand blocks. The discovery of the properties of chlorine by the French chemist Berthollet meant that days, instead of months in the sun, would suffice for the bleaching of cloth. The Frenchman, Jacquard, invented a pattern-weaving loom in 1801, and developments in dyeing techniques still further increased the efficiency of the industry.

The modern localisation of the English cotton industry in Lancashire and the adjoining parts of Derbyshire and Cheshire has been explained by the existence in the region of a suitable climate, coal, and a convenient port, Liverpool. Less easy to account for is the geographical separation of the spinning and weaving sides of the industry. By the early years of the nineteenth century power spinning was tending to concentrate in the southern part of the region around Manchester. In 1811, from an incomplete census of the cotton industry compiled by Samuel Crompton, we learn that there were 4,600,000 mule spindles in use, 310,516 water-frame spindles and 155,880 jenny spindles. Most of these were to be found within a 60 mile radius of Bolton. The sizes of the mules varied from one with 500 spindles to some with 50. Water-frames ranged from 48 to 160 spindles and jennies from 48 to 208, the most common being listed as having 120 to 126 spindles. This evidence of the extensive use of the mule persuaded Parliament in 1812 to grant Crompton £5000.

During the first two decades of the nineteenth century, handloom weaving had not yet been replaced by power looms. Handloom weavers were widely dispersed, but their "golden age" ended owing to the introduction of power-loom techinques and post-1815 trade dislocations. Hand-looms continued to survive, as hand-looms wove fabrics beyond the capacity of the early power-looms, but with decreasing profitability. After 1830 the numbers of hand-loom workers began to fall rapidly. Factory inspectors estimated that there were 220,000 hand-looms working in 1830 and 60,000 in 1844-46. By 1856 their numbers had become insignificant.

Most of the early power-looms were introduced into the industry by existing spinning firms. In the mid-nineteenth century there were many firms engaged in both spinning and weaving, men usually being employed in spinning and women in weaving. Other firms specialised in either spinning or weaving. Two-thirds of the workers employed lived in Manchester and adjacent towns. The remainder worked in the northern part of the region where a number of spinning and weaving firms, and weaving-only firms, had been established. A generation later a significant change was taking place in the geographical location of the spinning and weaving sections of the cotton industry. In 1884 the southern area possessed 78 per cent of the spindles and 38 per cent of the looms. In the northern area were to be found 62 per cent of the looms and 22 per cent of the spindles. There was a considerable amount of migration from neighbouring agricultural areas into such weaving centres as Burnley, Accrington, Blackburn, Nelson and Colne. After the 1880s fewer firms engaged in both spinning and weaving, and the geographical separation of spinning and weaving firms became more marked. In 1928 73 per cent of the looms and 12 per cent of the spindles were to be found in the north while in the south were located 27 per cent of the looms and 88 per cent of the spindles.

The Woollen Industry

The machinery which created the Lancashire cotton industry was capable of modification for use in the woollen industries. But power-driven machinery was introduced much later into them than into the cotton industry. Reasons for this state of affairs are not hard to discover. The cotton industry was localised, the woollen more widely scattered, hence knowledge of the new techniques spread more slowly. Kay's "Flying Shuttle" was known in Lancashire in the 1730s, but did not reach the West Riding until the 1760s, and the West Country until the end of the century. The cotton industry was a young one, owing its very existence to machinery. It was therefore less conservative in outlook, and unhampered, as were the wool crafts, by traditions, centuries old, and legislative restrictions. In the woollen areas independent-minded craft workers were very reluctant to operate the new inventions. To them, labour-saving machines were not a means of increasing productivity, and thereby standards of living, but a cause of grave unemployment. This point is well made by the workman in Charlotte Brontë's *Shirley*. "Invention may be all right, but I know it isn't right for poor folk to starve." In addition there was good cause for complaint that the pioneer spinning mills supplied unsatisfactory yarn, as wool, with its softer fibres, was less easy than cotton to spin on the early jennies and mules. Above all, however, the earlier use of machinery in the cotton industry can be explained by the availability of unlimited supplies of cotton from American slave plantations. The woollen industries, on the other hand, were dependent on a relatively scarce, home produced raw material, supplemented by a small import from Europe. During the war years (1793-1815), owing to the high price of corn, home wool supplies actually diminished, there being a serious deficiency in 1794-96.

The shortage of wool was eventually overcome, firstly, by crossing English breeds with Spanish merino sheep, and secondly, by the importation in 1797 of merino sheep from the Cape into New South Wales, Australia. By using scientific breeding techniques, Captain John Macarthur produced a fine wool of excellent quality. The crossing of the Blue Mountains in 1813 opened out vast pasture lands on the Bathurst Plains on which flocks increased rapidly. Some time had necessarily to elapse before Australia could supply wool, suitable in quality and adequate in quantity. In 1820, 190,000 lb of Australian wool was imported, 1,000,000 lb in 1826 and 2,000,000 lb in 1828. Thereafter, imports rose rapidly, making possible the mechanisation of the British woollen industries.

The use of the new machines was at first almost entirely confined to the West Riding. As records of individual enterprise are not always readily available, it is by no means easy to trace the process of machine introduction. It was in the preliminary and final processes of wool manufacture that changes first came. Lewis Paul was using a carding machine at Northampton in 1748. Although its use meant a considerable displacement of workers, no evidence has survived of mass resistance to its use. It does not appear to have come into general use in the West Riding until 1790. There was very great opposition, however, to Cartwright's wool combing machine, patented in 1789. Its use brought about a considerable saving in time and in labour costs, while it was technically an improvement on hand combing. Parliament was unsuccessfully petitioned to prohibit its use. After the repeal of the Combination Acts in 1824, a 23-weeks strike was organised in Bradford in association with the weavers, but to no avail. From 1853, following the patenting of James Noble's combing machinery, the combing section of the industry became fully mechanised and came to be located almost wholly in the West Riding.

The spinning jenny was introduced into the West Riding in the 1770s, being used in 1776 in Holmfirth near Huddersfield. By that time, jennies were becoming obsolete in the cotton industry. In the West Country, the jenny, although it was not unknown at this time, did not come into general use until much later. It was being used at Barnstaple and Ottery St Mary in 1790, and also in Kendal. At the end of the century the traditional hand spinning wheel and the jenny were competing with one another. The introduction of the jenny was bitterly resented in the West Country where low wages made the single spindle wheel economically unprofitable, even as a by-occupation. But steadily the jenny gained ground, and being a more elaborate machine made spinning a full-time occupation for men, instead of a part-time one for the women of the family. Being a hand machine, the jenny did not make a factory economy essential. Nevertheless, in the early nineteenth century in Trowbridge and other West Country woollen centres, production was organised by capitalist employers in mills in which handicraft workers laboured under strict supervision. Some of these buildings, still standing, have since been adapted to other uses. In this intermediate stage, between the older domestic and the modern factory economy, there was considerable labour unrest which expressed itself in rioting.

Power driven machinery was introduced very slowly, and first into the West Riding worsted industry. Early ventures in the Halifax area were failures owing to the unsatisfactory quality of the yarn produced. Worsted spinning factories were in existence in 1784 near Lancaster, and in 1792 at Mytholmroyd near Halifax. The Yorkshire spinner, Benjamin Gott of Leeds, was the first to use steam power for spinning, purchasing his engine at the end of the century from Boulton and Watt. By 1800 ten spinning mills were operating in Bradford, constituting a grave threat to the former East Anglian supremacy in the worsted trade. Thirty years later, Bradford was described by a lady diarist, Miss Lister, as the smokiest place she had ever seen, a marked contrast, she noted, to the fine, clean air of her native Halifax. Alas, time marches on. In 1837 she sadly recorded that Halifax in its turn was becoming smoke begrimed as steam engines were being used by local industry.

The general use of power looms was even longer delayed. Weaving sheds, powered by water, were in existence in Halifax in the 1820s but for many years afterwards good quality fabrics were a hand-loom monopoly. Power looms were being operated in Bradford in 1825, but ten years later of the 116,801 power looms in the United Kingdom, all but 7175 were being used in the cotton industry. The worsted trade was first taken over by the power loom. It was not until the second half of the nineteenth century that the woollen industry followed suit. Yet although many steam-powered mills, owned by family business units were erected, hand-loom weavers were still working in the West Riding in the early years of the twentieth century.

The introduction of power-driven machinery had more serious consequences for workers in the woollen than in the cotton industry. The latter, being an "infant industry," was capable of great expansion. The new machinery created employment, particularly as at first it was not backed by power. But there was no "golden age" for the woollen workers. When the woollen industry travelled the same road hand workers had to compete with both machinery and power. Distress was particularly severe in areas like East Anglia in which the industry was declining. Further, the country was at war, European markets being closed by Napoleon's Berlin and Milan decrees and trade relations with the United States cut off by the American Non-intercourse Act (1809). With trade stagnant and food dear, the price of wheat rising to 130s. and more in 1812, no wonder the lot of the workers was bad.

Not surprisingly the workers considered that the use of labour-saving machinery was the principal cause of the industrial depression. When their livelihood was threatened, woollen workers, as in past times, expected the Government to intervene to safeguard their craft. To quote again the workman in Charlotte Brontë's *Shirley*, "Them that governs mun find a way to help us." In the reign of Edward VI Parliament had forbidden the use of gig mills, simple machines which threatened serious redundancy among the shearmen, workers who finished woven cloth using teazles and hand shears. When similar machines were re-introduced into the West Country and the West Riding in the eighteenth century, there was a demand for the enforcement of this Tudor legislation. Instead, however, of following the precedents set by their Tudor predecessors, Parliament, after a House of Commons Committee enquiry, decided to favour the policies advocated by West Country capitalist employers. By an Act passed in 1809 the old protective laws were abolished. In other words Parliament had taken the view that it was in the national interest to give free rein to private enterprise.

As might have been expected the workers' resentment and despair erupted into violence. What are known as the "Luddite" riots began in Nottingham in the autumn of 1811. Here stocking frames were smashed by starving employees. The unrest spread into Derbyshire, Leicestershire, Yorkshire and Lancashire, where owners were threatened and their machinery destroyed by "Enoch," the name given to the sledge hammer used by the rioters. One employer,

William Horsfall, who had installed shearing frames in his Ottiwells Mill at Marsden, was shot as he was riding home from Huddersfield. To deal with the situation the Government made frame-breaking a hanging offence, increased the powers of the magistrates, and drafted troops into the disturbed areas. Many rioters were tried and convicted, 16 of them being sentenced to die at York Assizes. Social and economic unrest, however, continued after peace came in 1815, notable events being the Spa Fields riot (1816) and the "Peterloo" or "Manchester massacre" (1819). The Tory government of Lord Liverpool therefore continued its policy of savage repression which culminated in the passage of the Six Acts in 1819.

Distress and unemployment proved to be short-term consequences of the introduction of labour-saving machinery into the woollen industries. More permanent were the changes in the location of the industry. In 1700 there were three specialised areas, the West Country, East Anglia and the West Riding. In 1800, when machinery had not made any markedly visible impression, the West Riding was at least as important as its rivals. By 1914 the West Riding was far ahead, possessing 50 per cent of the looms. Its nearest rivals were the towns in the Tweed Valley, Hawick, Jedburgh, Galashiels and Selkirk. The industry also survived in Kendal. In the West Country and East Anglia the workers clung more tenaciously than those of the West Riding to the older methods of production. In the West Country, still notable for the manufacture of broad cloth, the industry died out in many towns and villages, surviving only in the Stroud Valley and in Wiltshire at Bradford and Trowbridge.

When steam was first used in the production of textiles mills only produced coarse quality goods. In these circumstances the high quality fabrics produced by East Anglian handworkers competed successfully in both home and overseas markets. This advantage was lost once the power-looms of the West Riding, Lancashire and Paisley were capable of producing cloth of the highest standards. Lacking coal, and increasingly dependent on Yorkshire for yarn, East Anglian producers never used the jenny and mule. Their industry, therefore, after 1860 succumbed to mass production competition. Its decline, however, was a relatively slow process. In 1861 more than 10,000 operatives were employed in Norfolk and Suffolk, Norwich being the main centre of the industry. By 1901 their numbers had fallen to about 3500, despite the application of steam power to spinning and weaving and the excellence of the hand-woven fabrics produced. It was on East Anglian looms that the lavishly dressed upper classes had depended in the eighteenth and early nineteenth centuries. The garments of later generations were fashioned from cloth produced in northern mills.

PART II

MEANS OF COMMUNICATION IN THE PRE-RAILWAY AGE

Chapter VI

ROADS

The economic order created by the use of steam power in industry was one characterised by a much greater degree of regional specialisation than had been customary before 1700. The new economy, however, could only function, provided means were found to ensure that raw materials were assembled for processing, and for the subsequent carriage of manufactured commodities to markets at home and overseas. Improved locomotion was obtained in four ways, by the construction of better roads, canals and railways, and by the application of steam power to river and ocean navigation. To these must be added, as major formative influences in establishing the modern inter-dependence of nations, the telegraph, telephone, submarine cable, wireless, films, broadcasting, the internal combustion engine and an unprecedentedly wide extension of the printed word.

Ruskin has reminded us that "all social progress resolves itself into the making of roads." There is no disputing that isolation is a potent cause of backwardness in any community, but we must not fall into the error of assuming that the absence of modern transport facilities in past centuries condemned our forefathers to a fossilised state of existence. The intricate communications network we possess meets the needs of a highly industrialised society. Pre-eighteenth-century transport systems, though less intricate and efficient than our own, were by no means wholly primitive. By and large they were adequate to the need of the time.

Internal transport before the eighteenth century was confined to roads and trackways, and to rivers, supplemented by coasting vessels for very bulky commodities. As road transport conditions, by modern standards, must be classed as poor, regional diversities were much more apparent than nowadays. In speech, folklore, customs, diet, recreations and weights and measures, there were marked regional differences. When travellers left their native heath, their distinctiveness became very obvious both to themselves and to those among whom they sojourned. Paucity of means of communication largely explains the poverty and backwardness that characterised social conditions in such regions as the northern counties of England and the Scottish Highlands. In the closing years of the eighteenth century when Englishmen were experimenting with steam-powered machinery, oxen were being used for ploughing in Cumberland, and relics of medieval villein tenure still existed in the western part of the same county. These examples may serve to remind us that generalisations about pre-eighteenth-century transport facilities in Britain, as in much else in economic history, can be misleading. Differences in economic development, and variations in soil and physical features, dictated much unevenness in the quality and quantity of road provision. The deep, stiff clays of the Midlands long delayed the construction of good roads, in contrast to the hard, firm surfaces of the chalk, limestone and sandstone regions. Areas concerned with trade with Europe, as one might expect, were better served with means of communication than those where traffic was purely local in character.

The earliest routeways are to be found in such areas as the chalk uplands of southern and south-eastern England. These ancient trackways, formed by the feet of men and beasts, were used by cattle drovers before the railway age in preference to turnpike roads. That Britain was far from being roadless before Roman times is obvious from the evidence of Julius Caesar that his legions fought against opponents who used wheeled chariots. Upon this network of ancient trackways was superimposed the Roman road system. Many Roman roads followed the lines of the older British routeways. Built on firm foundations with surfaces as impervious as possible to water, they lasted for centuries. From London, sited where the Thames was fordable, a number of highways ran, as they do today, to all parts of the country.

After the departure of the Romans the engineering of roads with a "hard" surface was a lost art until the eighteenth century. But the notion that the road system was completely neglected is erroneous. New roads were not built, but during the Anglo-Saxon period the main Roman roads were kept in reasonable condition. The speed with which King Harold in 1066 marched from Stamford Bridge to Hastings would only be credible on the assumption that his army travelled on a paved highway. After the Norman Conquest there was a considerable amount of internal traffic, regular royal progresses, pilgrims travelling in company to religious shrines, landed magnates with their retinues visiting in turn their scattered manors, royal judges on their way to hold assize courts, and merchants and pedlars transporting their wares to fairs and markets. For the most part, travellers of both sexes would use horses, mules or donkeys, the rough, uneven nature of the roads and the narrow width of bridges making the use of wheeled vehicles unusual.

During the Middle Ages the responsibility for the repair and upkeep of the highway was in some measure the responsibility of landowners. The Church admonished the faithful that bridge construction was meritorious, and it was not unusual for people in medieval times to make provision in their wills for the upkeep of roads and bridges. This was certainly not a responsibility assumed by the central government. Highway legislation in medieval times is concerned more with the safety of travellers than with providing good road surfaces. Edward I's laws, the Statute of Rageman (1276), the Statute of Gloucester (1278) and the Statute of Winchester (1285), all contain clauses designed to protect wayfarers from robberies and assaults. Recurrent controversy, however, as to who should pay for highway maintenance is a feature of the history of road transport. Royal intervention in the Middle Ages was usually in favour of the principle that travellers should foot the bill. The first two Edwards (1272–1327) made grants of "pavage" and "pontage" to landowners, monasteries and boroughs, which empowered the recipients to collect tolls to be used for road and bridge maintenance. Edward III in 1346 continued this policy, granting similar powers to certain corporate bodies and individuals.

These anticipations of the turnpike system of later centuries provided means of communication insufficient to meet the demands of expanding trade and industry in Tudor times. It was therefore decided to make the parish the unit of highway administration. In other words, ratepayers, not users, were to finance road upkeep. The Highways Act of 1555, as modified by clause XXV of Queen Elizabeth's Injunctions of 1559 and the Highways Act of 1562, became the statutory basis of a system of parochial road maintenance which lasted until 1835. Justices of the Peace, meeting in special annual Highway Sessions, chose two surveyors from lists submitted by parishes. The surveyors' duties were to "amend" roads, conscripting for this purpose, for six days each year, parishioners whose incomes were less than £50 per annum. Parishioners with larger incomes, in lieu of manual labour, were obliged to provide a man, a horse and a cart. Statutory authority was also given for the levying of a highway rate.

As far as local traffic was concerned this system of administration, according to current ideas, was productive of satisfactory results. Surveyors, usually local farmers and tradesmen, would have sufficient regard to local convenience to keep parish roads in a passable state of repair. Far different would be situations where main highways crossed parochial lands. It would be beyond the capacity, or the desire, of the inhabitants to cater for the needs of travellers and freight passing through. Not unreasonably parish vestries failed to levy highway rates and conscript labour for the benefit of "foreigners." A change of policy was therefore suggested. Why should not travellers, it was asked, pay for main roads? This solution was adapted from 1663 onwards. At their own request the Justices for the counties of Hertford, Huntingdon and Cambridge were authorised by statute to form a highway board. Under the Act of 1663, they were empowered to supervise the uniting of parish highway authorities on a section of the Great North Road, and to levy tolls. Three toll gates were erected, at Stilton, Wadesmill and Caxton. The experiment, not very successful, was repeated in 1695 by the creation of a turnpike trust on the London to Harwich road, an indication of the importance of traffic with Holland following the accession of William III. In the following years, in response to petitions from justices and others, Parliament authorised an extension of the system to other areas. Two Acts were passed in the reign of Charles II, six in the reign of William III and 28 in the reign of Anne. The roads affected before 1714 by this legislation consisted of detached portions of the main highways from London through the difficult clay region of the Midlands, and short isolated stretches of highway elsewhere, where commercial enterprise or public spirit stimulated local initiative.

In the main, turnpike trustees were concerned not with making new roads but with improving existing tracks. The word "highway" to modern ears conveys the meaning of a hard surface fit to travel on. To our forefathers it implied not a prepared surface but a right of passage, very liberally interpreted. The language of Highway Acts is significant. The Royal Injunctions of 1559 direct that the alms, subscribed by parishioners, were to be used, not for making roads but "for the reparation of the highways." Lord Macaulay in Chapter III of his *History of England* has graphically described the evil nature of English highways during the reign of Charles II. They were no better when the first Hanoverian king arrived in 1714. Not until the late eighteenth century were there signs of real improvements. Except in the summer months transport of goods was well nigh impossible. Timber going to the coast for shipbuilding had to await a hard frost. Farmers were for the most part restricted to supplying local markets. All too often they were requested to loan animals to extricate coaches stuck fast in quagmires euphemistically called "roads." Oxen were used in parts of Sussex to pull wheeled vehicles. In an age when Princess Anne's husband, George of Denmark, took six hours in wet weather to travel nine miles, more humble folk must have fared very badly. In 1685 the Viceroy of Ireland on the main road to Holyhead travelled fourteen miles in five hours. Even the King's coach in 1730 overturned at Parson's Green. Travellers could lose their way even on major highways like the Great North Road. In regions unenclosed it was hard to distinguish the highway from the heath and fen which bordered it. In 1676, Charles II's cosmographer, John Ogilby, published *Britannia*, an invaluable road book. All too often, however, what he listed as a road on close acquaintance became a narrow track, deeply rutted, contained on either side by bog and mud. British soldiers during the First World War, by superhuman efforts hauling transport and howitzers out of the mud of Flanders, were engaged in tasks very familiar to the subjects of the Stuart and early Hanoverian kings.

It must not be supposed, however, that all roads at this time were seas of mud. So much depended upon the character of the soil, the adequacy of the drainage and the whims of parish surveyors, who quite understandably made passable only those tracks used by themselves and their neighbours. About road conditions at the end of the seventeenth century much can be learned from the *Journal* of Celia Fiennes. She travelled on horseback through many counties, sometimes in winter, and did not invariably find progress impossible. She does comment on the many narrow lanes, and in hill country, on the steepness and stoney surfaces. Descriptions of eighteenth-century roads can be found in the books of Daniel Defoe and Arthur Young. They are both highly critical. Young writes of travelling "at the hazard of my neck," but even he, like Celia Fiennes, was pleased with road conditions in the chalk country on the way to Winchester.

Before the seventeenth century, the most convenient form of transport for travellers was on horseback, and for goods, long trains of packhorses or transit by river. The poor usually walked, as they could not afford the capital and maintenance costs of a horse. With the growth of urban centres needing food, great droves of cattle, sheep, pigs and even geese, turkeys, ducks and hens became a common sight on the highway. In the eighteenth century cattle from distant Anglesey, Wales and Scotland were driven by slow stages into England to be fattened for the market, no doubt exasperating travellers by impeding their progress and by the constant beating of their hooves churning up road surfaces. From the middle of the sixteenth century wheeled vehicles were used both in towns and on rural highways. In the seventeenth century the rich rode in private coaches, learning by experience that four or even six horses would not suffice on bad roads, and that in some areas narrow roads and bridges made progress impossible. Many parts of the kingdom from the middle of the seventeenth century were served by regular stage coach transport. This method of travelling was recommended by Edward Chamberlayne in *Anglia Notitia* (1669). Journeys could be made, he assured his readers, "sheltered from foul weather and foul ways, free from endamaging one's health and one's body by hard jogging or over violent motion on horseback." By stage coach, York or Exeter could be reached from London in most favourable circumstances in four days, but not all their patrons shared Chamberlayne's opinion about the comfort of ill-sprung coaches on uneven road surfaces. "Hell carts" was one description of them. Those who could not afford expensive coach transport travelled by slow moving stage wagons, used also for the transportation of bulky merchandise. All travellers, however, had to contend not only with the natural hazards of climate and terrain, but with highwaymen, criminals as difficult to apprehend as modern wages and motor lorry bandits, and despite popular legend, no more romantic.

The increase in wheeled vehicular traffic provoked complaints about congestion in towns and deterioration of road surfaces. Our forefathers, like ourselves, dealt with these problems, not by building roads to suit the traffic, but by imposing restrictions on their use. In 1601 a Bill to limit their excessive use by coaches was suggested. Legislative measures in the seventeenth and eighteenth centuries included limitations on numbers of horses and oxen, and on loads, regulations prohibiting narrow wheels, and stringent rules on vehicle design. The laws passed were numerous, of extreme complexity, incapable of enforcement and useless to achieve their main purpose, the prevention of damage to road surfaces. The opinion expressed in the early eighteenth century that road conditions were worse than formerly was possibly as true as a similar opinion voiced nowadays. The expansion of vehicular traffic on roads not designed for it presented the subjects of Queen Anne with a problem similar in nature to that caused by the rapid growth in popularity of motor transport during the reign of Queen Elizabeth II.

The increase in the numbers of wheeled vehicles, and of traffic on the highway, was, however, a symptom, not the basic cause, of traffic congestion. The root of the trouble, not as obvious then as now, was that Britain was on the threshold of the industrial age. The movements of vast numbers of animals, fish and foodstuffs to growing urban centres, of coal to industrial and domestic consumers, of raw materials to producing centres and manufactured goods to home consumers and the docks, were imposing strains on roads incapable of taking them. In other words, advances in other aspects of economic life had outstripped means of communication. The answer came in the second half of the eighteenth century in the form of improved roads, improvements in vehicular construction and in waterways.

In solving her transport problems, Great Britain, except in the Scottish Highlands and in the neighbourhood of Hadrian's Wall, relied upon private enterprise. In contrast, France in the reign of Louis XV planned a national road network using conscript peasant labour known as corvée. All who paid taxation, except nobles, clergy and burgesses of corporate towns, worked for 30 days each year on the highways, a practice which before the Revolution of 1789 in most regions had been commuted for a money payment. In England, parochial roads until 1835 were in the care of unpaid surveyors and conscripted labourers who carried out their statutory duties with ill will and inefficiency. For improvements in the main roads, reliance was placed on extensions of the turnpike system. The initial success of the Jacobites in 1745 opened the eyes of the Government to the need for improving communications, hence a rapid increase in the number of turnpike trusts. Between 1760 and 1774, 452 turnpike trusts were formed, and in 1773 a general measure affecting all main highways came on to the statute book. By the beginning of the nineteenth century the main roads were being maintained by approximately 1100 turnpike trusts.

The turnpike system was ill-designed to provide Great Britain with a decent network of main roads. There was a lack of uniformity in the powers and duties of trustees. The number of members of individual turnpike trusts was too large for efficient working. In many counties the J.P.s were members of all turnpike trusts in the county. Their regular presence at all meetings they were supposed to attend was an obvious impossibility. As individual bodies of trustees were responsible for relatively short stretches of road, uniformity in road design and construction was impossible of attainment. Roads were not well planned on a county, let alone a national, basis, as trustees rarely worked in unison with their neighbours and often in opposition.

Road development and administration was haphazard, dependent upon the whims, wishes and capabilities of local interests. Foot passengers did not pay tolls, but those for other forms of traffic, vehicles and driven animals showed marked diversities. Within the framework of the Acts creating them, trustees constructed tariff schedules and drew up rules and regulations. General statements about the finances of turnpike trustees are impossible to make. Some made a profit; others were heavily in debt. Not all carried out their duties honestly and efficiently. As a general rule, they did not build new roads but merely maintained existing ones, very often with a degree of efficiency not markedly superior to that of the parish surveyors. After years of control, some roads were little better than when first committed to the care of turnpike trustees. This state of affairs, however, was often due, not to lack of effort, but to daunting geological factors—for example on "the clayey dirty parts" along the trunk roads radiating from London—and to sheer ignorance of sound methods of road construction.

Fortunately competent road engineers, the first known in Britain since Roman times, provided remedies for the national transport emergency. The first, Field Marshal George Wade, has not received adequate recognition as a pioneer in the art of road construction. After the 1715 Jacobite Rebellion he built 250 miles of excellently surfaced military roads in the Scottish Highlands, a region previously traversed by tracks through moor and bog and along giddy precipices. Lessons could be learned from the Frenchman, Pierre Trésaguet, whose ideas were put into practice by the incredible John Metcalfe, Blind Jack of Knaresborough (1717–1810). Blinded by smallpox when six years old, he tried his hand at many occupations. He built 180 miles of road for West Riding turnpike trusts, the first being a three mile stretch on the Harrogate to Boroughbridge road (1765). He surveyed the routes and provided where needed culverts, bridges and embankments. In the more than two score years in which he earned his living as a road contractor, retiring at the age of 75 in 1792, Blind Jack left his imprint not only in Yorkshire but in Cheshire, Lancashire and Derbyshire. He stressed the need for sound foundations. Where the chosen routes led over bog country, he met the problem by laying bundles of whin and ling on the ground, covering this with stone and gravel. One of his roads, so constructed across the swamps of Pule Hill near Marsden in the West Riding, lasted twelve years without repair.

The two best-known road-makers of the period were Thomas Telford (1757–1834) and John Loudon Macadam (1756–1836). The son of an Eskdale shepherd and first apprenticed to a stonemason, Telford became a civil engineer of astonishing versatility. He built not only roads but canals, including the Gotha Canal in Sweden, aqueducts, harbours, bridges, houses and churches. He was appointed Surveyor of Public Works for Shropshire and from 1787 built 42 bridges and the Ellesmere Canal, joining the Mersey, Dee and Severn. In Scotland after 1802 he constructed the Caledonian Canal, made 920 miles of new roads and built 1117 bridges. It was Telford, Samuel Smiles wrote in his *Lives of the Engineers,* who "by his roads bound England and Scotland ... into one, and rendered the union a source of wealth and strength." In 1810 he was commissioned by the Postmaster General to survey the London to Holyhead road, then controlled by 23 turnpike trusts. The road was rebuilt, harbours made at Holyhead and Howth and the Conway and Menai bridges opened in 1826. The Menai Bridge, an exceptionally graceful structure, is particularly noteworthy because in building it Telford demonstrated the advantages of using iron instead of timber and stone in bridge construction. Unfortunately, his death and the coming of the railway prevented Telford from transforming the Great North Road. His roads were carefully made, particular stress being laid on the importance of firm foundations.

Telford's methods were challenged as unnecessarily expensive by his contemporary, John Macadam. He taught that the subsoil was a satisfactory foundation for a waterproof surface. His methods, expressed in his own words, were "to put broken stone upon a road, which shall unite by its own angles, so as to form a solid hard surface." He used stones broken into even-sized pieces, not more than 6 ounces in weight, filling in the gaps with powder ground off the stones themselves. To this day we use the word " macadamised" to describe a road surfaced with small stones. From about 1869 Trinidad bitumen or asphalt was used as a surface covering, and nowadays, to reduce the dust nuisance, "tarmac" is added, usually limestone dipped in coal-tar. Macadam's ideas were opposed by road engineers who preferred Telford's methods, but ultimately they gained general acceptance. Macadamised surfaces lasted longer and the springy nature and less solid foundations of his roads permitted an increased working life for coach horses. Macadam's appointments included that of Surveyor to the Bristol (1816) and more than 30 other turnpike trusts. In 1826 he became Surveyor General of Metropolitan turnpike roads. But although his methods were widely followed, control of highways by very large numbers of autonomous trustees hindered their universal acceptance. Apart from the interest shown by the Post Office and the Board of Agriculture, there was an absence of central direction in the development of the road network.

Contemporaneously, the revolution in the iron industry made possible improvements in vehicular construction. John Palmer, a one-time theatrical manager in Bristol and Bath who became Comptroller of the Post Office, inaugurated in 1784 fast mail coach services. The "flying coaches," running on turnpike roads improved by Telford and Macadam, reduced considerably the time spent on travel. The first 30 years of the nineteenth century were pre-eminently the hey-day of coaches and coachmen. In the reign of George II (1727–60) the London to Edinburgh journey was scheduled to take 16 days. When his great-grandson George IV died in 1830 it took two days. In the same year there were some 3000 stage coaches, half of which were based on London. Manchester could be reached in 19 hours, Exeter in 17 hours and Brighton in 4½ hours. As one might expect, the London coaching services were

MEANS OF COMMUNICATION IN THE PRE-RAILWAY AGE 73

more highly developed than those connecting provincial centres. But private enterprise did not neglect to provide provincial coach facilities, particularly in the newly developing manufacturing areas. By 1822, for example, daily coach services connected Huddersfield with Manchester, Leeds, Wakefield, Halifax and Sheffield. Along the five turnpike roads serving Huddersfield travelled also the large wagons of the carriers who transported the products of local industry as far afield as London, Liverpool and Bristol. Many of the inns where their journeys commenced and ended, such as the Pack Horse, the Ramsden Arms and the Swan, have survived to our own day.

Those who are curious about the joys, not to mention the discomforts and miseries, of coach travel will find the pictures of contemporary artists and the books of contemporary writers a mine of information. In the pages of De Quincey, Leigh Hunt, George Eliot, Charles Dickens and in *Tom Brown's Schooldays*, vivid word pictures can be found of the coachmen, the inns, the magnificent horses and the excitements of departure and arrival. Coach transport, like motor transport today, was a major industry, affording a livelihood to many thousands, coach drivers and postillions, innkeepers and their employees, farmers who supplied oats, horsebreeders, coach builders, harness makers, blacksmiths and wheelwrights. It is readily understandable, therefore, that the coming of railway competition after 1830 brought about a major economic upheaval.

When the railway era began there were some 22,000 miles of main road maintained by 1100 turnpike trusts and approximately 125,000 miles of parish-maintained roads. Both types were incompetently administered and financed. Interest in the creation of a national road system was diverted after 1830 when passenger and mail traffic was lost to the railways. The Road ceased to be a great industry, when what Thomas Hardy described as "a tomb-like stillness" had descended on highways used only by a trickle of pedestrians, and local, private vehicular traffic. The consequent loss of revenue made administrative changes inevitable. By the Highways Act of 1835 compulsory labour on parochial roads was abolished. Instead, parishes were empowered to levy a highway rate and appoint salaried surveyors. Not all parishes took full advantage of the Act. In Huddersfield, for example, at a meeting of ratepayers held at the Ramsden Arms Inn, it was only after a long discussion as to whether there should be two Surveyors as usual, or one with a salary, that Mr James Hanson, wool stapler, was appointed Surveyor (under the Act), with a salary of £100 a year. Most of the 1500 parishes in England and Wales were too small to serve as efficient units of highway administration, especially those called upon to maintain important roads. In 1862–64 Justices at Quarter Sessions were empowered to combine parishes in Highway Districts. In 1878 grants were given by the central government towards the cost of parish road maintenance which under the Local Government Act of 1894 became the duty of the newly created district councils aided by grants from the county rate.

The abolition of the turnpike system was made inevitable by its unpopularity and by railway competition which bankrupted many trustees. Much rioting, notably the "Rebecca Riots" of 1842–43, resulted in the roads of South Wales being taken over by County Road Boards. Elsewhere, after 1864, they were abolished piecemeal. Toll bars in Ireland had ceased to exist by 1857. The Roads and Bridges Act (1878) abolished tolls in Scotland, the last being levied in 1883. The 854 trusts existing in 1871 in England and Wales had been reduced to 71 in 1883. The last, on the Anglesey portion of the Holyhead road, ended in 1895. The only survivals of the turnpike system are the pier, bridge and tunnel tolls still levied in various parts of the United Kingdom.

Under the Local Government Act of 1888, main road maintenance became the responsibility of the newly created county councils. The invention of the internal combustion engine has, however, created an entirely new situation. Owing to the tremendous rise in the number of motor vehicles, the problem of road transport became incapable of solution except on a national basis. In 1903 motor taxation duties were used to assist ratepayers. In 1909 a Road Board was created, empowered to make grants to county councils from the proceeds of motor vehicle and petrol taxation. Finally, in 1937, the Ministry of Transport took over responsibility for main roads.

Chapter VII

CANALS

If eighteenth-century transport changes had been confined to road improvements, the demands of an expanding trade and industry could not have been satisfied. But in fact reliance had never been placed wholly on land transport. For the movement of heavy and fragile freight water transport was used from the earliest times. It was by waterways that the builders of our most imposing historic monuments, cathedrals, monasteries and castles, transported their building materials. In the Middle Ages there was a considerable traffic by sea and river in such commodities as coal, building materials, foodstuffs and salt. The most highly developed areas before the eighteenth century were those to which access was possible by water. Conversely, those not so endowed remained uninhabited wildernesses until the canal era. The beneficent effects of canal construction were noted by John Wesley on a visit to North Staffordshire in 1781. "The wilderness," he wrote, "is literally become a fruitful field," evidence confirmed by Josiah Wedgwood's statement that between 1760 and 1785 the number of workers in the pottery industry increased from 7000 to 15,000.

England is fortunate in as much as nature has endowed her with many navigable rivers and numerous coastal harbours. Even the hilly country was not without means of transport, as many rivers, for example those flowing from the Pennines, were navigable. Many inland urban centres in the Middle Ages were seaports, the shallow draught vessels of the period being able to reach places like York, Norwich and Gloucester. In fact before the railway era much of the traffic in heavy and bulky commodities was by sea. Conditions of overland transport were such that it would have been impossible otherwise to have transported, for example, coal from Tyne and Wear to London and other places, or china clay from Cornwall via the Mersey to North Staffordshire.

A very marked feature of economic development during the seventeenth and eighteenth centuries was the very considerable expansion of coastal traffic. Nevertheless, serious limitations on the expansion of trade and industry were being imposed by the lack of adequate transport facilities. Many parts of the country were not easily accessible to goods carried by sea transport. The alternative, transport of heavy freight by wagon or on pack horse, was costly and slow, if not impossible. The iron industry needed iron ore and coal and a means of moving bulky finished products. Poor transport facilities are one if not the only explanation of the decline of the iron industry in the Sussex Weald. The North Staffordshire pottery makers needed coal, china clay from Cornwall, flint from the eastern counties and a means of transporting fragile wares, safer than that in use, pack horses struggling through mire and mud. The Lancashire cotton industry was manufacturing increasing quantities of cotton imported through Liverpool. Coal, for household fuel, could only be made universally available provided an alternative was found to costly pack horses and wagon transport. Further, the new industrial centres were developing in areas where transport conditions were less satisfactory than in the older, settled districts.

The first solution to these problems was the deepening of river beds and the making of artificial channels where rivers meandered. After the Restoration Andrew Yarranton improved navigation facilities on the Stour between Stourport and Kidderminster, and on the Warwickshire Avon between Stratford and Tewkesbury. In the late seventeenth and early eighteenth centuries, Parliament sanctioned the deepening of river beds, though not without opposition, in some instances from local vested interests, and from landowners who considered that alteration in river levels would result in the flooding of their land. Schemes successfully carried out included those on the Weaver, Sankey Brook, the Aire–Calder Navigation, the Don, the Dee and the Bedfordshire Great Ouse.

In the development of waterways Great Britain lagged behind some continental countries. In France, for example, the ministers of the first three Bourbon kings, Sully, Richelieu and Colbert, did much to develop river navigation in the seventeenth century, an example followed by Napoleon. In the reign of Louis XIV (1681) Paul Riquet constructed the Canal du Midi between Toulouse on the Garonne and Cette on the Mediterranean, traversing at a height of 625 feet the Carcassonne Gap between the Central Plateau and the Pyrenees. Two other French waterways dating from the seventeenth century are the Seine–Loire Canal (1640) and the Orleans Canal (1692). But in Britain, smaller in size than France, and with all her urban centres relatively near the sea, no such initiative was taken by the Government, apart from the building of the Caledonian Canal and the short Crinan Canal. These, however, were not truly inland waterways, but a means of avoiding the perils of navigation along the Highland coast. For the development of inland waterways, as also later of railways, Great Britain relied upon the promptings of private enterprise. On the other hand, it was advantageous to traders that traffic on British rivers was not subjected to the vexatious tolls and duties which had to be paid by users of European rivers.

According to Defoe, at the beginning of the eighteenth century there were about 1160 miles of navigable river. Particularly important were the Thames, Severn, Warwickshire Avon, Mersey, Yorkshire Ouse and Tyne. But many parts of the country were not served by navigable rivers which in any case were sometimes too shallow in dry weather, while at other times their usefulness was impeded by floods and tides. Despite the high costs of road carriage, bad as they were, roads were sometimes a better means of communication. To send goods from Manchester to Liverpool cost 40s. a ton, but only 12s. by river, the barges being pulled by men. Cheshire salt was distributed by pack horses. Coal reached Manchester in panniers, each pack-animal carrying 280 lb. The solution to these problems was found in canals, which, before the railway era, became the principal inland means of transporting heavy goods like coal and grain, and breakable articles such as pottery.

Canal construction in level country is relatively easy given the labour and knowledge of how to construct a bottom that will not leak. But as water will not run uphill, canals could not be built in hill country until the lock system was invented, credit for which is disputed by Dutch and Italian engineers. In Great Britain, the pioneer in canal building was the Duke of Bridgewater, who was looking for a cheaper means of transporting coal from his Worsley pit to Manchester, seven miles away. The construction problem of this first canal was solved by the Duke's engineer, the almost illiterate James Brindley (1716–72). Brindley was born at Thornsett in Derbyshire. As a wheelwright in business in Leek he attracted attention by the ingenuity and skill he displayed in repairing machinery. In 1752 he designed an engine for draining coal pits at Clifton in Lancashire, and in 1756 made machinery for the manufacture of tooth and pinion wheels for a silk mill at Congleton in Cheshire.

Acting on Brindley's advice the Duke of Bridgewater decided to finance the heavy capital costs of constructing a canal from Worsley to Manchester along a route marshy in places and impeded by the River Irwell. The latter obstacle Brindley overcame by constructing the Barton Aqueduct which carried the canal over the river at an elevation of 39 feet. Opened in 1761 the Bridgewater Canal was an immediate success. The price of coal in Manchester fell from 7d. to 3½d. a cwt. It was followed in 1767 by the Duke's Canal, a continuation of the Bridgewater Canal from Longford Bridge to Runcorn on the Mersey, thereby providing a water route between Manchester and Liverpool.

Brindley's achievements are amazing especially in the light of the difficulties he had to overcome. He had no body of experience on which to draw. He had to train workmen to carry out tasks never previously attempted in this country, thereby calling into existence "navigators," or "navvies," whose skills were to prove invaluable to the builders of railways. He had to do his own surveying and his own contracting, to solve, unaided, difficult engineering problems and invent tools to perform novel tasks. Modern civil engineers, assisted by earth-moving equipment of massive capabilities may well admire Brindley's achievements—such as, for example, the 3000-yard tunnel he commenced in 1766 to carry the Trent and Mersey Canal under Harecastle Hill. But technical problems were only some of the obstacles he had to surmount. He had also to battle against the scepticism of contemporaries. Most of the canal network was built after his death. During his lifetime very few, apart from the Duke of Bridgewater, believed in the practicability of his ideas. The £220,000 the Duke spent on the first two canals was all he could afford to invest. It was only later, after the Duke and Brindley had demonstrated the profitability of canals, that investors, sometimes unwisely, made available capital for canal construction.

Brindley planned and nearly completed before his death from overwork about 365 miles of canals, including the Grand Trunk Canal, connecting the Mersey and the Trent, and the Staffordshire and Worcester (1766), and Oxford and Chesterfield Canals (1769). The linking of Manchester and Liverpool by waterway led to rapid development of the Lancashire cotton industry. The Grand Trunk Canal, completed in 1777, justified Josiah Wedgwood's advocacy of the project, as it transformed the Potteries, provided Cheshire salt mines with improved transport facilities and Cheshire farmers with new markets in industrial Lancashire. But the most active period of canal construction, between 1780 and 1800, occurred after Brindley's death. Between 1791 and 1794 81 Canal Acts were passed, many investors risking their savings in projects which had little or no hope of success. The existing canal network, with the notable exception of the Manchester Ship Canal, was built before 1830. In that year there were about 3000 miles of canals in England and Wales, 183 miles of canals and improved waterways in Scotland, and 848 miles in Ireland. The waterways of 1830 were immensely more useful than the road facilities available in 1700.

The three canals which spanned the Pennine hills and moorlands provided water routes between Liverpool and Preston on the west, and Goole and Hull on the east. The first followed the Aire valley through Leeds and Skipton, descending on the Lancashire side through Burnley and Blackburn to Preston. The second was routed in the Calder Valley from Wakefield to Halifax, thence to Rochdale, joining the Irwell in Manchester. The third, the Huddersfield to Ashton canal, linked the Calder valley by way of Huddersfield and the Colne valley with Ashton-under-Lyne and Manchester. The watershed was crossed by the building of the three-mile-long Standedge tunnel between Marsden and Diggle (1811), the longest canal tunnel in the world. Slightly lengthened in 1893 it was fed by water drained from the moors into two reservoirs.

Many canals opened out the Midlands, Birmingham becoming the centre of an intricate system of waterways with the consequent enhancement of its industrial prospects. The Trent and Mersey were linked to the Thames by the Coventry Canal (1768) and the Oxford Canal (1790). The Grand Junction Canal (1793–1805), running from the Oxford Canal near Northampton to London, was of inestimable value to the West Midlands. The Thames–Severn Canal (1783–89), constructed through a gap in the Cotswolds, provided a water route between London and Bristol. The inland waterways of the Midlands were linked to Bristol by the Wolverhampton Canal (1772) connecting the Trent at Haywood with Stourport on the Severn. The coal and iron industries of South Wales depended upon canal transport, the most important being the Glamorgan Canal connecting Cardiff with Merthyr Tydfil (1798). From England and Wales, canal building spread to Scotland. In 1768 work was started on the construction of the Forth–Clyde Canal. The largest of all the canals, the Caledonian Canal, linking the lochs in the Great Glen, was built by Telford between 1804 and 1822. Lastly, in Ireland, where the absence of hills and the rainy climate made canal building relatively easy, canals were built which commercially proved to be of little or no value.

Canals did not replace but supplemented long-used river transport facilities. Their construction, coupled with the pre-1750 improvements in river navigation, provided a system of inland water routes without which agricultural and industrial commodities could not have reached the market. The economic and social gains from canal building were immense. Transport costs were reduced to between one half and one quarter those of road carriage. Not only was merchandise carried more cheaply, but also more easily and more safely. Bulky commodities such as grain, coal, and building materials now entered into general trade. Coal was made available to all parts of the kingdom for both industrial and household consumption. Rural areas, hitherto dependent on wood or even dung for fuel, found coal, transported in canal barges, a welcome alternative. In fact the demand for coal was a major stimulus to canal construction. The expectation, however, that canals would end the Tyne–Wear monopoly in London was not realised as Northumberland and Durham coal interests had too firm a monopoly grip on the market.

The lowering of costs of distribution and manufacture made possible large-scale production in thickly populated urban centres. The concentration of population in large, urban, inland centres is a characteristic feature of modern British economic development. Before the canal era, the only large cities were ports or inland towns located on river banks at the head of navigation, at points where streams converged or at fording places. It was canals that made feasible the transportation of food, stone, brick and timber for building purposes, and fuel and raw materials to sites hitherto thinly-peopled. Birmingham, for example, where we learn from Leland's *Itinerary* iron and hardware manufacturers were thriving in 1538, grew rapidly after it had become the nodal point of the Midland system of canals. Its 17,000 inhabitants in 1700 had expanded to 73,000 in 1801. An explanation of much modern industrial location may be found in canal routings, as their banks were naturally favoured in the choice of industrial and commercial sites. Later, as they had become well established, railways were routed to serve them. Later still, in the motor age, roads were re-modelled to transport their products.

Canals played a very important part in opening up the Midlands, previously isolated by the detestable trackways that traversed the heavy clays of the region. Particularly noticeable was the transformation in the Potteries once transport by water was available for the carriage of china clay from Cornwall, flint from the eastern counties and coal from neighbouring collieries. A primitive peasant industry based on local clays was, during the reign of George III (1760–1820), changed into one exporting high quality earthenware and china to Europe, the West Indies and North America. Much of the transformation was due to the innovations of Josiah Wedgwood (1730–95), Josiah Spode (1733–97) and others. But their ingenuity could not have reaped its full reward without the two turnpike roads and canal links for which Josiah Wedgwood campaigned.

The development of the ports, consequent on the enlargement of their hinterlands, was a striking result of canal construction.

Liverpool at the beginning of the eighteenth century had some 5000 inhabitants, the slave trade being its principal activity. Later in the century its merchants took to privateering as a profitable investment. But before the slave trade was abolished in 1807 new prospects had opened out. Canals made Liverpool the chief outlet for industrial Lancashire and the Midlands. New docks were built, and the city expanded beyond its original limits, spreading up the slopes beyond the Pool. A visitor to modern Liverpool can see on the high ground in the neighbourhood of the modern university much evidence of the large amount of building activity in the early nineteenth century.

The trade of Liverpool, like that of Hull and Goole, also increased as the port handled much of the merchandise previously carried by coastal shipping. In the pre-steamship age a steady stream of barges poured through the Aire, Calder and Colne Valley Pennine gaps, laden with goods from the continent invoiced to Ireland, North America and the West Indies. Canals and better roads also changed methods of trading. Chapmen, or travelling merchants, with their trains of pack animals disappeared from the roads. They were replaced by commercial travellers with their samples. Farmers in regions served by canals, no longer restricted to selling in local markets, were encouraged to adopt the new agricultural techniques. Their customers, no longer wholly dependent on locally-grown foodstuffs, ceased to suffer the inconveniences of local scarcities and high prices, and were able to enjoy a more varied diet. To sum up, canal and improved river communications provided safe and easy, if slow, means of transport which stimulated trade, industry and agriculture, and opened up large areas hitherto backward and under-developed. Without the means of transporting bulky commodities along inland water routes the first phase of the British Industrial Revolution could not have taken place, a phase characterised by the revolution in the textile industries, an increasing importance of coal and iron, and the first steps in the use of steam power. The second phase, which came after 1830, was based on a new form of transport, the railway.

The methods of financing turnpike road improvement schemes differed from those used in canal construction. Turnpike trustees possessed statutory powers to levy tolls to meet road costs. Finance for the construction of the first canals was provided by wealthy individuals. But as wealthy persons able and willing to undertake such speculative ventures were in short supply, after 1780 joint stock companies were formed, subscribers investing their capital in the expectation of dividends. Some of the canals were very remunerative. In 1824 the Grand Trunk paid a dividend of 75 per cent, and the Loughborough Canal 197 per cent. In the same year the dividend on Grand Junction stock was 10 per cent. On the whole, however, canal speculators did not get large returns on their investments. Some, built through difficult country, were encumbered with unduly large capital costs. During the 1791–94 period many ill-advised projects were undertaken, from which speculators learned that the mere provision of transport facilities will not by itself create trade when the potentiality is absent. But those canals servicing areas where transport provision was urgently needed, owing to the slow growth of the railway network after 1830, continued to handle the bulk of the internal wholesale trade until about 1840. After 1840 they declined. In the first decade of the twentieth century, although canals carried more merchandise than in the nineteenth century, the percentage of the whole they attracted was much smaller. The bulk of the inland traffic had passed to the railways.

The decline of the canals was due, firstly, to the development of new means of transport, secondly, to the drawbacks of the canal network which remained unremedied, thirdly, to dissatisfaction of customers with the services provided by carriers enjoying a virtual transport monopoly, and fourthly, to changes in the nature of internal trade. Steamships regained much of the coastal trade. Railways provided a quicker and more efficient means of transport in contrast to the comparatively shorter hauls and lack of flexibility of canals which could only serve places situated on their banks. The belated introduction of express services by "fly boats," travelling at about 3 miles per hour, did little to improve their competitive capacity. Other than for the carriage of heavy commodities, when the time factor was unimportant, canal transport had little if any advantage over carriage even along the improved roads. Canals were ill-adapted for speedy carriage as, being narrow, the wash of quickly moving barges undermined their banks. The many locks and tunnels in hill country impeded traffic and made British canals costly both to construct and operate. Some passed through areas of mining subsidence, others, particularly in chalk and limestone regions, had difficulties in obtaining sufficient water.

Much of the failure of canal companies to offer effective resistance to railway competition can be traced to the circumstances in which they were built. Owing their existence to private enterprise and concerned to satisfy local needs, they were designed for comparatively short hauls. The many short canals were never unified. The construction of very large canals, in any case, would have been, both for technical and economic reasons, impracticable. What would have been possible, and highly desirable—a greater degree of co-operation in the construction and operation of canals—was not forthcoming. They varied in gauge, depth, sizes of locks and tunnels, height of bridges and in toll charges. As canal companies themselves did not carry the goods, the inconvenience and economic folly of frequent transhipments and no quotations for through rates for the whole journey was not brought home to them. A major factor in transport costs is the transfer of goods from one means of transport to another. A system of transport which offers long hauls and avoids numerous handlings of merchandise has obvious advantages. This canal companies, unlike the railways, did not provide. When in 1845 canal companies were given statutory powers to act as carriers it was too late to introduce more economical methods. On the contrary, faced with railway competition, canal companies tended to adopt defeatist attitudes.

No attempts were made by combinations to meet the railway threat. In any case a large part of the system was of narrow dimensions, impossible to widen, as on canal sides much industrial building had taken place. No help was forthcoming from the Government. In contrast, other European governments took positive action to modernise their national waterways. Being more interested in recovering their investments than in improving canal competitive capacity many canal companies sold their undertakings to railway promoters. Some directors even insisted on railway promoters buying them out as the price of non-resistance to the passage of railway bills through Parliament. According to the Report of the 1906 Commission on Canals and Inland Navigation, canal ownership was distributed as follows:

Independent waterways	3310 miles
Waterways owned by railways	1145 miles
Waterways controlled by railways	218 miles

Railways owned some of the strategic links in the canal system, a circumstance that could have militated against plans to unify it. But the common belief that railway companies of set purpose discouraged the diversion of traffic to their canals is hard to credit. It is certainly not easy to understand why they should have deliberately destroyed useful assets. That they had not done so was the conclusion of the commissioners appointed in 1888 and in 1906 to report on British waterways. In fact, the Birmingham canals, which during this period carried more traffic than any others, were controlled by the London and North Western Railway.

An explanation of why Victorian merchants welcomed an alternative to canals is to be found in the failure of the carriers to deserve public confidence. There was congestion at busy times and poor service when freight was scarce. Theft of goods in transit, lack of standardised freight charges, non-availability of quotations for through journeys and uncertainty of delivery dates were complaints all too often justified. The Royal Commission of 1906 reported that the greater part of the canal network was little used, and that many canals were derelict. But the dishonesty and inefficiency of carriers would not alone have accounted for this state of affairs. Railways triumphed owing to changes in the character of internal traffic. Much modern freight consists of small parcels. Farmers producing milk, fruit, vegetables, eggs, butter and meat need quick transport to markets. Coal distribution is more efficient by rail than by water. All in all, the railways met the needs of traders more efficiently than the canals.

Bulk commodities, it has been argued, can be transported by water carriage very cheaply. Unfortunately, the hundreds of private companies who built the canals did so with an eye to contemporary local needs, and with no thought of future expansion. The capital costs of modernising the canal network would be immense. The Royal Commission on Canals and Inland Navigations (1906) recommended the creation of a Central Waterways Board and the construction by the State of four trunk canals. But although the canal system was nationalised in 1948 no steps have been taken to implement these proposals. Some carriage of minerals, and bulky non-perishable commodities, still passes along a restricted number of canals at low costs. Bargemen sail barges which are also their homes. But they are fewer than a century ago when over 40,000 of them, with their womenfolk and children, many illiterate, carried on their occupation isolated from the rest of the community.

Nowadays there is a substantial amount of commercial traffic on about 800 miles of the canal network controlled by the British Waterways Board, mostly carried on such wide waterways as the Gloucester and Sharpness, the Weaver and the Lea below Enfield Many of the canals, suitable only for narrow boats, are choked by vegetation, and in urban areas are used as rubbish dumps. The remainder of the canal network is used only by pleasure craft and a handful of private carriers. Critics complain that the Waterways Board is wasting a national asset by failing to follow the example set by Holland, France and Germany in modernising waterborne transport facilities. Unfortunately, the Board's officials reasonably reply, many canals provide waterways into rural retreats. The only profitable use, therefore, of a canal system designed to meet the needs of the country in the early stages of the Industrial Revolution, is the sale of water. If there is to be a profitable use in the future for canal transport it may result from the urgent need to divert traffic from overcrowded roads and in the development of its cruising potential for those who enjoy holidays pottering about on canals and rivers. At the moment, however, all is as quiet on the waterways as it was on the roads in late Victorian times.

PART III

OVERSEAS COMMERCE AND FISCAL POLICIES, 1700–1850

Chapter VIII

THE COMMERCIAL REVOLUTION

Pre-1700 Trade Trends

Until comparatively recent times men relied upon the resources of their immediate neighbourhood for the greater part of what they need to sustain life. Primitive communities, living under conditions of local self-sufficiency still exist, but nowadays most people are consumers of commodities produced elsewhere than in their own neighbourhood. Twentieth-century man's demands on the products of the earth are such that they can only be satisfied by an intricate system of distribution and exchange. In the modern world local or even national and continental self-sufficiency is impossible of attainment. Climate, and physical and geological conditions vary considerably over the Earth's surface. As we live in an age where there is a division of labour between urban and rural societies, between craftsmen and agriculturists, and between those who produce primary and secondary goods, commercial relationships are necessarily organised on a world-wide scale.

The earliest form of trade was by barter. From such primitive beginnings our own complex system of exchange and distribution has grown. But trading can only take place provided transport by land and water is possible, and governments are powerful enough to ensure safe passage for merchants. For many centuries in Western Europe, after the fall of the Roman Empire, trade was restricted, because neither by land nor by sea could safe passage be guaranteed. Hence in the so-called "Dark Ages" the peoples of Western Europe were organised in village communities possessing a high but not a complete degree of self-sufficiency. These conditions of self-sufficiency were partially removed after A.D. 1000 by a considerable growth of maritime commerce, a complicated network of trading routes coming into existence.

Until the close of the Middle Ages England's import trade was for the most part in alien hands. Italians brought the products of the Levant and the Orient, spices, drugs, perfumes, precious stones, dyestuffs and eastern Mediterranean wines. In the ships of the Hanse merchants came more utilitarian wares, herrings, furs, hemp, iron, timber and naval stores, that is, pitch, tar and turpentine. From Bordeaux the Gascons, for three centuries subjects of the English king, exported claret. From Malaga and Tarragona came Spanish wines and from Flanders high quality cloth made from English wool. The manufacturing towns of the Netherlands, the principal industrial area in Europe, depended upon wool, the most lucrative English export. Wool and the other staple exports—wool fells, hides, leather and tin—were exported by the Merchants of the Staple to Calais until it became a French possession in 1558. Numerous magnificent brasses in Cotswold churches perpetuate memories of the many Staplers who made large fortunes following "the honourable" trade in wool. As Professor Eileen Power has shown in her account of one of them, Thomas Betson, their daily life is not difficult to reconstruct. But in the fifteenth century, when Thomas Betson was alive, England was entering on a new phase in her history. Another company, that of the Merchant Adventurers, was exporting *cloth*. Their bitter rivalry with the Staplers and Hanse merchants marked the beginning of an era when Englishmen were themselves becoming traders overseas. The Steelyard, the Hanse settlement in London, was closed in 1598, and the annual visit of the Venetian "Flanders Galleys" ceased in 1587. The Merchants of the Staple maintained a shadowy existence, in name only, until the eighteenth century. Their active participation in trade had vanished when the exports they had specialised in were needed by English manufacturers at home.

England began this new phase of her commercial history with considerable advantages. The decay of serfdom and restrictive guild practices removed obstacles to the development of England's natural resources by men of foresight and ambition. Home produced wool became the basis of a considerable woollen cloth export trade. Under the Tudors national unity was attained, baronial anarchy overcome and active encouragement was given to the development of national resources. England's many excellent harbours and tidal estuaries, navigable far inland, were solid assets for the development of overseas trade. In the enjoyment of peace and internal security England fared better than contemporary sixteenth-century countries. Italian disunity was perpetuated and Italian prosperity destroyed by the foreign wars fought on her soil from 1494. The prosperity of the Low Countries was undermined by "the Spanish fury," the Inquisition and the generation-long war of Dutch Independence. In France, during the second half of the sixteenth century, economic progress was interrupted by civil war, while in Germany disunity culminated in the appalling horrors of the Thirty Years' War (1618–48). The war with Spain during the second half of Queen Elizabeth I's reign did have dire effects on England's overseas trade, but at least the Queen's subjects were spared the damaging consequences of armed conflicts over their own fields.

The opportunity to make profitable use of these advantages was afforded by the geographical revolution of the late fifteenth and sixteenth centuries. The exploratory voyages of Christopher Columbus (1492), Vasco da Gama (1497–98) and many other European sailors resulted ultimately in the displacement of the Mediterranean by the Atlantic as the chief highway of commerce. Ports on the Atlantic seaboard fetched and carried the wares of distant countries, while those on the Mediterranean lost monopoly control of the trade between the Orient and the West. The early predominance of Spain and Portugal was later challenged by France, Holland and England, each of whom, in vigorous competition with one another, developed world-wide trade connections and extensive colonial empires. As freight costs by sea are considerably lower than those by land the prices of Oriental commodities fell. Costly wares imported for the very wealthy ultimately became commodities of mass consumption, while new commodities became commercially more important than the older luxury staples.

Chartered Trading Companies

For Britain, the new commercial order had momentous consequences. No longer isolated on the circumference of the known world she came to occupy a central position in the land mass of the northern hemisphere. Instead of having a small share of maritime trade in European waters only, she was destined to become an international trading power of the first rank. Credit for pioneering this commercial expansion belongs to the chartered trading companies founded in the sixteenth and seventeenth centuries. When James I came to the throne in 1603, trade with countries other than Spain, Portugal and France was restricted to members of trading companies granted by the Crown monopoly rights in specified regions. A list of the names of these countries demonstrates that long before 1700 English trade was world-wide in extent. By the end of Elizabeth I's reign, the Merchant Adventurers, the Eastland Company and the Russian or Muscovy Company were active in northern and eastern Europe. The latter traded with Russia at first through Archangel and later through Narva. Some of its members even voyaged by way of the Volga and Caspian Sea to Persia in search of Oriental wares. Members of the Levant or Turkey

Company (1581) traded in the territories of the Ottoman Empire where they encountered the bitter opposition of the Venetians. The Morocco and Guinea Companies traded in Africa. The members of the Guinea Company, originally attracted to Africa about 1533 by ivory and gold, became notorious after 1562 for the development of the iniquitous slave trade, monopolised after the Restoration of 1660 by the Royal African Company. The most important of all, the East India Company, received in 1600 monopoly trading privileges east of the Cape of Good Hope and west of Cape Horn. The East India Company had a long and extraordinary history, becoming the ruler of the Indian sub-continent until its abolition in 1858.

The colonisation of the North American seaboard was pioneered by the Virginian (1607) and Plymouth (1620) Companies. The only one of those early chartered trading companies still in existence, the Hudson Bay Company, was founded in 1670 by Prince Rupert, the Duke of York and sixteen others "for the finding some trade for furs, minerals, and other considerable commodities" in the vast territories watered by rivers flowing into Hudson Bay. Many of its rights were ceded to the Dominion of Canada in 1869. Scottish efforts to colonise the Panama Isthmus in the Darien Scheme (1695), in the expectation of a share in the eastern trade, ended in disastrous failure. The South Sea Company, founded in 1711, took over the Asiento trade privileges acquired from Spain by the Treaty of Utrecht (1713). As a trading company it was a failure, even more disastrous being its involvement in the South Sea Bubble, the gigantic financial crash of 1721.

In entrusting the development of trade to monopolistic companies Britain pursued a policy favoured also by her rivals, Spain, Portugal, Holland and France, and by the rulers of Brandenburg–Prussia, Peter the Great and the Habsburg Emperors. But unlike the European companies, the British companies were not state controlled. They owed their existence to the promptings of private enterprise aiming at making a profit for shareholders. The granting of monopoly privileges to associations of merchants was a sound policy. Not otherwise, in prevailing conditions, could trade with distant lands, politically unsettled, have been developed. Commerce was a very risky venture in which bankruptcy was as likely a consequence as the acquisition of a large fortune. Few merchants were as fortunate as Shakespeare's *Merchant of Venice*, who, if his "wealthy Andrew docked in sand" would take comfort in the thought: "my ventures are not in one bottom trusted, nor in one place, nor is my whole estate upon the fortune of this present year."

The natural perils of the sea, real enough today, were much greater hazards to the wooden sailing vessels in which the contemporaries of Lord Clive took eighteen months to make the return journey to India. Two generations later, after Queen Victoria was born, travellers spent one month on the return journey to Hamburg, and three months if they visited New York. Return journeys to Canton or New South Wales involved absence from home of almost a year. The life of a sailor was one of extreme hardships and privations. Very cramped quarters, unwholesome, loathsome food, tainted unsavoury water and the risk of death from disease, including the ever-prevalent scurvy, were his lot. Ships usually returned from long voyages with large numbers of sick, exhausted hands on board. Defective sea charts, unlighted coasts, rocks, sandbanks and "wreckers" who lured ships to rocky coasts by false lights, were hazards threatening mariners with watery graves. Those who sailed in the proud Venetian "Flanders Galleys" no less than modern seamen dreaded the Goodwins, described in the *Merchant of Venice* as "a very dangerous flat and fatal, where the carcasses of many a tall ship lie buried."

At journey's end ships tossed at anchor in open roadsteads, their cargoes being unloaded by lightermen on the riverside quays. Here they were piled up, exposed to the hazards of weather and the depredations of innumerable river thieves. At sea, privateers molested merchant vessels in European waters, Barbary corsairs in the Mediterranean, buccaneers in the West Indies and hostile natives elsewhere. Protection of British commerce by permanently stationing naval forces in the Mediterranean and elsewhere was impossible until such bases as Gibraltar, Minorca and Malta were acquired in the eighteenth century. Therefore merchant ships had to be armed. In distant seas European traders fought unofficial wars with one another. Ashore, in non-European lands, where native governments were either unable or unwilling to guarantee aliens protection, trading posts or factories had to be fortified and manned by soldiers. Forts were built, for example, on the Gold Coast and on the Gambia River in West Africa. The East India Company founded Fort St George, Madras, in 1640. Bombay was acquired in 1668 and Fort William, Calcutta, in 1690. Such essential conveniences could obviously only be provided from the resources of powerful associations.

In addition to the risks of trade there were many other sound reasons for the granting of trade monopolies. An unscrupulous lone trader, interested only in a single quick profit, could spoil the market, a state of affairs less likely to arise if trade was carried on by responsible companies with long-term interests to safeguard.

Interlopers were numerous, but at least they could not operate under a cloak of legality, and, if caught, were severely punished. It was also only fair that pioneers should be protected. Commercial investment was only likely to take place provided reasonable guarantees were given that those who took the considerable risks would enjoy the profits. Further, it was taken for granted by our forefathers that commerce should be regulated. From medieval times foreign trade was carried on under royal control. Kings depended for revenue upon customs duties, and, after the Civil War, upon excise duties also. It was easier to collect revenue from companies than from large numbers of individuals. But apart from fiscal considerations rulers also considered that they had a duty to ensure that economic policies were enforced that were beneficial to national interests. It was unthinkable that untrammelled rein should be allowed to the promptings of private enterprise. The monopoly privileges of the chartered companies were often attacked, but they were not abolished until the nineteenth century. By then, free competition was accepted as a paramount national interest, monopoly being thought of as an impediment to enterprise and expansion.

Chartered trading companies were of two types, regulated and joint stock companies. The earlier companies, the Merchant Adventurers, the Eastland, Muscovy and Levant Companies, were of the Regulated type. These did not trade as corporate bodies. A group of members provided capital for "a venture" and at its conclusion shared the profits or suffered the losses. But they conducted their affairs according to the rules of the company as, for example, do members of Lloyds or the Stock Exchange nowadays. Experience, however, soon showed that for the development of a permanent trade, such a form of association had its limitations. It became customary, therefore, for members to take shares in a series of ventures. In this way joint stock companies gradually came into existence. Members were shareholders, the practical management of affairs being entrusted to directors. The East India Company, in origin a regulated company, had by the Restoration of 1660 become one of the joint stock type. Other joint stock companies were the Virginia, Royal African, Hudson Bay and South Sea Companies. The advantages of this form of organisation were many. Capital could be obtained from a larger number of investors, not restricted to those with practical commercial experience. As joint stock companies had a greater degree of permanency, plans for expansion could be made, and the provision of ships, trading facilities and military protection overseas be more efficiently guaranteed. Investors, desirous of realising their assets, found the sale of shares a more practical possibility than the sale of rights in "a venture," the completion of which might be months ahead.

Overseas Expansion and its Causes

The enterprise and courage of members of chartered trading companies had made Great Britain by the eighteenth century not only an important commercial power, but also a colonial power. The companies, granted monopoly rights in North America, had to send settlers there to develop the resources of the territory as a preliminary to the establishment of commercial relations. The pioneer settlement made in Virginia (1607) had by 1732 become thirteen colonies, the nucleus of the modern U.S.A. From forts built on the Hayes and Churchill Rivers in what was then known as Rupertsland on James Bay, a few score hardy employees of the Hudson Bay Company collected beaver skins and furs from the Indians. Nova Scotia, New Brunswick and Newfoundland were acquired by 1713, and Quebec during the Seven Years' War (1756–63). In the seventeenth century a number of West Indian islands became English possessions, and trading posts were established on the coasts of India, and on the Gambia River and the Gold Coast in West Africa. In other words, by the beginning of the eighteenth century English merchants had established trading posts in close proximity to the sea in the New World, Asia and Africa. From these vantage points, after the middle of the eighteenth century, inland penetration took place, first by river and in the nineteenth century by railways.

The causes of this overseas expansion were many. Religious persecution and trade depressions explain the foundation of settlements in North America before the outbreak of the Civil War (1642). More important after the Restoration were political and economic motives. These included rivalry with Spain, France and the Dutch Republic, the desire to avoid dependence on foreigners for supplies of overseas commodities, and the ambition to develop shipping to strengthen the defences of an island power. Other influences at work were transport improvements, both by land and sea, and the not inconsiderable industrial developments in eighteenth-century Britain.

Major changes in the pattern of British trade were a consequence of the establishment of overseas settlements. There were changes in the geographical distribution of British trade and also in trade commodities and their relative importance. British trade, both on its export and import sides, expanded after 1700, but it is not possible to obtain precise estimates of the amount or rate of commercial expansion. The statistical information which exists is incomplete and hard to interpret. As far as imports are concerned, we must also note that very considerable quantities of luxury commodities were brought in by smugglers, estimates of the volume of which are impossible to make. It must also be borne in mind that between the outbreak of the War of Spanish Succession (1702) and the Battle of Waterloo (1815) there were more years in which Great Britain was at war than enjoying peace. War conditions inevitably affected trade. Trade with Europe was naturally impeded. Freight charges and prices rose. Higher tariffs, the imposition of wartime taxation and the activities of privateers, could not have had other than harmful consequences.

Commercial expansion between 1700 and 1780 took place at a relatively modest rate. Europe was the chief market, woollen cloth, and in years of good harvests corn, being exported to the continent. Of growing importance was the re-export trade in Asiatic and American wares. By 1784 more than a quarter of British exports to Europe were colonial wares, tobacco, sugar and spices, which by the provisions of the Interregnum (1650–51) and Restoration (1660) Navigation Acts, had to be sent to England before being despatched to their ultimate destination. This growing re-export trade is an indication that British commercial interests had ceased to be confined to Europe. Trade relations with Asia and the New World became increasingly important after the Restoration, bringing in their train changes in diet and fashion, improved standards of living and a revolution in popular consumption.

Trade with Asia

The Asiatic trade provoked much criticism from the woollen manufacturing interests. The Levant Company, which exported much cloth to the Mediterranean, and resented East India Company competition in the eastern trade, argued that lowly paid Indian workers, producing calicoes, muslins and silks, were ruining English woollen cloth producers. It was certainly true that European craftsmen could not compete with those of Dacca and Surat, hence the passage of Acts in 1700 and 1721 prohibiting the importation of Indian high class quality fabrics. These Acts were followed by the so-called "Manchester Act" (1735) protecting Manchester and Bolton "fustian manufactures," partially made of cotton. Government policy was certainly disliked by "our stately fops" and their ladies, for whom the decrees of fashion did not dictate reliance on good old English homespun. Fortunately for them, the textile inventions of the eighteenth century, making possible the production of high class cotton fabrics at home, led to the repeal in 1774, at the instance of Sir Richard Arkwright, of this prohibitive legislation.

Eighteenth-century industrial invention in Britain brought about a fundamental change in the centuries-old pattern of East–West commercial relationships. From at least the commencement of the Christian era India's exports to the west, owing to the difficulties of land transport, had been commodities small in bulk and costly in price. In payment she received corals, copper, tin, lead and precious metals. From the very earliest of times to the present day, the importation of precious metals has been an outstanding feature of India's foreign trade. The East India Company was criticised for its bullion exports, a harmful practice according to the economic ideas of the age. In the first half of the eighteenth century exports of bullion to India reached £27 million, the value of goods sent being only £9 million. To meet the criticism that its trade did not sufficiently enlarge the market for English woollen cloth, the East India Company did on occasions export to India more cloth than Indian demands justified, but selling at a loss.

In the second half of the eighteenth century there was a significant change in Anglo-Indian trade trends. After the Battle of Plassey (1759) the Company obtained control over the revenue of Bengal and embarked on a policy which made it the ruler of the Indian sub-continent. This change in the relationship of the Company with the people of India coincided in time with the rise of the Lancashire cotton industry. Between 1760 and 1809 the total value of bullion exports to India was £14 million and of other merchandise £48·5 million. Cotton piece goods which had once bulked so large in Indian exports had by the early nineteenth century become major imports. In the middle of the nineteenth century Lancashire cotton piece goods accounted for nearly half of the Indian import trade. Unbleached dhoti and sari, worn by millions of Indians, had ceased to be native woven, but a staple import from Manchester. The Indian export trade was also transformed. She became primarily an exporter of raw materials considerable in bulk and relatively low in value. These eighteenth- and early nineteenth-century trade trends were strengthened by the later application of steam power to sea transport and the opening of the Suez Canal in 1869.

The production of indigo, a one-time Portuguese monopoly in Western India, was revived in Bengal by the East India Company about 1778. India held the foremost place in the production of natural indigo until German chemists learned in 1897 how to produce synthetic indigo on a commercial scale. Raw jute, on a small scale, was exported from the Ganges–Brahmaputra delta in Bengal and Assam from 1795. It became a considerable export when the flax and hemp spinners of Dundee began to compete with the Bengal hand loom industry by manufacturing jute fabrics on power looms. The Dundee industry developed slowly until the Crimean War (1854–56) when, owing to the cutting off of supplies of Russian flax, the manufacture of jute fabrics on a commercial scale received a considerable stimulus.

Other important exports from India in the days of the East India Company were raw silk, pepper, opium and tea. In the time of Warren Hastings (1772–85) the raw silk trade of Bengal, although subject to great fluctuations, averaged 500,000 lb of reeled silk alone. The monopoly export of pepper to the west from the Malabar Coast was for centuries an important branch of commerce. By the early nineteenth century the trade was declining owing to competition from the Malay Archipelago. The opium trade, chiefly with China, was made a government monopoly in 1773 and the cultivation of the opium, other than for the East India Company, was forbidden in 1817.

The most profitable trade of the East India Company, in the second half of the eighteenth century, was the tea trade with China. Heavily taxed, tea naturally attracted the attention of smugglers, but its growing popularity as a beverage was not approved by everybody. Justices of the Peace in Hampshire in 1795 considered it a very unsatisfactory substitute for malt liquor and recorded in their minutes their concern at its popularity among the poor. Its consumption, in their view, was injurious to both body and mind, and "though perhaps beginning in elevation, certainly ending in depression." The Kent justices, on the other hand, authorised good fires in the workhouses, to be kept burning all night, so that paupers might boil their tea kettles. The trade was a considerable one, 20,000,000 lb being shipped to England from China in 1787. In the same year the authorities at Kew Gardens suggested that tea cultivation should be undertaken in India but it was not until 1834 that the idea was acted upon. The first shipment was made from Assam in 1838, and by 1852 Indian tea had become a serious competitor on the London market with that from China. By this date India's commercial relations with the west were markedly different from those that prevailed in 1700. The Indian trade had been opened to private traders in 1813 and that with China in 1833. The East India Company gave law, order and political security to the Indian sub-continent, but it was to the enterprise and initiative of the private traders that the new economic developments were primarily due.

The Trade with North America

The pre-1780 period saw also an increase in British trade with North America. But this trade, unlike that with the Far East, was not centuries old, but of comparatively recent origin. Before trade with America could begin a wilderness had to be made productive. To this end England during the seventeenth century exported men and capital across the Atlantic, a process stimulated by trade depression in the first half of the century. Some time had necessarily to elapse before the Plantations could develop to the point where their products and needs could have an appreciable effect on British trade. Attention to the American mainland was first prompted by the desire to find precious metals. To this was added the hope of a source of supply of naval stores which would make England independent of the Baltic, where Dutch and Danish competition was keen. In the first colony, Virginia, gold was not found, and supplies of naval stores did not materialise. Instead, the colony came to rely on the export of tobacco, produced on large plantations by Negro slave labour and that of indentured servants, for the most part transported paupers and criminals.

At first, by James I and many of his subjects, tobacco smokers were denounced in language which would be regarded as appropriate nowadays for criticising drug addicts. They were warned that "Men beganne to grow mad and crazed in the braine in that they would adventure to suck the smoke of a weede." Governments, however, soon discovered that heavy duties on tobacco were a welcome source of revenue. Those levied on foreign-grown tobacco were much greater than those on Virginian tobacco, ensuring to the latter a virtual monopoly of the home market. In the last year of James II's reign, for example, 15 million lb of Virginian tobacco were imported and only 16,000 lb. from the Spanish empire. In addition, home production of tobacco was sternly suppressed.

The tobacco exporting colonies, Virginia and Maryland, were regarded as valuable possessions. They could only legally export tobacco to Britain, seven-eighths of it, after being heavily taxed, being re-exported to Europe. On the continent, it found a ready sale as smoking habits spread rapidly despite threats of excommunication by the clergy and punishments by the knout and even death decreed by rulers. The planters themselves, however, were far from satisfied with arrangements which, in their view, permitted Bristol and Glasgow merchants, by whom they were financially controlled, to grow rich at their expense. Following the Act of Union with Scotland (1707) Glasgow enjoyed the same privileges in respect of trade as English ports. By 1772 more than half British tobacco imports were handled there, the large mansions of the tobacco merchants being a noteworthy feature of contemporary architecture in the city. Two other products exported to Britain from the southern colonies were rice and cotton, grown in Carolina.

The slave-owning tobacco planters who so loudly complained that Glasgow and Bristol merchants paid low prices for tobacco and sent trashy merchandise for sale in the colonies were loyalists during the American War of Independence. The U.S.A. emerged from the war in 1783 an independent nation, but independence did not result in a reduction in Anglo-American trade. As far as the southern states were concerned commerce with Britain increased. In the post-war period tobacco growing expanded into Kentucky and Tennessee. Even more important, during the early years of the nineteenth century short staple cotton became the chief cash crop of the South, whereas previously the long fibre or sea island cotton only had been grown in North Carolina. The invention of the cotton gin by the Yankee, Eli Whitney, made possible the production on a commercial scale of the short staple variety. Unskilled Negro slave labour being available, the "Black Earth" areas of the South were opened up. The price of cotton fell, and exports from the U.S.A. rose from under 500,000 lb in 1795 to over 300 million lb in 1832. Over two-thirds of that exported in 1832 was sent to Britain, France taking most of the remainder. These imports Britain supplemented by purchasing much smaller quantities from the East Indies, Mauritius, Brazil, Turkey and Egypt. Britain, which in the eighteenth century had competed with France for scanty supplies from the West Indies, the Levant and Portuguese and Dutch colonies, was now able to make full use of the technical innovations in the textile industries. The woollen industries after 1800 ceased to provide Britain's chief exports. Cotton piece goods, produced in Lancashire and the Clyde Valley came to occupy first place, by 1854 accounting for about half the total British export trade. Cotton exports went far afield, to Europe and the U.S.A., smaller markets being opened up in Asia, Latin America, the West Indies, the British North American colonies, Africa and Australia.

In New England, owing to geographical, geological and economic factors, a civilisation very different in character developed from that which had taken root in the southern lands. The notion that all New England pioneers were persecuted Puritan refugees is far from the truth. Many who settled there were men who sought a better life than was offered by an England which before the Civil War suffered acute economic depression. They settled in a land of poor, glaciated soils, with a harsher climate than that of the warmer south, and cut off by mountain barriers from easy access to the western interior. They lived in small townships, not on large plantations, laboriously clearing the land of forest to make farms on which subsistence crops were grown. Living close to the sea, many became fishermen, shipbuilders and traders. Their trade links tended to be with the southern and middle colonies, and with the sugar planters of the West Indies, rather than with England. Before 1700 a thriving trade was being carried on by Boston merchants in West Indian rum and African slaves, and in the exporting of temperate foodstuffs, fish and pork to feed the plantation workers. Apart from timber for shipbuilding, the New England colonies produced little considered valuable by Englishmen, who regarded colonies as useful only to the extent to which they assisted in making the Mother Country economically independent of her commercial rivals.

Trade with the West Indian Islands

Far more valuable, according to contemporary opinion, were the islands of the West Indies. So much so, that many subjects of George III thought that his ministers would have been well advised to have insisted that the French, in the Treaty of Paris (1763), should cede Guadeloupe instead of snow-covered Canadian waste lands. In the sixteenth and seventeenth centuries the islands were convenient bases, used to harass Spain in the New World and capture her treasure ships. Their real importance began with the introduction of sugar cultivation from Brazil. In addition, cotton and tobacco were grown and from Honduras logwood was obtained and used in making textile dyes.

The eighteenth century was the golden age of these fever-haunted islands in which countless thousands of European soldiers and sailors perished. The presence of the fleets and armies of European powers brought prosperity, but their major wealth came from sugar-cane plantations. Many were owned by absentee London and Bristol merchants whose large fortunes rivalled those of the notorious Indian nabobs of the Clive and Warren Hastings era. As a political interest the West Indian lobby was very important, commerce with the West Indies in the eighteenth century employing more shipping and yielding greater profits than that with the American mainland. Labour for the plantations was obtained by the importation of African slaves and indentured "whites," paupers, criminals and political offenders. After the Restoration even kidnapping in England was resorted to as a means of obtaining labour for the planters. During the Interregnum, royalists captured at the Battle of Worcester, and prisoners taken in Cromwell's Irish campaign, were despatched to Barbados. At the Bloody Assizes, following Monmouth's Rebellion, 841 of his followers were sentenced to transportation, the Lord Chief Justice deliberately ruling that their destination should be the West Indies to make their punishment harsher. According to Macaulay one-fifth of those shipped were flung to the sharks, while those who remained alive needed to be fattened to make them saleable at a worthwhile price.

Slavery and the Slave Trade

The trade in Negro slaves from Africa was begun by the Portuguese in 1441. It ended in 1865 when the Spanish authorities set free the human cargo on a slaveship which had arrived in Cuba. In addition to the Portuguese, British, Dutch, French, Danish, Spanish and American traders took part in it. Exact statistics of the numbers of human beings forcibly transported from Africa to the New World between 1441 and 1865 do not exist. One estimate is 15 million, more than 50 per cent of whom crossed the Atlantic in British and Portuguese slave vessels. The acute shortage of labour on Caribbean sugar plantations explains why this trade in human beings assumed its most massive proportions in the eighteenth century. English involvement in the trade begins with the expeditions of Sir John Hawkins in the 1560s, but it was not until after the Restoration that English slave trading came to be organised on a really large scale. The Dutch before 1660 had imported Negro slaves into Virginia and the West Indies. To deprive them of so profitable a monopoly, the Royal African Company was formed in 1671, its shareholders including King Charles II and his brother, the Duke of York. The pattern of trade in which the slaves participated was a commercial triangle. From Europe were exported such commodities as beads, ironwork, copper bars, weapons, woollens and cotton cloth, rum and wine, used to purchase slaves brought from the interior. With the help of the North-east trade wind the human cargo was shipped by the notorious "middle passage" to the New World and exchanged mainly for sugar or cotton, tobacco and coffee, or Spanish silver. The sugar was refined in Britain, much of it being re-exported to Europe.

The miseries and cruelties associated with this lucrative traffic in human beings is nowadays universally condemned. But people in the seventeenth and eighteenth centuries did not judge the slave trade and slavery by our standards. Their world was very different from ours. The notion that all men should be legally free to choose their occupations and negotiate the terms on which they sold their labour did not gain widespread acceptance until after the French Revolution of 1789. The economic foundations of the ancient world were based on slavery. The legal status of slavery survived in

Europe for centuries after the fall of the Roman Empire, but even after it had vanished, few of the inhabitants of Europe before the nineteenth century were "free" in our sense of the term. Most were peasants, tied to the land, protected, or some might say, exploited, by overlords.

Serfdom disappeared in Britain earlier than elsewhere, but in the seventeenth and eighteenth centuries not all its peoples were "free." Debtors, vagrants, the very poor, orphaned children and press-ganged sailors lived under restrictions which made nonsense of the notion that all subjects of the Crown were free-born Britons. In some parts of Scotland, villeinage persisted until well into the eighteenth century, and miners were tied to the pits. In the colonies during the eighteenth century the distinction between "slave" and "free" was not synonymous with the terms "Negro" and "white." Not all those condemned to forced labour on the plantations were Negroes. Many were indentured "whites." American and West Indian planters frequently petitioned for "white" labour and most that was sent was involuntary. The political philosopher, John Locke, whose name is usually associated with concepts of political freedom, drew up a constitution for South Carolina in 1669, which provided for the institution of a system of "white" villeinage. In passing judgment on the practices of our seventeenth- and eighteenth-century forefathers, it ought to be remembered that unlike their descendants, they did not think of a life of legal servitude as one the Almighty had ordained for the sons of Ham alone.

Europeans did not begin the slave trade. It had always been a feature of the African scene. Rather, European intervention made an existing evil worse. The horrors of the notorious "middle passage" were real and awful, but some of its appalling discomforts were shared by the crew. There were those who sincerely believed that Africans benefited by being transported from a pagan to a Christian environment, but that Europeans were primarily actuated by motives of philanthropy is hardly a point of view that can be taken seriously. The slave trade was very profitable, and men can usually find reasons to justify practices that put money into their pockets. Certainly from a material point of view Britain gained much, the economic benefits being very widespread. Some of the owners of slave ships, who included merchants highly respected in Bristol and Liverpool and also in Lisbon, Nantes and Copenhagen, accumulated large fortunes. Their gains, when reinvested, played a part in financing industrial expansion in eighteenth-century Britain. In Birmingham, Manchester and other Lancashire cotton towns, many workers found employment manufacturing goods used to purchase and shackle African slaves and to equip the plantations. Not unnaturally, proposals to abolish the slave trade roused apprehension in such towns of considerable unemployment. A profitable sugar-refining industry was built up. From the sale of slaves in Spanish America, silver was obtained, used to purchase Indian wares, while the transport of slaves and the commodities obtained by their sale created employment for seamen and British ships.

Before the end of the eighteenth century both the slave trade and slavery were being denounced as wholly immoral and inexcusable, by Quakers, Methodists and supporters of the Anglican Evangelical movement. In America during the Seven Years' War, the Quaker itinerant preacher John Woolman had roused his fellow co-religionists, some of whom possessed slaves, to campaign against slavery as a violation of human rights. The 10,000 slaves in Britain became free men as a consequence of Lord Chief Justice Mansfield's judgment, in Sommersett's Case, that a writ of Habeas Corpus must secure the release of a Negro slave from a ship on the Thames (1772). But due to the strength of the West Indian lobby in Parliament the prohibition of the slave trade was delayed. A society was formed in 1787 whose members included Granville Sharp, Thomas Clarkson, Zachary Macaulay, James Stephens and William Wilberforce, to campaign for its abolition. Only after years of propaganda did Charles James Fox and Lord Grenville in 1806 persuade Parliament to condemn the trade; in the following year, 1807, when Fox was in his grave, a Bill was passed prohibiting the slave trade after 1st January 1808. In France Napoleon decreed its abolition after his return from Elba in 1815. Other European powers agreed to do likewise at the Congress of Vienna in 1815. Slavery was abolished in the British Empire in 1833, £20 million being paid in compensation to the owners.

For the West Indian islands the economic and social consequences of these measures were catastrophic, coinciding as they did with the fall in sugar prices following the creation of the European sugar beet industry, and the abolition of preferential duties for Empire sugar in the United Kingdom. As the freed slaves were reluctant to work plantations went out of cultivation and their owners were ruined. Not until the end of the nineteenth century, with the importation of Asiatic coolies, the introduction of new agricultural products, cocoa, cotton and bananas, and the opening of the Panama Canal (1914), did economic revival begin. But the social legacies of slavery are still unresolved. In modern racial problems we are reaping the harvest from the seeds sown by our ancestors. Few of the descendants of the one-time slaves have as yet succeeded in securing for themselves a decent standard of living, as the inhabitants of the British towns, into which in recent years they have immigrated, have good cause to know.

Chapter IX

BRITISH OVERSEAS TRADE, 1780–1850

Before the Industrial Revolution a high degree of self-sufficiency had been a feature of Western European economic life. As commerce was mainly concerned with luxury products the market was very limited in scope. But as the British economy became increasingly industrialised and urbanised the major staples in trade came to be those in popular demand. Britain exported the products of her industries taking in payment food and raw materials. Under the new conditions commercial expansion was unprecedented but subject to considerable fluctuations. Although not unknown in earlier times a significant feature of the new industrial society was the trade cycle, the alternation of booms and slumps. Trade expansion was most in evidence in periods of prosperity but it must also be noted that exports and imports did not expand at equal rates. Before 1840 exports tended to expand more rapidly than imports, the reverse being the case in the second half of the nineteenth century.

Any consideration of trade trends before 1850 must take into account the unique position in which Britain found herself at this time. Her economy was not isolated from that of the rest of the world. Economic growth and trade expansion are dependent upon both internal and external influences. The major adjustments Britain was making in the use of her natural resources took the form of diverting capital towards industrial expansion at a time when her European rivals were still laggard, living for the most part under self-sufficient rural economy conditions. Opportunities were also available for investment overseas to exploit the natural resources of hitherto empty territories in which emigrants from Europe were settling. In these circumstances Britain by the mid-nineteenth century had become the workshop of the world.

As already indicated, the resultant commercial expansion was not continuous but subject to major fluctuation. Expansion was taking place before the outbreak of the American War of Independence, interrupted in time of war by trade embargoes and enemy fleet action, nullified partially by smuggling. This expansion was the prelude to very rapid commercial growth in the last twenty years of the eighteenth century. The export trade boom was due to transport improvements at home (roads and canals), to increased industrial production as new productive processes came into use, to an increase in Anglo-American trade and to an expansion of the re-export trade to Europe.

The outbreak of war with France in 1793, although it slowed down the rate of expansion, did not eventuate in any significant reduction in exports. Embargoes on British trade with European countries under French control were offset by British sea power. This made possible increased trade with the Americas and Asia unhampered by French and Dutch competition. For the Dutch, the commercial loss was permanent as they never recovered their carrying trade. Napoleon I's extension of economic warfare by his Berlin (1806) and Milan Decrees (1807) was countered by the British Orders in Council (1807-8), prohibiting the carriage of goods to French-controlled Europe other than from British ports. Napoleon's attempts to destroy British trade and industry were unsuccessful, the number of British ships on the high seas increasing, not diminishing. They did restrict British trade with Europe, but not completely. The Baltic was open to our shipping after the seizure of the Danish fleet in 1807 and Napoleon's disastrous Russian campaign in 1812. Trade with the Iberian Peninsula increased with the outbreak of the Peninsular War and the subsequent expulsion of the French from Spain and Portugal. In fact the Continental System, which can be listed as one of the major causes of Napoleon's downfall, did more harm to Europe than to Britain. Starved of raw materials, continental industry languished, so much so that Napoleon's officials had to connive at smuggling through Hamburg to obtain the cloth needed for uniforms for the Imperial army. The United Kingdom authorities, similarly worried by the depression in the woollen industry, issued thousands of licences authorising merchants to ignore the Orders in Council.

Unfortunately, the enforcement of the Orders in Council interfered with the very extensive American carrying trade between the New World and continental Europe. British seizure of American ships on the high seas and the confiscation of their cargoes was denounced by President Jefferson as a breach of international law. Congress retaliated by passing the Embargo Act (1807) prohibiting American ships from sailing to foreign ports. As the Act proved to be both unpopular and unenforceable, it was replaced in 1809 by the Non-Intercourse Act, prohibiting trade with both Britain and France. This Act expired in 1810, American resentment finally leading to a declaration of war against Great Britain. The Anglo-American War of 1812–14 had adverse effects on British trade. The cessation of trade with our largest single market caused industrial dislocation in both countries. The Lancashire cotton industry, starved of cotton, stagnated. One significant result of the war, an omen of future trends, was the development of manufacturing industries in New England, making goods hitherto imported from Great Britain. When the war came to an end, these "infant industries," threatened by a flood of cheap imports from Britain, demanded protection. They got it—the first American protective tariff being introduced in 1816.

In Europe the war ended with Napoleon's defeat at Waterloo in 1815. In the transition from war to peace Britain fared worse than continental Europe. Economic organisation in the greater part of Europe was too simple to be easily thrown out of gear. The problem of demolishing the armies was relatively easy to solve, the peasants simply returning to their holdings. Britain had more difficult transition problems, because her economy being more complex, she was dependent upon foreign trade. The expectation that British superiority in industrial equipment would ensure an immediate resumption of profitable commercial relations with Europe and America was not realised. Exhausted by nearly a quarter of a century of warfare Europe was slow in recovery. Instead of opening their markets to British merchants, European countries, led by France, followed high protectionist policies. In doing so they were copying the example set by Britain herself. After 1815, therefore, the free flow of trade was hampered by high tariff barriers which operated adversely against the interests of a country like Britain possessing the capacity to produce more than her home market could absorb.

By erecting obstacles to the free flow of imports, Britain inevitably reduced her volume of exports. Commercial enterprise was also impeded by the fall in prices, a consequence of the sudden cessation of government wartime spending, and of the deflationary monetary policies pursued after 1815. Customs duties levied at a fixed rate became more burdensome as prices fell. Such conditions inevitably discouraged private enterprise from embarking on new ventures either at home or abroad. Hence a very short-lived commercial boom, on the coming of peace, ended in 1816 in an acute trade depression which lasted until 1822. The trade revival in the early 1820s followed the resumption of cash payments by the Bank of England in 1821. There was much overseas investment in South America where revolts against Spanish rule were taking place, and in the U.S.A., much of it speculative in character. The sequel was the financial crisis of 1825, many banks closing their doors. Recovery was slow, trading conditions not improving until the boom period between 1832 and 1836. During these years there was considerable investment in the U.S.A., followed by a severe depression between 1836 and 1842. It was in the latter year, 1842, that Sir Robert Peel began the fiscal reforms which ended in Britain becoming a free trade country. The improvement in trading conditions that took place during Peel's ministry came to an end with the severe financial crisis of 1847.

Despite the regular occurrence of trade depressions between 1822 and 1850, the expansion of British overseas trade was very great, both in bulk and value, being most marked in the years of prosperity. As prices tended to fall during this period, the increase in bulk was all the more impressive. An examination of trade trends reveals how momentous were the changes taking place in the British economy. We were becoming a highly industrialised people, living in a small coal-producing island, and dependent upon imports for raw materials and for food for a growing urban population. By the 1840s imports exceeded exports in value. This dependence upon imports explains the campaign against current protectionist policies which persuaded statesmen after 1842 to pass free trade legislation.

Heading the list of imports in the 1840s were raw materials, cotton, wool, timber, silk, flax and hemp—cotton being easily the largest item. The wool industry, now much less important than the cotton industry, was relying increasingly on supplies from Australia. The second most important group of imports were foodstuffs, which expanded with the rising purchasing power of a growing population. Between 1828 and 1846 wheat was taxed according to a sliding scale of duties, less on colonial than on foreign wheat. The imports fluctuated according to home harvest yields and prices, being only 3,379 metric tons in 1835, 550,350 in 1839, 29,648 in 1845 and 559,954 in 1847. Wheat imports increased rapidly after the duties on corn were abolished. Butter, cheese and eggs were imported, subject to customs duties, but in relatively small quantities. Their consumption as regular articles of diet by the bulk of the population only became possible in the second half of the century, following the abolition of import duties on them between 1846 and 1860.

A survey of the mid-nineteenth-century export trade of the United Kingdom shows the close connection between industrial development and trade expansion. British exports were manufactured goods, re-exports of colonial wares and coal. The output of the most highly developed industry in the United Kingdom, textiles, was of overwhelming importance as export staples. In value, textiles in 1827–29 accounted for 78·2 per cent of British exports and for 78·7 per cent in 1840–42. But there was one significant difference from the former trade pattern. After 1802 woollens yielded pride of place to cotton goods as the leading export item. In 1816 two-fifths of British exports had consisted of cotton goods, and just over one-fifth of woollens. By the middle of the century the gap had widened, nearly half the country's exports coming from the cotton mills. The exports of other manufacturing industries at this time, pottery and porcelain, hardware and cutlery, for example, were of minor importance. The re-export trade in colonial wares was considerable, but relative to total British exports, much less than it had been in the eighteenth century. Two other exports, iron and coal, were less important before 1850 than they were destined to become in the second half of the century. The iron industry after 1815 exported its products to the U.S.A., where there was a growing demand for capital equipment. Coal exports to European markets were on a relatively small scale. Rapid expansion of coal exports came later in the nineteenth century, when European countries were entering on the industrial phase of their development.

The eighteenth-century tendency for British trade to become world-wide in geographical distribution continued during the first half of the nineteenth century. Europe continued to be the most important market for United Kingdom exports, but as their increase was impeded by the protectionist policies of continental governments, British trade expansion was mainly due to the development of commercial relations with America, Asia and Australia. The U.S.A., although its population was small, needed capital equipment, and supplied three-quarters of British cotton imports. Brazil was a growing market. As has been explained in the previous chapter trade with the Far East was expanded considerably by private merchants after the East India Company had been deprived of its monopolistic privileges. The cession of Hong Kong and the opening of Chinese ports to British traders in 1842 led to an increase in Anglo-Chinese commerce. Australia, with its growing sheep-rearing industry, imported manufactures in exchange for wool. One other feature of mid-nineteenth-century trade remains to be noted, namely the tendency for imports to increase more rapidly than exports. In other words, British exports did not earn all the foreign exchange needed to pay for imported commodities. The gap was bridged by interest payments on the considerable, if somewhat speculative, overseas investments, by the profits of British shipowners in the carrying trade and by those of Lloyds underwriters in the international marine insurance business, developed in the first half of the nineteenth century.

Chapter X

THE STATE AND ECONOMIC POLICY

From very early times English economic and social life had been subject to regulation. In the Middle Ages, when trade and industry were organised on a local basis, control was exercised through municipal, guild and manorial authorities. By the sixteenth century, as economic life was tending to be organised on a national basis, the central government took over responsibilities formerly entrusted to town and municipal agencies. The reign of Elizabeth I became a period of reconstruction in which there was much systematic and effective legislation. What did the law try to do? A short answer to the question would be that it attempted to regulate employment, methods of manufacture, price levels and overseas trade.

Conditions of employment were regulated by the Statute of Artificers and Apprentices in 1563, a complete code of industrial regulation that lasted for more than two centuries. It was not novel, but contained the fruits of previous experience. Elizabeth's ministers were simply applying on a national scale regulations previously enforced by the guilds. Among the 35 clauses of the Act were clauses making apprenticeship obligatory in the crafts listed in the Act, instructing Justices of the Peace to determine wages annually, according to the prices of bread and ale, and providing security for the workers by long hirings, one year being the minimum. The compulsory apprenticeship rule never covered the whole field of industry. The Act did not apply to such trades as cotton manufacture and framework knitting, which did not exist in 1563, and it was only enforced in the older boroughs. Industries in the new towns and in villages were outside the scope of the Act. Exemptions were sometimes permitted. For example, soldiers demobilised after the War of the Spanish Succession were excused the necessity of serving an apprenticeship.

The enforcement of the apprenticeship clauses of the Act of 1563 became increasingly lax during the seventeenth and eighteenth centuries. There was also in existence a system of non-statutory apprenticeship governing most child labour. As a system of industrial training, it was, to say the least, open to criticism. Records of proceedings in Courts of Assize and Quarter Sessions provide ample evidence of ill treatment by masters, and rebellious conduct by apprentices. Exceptionally barbarous, Charles Kingsley reminds us, was the fate of the pathetic children apprenticed to chimney sweeps. Elizabethan poor law legislation empowered parish authorities to apprentice pauper children. In the early days of the Industrial Revolution wagon loads of children were transported to work in Lancashire mills from as far afield as London. Many became unpaid, half-starved drudges. But the idle apprentice and the brutal master are only one side of the story. There were industrious apprentices and conscientious employers such as the cotton spinner Samuel Oldknow of Mellor in Derbyshire, the Greg family of Styal in Cheshire and Robert Owen in New Lanark. It must also be remembered that hard toil by children was not judged as an evil by our eighteenth-century forefathers, but as beneficial to the children and necessary to ensure national prosperity.

With the extended use of power-driven machinery a seven years' apprenticeship ceased to be essential to acquire industrial skills. Employers, therefore, were in favour of abolishing the apprenticeship clauses of the Act of 1563. Employees, on the other hand, concerned to keep labour scarce and wages high, petitioned Parliament for an extension of compulsory apprenticeship. It was the view of the manufacturers that prevailed. In 1814 the apprenticeship clauses of the Act of 1563 were repealed. In some crafts employees were strong enough, however, to restrict employment to those who had served an indentured apprenticeship. Parish apprentices also remained until 1844, when this relic of the Elizabethan poor law was abolished.

Clauses XI, XII and XIV of the Act of 1563 instructed Justices of the Peace in each shire to meet annually to draw up wage rates for submission to the Court of Chancery. These clauses were the most short-lived part of the Act. Wage assessments are known to have been made after 1750, but before the end of the eighteenth century the practice of fixing wages in this way had fallen into disuse. It was even forgotten. In 1795, wages fixed in 1725 were published as "an historical curiosity," with the remark that readers would be surprised if any magistrate in 1795 "ventured on so bold a measure." It is impossible to pass sound judgment on how the system worked, but we may suspect that awards, from the labourer's point of view, did not err on the side of generosity. Further, the rates laid down were the maximum it was permissible to pay or receive. After wage assizes had become obsolete, however, they came to be thought of by low-paid workmen as worth reviving. Petitions to the Government for this to be done were countered in 1813 by the repeal of the wage clauses of the Act of 1563. Evidently the Tory government of Lord Liverpool did not consider that it was the duty of the State to safeguard the weaker members of the community against the possibility of exploitation.

Of great complexity and doubtful value were the methods by which, to protect consumers, governments regulated manufacturers. Such supervision, undertaken originally by the craft guilds, was a function assumed by the State after their decay. Various methods were tried, supervision by companies, by individuals, and, in the case of the cloth industry, by a royal official, the Aulnager. The office of Aulnager dates from the reign of Richard I. From the "ulnage returns", still surviving, much can be learned about the early history of the woollen cloth industry. Supervision under the "ulnage" system continued into the seventeenth century, but with the growing complexity of the industry and the greater diversification of its products old standards had to be revised. An Act passed in 1665 extended the system to the "new drapery" as a measure of protection against fraud. After the abolition of the office of Aulnager in 1699, attempts were made to protect consumers against dishonest workmen by giving powers of "search" to Justices of the Peace. This was done, for example, in 1727 in Wiltshire, Somerset and Gloucester, and in 1767 in Yorkshire.

These methods of control proved ineffectual, and with the extended use of machinery the old regulations became harmful and an anachronism. The machines did not work to the regulations governing the length, breadth and weight of cloth. Government attempts to control prices met a similar fate. In 1709 it was laid down that the price of bread must fluctuate with the price of corn. A statute of 1757, a time of scarcity, extended price control to oatmeal, rye and pea flour. Attempts by the London magistrates to enforce the regulations broke down, experience showing that free competition was more in the public interest than state interference.

By the eighteenth century few of the paternalist measures introduced by sixteenth- and seventeenth-century governments to control the economic life of the community were being implemented. One notable exception were those designed to regulate overseas commerce. From the sixteenth to the nineteenth centuries politicians took the view that industry and trade should be controlled with the objective of making the community strong. "Power" was preferred to "plenty." To this end governments here and elsewhere in Europe did not scruple to trample on private interests and preferences. The name given to what can more accurately be described as "a trend of thought," rather than a "policy," is Mercantilism. The notion that communal interests should be paramount over those of the individual is many centuries old. In the sixteenth century, with the formation of nation states and the emergence of despotic monarchies, there began an era of competitive struggle between European countries in both the political and economic fields. Economic policies were therefore favoured which would increase national strength. To that end steps were taken to accumulate treasure, to develop shipping and to maintain a large and well-nourished population. In other words, to secure money, ships and people, tillage and trade, it was argued, must be controlled by the State. The accumulation of treasure was a major objective of mercantilist policy. As England, unlike Spain, did not possess overseas territories yielding precious metals, they could only be obtained by trade. During the seventeenth century the balance of trade theory was developed. Its advocates taught that exports should exceed imports in value, the gap being bridged by the importation of gold and silver. For over 200 years the achievement of a favourable balance of trade was considered to be a desirable objective by all Western European governments.

To stimulate exports and discourage imports, prohibitions or high duties were placed on foreign commodities. Bounties were given to encourage the export of home manufactures and restrictions placed on the export of precious metals. Commercial treaties were negotiated. The Methuen Treaty with Portugal (1703) may be cited as an example. Under the terms of this treaty Portuguese wine was admitted at a lower rate of duty than French and German wines. Portugal in return gave a preference to English textiles. The treaty had far-reaching consequences. The demand for "Port" and "Madeira" was such that Portugal was encouraged to concentrate her productive energies on the wine and cork trades to the detriment of other forms of agriculture. Foodstuffs in consequence had to be imported from Britain. In England it was patriotic to drink port wine, the export of "our oldest ally," in preference to the wines of our ancient enemy, France. Whether the port-drinking English aristocracy of the period thought that the gout from which they suffered as a consequence was a price worth paying for a monopoly market for cloth in Portugal must be left to the imagination. At any rate, their contemporaries in Scotland, with Jacobite sympathies, who drank French claret, avoided gout.

The principal weapon of the mercantilists was the tariff. Imports which competed with native manufactures were heavily taxed, and raw materials like wool were kept in England by heavy export duties or even actual prohibitions. The free movement of commercial commodities was clogged by innumerable regulations of extraordinary complexity. To encourage the woollen industry people were forbidden to use printed calicoes for garments and bedding. In the reign of Charles II it was even made compulsory to bury the dead in woollen shrouds (1678), the clergy being required to certify that the law had been obeyed. The encouragement of manufactures was considered to be desirable as a means of obtaining a large population and a high value for exports. The introduction of new industries was therefore favoured. Tillage was encouraged, partly to make the country self-sufficing and partly on the grounds that a healthy and vigorous agricultural population would be good recruiting material for the army.

As a maritime state needed a strong navy, encouragement was given to the development of shipping. Lord Burleigh, in Elizabeth I's reign, extended the market for the fishing industry, the best school for seamen, by reviving the Roman Catholic practice of making fish-eating compulsory on Wednesdays and Fridays, and in Lent (1563). Measures were taken to obtain ample supplies of timber and naval stores for shipbuilding. Efforts were made to encourage afforestation. Forests near the coast were reserved for shipbuilding, a policy much disliked by the iron smelters of the Sussex Weald.

The best known of the measures designed to increase the size of the mercantile marine and to find employment for English seamen were the Navigation Acts. The Navigation Acts were a series of laws beginning in 1381, continued by the Tudors, and in the seventeenth century by the Interregnum and Restoration governments. The authors of the seventeenth-century legislation were concerned to weaken the Dutch carrying trade by forcing English shipping to sail in distant waters. Two Acts, often erroneously ascribed to Oliver Cromwell, were passed in 1650 and 1651. The Act of 1650 prohibited trade with the four American colonies which had refused to recognise the regicide government, and banned the carrying of goods from any English colony in foreign ships. The second Act, that of 1651, provided that goods, including fish, from Europe could only be imported in English ships or in ships of the country of origin. Goods from Asia, Africa and America could only be imported in English ships or in those belonging to "the plantations thereof." This policy was reaffirmed by the Navigation Act of 1660 which defined English ships as ships built in England, Ireland or the Colonies, of which the captain and three-quarters of the crew were English subjects. An Act passed in 1670 took away from Ireland the rights it enjoyed under the Act of 1660. Scotland, which had not been treated as a foreign country under the 1651 legislation, was treated as one by that of 1660. The Scottish Parliament retaliated in 1661 by passing a Navigation Act of its own, and in 1663 by imposing heavy customs duties on imports from England. These measures proved to be of no value to Scotland. After the passage of the Act of Union in 1707, however, Scotland ceased to be excluded from the colonial trade, her merchants enjoying the same trading privileges as those in England.

By the second half of the seventeenth century the American colonies had become sufficiently well established for the Government of Charles II to give serious consideration to the principles upon which colonial trade should be regulated. It was during his reign that the framework of the Old Colonial System took shape by the passage, in addition to the Navigation Act of 1660, of two other Acts, the Staple Act (1663) and the Plantations Duties Act (1673). Certain commodities, known as "enumerated goods," could be exported to England only. These included sugar, tobacco, dyewoods and ginger. As by the Staple Act all colonial imports were to be shipped from English ports, foreign merchants were excluded from colonial trade. To prevent smuggling of "enumerated" commodities to markets other than in England, the Plantations Duties Act laid down that goods shipped from one colony to another should pay on export the duty payable if they were landed at an English port.

In the eighteenth century with the growing demand for raw materials for expanding manufacturing industry in Britain, and to reduce dependence on foreign sources of supply, the list of "enumerated goods" was extended to include iron, copper, naval stores and hides. A further eighteenth-century development was restrictive measures on colonial manufactures. This was not part of the seventeenth-century policy for the very good reason that the settlers had not then reached the stage of development when they could have manufactured goods for themselves. But by the eighteenth century industrial development could have taken place. Nevertheless Britain enforced a policy designed to keep the colonies as producers of raw materials and purchasers of British manufactures. If the colonists wanted hardware, woollen cloth, beaver hats or agricultural implements they had to buy them from Britain. It would be mistaken to argue that before the American War of Independence such prohibitions were a major cause of unrest. But American economic development was certainly retarded and ill-will generated in the minds of the few who were ambitious to develop colonial industrial potential. A further eighteenth-century restriction on colonial enterprise was the Molasses Act of 1733. This made illegal the lucrative trade with the French West Indies in molasses, made into rum in New York and the northern colonies. The English West Indies sugar planting interests were sufficiently influential to persuade Parliament to pass the Act, but it proved impossible to enforce it. The shortage of molasses supplies from the British islands, and the low prices charged by the French, led to the development of a considerable smuggling industry which the authorities were neither desirous nor capable of suppressing.

By confining colonial economic development in a framework thought to be beneficial to the Mother Country, Britain was carrying out a policy similar to but less strictly enforced than that of France, Spain and Holland. The advantages of the Old Colonial System to Britain were manifold. They included the partial exclusion of the Dutch from the carrying trade, the development of a very profitable re-export trade with Europe, markets for her manufactures, access to supplies of raw materials, and a considerable increase in the size of her mercantile marine. To the colonies, particularly in the pioneering stage, the system had many advantages. As their exports paid approximately one-third of the duties levied on foreign commodities they obtained a near monopoly for them in the British market. The protection given by the British navy, and the military protection against the Indians and the French, relieved them of costly defence expenditure. The bounties given to encourage exports of naval stores made possible access to the British market, despite the distance factor which operated in favour of Baltic sources, while the cutting down of trees brought more colonial land under the plough. As colonial ships enjoyed the protection of the Navigation Laws, the northern colonies built up a considerable mercantile marine. During the eighteenth century commodities not on the "enumerated list" could be exported to countries south of Cape Finisterre. As these waters were those in which Barbary pirates operated, such trade could not have been safely carried on without the protection of British naval strength.

The Old Colonial System came into existence at a time when the colonies were pioneering settlements, dependent upon Britain for capital, labour and markets. Its continuance, without considerable modification, was unwise in the altered conditions that prevailed in the late eighteenth century. At the time when the American War of Independence began the colonists were no longer pioneers battling against hardship and insecurity in an untamed wilderness, menaced by savage Indians and threatened by French imperialism. They had become men of property, living in a country where land was plentiful and cheap. They were enjoying a standard of living that would have seemed opulent to the peasantry of Europe, Scotland and Ireland, and to the very poor in contemporary rural

England. Such citizens, well informed about the rights of man, ought not to have been expected to submit to controls which hindered the natural growth of their homeland's economic potential, and were enforced by aristocratic politicians separated from them by 3000 miles of ocean highway. In point of fact, the continuance into the second half of the eighteenth century of the old colonial policies was only made possible by lax administration and fear of France. The British acquisition of Canada (1763) removed a strong tie keeping the colonists subjects of George III. The attempts of the Bute government to check smuggling, followed by Grenville's ill-advised Stamp Act (1763), raised a storm of resistance which culminated in the issue of the Declaration of Independence in 1776.

The revolt of the American colonies was not the only indication that the existing system of state regulation of economic affairs was becoming discredited. At a time when Britain needed markets for expanding industries, trade was hampered by innumerable restrictions. Those imposed by nature were being removed by the provision of better roads, and improved water transport facilities. But the artificial restrictions, those imposed by governments, still remained. In fact the system of government regulation had become obsolete. As it had grown up haphazardly over the preceding centuries, there was a lack of coherent policy behind the multitudinous rules and regulations which acted as a deterrent to enterprise and economic expansion. As it had degenerated into the narrow protection of vested interests, mercantilist practice was functioning to the disadvantage of the community as a whole. Legislation prohibiting the importation of Indian fabrics, enacted to placate wool manufacturing interests, had no justification once a cotton industry had become established in England. The protection given to the older industries was apt to result in high prices and low wages. Tariffs had become hopelessly intricate and extremely costly to collect. Five separate duties, for example, were levied on nutmegs. High duties on such imports as silk and brandy made smuggling a major industry from the Thames estuary to Penzance. It has been estimated that in 1783 revenue officers and the military had to battle against 40,000 smugglers who brought in so many commodities that home industry ceased to be protected. Under such circumstances, it was only to be expected that some of the subjects of George III came to the conclusion that mercantilist practice did not meet contemporary needs. The Age of Scarcity was passing and the Age of Plenty was emerging; under what conditions, men came to ask themselves, could production be maximised? The answer to this question, given by the classical school of economists, was:

end government interference in economic affairs.

But had mercantilism assisted economic development and growth? It is impossible to give a completely satisfactory answer to this question. It is much easier to evaluate the benefits gained by particular interests than to pass judgment on how well the needs of the community as a whole have been catered for. With what confidence can decision on such deep matters be entrusted to politicians? Communal interests are not self-evident or easy to determine. All too often the apparatus of state power has been controlled by men with sectional interests to serve, or by ministers apt to be manipulated by powerful pressure lobbies. Further, decisions which appear to satisfy immediate needs may have unfortunate long-term consequences.

There is no doubt that some mercantilist practices were harmful. Others were beneficial, at least to some sections of the community. The Corn Laws were helpful to landowners. The encouragement of fish eating promoted naval strength and provided employment for fishermen. According to Adam Smith, "as defence is of much more importance than opulence, the Act of Navigation is, perhaps, the wisest of all the commercial regulations of England." Certainly shipowners favoured protectionist policies. On the other hand it could be shown that the Navigation Laws, by preventing foreign ships bringing in cargoes other than those of their own country, reduced the volume of trade and provoked discriminatory legislation against British shipping. A policy that made good sense to shipowners, enjoying state-conferred monopoly privileges, was denounced as foolish by exporting merchants who wanted low freight charges.

It has often been asserted that mercantilists were mistaken in thinking, firstly, that the wealthiest countries were those holding large stores of precious metals, and secondly, that the amount of bullion received was the profit on trading transactions. Their critics have argued that they failed to understand that money is a mere token and that the value of gold is psychological. Concentration upon acquiring and hoarding bullion unduly restricted trade to those regions and areas able to offer bullion for goods. The experience of Spain has often been cited as proof of the evil results that could flow from undue hoarding. The Spanish monarchy retained one-fifth of the precious metals mined in the Indies and prohibited the export of gold and silver. This policy led to prices rising more steeply in Spain than elsewhere and assisted in the decline of Spanish industry, unable to produce manufactured goods as cheaply as other countries. On the other hand it has been argued that mercantilist practice made good sense. In the sixteenth century, when mercantilist ideas were taking shape, and credit instruments were little developed, rulers needed money for political and military purposes. The maintenance of standing armies, and the need for cash to meet rising court and civil service expenditure, made it impossible for kings to live off their estates. To find additional sources of revenue they encouraged the development of trade and industry. The possession of a favourable balance of trade was the only means by which countries without gold and silver mines could obtain the bullion needed for currency, and to finance rising government expenditure.

Considerable economic expansion was taking place in England before the Industrial Revolution. To what extent this growth was assisted or hampered by government policies must be a matter of dispute. But that governments can inflict lasting harm on a national economy is all too evident from the English record in Ireland. The Earl of Strafford, Charles I's Lord Lieutenant, had increased Irish prosperity and established a linen industry in Ulster. After 1660, in the interests of English manufacturers and farmers, the Parliament at Westminster inaugurated policies harmful to the Irish economy. In the reign of Charles II heavy duties were placed on imported Irish cattle. Attempts by the Irish Parliament to foster a woollen cloth industry were handicapped by laws passed in 1670 and 1699 by the English Parliament prohibiting the export of Irish manufactures except to England. In other words the Irish were denied direct access to colonial and foreign markets. The Act of 1720, prohibiting the wearing of printed and dyed calicoes, was a serious blow to the Irish cotton industry. Dean Swift was provoked into publishing *A Proposal for the Use of Irish Manufacture in Clothes ... utterly rejecting and renouncing everything wearable that comes from England* (1720). Fortunately for the Dean the authorities failed to discover the author and an Irish jury refused to convict the printer.

Not only in industry but also in agriculture policies were enforced which kept Ireland poor and undeveloped. In 1667 the export to England of cattle, sheep and pigs was forbidden. The principal Irish export, wool, was prohibited in 1698, while the bounties given to stimulate English corn exports adversely affected Irish farmers. These measures coupled with a land system which encouraged the payment of very high rents to absentee landlords by an impoverished peasantry made impossible the introduction of improved farming techniques in Ireland. In consequence, eighteenth-century Ireland was a country inhabited by a poverty-stricken people, bitterly resentful of the English connection.

Chapter XI

THE GENESIS OF THE FREE TRADE MOVEMENT

The momentous changes that took place after 1700 in British economic life were due, not to the initiative of politicians, but to the promptings of private enterprise. Under these circumstances the idea was questioned that governments were the proper depository of the duty of guiding and manipulating the use of economic resources. Those who did so argued that the main objective of economic activities should be to secure national plenty by maximising production. This objective, it was thought, could only be achieved provided there was open, unregulated competition between producers. As governmental interference impeded the productive process, the many old, obsolete laws which littered the statute book, in the opinion of these critics, ought to be swept away.

The leading eighteenth-century economist who challenged the economic practices known as mercantilist was Adam Smith (1723–90). Surprisingly little is known about his private life. Educated at Glasgow and Oxford Universities, he was a Professor at Glasgow for fourteen years. As tutor to the young Duke of Buccleuch he was given the opportunity of travelling on the continent. Here he met Voltaire and members of the school of thinkers, the Physiocrats, who criticised Colbertism and put forward ideas of non-intervention by the State in industrial and commercial affairs. On his return home he was appointed Commissioner of Customs in Scotland and went to live in his birthplace, Kirkcaldy. It was during these latter years that his epoch-making book, *The Wealth of Nations* (1776), was written.

Adam Smith has been described as "the Founder of Political Economy" but this description of him must not be read to imply that he was the first economist. Economic theories are as old as man's necessity to earn a livelihood. Similar statements could be made about Copernicus and astronomy, or Sir Isaac Newton and physics, with the qualification that like Smith and other original thinkers, they added to a store of knowledge acquired by their predecessors. Smith owed much to Francis Hutcheson, his predecessor in the Chair of Moral Philosophy at Glasgow, and to his friend David Hume, the eighteenth-century essayist who expounded free trade ideas and exposed the absurdities of mercantilist policies.

Of Adam Smith it can be said that, as a result of his researches, economic thinking developed on new lines. Much economic thinking before 1776 was concerned with considering how wealth should be consumed. Mercantilists investigated means of strengthening national power. The full title of Smith's book, *An Enquiry into the Nature and Causes of the Wealth of Nations,* makes clear that he provided economists with a new objective, namely, how to maximise production. It was only common sense, in his view, that economists should search for the conditions which favoured the production of wealth before considering what to do with it. The mercantilists thought that wealth had its source in foreign trade. Smith explained that wealth is created by labour. One of the most interesting parts of his book is that in which he demonstrated that production can be increased enormously by the division of labour, an idea so familiar nowadays that we find it difficult to appreciate its originality in 1776.

For our immediate purpose the most important part of Smith's book is that in which he criticised mercantilism. He compiled a detailed history of tariffs, bounties and monopolies to demonstrate that government interference with the economic process had been unfortunate in its results and harmful to the best interests of the community. A hopelessly complex system of tariffs, a poor law which hampered the free mobility of labour, limitation of the right to trade to members of privileged companies, were some of the obstacles Smith pointed out which restricted the production of wealth. Smith was not the only eighteenth-century critic of the contemporary protection system. But whereas most of the critics were hopeful of discovering a system of regulation free of abuses, Smith argued in favour of the abolition of controls. As individual enterprise is the most potent factor in economic expansion, governments in their dealings with trade and industry should, he taught, follow *laisser-faire* principles. A plentiful subsistence for all could only be obtained by getting rid of government regulations which acted as a brake on the natural human impulse to acquire wealth.

The *Wealth of Nations* gained for its author an international reputation. His opinion that untrammelled private enterprise and free trade were the foundations upon which men should build if they wished to be prosperous influenced the thinking and practice of his own and future generations. It was this aspect of Smith's teaching that was the most influential. As interpreted by later generations, the thesis that state activity ought to be reduced to a minimum was quoted to obstruct the abolition of child labour, the passage of sanitary legislation, and state action to protect the weak against ruthless exploitation. Smith had been primarily concerned with exposing the unwisdom of retaining rules and regulations which impeded the free flow of trade. He certainly never thought that all government activity was harmful. He defended the Navigation Laws and state provision of services such as education, which private capitalists would not have found profitable.

As in Smith's lifetime Great Britain was not a highly industrialised country, his teaching mainly affected contemporary mercantilist commercial practice. Lord North, Lord Shelburne and the Younger Pitt were influenced by the *Wealth of Nations*. North, who had to raise money to finance the War of American Independence, adopted some of Smith's ideas. It was North who, in 1779, removed the restrictions on Irish trade and allowed Ireland to trade with the colonies. Shelburne wished to promote free trade between Britain and the U.S.A. Suggestions for a commercial agreement between Britain and France were included in the text of the Treaty of Versailles (1783) but Shelburne lost office before he could take steps to implement them. It was therefore the Younger Pitt who in 1786 entrusted William Eden, later Earl of Auckland, with the task of negotiating the Anglo-French commercial treaty, which was signed by the French Foreign Minister, Vergennes, in March 1787. Under the terms of the Eden Treaty both countries agreed to reduce duties on most imports, silks being excepted. French wines could henceforth be imported but the preference given to Portuguese wines by the Methuen Treaty (1703) was maintained. The Treaty was one consumers approved, as it led to lower prices, but it was much disliked by smugglers whose activities became much less profitable. Unfortunately, this experiment in free trade came to an end on the outbreak of war in 1793.

We must be careful not to exaggerate the support for free trade policies in the days of the Younger Pitt. The manufacturing interest was still on the whole protectionist minded. This was shown in 1785 when Josiah Wedgwood and Lancashire manufacturers opposed Pitt's proposal to establish free trade with Ireland. Selfish manufacturers, fearful of competition from cheap Irish labour, were certainly not converts to the idea that universal free trade is a desirable state of affairs.

When the Younger Pitt took office in 1783 he did so at a time when national credit was low, the National Debt having reached the unprecedented amount of £250 million. He partially put into effect two of the reforms suggested by Adam Smith, a reduction in indirect taxation and a simplification of the system of tax collection. In 1784 duties on tea and spirits were reduced, the tea duty being cut from 119 to 12½ per cent. A "Hovering Act," in the same year, empowered revenue officers to seize vessels containing dutiable goods. In 1787 the very complex range of customs duties was reduced to a single tax on each commodity, payable into a Consolidated Fund. This administrative reform was a major improvement on previous practice, under which separate accounts had been kept by the Exchequer for each duty, items of expenditure being a charge on particular taxes, Smith had also criticised inequalities in the distribution of taxation, pointing out that an unfair share was paid by the landed classes. Pitt aimed at relieving the less well-to-do by increasing the proportion falling on the richer classes. In 1792, for example, the tax on women servants was repealed, and taxation was reduced on wagons, carts, candles, malt, and on houses with fewer than seven windows.

The late eighteenth-century challenge to mercantilist practices was not confined to Britain. In France the Physiocrats, inspired by François Quesnay, propagated doctrines of economic liberation. Reforms were made by Turgot between 1774 and 1776, but unfortunately his measures did not survive his dismissal, hence the destruction of privilege and the removal of economic abuses was postponed until the outbreak of revolution in 1789. The opening phase of the Revolution of 1789 in France was liberal. Provincial tariffs were abolished. The moderate external tariff was a continuation of that of the 1787–88 period when France had sought to encourage trade by negotiating commercial treaties and reducing customs duties. Low customs duties were supported by the agricultural and wine producing areas in the south of France that needed cheap British manufactures. The north, however, where industry was expanding, favoured protective duties to keep out the products of British industry.

The outbreak of the French Revolutionary Wars in 1792 brought to an end these late eighteenth-century tendencies towards more liberal commercial policies. Between 1792 and 1815 trade policies on both sides of the Channel were dictated by mutual hostility, particularly after the expansion of economic warfare by Napoleon I's issue of the Berlin and Milan Decrees. In time of war governments must obtain large revenues. To raise the major proportion of what is needed from direct taxation is politically impossible. They, therefore, take the line of least resistance—higher customs duties and extensive borrowing. This is the situation that has prevailed during all the major European wars since 1689. As a result of the wars waged between 1792 and 1815 the system of state regulation of trade got a new lease of life, Great Britain in 1815 having a tariff system, higher and more complex than that of 1792.

Even on the assumption that Britain after 1815 would remain a protectionist country, reforms would have had to be made in the existing structure. The end product of many years of legislative activity, the post-1815 protective system, was not a unified one, carefully designed to promote national wellbeing. In any case what is truly a national interest is much less easy to determine than sectional interests which are only too obvious. There had been a tendency to deal with trades separately without due regard to the effects which the imposition of a protective tariff might have upon other industries. Actually human society is a jungle of conflicting interests. There was even conflict between branches of the same industry. Smelters did not favour free admission of pig iron, while hardware manufacturers did. In the textile industries spinners were anxious to exclude foreign yarns, weavers to import them. Shipbuilders wanted cheap foreign timber, but timber owners protested against its importation.

It has been estimated that in 1815 there were about 2000 regulations controlling trade. Many had been issued in reply to Napoleon's Continental System, and as all too often happens, laws framed to meet wartime needs had been continued into the years of peace. The necessity and desirability of many of the regulations could be questioned at a time when British manufacturing potential was greater than that of any other country and there was a need to import raw materials. The importation of some manufactured commodities was prohibited. These included silks, cottons, woollens, tobacco, and gold and silver wares. Other manufactured goods were subject to penal rates of taxation, averaging 50 per cent of their value. The imposition of import duties on such raw materials as timber, hides, wool and silk were hard to justify. Tea, coffee, sugar, bacon, butter, cheese and even potatoes were heavily taxed, putting them out of the reach of working class consumers. The need for navigation laws was certainly questionable after 1815 when British shipping enjoyed an ascendancy over that of all other maritime nations. Fiscal legislation was so complex and intricate that merchants had grave difficulty in interpreting the law, breaches of which could mean liability to the seizure of their cargoes and vessels. Neither was it easy to decide whether a duty was imposed for revenue or protective purposes. Where revenue was the prior consideration the system was very inefficient. Much of the money collected was absorbed in paying the salaries and expenses of the numerous revenue officers, while the stimulus given to smuggling meant that many commodities reached consumers free of duty.

That the years following the defeat of Napoleon in 1815 saw much acute social distress can in fact be attributed to legislative restrictions on trade in foodstuffs. From 1770 to 1842 the import of livestock and beef, mutton, lamb and pork was forbidden. In addition severe restrictions were placed on the importation of corn. Legislation affecting corn was centuries old. From the eleventh to the fifteenth century its export was not allowed except in years of plenty. But the history of the corn laws really begins in 1436. For over 400 years, commencing with an Act passed in that year, the landed classes kept on the Statute Roll legislation giving home producers a near monopoly. After the Restoration of 1660, when the landed interest controlled Parliament, a policy of agrarian protection was followed. An Act passed in 1689 gave a 5s. bounty on corn exports when prices fell below 48s. a quarter. Duties on the export of corn were abolished, those on imports being retained.

The Act of 1689 did not give the landed classes the hoped for advantages. This was due partly to the debased state of the coinage and partly to legislation prohibiting the export of wool which eventuated in an increase in the area under the plough. The evil of a debased coinage was overcome in the reign of William III, new coins being minted worth their face value. But the circulation of a reliable currency led to a fall in the price of corn, as prices were now calculated according to the face value of coins. Between 1690 and 1699 the average price of wheat at Winchester was 50s. a quarter but only 21s. 2d. between 1746 and 1755. From the consumers' point of view the bounty system was an objectionable one. But had the bounty on exports been beneficial to agriculture? Experts differ in their answers. It has, however, been pointed out that the encouragement given to exports enlarged the area of cultivation and that some growers did export corn. Between 1740 and 1751, £1,515,000 was paid out by the Exchequer in bounties, of which £324,000 was paid out in 1749 alone. But the export trade was never large, and was not permanent, the quantity exported falling in the second half of the century.

Following a series of bad harvests, Parliament again took up the question of the corn laws in 1773. Burke's Act of that year was designed to facilitate imports and restrict exports. Between 1773 and 1793, when the average price of wheat was 46s. 3d. a quarter, imports exceeded exports. Home production increased as a result of enclosures and reclamation of waste land. But the liberal commercial policy of 1773, approved by Adam Smith, was of short duration owing to the demands of the landed interest for protection. An Act was passed in 1791 to encourage home production, and after the outbreak of war in 1793 the old corn law policy was revived. During the war years, however, instead of remaining constantly high, prices fluctuated violently, being 119s. 6d. a quarter in 1801, 58s. 10d. in 1803, 49s. 6d. in 1804, 89s. 6d. in 1805 and 120s. in 1806. Such fluctuations were a strain on the resources of consumers and not beneficial to producers. If farmers plan on the assumption that crops will sell for high prices, and prices slump, they are not fully compensated if in following years they rise to record heights, not to mention the possibility of prior bankruptcy.

The fall in wheat prices in 1803 led to the passage of an Act in 1804 providing that free imports should only be permitted when the price had reached 66s. This Act, however, was never operative as prices rose above 100s. The landed classes realised that high wartime price levels would not be maintained once peace came. Their fears were sharpened in 1814, when during the temporary peace the price of wheat fell to 55s. 8d. The sequel was the passage of the Act of 1815 prohibiting importation when the home price was less than 80s.

The authors of the Act of 1815 have been often criticised for raising the price at which imports were allowed from the wartime level of 66s. to 80s. Two points, however, may be made in their defence. Firstly, farmers, as was pointed out during the debates on the Bill, were as much entitled to protection as manufacturers. Import duties on all classes of merchandise had risen during the war considerably above the levels of the Younger Pitt's Consolidation Act of 1787. Conversely, those on farm products had only been moderately increased. It ill became industrialists to criticise high protection for corn when the duty, for example, on cotton goods was 85 per cent, on glass 114 per cent, and that on iron was £7 18s. 4d. a ton. Secondly, unless farmers obtained profitable prices, Britain would not produce sufficient food to feed an expanding population. In the first half of the nineteenth century the major part of food had to be home produced. Neither overseas suppliers, nor transport facilities then in use, were capable of doing more than supplementing domestic production.

Chapter XII

THE ACHIEVEMENT OF FREE TRADE

In the immediate post-war period Great Britain was, like her commercial rivals, a highly protectionist country. In France, for example, there was a high tariff, which by 1826 had been raised to prohibitive levels. But owing to differences in political, economic and social conditions, British and French commercial histories followed divergent courses. In France, apart from a short interlude during the reign of Napoleon III, protectionist policies were favoured. France was a peasant democracy whose politicians were obliged to follow policies agreeable to small farmers, who demanded protection for agricultural products, and to small industrial producers concerned to safeguard the home market against a flood of cheap imports from industrialised Britain.

In contrast the free trade movement in Britain was revived in the 1820s. British commercial history diverged from that of France and other countries, because in the nineteenth century it was in the interests of the most vigorous elements in the economic life of the nation to promote the greatest possible freedom in trading relationships. Britain emerged from the war period the dominant shipowning country. Being the first to use power-driven machinery on an extensive scale, she had obtained a near monopoly in textile and hardware production and could undersell native producers everywhere. Capitalist employers, who superseded the landowners as the mainstay of the resources and revenue of the realm, naturally expressed the opinion that the prosperity of manufactures was the primary need of the community, as population growth had made it impossible for Britain to remain self-sufficing in foodstuffs. By the mid-nineteenth century, therefore, the interests of certain groups of employers, notably in the textile industries, needing cheap labour and imported raw materials, coincided with those of their employees who wanted cheap food. The realisation that a tariff high enough to keep imports out is high enough to keep exports in, convinced both masters and men that the removal of artificial hindrances to trade would best serve the national interest. By both, protective corn law legislation was attacked as a device to make a selfish, aristocratic, landowning class rich by artificially raising the cost of living. Why, the industrial classes asked, should not measures be passed to facilitate trade with the primary producers of Europe, who in exchange for British manufactures could supply food and raw materials?

A notable victory was gained by those who advocated the throwing open of commerce to free enterprise when the East India Company lost its monopoly privileges. In 1815, the leading economist of the day, David Ricardo (1772–1823), criticised "restrictions on importation" in his *Essay on the Influence of a Low Price of Corn on the Profits of Stock*. But the business world was slower in discarding protectionist ideas than the economic theorists. Thomas Tooke, the London merchant who organised a petition to Parliament in 1820 in favour of the adoption of free trade principles, did not find that his mercantile colleagues were easily persuaded to sign. Nevertheless the London Merchants Petition of 1820 is a notable landmark in the history of the free trade movement. It led to the appointment of a House of Commons committee which in its report listed the disadvantages of existing restrictions on trade, and the extent to which foreign countries were copying British fiscal practices. After 1822, younger, more liberal-minded Tories became members of Lord Liverpool's government. William Huskisson, the member of Parliament for Liverpool, in 1823 became President of the Board of Trade. It was Huskisson, in association with the Chancellor of the Exchequer, Cobbett's "Prosperity Robinson," who laid the foundations of British free trade policies.

Huskisson, a member of Parliament since 1796, had a deserved reputation as an expert in financial matters. He aimed at increasing national wealth by removing restrictions on trade. The Navigation Laws were modified by the Reciprocity of Duties Act (1823), which empowered the Government to negotiate treaties on a basis of reciprocity in shipping matters. In the same year British colonies were allowed to trade direct with Europe.

In his reform of the customs duties Huskisson was not in practice a tariff abolitionist. He could not have abolished customs duties, as with the abolition of Pitt's wartime Property and Income Tax in 1816, customs duties provided three-fifths of the revenue. What Huskisson did was to substitute moderate for prohibitive or high duties on a wide range of imported manufactured commodities. These included cotton, linen, woollens, earthenware, paper and printed books. Reductions in duties on raw materials compensated manufacturers deprived in some measure of protection. The duty on raw silk was abolished and those on copper, tin, zinc and wool were considerably reduced. These measures, he explained, would make smuggling unprofitable. "Let the State," he told the House of Commons, "have the tax which is now the reward of the smuggler."

The long-term effects of the fiscal reforms of Huskisson and Robinson were good. Both exports and imports were substantially greater in 1830 than in 1820. The immediate effects were less happy. A wild fever of speculation brought about a financial crisis in 1825 and 1826 more ruinous than any Britain had known since the bursting of the South Sea Bubble in 1720. Yet despite the reforms of Huskisson and Robinson the British tariff remained a formidable obstacle. Whig governments between 1830 and 1841 were responsible for political and social reforms, but they did not risk challenging vested agricultural and industrial interests. There was a severe trade depression between 1836 and 1842. From the Government's point of view, lowering of customs duties in such circumstances appeared to be a hazardous venture, as the recession in trade had calamitous consequences, including revenue deficits of £1½ million in 1838, £½ million in 1841 and £2 million in 1842.

In 1840 the Hume Committee was appointed "to inquire into the several duties levied upon imports." The Hume Committee reported that the tariff system had not unity of purpose and that it often aimed at incompatible ends, to raise revenue and to give protection. It could not do both. If foreign goods were kept out, there would be no revenue; if they were brought in there would be no protection. The report revealed that there were more than 1150 dutiable commodities and that 95 per cent of the customs revenue was derived from the duties on seventeen of them. These seventeen included foodstuffs and beverages, some raw materials, cotton, wool, timber and tallow, and manufactured articles such as silks, tobacco, wines and spirits. The Hume Committee was very impressed by what was happening in Germany where since 1834 Prussia had taken the initiative in negotiating an economic union of the German States, the Zollverein. In its external tariff the Zollverein was pursuing a liberal trade policy, free imports of raw materials and low duties on manufactured articles. There was a lesson to be learned from German experience. The cost of living was lower than in Britain, and, although Germany was still mainly an agrarian country, the foundations of industrial expansion were being laid in the Rhinelands, Silesia and Saxony.

Sir Robert Peel became Prime Minister in 1841. Inheriting a serious financial problem at a time of acute trade depression, he came to the conclusion that fiscal policy needed a thorough overhaul. The principles upon which he acted were those recommended by Sir Henry Parnell in a treatise published in 1830 *On Financial Reform*. Peel was the first statesman to understand the intimate connection between the import and export trades. Hitherto each had been dealt with separately. Protectionists thought that if foreign goods were excluded the home producer would be fully employed. Peel, on the contrary, maintained that home producers would benefit if tariffs were reduced, as in the long run exports pay for imports, and imports for exports. Peel also believed that full economic activity would only eventuate if prices were lowered. In his own words, "We must make England a cheap country to live in. Enable them to consume more by having more to spend." Artificially high prices, particularly those on foodstuffs, had the opposite effect. The cost of food and drink was so high that the masses had little or no purchasing power left over to buy the products of British industry. Peel's budgets, therefore, were designed to lower the cost of living and to permit fair competition between our own producers and those overseas.

The financial measures introduced by Peel in 1842, 1843 and 1845 provided that duties on raw materials were not to exceed 5 per cent, those on partly manufactured goods 12 per cent and those on wholly manufactured goods 20 per cent. Manufacturers were compensated by reductions or abolitions of duties on their raw materials. Some export duties were repealed with the notable exception of those on coal and wood. Breaches were even made in the system of agricultural protection. The sliding scale of 1828 on corn was modified, the prohibition on the importation of livestock was replaced by duties, and the duties on ham, bacon, meat and butter were reduced. In all, 750 dutiable commodities were affected. The resultant loss of revenue and the current revenue deficits, totalling about £10 million, made it necessary to find a new source of revenue. As a temporary measure, to last for three years, Peel imposed an income tax of sevenpence in the pound on persons enjoying annual incomes of £150 and more.

Peel's budgets were very successful. Trade revival, increasing customs revenues, and the yield from income tax provided the Exchequer with a surplus of over £2 million in 1844. This made possible further reductions in indirect taxation including the abolition of the export tax on machinery. In 1845 a revenue surplus of nearly £3½ million permitted further extensions to the policy of 1842. Instead of simply reducing duties, Peel embarked on a policy of abolitions, 430 in all, which included the duties on cotton, silk, hemp and flax, and the irritating excises on glass and the proceeds of auctions. The remaining export duties disappeared and the sugar duty was considerably reduced. In 1846 duties on manufactures were reduced and on some abolished. Duties on timber and tallow were reduced and the cost of living was significantly lowered by reductions of those on soap, candles, footwear and foodstuffs. But the budget of 1846 was above all noteworthy for its agrarian content. Duties were reduced on seed and maize, giving partial compensation to farmers for the abolition of the duties on imported livestock, and on meat, ham, bacon, butter and cheese. More significantly, the duty on corn became purely nominal. Britain was not a free trade country when Peel resigned in June 1846, nevertheless his budgets had inaugurated a revolutionary change in fiscal policy. He had in all abolished 605 customs duties and reduced 1035. Yet, despite these remissions the public revenue had been increased and the public debt decreased.

Of all his many achievements that for which Peel is above all remembered is the 1846 legislation dealing with the importation of corn. As explained in the previous chapter, Parliament in the first half of the nineteenth century had legislated to keep corn above the level of a free market price. Under the provisions of the Act of 1815 wheat could be imported from foreign countries, free of duty, when the price of home produced wheat was 80s., and from the British North American colonies when it was 67s. Lower price levels were fixed for free-of-duty imports of barley, rye and oats. In 1822 a new system was introduced, a sliding scale of duties. The price at which free imports of wheat were permitted was reduced to 70s. for foreign wheat and 50s. for British North American wheat. The price level for barley was reduced to 35s. and for oats to 25s. Import duties varied with price levels, being 17s. when wheat was 70s., falling to 10s. when wheat was 85s. The Act of 1822 was a dead letter as prices never reached the expected levels. In seasons of scarcity it was even necessary to empower the King in Council to override the Act. In 1825 wheat from the colonies was allowed in at a fixed duty of 5s. whatever the home price. This concession, though no doubt important politically, made little difference economically, as the amount available for export to Britain was very small.

In 1828 the practice of fixing a price level at which imports were prohibited was abandoned. Instead all wheat imports were made liable to duty, calculated according to a sliding scale. When the home price was 73s. or more the duty was 1s. and 39s. 8d. when the price was 47s. For every shilling decrease in price below 47s., an additional shilling was added to the duty. This sliding scale was modified by Peel in 1842. A duty of 1s. was levied when wheat prices were 73s. or more, 4s. when the price was 70s., rising to 20s. when prices were lower than 51s.

Before Peel became Prime Minister public opinion in some manufacturing areas was becoming increasingly critical of the wisdom of legislative action to keep food prices at artifically high levels in defiance of economic trends. The first motion for the abolition of the Corn Laws was moved in the House of Commons in 1838 by Charles Pelham Villiers, the member for Wolverhampton. It was rejected by an overwhelming majority. In the same year an Anti-Corn Law Association was formed in Manchester, its title being changed in 1839 to the Anti-Corn Law League. The driving force behind the League was Richard Cobden (1804–65). Born near Midhurst in Sussex, Cobden published free trade pamphlets in 1835, took a leading part in Manchester political life and in 1841 was elected member of Parliament for Stockport. It was to Cobden, as Peel later testified, that the victory of free trade principles was due. He won his audiences over by appealing to reason not to emotions, as he had a genius for lucid exposition, in simple words and phrases, of abstract, difficult economic concepts.

Cobden secured for the League the services of the Quaker cotton spinner, John Bright of Rochdale (1811–89). Both were opponents of state controls. Bright at the beginning of a long political career opposed the levying of a church rate at Rochdale, and to the end of his life opposed factory legislation and laws to improve public health amenities. But every political cause he championed he saw as a moral issue. Repealing the Corn Laws, he said, was putting "Holy Writ into an Act of Parliament." As a public speaker his abilities were outstanding, being described, even though he was a contemporary of Gladstone, as "the greatest master of English oratory" of his generation. His speeches abounded in memorable phrases, for example "a free breakfast table," that became popular programmes. Bright's rhetorical speeches and Cobden's lucid arguments stirred the country to its depths. The Penny Post (1840) and the newly constructed railways enabled the movement to grow to unheard-of dimensions, hence when in March 1839 Villiers moved his second repeal motion he got 195 votes.

The opposition of the agricultural classes and the Chartists would have to be countered before the League could hope for success. The landowners never became free traders. Many farmers, on the other hand, were won over by Cobden's lucid analysis of how the corn duties affected them. Farmers above all wanted steady prices, as rotation of crop practices compelled them to plan land use years ahead. Cobden convinced many that the Corn Laws were the cause of price fluctuations and that high prices were absorbed by high rents. Farm labourers, who did not possess parliamentary votes, regarded themselves as consumers rather than as producers. They wanted cheap bread, but although they were supposed to be protected, they were starving. The Chartists, for their part, distrusted the Anti-Corn Law League as a middle-class movement, the class which had betrayed the workers during the Reform Bill agitation of 1832. They further disliked the League agitation for the very understandable human reasons that it distracted attention from their own and was carried on much more effectively. To Cobden's arguments they replied that a fall in the price of bread would be followed by a reduction in wages. Repeal would increase millowners' profits, not their employees' standard of living, a point of view which had the merit of being sanctioned by the "iron law of wages" of contemporary economists.

What were the effects of the Corn Laws? From the consumers' point of view they were bad. Before 1793 corn duties had practically no effect on prices, as England was on balance a corn-exporting country. After 1815 the position was different, an expanding population making corn imports essential. Prices fell on all classes of commodities, but wheat prices were kept artificially high. In 1839, when wheat prices were at their highest during the 1825–46 period, the effect of the duty on foreign wheat was to raise the price by 15 per cent. In that year 550,000 tons were imported. The lowest price for wheat during the same period, 39s. 4d., was reached in 1835. Only 3379 tons were imported as the import duty, 121 per cent of the price, was almost prohibitive. For the consumer, even more distressing than high prices were fluctuations in prices. Given steady prices wage rates would inevitably have been adjusted to meet them. This was prevented by the way in which the sliding scales operated. When prices were rising, owing to poor harvests, corn dealers kept imported wheat in bonded warehouses until prices reached 73s., the price at which under the 1828 and 1842 scales the import duty was at its lowest level, one shilling. The subsequent release of wheat on to the market caused prices to fall, to the profit of corn dealers who had paid a low duty, and to the disadvantage of home producers who had failed to obtain high prices in years of poor harvests. A situation could, and did arise, for example in 1841, when although people were starving, immense quantities of foreign wheat filled the bonded warehouses. The high cost of wheat often led to a desperate competition for work at any price, a situation which had a tendency to lower wages. It is also worth noting that bread formed a larger part of the diet of working men than nowadays, hence high prices, and especially fluctuating ones, were particularly distressing.

There was a genuine belief that the corn duties were beneficial to producers. High rents were regarded as evidence of good and careful farming. But were the Corn Laws really beneficial to producers? They were without question not beneficial to farm labourers. Ample evidence is available to prove that they lived under conditions of extreme wretchedness. Small farmers were little better off. Many had difficulty in paying their rents. Fluctuating prices drove some from the land. In parts of the country untilled land and untenanted farmhouses were eloquent of the parlous state of English farming. The periodical depression in trade and industry and low wage rates put the purchase of such farm products as bacon, cheese, eggs, milk, meat and butter beyond the reach of town consumers. With good reason, advocates of free trade contended that their policy, by increasing the spending power of the urban masses, would do more to increase agricultural prosperity than the maintenance of high duties on foreign imports. Lastly, as a tax, the corn duties were grossly unfair. A tax on bread placed the heaviest burden on the shoulders of those least able to pay.

The Anti-Corn Law League drew strength from the *laisser faire* intellectual atmosphere of the age. The considerable reduction in the protection given to industry, brought about by Peel's fiscal reform, made agricultural protection less defensible. But Peel was not easily convinced that it would be in the national interest to pursue a policy which would result in Englishmen becoming dependent upon overseas farmers for most of their food supplies. His first essay in agricultural reform, the sliding scale of 1842, only slightly modified that of 1828. The subsequent repeal campaign of Cobden and Bright did not, as Disraeli and Lord George Bentinck later pointed out, gain mass approval for their programme. The League was successful, not because it could be shown to have obtained overwhelming public support, but because Peel was won over. The events which forced Peel's hand and split the Tory Party were the bad harvest of 1845 and the disastrous failure of the Irish potato crop. When Peel failed to get Cabinet support, and resigned, the Whig leader, Lord John Russell, published the "Edinburgh Letter" in which he committed the Whigs to repeal the Corn Laws. Russell, however, did not become Prime Minister, but, to quote Disraeli, "passed the poisoned chalice to Sir Robert." Peel returned to office and supported by Whigs and Peelites introduced the Bill which paved the way for the abolition of the Corn Laws. Peel's Act of 1846 provided for a duty of 10s. where wheat was less than 48s. falling to 4s. when the price was 54s. This modified sliding scale was to continue until 1st February 1849, when the duty on wheat, oats and barley was to become a nominal levy of 1s.

Russell's government, which succeeded that of Peel, repealed the Navigation Laws in 1849. Some concessions to foreign shipping had been made earlier. In 1796 the U.S.A. was permitted to send her exports to Britain in her own ships. In the same year trade between the U.S.A. and the West Indies was allowed, and with Canada in 1807. In 1808 Brazil, and in 1822 the new Latin American republics were granted the same concessions in shipping matters as the U.S.A. As already explained, Huskisson in the 1820s had relaxed the Navigation Laws in favour of those countries willing to conclude reciprocity treaties, but in actual fact only a limited number of reciprocity treaties were signed. The Navigation Laws were consolidated in an Act passed in 1845, certain restrictions still being maintained. The colonies were allowed to trade with foreign countries but goods of non-European origin could not be imported from Europe. Inter-imperial trade was still reserved to British or colonial ships, and goods from Asia and Africa could only be imported in British ships or in ships of the country of origin. Further, restrictions still remained on the employment of foreign seamen.

The abolition of these protective measures was only a matter of time. Merchants pressed for their removal as they wanted to charter the cheaper and faster American vessels. Canadian corn exporters, deprived of preferential treatment by the repeal of the Corn Laws, protested at being compelled to pay high freight charges to protected British shipowners, while the Zollverein was threatening to penalise British shipping. But repeal was stoutly resisted in the House of Lords by members who doubted the ability of British ships to compete on equal terms with the fast American "clippers." Tory speakers reminded the House that even Adam Smith had approved the Navigation Laws. But as a matter of fact they had outlived their usefulness. The repeal went through but the Tories did succeed in delaying, until 1853, the admission of foreigners to a share in the coasting trade, and the removal of the obligation to man British ships with British seamen.

In 1852 Lord Derby became Prime Minister and Disraeli Chancellor of the Exchequer. The Tories made no attempt to repeal the free trade legislation. "Protection," as Disraeli afterwards admitted, "was dead and damned." The Derby–Disraeli Government was succeeded by the Aberdeen coalition of Whigs and Peelites. Gladstone became Chancellor of the Exchequer. In a series of masterly budgets, beginning in 1853, Gladstone completed the task of making Britain a free trade country, import duties being retained for revenue purposes only. In the budget of 1853 Gladstone swept away the excise duty on soap, a tax on cleanliness, and removed the tax on newspaper advertisements. In all, he repealed duties on 123 articles and reduced those on 133. The tea duty, for example, was reduced from 2s. 2¼d. to 1s. a pound, and the tax on life assurance from 2s. 6d. to 1s. per £100. He paid for these reductions by increasing the duty on whisky, extending the legacy duty to real and personal property passing by will, and renewing the income tax for seven years on incomes exceeding £100 per year.

The budget of 1853 was a brilliant success, the revenues from customs and excise actually increasing. It had been designed as the beginning of a great scheme of reform but unfortunately Gladstone lost office shortly after the outbreak of the Crimean War. He returned to the Treasury in 1859 where he remained as Chancellor of the Exchequer until 1866. In 1860 he introduced the first of a series of budgets, which, although they excited keen opposition at the time, ultimately proved beneficial. The budget of 1860 was preceded by the Cobden Commercial Treaty with France (1860). The intellectual leader of French free traders had been Frederic Bastiat (1801–50), a friend of Cobden and Bright. About 1844 Bastiat attempted to organise in France a movement modelled on the Anti-Corn Law League. Free traders, however, were a minority in France, so the movement made little headway until the accession of Napoleon III. Owing to the opposition of the protectionists the Emperor failed to get his tariff reforms accepted by the legislature. He decided, therefore, to circumvent the opposition by using his executive authority to conclude commercial treaties. In absolute secrecy a commercial treaty was negotiated between Cobden and Michel Chevalier the economist and adviser of Napoleon III. It was to last for ten years. France and Britain agreed to abolish all prohibitions and to guarantee "most favoured nation" treatment to each other. The treaty paved the way for a substantial reduction in duties. France agreed to levy moderate duties, not exceeding 30 per cent on British coal and manufactures. Britain agreed to abolish duties on French manufactures and to reduce those on wines and brandy. The Cobden Treaty was the prelude to a great European movement in the same direction. Anglo-French trade increased nearly four-fold in the next twenty years. Indeed in the 'sixties it looked as though Cobden's prophecy, that free trade would usher in an era of prosperity and universal peace, was on the verge of realisation even though high tariffs continued in Austria and Russia and also in Spain. Unfortunately, this did not prove to be the case, as after 1870 European States embarked on policies of high protectionism and militarism.

Gladstone in his 1860 budget had to provide for the remission of duties agreed in the Cobden Treaty. In drawing up the budget he was guided by two principles: firstly, no protective duties on raw materials, food and manufactured commodities; secondly, revenue should be raised from the smallest possible number of articles.

Before 1860 there were 419 dutiable commodities. Gladstone reduced the number to 48, of which only 15 made any significant contribution to the revenue. These were spirits, sugar, tea, tobacco, wines, coffee, currants, timber, chicory, figs, hops, pepper, raisins, rice and the 1s. registration duty on corn. By far the most lucrative were the taxes on tobacco, tea, spirits and wines. Taxes on manufactured goods were abolished and a number of foodstuffs, including butter, cheese and eggs, were henceforth duty free.

Gladstone in 1860 had also hoped to abolish the lucrative duty on paper. The proposal, sent to the Lords as a separate Bill, was thrown out, but Gladstone ultimately got his way by including the abolition as an item in the 1861 budget, thus making possible cheap books and newspapers. Gladstone's budgets completed the work begun by Huskisson and Peel. After 1860 Britain was a free trade country. A few minor reforms were made after 1860. Robert Lowe repealed the 1s. registration duty on corn in 1866, and Gladstone the timber duties in the same year. The sugar duty was repealed in stages, in 1864, 1870 and 1873, being finally abolished in 1874. The achievement of free trade coincided with a massive expansion in British trade. It would be a mistake, however, to attribute this expansion wholly to the adoption of free trade policies, as much of it was due to other factors. Nevertheless, given world trading conditions prevailing at the time, the wisdom of Gladstone's policies was amply demonstrated. Their suitability, a generation later, when British industrial supremacy was no longer unchallenged, could not be taken for granted. These are matters, however, that will have to be left for consideration in a later chapter.

PART IV

THE NINETEENTH-CENTURY REVOLUTION IN MEANS OF COMMUNICATION

Chapter XIII

RAILWAYS

"The dominant fact of our own age," the famous economist Professor Alfred Marshall once wrote, "is the development not of manufacturing but of the transport industries." Marshall witnessed during his long life revolutionary changes in transport facilities. Until just before he was born, in 1842, the fastest speed at which men and commodities could be carried on land was that of the horse. Before his death, in 1924, steam locomotion had brought about far-reaching changes in human society. Canals and improved roads and bridges had, in the eighteenth century, enabled human beings and freight to be transported more cheaply and expeditiously than ever before. But the transport facilities created by the genius of Metcalfe, Telford, Macadam, Brindley, Smeaton and Rennie had only a limited potential because they were restricted to the speed of horses. Before the British industrial potential could be fully realised new means of transport would have to be found. They were found in the nineteenth century. The communication of news and commercial intelligence was dramatically speeded up by the telegraph, submarine cables and the telephone, and the carrying of people and commodities was revolutionised by railways and steamships.

The far-reaching consequences of railway construction, on both the British and world economies, cannot be exaggerated. To railways is due the creation of modern industrial civilisation built upon the twin foundations of coal and iron. Steam locomotion transported commodities, manufactured in urban industrial centres, more speedily, and in vastly greater quantities than was possible in barges pulled by horses. Railway construction and operation made unprecedented demands upon the iron, steel and coal industries, about 150 tons of iron being needed to build a mile of track. Railways opened up the interiors of continents previously inaccessible. As much of the equipment and "know how" for railway construction overseas was provided by Great Britain, capital investment overseas expanded considerably. Railways were built in India by

John Brunton. Better known are the railway contractors, Thomas Brassey (1805–70) and Sir Samuel Morton Peto (1809–89). Brassey built railways in England, Scotland, most European countries, India, Australia and South America. At one time he had 75,000 men on his payroll and contracts worth approximately £36 million. He was associated with Peto in building the Grand Trunk Railway in Canada, in the construction of a magnificent bridge over the St Lawrence, and in building railways in the Crimea during the Crimean War. In England, Peto built the London, Chatham and Dover line, and in association with Brassey, the London, Tilbury and Southend Railway. The railway engineers not only pioneered the development of an export trade in locomotives and rolling stock but also opened up for settlement and trade new overseas areas. The first steamships made possible emigration into these territories on a previously unknown scale. The British economy, which before the railway era had been dependent upon overseas markets, became even more so. Access was gained to raw materials and foodstuffs produced by the emigrants who received in payment manufactured commodities.

An important consequence of railway construction was an enlargement of the field of joint stock company enterprise. Before the nineteenth century this had been largely confined to the Bank of England, to chartered trading companies, and in the last two decades of the eighteenth century, to the financing of canal building. The capital outlay to build, equip and operate a railway is very large, and the return on it, in the form of profits, is not immediate. Capital on the required scale could only be provided by the State or from the savings of very large numbers of its citizens. In some countries governments have financed railway construction. In others, governments have offered inducements to investors, such as guarantees of interest payments or free or cheap land. But in Britain state help was not forthcoming. Railway promoters obtained the capital they needed by persuading members of the upper and middle classes to invest their savings in joint stock companies. This extension of the opportunities for speculative investment made necessary a revision of company law, and provided a model, in the second half of the nineteenth century, for financing other forms of productive enterprise. From the 'sixties onwards, business units, owned and managed by individuals or small partnerships, gave way to large joint stock companies, nominally owned by shareholders, but managed and controlled on their behalf by boards of directors and professional managers.

On 27th September 1825, the first public railway operated by a steam locomotive, the Stockton to Darlington line, was opened. An engine, "Locomotion," made and manned by George Stephenson (1781–1848), engineer of Killingworth, Northumberland, pulled a long train consisting of wagons, loaded with coal and sacks of flour, and passenger wagons. In the following year, 1826, Parliament passed "an Act for making and maintaining a Railway or Tram-road from the Town of Liverpool to the Town of Manchester with certain branches therefrom." The Liverpool to Manchester Railway was opened on 15th September 1830. The same George Stephenson was the engineer in charge. Still to be seen on exhibition in the South Kensington Museum is the forerunner of the present day steam locomotive, the "Rocket," built at Newcastle by Messrs Robert Stephenson and Company. Fitted with a multitubular boiler and capable of travelling at 35 miles an hour, the "Rocket" had gained a decided triumph at the Rainhill Trials in October 1829. The day on which the Duke of Wellington travelled in "the State Coach" from Liverpool saw the beginning of the first passenger locomotive railway, and of the first commercially successful railway in the world.

In its obituary notice on George Stephenson, the *Athenaeum* paid tribute to a mechanical genius, the "Author of the British Railway System." But this tribute must not be taken to imply that he invented the railway. Others, before and after Stephenson, contributed ideas. Four main elements had to be combined to form a railway, the road, the rail, steam power and the duty of functioning as a "common carrier." Railways originated in the "tram roads" or waggon ways, levelled surfaces on which coal was transported from collieries to riverside wharfs. Consisting of log roads, raised slightly above ground level, they existed in Durham in the sixteenth century. On Tyneside, before the Restoration, wooden rails were clamped on to these log roads along which wagons with grooved wheels were pushed. From Arthur Young we learn that some of these "tram roads" in the North of England were "great works," nine or ten miles long. At Coalbrookdale in 1767, and possibly earlier elsewhere, cast iron rails were substituted for wooden ones. In the early nineteenth century "tram roads" were also used for passenger carriage. About 1799 a railway company, using horse drawn vehicles, transported passengers and coal for about three miles between East Ardsley in Yorkshire and the River Calder. The Surrey Iron Railway, authorised in 1801, was opened in 1803 between Wandsworth and Croydon, horses being used to pull passenger wagons along iron rails.

The next development was the use of steam power. Between 1772 and 1812 experiments were made in designing steam carriages for use on the highway, notably by the Frenchman, Cugnot (1771),

William Murdock at Redruth in Cornwall (1784), and by Richard Trevithick (1802). A second line of invention, the use of steam traction on rails, at first made slow progress. The Cornish engineer, Trevithick, one of the most brilliant inventive geniuses of his time, built a locomotive in 1804 for use on a "tram road" in South Wales, which was later converted into a stationary engine. The first really successful experiments were made on Tyneside. At Wylam, the local colliery manager demonstrated that smooth wheels would not slip on smooth rails. At the same colliery, the owner, Blackett, and his engine-wright, Foster, designed "Puffing Billy" and "Wylam Dilly," two engines used for hauling coal. Stephenson followed with his "Blucher" (1814), the first locomotive to have a blast pipe and to send out steam with a succession of puffs. The promise of a revolution in transport, implicit in what was happening on the banks of the Tyne, was long in being realised elsewhere. The real breakthrough came in 1821, the year in which George Stephenson walked barefoot to Darlington and persuaded the Quaker, Edward Pease, to use a "steam horse" on the projected Stockton–Darlington tramway.

The initiative in the building of railways in Great Britain was taken by business men, keen to promote local prosperity. Edward Pease and his fellow promoters were looking for a cheap means of transporting coal from the West Auckland coalfield. In Liverpool the initiative was taken by the corn merchant, Joseph Sandars. In contrast to Bristol whose rich merchants were too indolent to take advantage of the opportunities of the age, Liverpool was a rapidly expanding city. Telford noted in 1799 that while Bristol was declining in importance, Liverpool was "young, vigorous and well situated." Liverpool's population rose from 60,000 to 165,000 between 1792 and 1831 and its customs revenues from £80,000 in 1780 to £1,808,423 in 1823. This growth was based not upon industrial expansion but upon shipping. No port profited more than Liverpool from the industrial changes taking place in northern England. Its rise in commercial importance from about 1780 was due, as Telford saw in 1799, to the system of inland waterways linking it with a hinterland undergoing social and economic transformation.

Long before 1830, Liverpool merchants were complaining that the transport facilities provided by the canal companies were not keeping pace with business expansion. Proposals for a railroad between Liverpool and Manchester were made as early as 1796. In 1820 Thomas Gray of Nottingham, a writer of unusual prophetic insight, published *Observations on a General Railway*, in which he suggested that all the principal towns of England should be connected by rail, beginning with one between Liverpool and Manchester. But it was not until Sandars showed interest that progress was made. In 1822, following a refusal by the Bridgewater Canal Trustees to reduce charges, Sandars began to seek support for a railway link. He had embarked on no easy task. There were serious physical hazards to overcome, including the crossing of Chat Moss. It was only after many set-backs that Stephenson built a firm but elastic causeway across its peaty, sodden surface. More difficult to cope with were the political and human obstacles. Ignorance, prejudice and greed obstructed the promoters. In 1825 the first parliamentary Bill was wrecked by the opposition of canal companies, turnpike trusts and powerful landed magnates including Lord Derby and Lord Sefton. The rejoicing of the opposition, however, proved to be short-lived, as a second Bill was passed by Parliament in 1826 with the aid of Huskisson.

The Liverpool to Manchester Railway exceeded the expectations of the promoters. Contrary to original forecasts railways obtained considerable profits from passenger transport. A further discovery was that railway companies must become common carriers. At first the right to use the line was leased to private individuals who used either locomotives or horse-drawn wagons. In 1832 as such arrangements created impossible situations the Company took over responsibility for transporting both passengers and freight. The success achieved encouraged railway construction elsewhere. By 1840, 1331 miles had been built, most of the lines being very short in length. In 1846 the average length of English railways was only 15 miles.

No form of economic enterprise was more prolific in the use of resources of labour and capital than railways. Their construction, the production of materials needed to build them, and their operation when completed provided gainful employment for hundreds of thousands. Huge amounts of capital were subscribed by noblemen, bishops, members of the professions and middle classes, all hopeful of becoming rich overnight. A mania for railway speculation, beginning in 1836, endowed the country with 1000 miles of track. In the 'forties the investing public was even more eager to give financial backing. Parliament authorised railway projects estimated to cost £17$\frac{3}{4}$ million in 1844, £60 million in 1845 and £132 million in 1846. If Parliament could have been persuaded to agree subscriptions would have been solicited for much greater amounts. Five companies, for example, proposed to build lines to Brighton and three to Norwich.

Despite the refusal of Parliament to approve a majority of the schemes submitted, Great Britain came to possess the most closely built railway network in the world. Railway mileage increased from 2036 in 1843 to 5900 in 1850, to 9100 in 1860 and to 13,600 in 1870. After 1870, the rate of increase diminished, the mileage being 15,500 in 1880, 18,600 in 1900 and 20,100 in 1913. The creation of this mileage is a tribute to the skill and foresight of pioneer Victorian civil engineers, and to the barely credible muscular powers of the "navigators" or navvies who could move 20 tons of earth a day, and with picks and shovels built the London to Birmingham line in less than five years. To these superb labourers, brutalised and coarsened by the squalid, appalling conditions in which they lived and worked, we owe the massive earthworks, cuttings and embankments still to be seen blending into the countryside.

As the direction of British resources in men and money into railway construction was directed by private, commercially inspired local enterprise, the system was not planned on a national basis. Railway development elsewhere followed a different course. Belgium was the first European country to build railways, as its coal industry created a demand for cheap transport. In France railways came later as the economic insistence was not so great. Their development in France was hindered by the same scepticism as in Britain, and by dispute between advocates of public and private enterprise. But when action was finally taken it was under a considerable degree of state control. Building and operating the lines was entrusted to private companies, the Government paying a subsidy, owning the road bed and deciding the geographical plan of the system. Monopoly franchises were awarded to six companies and all main lines were designed to converge on Paris. As Germany before 1870 lacked political unity, the first railways were built separately in each State. There was no radiation from Berlin, as from Paris, but a multitude of focal points, the state capitals. Bismarck's intention of creating after 1870 a single, imperial system, broke down owing to the opposition of the States. Development, however, was not as haphazard and chaotic as in Britain. The first German railways were built by private enterprise but except in Prussia this phase did not last very long. In Prussia also, however, the railways were eventually nationalised by a process of systematic purchase. Generally speaking as *laisser-faire* traditions on the continent were less dominant and private capital was more scarce, the State played a more active role in railway affairs. In East Prussia, where defence considerations were paramount, the Government built lines that could never hope to be commercially profitable. In Russia, railways were built for both military and commercial reasons. Construction began on a big scale after the

Crimean War, the building programme of the State culminating in the construction of the Trans-Siberian Railway, opened in 1901. In the U.S.A. where railways, as in Russia, provided the best means of opening up inland areas not readily accessible from the sea by navigable waterways, state governments played a major role, making grants of land and loaning money to private enterprise.

In contrast, Victorian Britain, with its strong *laisser-faire* prejudices, built railways haphazardly in the teeth of considerable opposition. John Francis in *A History of the English Railway* (1851) has recorded contemporary opinion. "The country gentlemen were told that the smoke would kill the birds as they passed over the locomotives ... the manufacturer was told that the sparks from its chimney would burn his goods.... Foxes and pheasants were to cease in the neighbourhood of a railway. The race of horses was to be extinguished. Farmers were possessed by the idea that oats and hay would be no more marketable produce; ... cows even, it was said, would cease to yield their milk in the neighbourhood of one of these infernal machines."

The opposition the railway pioneers had to contend with has had serious economic consequences, not the least being incurring the highest capital costs in the world. Building a railway involved considerable interference with private property rights, and with vested interests in the older forms of transport. Canal companies, turnpike road trustees, landowners, coaching establishments and prejudiced individuals combined to make the passage of Railway Bills prolonged and expensive. The legal costs of British railways have been estimated at £4000 a mile. Land costs were also very high. Parliaments, dominated by landed interests, safeguarded private property rights. Parliamentary sanction for the Stockton–Darlington line, for example, was delayed because the Duke of Cleveland opposed a route through his fox-covers. Land for the London to Birmingham railway cost £750,000, and that for the London to Brighton line £8000 a mile, to which must be added £4000 a mile for legal and surveying costs.

Lines had to be re-routed because landowners and municipal authorities objected to the noise and smoke of steam traction. In consequence stations were sometimes sited at a distance from urban centres to the subsequent regret of their inhabitants. As Britain was the pioneer in railway construction, costly mistakes were made that other countries avoided, profiting by our experience. On some of the lines, laid down in the railway boom of the 'forties and 'fifties, curves and gradients were too sharp to allow high speeds. As the early lines were designed to serve local traffic much of the mileage had to be re-laid to integrate it into a national system. The development of railway transport was hindered by ideas and methods taken over from roads and canals. As has been well said, "the ghost of the horse and coach runs before the modern locomotive." It seemed natural that traders should put their own wagons on the line, hence railway companies did not at first undertake the duties of a common carrier. In consequence, until the railways were nationalised in 1948, private traders owned more than half the trucks, a state of affairs which reduced efficiency and increased working expenses.

The high capitalisation of British railways can also in part be attributed to mountain and river obstacles to communication. Costly engineering achievements of the early railway builders included Stephenson's Sankey Viaduct near Warrington, the Woodhead and Standedge Tunnels through the Pennines, the Kilsby Tunnel near Rugby and the tunnels built to overcome such water obstacles as the Thames, Mersey and Severn. In contrast, railway construction costs were much lower in other countries with flat terrains where standards of construction were much inferior. Capital costs per mile in Great Britain have been estimated to be £54,152 but at only £21,000 in Prussia and £13,000 in the U.S.A.

Regarding railways as dangerous innovations, Parliament added to their constructional and operating costs by insisting on the fencing of all railway routes, and, in the interests of public safety, making regulations governing braking and signalling systems. At first semaphore signalling was in use during the day and coloured lamps at night. In 1839 the Great Western Railway experimented with the newly invented electric telegraph, its use gradually becoming universal. A system of signals invented in 1846 by Charles Gregory was improved ten years later by John Shaxby.

The early railways were short, local ones, the 112-mile London to Birmingham line, for which Robert Stephenson secured the contract, and Isambard Kingdom Brunel's Great Western, being notable exceptions. Many lines connected unimportant places and were never a profitable investment. The money and enthusiasm of which our forefathers were so prodigal partly explains the need for the Beeching Plan in the 1960s. The wonder is, not that the Plan recommended the closure of many lines, but that so much unremunerative mileage has survived to need surgical attention. That Britain today possesses a system of main trunk lines, like the Roman road network centred on London, is not due to the implementation of a national plan. Rather it is a consequence of piece-meal amalgamations of small railway companies. In 1839, the Manchester Quaker, engraver and printer, George Bradshaw, published the first edition of *Bradshaw's Railway Timetables*. The 1840 edition lists about 200 railways which by 1848 had been reduced to 22 large ones and a few smaller concerns.

Amalgamations were unavoidable in the interests both of the public and the companies themselves. Only under unified management could long distance transport be efficiently provided, better services and reduced fares be made possible, and ruinous competition ended. In the Midlands, for example, there were three lines terminating at Derby, varying in length from 50 to 73 miles. They were unified in 1844 to form the Midland Railway. A much larger grouping was achieved in 1846 when the London–Birmingham, the Manchester–Birmingham and the Grand Junction (Warrington to Birmingham) lines were amalgamated to form the London and North Western Railway Company.

Although very necessary, amalgamations were not easy to bring about, directors and officials resisting proposals which might make them redundant. Parliament viewed with concern the formation of transport monopolies, its fears being increased in the 1840s by the "take over" by railway companies of hundreds of miles of the canal network. Neither was it easy to determine the values to put upon the shares of the companies concerned. Nevertheless, the amalgamation movement inevitably gained in momentum. George Stephenson, realising from the start that railways would have to be organised on a national basis, had recommended that there should be a standard gauge. His own was 4 ft $8\frac{1}{2}$ in., the gauge of the colliery tram-roads. Brunel, to permit the use of locomotives of higher speeds and power, adopted a 7 ft gauge on his Great Western Railway. The desirability of a standard gauge became obvious in the 1840s when there was a possibility of the Great Western absorbing the Grand Junction. The issue of "the battle of the gauges" was determined by Parliament in 1846. Stephenson's narrow gauge was made the standard for Great Britain, that for Ireland being fixed at 5 ft 3 in. The Great Western Railway had to conform, the conversion being completed by 1892.

The leading advocate of railway amalgamation in the 1840s was the "Railway King," George Hudson (1800–71), denounced in Carlyle's *Latter Day Pamphlets* as "the big swollen gambler." His career was meteoric. Apprenticed to a linen draper in York, he founded the York Banking Company in 1833, became Lord Mayor in 1837 and between 1845 and 1859 was Tory M.P. for Sunderland where there still exists a statue to his memory. Like his friend, George Stephenson, he realised that railways must be organised as a national network. The development of York as a major railway junction owes much to his initiative. In his hey-day he had some 1000 miles of line under his control. Amalgamations had taken place as early as 1834, but the real movement for railway unification began with Hudson's formation of the Midland Railway in 1844 and the later linking up of York with Newcastle and Berwick. He built up his financial empire by offering higher dividends, paid out of capital, than his rivals. The end came in 1849 when his dishonest private transactions with the Great Northern Railway promoters, the rivals of his North Midland lines, were exposed, to the wrathful dismay of the thousands of titled and untitled script holders who had looked to Hudson to make them rich. Hudson did realise the need to bring order out of chaos in railway affairs, and deserves credit for the many improvements he introduced into their working. Unfortunately, he was the first, but by no means the last company promoter, operating on a colossal scale, who by either unwise or dishonest methods, in an era of inadequate accountancy techniques, brought financial ruin on himself and many others.

Amalgamations were accelerated by the formation of the Clearing House and by the practice of negotiating "running powers" over neighbouring lines. The Clearing House was established in 1847 to arrange co-operation between companies and the basis on which receipts should be shared. It thereby facilitated through bookings a public convenience which canal companies had failed to provide. "Running powers" over neighbouring lines were sometimes arranged by mutual agreement. For example, until it built its own terminus in London, St Pancras, in 1863, the Midland used the Great Northern line from Hitchin to Kings Cross. But as railway companies were not always willing to co-operate, Parliament in 1854 passed the Railway and Canal Traffic Act. This Act, sometimes referred to as Cardwell's Act, made it mandatory for companies to provide facilities for through traffic.

Nineteenth-century railway history may be divided into well-marked periods. Firstly, the Experimental Period, before 1844, and secondly, the Period of Amalgamation and Consolidation, 1845 to 1872. The third period, 1873 to 1894, witnessed a considerable extension of state control. Although railways came into existence at a time when it was accepted policy to leave economic enterprise free from state interference, they had from the first been subject to parliamentary regulation. They were statutory joint stock companies possessing privileges and obliged to assume obligations. Otherwise, in the early days Parliament contented itself with a minimum of interference.

After the railway panic of 1836 the opinion was expressed that some degree of control over railways would be desirable. Lord Seymour's Act (1840) added a Railway Department to the Board of Trade, empowered by the Railway Act of 1842 to approve new lines. Gladstone's Railway Act in 1844 gave authority for compulsory state purchase of all future railways, an option it would have been futile to take up without also purchasing existing lines, for which statutory provision was not made. Railway charges could be revised, if profits exceeded 10 per cent, which they never did. These clauses of the Act of 1844 were not implemented, but there was enforced the clause in the Act instructing the companies to provide at least one train daily at a fare not exceeding one penny a mile. This, the so-called "parliamentary train" was immortalised by W. S. Gilbert in the *Mikado* when he wrote about:

> *The Idiot who, in railway carriages*
> *Scribbles on window panes.*
> *We only suffer*
> *To ride on a buffer*
> *In Parliamentary trains.*

The early attempts at public control of railways included the setting up in 1846 of an ineffective Railway Board composed of five Commissioners which was abolished in 1851. Indeed it would have been surprising if measures conceived by statesmen opposed to governments meddling in business affairs had brought railways under effective state control. What stimulated politicians to more drastic action was the fear that with the decline in other forms of transport amalgamations would enable large railway companies to profit at public expense. This belief explains why the railways were the first sector of the economy in which a major breach occurred in *laisser-faire* principles. In other words, the railway policy of the Government which originated in the desire to foster competition resulted in the breakdown of *laisser-faire*. Legislation was enacted, firstly, to limit freight charges and fares, secondly, to ensure the safety of the travelling public, and thirdly, to protect railway employees against undue exploitation.

At first, three-quarters of railway revenues were derived from passenger fares, the proportion falling sharply later. Nevertheless governments in the main concerned themselves with fixing freight rates rather than passenger fares. The private Acts incorporating railway companies contained clauses fixing the charges companies could levy. As the amalgamation movement gained in momentum parliamentary interest in the problem of determining fair rates became greater. Following the disappearance in 1851 of the 1846 Railway Board, the Railway and Canal Traffic Act was passed in 1854, making illegal preferences to individual traders.

There was no easy solution to the problem of determining fair and reasonable rates. Passenger fares were fixed according to the mileage travelled, but no such simple formula could be used in deciding freight charges. Litigation between traders and railway companies raised issues too technical for the common law courts. In 1872 a Joint Committee on the Amalgamation of Railway Companies reported, firstly, that competition between railway companies could not be maintained by legislation, and secondly, that amalgamations had not been as damaging to the public interest to the extent anticipated. The report was followed by the setting up in 1873 of the Railway and Canal Commission, with limited supervising powers, which in practice failed to provide effective safeguards for traders. It was therefore reconstituted with wider powers by the Railway and Canal Traffic Act of 1888. Provision was made for public revision of rates which were to become the maximum charge. The new maxima and the agreed classification of goods were given statutory authority in 1893 by the Railway Rates and Charges Orders Confirmation Acts.

This legislation is an important landmark on the road to a new theory of the functions of the State. By fixing prices of services in a major industry the Government was abandoning the idea that prices should be allowed to find their own level through competitive processes. Although not generally realised at the time, precedents were being created which would end in the organisation of many aspects of economic life on a collectivist basis. The immediate sequel to this legislation was certainly not foreseen. Railway companies responded in 1893 by enforcing the new maxima, the storm of protest which followed leading to the hurried passage of the 1894 Railway and Canal Traffic Act. This laid down that the 1892 rates should be the future maxima. Upon the companies was placed the onus of proving that increases were reasonable. Neither in future dare they experiment by reducing rates as the Act of 1894 had deprived them of the authority to raise them subsequently, if reductions had proved to be financially not worth while. This legislation, therefore, had the effect of ending rate competition between railway companies, the companies after 1894 attempting to attract traffic, not by lowering their charges, but by offering better facilities.

To protect the travelling public, the Regulation of Railways Act (1871) laid down safety rules, required the notification of all accidents, and empowered the Board of Trade to hold enquiries into their cause. An Act passed in 1883 required companies to use "the block system" of working, to arrange for "the interlocking" of signals and points and to fit trains with automatic continuous brakes. The Notice of Accidents Act (1884) obliged the companies to report all accidents to its employees, and following the report of a Royal Commission in 1899, Parliament passed in 1900 the Railway Employment (Prevention of Accidents) Act. The legislation enacted to safeguard the employees was prompted more by concern for public safety than workers' welfare. Unduly long hours could be a cause of accidents. In 1893 the Board of Trade was empowered to fix the length of a reasonable working day for railway employees, the Railway and Canal Commission being authorised to hear appeals from the companies.

Between 1894 and 1914 the expenses of the railway companies increased and their profits fell. This situation was aggravated by the expensive competition in the provision of improved facilities such as dining cars, sleepers, corridor trains, cheap excursions and faster speeds. The companies attempted to cut operating costs by negotiating a limited number of amalgamation agreements. In 1899 the Chatham and South Eastern Railways united and in 1908 the London and North Western and the Lancashire and Yorkshire Railways formed a working alliance. Further progress on these lines, however, was impeded by Parliament which refused in 1909 a closer union between the Great Northern, the Great Eastern and the Great Central lines. The companies also had to deal with the growing militancy of railway trade unionists. A railway strike in 1911 was settled by government intervention which secured for the men a wage increase, and for the companies permission in 1913 to increase their charges. In 1913 the N.U.R. was formed, a union of all railway workers except the locomotive men and the clerical staff.

During the First World War the railways were operated under government control. It was confidently expected that benefits of unified management would be retained after the war by the implementation of the pre-war nationalisation proposals of the N.U.R. These hopes were encouraged by the formation in 1919 of the Ministry of Transport with extensive powers. A return to the pre-1914 position was out of the question as the financial position of the railways was critical. During the war, railway employees had obtained wage increases and an eight-hour day, while costly arrears of maintenance and repairs had accumulated under wartime conditions. After considerable discussion the Government decided against nationalisation. Instead the railways were returned to private control by the Railways Act of 1921.

The Act of 1921 made changes of considerable importance as it reduced the number of railways, settled the terms of compensation for wartime neglect, laid down principles governing railway charges and set up machinery to improve relationships between managements and staff. Some 120 companies were combined to form four large companies, the Southern, the Great Western, the London, Midland and Scottish and the London and North Eastern Railways. £60 million was awarded to cover expenditure on arrears of maintenance and repairs. An important innovation was the setting up of the Railway Rates Tribunal, empowered to vary and fix rates, fares and charges, to enable the companies to earn a "standard revenue." This was defined as the aggregate revenues earned in 1913 plus 5 per cent on certain items of recent capital expenditure. The "standard revenue" was eventually fixed at £50 million. Lastly wages and conditions of service were to be dealt with by a National Wages Board and local conciliation machinery was set up to settle disputes between management and workers.

The Act did not wholly fulfil the expectations of its authors. Wasteful competition was not entirely eliminated as rival routes between important centres continued to exist. Neither was the hope realised of a profitable return from capital investment in railways. The companies never earned the standard revenue, a failure in part due to competition during the inter-war years from motor transport. In 1928 the Railway (Road Transport) Act empowered the railways to establish transport services to "convey by road passengers and passengers' luggage, parcels and merchandise." The notion that Parliament ought to intervene to safeguard the public from the dangers of a railway transport monopoly had become out of date, as the establishment of motor services on long distance routes by private enterprise had made road transport a serious rival to the railways. Then came the outbreak of the Second World War. By an order made under the Defence Regulations on 1st September 1939, the Minister of Transport assumed control of the four principal railway groups and of the London Passenger Transport Board. The revenues of the four companies were pooled, each receiving a guaranteed minimum equivalent to its average net revenues in 1935, 1936 and 1937.

As a Labour Government took office when the war ended the restoration of the railways to private enterprise was never contemplated. Instead the advocates of state socialism got their way. A Transport Bill introduced in 1946 provided for the creation of a British Transport Commission to provide "an efficient, adequate, economical and properly integrated system of public inland transport and port facilities for passengers and goods." The railways, docks and inland waterways, road transport undertakings engaged in haulage for a distance of over 40 miles and London Passenger Transport, became publicly owned. Compensation for assets taken over was made in the form of transport stock guaranteed by the Treasury.

Chapter XIV

SHIPPING

From the earliest of times men have made vessels to cross stretches of water. But until the coming into use of the mariner's compass and the chronometer, the invention of the sextant in 1731, and the publication of reliable nautical almanacs and charts, sailors rarely ventured far from land. When they did so, they had to find their way by guess and by God—navigational aids that proved to be very unreliable. Mistaking their latitude, for example, the ships of Sir Cloudesley Shovell's squadron foundered off the Scilly Isles in 1707. When and by whom the mariner's compass was devised is uncertain. What is certain is that those in use were of a very primitive character. As late as 1820 the Admiralty was advised that more than half of those possessed by the Navy could be written off as almost useless. The invention of the chronometer can be dated with more certainty. Latitude could be found by measuring the altitude of the sun at mid-day. Longitude had to be guessed by "dead reckoning." Suggestions for finding the time at sea with watches were made before the eighteenth century, but it was to a Yorkshire carpenter, John Harrison, in 1736 that navigators were indebted for the first satisfactory means of determining Greenwich time in any part of the world.

Until the nineteenth century men used sails or human muscle to propel their vessels, large and small. But the increase in commercial enterprise during the seventeenth and eighteenth centuries necessitated considerable changes in the design of vessels. Oar-propelled ships, developed for use in inland seas like the Mediterranean, were unsuitable for use on ocean highways. Hence the construction during the period of increasingly large sailing ships. By the early nineteenth century some of those belonging to the East India Company exceeded 1500 tons. On other shipping routes, where traders did not enjoy monopoly rights, and where the volume of trade was much less, smaller and cheaper ships were used. Typical of these were the West Indiamen, some 300 to 500 tons in size, in which sugar was transported from the West Indies. Smaller still were the colliers used to transport coal from Tyneside to London and the North Sea and Mediterranean ports. Sir Joseph Bankes complained bitterly about the discomforts he endured in the Whitby collier, the *Endeavour*, which Captain Cook commanded in his 1768-71 voyages of exploration.

In the second half of the eighteenth century British shipping gained a lead over that of her European rivals. After Trafalgar (1805) French maritime power was seriously weakened. The trade of Amsterdam and Rotterdam declined as sandbanks prevented access to them by the larger vessels built in the eighteenth century, experiments made with flat keels proving to be of little value. Further, annexed by France, Holland lost its profitable carrying trade and its overseas bases at the Cape and in Ceylon. In contrast, there was a great boom in American shipping. The American coasting trade had always been important, particularly so in the early days when land transport was inefficient. Following the outbreak of war in Europe in 1792, the U.S.A. became the world's second carrier, a considerable trade being developed by New England shipowners with Europe. Unfortunately, the Embargo and Non-Intercourse Acts, followed by the outbreak of the Anglo-American War in 1812, resulted in a shipping depression which lasted until the 1840s.

The American challenge to British mercantile supremacy became a cause for concern during the American shipping boom between 1840 and 1860. Various factors, in addition to the expansion of world commerce, explain the rapid growth of American shipping at this time. The vast forests of the U.S.A. yielded excellent shipbuilding materials whereas in Britain the shortage of oak was a severe handicap. During the 1850s American railway mileage increased from 9000 to 30,000. As these new lines of communication ran east to west, instead of north to south in the valley of the Mississippi, the Atlantic ports and not New Orleans became the outlet for the Middle West. The Californian gold rush (1849) increased trade with the Pacific round Cape Horn. To handle their rapidly expanding trade the Americans designed a new type of vessel, the great clippers, speedier and cheaper to build than any hitherto known.

British ship designers were much more conservative than the American. Throughout the eighteenth century the monopoly rights of what was known as "the Marine Interest" checked advances in the design of the vessels chartered by the East India Company. Following the abolition of the Company's monopoly, East Indiamen were replaced by the smaller but speedier Blackwall frigates, which until sail gave way to steam handled much of the British trade with the Far East and Australia. On less remunerative trade routes the British relied on the West Indian Free Traders, slow vessels, their breadth or beam being excessive compared to their length. But their carrying capacity was high, they could be manned by a small crew and were relatively safe.

American shipowners prospered after 1840 because they preceded the British in meeting the current demand for speed. Fast sailing ships built in Maryland and Virginian shipyards at the end of the eighteenth century for use by smugglers, slavers and privateers were the forerunners of the clippers of the 1840s. The Americans sacrificed safety to speed, the length of their clippers being five or six times the beam. By 1860 American tonnage all but equalled that of Great Britain. That the American challenge was formidable was demonstrated when the first American tea clipper, the *Oriental,* launched at New York in 1849, made the journey from Hong Kong to London in 97 days. Her revolutionary design astonished British shipwrights, while the freight rates she quoted were approximately half those of British shipowners.

The American challenge proved to be short-lived. The failure of the Americans to stay the course can be explained, firstly, by the outbreak of the American Civil War, secondly, by the building of British clippers on the Thames, the Clyde and in Aberdeen and thirdly, by the substitution of iron for wood as ship construction material. The Civil War almost destroyed American cotton exports. Much American shipping was sunk and while Americans were fighting the British expanded their carrying trade. After the war American capital resources and investments were diverted not into shipping but into railway construction and into internal development projects. But even before the outbreak of the Civil War the British had begun to build ships designed to meet the demand for speedy passages, essential in the China tea trade to avoid deterioration in quality. The British responded to the American challenge with first wooden, and later iron sailing vessels. In 1850, Richard Green, a member of the firm which built the Blackwall frigates, launched on the Thames the *Challenger* and the Aberdeen firm of Alexander Hall built the *Stornaway* and the *Chroysolite*. These British clippers were stronger and more economical to man than any previously produced. The subsequent competition between the British and the Americans to be the first to reach United Kingdom ports with the costly China teas was productive of many memorable races. By the 'sixties, however, British ships alone were engaged in the tea races, one of the most exciting being that in 1866 between the *Ariel* the *Taeping* and the *Serica*. All arrived 99 days after leaving Foo-chow.

Following the Australian gold discoveries in 1851 Anglo-American competition spread to the Australian trade. After the opening of the Suez Canal steamers took over the China trade, such famous China tea clippers as the *Thermopylae, Sir Lancelot* and the *Cutty Sark* being transferred to the Australian wool run. Built in 1869 at Dumbarton, the *Cutty Sark*, one of the most beautiful of sailing ships, could, if given a suitable wind, outpace the mail steamers. The Australian wool clippers were as justly renowned as the China tea clippers, but were bigger, more seaworthy and carried passengers as well as cargo. Clipper crews were better paid and worked under more favourable conditions than sailors in former times. To the onlooker, the clippers were magnificent vessels especially when viewed at sea in full sail. Nevertheless they had their drawbacks. Life on board was strenuous, discipline was strict and discomforts many. As carriers of bulk cargoes they were less profitable than the West Indian Free Traders. Their strength lay rather in their suitability for the transport of perishable cargoes and passengers at great speed. They played a memorable part in making available for popular consumption commodities which the East Indiamen had brought to Europe for the wealthy.

Some of the clippers had iron frames and wooden plankings. The substitution of iron for timber in ship construction is a major reason why Great Britain and not the U.S.A. had maritime supremacy in the 1870s. Britain, at this period being the principal iron-manufacturing country in the world, had many workers skilled in iron construction techniques, iron ships being first made possible by Cort's innovation of the rolling mill at the end of the eighteenth century. In 1787 Wilkinson built an iron canal barge, the *Trial*. Thirty years later the Forth and Clyde Canal Company commissioned the *Vulcan* which gave excellent service for 70 years. In 1820 Vice-Admiral Sir Charles Napier voyaged from the Thames to Paris in the *Aaron Mamby*, the first iron steamer. Yet despite these demonstrations neither the Admiralty nor shipowners were easily convinced that iron was suitable for use in ship construction. Sceptics were many, using arguments which they were convinced only fools would reject. Being heavier than wood, they argued, it was an impossible constructional material. Fouling of iron hulls by weeds and barnacles was a problem not admitting of an easy solution, while the magnetic attraction of iron caused compass deviations.

With the passage of time and experience these early prejudices were overcome. Iron ships in fact weigh less than wooden ones of the same tonnage. As the structural limit of wooden vessels is much smaller, given the urgent need for ships of much larger carrying capacity, iron had a positive advantage. Experience showed that in rough weather, or on being driven ashore, iron ships were less likely to suffer irreparable damage. The problem of fouling was overcome by frequent cleaning and re-painting, and by the use of anti-fouling devices, while Sir G. B. Airy in 1839, and later Sir William Thompson, introduced methods of countering the dangers from compass variation. A spectacular demonstration of the possibilities of iron was Brunel's *Great Eastern* (1858). The largest vessel afloat before 1858 was 3438 tons. The *Great Eastern* was designed to be 18,914 tons, and in length 192 ft. Following the discoveries of Bessemer and Siemens, steel was substituted for iron, first in the *Rotomahano* launched in 1879, ensuring greater durability, economy in weight and higher cargo carrying potential.

The earliest metal-hulled vessels were sailing ships or vessels with iron frames and wooden planking. Coincident in time with this development came the introduction of steamships. The ready acceptance of steam, however, was hindered by the degree of perfection reached by sailing ships. Although experimented with as early as 1543 by Blasco de Garaz of Barcelona, the idea that steam could be used instead of wind and sail did not become a practical proposition until James Watt had patented the steam engine. Adaptation of Watt's engine for boat propulsion was pioneered by a Scotsman, Patrick Miller, in 1786. In the same year the Connecticut Yankee, John Fitch, sailed a steamboat on the Delaware River. It was left to others, however, after his death, to prove that steam propulsion had a future. Steamboats first appeared on inland waterways in America, Europe and Britain. William Symington's *Charlotte Dundas* (1802), the first steam tug, threatened the stability of the banks of the Forth–Clyde Canal. In America Robert Fulton fitted an engine supplied by Boulton and Watt to the *Clermont*. Popularly ridiculed as "Fulton's Folly," it inaugurated in 1807 the first commercially successful steam passenger service on the Hudson River. Within ten years there was a fleet of steamers on the Hudson, and by 1816 timber-fuelled boats were capable of sailing against the strong Mississippi current from New Orleans to Pittsburg. Two hundred such boats were in service on the western rivers of the U.S.A. by 1830, stimulating a rapid growth of population and providing material for the writings of Mark Twain, the American humorist and one-time Mississippi pilot.

The first passenger steamboat in Europe was the 40-ft *Comet* built by Henry Bell of Glasgow for use on the Clyde (1812). Three years later the *Marjory* was carrying passengers between London and Gravesend. The Americans pioneered steamboats on the sea with the James River boat the *Powkatan*, built in 1816. At the same time, services were started between Holyhead and Ireland, and Brighton and Le Havre. By the early 1820s, paddle steamers were operating between Hull and Rotterdam and foreign steamers were trading in British ports. Then in 1819 the American *Savannah* crossed the Atlantic from New York to Liverpool in 25 days, but using sail for most of the way for the very good reason as its captain recorded, "no cole to git up steam."

The first steamers can more accurately be described as sailing ships using auxiliary steam power to drive paddle wheels, which being portable, could be stacked on deck when not in use. The paddle wheel arrangement necessitated placing the engine inconveniently in the hull, and in heavy seas when ships rolled badly, the paddles ceased to grip the water. The reluctance of the British Admiralty to jettison sail for steam was not wholly due to the innate conservatism of their lordships. In their defence it ought to be noted that paddle wheels, located on either side of the ship, made it impossible to mount guns where they were most effective, on the broadside.

Greater efficiency was obtained by the substitution of the underwater screw propeller. This followed experiments by the American, Colonel John Stevens, in 1804, and in 1836 by a Swede, Captain John Ericsson, remembered also as the designer of the *Monitor*, the iron-clad which by winning its duel with the Confederate ironclad the *Merrimac* in 1862 saved the North from possible defeat, and demonstrated that wooden warships were obsolete. Screw propeller propulsion, however, came into favour very slowly. It was not until the 1850s that side paddle wheels were becoming obsolescent. The first ship fitted with a screw propeller to cross the Atlantic was Brunel's *Great Britain* launched in 1842. His *Great Eastern* used both screw propellers and paddle wheels in addition to being fitted with six masts carrying an enormous spread of canvas. But before the *Great Eastern* was launched in 1858, steamers were challenging sail in the North Atlantic. Credit for making the first trans-Atlantic crossing wholly by steam belongs to a Dutch wooden paddle vessel, the *Curacao*, which in 1827 voyaged from Rotterdam to Paramaribo in Surinam in one month. The second was that made by the *Royal William* of Quebec in 1833.

Modern trans-Atlantic services really began in 1838 when the wooden steamers *Sirius,* owned by a London company, and the *Great Western* crossed the Atlantic in seventeen and fifteen days respectively. The *Great Western* was the brain child of Brunel, the engineer of the Great Western Railway, who hoped that his Great Western Steamship Company based on Bristol would capture a major share of North Atlantic traffic. Brunel's dream did not materialise as rail hauls in Britain are too short to enable a railway company to divert traffic through a port of its own choosing. Unfortunately also for Brunel the tender for the mail contracts accepted by the Government in 1839 was that of the British North American Royal Mail Steam Packet Company, based on Liverpool, the predecessor of the Cunard Line. Its founders were Samuel Cunard, a merchant of Halifax, Nova Scotia, and his associates, George Burns of Glasgow and David McIver of Liverpool.

The Canadian financier Sir Hugh Allan (1816–82) founded in 1853 the Allan Line of steamships plying between Montreal and Liverpool and Glasgow. Determined not to be outdone the American Government from 1850 lavishly subsidised the Collins Line. Its four steamers beat the Cunarders for speed on the New York to Liverpool run but at a cost, coupled with the loss of the *Arctic* and *Pacific*, which proved ruinous. The government subsidy being withdrawn the Collins Company was wound up in 1858. One of the most notable shipowners associated with North Atlantic travel was Thomas Henry Ismay (1837–99). In 1868 he and William Imrie founded the White Star Line. Ismay sought to attract custom not only by speed but also by providing improved passenger accommodation, the rivalry between the White Star and Cunard companies resulting in the North Atlantic crossing being served by the fastest, largest and most luxurious ships afloat.

Over greater distances sailing ships retained their dominance longer than in the North Atlantic. For many years reliance on steam only was not a commercial proposition. There was a lack of coaling and repair stations, and steamers consumed so much coal that there was little room left for cargo. The first break-through came in the passenger and mail services. Steamers became a commercial success only after progress had been made in marine engineering. Improvements in iron- and steel-making techniques made possible the generation of steam in ships' boilers capable of withstanding very high pressures. The early steamers had one-cylinder engines. A significant reduction in fuel consumption was achieved by John Elder's compound engine (1854), the triple expansion engine (1881) and the quadruple expansion engine (1894). But the piston and cylinder marine engines in use at this time were responsible for considerable vibration which those travelling on large liners had good reason to dislike. This drawback did not exist on steamers fitted with steam turbines. The steam turbine, originally used to drive electric generators in power stations, was adapted for marine purposes by Sir Charles Parsons. His steamship the *Turbinia* was given its first trials in 1894. It can still be seen in the museum at Exhibition Park at Newcastle upon Tyne. Its advantages were reductions in steam, fuel consumption, weight and bulk, no internal lubrication and lower maintenance costs. The decision in 1907 to fit turbine engines instead of the older reciprocating type in the *Lusitania* and *Mauretania* enabled the Cunard Company to regain from Germany in 1910 the blue riband of the Atlantic.

The invention of the screw propeller, improvements in marine engineering and the opening of the Suez Canal were the decisive factors in the conversion of shipping from sail to steam. In 1860 sailing ships predominated. In 1880 sailing tonnage was slightly less than steam tonnage, but by 1900 four-fifths to three-quarters of the tonnage of merchant shipping owned by United Kingdom shipowners consisted of steamers. The twentieth century witnessed a further development pioneered by the German engineer, Dr Rudolph Diesel. Born in Paris in 1858, he invented the diesel oil engine, but when he was drowned in 1913 its marine possibilities had not been fully exploited. The first commercial diesel engine was made in Germany in 1897 and the first marine diesel engine in Paris in 1902 to drive a canal boat. Oil fuel has many advantages, including a considerable saving in boiler-room staff, a reduction in bunker space, absence of coal dust and ashes and increased radius of action. The use of oil fuel and diesel oil engines in ocean steamers was a post-1914 development. British shipowners were slower to change than some of their foreign competitors. Despite its great advantages at sea, oil was dearer than our only significant indigenous source of fuel, coal, and at the time there was greater uncertainty in obtaining supplies of oil than nowadays. But with the passage of time oil has increasingly taken the place of coal. Two disadvantages of this may be mentioned: the serious unemployment in the South Wales anthracite industry and the widespread contamination of beaches and ocean waterways.

Over the world as a whole the recent change in types of vessels and in fuel consumed has been remarkable. In 1914 nearly 90 per cent of all the tonnage listed in *Lloyd's Register Book* used coal. In 1938 the percentage was $46\frac{1}{2}$. Oil burning steamers rose during the same period from $2\frac{1}{2}$ per cent to 30 per cent, and motor ships from $\frac{1}{2}$ per cent to $22\frac{1}{2}$ per cent. Using only half the daily fuel consumption of a steam turbine ship of a similar size, it is not surprising that the world-wide trend from steam propulsion to diesel motor continued after the Second World War. Of the 2147 merchant ships launched in 1966, 2063 were motor ships. While these changes were taking place in ship design Great Britain remained the dominant shipowning country. In 1901, 44·63 per cent of world tonnage was registered under the British flag. Subsequently, the British share of world tonnage shrank to 41·6 per cent in 1914 and to 26·4 per cent in 1938. But the British merchant fleet in 1938, with 17,675,000 tons, was nearly twice as large as that of the next biggest, that of the U.S.A. (excluding vessels on the Great Lakes), 8,936,000 tons.

British ocean-going tonnage consisted of two main types of ships, liners and cargo vessels or "tramps." Four specialised cargo steamships came into use, colliers, refrigerator ships, oil tankers and banana boats. The trade in foreign meat began in earnest in 1879 with the arrival at the London docks of supplies from Australia. Oil at first was transported in sailing ships, the first, the *Atlantis*, being built in Britain in 1863. Twenty years later the first British oil tanker steamer was built at West Hartlepool. Of oil tankers, Great Britain owned in 1938 2,672,000 tons and the U.S.A. 2,760,000 tons, out of a total world tonnage of 10,716,000. Norway was the remaining big owner, with nearly 2,000,000 tons. Banana boats were in use from the early twentieth century to transport fruit from the Caribbean and Canaries to Liverpool and Bristol, and to New Orleans and New York.

In the second half of the nineteenth century fundamental changes took place in the ownership and management of shipping. In earlier times shipowners ceased to exercise control once ships had left port. Their business interests were entrusted to agents known as supercargoes. Changing trading conditions after 1850 made the supercargo unnecessary. Trade ceased to be a "venture" as it became more regularised, the laying of submarine cables from 1851 onwards and the appointment of agents and the establishment of branch offices in foreign ports permitting a much greater degree of control from home.

The British mercantile marine in the early nineteenth century consisted of ships owned by the chartered trading companies and of those belonging to capitalist firms or small partnerships. With the going out of existence of the chartered trading companies their place was taken by substantial commercial companies. These were able to make steamship services profitable because it became government policy to discontinue Post Office packets for the transmission of mail. Vessels owned by the Crown were suitable for the short sea services to Ireland and Europe, but could not provide a service as speedy as that of steamers on long distance ocean routes. The Post Office therefore decided to pay commercial companies to carry mail. In 1853 the mail subsidies totalled £853,146, three-quarters of which was paid to the Peninsular and Oriental, Royal Mail and Cunard lines.

Uncushioned by mail subsidies, the appearance on the high seas of commercially profitable cargo steamers was delayed until the

1870s. These were owned by joint stock companies, a development assisted by the passage of the Limited Liability Acts of 1855 and 1862. Some of these companies had their head offices in Liverpool, Glasgow and in the ports of the North East. In Glasgow the Donaldson Line operated from 1854. Liverpool firms included the Booth Line (1866) and the Elder Dempster Line (1852), which at the end of the century extended its activities under the direction of Sir Alfred Jones. The Bibby family instituted in the mid-nineteenth century a service between Liverpool and the Mediterranean and later with Rangoon. On the east coast the Wilson Line, which became the largest private steamship company in the world, was founded in 1835 by Thomas Wilson and two partners. As a result of the pioneering activities of these and many other shipping companies, shipbuilding and shipping had before 1914 come to occupy a position of major importance in the British economy. In the years preceding the outbreak of the First World War, some 60 per cent of the world's new tonnage was launched in British yards.

After 1870, as there was more tonnage available than the volume of trade justified, the evils of unrestricted competition appeared. The regular lines, guaranteeing services at fixed times, had to meet tramp steamer cut-throat competition when prospects of obtaining cargoes were good. To protect their interests the regular lines introduced the Conference System. Freight rates were fixed and arrangements made to ensure that only one ship was available at a time, but as the tramp steamers were not parties to these agreements they proved to be ineffective. In order to obtain shippers' fidelity some Conferences introduced two-tier rates, that is a system of deferred rebates. At the end of a period, varying from three months to a year, as much as 10 per cent of the freight charges paid were refunded to shippers who had remained loyal. The Conference System came to cover most of the export routes from the United Kingdom with the notable exception of the North Atlantic cargo trade. The system of deferred rebates was less used in the import trade as much of it was in the hands of tramp steamers transporting bulky cargoes. On the whole, the Conference System has proved to be advantageous to both shipowners and their customers. Stabilised freight charges are desirable while the guarantees of regular sailings enable exporters to meet contractual delivery dates.

From the late nineteenth century, in addition to the competition between British steamship companies, there was also competition to be faced from foreign countries. Foreigners adopted various methods to stimulate the growth of their mercantile marines. These included payment of bounties on construction and mileage worked, excessive mail subsidies, reductions in tariffs levied on shipbuilding materials, loans, payment of port and canal dues and the reservation of coasting trade to national shipping. France, for example, in 1881 introduced a system of tonnage bounties on voyages. German shipping made considerable progress in the North Atlantic. The Americans challenged British dominance in the same area by the formation in 1902 of the International Mercantile Marine Company. Financially backed by the New York banking firm of Pierpont Morgan, it included several British companies, among them the White Star and Leyland Lines, and had a fleet of 126 ships totalling 1,053,238 tons of shipping. As the Morgan syndicate had a working agreement with the German lines and controlled the main trunk railways between the eastern American seaboard and the West, it was a powerful threat to British marine interests. The British met the challenge by forming two shipping combinations headed by the Royal Mail and Cunard companies.

British governments gave less assistance to shipping companies than foreign governments did. A loan of £2,600,000 at $2\frac{3}{4}$ per cent interest was made to the Cunard Company to build the *Mauretania* and *Lusitania*. The Colonial Office gave an annual subsidy of £40,000 to the Elder Dempster Line between 1900 and 1910 to develop West Indies trade by improving steamer communications. Otherwise, apart from the payments made for the carriage of mail on a strictly commercial basis, British shipping was dependent upon the promptings of private enterprise. This *laisser-faire* policy towards shipping is a marked contrast to the increasing interference in the affairs of railways before 1914. In shipping, after the repeal of the Navigation Laws, there was an absence of legislative interference, with two notable exceptions, the passage of laws to safeguard life at sea, and legislation to protect seamen against undue exploitation.

In 1850 the supervision of maritime affairs was entrusted to the Board of Trade. Examinations in seamanship for ships' officers were introduced and seamen were to be engaged under signed agreements. These regulations were followed by the passage of the Merchant Shipping Act of 1854 whose 548 clauses contained regulations governing pilotage, lighthouses, buoys and beacons. The dangers to life at sea, however, were increased by an unscrupulous minority of owners who sent to sea over-insured, overloaded "floating coffins." It lies to the credit of one man, Samuel Plimsoll (1824–98), that the scandal was exposed and seamen given legislative protection. Plimsoll published in 1872 a popular book on *Our Seamen*. On his motion a Royal Commission was appointed in 1873 to investigate the conduct of the owners of "coffin ships." Its report in 1875, action on which the Disraeli government proposed to delay, roused Plimsoll to create a scene in the Commons and to denounce the "villains who send men to death and destruction." Public opinion was sufficiently roused to force the passage of a temporary act, the Unseaworthy Ships Act (1875), the provisions of which were amended, enlarged and made permanent by the Merchant Shipping Act of 1876. This legislation strengthened the powers of the Board of Trade to detain unseaworthy ships and obliged shipowners, not the Board of Trade as Plimsoll wished, to fix a loadline, popularly known as the Plimsoll Mark. It was not until 1894 that responsibility for determining the position of the loadline was entrusted to the Board of Trade. Plimsoll later became President of the Sailors' and Firemen's Union and the author of *Cattle Ships* in which he exposed the cruelty associated with the shipping of live cattle.

The expansion of steamship services and the increase in the size of ships necessitated an increase in accommodation and shipping facilities at the ports. Private ownership of small docks created a state of affairs that called for drastic remedies. A number of new docks were opened in London, and in 1908 all the docks and the tidal part of the Thames were handed over to a public trust, the Port of London Authority. The Liverpool and Birkenhead docks were placed under the control of the Mersey Docks and Harbour Board in 1857. Hull, one of our oldest ports, transformed since the mid-nineteenth century, owes much to railway company enterprise, culminating in the opening in 1914 of the King George V Dock by the Hull and Barnsley and North Eastern Railway Companies. The Manchester, Sheffield and Lincolnshire Railway began the transformation of the fishing village of Grimsby in the 1860s.

In the early nineteenth century the task of making the Tees capable of providing transport facilities for the pig iron and other products of the Cleveland district was begun by the Tees Navigation Company, a duty taken over in 1852 by the Tees Conservancy Commission. Massive industrial development subsequently resulted in Middlesbrough and the Hartlepools becoming major ports. Before the nineteenth century the Tyne was navigable only by "keels" of light draught, which carried coal to Shields where it was transferred to sea-going colliers. The development of the Tyne as a great commercial waterway began in 1857 when the Tyne Improvement Commission was incorporated by Act of Parliament.

Southampton, the second port of England in the Middle Ages, decayed in Tudor times. Revival came in the nineteenth century and with the creation of dock facilities in 1912 providing accommodation for the largest liners, enabling it during the inter-war years to take over much of Liverpool's passenger trade.

Southampton, with its double high tides, enjoys advantages nature has not given to the Clyde, originally a small stream impeded by sandbanks. Glasgow began its history as a port in Charles II's reign. Constant dredging, widening, deepening and straightening of the Clyde has made Glasgow one of the main ports and shipbuilding centres of the United Kingdom.

Life at sea will always be perilous. It was more so to our forefathers who had to rely on defective charts or sail in seas where none existed. That it is less perilous today is due to seventeenth- and eighteenth-century Dutch, French and British mariners and cartographers, who began to map and locate the hazards of treacherous coasts. Shoals, sandbanks and submerged rocks will always be hazards, but less so than formerly, owing to the invention of lifeboats and the erection of lighthouses, and of buoys to mark navigable channels. The first lifeboat was designed in 1785 by a London coach builder, Lionel Lukin. In 1824 Sir William Hillary founded what was later named the Royal National Lifeboat Institution, a voluntary society maintaining lifeboats at various stations.

Lighthouses were not unknown even in ancient times, but before the eighteenth century the few lighthouses existing round the coasts of Britain were privately owned, fees being levied on passing vessels. Trinity House, founded in 1514, was given authority in 1575 to erect beacons and marks for the guidance of mariners. But it was not until the eighteenth century that the modern lighthouse era may be said to have begun. The first two of the four Eddystone lighthouses were erected in 1695 and 1706. Made of wood they were replaced by one erected in 1759 that lasted until 1878. Its builder, the Yorkshireman John Smeaton (1724–92), was the first man to describe himself as a civil engineer. Smeaton constructed the Calder and Hebble Navigation between Wakefield and Sowerby Bridge (1758–65), the Forth–Clyde Canal and many bridges. He insisted on the use of stone for the Eddystone Lighthouse and built it so well that its demolition was necessary, not because of any fault in its construction and design, but because of the undermining of the rock on which it stood. In 1836 statutory powers were given to Trinity House to purchase all interests in coast lights, the corporation still being responsible for the erection of lighthouses, buoys and beacons. Improvements in methods of illumination were also introduced, the wood and coal fires, and tallow candles used in the eighteenth century being superseded by vegetable oils and coal gas, and in modern times by electricity and oil.

The story of shipping would be incomplete without reference being made to Lloyds, the association of underwriters and marine insurance brokers. Doubtless marine insurance existed in very ancient times but the earliest known English policies were taken out in 1555 and 1557. In the early seventeenth century those concerned with marine insurance met at the Royal Exchange, and after the Great Fire of London (1666) at a coffee house in Tower Street, kept by a Welshman, Edward Lloyd. In 1692 Lloyd moved to Lombard Street and began the publication weekly of commercial and shipping news. *Lloyd's News* was the predecessor of the later *Lloyd's List*, apart from the *London Gazette*, the oldest British newspaper. Subsequent increase in business led in 1774 to brokers and underwriters finding a new home in the Royal Exchange. A very great increase in marine insurance business for both British and foreign clients was undertaken during the French Revolutionary and Napoleonic Wars. The association was reorganised in 1811, and in 1871 by statutory authority it was given the rights and privileges of a corporation. By Lloyds Act (1911) members were authorised to accept all forms of insurance, except life, the non-marine business nowadays exceeding shipping insurance. Insurance policies are taken out, not with Lloyds, but through brokers with underwriters who are required to deposit with the corporation securities as a guarantee their contracts will be honoured. A separate organisation, Lloyds *Register of Shipping*, dating from the latter years of the reign of George III, is responsible for compiling lists and particulars of all ships in the world. It employs surveyors in all parts of the world, who classify ships, those in first class condition being placed (since 1771) in class 100 A.1. Issued annually, *Lloyd's Register Book* contains accurate details of every ship in the world.

PART V

FINANCE

CHAPTER XV

BANKING AND FINANCE

Nowadays economic expansion is financed by governments, overseas borrowings, finance houses and joint stock company investment. Such means of financing capital development were not normal in eighteenth-century Britain, the capital needed for business enterprise being in the main provided by single individuals or small partnerships. Business units, local in character and relatively small in size, were managed by their owners, who before 1855 did not operate under limited liability conditions. Business risks were considerable, proprietors risking the loss of all their assets. Without the contemporary development in banking and credit facilities, however, private investment unaided could not have sufficed to promote the unprecedented expansion in industry, agriculture and commerce, so marked a feature of British history after 1700.

Banks may be said to have three main functions: to receive deposits, to lend money and to issue bank notes. As before 1546 usury was illegal, banks as we know them today could not have existed. In the Middle Ages the business of money-changing and money-lending was carried on by Jews and the Lombards, merchant bankers of North Italy. Public banks, chiefly concerned with money-changing and discounting bills of exchange, existed in Venice in the twelfth century, and later in Barcelona, Genoa, Hamburg and Amsterdam.

English banking really begins with the goldsmiths, originally dealers in gold and foreign currencies, and intermittently, from the reign of Henry VIII, money-changers. To these functions they added in the seventeenth century that of safeguarding the coin, plate and bullion of wealthy clients, giving in return receipts, in effect promises to repay on demand. Acting on the reasonable assumption that all their clients would not simultaneously demand repayment, the goldsmiths made loans which took the form of documents entitling their holders to immediate payment in coin. These notes, passing from hand to hand, served as a useful form of currency, obviating the necessity of carrying stocks of coin, and were in effect the first English bank notes. In the reign of Charles II the banking activities of some goldsmiths were very considerable, for example, those of Edward Blackwell and Robert Viner, the former numbering among his customers the King, the Duke of York, Samuel Pepys and various City companies including the East India Company. Goldsmith bankers, listed as in business in 1677, founded banks which have continued into modern times, Childs of Temple Bar, Martins of Lombard Street and Hoares of Fleet Street. They made their profits by charging borrowers a higher rate of interest than was paid to depositors. Charles II, whose expenditure, like that of Oliver Cromwell, tended to exceed his revenues, borrowed extensively from the goldsmiths at high rates of interest. When, on the outbreak of the third Anglo-Dutch War in 1672, he temporarily suspended interest payments out of the Exchequer, business confidence was severely undermined, government credit was damaged and several goldsmiths, including Blackwell, became insolvent.

Modern banks provide a number of services. One, the issue of bank notes is restricted today in England and Wales to the Bank of England. Banks which issue notes are known as "banks of issue." In the eighteenth century a second type of bank came into existence, "banks of deposit." These did not issue bank notes but provided depositors with cheque books. When payment by cheque first began is not known with certainty. It was anticipated in the business practices of the seventeenth-century goldsmiths, and had become standard practice by the London bankers from about 1781. By the middle of the reign of George III, therefore, there were two types of banks in England and Wales. The Bank of England and the provincial banks were "banks of issue." The London banks, having ceased to issue notes, were "banks of deposit."

With the increasing use of cheques to settle business transactions organised Clearing House facilities became essential. Clerks used to meet in Change Alley to exchange cheques, settling the balance in notes or coin. Then from about 1775 a room was hired for the transaction of such business. Until 1854 Clearing House facilities were used only by the private London banks but in that year the joint stock banks were admitted. In 1858 Sir John Lubbock (later Lord Avebury) made arrangements for the Country Clearings to deal with cheques drawn on London banks outside London. In 1907 Metropolitan Clearings were arranged and in the twentieth century Clearing Houses were established in important urban centres.

During the seventeenth century "exchange banks" were founded in Amsterdam (1609), Middleburg (1616), Hamburg (1619) and

Rotterdam (1635) to overcome the hindrances to international trade caused by the circulation of national currencies of uncertain and varying values. These banks had no capital of their own but merely accepted deposits in foreign currencies, the value of which they assessed as "bank money." This "bank money" could be used to settle international indebtedness, the banks obtaining their profits from the small charges they made for the service. England did not possess a public bank rivalling in status the continental exchange banks until after the accession of William III. The Bank of England, founded during his reign, however, was not modelled on the continental exchange banks, as it had a capital of its own, issued notes and made loans.

William III was at war with Louis XIV, a war too costly to be financed wholly out of the proceeds of taxation. The alternative, borrowing, was not easy owing to the possibility that the exiled James II might return and repudiate his nephew's debts. The problem was solved by a Scotsman, formerly resident in Holland, William Paterson, who suggested the formation of a joint stock bank. Its capital, £1,200,000, raised by public subscription in ten days, was loaned to the Government at 8 per cent interest. In return the subscribers were incorporated by Act of Parliament as a banking corporation, the first Governor being Sir John Houblon, the descendant of a Flemish refugee who had settled in England in the reign of Elizabeth I. The Charter gave the Bank limited liability privileges, denied to other banks until 1862, and the right to issue notes on government security. The interest payment, £100,000 a year, was made the first charge on the proceeds of specific taxes. As coins in 1694 were rarely worth their face value Bank of England notes were a boon to the business community. Passing from hand to hand they were readily acceptable in payment for goods and services as people were confident that they would be exchanged on demand at the Bank for gold.

The Bank of England was strictly limited to carrying on banking business, trading only in bullion, bills of exchange and goods deposited as security and not redeemed. It was not, however, given a monopoly in 1694. In fact the success of the Bank, whose propprietors were Whigs, provoked Tory jealousy, and a futile attempt to found a land bank in 1697. But in return for a further loan in 1697, the Bank received further privileges and a guarantee that until after 1711 no other bank would be incorporated by Act of Parliament. The monopoly was reaffirmed in 1707 and again in 1708 by an Act of Parliament which enacted that no corporate body or partnership of more than six persons should "borrow, owe, or take up any sum or sums of money on their bills or notes payable on demand or at any time less than six months from the borrowing thereof." This legislation was universally believed to prohibit the formation of joint stock banks, until it was pointed out in 1833 that by it the Bank of England monopoly only extended to joint stock banks of issue, and not to joint stock banks of deposit.

The Act of 1708, reaffirmed by Parliament in 1800, explains why before 1833 banking establishments in England and Wales were family businesses or private partnerships. In contrast, in Scotland, where private banking firms were relatively unimportant, three joint stock banks were incorporated, the Bank of Scotland (1695), the Royal Bank of Scotland (1727) and the British Linen Company. The last, founded in 1746 to encourage linen manufactures, after 1763 confined its activities to banking. In England and Wales there were two types of private banks, firstly, those with offices located in the Lombard Street district of London, and secondly, the provincial or country banks. The London banks, some 28 in number in 1740, and about 60 in 1832, were well-managed concerns with considerable resources, handling cheques and such negotiable instruments as bills of exchange on a country-wide basis.

The country banks were family businesses or small partnerships. Traders added to their usual occupation the discounting of bills of exchange, and sometimes a note issue. No licence was needed for enterprising business men, often possessed of limited resources, to solicit deposits and to issue notes on the volume of which no legal restriction was placed other than the obligation to exchange for cash on demand. As Bank of England notes rarely circulated more than 30 miles from the metropolis notes issued by country bankers were the principal paper currency. In areas where bank notes were not issued the shortage of currency led to the use of endorsed bills of exchange to settle accounts.

That economic life in eighteenth-century England was tending to be organised on a national rather than a local basis can be attributed not only to transport improvements, but also to the new credit and banking facilities. Savings at harvest periods in the prosperous agricultural areas of East Anglia and the West Country were channelled to the capital-hungry industrial areas in the North and the Midlands. The link between the capital-surplus agricultural areas and the capital-demanding industrial regions was provided by the Lombard Street bankers. They held on deposit the reserves of the country banks, did an extensive business in inland bills of exchange and made loans to manufacturers and traders. Manufacturers, therefore, needing capital for development projects were not constrained to rely wholly on scarce local sources of supply.

At the apex of the credit network which evolved in eighteenth-century England was the Bank of England. It held the reserves of the London banks and hence became the custodian of the final reserves on which the paper currency was based. Paper money was used in an increasing volume of commercial transactions during the eighteenth century, but its acceptability rested on the premise that it could, on demand, be exchanged for cash. Before 1774, both silver and gold were legal tender. In 1774 silver ceased to be legal tender in settlement of debts over £25, lowered in 1816 to £2. In other words, by 1816, Great Britain had adopted a gold standard, the standard coin being the guinea which since 1717 had equalled 21s.

In theory, a bank note is a promise to pay the holder cash on demand. In practice, the volume of notes in circulation was far in excess of the amount of gold held by the issuing banks. Hence on the occasions when there was a loss of confidence bankers risked insolvency. In the event of a sudden demand for more than they held in reserve the country banks drew on their deposits in the London banks and the latter in turn sought cash from the Bank of England. There were runs on the banks, for example, at the close of the Seven Years' War in 1763, and of the American War of Independence twenty years later. This was the state of affairs which forced the Bank of England into occupying the position of a central bank.

The men responsible for the foundation of the Bank had no such ambitions, as they saw themselves as bankers operating to make profits for their stockholders. But the blunt truth was that in times of financial panic the directors of the Bank had to assume responsibility for the proper functioning of the national credit structure. The need for the assumption of such responsibilities became pressing as a result of the severe financial crisis which followed the outbreak of war in 1793. Between 1792 and 1797 the price of 3 per cent consols fell from 97$\frac{1}{8}$ to 47$\frac{3}{4}$, and of bank stock from 219 to 121$\frac{3}{4}$. In 1797 as the reserves of gold held by the Bank were threatened with exhaustion, the Prime Minister authorised the issue of an Order in Council, subsequently confirmed by Act of Parliament, permitting the Bank to suspend cash payments. As these were not resumed until 1821, Great Britain between 1797 and 1821 had an inconvertible note issue.

After 1797 banks played an increasingly responsible part in economic affairs but the lack of stability in the economy inevitably focused attention on weaknesses in the banking system. Attempts were made to put English banking on a sound financial footing by legislation permitting joint stock banking and restricting the issue of notes not backed by gold. Changes in banking law were assisted by the objections to the existence of a state-favoured monopoly. Why, it was asked, should the Bank of England be the only joint stock bank permitted to issue notes? In 1822, a Newcastle stockbroker, Thos. Joplin, published an *Essay on the General Principles and Present Private Practice of Banking in England and Scotland*, in which he drew attention to the absence of bank failures in Scotland, where joint stock banks were legal. In England, about 300 country banks failed during the 1797–1819 period. There was a serious financial crisis in 1825 mainly due to unwise speculative loans to the newly-independent South American countries. Nearly 60 country banks and a large number of finance houses in London became insolvent.

As it believed that "the rash spirit of speculation" was supported, fostered and encouraged by the country banks, the Government decided to repeal the law limiting co-partnership in banking to not more than six persons. In a speech in the House of Lords, Lord Liverpool, the Prime Minister, discoursed on the irrationality of keeping on the statute book a law which prevented the formation of banks with resources adequate to supply the country with a secure paper currency. Two Acts were therefore passed in 1826. The first legalised joint stock banks of issue "except in London and within a distance of 65 miles thereof." The second, despite the protests of the country bankers, authorised the Bank of England to establish branch banks outside the metropolitan area, a concession of which it actually took very little advantage. In addition, acting on the dubious theory that the suppression of small notes would prevent an over-issue, and afford some measure of protection to the less well-to-do, Parliament forbade the issue of bank notes of a lower denomination than £5. The sequel to this legislation was the establishment of provincial joint stock banks of issue, mainly at first in the expanding industrial districts. In October 1826, for example, the Lancashire Banking Company opened its doors and in June 1827 the Huddersfield Banking Company.

The commencement of joint stock banking in London followed the revelation of James William Gilbart that there were no legal obstacles to the functioning of joint stock banks of deposit, an opinion in which the law officers of the Crown concurred. An Act of Parliament passed in 1833 settled the matter, its enactment being followed by Gilbart's foundation of the London and Westminster Bank in 1834. The London Joint Stock Bank was founded in 1836 and the Union and County Banks in 1839. For many years, however, joint stock banks operated under severe disabilities. The Bank of England refused to accept bills endorsed by them. The

London joint stock banks were denied admission to the Clearing House and until 1844 could not sue or be sued. The unlimited liability of bank stockholders was not removed until 1858 and even then not in respect of the note issue. Unlimited liability on the note issue could be disastrous to stockholders in the event of a bank failure, as was demonstrated when the Western Bank of Scotland in 1858 and the Glasgow Bank in 1878 failed to meet their obligations. The Glasgow Bank failure led to the passage of the Companies Act in 1879. This Act did not remove stockholders' liability in respect of the note issue, but by 1879, this was becoming a disability of little practical importance, as, owing to the Bank Charter Act of 1844, notes other than those of the Bank of England were ceasing to be issued in England and Wales.

The passage of the Bank Charter Act in 1844 marked the culmination of a controversy over many years about the paper currency. In 1809 the price of gold rose and the value of British currency on the foreign exchanges fell. The opinion that this state of affairs was the result of an excessive issue of inconvertible paper money was expressed by David Ricardo in *The High Price of Bullion: a Proof of the Depreciation of Bank Notes*. This publication was followed by the setting up by the House of Commons of the Bullion Committee (1810) which heard evidence from bankers and merchants challenging Ricardo's views. They made out a good case against the Bullionists' theory that an excessive issue of notes was a sufficient explanation of the rise in internal price levels and of the fall in the value of the pound on the foreign exchanges. Nevertheless, the Bullion Committee recommended the repeal of the Bank Restriction Act of 1797, a recommendation which, perhaps wisely, the Government refused to act upon. Instead it decided in 1812 to make Bank of England notes legal tender. The Bullionists, however, continued their agitation, and got their way in 1819 when the Bank of England was ordered to resume cash payments by 1st May 1823. In the event its notes were made convertible into gold in 1821.

In 1816 Ricardo published *Proposals for an Economical and Secure Currency*, advocating a paper currency linked to gold. After 1826 three classes of bank notes were in circulation, namely, those issued by the Bank of England, the country banks, and the provincial joint stock banks. Commercial crises, notably those of 1825 and 1836–39, when many banks failed to honour their obligations, inevitably raised the question of placing restrictions upon bankers' note-issuing powers. A Committee of Enquiry in 1840–41 heard the views of two schools of thought, the Currency and Banking schools. The Currency school led by Samuel James Lloyd (later Lord Overstone) argued that the volume of notes in circulation should be strictly tied to gold. The Banking school, whose leading spokesman for many years had been Thomas Tooke, favoured giving greater latitude to bankers. The Prime Minister, Sir Robert Peel, decided to accept the advice of the Currency school in the Bank Charter Act of 1844.

The Act of 1844 had two objectives, firstly, to make Bank of England notes secure, and secondly, to impose limitations on the amount of paper currency issued by all other banks in England and Wales. The second objective was achieved by prohibiting the formation of new banks of issue and restricting the note issue of those already in existence. After 27th April 1844 the note issue of banks, other than the Bank of England, was not to exceed the average of the preceding twelve weeks. The banks could lose their issue rights in one of three ways; by ceasing to exercise them, by opening a London office, and lastly, if restricted by law to six partners, by increasing the number beyond six. The aggregate value of the note issue in 1844 of the private banks, which was not legal tender, was £8,648,553. This was bound to diminish with the passage of time. It was £2,958,000 in 1900 and by 1914 had fallen to £84,831. The last private bank of issue, Fox, Fowler & Co., lost its issue rights in 1921 when it amalgamated with Lloyds Bank.

To secure the first objective, a limitation on the note issue of the Bank of England, the Bank was divided into two departments, the Issue and Banking Departments. The Issue Department was authorised to issue notes to the value of £14 million. This, known as the "Fiduciary Issue," was backed by the government debt to the Bank (£11,015,100) and interest-bearing securities. All other notes were to be backed by gold and silver. Silver was included to meet the need for silver in settling accounts with bi-metallic and silver standard countries, but it was not to exceed one quarter of the combined bullion and coin holding. Actually, however, before 1928 the Issue Department did not take advantage of the authority to issue notes backed by silver. When a private bank note issue lapsed the Issue Department was empowered to ask for an Order in Council authorising it to increase the fiduciary issue by two-thirds of the lapsed issue. The fiduciary issue was ultimately raised to £19,750,000, the last Order in Council being issued in 1923, permitting the Bank to take over two-thirds of the lapsed issue of Fox, Fowler & Co. The Bank also became the intermediary between the public and the Mint. It purchased gold bullion at the rate of £3 17s. 9d. per standard ounce, receiving in return from the Mint gold coin to the value of £3 17s. $10\frac{1}{2}d$.

Each week the Issue Department published a statement showing that it was carrying out its obligations. The following is a typical example:

BANK OF ENGLAND RETURN
ISSUE DEPARTMENT, 2ND JULY 1908

Dr.		Cr.	
Notes issued	£55,484,385	Government debt	£11,015,100
		Other securities	7,434,900
		Gold, coin and bullion	37,034,385
		Silver bullion	—
	£55,484,385		£55,484,385

This return shows that before 1914 the aggregate value of the note issue was not large. Bank of England notes were not commonly used by the public being primarily held as a reserve by other banks. Until 1914 gold coins were used as currency. The outbreak of war in Europe, however, in July 1914, provoked a serious international financial crisis which the Government met by raising the Bank Rate to 10 per cent and making Bank of England notes inconvertible. Gold coins ceased to circulate, their place being taken by one pound and ten shilling Treasury notes. These continued in use until the passage of the Currency and Bank Notes Act in November 1928 which authorised the Bank of England to take over the Treasury issue. To enable it to do so the fiduciary issue was raised to £260 million, not to be exceeded without Treasury permission, backed by securities, and by silver coin not greater in value than £5,500,000. The obligation of the Bank to change its notes into gold still remained after passage of the Act of 1928 but as modified by the Gold Standard Act of 1925, "only in the form of bars containing approximately 400 ounces troy of fine gold." This was designed to discourage the use of gold as a circulating medium as the minimum amount of gold obtainable would cost £1700.

The second of the two departments, the Banking Department, in theory operated to make profits for stockholders. Actually, it had major public responsibilities. It managed the National Debt, and had since 1694 been the agency through which the Government raised long- and short-term loans. It was the depository of public monies and of the reserves which the other banks could withdraw in emergencies. The Banking Department was therefore required by the Act of 1844 to make a weekly statement showing its current assets and liabilities. These show that like all other banks it converted part of its assets into interest-bearing securities. In the event of a financial panic, therefore, it would not be able to meet all its obligations to pay coin or notes on demand. But the Bank Charter Act of 1844 did not fulfil the expectations of its promoters that financial crises would be avoided. On four occasions after 1844, in 1847, 1857, 1866 and 1914, the reserves of the Banking Department were threatened with exhaustion. The situation was met by what is known as "suspending the Bank Act," that is permitting an increase in the fiduciary note issue. The 1847 monetary crisis followed a failure of the Irish potato crop, a series of poor English harvests and over-investment in railways. The crisis of 1857 was the consequence of banking and railway failures in the U.S.A., in which large amounts of British capital were invested. More serious was the crisis of 1866. The passage of the Limited Liability Companies Act in 1862 encouraged some banks and discount firms to extend themselves beyond the bounds of prudence. A number of banks and the very important discount company, Overend, Gurney & Co., failed, the latter with liabilities totalling over £19 million. On each of these three occasions, with the Government promising to introduce a Bill of Indemnity, the Bank of England arranged to exceed the legal limit of the fiduciary issue. Actually, the power to over-issue was only used in 1857, confidence being restored in 1847 and 1866 without its exercise.

Heavy speculative investment in the Argentine was responsible for a severe monetary crisis in 1890. The merchant banking firm of Baring Brothers, which had underwritten too many shares, was saved from liquidation by action taken by the Bank of England and the Bank of France. On this occasion, therefore, resort was not made to a suspension of the Bank Act. Without government intervention, however, the bank could not have dealt unaided with the international monetary crisis following the outbreak of war in 1914. The Government went further than merely promising to introduce a Bill of Indemnity. A Moratorium was declared on 3rd August. On 6th August an Act was passed empowering the Bank to issue notes in excess of the legal maximum, "as far as temporarily authorised by the Treasury and subject to any conditions attached by that authority."

Government policy in 1914 marks the end of an era in monetary policy. The terms of the Bank Charter Act of 1844 had ensured an absence of State determination of monetary policy by strictly limiting the size of the note issue to gold holdings. From 1914 the volume of notes in circulation was decided by the State. As their numbers increased, their value fell. Inflationary tendencies were a marked feature of monetary history in all the warring countries. In

Britain, however, from 1920 government policy was directed towards raising the value of the depreciated pound. In other countries, where deflationary policies were not followed, paper currencies became worthless, much more so in Russia and Germany, and less so in France, Italy and Belgium. Cobbett in the early nineteenth century violently denounced the Government of his day as a coiner of false money. All too many citizens of modern states have much more cause to condemn their governments than he had his.

A notable aspect of post-1844 banking history was the replacement of the local country bankers by branch managers of national joint stock banks. Since the passage of the Bank Acts of 1826 and 1833 the private provincial banks had been losing ground to their joint stock rivals, a process accelerated by the Act of 1844. Local bankers were inevitably adversely affected by the opening of branches of joint stock banks in their neighbourhoods, while some joint stock banks came into existence as a result of amalgamations of private banks. After the passage of the Limited Companies Act in 1862, the tendency towards amalgamations accelerated, continuing to the end of the First World War. By that time, English banking had come to be dominated by "the Big Five," Barclays, Lloyds, the Midland, the National Provincial and the Westminster. Smaller joint stock banks also existed, for example, the Liverpool-based Martins Bank, the Manchester-based Williams Deacon and the four-branch Glyn Mills in London. The fear that concentration of financial power in few hands might militate against the public interest led to State intervention. In 1918 the Colwyn Committee recommended that further amalgamations should be subject to Treasury control and hence in 1928 the Treasury announced that further amalgamations would not be permitted.

In recent years, however, as their customers, the great industrial combines, have expanded by mergers, the smaller banking firms, possessing relatively small deposit holdings, have been handicapped in maintaining a share of big company banking business. Amalgamations would permit of some rationalisation of existing branch networks. Even now important mergers are advocated as necessary to enable the clearing banks to meet increasing competition at home and abroad. They have to meet the challenge of the Post Office Giro in addition to the growing competition from American and other overseas banks in London, and from other financial institutions such as merchant banks and trustee savings banks. In risky overseas business size is necessary for success. Lastly, so numerous and expanding are the services offered by banks, new business techniques have had to be introduced. The new way is automation, the chief investment in which is the computer. A computer can do in less than five minutes what formerly took a machinist fifteen hours, while all the details of an account may not occupy more than an inch of magnetic tape. Already an increasing number of branches are being automated. The era of ledger clerks making entries is rapidly vanishing. Instead the day's work is reduced to a computer message and transmitted to centres in London and large provincial cities where the information is processed and the following day returned in the form of balance and statements. Such an approach to banking processes can only be economically introduced in a large organisation.

For these reasons mergers are today transforming British banking. In January 1968 the Westminster and National Provincial Banks announced that they proposed to merge. This was followed by the news that the National Bank of Scotland and the Royal Bank of Scotland were to join forces. The latest and biggest merger proposed was that of Barclays Bank, Great Britain's largest, and Lloyds, the third largest, which would also have taken in Martins. At this point the Government decided to review the situation by referring the Barclays–Lloyds–Martins proposed merger to the Monopolies Commission. In the summer of 1968 permission for the merger was withheld, but a Barclays–Martins merger was allowed. The other clearing banks are already owned by the bigger ones, the District Bank and Coutts by the National Provincial, Glyn Mills and Williams Deacon's by the Royal Bank of Scotland and the National Bank by the National Commercial Bank of Scotland.

For sentimental reasons, one might regret the passing of the old-time private banker with his intimate local knowledge and associations. But his ending was inevitable. In no other way could finance have been provided for the rapid economic expansion, both at home and overseas, of the second half of the nineteenth century. Joint stock banks, with their massive resources and widely spread branches, ensured greater banking stability. Failure of joint stock banks were not impossible, as was shown by that of the City of Glasgow Bank in 1878, but were very unusual, especially when compared with the numerous pre-1844 country bank collapses.

We must also note the rising importance in the second half of the nineteenth century of London as an international financial centre. Joint stock banks established branches overseas, and banking firms, known as merchant bankers, expanded their activities. The older merchant banks originated in firms which earned fees by underwriting the bills of business men. By the early nineteenth century such merchant banking firms as the Rothschilds, Barings, Hambros, Brandts and Schroders were loaning money to overseas borrowers, the Rothschilds, for instance, providing the finance for the army of Wellington fighting the Peninsular War. The oldest merchant bank in London, that of the Baring Brothers, which during the Napoleonic Wars shipped gold and arms to Britain's continental allies, was described by the minister of Louis XVIII, the Duc de Richelieu, as one of "the six great Powers in Europe" the other five being Britain, France, Russia, Austria and Prussia.

At first the merchant banks were primarily concerned with the acceptance of bills and the issue of sterling bonds for foreign governments. But from the mid-sixties, when new merchant banking houses came into existence, they extended their activities, becoming the intermediaries through which finance was provided for home and overseas economic development. After the First World War, with the decline in London's pre-eminence as a world financial centre, merchant banking firms played an important role as issuing houses, directing the savings of the investing public into British companies.

With their offices located in the City the approximately twenty merchant banking firms are still controlled by descendants of the original founders. As the author of *Anatomy of Britain*, Anthony Sampson, reminds us, the merchant banks have been dynastic, passing down know-how, wealth and sometimes brains. Members of their firms are directors of big business corporations while Lord Cromer, until recently Governor of the Bank of England, is a Baring. Since 1945 new merchant banking firms have been founded such as Hill Samuel and S. G. Warburg. These, together with the older houses, are nowadays playing a major part in the rationalising of British economic enterprises and in the arrangements of mergers and the conduct of "take-over" battles.

The dominance of London as a financial centre owes much to their expertise, and to that of the discount houses, members of the Stock Exchange, dealers in commodities, insurance companies and Lloyds underwriters, with all of whom they worked in close relationships. The invisible earnings of the City came as a result to play an important part in the national economy. Improved means of communication in the nineteenth century opened up new possibilities for commercial development which stimulated an extension of banking and financial facilities centred in London. At the beginning of the century Europe had been the chief area in which British capital was invested. Later, considerable investment, much of it in railway construction, was made in South America, the U.S.A., the colonies and the Far East. Britain became a world banker, many countries holding sterling balances in London which were used to settle multilateral trade transactions.

No accurate information exists on the extent to which Britain invested capital overseas during the first half of the nineteenth century. By 1870, however, British overseas investment holdings have been estimated to be worth £1000 million, yielding an annual income of £44 million. The amounts by 1913 had risen to nearly £4000 million, yielding an income of £200 million. But it would be erroneous to conclude that during the 1870–1913 period Britain was exporting large amounts of capital. In most of the years between 1870 and 1913 Britain did not export more than she imported. Rather, there was an excess of imports over exports. The increase in the capital value of British overseas investments was in the main due to the re-investment of the income due on investments already made.

The chief areas in which British capital was invested after 1850 were the newly-settled territories, with large, unused resources, into which millions of European emigrants were moving. That this was the case can be illustrated by the following statistics:

DISTRIBUTION OF BRITISH OVERSEAS INVESTMENTS, 1913

PUBLICLY ISSUED SECURITIES IN 1913

	£'s million	Percentage of total
Canada and Newfoundland	510	13·6
Australia and New Zealand	420	11·2
U.S.A.	750	19·9
Latin America	760	20·2
India and Ceylon	380	10·1
Others	940	25·0
TOTAL	3,760	100·0

British overseas investment during the period was profitable because it was in the main directed to lands with unexploited agricultural and mineral resources which skilled European settlers were able to develop. Contemporaneously, Britain, with an expanding population and rapidly growing industries, was able to absorb the food and raw materials produced by the labour of these European emigrants. Britain, therefore, before 1914 had a surplus of imports over exports because part of what she imported represented payment of interest on overseas capital investment. Other European countries before 1914 possessing substantial overseas capital investments, for example, France and Germany, found themselves

178   BRITISH ECONOMIC AND SOCIAL HISTORY

in a similar position. Like Britain, they were importing more than they exported, the increase in their capital investments overseas being due to re-investment in part of the interest income due to them.

PART VI

SOCIAL REFORM

CHAPTER XVI

THE POOR LAW

In 1843, Thomas Carlyle wrote in *Past and Present*, "this rich English nation has sunk or is fast sinking into a state to which ... there was literally never any parallel." A year earlier there had been published Edwin Chadwick's *Report on the Sanitary Condition of the Labouring Population* which showed that the lower classes lived under conditions that were destructive both to morality and health. The conclusion of some historians, that the Industrial Revolution was responsible for a marked deterioration in the lot of the working classes, can be supported by contemporary descriptions of rural and urban slums, by well documented accounts of the brutalities and excessive hours associated with the employment of women and children and by the undoubted distress among handicraft workers whose skills machine methods of production made obsolete.

That both before and after 1815 British governments did not introduce ameliorative measures to deal with what Carlyle called the "condition of England question" was largely due to the French Revolution, which, as has been said, "made Pitt a Tory." Pitt's and successive governments contented themselves with repressive measures, at a time when revolutionary theories emanating from Paris threatened to destroy the existing political order, and war perils made the maintenance of national survival the prime consideration in government thinking and policies. This defensive reaction against the principles of the French Revolution militated against the adoption of reform policies for many years after Napoleon had been transported to St Helena, adherence to static policies in a dynamic world delaying political reform until the passage of the Parliamentary Reform Act of 1832. Social reform was impeded by doctrines of *laisser-faire* taught by academic economists and accepted uncritically by politicians, capitalist employers and even trade union leaders. Until after the passage of the Parliamentary Reform Act of 1867, parliamentary candidates had not to canvass votes from working men, while the areas in which industrial expansion was taking place were remote from Whitehall, and, at first, sent relatively few representatives to Westminster. In fact, sheer ignorance of conditions in little visited industrial centres goes far to explain aristocratic laxity in providing remedies for social evils. "Nine hundred and ninety-nine thousandths of the people of England," Cobbett said, "have not the most distant idea that such things are carried on in a country calling itself free."

It is significant that much of the evidence, cited in support of the theory that the social environment had worsened, is culled from official government publications. This indicates that the governing classes were not wholly unwilling to sponsor social legislation and were aware of their responsibilities to do so. The truth is that degradation, poverty and misery were not peculiar to the nineteenth century. Such evils had always been the lot of mankind. What distinguishes the nineteenth from preceding centuries is that there was an awareness of them and a realisation that remedies ought to be searched for and could be found. It was economic growth, a consequence of industrialisation, which enabled Great Britain to feed and clothe an expanding population, and provided the resources to improve social conditions. The economic and social dislocations during the early years of the nineteenth century were not so much a consequence of power-driven machinery but in the main a product of war.

The notion that economic changes before 1850 were wholly harmful to the workers is one that must be rejected. On the contrary, the post-1820 period was one of economic growth and falling prices and one in which the first legislative steps were taken against the evils associated with early industrialisation. Further, although for many years denied a parliamentary vote (the town artisans until 1867, and agricultural labourers until 1884), the workers were not helpless. The Industrial Revolution brought into existence a social order making it easier than formerly for the workers to protect their interests. Artisans, massed in urban communities, working in factories and mines, were better able to combine for their own defence than were the agricultural labourers and scattered handicraft workers in eighteenth-century rural society dominated by squire and parson. In other words, industrialisation created a form of society in which social reform could be achieved, partly by the State and partly by worker self-help. Governments reformed the poor laws and passed legislation dealing with factories, mines, education and public health. The working classes founded trade unions, co-operative societies and mechanics institutes, and supported Chartism, the Ten Hours Movement and the Anti-Corn Law League.

The first Parliament elected after the reform of the franchise in 1832 passed the Poor Law Amendment Act in 1834. Its enactment followed the astonishing revelations of the Royal Commission appointed in 1832 to examine methods of poor law administration. A review of previous legislation and administrative procedures, and of the changing attitudes in preceding centuries towards those unable or unwilling to maintain themselves, will assist towards an understanding of the nature of the problem the Whig government in 1834 sought to solve. There existed four classes of persons dependent upon public assistance, the sick and the aged, destitute children, industrious able-bodied adults unable to find work and lastly incorrigible rogues and vagabonds. Modern conceptions of social welfare are based on the recognition that each of these classes needs separate treatment. This unfortunately has not always been the case.

1388–1601

Poor law legislation began in 1388 when the first of a long series of laws was enacted concerning the impotent poor. Apart, however, from recognising the existence of a class of persons unable to provide for themselves, the Government provided little practical help until the end of the Tudor period. During the sixteenth century social and economic changes were associated with a disturbing increase in the numbers of vagabonds who terrorised peaceable folk on the dirt tracks that passed for highways. Early Tudor rulers dealt with this menace by enacting laws of merciless severity in 1495, 1503, 1536 and 1547. After the accession of Elizabeth I effective measures were passed to assist the large numbers of those not gainfully employed who could not be described as "sturdy vagabonds." Poor Law Acts were passed in 1563, 1572 and 1576, this experimental legislation being consolidated by the Act of 1597–98 which was re-enacted with slight amendments in 1601. The system of poor law administration outlined in the Act of 1601, in its main essentials, remained the law of the land until the Poor Law Amendment Act 1834.

1601–1782

The unit of administration was the parish. Yearly in Easter week each parish had to nominate overseers who, with the churchwardens, and under the supervision of the J.P.s, were to levy a poor rate on all householders and occupiers of land, and to apply the proceeds to the relief of the indigent. The impotent poor, the old, lame, blind and sick were to be given "competent sums of money." Children were to be apprenticed, boys till they were 24 and girls to the age of 21. To provide work for unemployed adults, "a convenient stock of flax, hemp, wool, thread, iron and other stuff" was to be purchased. Lastly, those unwilling to work were to be harshly punished and made "to labour as a true subject ought to do."

The intentions of the Queen and her ministers were humane. Their scheme was complete on paper, but did it ever become an administrative reality? The parish authorities were supervised by a Committee of the Privy Council, but as far as we can judge, drastic action was not taken against those remiss in carrying out their statutory duties, even before the Civil War when conciliar government was strong. But apart from lax administration, real difficulties were experienced in administering the scheme. Elizabethan legislators had acted on the assumptions that the numbers of unemployed would be small and temporary, that the parish would not be overburdened and that conditions of economic life would remain unchanged. But during the seventeenth century, when employed workers were condemned to a low and uncertain standard of living, the number of persons on occasional relief has been estimated at one in four of the population. The parish, as a unit of administration, was ill-suited to deal with such a situation. It was even less capable of coping with the problem of indigency that resulted from the social and economic changes brought about by the Industrial and Agrarian Revolutions.

The methods devised to cope with the problems of the able bodied unemployed were difficult to implement. It was never easy to discriminate between those willing to work and those who "shall be deemed rogues, vagabonds, and sturdy beggars." What was to be done if recipients embezzled the raw materials or if the work was done badly, a likely result as paupers tended to be the least skilled of the population? The marketing of manufactured articles was difficult, and parish subsidised labour could throw others, gainfully employed, out of work. In the early eighteenth century the practice of farming out pauper labour to private employers proved to be an unacceptable solution. Finally, where were the poor to do the work?

In the seventeenth century transepts of churches were sometimes used and private Acts were passed permitting some municipalities, for example, Bristol, King's Lynn and Norwich, to build workhouses. In 1723 an Act was passed permitting parishes or unions of parishes to build workhouses and to deny relief to those refusing to enter them. The Act was administered harshly, most overseers regarding it as their primary duty to keep down the rates. As a result rates fell from £819,000 in 1698 to £689,000 in 1750. The term "workhouse," as the name of the buildings erected under the

Act of 1723, proved to be a misnomer. They were in fact "poorhouses" in which all classes of the destitute were confined under conditions of acute shame and degradation.

The law laid down that every parish should make compulsory provision for the maintenance of the poor. But who were "the poor of a parish"? Were they people born in the parish, people who had lived in it for periods of months or years, or just people who happened to be there when misfortune befell them? Parliament's solution to this problem was the Settlement Act of 1662, amended in 1685 and 1691. These statutes, aimed at the vagrant class, empowered overseers to remove from the parish any persons who had not resided there for 40 days if they did not hold a tenement worth £10 a year or had not become apprentices. This legislation had disastrous effects on English labour. Men who had lost their jobs could not seek employment elsewhere. Enforcement led to endless difficulties. Special Acts had to be passed to deal with particular classes of workers, for example, gangs of reapers and discharged soldiers. Later, a system of certificates was introduced permitting artisans to live in parishes where employment could be obtained but denying them the right to acquire a legal "settlement," and thereby qualifying for assistance if misfortune overtook them. One other law enacted in the seventeenth century may be mentioned, that of 1691. This forbade overseers to give relief unless they had obtained permission from a J.P.

Two other classes of the poor are often mentioned by contemporaries. These were, firstly, squatters who grubbed a livelihood on village commons, following what respectable folk regarded as an idle and ill-disciplined way of life, and secondly, prisoners for debt. These latter tended to be regarded as men who by fraud or carelessness had cheated honest creditors of their just dues. Debt prisoners, however, were not always the victims of relentless creditors. Many chose prison as a means of evading their just obligations.

1782–1834

From the closing decades of the eighteenth century there was a marked increase in unemployment, both in rural and urban areas. This increase in the numbers of unemployed adults made necessary a relaxation of the rule restricting outdoor relief to the impotent poor. By Gilbert's Act (1782) parishes were allowed, if they wished, to combine to form poor law unions, less than one-fifteenth of them actually doing so. Workhouses could become places in which the impotent poor were housed rather than centres in which employment was found for able-bodied adults. Oudoor relief was permitted for adults, but they were to qualify for it by working. Justices of the Peace were permitted to supplement inadequate wages out of poor law funds and to appoint paid officials called Guardians of the Poor, whose duties in some respects approximated to those of relieving officers of later times. In 1795 the Settlement Laws were relaxed by an Act laying down that overseers were not to banish newcomers until they actually made application for parochial assistance.

Gilbert's Act, being merely permissive, depended upon local initiative for its implementation. Intended as a temporary measure, at a time of acute distress, it lasted, with dire results, for more than a generation. In 1795 the Berkshire Justices meeting in Quarter Sessions at the Pelican Inn, Speenhamland, sought a remedy for the appalling poverty of the agricultural labourers in the county. Rejecting as impracticable the use of their statutory powers to fix wages, they decided to supplement wages out of the poor fund. The amount payable was based on the price of a quartern loaf and the size of the family. In 1796 Parliament ratified this method of aiding the poor by legalising the payment of allowances to wage earners and abolishing the workhouse test. The policy of the Berkshire J.P.s, the beginnings of what came to be known as the "allowance system," was widely copied in the southern counties, but not in the northern counties which were becoming industrialised.

The widespread adoption of the allowance system brought in its train many abuses. The best account of them is to be found in the Report of the Royal Commission appointed in 1832 to investigate poor law administration. The report, published in 1834, is one of the most astonishing documents ever penned. Much valid criticism was passed on the officials who administered poor law services, overseers, parish vestries and J.P.s. The overseers, who collected and disbursed poor law monies, were drawn from the farming and shopkeeping classes. The office was disagreeable, unpopular and unpaid. As overseers usually held office for short periods they rarely became efficient. Proper accounts were not kept, and no adequate checks existed against partiality, favouritism and jobbery. Many were illiterate, and many exposed to intimidation by lazy, mutinous and imperious paupers. Tradesmen were vulnerable to threats of loss of custom if they refused the doles demanded.

Members of parish vestries, the local governing bodies, belonged to the same strata of society as overseers. They rarely kept proper minutes and many had a direct interest in giving relief in aid of wages. Shopkeepers and cottage landlords attended vestry meetings to make sure their interests were protected. Farmers were concerned to make sure that a minimum proportion of labourers' incomes were paid in wages and a maximum from poor law funds. Wages were deliberately reduced in order to place the larger share of the cost of maintaining labourers upon the gentry, clergy and non-employer householders. The J.P.s fixed the relief scales and adjudicated in disputes between overseers and applicants for relief. Methods of giving outdoor relief varied. In some parishes it was given in kind, payment of rents, and in vouchers which could be exchanged for goods in shops owned by overseers and members of vestries. Other parishes gave monetary relief without labour, two or three shillings a week, recipients being required to remain in one place in order that they might be contacted, it was explained, if work became available. A more likely reason was to make conditions as disagreeable as possible for the paupers. A common form of relief was the payment of allowances, the amounts added to wages to bring them up to the Justices' scale. In some parishes farmers were paid to employ labourers, in others labourers were employed by the parish, usually on road maintenance work. Such tasks, however, were never easy to enforce, paupers spending most of the day in idleness. Finally there were parishes in which ratepayers were required to employ paupers, or alternatively pay their wages to the overseers. In these parishes farmers were tempted to discharge their regular employees in order to find work for the paupers assigned to them.

There was also much maladministration associated with indoor relief. Some of the workhouses built under Gilbert's Act were massive and costly. Generalisations about conditions in them are not easy to make, but there is no doubt that in some paupers were better housed and fed than were independent labourers living in insanitary hovels on starvation rates of pay. In one workhouse, it was reported that paupers who spent the day sitting round the stove had an overfed mutinous and insubordinate appearance. Certainly, however, the conditions in many workhouses left much to be desired, the sick, lame and blind being herded together, with children exposed to the filthy talk and vile language of adult inmates.

The effects of such a system of poor law administration could not be other than harmful. So heavy was the burden upon rateable property that land went out of cultivation. An extreme case was Cholesbury in Buckinghamshire where the amount collected rose from £10 18s. 0d. in 1801 to £367 in 1832. The rate burden upon non-pauper labourers of good character was crippling. As the poor rate was levied upon property and tithes, and not upon employers as such, wage rates were deliberately reduced. Officials were demoralised. Paupers deteriorated in skills, and indolence and dependence sapped the moral fibre of countless thousands. There was a destruction of family ties. Paupers looked to the parish to maintain the aged, and it was commonly and probably untruly claimed that the allowance system encouraged improvident marriages and stimulated increases in the size of families.

The Royal Commission of 1832 had been given a dual task, "to inquire into the practical operation of the laws for the relief of the poor" and "to report their opinion as to what beneficial alterations should be made." The report, drafted by Edwin Chadwick and the Oxford economist, Nassau Senior, was noteworthy for its length, over 8000 folio pages, for the meticulous detail in which abuses were listed, and for the far-reaching changes it recommended in poor law administration and practice. Legislative effect was given to the substance of their proposed "beneficial alterations" by the Poor Law Amendment Act of 1834. Changes were made, firstly, in the machinery of poor law administration, and, secondly, in the principles of relief.

The report had amply demonstrated that as a unit of administration the parish lacked adequate financial resources and administrative talent. As in 1834 the modern machinery of government did not exist, a special *ad hoc* authority was set up. The 15,000 parishes in England and Wales were combined to form 640 Poor Law Unions administered by Boards of Guardians and their salaried officials. The members of the Boards were Justices of the Peace, *ex officio* members and unpaid members elected by ratepayers. The principle of one ratepayer, one vote, was not conceded until 1894, but a democratic beginning had been made (which in the twentieth century created difficulties in poor law administration). Each parish was assessed to make a contribution to the income of the Union of which it formed a part.

To ensure uniformity in the treatment of the indigent, a Poor Law Commission, consisting of three Commissioners, was set up, initially for five years. Chadwick became its Secretary. The extent of central government control was considerable but less than Chadwick, who was primarily concerned with administrative efficiency, had advocated. If he had got his way poor law administration would have been brought more strictly under central control through a bureaucracy appointed by the Poor Law Commissioners. Instead, England and Wales were divided into 21 Poor Law Districts, each under an Assistant Commissioner, upon whom was laid the duty of seeing that Boards of Guardians implemented the policies of the Poor Law Commission and obeyed its numerous orders and regulations.

The Report of the Poor Law Commission had exposed outdoor relief to able-bodied adults and their dependants as "the great source of abuse." Chadwick and his colleagues were influenced by the political psychology of Jeremy Bentham's school of utilitarian philosophers, according to which men will always choose the lesser of two evils. Conceding that this is a characteristic of human behaviour, a reduction in the number of paupers could be secured by making conditions under which relief was given "less eligible" than those enjoyed by the least poorly paid workers. In 1835 the Outdoor Relief Prohibitory Order was issued. Henceforth paupers were either to do an honest day's work or submit to the humiliations and rigours of life in the workhouse. Outdoor relief was only to be given, with the consent of two J.P.s, to the aged and infirm.

1834–1909

It would be a gross under-statement to describe the new poor law as unpopular. The proposal that wide powers of supervision should be entrusted to Whitehall provoked the same bitter hostility that had been roused against conciliar government in Tudor and Stuart times. Traditionally central control had been minimal, such government as Englishmen possessed being for the most part in the hands of J.P.s, parish vestries and town councils. That these could not function as efficient organs of government in the newly industrialised society was all too obvious. Equally so were local prejudices against interference by a bureaucracy with dictatorial tendencies controlled by Whitehall. Chadwick and those who thought like him saw clearly that social abuses could only be effectively removed by extending the powers of the State and entrusting their exercise to a technically efficient civil service. The nineteenth century witnessed the beginnings of an administrative revolution which was strongly resisted by men who thought of themselves as fighting a battle for liberty against centralised despotism. It might also be noted that their opposition was reinforced by dislike of paying higher rates to meet the costs of the changes insisted upon by the social reformers. The sphere of poor law administration was the first in which the protagonists of central control sought to achieve their objective. Particularly in the North of England resistance was strong, the assistant commissioners, attempting to reorganise poor law administration, meeting both deep hostility and lack of co-operation from those who controlled the organs of local government.

To the opposition of local gentry, town councillors and well-to-do ratepayers to the Act of 1834 as a threat to the liberties of Englishmen, was added the working class dread of the "workhouse test." Many contemporaries of Chadwick of course considered that the drastic remedies of the Poor Law Commissioners were necessary. The burden on the ratepayers was noticeably lightened. The cessation of parish employment and of the practice of subsidising wages did result in a fall in the numbers of unemployed persons and in a rise in the level of wage rates. Some of the rural unemployed found work in agriculture, and in the months following the passage of the Act assisted migration of others took place to the factory districts. The numbers of unemployed found work in these ways, however, was small. Far more important was the growth of the railway network, the construction and operation of which brought gainful employment of a permanent nature to many thousands.

Conversely, much can be said against the policies of the Poor Law Commissioners. They were framed to solve the problems of pauperism in the rural areas of the southern counties and had little relevance to the far different conditions prevailing in the Midlands and the North. The institution of a "workhouse test" could not and did not solve the problem of unemployment in industrial areas. The numbers of under-employed artisans were too great for all to be housed in what *The Times* dubbed "the new Bastilles," which were bitterly disliked both by handworkers whose skills powerdriven machinery was making obsolete, and by factory workers who formed a pool of the unemployed during trade depressions. Workhouses were administered, as Charles Dickens tells us in *Oliver Twist*, on the principle "that all poor people should have the alternative of being starved by a gradual process in the house, or by a quick one out of it." The separation of married couples, and the housing of their children separately, were practices bitterly resented. In fact, when Dickens was writing *Oliver Twist*, in 1837 and 1838, he was exposing poor law inhumanities, some of which survived into the twentieth century.

Relaxation of the harshness of the rules of 1834 came very slowly and reluctantly. In 1842 outdoor relief for adults was authorised, provided work was done by the recipients. But two years later Boards of Guardians were instructed that outdoor relief to adults was only to be given in very unusual circumstances. A circular in 1869 advised Guardians against laxity in providing it. An Act passed in 1847 permitted workhouse authorities to exempt married couples over 60 from the separation rule, provided their sleeping accommodation was separate from that of other inmates. In 1876 the discretionary powers of Guardians was extended to cover cases where husband or wife was infirm, sick or disabled, but all such cases had to be reported to the Local Government Board.

Workhouses had long been a feature of poor law administration but their existence in all parts of England and Wales dates from 1834. In theory, conditions in them were governed by rules and

SOCIAL REFORM

regulations emanating from the Poor Law Commissioners and their successors, the Poor Law Board (1847) and the Poor Law Department of the Local Government Board (1871). In practice, the interpretation and implementation of the law was left to Boards of Guardians and their salaried officials. Inevitably, therefore, conditions varied considerably, but even the best-regulated workhouses were dreaded and shunned. A circular issued by the Local Government Board in 1886, when very many people were out of work, recognised that there were many unemployed persons who refused to suffer the stigma of pauperism and apply for relief. To assist such the Board recommended Guardians to co-operate with local authorities in arranging relief work at rates of pay lower than current wage levels. Many sensibly decided to take no action.

The poor law system of 1834, with modifications, lasted until 1929. Experience showed, however, that "the principles of 1834" were inadequate to solve the problems of unemployment and destitution. The authors of the Act of 1834 had been primarily concerned with only one aspect of the problems, the able-bodied adult unemployed. Their remedy, "the workhouse test," did not find gainful employment for these. Still less did deterrent methods provide solutions to the problems of other classes of the pauper host, the children, the deserted wives, the widows, the aged, the infirm and the mentally unbalanced. These unfortunately constituted three-quarters of the destitute, for whom during the nineteenth century Boards of Guardians were compelled by force of circumstances to make special arrangements. Pauper children were cared for and educated, unfortunately all too often in institutions or foster homes where the pauper taint was very much in evidence. Workhouse infirmaries were provided for the sick, asylums for the mentally afflicted and dreary shelter in workhouses for the aged and the vagrants. These costly services were supplemented by those provided by the local authorities created by Parliament in the nineteenth century. Yet, despite this very considerable expenditure, there still existed in the early twentieth century an appalling amount of preventible destitution. Beginning with the report in 1909 of a Royal Commission appointed in 1905, successive governments introduced measures which resulted in the final break-up of the Poor Law System, and the creation of new services founded on modern conceptions of social welfare. These will be described in a later chapter.

Chapter XVII

FACTORY AND MINING LEGISLATION

The history of factory legislation is complex and spread over a long period of time because parliaments in the nineteenth century did not enact laws based on a previously thought out, comprehensive code of general principles: instead, there was piecemeal legislation. In the first half of the century restrictions were placed upon the employment of children and women in the coalmining and textile industries. Although many other trades in the second half of the nineteenth century were brought within the scope of factory law, at the beginning of the twentieth century there still remained industries in which the workers lacked legislative protection.

The amount of protection conceded tended to be inadequate, as legislative proposals had to be enacted in the teeth of influential opposition from employers resentful of any interference with the rights of private property. The same arguments were repeated in all Factory Bill debates. The proposed legislation would be injurious to both capital and labour. If the Bill passed, production would fall, costs of production would rise, trade would decrease and workers would become unemployed. Employers derived their profits from the last hour of the working day. Only if there was unregulated competition between men of business, free to use their capital and employees as they chose, would production be maximised and commodities be marketed at the lowest possible prices. In *Hard Times* (1854) Dickens sarcastically commented on the opposition to extension of State power by the employers in Coketown, identified as Preston. "Surely," he wrote, "there never was such fragile china-ware as that of which the millers of Coketown were made.... They were ruined when they were required to send labouring children to school; they were ruined when inspectors considered it doubtful whether they were justified in chopping people up with their machinery; they were utterly undone when it was hinted that perhaps they need not always make quite so much smoke."

In support of a freely competitive or *laisser-faire* policy, were cited what were taught as natural laws by contemporary economists, including the preposterous notion that wages could never rise above a subsistence level. Neither parliamentary interference nor collective action by trade unions could remedy this unfortunate state of affairs. God had ordained the division of mankind into the rich and the poor, the "two nations" of Disraeli's *Sybil*, or perhaps more accurately, the three classes, the upper, middle and lower, described by *Punch* in 1841. Class distinctions were fixed and immutable.

> *The rich man in his castle,*
> *The poor man at its gate,*
> *God made them high or lowly,*
> *And ordered their estate.*

It was fitting that leisure, wealth and happiness should be enjoyed by the upper classes, and inevitable, if unfortunate, that the lower must endure, uncomplainingly, poverty and hard toil. It was assumed that workers were inferior beings, incapable of spending leisure hours profitably. If they were not compelled to work hard, their betters complained, to quote from *Hard Times* again, "these same people would get drunk, take opium or resort to low haunts."

It was commonly argued that it was unfair to pass legislation affecting all manufacturers simply because investigations revealed inhuman treatment of employees in some mills. There were of course enlightened employers, for example, the Strutts of Belper, the Ashtons of Hyde, the Gregs of Styal and David Dale and his son-in-law, Robert Owen. There were also many occupations in which conditions were worse than those in textile mills. Thomas Hood's "Song of the Shirt" published anonymously in *Punch* in 1843 is a vivid reminder of the degrading conditions under which many Victorian women lived.

> *With fingers weary and worn,*
> *With eyelids heavy and red,*
> *A woman sat in unwomanly rags,*
> *Plying her needle and thread—*
> *Stitch—Stitch—Stitch!*
> *In poverty, hunger and dirt,*
> *And still with a voice of dolorous pitch*
> *She sang the Song of the Shirt.*

Hood's needlewoman had to wait many long years before Parliament took notice of her plight. Nevertheless, her existence, and that of many humane millowners, cannot be accepted as a reason for not taking legislative action to abolish inhumanity from the mills of bad employers. It is also worth noting that some of those who campaigned for the abolition of slavery on West Indian plantations were insensitive to the plight of workers at home. The incredible labours of English girls in coal mines, according to Disraeli in *Sybil*, seemed to have escaped the notice of the Society for the Abolition of Negro Slavery. "These worthy gentlemen too," he added, "appear to have been singularly unconscious of the sufferings of the little trappers, which was remarkable, as many of them were in their own employ."

The weak point in the employers' case was that they were too concerned with monetary values and profits. An increasing export trade was assumed to be proof that the nation was prosperous, and the payment of minimum wages for the longest possible working day was considered to be the soundest way to build up a profitable business. But victory in the end was gained by men who thought it right to use legislative authority to solve Carlyle's "condition of England question." There were many good reasons to account for their triumph. The development of trade unions, and after 1867 the growth of the political power of the working classes, made it impossible for governments to adhere permanently to policies based on the idea that self-help was the only sure means of promoting commercial prosperity and social wellbeing. It proved easier to enact factory legislation than, for example, to persuade M.P.s to ameliorate the lot of paupers. Millowners were fewer in numbers and more susceptible than ratepayers to the pressures of public opinion. Hence laws were passed limiting the right of factory owners to employ labour for as many hours as they pleased. Conversely, the complaints of paupers received scant consideration because ameliorative measures would increase poor rates.

Legislative protection was first given to women and children. But it is not easy to determine whether or not from their point of view the factory system was invariably a change for the worse. The evidence is conflicting as it is dependent upon individual experiences. Knowledge of conditions prevailing in private households is hard to obtain, and childhood memories of the aged cannot always be accepted as wholly reliable. No doubt heads of households in the pre-machine age could be the hardest of taskmasters, but some doubtless were kind and considerate. But one generalisation may be made with firm assurance. In the eighteenth and earlier centuries, the productive capacity of hand workers was too low to permit exemption of women and children from participating in producing what was essential to sustain life. That children should earn their livings was therefore a state of affairs our forefathers accepted without question. Power-driven machinery, with all its faults, brought mankind into the Age of Plenty and ultimately made it possible to make child employment illegal.

There was one class of workers many of whom were mercilessly exploited, namely pauper apprentices. The philanthropist, James Hanway (1712–86), sometimes remembered as the first Londoner to carry an umbrella, publicised their sufferings in a pamphlet entitled *The Importance of the Rising Generation*. In the late eighteenth century the investigations of Dr Percival, a Lancashire doctor and a pioneer in sanitary and public health work, persuaded the Lancashire J.P.s to refuse to apprentice pauper children without guarantees that night work was not allowed and the working day was limited to 10 hours. The Greg family, who had a mill at Styal in Cheshire, employed children born in London, Liverpool, Newcastle-under-Lyme and many Cheshire parishes. In 1823 they were employing 91 apprentices and had deservedly earned a reputation for kind and considerate treatment of the children. Two boys prosecuted in Middlesex for deserting "the service of Samuel Greg," testified that they had no complaints to make against their master. They were merely two homesick youngsters who had left him because they wanted to see their mothers. Unfortunately, there is ample evidence to support the opinion that conditions in the apprentice house at Styal were the exception. More usually, the indenturing of pauper children to millowners was a sentence to industrial slavery. Ill-treatment of pauper apprentices was an old story. It was their concentration in large numbers in textile factories which brought its evils and horrors into public view and thereby made parliamentary intervention inevitable.

The Health and Morals of Apprentices Act (1802) was the first of a long series of laws enacted to improve conditions of employment. Its passage was due to the initiative of Sir Robert Peel, a wealthy cotton spinner in Bury, and father of the future Prime Minister. Strictly speaking, the Act of 1802 was not a Factory Act but an amendment to poor law legislation. Apart from the clause making mandatory whitewashing and ventilation of cotton and woollen mills, the Act only applied to pauper children employed in cotton mills. These in future were not to work more than 12 hours a day, and after 1804 were not to be employed in night shifts. They were not to sleep more than two in a bed and were to be given religious instruction, an elementary education and adequate clothing. The sponsors of the Act were well aware of the need for a more comprehensive measure but wisely decided that if they attempted to obtain more, they might achieve nothing. The enforcement of the Act was entrusted to J.P.s and parish overseers. These, through neglect and ignorance, made it a dead letter in most districts.

After 1802, with the increasing use of steam power, factories were built in urban centres, "free labour children" being employed, that is children who lived with their parents. Millowners naturally preferred such children to parish apprentices who, if employers carried out their moral and statutory obligations, had to be housed, fed and clothed at considerable expense and trouble. As a result of the initiative of Robert Owen and Sir Robert Peel, the first true factory Act was passed in 1819. In the New Lanark Mills, Owen had set an example by not employing children under 10 years of age, and limiting the working day to 10 hours. But a committee of enquiry revealed that in many mills children of 7 years of age were working 14 hours a day, and were being subjected to brutal ill-treatment. Despite these revelations, owing to the submission of employers that child labour was essential to the profitable functioning of the cotton industry, the draft legislation of Peel and Owen was not fully enacted. Nevertheless, though limited in scope, the Act of 1819 was a significant improvement on that of 1802. It protected all children in cotton mills. Child labour under 9 was made illegal, and a 12-hour day was fixed as the maximum for young persons under 16 years of age. There was, however, no certainty that effective action would be taken in the courts of law against errant millowners, as enforcement of the law was entrusted to J.P.s. Further, until after the passage in 1836 of an Act making compulsory the registration of births and deaths, the true age of children was hard to prove. Slight amendments to the law were made by Acts passed in 1825 and 1831, still applying only to cotton mills. Sir John Hobhouse's Act (1825) shortened the working day for workers under 16 to nine hours. The Act of 1831 revised the age limit for the 12 hours working day to 18 and permitted only workers over 21 years of age to be employed on night shifts.

When the factory form of industrial organisation appeared in other textile occupations, the same abuses became manifest which had provoked parliamentary interference in the affairs of Lancashire cotton millowners. Coincident in time with the agitation for the reform of the parliamentary franchise, a campaign was started in Lancashire and Yorkshire for the passage of a Ten Hours Bill. In Lancashire, John Doherty, the Secretary of the Cotton Spinners Union, was a prominent figure, but the leaders for the most part came, not from among the ranks of illiterate working men, but from the middle and upper classes. A minority of enlightened millowners, including a wealthy Todmorden cotton spinner, John Fielden, and John Wood, a leading worsted spinner in Bradford, actively supported the movement and subscribed lavishly to finance it. It was Wood who in 1830 first interested the "Factory King," Richard Oastler (1789–1861), in the evils of child employment. Oastler, a Tory in politics, was the land agent on the Fixby estates near

Huddersfield, of the Thornhill family. That Oastler was a Tory is not without significance. The passage of factory laws can in part be attributed to the conflict between Whig industrialists and Tory landowners, the latter supporting factory reform in retaliation against the parliamentary reform and free trade policies of the former. A fiery orator, tall, commanding in appearance, Oastler, with reckless disregard for personal consequences, became the leader of the Ten Hours Movement in the West Riding. His rewards were the loss of his stewardship and imprisonment in the Fleet Prison for debt, against which can be set the regard in which he was held by many thousands of working class Yorkshire folk, symbolised by the erection in 1869 of a statue to his memory in Bradford. Worth recalling is the great rally Oastler addressed on 24th April 1832, on York Racecourse, attended by thousands of men, women and children, who in atrocious weather had walked to York from all parts of the West Riding. Others prominent in the mass agitation which followed Oastler's revelations in the *Leeds Mercury* were the Vicar of Bradford, the Rev. G. S. Bull, and the fiery Wesleyan minister and Chartist leader, the Rev. J. R. Stephens. In Lancashire, leading parts were played by a Manchester editor, George Condy, and by the author of a history of the movement, Philip Grant.

The factory reform spokesman in Parliament was Michael Sadler, M.P. for Newark, who in 1831 introduced a Ten Hours Bill. The Bill was dropped after its second reading, but the House of Commons agreed to the appointment of a select committee under Sadler's chairmanship to investigate child employment in factories. The evidence collected by the Sadler Committee, from the workers, showed that Oastler had not exaggerated when he wrote in the *Leeds Mercury* that thousands of "the miserable inhabitants of Yorkshire towns are this very moment existing in a state of slavery." Children from 6 years of age were working, sometimes 16 or even 20 hours a day, in steamy, overheated mills for two or three shillings a week. When they were overtaken by fatigue, brutal overlookers used the strap, harsh blows and cold water to keep the children on their feet. As safety precautions did not exist, many were maimed for life by dangerous machinery.

The publication of the Report of the Sadler Committee ended its chairman's connection with the factory reform movement. In the general election of 1832, as Sadler was defeated at Leeds by Macaulay, he was replaced as the parliamentary spokesman of the factory operatives by Lord Ashley, better known as the seventh Earl of Shaftesbury (1801-85). A Tory in politics, Shaftesbury's religious beliefs were those known in Victorian England as Evangelicalism, whose adherents combined literal belief in the Bible with unrelenting opposition to the ritualistic and sacramental form of Christianity inspired by the Church Tractarian Movement led by John Keble, Edward Pusey and the future Cardinal Newman. Evangelical Christianity, a religious outlook shared by Anglicans and nonconformists, with its insistence on high standards of moral conduct, inspired the anti-slavery crusade and movements to abolish the social evils of Victorian society. When he was approached by the Rev. G. S. Bull to take Sadler's place, Shaftesbury was ignorant of the state of affairs in textile mills. Acquaintance with the facts began for him a half century of public service directed towards improving conditions in factories and coal-mines, and in the fields of public health, housing and education. To him also was due the reform of the lunacy laws and the abolition of the scandals associated with the employment of boy chimney sweeps.

When Shaftesbury agreed to take Sadler's place, it was on the strict understanding that factory reform should be restricted to limiting the working hours of children and young persons, to be achieved by constitutional and lawful means. Although active in the field of social work, Shaftesbury's aristocratic sympathies and dread of political democracy made him an opponent of many worthy causes, for example, parliamentary reform, trade unionism, legislative interference with wages and capital and agrarian reform in Ireland. The evangelical conflict with High Church ritualism absorbed much of his time. After the passage of the Ten Hours Act in 1847 he never attempted to organise a political movement, based on mass support, dedicated to using the power of the State to remove the scandals and abuses which defaced Victorian industrial society. Rather, he was a philanthropist, impelled by religious conviction to help particular groups of unfortunates, chimney boys, street arabs and lunatics. Deservedly, to quote the inscription on the monument erected to his memory, "by serving his fellow men," he left behind "a name to be by them very gratefully remembered."

In the first Parliament elected after the 1832 franchise reform, Shaftesbury, then Lord Ashley, introduced a Bill to forbid employment of children under 9 and to limit the hours of those under 18 to 10 a day. The Government countered by setting up a Royal Commission. The Commissioners—Edwin Chadwick, the economist Thomas Tooke and Dr Southwood Smith, the public health reformer —reported that legislation as drastic as that proposed by Ashley would bankrupt millowners. "Now it was admitted," Cobbett sarcastically commented during the subsequent debates, "that our great stay and bulwark is to be found in 30,000 little girls." The consciences of M.P.s were stilled by statements in the report, attributed to doctors and even to young persons themselves, that long hours of labour were not harmful to health. Ashley's Bill was therefore dropped in favour of one introduced on behalf of the Government by Lord Althorp. Althorp's Bill, which became the Factory Act of 1833, applied to all textile factories. The employment of children under 9 was prohibited except in silk mills, and the working hours of young persons under 18 were limited to 12 a day and 69 a week. After 1834, no one under 13 was to be employed more than 9 hours a day and 48 a week. Night work was made illegal for all under 18 and children under 13 were to attend school for at least 2 hours a day. But the most important clause in the Act was that which provided for the appointment of four full-time inspectors.

The Act of 1833 both exceeded the intentions of its promoters and disappointed the workers. The appointment of central government officials to enforce factory legislation was to have far-reaching consequences. The inspectors were empowered to enter factory buildings, collect information and fine offenders. There was now an external authority, which proved to be free from local bias and influence, whose reports were an authoritative source of information upon which future legislation could be based. At first, however, the law was not easy to enforce. The shift system of employment made it difficult to determine how many hours protected persons worked. Until birth registration became compulsory in 1837 ages could not be checked. The educational clauses were largely ignored. In some mills children were packed in coal-holes and taught by illiterates, incapable even of writing their own names. The agitation for more drastic reforms therefore continued. Fielden planned a general strike which failed, except in Oldham, where the workers stayed away from work for one week. Ten Hours Bills introduced in 1836, 1838 and 1839 were all rejected.

Factory reform became a major issue in the 1841 election won by Peel's Tories. In office, however, the Tories were as obstructive as the Whigs had been. Meanwhile, industrial depression in the early 1840s was responsible for acute distress in the industrial areas. Exasperated, starving workers in Lancashire removed the plugs from mill boilers. Those who agitated for factory reform made common cause with Feargus O'Connor's Chartists, troops having to be used in the summer of 1842 to quell rioting in Lancashire and Cheshire. But legislative action was difficult to avoid after the publication of the Reports of the Second Children's Employment Commission which, since 1840, had been enquiring into the conditions women and children worked under in mines and factories. The Commissioners, Tooke, Southwood Smith and two factory inspectors Leonard Horner and R. J. Saunders, published a first report in May 1842, revealing in words and pictures to a horrified public, working conditions in coal-mines. Underground, in darkness and solitude, except in North Staffordshire, 4- and 5-year-old children, boys and girls known as "trappers," were responsible for the functioning of the ventilation system. Spending hours in darkness and solitude, they had, to quote from Disraeli's *Sybil*, to "endure that punishment which philosophical philanthropy has invented for the direst criminals, and which those criminals deem more terrible than death." In Scotland, South Wales, Yorkshire, Cheshire and Lancashire, older children of both sexes, and women, pushed coal tubs through low, narrow passages or pumped water. In Scotland, women and children carried coal up steep ladders. Particularly inhuman was the treatment of workhouse apprentices in South Staffordshire, Lancashire and the West Riding, hours of labour being 12 hours a day and sometimes more.

The Bill Ashley introduced to deal with these evils passed the Commons, but its rejection was moved in the Lords by the Durham colliery owner, Lord Londonderry. "I conceive my colliers," he had on another occasion claimed, "were really attached to my family." The Report, he told their lordships, with its "disgusting pictorial illustrations," conveyed a false picture of conditions in coal-mines. With amendments, however, the Bill was subsequently enacted as the Mines Act of 1842, the most drastic legislative interference hitherto with industry in the nineteenth century. The Act laid down regulations for the prevention of accidents, but its most significant clauses were those prohibiting the employment underground of women, and of children under 10 years of age. The first inspector of mines (H. Seymour Tremenheere) was appointed on 28th November 1843. From 1844 onwards he made annual reports on the enforcement of the Act of 1842 which came into force on 1st March 1843.

The Act of 1842 was followed by legislation compelling colliery owners to obey safety rules. In an explosion in 1812 at Felling Colliery, near Gateshead, 92 men and boys were killed. The Vicar of Felling, the Rev. John Hodgson, braved the displeasure of the owners by publishing an account of the tragedy which led to the formation of the Sunderland Society to study its causes. But more than a generation elapsed before the Felling and other comparable disasters provoked the authorities into taking steps to reduce the death rate in mines. The first safety law was the sequel to a dreadful explosion in September 1844 at Haswell Colliery in Durham. W. P. Roberts, the Bristol solicitor, known in his day as "the Miner's Attorney," pressed Sir Robert Peel, the Prime Minister, to have the disaster scientifically investigated. A report, drawn up by Sir Charles Lyell, the leading geologist of the time, and the eminent physicist, Michael Faraday, was supplemented by further investigations in

1845 and 1849. But it was not until 1850, in the teeth of bitter opposition by colliery owners, that the first safety law, the Mines Regulation Act, was passed. As Lord Londonderry had publicly stated that he would not allow inspectors to enter his mines, a clause was inserted in the Act giving government inspectors statutory rights to enter and leave mines freely.

Women, it is worth noting, were forbidden to work underground two years before there was legislative interference with their employment in textile factories. By the Factory Act of 1844, although the age for the employment of children in textile mills was reduced from nine to eight, the half-time system was introduced. Children under 13 were to attend school 3 hours a day and their daily hours of labour were reduced to $6\frac{1}{2}$. The 12-hour day was retained as the legal maximum for young persons, but henceforth this was to apply to women also. Realising that there was no hope that Parliament could be persuaded to restrict the hours of labour of adult males, the factory reformers decided to concentrate on obtaining concessions for women and young persons. As Ashley was not returned as an M.P. in 1846, it was Fielden who introduced the Bill which was enacted as the Ten Hours Act in 1847. The Bill, which was passed with relative ease, at a time of acute trade depression, limited the hours of labour of women and young persons to 58 a week.

The Act of 1847 proved difficult to enforce, as Parliament had not laid down precisely the hours between which "protected persons" might be employed. Millowners, in order to run their machinery for more than 10 hours a day, introduced the relay system, under which women and young persons were employed in shifts, the intervals between which were too short to permit of them leaving the mill premises. This was prevented in 1850 by an Act fixing a normal working day, for women and young persons, between 6 a.m. and 6 p.m., or between 7 a.m. and 7 p.m. One and a half hours were allowed for meals, and on Saturdays work was to cease at 2 p.m. In 1853 the normal working day principle was extended to cover children. By 1853, therefore, a uniform working day had been laid down for all protected persons in textile mills.

No significant reduction of the legal length of the working day, fixed in 1847, was made until 1937. The Factories Act of 1937 provided that the hours worked by women and young persons were not to exceed nine in a day and 48 in a week. In the intervening years, the chief changes in factory law were extensions of the principles of factory legislation to industries other than textiles. These changes were made partly by statutes and partly by rules, regulations and orders issued by the Secretary of State for Home Affairs. The second report of the 1840 Children's Employment Commission (1843) revealed that the textiles and coal industries were not the only ones in which child labour was mercilessly exploited. Conditions were even worse in the calico printing, pottery, hosiery, needles, nail and tobacco trades. With considerable difficulty, Ashley in 1845 persuaded Parliament to forbid the employment of children under 8 in calico printing, and to make night work illegal for children and women. Factory regulations were applied to bleach and dyeworks in 1860, and to lace factories in 1861, by which date many influential politicians, among them Gladstone and Sir James Graham, had recanted their earlier opinion that factory legislation was unwise.

The need for further legislation was made plain by the Report of the Third Children's Employment Commission appointed in 1861. As a result of its findings an Act passed in 1864 extended factory regulations to pottery, lucifer matches, fustian cutting and other trades. Special regulations were drawn up governing dangerous occupations such as lucifer match making, in which workers were liable to suffer from "phossy jaw." In 1866 local authorities were empowered to enforce sanitary regulations in factories and workshops not subject to factory regulations. Two important Acts were passed during the Derby–Disraeli ministry in 1867. The first, the Factory Acts Extension Act, applied factory regulations to premises in which 50 or more persons were employed in a manufacturing process. Special rules were drawn up for dangerous trades, and it was made illegal to employ women and children in some processes. Unfortunately, a long list of exemptions reduced considerably the effectiveness of the Act. The second Act, the Workshops Regulation Act, applied to all premises where less than 50 persons were employed in a manufacturing process. In these, factory regulations were to be enforced with two significant differences. Firstly, earlier and later times for commencing and ending the working day were allowed, creating thereby the same difficulties in enforcing the rules which had been experienced in textile factories before the 1850 abolition of the relay system. Secondly, administration was entrusted to local authorities who proved to be remiss in enforcing the law. Fortunately, in 1871, administration of that part of the Act concerned with hours of labour was transferred to Home Office inspectors.

Proposals for further reductions in the length of the legal working day were made soon after the passage of the Ten Hours Act in 1847. Experience had shown to be false prophecies of industrial disaster and of inevitable falls in production and wages earned. On the contrary, less overworked operatives, tending machines running at higher speeds, were able to produce more at lower labour costs, and to earn higher wages. Similarly, the fears of women workers proved to be groundless. Laws reducing their working day, which did not apply to adult males, did not result in men workers being offered women's jobs. But as it was still hopeless to try to persuade Parliament to limit the legal working day of adult males, the demand for a shorter working day continued to be made on behalf of women only. In 1872 the Factory Acts Reform Association was formed to organise propaganda for a 54-hour week in textile factories. A Home Office investigation in 1873 was followed by the introduction of a Bill to reduce the length of the working day. This, the Factories (Health of Women) Bill, was rejected by the Liberals. In the following year, 1874, Disraeli's Tory ministry replaced that of Gladstone, and the Lancashire banker, Richard Assheton Cross, became Home Secretary.

The achievements of Cross in the field of social reform were such that in Shaftesbury's opinion, "two millions of people of this country would bless the day" he became Home Secretary. His first Act, that of 1874, applied to textile mills only. The 12-hour working day was retained, but the age for commencing work was raised to 9, and to 10 in the following year. In 1875 the abominations associated with the employment of boy chimney sweeps at last ended. Jonas Hanway in 1773, Dickens in *Oliver Twist* and Charles Kingsley in *Water Babies* had exposed the scandals associated with the trade, but an Act passed in 1840 had proved ineffective, although some masters were found guilty of manslaughter. For many years Shaftesbury had campaigned on behalf of the boys, but without success until 1875, when he introduced the Bill which empowered the police to take court proceedings against offenders.

As the Cross Act of 1874 was passed at a time when the desirability of State regulation of industrial conditions was coming to be more widely acceptable, the practice of dealing separately and in piecemeal fashion with a limited number of industries came to be thought of as unsatisfactory. There was an urgent need to codify the law and to treat all industries with some degree of uniformity. A Consolidation Commission was therefore appointed in 1876 whose recommendations were given statutory force in 1878 by the Factory and Workshops Act. The Act of 1878, an impressive legislative achievement, replaced sixteen Factory Acts. The unreal 1867 distinction between factories and workshops was abandoned. Instead, factories were defined as places in which power was used and workshops as places in which manufacturing was performed by manual labour. Women were not to work more than $56\frac{1}{2}$ hours a week in textile factories, and not more than 60 in other establishments. Child labour was prohibited under 10 years of age. Regulations were laid down governing such matters as ventilation, safety and arrangements for meals. Unfortunately, the Act did not provide protection for all wage earners. Workshops in which adult males only were employed were outside the scope of the Act. In workshops where only women were employed, and in places where work was carried on in private houses, hours of labour could fall between 6 a.m. and 9 p.m.

The neglect to regulate conditions of employment for the large number of workers paid starvation wages, and working in small workshops in which trade unionism had not found a footing, is a major defect of the Act of 1878. The need for further legislative action was made plain by the Report of the House of Lords Committee on the Sweating Systems (1889), Charles Booth's researches on *The Life and Labour of the People of London* (1886-93) and the Report of the Labour Commission (1894). The Factory and Workshop Act (1891) applied sanitary regulations to premises in which adult males only were employed, empowered the Home Secretary to draw up special regulations for dangerous occupations, and raised the employment age to 11, subsequently raised to 12 in 1901 and to 14 in 1920. Further Factory Acts were passed in 1895 and 1901. The Factory and Workshop Consolidation Act of 1901, which codified and amended previous legislation, remained in force until the enactment of the Factories Act of 1937.

Between 1901 and 1937 considerable progress was made in protecting workers in industries in which there are major risks to health and safety. The Notice of Accidents Act, for example, was passed in 1906 and the White Phosphorous Matches Protection Act in 1908. Medical inspection, research and the enforcement of Home Office regulations have markedly reduced the numbers of victims of lead poisoning, anthrax, silicosis and other industrial diseases. Legislation has also been passed dealing with occupations previously unregulated, for example, laundries in 1895 and 1907, and retail shops in 1892 and 1911.

The scope of protective legislation was widened considerably during the twentieth century. As early as 1831 the Truck Act forbade payment of wages in kind, but its effective enforcement had to wait until trade unions had grown strong, and mines and factory inspectors in 1887 were given powers to prosecute offenders. A noteworthy precedent was created by the passage of the Trade Boards Act in 1909, the first attempt by the State in modern times to devise machinery to raise the wages of very poorly-paid workers. Trade Boards had existed in New Zealand since 1894 and in Victoria, Australia, since 1894. The Act of 1909 was preceded by the *Daily News* exhibition in 1906 at Queens Hall, depicting the evils of the sweating system, and by the report in 1908 of the Select Committee on Homework. The Trade Boards were given statutory powers to fix wages and determine working conditions in four trades, tailoring, box-making, lace-making and chain-making. Food-preserving, sweet-, shirt- and hollow-ware-making were added in 1913. Considerable extensions were made in subsequent years, the Trade Boards being renamed Wages Councils in 1945. The precedent created in 1909 was followed in the Coal Mines Minimum Wage Act (1912) and the Agricultural Wages Act (1924).

The results of factory legislation have been good, the working population of modern Britain being healthier, and enjoying more leisure time than any previous generation. The last important comprehensive measure, the Factories Act of 1937, deals with a much wider range of industries than its predecessors and confers extensive powers on the Home Secretary. Much of the Act is concerned with simplifying, consolidating and amending previous legislation, but it does, in one respect, contain important innovations, namely, the clauses dealing with welfare. Part III of the Act makes obligatory the provision in all factories of certain amenities, such as accommodation for clothing, first aid, ambulance and rest rooms, facilities for sitting for the use of all female workers, and arrangements for preparing and taking meals. The number of workers given legislative protection was increased from about $5\frac{1}{2}$ to 7 millions. The Act, however, did not affect the large number of persons employed in the one million shops and offices in Great Britain, in more than half of which inspectors found inadequate heating, no running hot water, poor lavatory accommodation, crumbling stairs, dirty walls and ceilings, broken washbasins and poor lighting. In shops, many hundreds of unprotected bacon slicers were seen. Solicitors' offices were listed as among the worst, the inspectors reporting that clerks were discovered working under dimly-lit staircases, handling files smothered in dust. Obviously, the Offices, Shops and Railway Premises Act of 1963, which was designed to enforce minimum standards in such premises, was long overdue.

Chapter XVIII

PUBLIC HEALTH AND HOUSING

Public Health

In 1865 the City of Bristol appointed its first Medical Officer of Health at a salary of £200 a year. He faced a formidable task. The average age at death of Bristolians was 32, the death rate was 23 per thousand and the infant mortality rate was 16. His biggest problem was to control the frequent epidemics of cholera, smallpox, typhoid and scarlet fever. Nowadays, citizens of Bristol can expect to live to 70, and infectious diseases are at their lowest ebb. A century of public health services explains why modern Bristol, like other urban centres, is a much healthier city than it had been in mid-Victorian times.

In 1800 most people lived in a rural environment. As urbanisation proceeded at a very rapid rate, by 1900 one-third of the population of England was living and working in the great conurbations located around London, Manchester, Liverpool, Leeds, Birmingham and Tyneside. Rapidity of growth partially explains why town planning was conspicuous by its absence. Speculators bought or leased land, on which jerry-built houses were erected, crowded as close together as the builders' ingenuity could devise. Outside London, two- or three-roomed back-to-back houses were common, built round courtyards connected with the street by a narrow entry, or alternatively, dreary streets containing houses of identical design were built.

In most areas no public water authority existed. In Huddersfield, until 1828, the water supply was that constructed by the lord of the manor in 1743. Water was pumped from the River Colne, through pipes made of tree trunks pierced by a $3\frac{1}{2}$-inch bore, but the engine used was so feeble that the higher parts of the town were inadequately supplied. In Halifax, some of the inhabitants had to travel half a mile for water which was so scarce that people were known to steal it. In some places water had to be purchased from carriers. Fortunate indeed were householders with an interior supply. More usually, an outside tap or pump served several dwellings, or rain water was collected in wooden tubs. All too often, the supply was contaminated, as when an outside privy shared by several families emptied into a cesspool from which filth seeped into the well. In 1850, 640,000 Londoners living in 80,000 houses were without adequate supplies, and women in Bermondsey were drawing water from "a foul foetid ditch, its banks covered with a compound of mud and filth and with offal and carrion—the water to be used for every purpose."

Despite laws and ordinances the paving of streets was far from being tolerably efficient. Sewers were defective or non-existent. In London water closets came gradually into use after 1800, discharging into cesspools. When later it became the practice to discharge sewage through street drains into the Thames, the river, the main source of London's water supply, became dangerously impure. In many towns fly-invested refuse from kitchens and privies littered muddy highways, courtyards and alleys, removed sometimes by pauper labour or for sale as manure by the "night soil" men. In Greenock in 1840, reputed to be dirtier than other Scottish towns, a hundred cubic feet of manure was piled up in the centre of the town, while the open sewers of Royal Windsor were at least as bad as anything to be found in the newly industrialised North, and possibly worse. At any rate Yorkshire housewives were house proud, visitors in 1845 commenting on their constant battle "for decency and cleanliness amidst adverse circumstances ... the steps made white with the hearthstone, when the first persons coming in to the house must spoil their labours, with the mud from the street kept filthy by neglect of pauper scavenging."

Before private enterprise built gas works, oil lamps were in use for street illumination. Indoors, the inhabitants were dependent at night upon costly ill-made candles or dangerous portable lamps. Oil lamps were installed in the City of London from 1736, and gas lighting from 1807. The latter method of illumination spread into the provinces, the first gas works in Huddersfield, for example, opened in 1842, providing dim illumination only in a very limited number of main streets.

Burial grounds were a serious menace to health. Rain falling over graveyards percolated into wells from which the living drew water. Highgate cemetery drained into a well in Clerkenwell. Dickens, in *Bleak House* describes an early Victorian graveyard as "a beastly scrap of ground which a Turk would reject as a savage abomination, and a Caffre would shudder at." Ancient churchyards had become grossly inadequate for now populous parishes. There were only 1½ acres for Whitechapel's 30,000 people, and 3½ acres for the 75,000 inhabitants of Bethnal Green. The 1¼ acres of St Margarets, Westminster, was denounced by a parliamentary committee as "a place which could not be kept up, affecting the cellars of neighbouring houses." Here, as elsewhere, the grave diggers, a drunken, savage crew, suffered illness and sudden death. The soil of the Green Ground, Portugal Street, belonging to the parish of St Clement Danes, was described in 1839 as "absolutely saturated with human putrescence." Conditions were even worse in the private burial grounds and charnel houses run for profit. Enon Chapel, in Clements Lane off the Strand, was opened in 1822. The upper part of the building was used for public worship, the cellar as a burial ground. Over 10,000 bodies were deposited there in sixteen years, the reverend proprietor receiving over £950 between 1822 and 1828. As the cellar filled he made room for more by putting surplus bodies down a sewer, burning the coffin wood on his household fires.

Few towns possessed parks or open spaces. Preston had a park and Newcastle upon Tyne was fortunate, and still is, in having within its boundaries a very large open space, the Town Moor. But Manchester folk in 1833 had to confine their walking to turnpike roads. Round Halifax, in the closing decades of the eighteenth century, it was possible to roam for miles across unspoilt, open country. By the early nineteenth century, access was barred by stone walls, travellers being restricted to field paths and highways. In 1840, Fairweather Green, near Bradford, was enclosed, the plea that it was the only open space available for the recreative activities of 120,000 people being dismissed with laughter in the House of Commons. Near London, many commons, open spaces and heaths were lost. Epping Forest was reduced to 3000 acres, Finchley Common vanished and Hainault Forest was destroyed. Fortunately, however, much was saved, including some royal property, Hyde Park, St James's Park, Green Park and Kensington Gardens.

Illiterate, brutalised by squalor, ignorance and vice, the inhabitants of urban slums were much less law-abiding than their twentieth-century descendants. Young ruffians, larrikins and hooligans, armed with knives and guns, waged gang warfare and molested respectable folk with impunity. In *Oliver Twist* Dickens described Field Lane, Clerkenwell, "the emporium of petty larceny," where wares snatched by pickpockets were displayed for sale. There were large areas in London, labyrinths of narrow courts and alleys which officers of the law dared not patrol except as members of a posse. In Soho, Drury Lane, Whitechapel, St Giles, parts of Westminster, and in other metropolitan areas scores of thousands lived in depraved, squalid misery. Fortunately, our Victorian forefathers, needing space for great public works such as the High Courts of Justice, and main line railway termini, pulled down many of these monuments of past human degradation.

The preservation of law and order was made difficult by the lack of an organised police force. In Huddersfield down to 1820 the governing body of the town, the Court Leet, appointed a Chief Constable. One holder of the office, on the frequent occasions when midnight rioting took place, gave the combatants time to exhaust their energies before venturing into the streets to assert his authority. As the Chief Constable was evidently not carrying out his duties satisfactorily, the Huddersfield Vestry in 1816 appointed an Assistant Constable who was instructed in the following year "to visit the public houses frequently." There was certainly need for him to do so. In 1825 pressure by agricultural interests induced Parliament to relax restrictions on the issue of liquor licences. By the Beer Act of 1830 a licence to sell alcoholic beverages could be obtained by any ratepayer on payment of two guineas. According to Sydney Smith, the clerical wit and first editor of the *Edinburgh Review*, 75,000 licences were taken out in 1830. "The new bill has begun its operations," Smith wrote, "Everyone's drunk.... The sovereign people are in a beastly state." Such alarming consequences led to the imposition of restrictions on granting licences in 1834 and to the foundation in 1835 of the British Association for the Promotion of Temperance.

Insanitary conditions inevitably led to outbreaks of diseases of epidemic proportions. There were cholera epidemics in London in 1832, 1849, 1854, 1866 and 1871. In 1849 cholera caused the deaths of 13,161 persons in London alone, and in 1866 of 5548. But sanitary shortcomings were not wholly due to industrialisation. Since Roman times towns had always been insanitary places. The slums of Bath, not a factory town, were notoriously bad. A lady diarist in 1781 described Ipswich as "altogether a most melancholy place," with "dreadful narrow streets" and "poor looking old houses." Bristol, in Queen Anne's reign, had possibly 50,000 inhabitants, many living in squalid hovels, shared sometimes with domestic animals. Constantly exposed to the onset of disease, the citizens of pre-industrial towns and cities lived in an environment made unpleasant by strong offensive smells. Industrialisation simply made worse long-existing evils and increased the filth, congestion and risk of infection.

Conditions in rural areas were little better and often worse. Overcrowding, which had always existed, was increased by the destruction of cottages by landlords concerned to keep poor rates low. The notion that eighteenth-century village folk inhabited picturesque dwellings set in charming locations is contradicted by contemporary accounts of rural housing. In some districts, eighteenth- and early nineteenth-century landowners built improved houses, but the bulk of the rural population lived in insanitary, damp, ill-constructed hovels, shared in some parts of the country with farm animals. Where stone and brick were costly, cob, clay mixed with straw, was used to build cottages consisting of one or two small rooms, with earthen floors. Many turf hovels on village commons, inhabited by squatters, were swept away by enclosures. Squalid dwellings were to be found in all parts of the country, rural housing conditions tending to be worse in the south-western and northern counties, and in Wales and Scotland. The truth is, many of the new stone-built houses in the industrial areas provided factory workers with better living conditions than those available to most farm workers.

Granted that living conditions for a very large proportion of the population were intolerable, why, we may well ask, were improvements so slow in coming? It would be unfair to explain the delay as being wholly due to the *laisser-faire* prejudices prevalent in Whitehall. Even when the consequences of urban social abuses made government action imperative, contemporary technical knowledge and financial resources were insufficient to provide adequate remedies. The knowledge and experience of modern sanitary engineers, and mass production methods of making cast-iron drainage pipes, were not available in the first half of the nineteenth century. The massive engineering projects, needed to provide immense supplies of purified water and to dispose of personal and industrial wastes, would have been costly undertakings, involving financial and technical problems that did not admit easy solutions. Further, their necessity, as the surest means of reducing the appalling mortality rates, was not understood until medicine and surgery had been revolutionised by researches into the nature and habits of bacteria.

Our early forefathers thought of diseases and epidemics as manifestations of divine wrath, or of demoniac agencies, but from the thirteenth century attempts were made to find natural explanations. The fourteenth-century Black Death, for example, was attributed to planetary motions. The solutions offered were wrong, but at least natural instead of supernatural explanations were being sought for. The notion that there was an intimate connection between pestilences and impure air naturally suggested itself to the inhabitants of urban communities, who had to endure nauseating stenches arising from the piles of refuse that littered streets, courtyards and alley ways. But although scientifically untrue, the theory was valuable in as much as it roused public opinion to the need for cleansing highways and preventing pollution of water supplies.

In 1854 John Snow demonstrated that the cholera outbreak in London during that year could be traced to the contamination of water supplies by human excreta. The germ theory of disease was subsequently firmly established by the researches of Louis Pasteur (1822–95) and emphasised by the lecture in 1870 at the Royal Institution delivered by Professor John Tyndall (1820–93) on "Dust and Disease." In 1865, the Quaker, Joseph Lister (1827–1912), the first member of the medical profession to be raised to the peerage, was inspired by Pasteur's paper, "Researches on Putrefaction," to introduce antiseptic techniques to the operating theatre. Mankind also owes an incalculable debt to Sir James Young Simpson (1811–70) whose advocacy of chloroform instead of ether as an anaesthetic banished the agonising pains associated with the use of surgeons' instruments. Improvements in the microscope led to further advances in biological and medical knowledge, notably Sir Patrick Manson's researches into the causes of elephantiasis (1877), and the discovery by Sir Donald Ross (1895) that mosquitos were the agency through which micro-organisms that caused malaria were spread. Before the end of the nineteenth century such diseases as cholera, typhus, typhoid, dysentery and diphtheria had been brought under control. To this list may be added smallpox, which, before Edward Jenner's (1749–1823) pioneering work on vaccination at the end of the eighteenth century, had killed or disfigured countless multitudes.

The new knowledge made possible advances in preventive medicine once the initial hostility of orthodox members of the medical profession had been overcome. Simpson, for example, encountered opposition to the use of chloroform to relieve pain in childbirth, but he himself dismissed Lister's germs as non-existent. But in addition to the conservative prejudices of doctors, a major obstacle in the way of public health reform was the lack of central and local government agencies with adequate powers to cope with insanitary problems. Two reforms were needed, firstly, the passage of public health and housing legislation, and secondly, the creation of local government authorities with a sufficient sense of social responsibility to enforce it. When George IV died in 1830 there was no central department of government specifically entrusted with the duty of initiating and superintending sanitary reform. Local administration was substantially as it had been under the Tudors. The smallest unit of local government, the parish, was primarily concerned with poor relief and the maintenance of roads. The counties were administered by J.P.s meeting in Quarter Sessions, and the boroughs by councils deriving their authority from ancient charters. The boroughs were dominated by corrupt oligarchies and, even if men of public spirit had sat on their councils, the powers they possessed were insufficient to ensure that public monies would be made available for lighting and paving streets, disposing of refuse and providing water. In many, populations had expanded beyond the original town limits, into areas where the borough council had no jurisdiction. The new urban communities, for their part, were not incorporated, being still subject to the authority of parish or manor. There were, however, a few lords of manors sufficiently public spirited, including the Earl of Stamford at Ashton-under-Lyne and the Duke of Norfolk at Glossop, to insist on town planning regulations.

In the new urban communities the need for more extensive powers was met by the passage of special Acts of Parliament. Huddersfield may be cited as an example. Until 1820 the governing body was the manorial Court Leet, which appointed a chief constable, a pinder, a bellman and a river conservancy officer, the latter having the duty of removing from local streams dead dogs, cats and vermin. In the early nineteenth century, the lord of the manor, Sir John Ramsden, was an enlightened landlord who saw that wide streets and sound houses were built, but as the town grew complaints were made that not all streets were "properly cleansed but are subject to vermin." In 1820, therefore, the Huddersfield Lighting and Watching Act was passed, putting the town under the control of a virtually self-elected body of well-to-do Commissioners. In 1848 the Huddersfield Improvement Act was passed under which the town was to be administered by a Board of Improvement Commissioners elected by the wealthier residents. But the powers of the Board to provide water, effective drainage and sewerage, and undertake road construction and maintenance, were hampered by the existence in the town of eleven local boards, each having separate and independent jurisdictions, a state of affairs that lasted until a charter of incorporation was granted in 1868.

The existence of a medley of authorities with conflicting jurisdictions was widespread. In the London area there were seven Boards of Commissioners of Sewers within 10 miles of the General Post Office. There was no uniformity or co-ordination in the way they carried out their duties, while important streets like Cheapside and Leadenhall Street had cesspools, not sewers. It was not until 1848 that an Act was passed creating the Consolidated Commission of Sewers with jurisdiction over an area 12 miles from St Paul's Cathedral, excluding the City of London.

The Municipal Corporations Act of 1835 abolished the charters of 183 ancient boroughs, replacing them with a uniform type of administration, a council consisting of a mayor, aldermen and councillors, the councillors elected by citizens who had paid poor-rates for three years. Several small boroughs retained their ancient charters until 1883, after which date the City of London remained as the only corporation of the ancient type. But the Act of 1835 did little to revolutionise urban administration. No change was made in boundaries to take account of urban expansion and such public powers as they possessed were permissive, not mandatory. In practice borough councillors were reluctant to increase rate demands to finance drainage, sewerage and water supplies undertakings. Newcastle ratepayers, Lord Palmerston discovered when he was Home Secretary, thought that a sixpenny increase in the rates was too high a price to pay to remove the dangers of infection to which their families and fellow citizens were exposed. But there were urban areas in which local initiative was responsible for improvement. A window in Liverpool Cathedral commemorates Mrs Kitty Wilkinson, who provided clothes washing facilities in her home for her neighbours, her public spirited example leading to the establishment in 1842 of public baths and workhouses in the City and to the passage in 1846 of the Baths and Washhouses Act.

An important influence in stimulating the Government to pass public health laws were the reports on urban conditions submitted to Parliament by the Poor Law Commission. Its Secretary, Chadwick, realised that sickness and ill health, products of bad sanitation, were major factors in keeping poor-rates high. In 1838 conditions in Bethnal Green and Whitechapel were reported on, based on evidence given by three doctors, Southwood Smith, Arnott and Kay. Parliament was sufficiently impressed to authorise the Poor Law Commissioners to investigate conditions in the country as a whole, resulting in the publication in 1842 of Chadwick's *Report on the Sanitary Conditions of the Labouring Population of Great Britain*. This was followed in 1844 by the Report of the Health of Towns Commission. These publications amply demonstrated that the failure of local authorities to introduce sanitary measures was the chief cause of the moral degradation of the urban masses. In the county of Rutland, although wage rates were about half those in Manchester, school attendance was higher, and the health and moral condition of the people was better than in Manchester. The average age of death among mechanics, labourers and their families was 38 in Rutland and only 17 in Manchester. The conclusion was inevitable that "Fever" was "a dirt, not a destitution disease."

Chadwick and his colleagues recommended two reforms, central government supervision and the assignment of sanitary duties in each area to a single local authority, armed with adequate powers. By the Public Health Act of 1848 a central government department, the General Board of Health, was created, initially for five years. The Board, whose members were Chadwick, Shaftesbury, Southwood Smith and *ex officio*, the Commissioner of Woods and Forests, was authorised to set up local Boards of Health, firstly, in places where the death rate was high, and secondly, in places where one was requested by 10 per cent of the inhabitants. In boroughs, the town councils became the health authority. Elsewhere, special sanitary boards were formed. Excellent work was done, about 200 local boards being brought into existence, but Chadwick's methods were too autocratic for popular taste. Impatient of criticism, and never capable of suffering fools gladly, instead of trying to stimulate local enthusiasm, he made sanitary reform unpopular by too much reliance on what his enemies denounced as bullying, autocratic control from Whitehall. In 1854, when the Board's authority was extinguished, *The Times* wrote, "we prefer to take our chances of cholera and the rest, than be bullied into health."

After the destruction in 1854 of determined central government control, experience showed that towns would never become healthy places to live in until Whitehall compelled the negligent to take action and simplified local administration by abolishing many of the local boards and commissions. A cholera outbreak in 1866 led to the appointment in 1868 of the Royal Sanitary Commission. Its report was followed by the formation in 1871 of the Local Government Board, which was given authority to compel local authorities to use their public health powers. In 1872 England and Wales were divided into urban and rural sanitary districts. In urban areas borough councils became the sanitary authority, in rural areas the Boards of Guardians. A Bill of outstanding importance, introduced by Disraeli's Home Secretary, Richard Cross, was enacted as the Public Health Act of 1875. This Act consolidated the laws relating to public health and increased the public health powers of local authorities, some of which were mandatory and some permissive. Supervised by the Local Government Board, the local authorities were henceforth compelled to appoint qualified medical officers of health and inspectors, to maintain, pave and light streets, and to ensure that dwellings' drains ran into sewers. Houses were not to be built unprovided with water and drainage, and landlords could be compelled to provide these amenities. The permissive powers given to the local authorities included the purchase of land for use as public parks, and municipal ownership of gas and water undertakings.

It is largely due to the effective use of these powers that "to the Industrial Revolution has succeeded a Hygienic Revolution." It had at last come to be accepted that it was a proper function of State activity to concern itself with matters of public health. This view of the function of government was reinforced during the Boer War, during which a large proportion of those medically examined for military service were rejected as unfit, as reported by the Select Committee on

Physical Deterioration (1904). Advances in medical knowledge have shown that, given a healthy environment, much ill health is preventable. The Government, therefore, sensibly came to the conclusion that a ministry with increased powers should be formed to supervise public health affairs. The Ministry of Health (1919) took over the powers of the Local Government Board, those of the Board of Education relating to mothers and children, the infant life protection and lunacy duties of the Home Office and the duties of the Health Insurance Commissioners. Much remains to be done before we are rid of the ugliness that industrialisation brought to our towns and cities. But at least we can be grateful that the filthy courts, tenements and alley ways in which decency and cleanliness were impossible have vanished. Instead, we enjoy clean streets, ample supplies of water, regular disposal of household refuse and a much healthier environment. Even those citizens who dislike paying rates, if they were honest, would have to admit that they get excellent value for their money.

Housing Reform

Full recognition that it is a proper use of State and municipal powers to see that all citizens are well housed in attractive environment was postponed until after 1914. In the mid-nineteenth century some town councils applied for and were given parliamentary authority to make housing bye-laws. Such powers were used to prohibit the building of back-to-back houses and to compel landlords to equip dwellings with water supplies and drainage to public sewers. Liverpool in 1864 was authorised to demolish insanitary dwellings and in 1869 to re-house slum dwellers. Under an Act passed in 1866 Glasgow set up an Improvement Trust which did excellent work. But it was not until 1925 that Parliament prohibited the building of back-to-back houses in the country as a whole.

In housing reforms attention was first concentrated on urban slums, the initiative being taken by private philanthropists. The movement began about 1841, Shaftesbury being one of its leading sponsors. A number of societies were formed to provide improved lodging-houses and tenement buildings, including the "Metropolitan Association for Improving the Dwellings of the Industrial Classes" (1841), the "Society for Improving the Condition of the Labouring Classes," of which the Prince Consort was President, and the "Guinness Trust" (1889). With £750 donated by John Ruskin, Miss Octavia Hill and her sister, Miranda, the granddaughters of Dr Southwood Smith, purchased the leases of three houses in a Marylebone slum court. These were repaired and used to re-house needy tenants. Later, with the aid of a group of voluntary workers, Miss

Hill was able to extend the scope of her operations. A wealthy American, George Peabody, gave £500,000 in 1864 for the erection of dwellings. The Peabody Trust by the end of the century controlled about a score of tenements housing 20,000 persons. In 1909 under the will of Mr W. R. Sutton, nearly £2 million was made available to improve working-class houses.

Apart from a limited amount of activity in a few provincial towns, for example Leeds, Newcastle, Hull, Salford and Dublin, the provision by private enterprise of tenement dwellings was for the most part confined to London. It has been estimated that by the end of the nineteenth century, improved accommodation had been provided for about 150,000 people. These figures show that the problem of slum clearance was too massive and complex to be capable of solution by the activities of private philanthropists. But really effective State and municipal intervention was slow in coming. The earliest housing legislation took the form of encouragement to private effort. In 1851 the Shaftesbury Act was passed and in 1855 the Nuisance Removal Act empowered local authorities to demolish premises unfit for human habitation. A significant advance was made by the Torrens Act (1868), which made owners responsible for keeping their property in a state fit for human habitation, and empowered local authorities to demolish, without compensation, property not repaired. The Artisans Dwellings Act (1875) gave to local authorities, in towns with more than 20,000 inhabitants, the power of compulsory purchase of insanitary houses and of arranging for erection on the site of improved dwellings.

The 1885 and 1890 reports of the Royal Commission on the Housing of the Working Classes revealed that, as much housing legislation was permissive and not mandatory, local authorities were not enforcing it. The Royal Commission therefore recommended that the Local Government Board should compel the laggards to use their statutory powers. Further recommendations included compulsory powers to buy land for housing, loans at low rates of interest for municipal housing schemes, and the provision of cheap transport facilities to stimulate housing development in suburbs. Local authority powers to demolish and replace insanitary dwellings were increased by the Housing of the Working Classes Act (1890). Much insanitary property was demolished in London and the larger provincial cities, but slow progress was made by local councils in building houses to be let at rents which the poor could afford. Further, very few local authorities used the powers, given by the Small Dwellings Acquisition Act (1899), to lend money to tenants for the purchase of their homes.

As its title indicates, a notable advance in government thinking on housing needs was made by the Housing and Town Planning Act of 1909, which authorised the preparation of "town planning" schemes by local authorities. The beneficial results of municipal town planning in Germany were available as an example of what could be achieved. After 1909, therefore, government housing policies ceased to be concerned only with the removal of insanitary conditions and the provision of dwellings for needy tenants. The cultural and aesthetic needs of citizens, and the siting of houses in pleasant well-laid-out environments, were in future to be given due consideration.

A new approach to the housing needs of the population became necessary as people deserted town centres for suburbs. Owing to the development of railways and newer forms of transport, the tram, the bicycle and later the motor car, people were no longer compelled to live in close proximity to their place of work. When the population was confined to city centres, authority had been concerned only to enforce housing bye-laws defining the minimum sizes of houses and rooms, the width of streets, and laying down ventilation and sanitary standards. Estate developers and speculative builders, adhering strictly to the minimum requirements of the law, built streets consisting of drab, ugly dwellings, many of which still disfigure the inner zones of our towns. The need for more communal control and for town planning was obvious if the drawbacks of "bye-law housing" were to be avoided as urban growth continued. The garden suburbs subsequently built, though not without their critics, certainly offer their inhabitants a cleaner environment and more privacy than is possessed by people still condemned to live in the drab, ugly, streets inherited from the nineteenth century.

Two important housing developments before 1914 were the housing estates built by employers, and those sponsored by the Garden City Movement. As the Industrial Revolution began with the use of water power, the first planned industrial settlements were rural, not urban. Sir Richard Arkwright provided good living accommodation for his workers at Cromford, as did Robert Owen at New Lanark. Owen's improvements in the physical environment of his employees impressed Marx and Engels, but his attempts to safeguard their moral welfare were sometimes resented. One old lady, Professor Jack Simmonds told a television audience in 1966, complained that although she did not mind working all day for Mr Owen, she did object to dancing all night for him.

More impressive than Owen's New Lanark settlement was the model industrial village built about a century ago at Saltaire, in Airedale, many of the buildings of which were listed in 1966 by the Ministry of Housing and Local Government as being of special architectural and historic interest. Its founder was the Yorkshire woollen manufacturer, Sir Titus Salt (1803–76), who in 1836 solved the difficulties of spinning alpaca wool. Sir Titus did not believe that industrialism must be associated with ugliness, a state of affairs that tended to be the normal after steam-powered factories were located in large towns. On the contrary, Saltaire Mills with its smoke-burning devices, and the village with its factory houses, congregational church, institute and library, high school and hospital, formed a model industrial community in a rural setting. Well designed also were the houses and mechanics institute built in the new town of Swindon by the Great Western Railway Company for the workers employed in its vast locomotive and wagon works. Later, Port Sunlight was started by the first Lord Leverhulme (1888), Bournville by the Cadbury brothers (1895), and New Earswick near York by Messrs Rowntree and Company (1904).

The founder of the Garden City Movement, Ebenezer Howard, published *To-morrow* in 1898. The first "Garden City," Letchworth, was started in 1901, followed by Welwyn Garden City in 1920. In conclusion, reference ought to be made to the Building Society Movement which has made home ownership possible for many, and to the part played by retail co-operative societies in building houses for working class people. By 1906, they had built over 46,000 houses in manufacturing areas, mainly in north-western England, and by lending money to their members had enabled many to become owner occupiers.

Chapter XIX

EDUCATION

Parliament voted the first state grant for education, £20,000, in 1833, raised to £30,000 in 1839. Obviously, a government responsible for making such meagre provision, less than the contemporary expenditure on the royal stables, did not consider that the State had a duty to educate its citizens. The system of national education ultimately established in England and Wales differed in three main respects from that in other European countries. Firstly, it was decentralised, a considerable amount of control being in the hands of local education authorities. Secondly, voluntary agencies retained a very large share in the provision of educational facilities and, thirdly, teachers remained free from official control in the construction of curricula and syllabuses, and in the choice of methods of instruction.

The absence of rigid, bureaucratic control from Whitehall can be explained by historical factors, and by the reluctance of the governing classes to provide educational advancements, which, they feared, might lead to social unrest. A dual system of education evolved in the nineteenth century. The sons of the newly emergent middle classes were given an education in grammar schools, designed to make them "gentlemen," or to satisfy the demand for increasing numbers of "white collar" workers in professional and administrative occupations. For the children of the rest of the population—the great majority—a cheap, elementary education only was envisaged, the training of skilled manual workers being provided, not in schools, but by a system of industrial apprenticeship.

The pioneer in educational progress, both before and long after the Norman Conquest, was the Church, the strength of the traditional view that education should have a religious basis explaining why schools controlled by clerically dominated voluntary bodies have continued into the twentieth century. But from the thirteenth century Church provision was supplemented by the foundation, often under secular control, of local free grammar schools. Some of these before 1700 had become "public schools," admitting pupils from various parts of the country. Others had remained day schools attended by fee payers. Both types of grammar schools educated the sons of upper and middle class Anglican families, condemning them, with liberal use of the birch, to spend most of their time construing Greek and Latin texts.

After 1660 the religious exclusiveness and curricular narrowness of the traditional grammar schools led to the foundation by the nonconformists of dissenting academies. Shut out of politics by the repressive legislation of post-Restoration parliaments, the nonconformists became active in commerce, industry and banking. Their schools inaugurated a new educational tradition, the children attending them being trained for careers as nonconformist ministers, and in business. Instead of unduly concentrating on the study of classical texts, pupils in dissenting academies were taught such "modern subjects" as English, history, geography, book-keeping, foreign languages and science—known as natural and experimental philosophy. Excluded until 1871 by theological tests from Oxford and Cambridge, nonconformists in search of higher education went to the more progressive Dutch universities of Leyden and Utrecht, or to Glasgow and Edinburgh. In the eighteenth century there also existed many privately-owned day and boarding schools, some of whose proprietors charged fees for an education that did not match the glowing terms in which they advertised their establishments in newspapers and prospectuses.

For children whose parents could not afford fees schools were founded by local benefactors. In the late seventeenth and eighteenth centuries the Charity School Movement was responsible for an increase in the numbers of such schools. Taking advantage of the joint stock principle, money was raised to finance a larger number than would have been possible by reliance solely on individual, private benevolence. The motives inspiring their promoters were partly religious and partly humanitarian. They taught Christianity to the children of the irreligious poor, and provided an elementary education designed to improve their prospects in life. The curriculum of the Charity Schools was therefore based on a study of "the three Rs" and included vocational training and instruction in Anglican doctrines. Girls were trained for domestic service, and boys, who learned to write like copperplate, that is form every letter perfectly, became clerks urgently needed in a fast developing commercial society. The most important of the religious societies founded to promote these ends was the Society for Promoting Christian Knowledge (1698), which encouraged the foundation of schools, financed by subscriptions and church collections, and managed by local boards of trustees.

In the early eighteenth century Charity Schools were established in Scottish parishes which lacked a school. In Wales an educational revival was pioneered by the Rev. Thomas Gough from 1674. A generation later a Carmarthenshire rector, the Rev. Griffith Jones, organised the provision of travelling teachers to educate both children and adults, Welsh being the medium of instruction. Griffith Jones died in 1761, the educational work he had pioneered being continued by Madame Bevan. Unfortunately after her death in 1779 the Welsh Circulating Schools declined, a fate which also overtook the English Charity Schools in the second half of the eighteenth century.

This decrease in popular education occurred at a time when increased facilities were needed for children in the rapidly expanding urban areas. Hitherto the parish had been the principal unit of administration catering for the social needs of the people. In the new industrial Britain it was ceasing to be so, and as the State did not take over the responsibility, reliance continued to be placed on voluntary effort. This took the form of the Sunday School Movement. Sunday Schools first became really important after the establishment in 1780 of Sunday Schools in Gloucester by the Rev. Thomas Stocks and Robert Raikes. The lawless behaviour of child workers on Sundays, their only free day, convinced Raikes, the editor of the *Gloucester Journal*, that only by bringing Christian influences into their lives would it be possible for the children to become lawabiding citizens. In 1785 the Society for the Establishment and Support of Sunday Schools was founded. The movement was encouraged by the Methodist preachers, John and Charles Wesley, and George Whitfield, and by members of the Evangelical Movement in the established Church. The cause was assisted by individuals, inspired by philanthropic and religious enthusiasms, among whom may be noted Hannah More, and her sister Martha, who taught children and adults in the Cheddar district, and Mrs Trimmer, who opened schools in Brentford in 1786 and wrote story books for children. To Mrs Trimmer and others was also due, at the end of the eighteenth century, a revival of schools of industry in which industrial training was combined with instruction in reading and writing.

The sponsors of the Sunday School Movement were not concerned to meet the educational needs of the industrial age, but to inculcate in the poor habits of thrift and piety, and contentment with their lot. Indeed, a more comprehensive approach to educational practice was considered unwise, as a well educated proletariat might become discontented, shun manual occupations and be attracted to revolutionary social and political programmes. In some Sunday Schools a small payment was made to the teachers, the children in return being taught reading and spelling by reciting passages from the Bible, the Church catechism and the Collects. Hymns were sung, one in use in the West Riding containing the following verses:

> *Why do we on Sunday meet*
> *At School, while others in the street*
> *Do run and play?*
> *It is that we may there be taught*
> *And learn to read as children ought*
> *While in their early days.*
>
> *Oh! see how many friends unite*
> *To teach us reading with delight,*
> *And make it all their care.*
> *They buy us books, their money spend,*
> *Give us their time and well attend*
> *For our instruction there.*

Despite their limitations, in a period of economic changes and rapid population expansion, the Sunday Schools did praiseworthy work. They gave to many thousands of children, at low costs, rudimentary instruction without withdrawing them from the labour market. It is impossible to estimate precisely the extent to which illiteracy existed in the mid-nineteenth century but it was, doubtless, considerable. The Registrar General in the 1840s reported that 40 per cent of those who married could not even write their names. A Huddersfield witness told a select committee of the House of Commons in 1832, "I don't think there is above one in a hundred in the factories that can write." But it is safe to conclude that most of those who could had learned to use a pen, not in a day school, but in a Sunday School.

At the beginning of the nineteenth century two religious societies came into existence to meet the demand for greater educational provision. The National Society for Promoting the Education of the Poor in the Principles of the Established Church (1811) adopted the pedagogic principles of Dr Andrew Bell, an army chaplain in Madras who in 1801 became Rector of Swanage. The educational methods of the Quaker, Joseph Lancaster, were used in the schools established by the Lancastrian Society (1808), renamed in 1814 the British and Foreign Schools Society. Between the two societies an acrimonious dispute was waged which impeded the creation of a truly national and unified educational system. Lancaster, who had nonconformist and Whig support, advocated a non-sectarian approach to education. Bible study was included in the curriculum but not the doctrinal teaching of particular churches. His schools were therefore criticised by Anglicans and Tories who believed that the Church of England should have monopoly control of education.

The resources of the voluntary bodies were hopelessly inadequate to educate all the children, particularly as the problem became more complex due to the population increases taking place in urban areas. Church schools tended to be built in rural parishes, while those provided by the British Society in towns could not enrol all in search of an elementary education. Parents whose children did not attend the schools of the religious societies, where as many as 1000 pupils might be packed on benches, and taught by monitors supervised by two or three teachers, could patronise those provided by private enterprise. These included Dame Schools, in which for three or four pence a week, elderly women taught or at least looked after young children. Older children, paying slightly higher fees, could attend Common Day Schools, in which educational standards were extremely low. Not more than a quarter of the children attending day schools learned to read and write. Many children, government inspectors reported, could read, but did not understand the meaning of the words they recited. We need not be surprised when the pedagogic methods in use are taken into account, together with the evil-smelling, ill-ventilated buildings used as schools, and the low academic equipment of the staff. Anybody could open a private school, while those maintained by the National and British Societies were staffed by masters and mistresses with very scant academic knowledge, supplemented by periods of teacher training of three to five months' duration.

In the eighteenth century there was an adult education movement whose sponsors wished to teach the poor to read the Bible. After 1789 the movement was discouraged by members of the upper classes who feared that literate workers might become interested in seditious literature. By the nineteenth century, however, such prejudices were offset by the need to train skilled engineers and artisans, and by the desire of the more ambitious workers to obtain an education which would enable them to rise in the world. Hence the development of what were known as Mechanics Institutions. The movement originated in Scotland with lectures on practical physics given to workmen in 1760 by Professor John Anderson, and classes for mechanics arranged by Dr George Birkbeck in 1799. After his removal to London Dr Birkbeck played a leading part in the foundation in 1823 of the London Mechanics Institute. By the 1840s Mechanics Institutes existed in many industrial centres. In Huddersfield, for example, an association of working men and voluntary teachers provided from 1841 evening classes in reading, writing, arithmetic, geography, art and French. These classes, after 1861, were housed in a Mechanics Institution, containing 18 classrooms, a library, reading rooms and a lecture and concert room, built at a cost of £4000 defrayed by voluntary subscriptions.

It has been estimated that there were 610 Literary and Mechanics Institutes in 1850, with more than 100,000 members. Few of them remained flourishing for long. Initial enthusiasm waned. Lecturers capable of holding the interest of ill-educated artisans, and of explaining in simple language difficult scientific concepts, were hard to recruit. Premises were dingy and endowments being meagre, money was scarce. No grants were made available from public funds and members' subscriptions were not easy to collect. In some, workmen for whom the institutes were originally designed ceased to attend, middle-class students taking places. The modern adult education movement, which dates from the institution of University Extension Lectures (1873) and the foundation of the Workers' Education Association (1903), possesses advantages not enjoyed by the early pioneers. These include money grants from the Government, local education authorities and the universities, a better educated population from which to recruit members, and student participation in the arrangement of classes. In some urban centres, however, classes arranged to give artisans elementary instruction developed into colleges of further education, teaching a variety of advanced studies and providing facilities for research. The Huddersfield Mechanics Institution, for example, became a technical school in 1884 and in 1896 a technical college.

The early adult education movement could not have provided growth in the field of technological education to match contemporary industrial progress. What has made possible the impressive developments in technological and scientific education in modern Britain has been the assumption by the State of responsibility for providing compulsory, free education. The first breach in the principle that education was primarily a spiritual concern came in 1802. The Health and Morals of Apprentices Act of that year and the Factory Act (1819) made it mandatory for owners of cotton mills to provide instruction in "the three Rs." But as no provision was made to ensure that the law was complied with the educational clauses of these Acts remained largely inoperative. Then followed the Factory Act of 1833 under which textile employers could only employ children between the ages of 9 and 13 who produced school attendance certificates. The children would normally attend the schools of the National or British Societies, and as the Act had provided for the appointment of four factory inspectors, there was some guarantee that its provisions would be carried out. In the same year, J. A. Roebuck, the member for Bath, proposed in the Commons what appeared to contemporaries the fantastic motion "that this House proceed to devise a means for the ... education of the whole people." Needless to say, the motion did not pass, but Parliament did vote the first education grant, to be distributed between the voluntary societies.

To later generations the parliamentary grant of 1833 marks the beginning of State responsibility for education. To contemporaries it had no such implications. The traditional view long continued to prevail that education should be the function of clerically dominated voluntary bodies. The vote of 1833 merely authorised the Treasury, until 31st March 1834, to make grants in aid of private subscriptions "for the erection of school houses for the education of the children of the poorer classes." As applications for aid proved to be greater than the £20,000 available for distribution, the grant was raised to £30,000 in 1839, to £100,000 in 1847 and £900,000 by 1849.

Of great significance was the decision in 1839 to entrust the distribution of the grant to a Committee of the Privy Council, and to appoint as its Secretary Dr James Kay, later known as Sir James Kay-Shuttleworth (1804–77). Kay-Shuttleworth, the first central government educational administrator in England, before he retired in 1849, despite overwork, inadequate powers and bitter resistance from religious interests, laid the foundations upon which the State system of elementary education was subsequently built. He led the way in studies of foreign educational practices and pioneered the foundation of teacher training colleges. The first, that at Battersea, was founded by him and E. Carlton Tufnell. That the English system of education came to be one in which schools were controlled by local authorities, advised, influenced and financially aided from Whitehall, can be traced to Kay-Shuttleworth's initiative. In a memorandum, circulated to the inspectorate in 1840, its members were told "that the inspection is not intended as a means of exercising control but of affording assistance." An inspectorate with authoritarian powers to issue orders was not permitted to come into existence. On the contrary, inspectors were instructed by Kay-Shuttleworth not to "offer any advice or information except when it is invited." Not all Kay-Shuttleworth's views prevailed. In particular, Treasury parsimony, sectarian jealousies and religious prejudices prevented the setting up of a non-denominational, unified system of State schools. But the inspectorate he created did very useful work, making the public aware of social evils, and of the desirability of taking steps to remedy educational deficiencies.

In 1858 the Newcastle Commission was appointed which published in 1861 a massive report in six volumes. To say the least the state of affairs revealed was unsatisfactory. According to the

Commission "a superior education" was given to 321,768 upper- and middle-class children. Of these 35,000 attended "collegiate and superior endowed schools," the rest, private schools. More than 120,000 children were reported as not receiving any school instruction, but as the methods used to compile the statistics included an element of guesswork, it is certain that the actual numbers were much higher. The 2,213,694 children of "the poorer classes" attending day schools did not, according to the Commissioners, obtain "a serviceable amount of education" owing to inefficient teaching and irregular attendance. The children, only one-fifth of whom were more than eleven years old, attending the 22,647 schools belonging to the voluntary religious societies did not get a satisfactory education. The majority of those attending private schools fared even worse. They were packed into small rooms, in which it was reported "though foul air may for a time make the children restless, it soon acts as a narcotic, and in keeping them quiet is as effective as Daffy's elixir." Many such schools had a short life, their owners being persons with sufficient capital to meet the cost of a notice to hang in the window, and their qualification failure to succeed in other occupations.

The Newcastle Commission, which had been instructed to consider and report on measures "required for the extension of sound and cheap elementary education," recommended continued reliance on voluntary efforts aided by monetary grants from the Education Department and the county rates. Despite the damning evidence it had collected about conditions in private schools, it even naïvely considered that they could be improved if they were grant aided. The report certainly did not offer a solution to the educational needs of the 'sixties. Subsequent government policy was similarly ill-designed to do so. This was embodied in the Revised Code of 1862 issued by Robert Lowe, the Vice-President of the Education Department, which inaugurated the widely condemned system of Payment by Results. The Revised Code certainly saved the Treasury expense but at the price of lowered educational efficiency. Despite the increase in the numbers of children attending school, the parliamentary grant fell from £774,743 in 1862 to £649,307 in 1866. But educationally the system was unsound. Teaching of "advanced" subjects was neglected in favour of the grant-earning "three Rs," taught by mechanical methods designed to keep the percentage of failures as low as possible. Attendance registers were falsified. The reduction in the size of the parliamentary grant was not compensated for by an increase in voluntary subscriptions, hence tuition fees had to be increased and teachers' salaries reduced. Recruitment to the teaching profession in consequence declined, both in quantity and quality, a process accelerated by economies in teacher training facilities.

During the period the Revised Code was in operation, many people, of all classes and parties, became convinced of the need for educational reforms. Meetings were held in large urban centres. The Manchester Education Aid Society was formed in 1864, followed by the Manchester Education Bill Committee, which agitated for a system of free, unsectarian, compulsory education in schools financed out of local rates. Joseph Chamberlain played a major part in the formation in 1867 of the Birmingham League which had a similar programme. The League campaigned all over the country, over a hundred branches being formed in important towns and cities. The Anglican Church countered its propaganda by forming in 1869 the National Education Union to agitate for increased grants to enable the voluntary societies to preserve the denominational character of the schools.

Prospects for educational reform were improved by the passage of the Reform Act in 1867 which enfranchised illiterate citizens. As Lowe said, "We must educate our masters." In Gladstone's first Liberal administration William Edward Forster (1818–86), the son-in-law of Dr Arnold of Rugby and a woollen manufacturer of Quaker origins, became Vice-President of the Education Department. Forster, who for many years had been active in the cause of educational reform, introduced an elementary Education Bill into the Commons in February 1870. Its introduction was preceded by an enquiry, authorised by Parliament in 1869, which revealed that nearly half the children in England and Wales did not attend school. The problem Forster therefore sought to solve was how to provide these children with an elementary education, all that was considered needful for the offspring of the labouring poor. The type of education given to the children of the well-to-do was considered to be inappropriate for all children. It never occurred to those who laid the foundations of the State system of education in Queen Victoria's reign that equality of opportunity for all was either desirable or possible.

In framing his Bill, Forster had to take into account the existence of the voluntary schools, the views of those who favoured unsectarian education and the impossibility of obtaining from Parliament money grants large enough to provide school places for all on a free and compulsory basis. As a solution to the religious problem the Elementary Education Act of 1870 instituted the dual system. The voluntary schools were given increased grants. In areas where voluntary provision was insufficient, elected School Boards were to provide school places financed by levies on ratepayers and by central government grants. The prejudices of the secularists were met by the Cowper–Temple clause which prohibited denominational teaching, but permitting Bible instruction, restricted until 1944 to the beginning and end of each school day. The School Boards were empowered to make education compulsory between the ages of five and thirteen, a power few exercised. Neither was education to be free, but fees were not to exceed ninepence a week, and those of necessitous children could be paid by the School Boards.

The dual system has lasted to our own day. Conflicts between school boards and denominational interests continued for long to hamper educational progress. After 1870 the churches made such strenuous efforts to provide school places, that at the end of the nineteenth century more children were attending denominational schools than board schools. Elections of School Boards became occasions for acrimonious disputes between clerical and non-sectarian interests, each seeking numerical supremacy on them. In some areas, Birmingham for example, School Boards refused to pay the fees of necessitous children attending religious schools. School Boards were elected in urban, industrial areas soon after the passage of the Act, that in Leeds, for example, in November 1870, and that in Huddersfield in February 1871. In rural areas progress was much slower owing to the determination of clergy to retain monopoly control, to parental apathy and to financial stringency, the product of a penny rate being in some places ludicrously small.

Free and compulsory education was long delayed in the sphere of elementary education and longer still in that of secondary education. Precedents for compulsory education were to be found in factory and mines legislation which had made part-time attendance at schools a condition of employment. In 1876 Lord Sandon's Act provided that parents had the duty of seeing that their children received an elementary education, but there were too many legal loopholes to make the Act effective. Mundella's Act in 1880 ordered School Boards to issue bye-laws making school attendance compulsory to 13, but children over 10, however, need only attend half-time if granted a certificate of proficiency. In 1893 the minimum age for full-time attendance was raised to 11 and to 12 in 1899. Although local authorities in 1900 were empowered to raise the leaving age from 13 to 14, a considerable number of children under 14 attended school part-time only. Not until the passage of the Fisher Act in 1918 was part-time attendance abolished, the compulsory school leaving age becoming 14, or at the discretion of local authorities, 15. Inevitably, compulsory education became free. In 1891 parents were given the right to demand free education for their children. A few fee-paying schools, however, survived, with parental approval, until 1918, when by the Fisher Act all fees in elementary schools were abolished.

The creation of *ad hoc* boards, charged with the duty of providing an elementary education for the under-privileged, was not a concession to the working class demands since the 1830s for equality of educational opportunity. After 1870 social class determined the education a child received: cheap, elementary education for the masses, secondary education in a boarding or day school for those who could afford to pay fees. The abandonment of *laisser-faire* traditions in higher and secondary education become essential when Britain had to meet the challenge of increasing competition from overseas countries in commerce, industry, science and technology. She could only do so successfully by making drastic changes in secondary and higher education structures geared to economic and social situations which no longer existed. Facilities were needed for the training of scientists, technologists and business men which the ancient universities and grammar schools were not providing. Religious discrimination was ended by the Universities Test Act (1871), and later the Oxford and Cambridge colleges were reformed and their curricula widened. New universities were founded, London and Durham in the 1830s and later the University of Wales and the great civic universities in Manchester, Liverpool, Sheffield, Birmingham, Bristol and Leeds, in which scientific, technological and modern studies played a prominent part.

The development of scientific and technological studies in the universities could not have taken place without changes in secondary and grammar school curricula. The influence and example of headmasters like Dr Arnold of Rugby and Edward Thring of Uppingham rescued the older public schools from degeneracy. In 1868 the Public Schools Act established new governing bodies for Eton, Winchester, Charterhouse, Harrow, Rugby and Shrewsbury. New boarding schools were founded to cater for the children of the *nouveau riche*, the leaders in commerce and industry, for example, Marlborough, Haileybury, Malvern and Wellington. Those imitated the older foundations in giving classical studies a very prominent place in their curricula but also provided tuition in science, modern languages and modern studies.

Many middle-class children attended as day pupils in old endowed grammar schools or in recently founded private, proprietary schools. The Taunton Commission, appointed in 1864, reported that many of the endowed schools were in an advanced state of decay and recommended an extension of public control over them. The Endowed Schools Act of 1869, however, went no further than the appointment of three commissioners to revise out-of-date trust deeds. It was not until the appointment of the Bryce Commission (1894) that the Government began seriously to consider the need to reorganise secondary school provision. The report of the Bryce Commission (1895) recommended the setting up of "a single central authority" to "supervise the interests of secondary education as a whole." The sequel was the formation of the Board of Education (1899) which took over the duties of the Education Department, responsible for elementary schools, and the Science and Art Department, originally attached to the Board of Trade, which administered grants for technical education.

The Board of Education remained in being until 1944. It was never given the power or the administrative structure which would have enabled it to organise educational provision as a whole. In theory it was "charged with the superintendence of matters relating to education in England and Wales." In practice it was never more than a President with inadequate powers and officials who could do little more than recommend. But despite the limitations placed on its authority the Board of Education did stimulate educational progress. In 1903, one of the most influential English educational administrators, Sir Robert Morant, was appointed its Permanent Secretary. Morant was associated with Mr A. J. Balfour in the framing of the Education Act of 1902. This abolished the School Boards, over 2500 in number, replacing them by 315 local education authorities. The new L.E.A.s, each of which appointed an education committee, were the county and county borough councils. Some smaller boroughs and urban councils, known as Part III Authorities, were given responsibility for elementary education only. The L.E.A.s were entrusted with full responsibility for what came to be known as Council or Provided Schools, and for the maintenance and secular instruction in Voluntary or Non-Provided Schools. The use of public monies to aid the voluntary schools was bitterly resisted by nonconformists and the Liberal Party. The Baptist preacher, Dr John Clifford, used his outstanding oratorical talents to denounce the policy of putting "Rome on the Rates." Lloyd George roused the Liberals to resist a policy which, in rural areas, forced nonconformist children to attend, in the absence of any other, Anglican schools. Dr Clifford founded the Passive Resistance League and many thousands of nonconformists were prosecuted for refusals to pay rates. In Wales some local authorities even neglected to carry out their statutory obligation to rate-aid voluntary schools. The Balfour Government countered their defiance by passing in 1904 the Education (Local Authority Default) Act. After the formation of the Liberal, Campbell-Bannerman Government, three Presidents of the Board of Education, Birrell (1906), and McKenna and Runciman (1908) unsuccessfully introduced Bills to modify the special privileges given by the Balfour Act of 1902 to the voluntary schools.

With the passage of time the passions roused by the religious quarrels between church and chapel abated. Seen in retrospect the most significant result of the Act of 1902 is that, by placing responsibility for elementary and secondary education under unified control, a breach was made in the Victorian notion that there should be two distinct systems of education, secondary for the privileged few and elementary for the unprivileged many. Although School Boards in some large urban centres had before 1902 organised what were known as "Higher Grade" classes, their development had been impeded by a London District Auditor who challenged the legality of financing classes for children over 15 out of the rate fund. In the Cockerton Judgment (1901) the High Court upheld his action. After 1902, however, the L.E.A.s, encouraged by Sir Robert Morant, built grammar schools for both boys and girls, and in some areas took over existing foundations. These grammar schools were attended by fee-paying pupils, but in 1907 the Board issued regulations requiring all publicly aided secondary schools to reserve a proportion of places for non-paying pupils from elementary schools. By 1914 six per cent of their pupils were boys and girls who had passed the "free place" examination, most of them drawn from lower middle class families as expenditure on textbooks, school uniforms, and keeping a child at school to 16 years of age and later was too great for working men.

There was before 1914 a rapid increase in the number of pupils attending L.E.A. secondary schools. Graduates were recruited to their staffs and very creditable educational standards were achieved. Largely owing to the influence of Morant they modelled their curricula on traditions handed down from the older endowed grammar and public schools. They sought to give their pupils "a liberal education," qualifying them for admission to university honours courses, rather than a training designed to be vocationally useful. Morant ceased to be Permanent Secretary to the Board in 1912, leaving behind him a network of very good secondary schools. He had not, however, created a really unified system of education, designed to ensure equality of opportunity for all. A majority of the boys and girls attending L.E.A. secondary schools left without taking the matriculation examination. Nevertheless there were many who did obtain a secondary school education which, without his reforms, would have been denied them, and who by passing the matriculation examination qualified for entrance to professional and university courses of study.

The policy of the Board during Morant's tenure of office has been criticised for its neglect of technical and commercial education. This long continued to be the case. As late as 1956 a White Paper on Technical Education noted that the U.S.A., the U.S.S.R. and Western European countries were "making an immense effort to train more scientific and technical manpower and that we are in danger of being left behind." In nineteenth-century Britain State aid for technical, scientific and commercial instruction was meagre. A Normal School of Design was opened at Somerset House in 1837, the beginnings of the Royal College of Art (1896), and schools of design were founded in other urban centres from 1841. The Great Exhibition of 1851 quickened interest in the need to extend technical and trade instruction. The Science and Art Department, controlled by the Board of Trade, conducted examinations and made grants to schools. Unfortunately the emphasis of its examinations was on theory, most of those obtaining certificates doing so without handling scientific apparatus. The teaching of science and technological subjects was encouraged by the London Society of Arts (1754) which from 1854 conducted examinations, and also by the City and Guilds of London Institute. The latter, from 1879, arranged examinations and awarded certificates to students attending both day and evening classes. The Technical Instruction Act (1889) empowered county councils to spend the product of a penny rate on technical instruction. The financial resources available for such instruction were increased in 1890 by the decision to allocate to it what was popularly known as "Whiskey Money," duties levied on wines and spirits.

After 1902 technical instruction was, for the most part, given in evening classes, much of it being very elementary in character. Improvements in standards were stimulated by examinations conducted by regional examination councils and, after 1921, by the institution of national certificate schemes. Papers set and marked by teachers in technical colleges were moderated by assessors appointed by the Board of Education and the professional institutions sponsoring ordinary and higher national certificate and diploma courses. But further education facilities, to quote the Crowther Report (1959), able to satisfy "the needs of the community to provide an adequate supply of brain and skill to sustain its economic activity," could not be provided unless far-reaching changes were made in Great Britain's educational structure.

In modern times there has been a need for larger numbers of highly skilled personnel in science, technology, commerce, administration and the professions. These would not be forthcoming from an educational system inherited from the Victorian era, secondary schools biased towards classical and literary studies and elementary schools providing little more than instruction in "the three Rs." Reforms needed to avoid the considerable wastage of human potentialities included the abolition of fees and the creation of a unified educational system. Elementary and secondary education would have to be treated as parts of a unified whole, not as separate entities designed for different classes. Further, the central government would have to lay down minimum standards to ensure that children living in areas where rate yields were low or local authorities were lax were not denied opportunities given to those living in richer and more progressive localities.

Both the First and Second World Wars generated atmospheres favourable to reform. The Fisher Education Act in 1918 raised the compulsory school leaving age to 14 and to 15 at the discretion of L.E.A.s. Fees in elementary schools were abolished and the employment of children under 12 years of age was prohibited. But the 1918 Act was not fully implemented, in particular the proposed setting up of day continuation and day nursery schools. Educational progress was checked by post-war depression and financial stringency. As a result of the "Geddes Axe" in 1921–22 teachers' salaries were reduced, their numbers decreased and the size of classes increased. Hope of an educational advance, however, was revived by the publication in 1926 of *The Education of the Adolescent*, usually referred to as the Hadow Report. This recommended the reorganisation of education in two complementary types of schools, primary from 5 to 11, and secondary from 11 to 15 or 16.

The proposal that all children over 11 years of age should be given a secondary education was not fully implemented. Reorganisation on Hadow principles had only been half completed when the Second World War began. Its outbreak had been preceded by a report of the Consultative Committee on "Secondary Education with special reference to Grammar and Technical High Schools." This, known as the Spens Report, recommended free secondary education, to begin at 11 years of age in grammar, technical and modern secondary schools. There was, however, no opportunity to reorganise the educational structure on Spens lines, as in September 1939 the Second World War began, the passage of a major educational statute being in consequence delayed until 1944.

Public opinion in 1944 was in favour of educational reform and the need was urgent, as during the war the existing system had broken down in some of the larger urban centres and in rural areas which had provided refuge for thousands of evacuee children. The Educational Bill, introduced by the President of the Board of Education, Mr R. A. Butler, was passed with a surprising absence of controversy, due to the painstaking consultations with all interested parties undertaken by Mr Butler and his parliamentary secretary, Mr Chuter Ede. The Board was replaced by a Ministry of Education with effective powers, the Minister being given statutory authority "to secure the effective execution by local authorities, under his control and direction, of the national policy for providing a varied and comprehensive service in every area." The Act of 1944 retained the partnership between the central and local authorities but the Minister was henceforth indisputably the senior partner. The 169 Part III Authorities, responsible for elementary education only, were abolished, and the number of L.E.A.s in England and Wales was reduced from 315 to about 140.

In the sphere of education, inequality, Professor Tawney has reminded us, "was a principle and a dogma. In origin a discipline, half redemptive, half repressive, for the lower orders, elementary education has been, throughout its history, not an educational, but a social category." The Butler Act was a genuine attempt to alter this state of affairs by putting into practice the principle embodied in the Hadow Report that primary education is merely a stage in a continuous process. Fees were abolished in all L.E.A. secondary schools, and each L.E.A. was required to submit to the Minister a development plan for primary and secondary education. In addition they were to provide further and adult education facilities for those over 18 years of age. The extent to which the system of public education that emerged after 1944 did give equality of opportunity has been a matter of controversy in recent years. The Act laid down that each child was to receive "efficient, full-time education suitable to his age, ability and aptitude." As children's aptitudes, abilities and home circumstances vary, secondary schools after 1944 were of three types, grammar, technical and secondary modern. The type of secondary school a child attended was decided by his or her performance at the "eleven plus" examination. Widespread criticism and dislike of this method of selection, has, in recent years, resulted in the proposal that all children should, on leaving the primary schools, be transferred to comprehensive secondary schools, a policy which the Minister is nowadays instructing L.E.A.s to follow.

The Butler Act did not provide a fully unified system of public education for all children. There still existed the two other school systems, older than the State system. Firstly, parents able and willing to pay fees could send their children to public and private schools or to one of the 232 direct grant schools which, in return for a Ministry grant, admitted pupils from L.E.A. schools. Secondly, there were the Voluntary Schools renamed Auxiliary Schools, which belonged to religious bodies, mainly the Church of England and the Roman Catholic Church. As the managers of these schools would have had difficulty in raising the money to comply with minimum Ministry standards they received additional financial aid. In these schools denominational religious teaching took place but children couldn't be compelled to attend the periods of denominational instruction. The future of the exclusively denominational schools, however, has nowadays become to some extent an open question. The social and economic influences bringing about the change to a system of comprehensive schools might mean that in the years to come there will be no place for completely separate religious schools.

PART VII

WORKING CLASS MOVEMENTS

CHAPTER XX

THE CHARTIST AND CO-OPERATIVE MOVEMENTS

Chartism

In the mid-nineteenth century the class structure of British society was much more complex than it had been in earlier times. The upper class or aristocracy consisted of a few thousand families owning land. Below it in social rank came what we have learned to call the middle classes. No precise definition of who belongs to the "middle class" order of society exists, but in Tudor and Stuart times it could be described as consisting of people following mercantile and professional occupations. From the latter part of the eighteenth century its ranks were reinforced by those engaged in a number of expanding old, and new, occupations—manufacturers, civil engineers, surveyors, land agents, lawyers, accountants and bankers for example. The remainder of the population belonged to what was thought of as the working-class strata of society.

Chartism was a product of working-class discontents but it had never more than minority support as the working class was far from being an equalitarian social order. It would be erroneous to think of the working class in early Victorian Britain as consisting in the main of manual workers employed by manufacturers, mineowners and iron-masters. It also included those employed on the land, in transport, in domestic service, in the retail trades, and independent craftsmen. Further, as the industrial changes set in motion by the use of steam power were far from complete, many handicraft occupations survived. The introduction of power-driven machinery had had a dual effect. New industries had evolved and new groups of workers had come into existence who enjoyed prospects of higher living standards. Conversely, power-driven machinery had made obsolete many ancient crafts. Workers employed in such industries as handloom weaving, wool-combing, nail-making and hosiery manufacture were finding it increasingly difficult to keep themselves and their families above starvation level. It was only to be expected, therefore, that although there was widespread acceptance among the working classes of the idea that government should be based on democratic foundations, there was no general consensus of opinion on the social and economic policies a "People's Government" ought to pursue. The Anti-Corn Law League, in part, owed its success to the circumstances that its members had a clearly defined objective, the abolition of taxation on imported corn. Not so Chartism.

It certainly was not the case that all who supported the political programme of the Chartists wanted to reverse the trends set in motion by the application of steam power to industrial processes. Rather, an outstanding characteristic of working class life in early Victorian Britain was the absence of regional and occupational uniformity. Hand-loom weavers in the West Country and the northern textile districts, whose skills were becoming obsolete, might favour burning mills and reversing industrial trends. But such a programme did not appear sensible to factory operatives, producing for overseas markets, whose prosperity was at the mercy of violent trade fluctuations. The Lancashire mill hands, who in the summer of 1842 removed plugs from factory boilers, were trade unionists concerned to raise wages, not demonstrators in favour of the "People's Charter." The self-educated artisans who were members of the London Working Men's Association had little in common with northern factory operatives. In the Midlands, where business units were small, catering primarily for the home market, the interests of small masters and their employees were less diverse than was the case in the textile areas of Lancashire and the West Riding. In reality Chartism was a movement with markedly diverse provincial and occupational aims, the victims of Chadwick's Poor Law helping to swell its ranks.

Since the Revolution of 1688, the bulk of the population had been denied a share in the determination of national policy as the machinery of government was controlled at the centre by the aristocracy, Disraeli's "Venetian Oligarchy," and at a local government level by the gentry. The movement for political reform was not in origin a working class one. Agitation for the reform of Parliament and the electoral system can be traced back to the early years of George III and even earlier. Proposals for reform were supported by the Elder and Younger Pitts, the Duke of Richmond, Major Cartwright, John Wilkes and many others, but following the outbreak of the French Revolution the movement flickered out, the cause only being kept alive in Parliament by Charles James Fox and a handful of Whig politicians. In the early nineteenth century working class discontent expressed itself in various ways, much of the agitation taking the form of a demand for annual parliaments and manhood suffrage, supported by Cobbett in his *Weekly Political Register* published from 1802 onwards. After 1815, with Fox in his grave, the democrat,

Sir Francis Burdett, championed a programme of parliamentary reform in the House of Commons.

The provisions of the Reform Bill ultimately passed in 1832 bitterly disappointed the radical and working class supporters of Earl Grey and Lord John Russell. Its title, "An Act to amend the representation of the People," belied its contents. Votes were given, not to men as such, but to holders of property, in boroughs to £10 householders, in counties, in addition to 40s. freeholders, to £10 copyholders, to £50 leaseholders and to £50 tenants at will. The ultimate, if not the immediate, effect of these franchise changes was that the landed classes had to admit the "moneyed interest" to a share in political power. The Whig government elected to office on the new franchise proceeded to pass legislation which worsened the lot of the working class. The Poor Law Amendment Act (1834) hardly pleased the people as it even aggravated certain grievances. The workers, whose hopes had been raised during the reform agitation, discovered that distress still remained, hence by the mid-1830s public feeling was fanned into a very dangerous flame.

The Chartist Movement came into existence at this time as an expression of popular discontent. Its leaders, men of strong personalities and passionate beliefs, quarrelled with one another, not only about policies but also about the means of implementing them. Two schools of thought emerged, the one advocating constitutional methods and reliance upon education and moral force, the other violence. The party which relied upon moral force had its home in the London Working Men's Association. That which advocated the use of physical force was strongest in the North where trade fluctuations were most severely felt. Too much, however, can be made of the difference between the moral and physical force wings of the movement. Although vehement expressions of opinion about the need for revolutionary action were frequently made, steps to procure arms were never taken. Rather, the authorities were to be terrorised into giving way by strong language, not by overt acts of violence. The most extreme of the Chartist leaders were only too well aware that an army to man the barricades could never have been recruited from a working class whose members lacked unity of aim and interests.

Reform proposals were put forward by three organisations, the Birmingham Political Union, the Northern Union, and the London Working Men's Association. The Birmingham Union, founded in 1816, was revived in 1830. Its purpose was to secure franchise reform, branches being opened all over England. One of its leading members was a Birmingham banker, Thomas Attwood (1783–1856), who used his considerable influence in favour of constitutional means to obtain both political and monetary reforms. In place of the existing currency Attwood proposed that inconvertible notes should be issued by the Government, the value of which should be altered as prices fluctuated. The idea, however, that in periods of bad trade economic activity could be stimulated by expanding the note circulation found no support in contemporary banking circles. The Northern Union was formed in the area where industrial changes were most advanced and social and economic dislocations were therefore greatest. Its most colourful leader, the demagogic Feargus O'Connor (1794–1855), M.P. for Cork in 1832, was the son of an Irish Protestant landowner claiming descent from Irish "kings." In 1837, O'Connor founded in Leeds the *Northern Star*, a newspaper that achieved a circulation of over 50,000. The huge crowds swayed by O'Connor's irresponsible oratory and seditious language became a cause of real concern to the authorities.

Typical of the Chartist leaders who considered that political democracy could only be achieved by constitutional agitation and educational methods was William Lovett. With Francis Place he founded in 1836 the London Working Men's Association whose membership consisted of self-educated artisans. It was Place who in 1838 drafted the "People's Charter" with its six proposals, annual parliaments, manhood suffrage, vote by ballot, abolition of the property qualification, equal electoral districts and payment of M.P.s. These proposals were not new. Three of them, manhood suffrage, annual parliaments and vote by ballot, had been suggested by political reformers in the seventeenth century. All of them had been included in 1780 in the programme of the Society for Constitutional Information founded by Major Cartwright and Horne Tooke and patronised by Charles James Fox.

In support of the Chartist programme a vigorous agitation was begun, and Lovett was elected Secretary of a People's Convention consisting of 53 delegates which met in London in February 1839. This promoted the preparation of a petition containing over $2\frac{1}{4}$ million signatures which was rejected by the Commons in July, its sponsors Attwood and Fielden only being able to muster 46 votes in its favour. Meanwhile, the Convention had adjourned to Birmingham where it discussed tactics to be adopted if the petition were rejected. Faced with threats of a general strike and mass uprisings, the authorities arrested Chartist leaders and placed General Sir Charles James Napier in charge of the troops stationed in disaffected areas in northern England. The threatened revolution finally resolved itself into a few isolated outbreaks, rioting in the Bull Ring, Birmingham, and in Shoreditch, and a clash between a handful of troops and miners at Newport in South Wales. Here some miners, led by John Frost, a former Mayor of Newport, attempted to release a Chartist leader, Henry Vincent, from Monmouth gaol. They were repulsed, ten being killed and 50 wounded. Frost was transported to Van Diemen's Land. Pardoned in 1854, he returned to England where he died in 1877 at the advanced age of 93.

The Battle of Newport marked the collapse of physical force Chartism. The movement, however, was reorganised at Manchester in 1840 with the foundation of the National Charter Association which claimed to lead some 400 societies in various parts of the country. A second petition was prepared, containing over $3\frac{1}{4}$ million signatures, which was refused a hearing in the Commons. In the same year, 1842, outbreaks of mob violence, triggered off by trade depression, unemployment and the harsh enforcement of poor law regulations, led to the imprisonment of some and the deportation of other Chartists. After 1842 revival of trade unionism and the activities of the Anti-Corn Law League diverted interest from the Chartist Movement. Its real strength became apparent in 1848, a year of revolutions in Europe, and of trade depression. A third petition was prepared, claimed to contain some five million signatures, and a mass demonstration was planned on Kennington Common from where a monster procession was to escort the petition to Westminster. Fearing the worst, the authorities stationed troops at strategic points under the aged Duke of Wellington, and enrolled thousands of special constables. But the anticipated mass uprising never materialised, the working classes showing no desire to emulate their continental contemporaries. At Kennington Common, instead of the hoped for half million, only 50,000 assembled to support O'Connor and Charles Ernest Jones. Hence, instead of defying the authorities, O'Connor and Jones took the petition unescorted to Westminster. When examined it proved to have less than half the number of signatures claimed, including many obvious forgeries.

After 1848 Chartism flickered out, overcome by ridicule, apathy and trade revival. Chartism was "a barometer of hunger," waxing and waning as trade was depressed and then recovered. Further, it lacked middle-class support without which success was impossible in mid-nineteenth-century Britain. It did not even possess the whole-hearted support of the working classes, many of whose members were more attracted to trade unionism, the factory reform and the co-operative movements and by Anti-Corn Law League propaganda. Improvements in the economic wellbeing of the people destroyed the economic basis on which the movement had rested. Its political programme, taken over by the radicals, with the exception of annual parliaments, ultimately became the law of the land. The property qualification for members of Parliament was abolished in 1858, voting by ballot was granted in 1872, payment of members of Parliament in 1911, and manhood suffrage and more equal constituencies by the 1867, 1884, 1885 and 1918 Franchise Acts.

From the short-term point of view Chartism may be judged as having failed. Regarded, however, as a stage in the growth of political awareness among the workers it may be said to have achieved much. The necessary conditions for the formation of a truly united working-class movement did not exist in the mid-nineteenth century. Nevertheless the movement afforded the opportunity of an apprenticeship in political activity to working men, traditions handed down to a later generation doubtless assisting in the formation of the Independent Labour Party at the end of the century. Further, Chartist agitation drew attention to social and economic evils and awakened public opinion to the need for ameliorative measures. That the State intervened more actively in the second half of the nineteenth century to promote measures of social and economic reform may in part, be attributed to the fears for the maintenance of public order which Chartist agitation aroused in the minds of the aristocracy and middle-class property owners.

Consumers' Co-operative Movement

The foundation in the nineteenth century of consumers' co-operative societies was one of the most noteworthy achievements of British working men. Nowadays the movement has millions of members in all parts of the world linked through the International Co-operative Alliance formed in 1896. In "Co-op shops" a wide variety of goods is sold, many produced by industrial enterprises owned by co-operative wholesale and retail societies. Co-operative societies have loaned money for house purchase and built houses. The movement provides banking facilities and engages in overseas trade, while the co-operative principle has been applied to farming in many parts of the world. The word "co-operation," one of the most familiar in our vocabulary, is used to convey two distinct ideas, a way of life and a particular method of organising business affairs. When used to describe a way of life, it implies that men should combine for their mutual benefit. Robert Owen, often referred to as "the father" of co-operation, used the word in this sense. The name "Socialists," first used about 1835, was given to Owen and his disciples.

In the sense that Owen interpreted the meaning of "co-operation" the co-operative movement is centuries old. Its use to describe a way of organising business affairs may be said to date from 1844. This was the meaning President F. D. Roosevelt had in mind when, in a centenary address in 1944 to the Co-operative League of America, he paid tribute to "the weavers of Rochdale who founded modern cooperative enterprise." The Rochdale Pioneers were inspired by Owenite ideals, but the movement they pioneered was based on principles very different from those of Robert Owen. It was democratic, whereas the organisations sponsored and financed by Owen and his disciples were autocratically governed by philanthropists, who thought that working men were too ignorant to be capable of taking wise decisions. To Owen the Rochdale experiment was not an Owenite co-operative enterprise but a method of shop-keeping.

Owen was born in 1771 in Newtown, Montgomeryshire. He died in 1858. Appalled by the living and working conditions of wage earners, he sought by precept and example to rid society of the abuses of the early factory system. In 1799 he married the daughter of a millowner and went to live in New Lanark where he tried out his first experiments in practical economics. Hours of labour were reduced to ten a day, housing improved, schools started and a shop was opened in which good quality commodities were sold at reasonable prices. Owen's teaching challenged that of the classical economists, that man is fundamentally selfish and competent to decide what suits his own interests. Communal wellbeing, they argued, would inevitably follow if each individual was allowed to make his own choices unhampered by his neighbours or the State. Owen on the contrary wanted the State to check the hideous abuses of the new industrialism. Communal wellbeing, he taught, would only eventuate if men make that their conscious aim. The flaws in human character, he insisted, were not innate, but rather the result of environmental factors. As human beings were malleable they could be transformed by education and a healthy environment. "We have learned to improve the breed of the lower animals," he wrote, "but in the much more important matter of breeding human beings we are content to leave all to chance." Modern psychologists may criticise Owen's neglect of hereditary factors. Not all who display anti-social and criminal traits are bred in slums. But at least it must be conceded that as an educational pioneer at New Lanark he deserves credit for the introduction of pedagogic methods better than those used in contemporary schools. Further, he demonstrated that well-paid, healthy employees were more productive than the under-fed, overworked hands who toiled in the foul, insanitary mills that were common in his day.

In 1817 Owen submitted a memorandum to a House of Commons committee appointed to investigate poor law administration. In it he analysed the causes of contemporary distress and submitted a "Plan for the Regeneration of the World." He proposed the setting up of "townships," visualised as self-sufficing communities in which labour was to be rewarded according to need. In these "townships" there was to be communal ownership of land and the means of production. Attempts were made by philanthropists to establish model settlements on Owenite principles. One by Abram Combe at Orbiston, near Motherwell, in 1825, lasted for two years. A settlement at Queenwood, Tytherley, Hampshire (1839), in a magnificent building costing £30,000 became bankrupt in 1845. The same fate within $3\frac{1}{2}$ years befell an experiment at Ralahine in Ireland in 1831. In 1824 Owen sank most of his capital in the "New Harmony" venture in Indiana which ended in 1828.

Owenite propaganda inspired groups of workers to found cooperative societies or "union shops," the accumulated profits of which were to be used to finance the foundation of communal "townships." Some of these societies engaged in productive enterprises, the Huddersfield Society, for example, manufacturing woollen cloth, remunerating one of its employees in 1832 with a suit of clothes, a hat, a shirt and a pair of shoes. It has been estimated that in the decade after 1824 between 400 and 500 "union shops" were founded. Thirteen were founded in the Huddersfield district between 1829 and 1840, four of which still exist. One, the Meltham Mills Society (1827), the sixth oldest in England, anticipated the Rochdale Pioneers in paying dividends on purchases. Periodicals were published and a British Association for Promoting Co-operative Knowledge was founded, the first of its seven national congresses being held in Manchester in 1831 and the last in 1835. George Jacob Holyoake, the contemporary historian of the movement, and Owen addressed numerous public meetings, implanting in the minds of uncounted thousands a vision of "the good times coming." In 1838 *Social Hymns for the use of the Friends of the Rational System of Society* were published. The visionary hopes of those who joined in the singing can be illustrated from one of the verses:

> The Skies are clearing from the gloom,
> Which have our spirits long oppressed;
> Old things are passing to their tomb,
> And brighter prospects cheer the breast;
> For Hark; We hear the millions cry,
> No more shall man dispairing roam,
> And weep beneath a foreign sky—
> The glorious Social Age has come.

The rules of the Owenite societies were usually prefaced by reminders to members of their moral obligations. Those of the Huddersfield Society contained a quotation from Isaiah, "They helped everyone his neighbour, and everyone said to his brother, be of good courage." Only applicants of sound moral character were admitted as co-operators, a sensible rule when the ultimate intention was a communal way of life. The Huddersfield Society, one of whose rules forbade members to swear or curse at meetings, expelled a member for "an obvious crime," not specified in the minutes. Co-operators were very conscious of the importance of education. Some societies would not accept husbands with unwilling wives, others ruled that wives could not withdraw money without the husband's consent.

The visionary hopes of the pre-1844 co-operators were never realised. Enthusiasm was hard to maintain. Members died or left the district. When profits accumulated some members decided to withdraw their share, preferring an immediate gain to distant prospects of life in a "New Jerusalem." The modern co-operative movement dates its foundation, not from the vain efforts of poor, working-class folk to inaugurate a "Rational System of Society," but from the opening of a little store in Toad Lane, Rochdale, one dark December evening in 1844. The Pioneers were young men of varied occupations, very familiar with grinding poverty and unemployment. Their capital, saved in coppers, was small, and their stock of goods could have been accommodated on a wheel-barrow. Jeers, laughter and hostility greeted their enterprise.

Like their Owenite predecessors the Rochdale Pioneers founded a Society "to form arrangements for the pecuniary benefit and improvement of the social and domestic condition of its members," to be achieved by the establishment of a self sufficing and self governing community. Their actual achievement was much grander. What they accomplished was the result of the adoption of four principles: open membership, anyone could join; democratic government, one member, one vote; payment of a fixed interest on capital, originally five per cent; and lastly, the distribution of surplus profits to customers as dividends on purchases. The payment of dividends guaranteed that ownership and control remained in the hands of member customers. The Pioneers adopted three other principles which became part of co-operative practice, the provision of educational facilities, strict neutrality in politics and religion, and the refusal of credit. Cash had to be paid for goods.

The business of the Rochdale Society expanded amazingly. Branch stores were opened and the range of goods was increased. By 1850 the Pioneers had opened a wholesale department to serve their own and neighbouring stores. Later they branched out into productive enterprises and provided Rochdale with Turkish baths. The Rochdale methods became the model imitated by other societies, the development of the movement becoming most marked in the North of England. It was one of the Rochdale members, Abraham Greenwood, who suggested the formation of the Co-operative Wholesale Society (1864). Its headquarters were located in Manchester, the relations between the retail societies and the C.W.S. being similar to those between the retail societies and their members. The Scottish C.W.S. was formed in 1869. At first the wholesale societies produced only the basic necessities of life, but later they expanded their activities to produce a wide variety of goods, for example, footwear and confectionery in 1873 and shirts in 1881.

In 1944, the centenary year of the movement, there were 1100 consumer societies in Great Britain with over 9 million members and about 25,000 shops. The Scottish C.W.S., owned a very large industrial estate near Glasgow. The English C.W.S. produced goods in its factories valued at £49,420,550, owned cargo ships and since 1902 tea plantations in Ceylon and South India, and an agency in West Africa which purchased cacao beans from local producers. In 1869 the decision was taken to form the Co-operative Union to look after the legal, parliamentary and educational interests of co-operators. In 1919 the Co-operative Union founded at Manchester the first Co-operative college to train British and overseas students in co-operative methods and practices. Other notable developments have been the formation of the Co-operative Insurance Society and the provision of banking facilities. In one respect, however, the modern movement has abandoned a basic principle of the 1844 pioneers, namely, neutrality in politics. In 1917 the Co-operative Party was founded which developed a close understanding with the Labour Party, and secured the election of the first of its candidates to the House of Commons in 1918.

These achievements are the more creditable when the difficulties the early co-operators had to surmount are borne in mind. They were short of capital. The Huddersfield Industrial Co-operative Society was founded by 13 members in 1860 with money borrowed without security, £200 from Mr Jonas Horsfall, and smaller amounts from friendly societies. Members were ill-educated, and lacked business experience, while their "socialist" sympathies provoked hostility. Faced with local prejudice, the Huddersfield co-operators prudently advertised their store on the shop sign as belonging to "Jonas Horsfall and Co." To convey the impression that the business was flourishing it was suggested that committee members should walk frequently in and out of the premises. As wholesalers often refused to supply co-operative shops with goods, even for cash, they were stimulated to undertake manufacturing for themselves. At first co-operative societies were registered under statutes governing friendly societies as Associations of "Rational Religionists." A sounder legal basis for the movement was provided by the Industrial and

Provident Societies Act of 1852, followed by subsequent legislation revised in 1893.

In recent years damaging competition from supermarkets and nationally-integrated multiple shops has forced "the Co-ops" to investigate means of modernising their buying methods and improving their "image." A committee, presided over by Sir Leonard Cooke, Chairman of the C.W.S., reported in 1965 that the movement could "never compete successfully with nationally integrated rivals on the basis of 600 separate retail societies ... and a wholesale society which merely competes for their trade like any other supplier." In November 1965 a majority of the retail societies accepted the recommendation of the Cooke Committee that all orders be placed through the C.W.S., which will negotiate with manufacturers for the goods it does not itself produce. Also endorsed was the plan to entrust the day-to-day business management of the C.W.S. to highly paid management executives under a chairman some co-operators have referred to as "the Co-op's Dr Beeching."

To judge the co-operative movement in economic terms, merely as a specific type of business organisation, would be to underestimate its contribution to humanity. Born out of discontent, it has succeeded in improving the standard of life of millions of working men and provided them with unadulterated foods. People were given opportunities to save and enabled to organise their household economy on a sound basis. Co-operative enterprise helped many to obtain education and to live with an ideal. Participation in managing co-operative business enabled working men to learn business methods and the arts of self-government. As employers they set an example when trade unionism was weak, in treating their employees fairly. Humanity owes a deep debt of gratitude to men, who, by preaching the gospel of mutual aid, laboured to ameliorate and improve the conditions of daily life for the masses. In truth, the co-operative idea was not the least fruitful of the gifts British working men gave to the world in the nineteenth century.

Producers' Co-operative Societies

The term "co-operative" is usually thought of in Great Britain as applying to the societies which adopted the "Rochdale Plan." There have, however, been other forms of co-operative enterprise, notably associations of producers, which before 1844 were more numerous than associations of consumers. Producers' associations existed in England from the end of the eighteenth century, few of them for long periods of time. From the 1840s the formation of producers' co-operatives was encouraged by the writings of John Stuart Mill and French socialists. John Stuart Mill (1806–73) published his

Principles of Political Economy in 1848. Mill's economic system in the main was that he had learned from the classical school of economists whose members included his father, James Mill, Malthus and Ricardo. They taught that economic laws, like physical laws, were imperative, not subject to control by human agency. The pressure of population growth compels recourse to the cultivation of poorer soils with consequent increases in food costs. The labourer can do little, apart from abstaining from marriage or limiting the size of his family, to improve his standard of living, as natural wages are determined by the cost of producing labour. In other words, wages can never rise above subsistence level. Although in later life Mill abandoned the "wage fund" theory, essentially, he gave a longer lease of life to the teaching of the classical school of economists.

Mill was appalled by the misery the lower order had to endure, so much so that in 1848 he wrote that mechanical inventions had not lightened the day's toil of any human being. But his influence on the economic thinking of contemporaries was immense, hence it is fortunate that he sought means by which the living standards of the masses could be raised. He did so by drawing a distinction between the laws governing production, which are imperative, and those determining distribution, which he pointed out, being man-made, can be changed. In his *Principles of Political Economy* he discussed "the probable futurity of the labouring classes," concluding that the wage system would not be permanent. In its place he suggested the setting up of co-operative associations of producers, an idea he borrowed from contemporary French socialists, Philippe Buchez, "the father of French co-operation," and Louis Blanc, whose *L'Organisation du Travail* was published in 1839.

Mill's contemporaries included a small group of well-to-do philanthropists who sought means of ensuring that the spirit of Christian fellowship influenced human affairs. They included the Rev. Frederick Denison Maurice, Charles Kingsley the novelist, John Malcolm Ludlow, Thomas Hughes, M.P., who presided at the first Co-operative Congress in 1869, and Edward Vansittart Neale, who founded the first co-operative store in London and gave generously, both in time and money, to co-operative causes. In France, following the abdication of King Louis Philippe in 1848, a proclamation was issued guaranteeing employment. To implement it national workshops were established. This experiment, though short lived and a failure, inspired the Christian Socialists in England to found in 1849 a Society for Promoting Working Men's Associations. Convinced, as Hughes later wrote, that a means of ushering in the millenium had been discovered, the Christian Socialists provided capital to finance self-governing producer associations. Twelve were formed, all confined to trades in which power-driven machinery was not used. All had collapsed by 1852, one or two becoming businesses controlled by small masters.

During the early 1850s a number of manufacturing enterprises owned by workers were founded in Lancashire and Yorkshire, all of which were unsuccessful. The outbreak of the American Civil War and the resultant cotton famine made impossible further experiments for the time being. But a new phase of activity began after the Civil War ended in 1865. Hundreds of producer societies came into existence, some financed by the Christian Socialists, others by trade unions and the workers themselves. The best known Christian Socialist experiment, the Cobden Mills, began in 1866 and lasted until 1890. At the end of the nineteenth century there were about 54 societies claiming to be run in the interests of the workers, but only eight were really self-governing organisations, appointing the manager and employing only members. Of the remainder, some were controlled by managers, others employed labour, usually at less than trade union rates, the rest being owned by shareholders or consumer co-operative stores.

The failure of the producers' co-operative movement is easy to explain. The societies were handicapped by shortage of capital, their members learning by bitter experience the unwisdom of producing goods for which there was no certain demand. Conversely, the manufacturing enterprises of the consumers' co-operative movement prospered because their products were readily saleable in co-operative retail shops. All too often producer societies were established in years of depression and in handicraft industries competing with steam-powered factories. The eighteenth-century world, in which it was possible for small producers to buy raw materials and sell the fruits of their industry, was fast vanishing. In its place had come an industrial system in which wage-paid workers operated machinery financed by shareholders and managed by expert executives. Workers' control henceforth would have to be exercised through trade unions.

The only industries in which producer societies might hope to survive were those not transformed by the new industrial methods. Even in these, however, Christian Socialist theories proved to be unworkable in practice. Workers were not in reality bands of brothers willing to subordinate individual interests to the common good. In 1850 the Rev. F. D. Maurice sadly recorded that the societies "were actuated by a thoroughly mercenary competitive spirit." Members were quarrelsome and undisciplined, all too often unwilling to submit to control by their servant, the manager. In societies that enjoyed some measure of business success, members made it difficult for newcomers to become members and as employees they proved to be less generous than capitalists. Trade unions, which invested funds in co-operative workshops became disillusioned, their losses being estimated at £60,000. The outstanding feature of the new economic order was the separation of workers from the control and ownership of the means of production. Inevitably, therefore, the search for social justice and improvement of the workers' lot by the establishment of "self-governing workshops" was doomed to failure.

Chapter XXI

TRADE UNIONISM TO 1876

Trade Unionism before 1800

Associations with some of the distinctive features of modern trade unions did exist before the Industrial Revolution, for example, the offshoots of the medieval craft guilds known as yeoman or journeyman fraternities. The members of the latter, however, did not constitute a "working class" in the sense that we use the term nowadays. The working class during the fourteenth and fifteenth centuries must be thought of as consisting of master craftsmen. Journeymen worked alongside their masters and could hope in time to become masters themselves. Disputes might take place between individuals but such conflicts cannot be listed as collisions between capital and labour. Unlike the modern working man the master craftsman was independent in as much as he worked on his own premises, with his own tools, and had personal relationships with his customers.

In the Middle Ages the guilds, under the general supervision of town authorities, exercised a wide control over industry, endeavouring to set standards of quality and limiting output and recruitment to the demands of the market. When they declined and Tudor governments took over the duty of regulating industry, combinations to secure higher wages and better conditions naturally came to be looked upon as illegal conspiracies. It was a principle of English law that a man should be able to carry on his trade freely, hence combinations "in restraint of trade" were illegal conspiracies, this common law rule being reinforced by over 30 statutes enacted between the reigns of Edward I and George IV. But by the eighteenth century, with the decline of subsistence agriculture and small-scale industries, conflicts between capital and labour became inevitable. The rise to power and influence of a "moneyed interest" coincided in time with the abandonment by the Government of the idea that it had a duty to safeguard the welfare of all citizens. Needing cheap, not highly-skilled labour, employers ignored the old regulations, while workers petitioned the Government to enforce them. But it was *laisser-faire* principles that prevailed, Adam

Smith's *Wealth of Nations* being misinterpreted to support the view that it was in the national interest that wages and prices should be determined by the "laws of the market place." As Parliament did not devise legal rules to settle industrial disputes equitably, the workers united to protect their interests and formed trade unions.

At the end of the eighteenth century the fear of revolution on the French model created a political situation in which opposition to organisations formed by the workers flourished. On the outbreak of war in 1793 there was naturally a tendency to minimise individual liberty. To quote Sir Erskine May, "the popular constitution was suspended." The Habeas Corpus Act was suspended between 1794 and 1801. The Treasonable Practices Act (1795) made printing, writing and speaking in addition to overt acts into treasonable offences, and in the same year the Seditious Meetings Act prohibited meetings of more than 50 persons without notice to a J.P. The stamp and advertisement duties were increased and in 1799 revolutionary societies, including the London Corresponding Society, were suppressed. In the same year, 1799, the first of the Combination Acts was passed reinforcing the common law rule proscribing combinations as conspiracies. By it, one magistrate, who might be the defendant's employer, could send to prison for three months a workman combining with others to obtain improved wages and conditions of employment. Protests followed, the workers' cause being championed in the House of Commons by Richard Sheridan, resulting in the passage in 1800 of the second Combination Act making necessary the concurrence of two magistrates, neither of whom could be an employer of labour in the trade of the defendants.

The 1799 and 1800 Combination Acts, the last of a long series making workers' trade combinations illegal, were repressive, but had at least the merit of laying down less severe penalties than those enacted earlier. Their main justification is to be found in the very real contemporary fears that the social and economic order was threatened by deadly war perils and widespread unrest at home. That the danger of a revolutionary upheaval was slight is a judgment easier for later generations than that of the Younger Pitt to make. Neither was Great Britain alone in making trade unionism illegal. The Le Chapelier law of 14th June 1791 in France prohibited workers' combinations, a proscription continued by Articles 414–16 of Napoleon's penal code and the law of April 1834. Strikes were outlawed by the General Civil Code in Prussia, which was followed by legislation against trade unionism in 1845, 1854 and 1860. In Austria the penal codes of 1803 and 1852 prohibited combinations for economic purposes.

The Combination Laws and Trade Unionism, 1800-25

Banned by the law, trade unionism was driven underground. Trade unions became secret societies admitting members by strange initiation ceremonies. Those of the Woolcombers' Union are described in a publication of 1834. Applicants for membership were admitted, blindfolded, into the meeting place. In the presence of the union officials, who were clothed in surplices, the bandages were removed and they were placed in front of a skeleton above which was a sword and a battle axe, and in front a table on which there was a Bible. The President, pointing to the skeleton, addressed the applicants in harrowing verse beginning:

> Strangers mark well this shadow which you see,
> It is a faithful emblem of man's destiny.

After promising to keep a secret, the applicants, with eyes bandaged, were marched several times round the room, being finally led to the table where placing their right hands on the Bible they took the oath to the union. Throughout this ritual hymns were sung, the proceedings ending with the President saying:

> "In the name of King Edward III [the reign in which wool manufacture was supposedly introduced into England], I declare this Lodge to be duly closed."

After 1800, although tolerated in some areas and trades, trade unionists had always hanging over them the threat of prosecution. "Bloody Black Jack," Sir John Sylvester the Common Serjeant of London, sentenced 19 printers of *The Times* who had gone on strike to terms of imprisonment varying from nine months to two years, after telling them they had "been convicted of a most wicked conspiracy to injure ... those very employers who gave you bread." Fortunately for trade unionists such views were not shared by all in a position to influence public opinion. The prosecution of *The Times* printers in 1810, and the attempt in the same year by the master tailors to obtain an Act of Parliament suppressing combinations in their industry, are noteworthy because they led to Francis Place (1771-1854) beginning his campaign for the repeal of the Combination Laws. If it had not been for the researches of Graham Wallas, who published a biography of Place in 1898, we would be unaware of his services towards the establishment of democracy in nineteenth-century Britain. A master tailor in business at No. 16 Charing Cross, Place was a genius in the art of practical politics, and in the use of propaganda, petitions, wire-pulling and bargaining. He was no orator, but he did know how to turn the dreams of visionaries into practical achievements. Place can be best described as an individualist radical, opposed to state intervention in economic and social affairs. He criticised both factory legislation and the Combination Laws as unwarranted restrictions on individual liberty. Although he was the father of fifteen children, and had in his early days known destitution and business misfortune, Place remained a disciple of Malthus, believing that only by limiting the size of their families could workers be rescued from acute poverty. Men were ignorant and ought to be educated as a means of improving their lot. But that the State might usefully play a part in educational provision was not a policy Place supported. To him, education belonged to the field of voluntary effort.

In working for the repeal of the Combination Laws, Place found an ally in Joseph Hume (1773–1855), a radical M.P. who became Chairman of a Select Committee appointed in 1824 to report on the working of the Combination Laws. Place organised the presentation of evidence by workers which persuaded the committee to report, that as the Combination Laws were a cause of friction, masters and men should be left free to negotiate terms of employment. The sequel was the passage in 1824, almost unnoticed through both Houses of Parliament, of a Bill which repealed all legislation since the reign of Edward I dealing with combinations. The immediate results surprised Place. He had assumed that it was the existence of the Combination Laws which made trade unionism essential and that if the law was changed trade unionism would wither away. The contrary happened. In a period of expanding trade the workers united to obtain higher wages, the masters countering with lockouts. Proposals to re-enact the Combination Laws led to the appointment of a second Select Committee, before which Place once again marshalled the evidence of trade unionists. The Act of 1824 was subsequently amended by a Bill piloted through the Commons by Huskisson in 1825. The Act of 1825 was in some respects less favourable to trade unionists than that of 1824. It legalised trade unions for the sole purpose of consulting upon and determining wages and prices, but whereas the Act of 1824 had prohibited "violence," "menace" and "molestation," that of 1825 laid down penalties for "obstruction" and "molestation."

The Trade Union Act of 1825 was the legal foundation of trade unionism in Britain for half a century. From 1825 the unions ceased to be illegal bodies, becoming "non-legal" associations, that is, they had no status in the eyes of the law. They therefore functioned under severe legal disabilities, being unable to enforce agreements in the courts, while their property and funds were at the mercy of dishonest officials. Workers had a legal right to join a trade union, but if they went on strike they might be prosecuted under the common law rule prohibiting "any action in restraint of trade." The law was also concerned to protect those who did not wish to join, against "intimidation" and "violence," words which judges could construe to cover almost any aspect of strike management.

The Trades Union Period, 1825–35

This period is one of intense political excitement, reforming zeal expressing itself in the agitation for Catholic emancipation, parliamentary reform, a ten hours day for factory operatives, the Chartist Movement and the propaganda of the Anti-Corn Law League. There were, however, pioneers of social reform who doubted whether really worth-while reforms could be achieved by political action. It was certainly less easy for people living at the time, than it is for ourselves, to think of the machinery of government as a possible agency of social reform. Government then was concerned with national defence, foreign and colonial affairs, the care of the destitute, the detection and punishment of criminals, and little else. Economic matters were the domain of private business interests. In these circumstances it was not unreasonable to hold the opinion that reforms could best be achieved by "direct action," that is, by strikes organised by militant trade unions. Such views naturally gained ground after 1832 as members of Parliament sent to Westminster by ten-pound householders were, from the workers' point of view, no better than those representing rotten boroughs.

The early trade unions, local and craft in character, had two main functions, to provide friendly society benefits and to secure improvements in working conditions. The first attempts to broaden the movement were made at the end of the 1820s. Inspired by Robert Owen, efforts were made to organise trade unions on a national basis and to create workers' organisations powerful enough to take over control of industry. In 1829 the Irishman, John Doherty, formed the short-lived Grand General Union of the Operative Spinners. In 1830 Doherty founded a National Association for the Protection of Labour and issued a widely-read newspaper, *The Voice of the People*. At Birmingham, on Owen's advice, a Grand National Guild of Builders was founded in 1834 which began the construction of a Builders' Guild Hall. Unfortunately, the members had insufficient money to complete the work themselves.

Owen's most spectacular achievement was the formation in 1834 of the Grand National Consolidated Trades Union, membership of which was open to all workers, both skilled and unskilled. Within a few weeks more than a million members were enrolled. What Owen proposed to do with the massive organisation he suddenly found himself leading is not clearly recorded, other than by threatening strike action to obtain workers' control over the means of production. Owen himself has been described as the forerunner of modern Syndicalists, social theorists who argue in favour of workers' ownership of industry. He had no faith in political measures as a sure means of improving the lot of wage earners. "It is not any mere political change in your condition," he wrote in a manifesto to the Chartists, "that can now be of any service to you or society." Social betterment, he thought, could not be expected to spring spontaneously from the ignorant masses, but could only be obtained by educating them and organising society under bureaucratic direction.

The possibility of using the Grand National to remodel society was not realised for it collapsed within six months as a result of government and employers' hostility, and its own internal weaknesses. The union was little more than the sum of very many little trades and craft unions, some of which tended to be secret societies with mystic and childish rites of initiation. It was this latter aspect of the movement that gave the Government the chance to prosecute successfully the six "Tolpuddle Martyrs." An informer, Edward Legg, testified that he had been compelled to take an oath on the Bible when he joined the National Friendly Society of Agricultural Labourers. This, the prosecution contended, was a criminal offence under an Act passed in 1797 prohibiting the tendering of oaths by private persons. Counsel for the defence argued that the Act had been passed to meet a specific and special case, the 1797 mutinies at Spithead and the Nore. But the judge, Baron Williams, after ruling that the statute applied to all societies the objectives of which were illegal, passed the savage sentence of seven years transportation. The Home Secretary, Lord Melbourne, refused to take action, but the state of public opinion was such that within two years the six were released and brought home at public expense. One of the immediate consequences of the conviction of George Loveless and his five companions, it may be noted, was that melodramatic rites ceased to be associated with membership of trade unions.

The prestige of the Grand National was severely damaged by the conviction of the "Dorchester Labourers" and by the failure of strikes sponsored by local unions. It was not the Grand National but local strike action that employers feared most. They refused to recognise trade unions and insisted that employees sign the "document," a profession of non-unionism. This, becoming part of the workers' contract, gave the employers a legal hold over the signatories. The failure of many costly local strikes inevitably generated among the men a feeling of disillusionment with "direct action" methods. The Potters Union, for example, spent over £6000 in ten months. Interest in trade unionism therefore waned. Owen himself appears to have henceforth taken little interest in trade union affairs. Instead, among militant unionists, his advice to work for more co-operative relations with employers earned him a certain amount of distrust and dislike.

The Period of Consolidation, 1835–60

A noteworthy feature of British working-class movements, after the failure of Owenite trades unionism, was the cleavage between its industrial and political wings. Not until the formation of the Labour Party at the end of the century did the industrial and political movements come together. The working-class movement in Britain can be sharply contrasted with that in France which drew its inspiration from the Revolution of 1789. As action at the barricades was the weapon of the French working class in 1830, 1848 and 1871, permanent and stable trade unionism did not come until after the formation of the Third Republic. In Britain the reverse was the case, trade unionism preceding political activity. The traditions of the French Revolution were of course not wholly absent in Britain, being expressed in the programmes of the radicals and the Chartists. A minority of the working class were interested in the co-operative movement, and fewer still in Christian-Socialist ideas. Christian Socialism, however, originated in the minds of intellectual, middle-class people, not in those of working-class origin. In Britain, in contrast to continental states, there never occurred the division between Christian and secular socialist trade unions.

The aspirations of post-Owenite trade unionists had nothing in common with those of the supporters of these other movements. After the collapse of the Grand National, British trade unionism was characterised by piecemeal growth and rigid conservatism. Weaknesses due to the lack of organised relationships between scattered groups of workers in different towns were removed by amalgamations, local craft unions constituting the nuclei round which trade unionism evolved into its later pattern. It must not be imagined that national unions were formed easily. Tact, wisdom and diplomacy were needed to form them. If there was to be an amalgamation, how much power was to be retained locally? Local unions were hard to convince that such a step was in their members' interests, while officials did not like losing their status and having their authority curtailed. There were problems of financial relations to be resolved, subscriptions, benefits and the sizes of reserve funds varying considerably.

Eventually, by perseverance and statesmanship, obstacles were overcome. In 1841 Martin Jude formed at Wakefield the Miners Association of Great Britain which soon had 100,000 members. But the new policy found its first complete expression in the formation in 1851 by William Newton and William Allen, of the Amalgamated Society of Engineers. To ensure that the resources of the union were not dissipated in local disputes, strike pay could only be given with headquarters' approval. Only skilled engineers were admitted to membership, an apprenticeships scheme being agreed with employers. This "New Model" of trade union organisation was imitated by workers in other industries. Robert Applegarth formed the Amalgamated Society of Carpenters and Joiners (1861), Daniel Guile the National Association of Ironfounders (1863) and Edwin Coulson the Bricklayers' Union.

Membership of the "New Model" unions was strictly confined to skilled craftsmen practising single or allied crafts. Relatively high rates of contributions were levied. A.S.E. members, for example, paid one shilling a week, part of which sum was devoted to the provision of friendly society benefits. The leaders did not challenge capitalist ownership of industry, and they were not ambitious to build "New Jerusalems," to re-model society or to coerce governments. A new type of paid trade union official emerged, radical individualists, not doctrinaire idealists, men of business capacity and high personal character, not irresponsible agitators. They aimed to build up large reserve funds, to convince public opinion that trade unionists were responsible citizens, and to secure better working conditions for their members by processes of negotiation and bargaining, rather than by strike action. One may instance the policy of the Durham miners in the 1840s. For a fee of £1000 a year they retained the services of the Bristol solicitor, Mr W. P. Roberts. The achievements of the "Miners' Attorney" were impressive. He did more to protect his clients from capitalist oppression than local strikes could possibly have done. For example, 68 miners of Thornley Colliery, imprisoned by the local magistrates for absenting themselves from work, were released when Roberts appealed on their behalf to the courts at Westminster.

Trade union officials living in London, among them Allen, Applegarth, Guile, Coulson and George Odger, used to meet from time to time at the Old Bell Inn near Newgate. Known as the Junta, they sought to formulate a policy for the whole trade union movement, their Trades Council being the forerunner of the Trade Union Congress (1868). They served the movement well for some 20 years, winning for trade unionism acceptance by public opinion and a permanent place in British life. By the 'sixties the number of trade unionists was increasing but membership tended to be limited to "the aristocracy of labour," whose leaders deliberately adopted a policy of conciliating public opinion. They incorporated in the rules of the amalgamated craft unions clauses favouring peaceful settlements of disputes, strike action being reserved for use as a last resort. On the "benefit" side of their activities they insisted on honest financial administration, with frequent audits.

The State and Trade Unionism, 1860–76

During this period, with public opinion becoming less hostile and with the increase in the political power of the workers following the passage of the Parliamentary Reform Act of 1867, trade unionists obtained amendments to legislative restrictions. Employers, hostile to trade unionism, could confidently rely on the judges to hamper trade union activities. In 1859 the Molestation of Workmen Act left the courts of law to decide what activities, other than the determination of wages and hours, were legal. Excuses to discredit trade unionism were easily found, as in addition to the national craft societies there were a number of local unions whose members were guilty of acts of violence against non-unionists. Press reports tended to discredit trade unionism as a whole, in particular, attention being drawn to events in Manchester and Sheffield. In Manchester brickfields, clay handled by non-unionists was filled with needles which lacerated their hands. In Sheffield, the Secretary of the Saw Grinders' Union organised violence against men who would not join his union, culminating in the explosion of gunpowder in a workman's cottage. In his anti-union novel, *Put Yourself in his Place*, Charles Reade vividly portrays these practices which sometimes took the form of "rattening," the temporary removal of the tools of non-unionists.

The publicity given to these irresponsible activities led to the appointment of a Royal Commission (1867–69) two of whose members, Tom Hughes, M.P., and the jurist and historian Frederic Harrison, were pro-union sympathisers. Largely owing to the obvious integrity and persuasive manner of the principal trade union witness, Robert Applegarth (1834–1925), the Report of the Commission exonerated trade unionism as a whole from complicity in the crimes of a small minority. The members of the Royal Commission accepted contemporary economic teaching that as the wage fund was a limited one trade unions could not improve a workman's lot. Nevertheless, as working-class opinion was that trade unionism was beneficial, the Commission recommended that measures should be passed to legalise it. In the event, two reports were published. Firstly, the majority report recommended that the Registrar of

Friendly Societies should be empowered to reject union rules which he considered to be "objectionable." Secondly, the minority report, signed by Hughes, Harrison and the Earl of Lichfield, recommended that the unions should be given the protection of the Friendly Societies Act.

Important amendments to the laws affecting trade unions were made both before and after the publication of these reports. Legislation, dating from Tudor times, enabling an employer to break a contract and be liable only to a civil action, while an employee would be liable to a criminal prosecution, was amended by the 1867 Master and Servant Act. Henceforth either party could summon the other in a civil action for breach of contract, and in default be fined. But in the same year, while the Royal Commission was sitting, the Court of Queen's Bench dismayed and astonished the Junta by its decision in the Case of Hornby v. Close (1867). The Treasurer of the Bradford branch of the Boilermakers' and Iron Shipbuilders' Society was accused of embezzling £24 from the branch funds. Trade unionists thought that their funds were legally protected by a statute passed in 1855 which enabled a friendly society to bring its internal affairs in cases of dispute or default before a magistrate. There were many independent societies, concerned only with the provision of benefits, who had deposited copies of their rules with the Registrar of Friendly Societies. To some extent, trade unions undertook thrift and benefit activities, but not all of them desired to be registered. Partly this was due to the wish for privacy, and partly to the suspicion that registration might lead to public interference in their rules and affairs. The legal point at issue in the Case of Hornby v. Close was the extent to which trade unions were protected by the Friendly Societies Act of 1855. The judges refused to convict, ruling that any trade union, having among its objectives the support of members on strike, could not take advantage of the Act. But following protests, the situation was eased by the Trade Union (Protection of Funds) Act, passed in 1869 which gave temporary protection to union funds.

After the publication of the reports of the Royal Commission two Acts were passed in 1871, the Trade Union Act and the Criminal Law Amendment Act. The Trade Union Act removed the possibility of trade unionists being prosecuted under the common law rule prohibiting associations "in restraint of trade." But the Criminal Law Amendment Act imposed serious limitations on trade union activities. A new offence was created, in effect making peaceful picketing illegal. Any person guilty of "watching or besetting" could be sentenced to three months' hard labour. The law was so elastic that it could be construed to cover almost every aspect of strike management as was shown in the Gas Stokers' Case in 1872. Five employees of the Gas, Light and Coke Company of London who went on strike were sent to prison for a year for "intimidating" the manager by refusing to work. In other words, though workers had a legal right to strike, the threat to do so was illegal.

That in the general election of 1874 the Tories, for the first time since 1841, were returned with an overall majority, was due in part to the opposition by organised labour to the conspiracy clauses in the 1871 trade union legislation. The Disraeli government responded by passing in 1875 the Conspiracy and Protection of Property Act and the Employers and Workmen Act, followed by the Trade Union Act of 1876. As a result of this legislation trade unions, which at the beginning of the century had been illegal associations, had by 1876 been given recognition as voluntary societies with the freedom of unincorporated bodies. As the Criminal Law Amendment Act of 1871 was repealed peaceful picketing was lawful. But threats, violence and intimidation were prohibited and breaches of contract likely to result in interference with essential public services, for example, the provision of water supplies, could be treated as crimes. In general, however, during a trade dispute, an act by a group of those taking part was not to be regarded as a criminal offence unless the same act by one individual could be construed as such.

In conclusion, it is worth noting that trade unions in Britain obtained legal recognition earlier than those in other countries. It was not until 1884 that French trade unions permanently secured full recognition of their right to exist. In Bismarck's North German Confederation the prohibition of workers' combinations was abolished in 1869, but only for industrial employees, restrictions still continuing to be placed on trade union activities. In Austria freedom to form trade unions was given in 1870, but they were denied legal status. Lastly, in Russia, with the introduction of modern industrial techniques in the 1880s the State assumed the duty of regulating industry. It therefore prohibited workers from uniting to protect their interests, trade unions in consequence taking on the characteristics of secret societies and short-lived militant organisations. To sum up, sufficient has been written to show that in Britain and elsewhere, the right of the workers in the new industrial society to combine for their own protection was only won in the teeth of bitter opposition by the State and by employers. It remains to consider in a later chapter the uses to which trade unionists put their hard-won freedom to exist.

PART VIII

GREAT BRITAIN IN THE ERA OF FREE TRADE, 1850-1919

CHAPTER XXII

SCIENCE AND TECHNOLOGICAL CHANGES

The unprecedented industrial growth based on the power of steam was highlighted by the displays of manufactured articles at the Prince Consort's Great Exhibition in 1851. A new civilisation had been created and three industries had been established, coal, textiles and iron, in which Britain was pre-eminent. After 1851 industrial expansion accelerated, ending in what has been described as "a second industrial revolution." This was markedly different from the first, as it was associated with new science-based inventions, the second half of the nineteenth century witnessing improvements in metallurgical practice, the use in industrial processes of chemical discoveries, the application to practical uses of investigations into electrical and magnetic phenomena, the development of the petrol-engine to drive motor-cars, and innovations in methods of farming. Continuing technological expansion has made twentieth-century man familiar with synthetics, plastics, electronics, automation and atomic power. Drudgery has been banished from the home by the invention of heating and cleaning appliances, the monopolies of rail and steamer have been challenged by air transport, and means of communication have been revolutionised by telephone, radio, radar and television. Man has even embarked on the hazardous task of seeking a solution to the problems of travelling in space. But science and technological ideas are international; hence, whereas Britain had led the world in the older industries like textiles and iron, she was not, in the newer science-based industries, "the workshop of the world."

Increasingly since the latter part of the nineteenth century industrial expansion has depended upon the solution by technologists of the problems involved in putting to practical uses the discoveries made in scientific laboratories. From the very earliest of times scientific investigations have yielded knowledge that could be put to practical uses. The observations of astronomers enabled men to make a calendar and navigate ships. As already explained in the introductory chapter, inventive activity during the first stages of the Industrial Revolution was linked with scientific curiosity. But for the most part industrial innovators in the eighteenth century were not scientists but ingenious, practical men. That scientific research, however, could be of value to industry was realised after the foundations of modern chemistry had been laid by Lavoisier, Priestley and Cavendish. Sir Humphry Davy's theoretical knowledge of gases was put to practical use when he invented the miner's safety lamp. In 1808, John Dalton (1766–1844), the son of a Cumberland weaver who had become a teacher of mathematics in Manchester, published his *New System of Chemical Philosophy*, in which he outlined the chemical atomic theory which Davy described as the greatest scientific advance of recent times. Ten years later, the Swedish chemist Berzelius compiled a list of the atomic weights of about two thousand simple and compound substances. By this time business men in industrial centres like Manchester and Birmingham were becoming aware of the need to encourage research in chemical science if progress was to be made in metallurgical, textile and soap manufacturing. It was not, however, until the latter part of the century that really considerable progress came to be based on discoveries in pure science.

In 1856 Sir William Henry Perkin, then a young man engaged on a chemical study of coal tar, accidentally produced from impure aniline the first cloth dye, "mauve." Hitherto textiles had been dyed with plant juices such as madder and indigo. The synthesis by two German chemists in 1868 of the colouring matter of madder, and the later synthesis of indigo, ruined French madder producers and India's indigo planters. Perkin's formula was commercially exploited at the dyeworks of Messrs Pullar at Perth, and by Perkin in 1857 at a small plant he opened at Greensford Green. Thousands of synthetic dyestuffs were subsequently produced, but in 1885 private enterprise in Britain was only manufacturing a sixth of the quantity produced by state-encouraged German firms from coal tar products, most of which incidentally were being imported from Britain. This surrender of the lead in organic chemistry, the chemistry of carbon compounds, was to have embarrassing and even dangerous consequences for Britain when war broke out in 1914. In addition to the dyestuffs industry, coal tar had become the basis of a number of chemical industries, disinfectants, synthetic perfumes and resins, drugs, fertilisers, and of crucial importance in 1914, high explosives. Not surprisingly the Government decided that it was in the national interest to protect certain chemical industries. By the Dyestuffs Import Regulations of 1920, dyestuffs could not be imported except under licence from the Board of Trade, concessions being made in respect of those produced in the Empire.

Improvements in metallurgical practice are associated with the names of Sir Henry Bessemer (1813–98), Sir William Siemens (1823–83) and Sidney Gilchrist Thomas (1850–85). Born in Hertfordshire, Bessemer was a self-taught, versatile inventor and a keen business man. In his later years, for example, he wrestled with the problem of designing a ship in which passengers would not suffer from sea-sickness. But his chief claim to fame rests on the revolutionary changes in steel production, announced to the world at a meeting of the British Association in Cheltenham in 1856. Steel, iron combined with from 0·3 to 2·2 per cent of carbon, has many advantages over iron. It is harder, more durable, more malleable, more homogeneous and can be polished. Since the Middle Ages, what was known as "blister steel" had been produced in small quantities for use in the manufacture of knives, swords and daggers, by the cementation process, which involved embedding bars of wrought iron in charcoal heated to a high temperature for up to ten days. In 1740 Benjamin Huntsman, a Doncaster clock-mender, needing a better material for springs than the German steel then available, refined Swedish iron in clay pots or crucibles. The resultant product, known as "cast steel" or "Sheffield pot steel," was of a quality much superior to any hitherto known. Huntsman's crucible steel was first used by the French metal workers, but later helped to make Sheffield a steel manufacturing centre with an international reputation.

The Huntsman process could only be used to make steel in small quantities and at a very high cost. What Bessemer learned to do was to mass-produce cast steel. Air was blown through molten pig iron in a large converter, impurities such as carbon, silicon, sulphur and phosphorous being thereby burnt out. By adding the correct amount of carbon to the resultant malleable iron Bessemer produced steel at his plant in Sheffield more cheaply, and in greater amounts, than had hitherto been possible. The first users of Bessemer's method obtained an unsatisfactory brittle steel, a fault remedied by using haematite, a non-phosphoric ore mined in Cumberland, Sweden and North Spain. Complete success followed the adoption of the metallurgist Robert Mushet's suggestion to add a small quantity of spiegeleisen, derived from iron ores rich in manganese, and found in Spain, the Siegerland district of Germany, and elsewhere.

An alternative method of making steel, the Siemens–Martin or open hearth process, dates from 1866. In this method, gas-heated air currents passing through regenerative chambers played on the molten metal instead of being blown through it, as in the Bessemer converter. Of German birth, Siemens came to England in 1843 to market an electro-plating process. His outstanding technological achievements stemmed from his ability to apply scientific principles to practical needs. He was a pioneer in the development of the dynamo, land and under-sea cables and in the use of electricity for lighting and locomotion. He built an electric furnace in 1879 and the first electric railway in 1883, that between Portrush and the Giant's Causeway. The open hearth process at first seemed to be less advantageous than that of Bessemer as it used more fuel and had less capacity. On the other hand, Siemens' steel was of better quality as a greater degree of control could be exercised during manufacture. By 1907 more steel was being produced by the open hearth method than in Bessemer converters, and by 1929 seven times as much.

A London magistrates' clerk, Sidney Gilchrist Thomas, and his cousin, P. C. Gilchrist, a works chemist, solved the problem of using phosphoric ores in the making of steel. Their solution was to line the converter with limestone bricks possessing heat-resistant properties. The chemical action of the lime was such as to remove the phosphorous, the slag left over being, owing to its high phosphoric content, a valuable fertiliser. The Gilchrist–Thomas method, initially used in 1879 at the Tees-side Bolchow–Vaughan iron works, still further cheapened steel. The end product, basic steel, by 1914 exceeded in quantity the production of acid steel by the Bessemer and Siemens–Martin methods. But from the British point of view the researches of Gilchrist Thomas may be regarded as unfortunate as they enabled the U.S.A. and Germany to produce more steel than Great Britain. The manufacture of steel in the U.S.A. began in 1865, the basic process being first used in 1890, steel tycoons like Andrew Carnegie exploiting Pittsburg fuels and Lake Superior ores. Germany built up her steel industry with Ruhr coal and low grade Lorraine ores annexed from France after the Franco-Prussian War.

Later researches in steel production, especially after the appearance of the electric furnace, were directed to investigating the effects of combining elements other than carbon with iron. Not the least of the influences stimulating these researches was the post-1870 arms race. Compounds of steel with nickel, chromium, tungsten and manganese have been devised to meet special needs. Nickel steel, used as armour plating for warships, was countered by the invention of chrome steel, used in the manufacture of armour-piercing projectiles. Corrosion-resisting steel, popularly known as stainless steel, and obtained by adding 12–14 per cent of chromium, was known before 1914, but did not come into common use until after the First World War. Who invented stainless steel is not known with certainty but in 1924 Dr Hatfield invented "Staybrite," an alloy containing ferro-chromium and nickel. A very wide range of articles in every-day use in the home and industry is made nowadays from this and other alloys.

Knowledge obtained from investigations into electrical and magnetic phenomena was applied to practical uses much later than that of the chemists and metallurgists. The Society of Telegraph Engineers, which later became the Institution of Electrical Engineers, dates from 1871, but the advances in electrical technology which have so profoundly affected the modern industrial and household economy took place for the most part in the twentieth century. The name "electricity," from the Greek word "electron," was coined by Elizabeth I's physician William Gilbert, who made contributions to the theory of the mariners' compass which no doubt were of interest to the Queen's sailors. In 1752 Benjamin Franklin showed that lightning and electricity are identical and that buildings could be protected by lightning conductors. Later in the eighteenth century the Italians Galvani and Volta experimented in the production of an electric current, Volta being responsible for making the first electric battery. In 1821 came the discovery of the magnetic field by the Danish Professor Oersted and the Frenchman Ampère. This made possible the transmission of messages over long distances, the initial experiments of Sir Francis Ronalds in 1823 being improved upon in 1838 by the telegraph instrument of Sir Charles Wheatstone and Sir William Cooke. The first message in Morse Code, now universally used, was sent out in 1844 by the American, Samuel Morse (1791–1872). Before that date Morse had also examined the possibility of transmitting messages by submarine cable. Dover and Calais were linked by the Brett brothers, Jacob and John, in 1851. The first attempt to lay a trans-Atlantic cable was made in 1857 but the project encountered many difficulties and disappointments before success was finally achieved.

Knowledge of electrical and magnetic phenomena was increased by the researches of Michael Faraday (1791–1867), James Prescot Joule (1818–89), James Clerk-Maxwell (1831–79), Lord Kelvin (1824–1907) and, on the continent, those of Heinrich Hertz (1857–94). But the immense practical consequences that have flowed from their studies benefited later rather than their own generations. Before electric power could be applied to the manifold uses of today, it was necessary to solve the problems of producing and transmitting it in large quantities at moderate costs. The theory which underlies the dynamo or electric generator was explained by Faraday in a lecture at the Royal Institution in 1831 but the construction of dynamos, technically and economically efficient, was not achieved until more than 20 years after his death. In the last two decades of the nineteenth century electricity was used on a very limited scale as a form of artificial light. Lord Salisbury installed Edison Swan lamps at Hatfield in 1880. His daughter subsequently wrote, "there were evenings when the household had to grope about in semi-darkness," and "others when a perilous brilliancy culminated in miniature storms of lightning ending in complete collapse." Electric lighting did not win the battle with incandescent gas lighting until after the 1920s, the technological progress making this possible being a twentieth-century development. The widespread adoption of electric traction was delayed by technical disputes on the rival merits of current transmission along overhead wires or through the rails, and by the discouragement given to private enterprise by the Tramways Act of 1870. Local authorities showed little zeal in using the powers given to them by the Act of 1870. Hence it was not until the reign of Edward VII that horse and steam tramways disappeared from urban streets and electric trams linked suburban areas with city centres.

Although much of the research on which the modern age of electricity is based was done by British scientists, Great Britain lagged behind in its commercial exploitation. In 1920 electricity production in the United Kingdom was only 4·275 millions of kilowatt hours, which may be compared with the 26·409 millions in 1939 and the 54·960 millions in 1950. The generation and supply of electricity from the late nineteenth century was in the hands of unco-ordinated private and municipal undertakings with resultant variations in voltages, frequencies and costs. The use of electricity instead of coal has many advantages in productive industry, railway transport, and in the home for heating, cooking and lighting, while it certainly guarantees a cleaner, less smoky environment. Nevertheless, Great Britain long continued to rely on productive methods based on cheap coal. In the new industries based on electric power which arose in the closing decades of the nineteenth century, she lost ground to countries like the U.S.A. and Germany which had industrialised themselves much later.

An interaction between technology and science after 1880 of momentous promise for the future was the metallurgical revolution brought about by advances in electrical and chemical knowledge. As early as 1807 Sir Humphry Davy had demonstrated that decomposition can be induced by passing an electric current through matter in a liquid form. Davy was able to produce two new metals, potassium and sodium, from caustic potash and caustic soda respectively. As very high temperatures had to be reached the exploitation of this knowledge on a commercial scale was delayed until after Siemens in 1879 had patented the electric furnace. The usefulness of the electric furnace was greatly enhanced at the end of the century by the researches of a French chemist, Henri Moissan (1825–1907).

Among the metals it became possible to produce on a commercial scale by the use of electro-chemical processes were aluminium and magnesium. Aluminium is the most abundant metal to be found in the earth's crust, existing in great quantities in common clay, but bauxite has proved to be the only ore from which it can be produced economically on a large scale. Aluminium in small quantities had been produced by Oersted in 1825. In 1886 Charles Martin Hall in America, using an electric furnace, and with the aid of cryolite, extracted aluminium from bauxite in large quantities and at a very much reduced cost. World production increased from 16 metric tons in 1886 to 19,800 metric tons in 1907. As cheap electricity is essential the most important aluminium-producing centres came to be located in countries with large resources of water power. One of the lightest of metals magnesium is widely used, sometimes alloyed with other materials, in aviation, motor manufacturing, railways and in structural industries. The German chemist Wilhelm von Bunsen, known to every schoolboy as the inventor of the "Bunsen burner" (1855), by electrolytic methods in 1852 produced magnesium in a metallic state. The first commercial plants for its production were built in Germany in 1886 and in the U.S.A. in 1915. These innovations indicated that the dominant position coal and iron had occupied in industrial affairs was not going to remain unchallenged. The twentieth century was destined to be one in which light metals and hydro-electricity were to be increasingly used to satisfy human needs. But in these new fields of human endeavour, Great Britain before 1914 was not, as she had in the age of coal and iron, taking the lead.

Agricultural practice also was considerably affected by scientific research. Advances made in chemical and biological knowledge provided explanations of natural phenomena and pointed the way towards improvements in tillage and animal husbandry, urgently needed owing to the unprecedented growth in the size of the population. During the eighteenth century population and food supplies had been kept in balance by enclosures, by an extension of the area of cultivated land, and by improvements in farming practices and crop rotation. Contemporary transport improvements made possible the movement of foodstuffs from agricultural to urban areas, a state of affairs that inevitably stimulated investment in agriculture. But, bearing in mind that the bulk of the food supply would have to be home produced, could agricultural output be increased to provide a sufficiency for an ever-increasing population? Admittedly there was ample scope for increasing output from British farms. In the first half of the nineteenth century, the improved farming techniques associated with the names of the eighteenth-century agricultural pioneers were unknown in many parts of the United Kingdom, and were not practised by many farmers even in the home counties. But even if all farmers had been as enterprising and successful as Coke of Holkham, there still remained limits beyond which agricultural output could not be raised. According to Ricardo's "Law of Diminishing Returns" the application of increasing quantities of capital and labour to land could not indefinitely ensure a worth-while increase in production. The contemporaries of Ricardo were haunted by fears of over-population because, as Malthus had argued, population tends to increase faster than the food supply. Hence a proportion of the population must be undernourished. The actual course of events, however, suggested that Malthusian fears were unjustified. England and Wales in 1901 were feeding 32,528,000 people, nearly four times as many as in 1798, on food imported from overseas, a possibility that Malthus can hardly be blamed for not foreseeing.

The current world population explosion has led many to express the opinion that after all Malthus was writing good sense. Be that as it may, Britain in the nineteenth century, before she began to import foodstuffs on a massive scale, had to learn how to increase supplies of home-grown food with the labours of fewer workers on the land. By choosing for its motto, "Practice with Science," the founders of the Royal Agricultural Society in 1838 demonstrated their opinion that to achieve this end scientific research ought to be encouraged on soil content, plant needs, stock breeding and mechanical aids designed to make output greater and less costly. The Society was founded at a time when farming was a depressed industry. In contrast, historians have described the third quarter of the nineteenth century as one in which agriculture enjoyed "a golden age" and as a time of "high farming." That they could do so was in part due to scientists and improvers who provided knowledge which enabled farmers to increase production. In the dissemination of this knowledge, and in encouraging research, the Royal Agricultural Society played a very important part. The Board of Agriculture, founded in 1793, also assisted farmers in increasing output by collecting statistics, encouraging research and sponsoring lectures. Under its auspices from 1803 Sir Humphry Davy delivered lectures on agricultural chemistry. In 1813 he published *Elements of Agricultural Chemistry*, a book which Lord Ernle in *English Farming Past and Present* described as "the foundation stone on which the science of agricultural chemistry has been reared."

Knowledge of the food supply needed by plants was increased by the investigations of Boussingault and De Saussure and by those of the German chemist, Baron Justus von Liebig (1803–73). Liebig toured England in 1842, his teaching, that cultivators should restore to the soil the minerals taken out by plant growth, attracting a great deal of interest. Field investigations into the value of fertilisers based on Liebig's theories were undertaken from 1837 by Sir John Bennett Lawes (1814–1900) on the family estate of Rothamsted in Hertfordshire. In 1843 he was joined there by Sir Joseph Henry Gilbert, a Deptford chemist born in Hull, who had been trained under Liebig. Major field experiments were planned and the famous Rothamsted Experimental Station was founded. The results of the experiments carried out on it were published in the *Journal* of the Royal Agricultural Society. To quote the late Sir John Russell, a former Director of Rothamsted, "Sir John Lawes made one of the greatest innovations in agricultural science, the invention of soluble phosphatic fertilisers," without which "Britain and the industrial countries of Western Europe could not have supported the dense populations that grew up during the nineteenth century."

Basic slag from steel furnaces and nitrogenous material obtained in distilling coal gas were also used as fertilising agents. Other inorganic sources of nitrogen that became available in the nineteenth century were Chilean nitrate of soda, imported from the late 1830s, and later Peruvian guano. In 1898 Sir William Crookes pointed out that as mineral sources of nitrogen were heading for exhaustion "the fixation of atmospheric nitrogen" was becoming an urgent necessity to meet the food needs of populations that were expanding rapidly. Commercial nitrogen fixation plants were built in Norway and Germany, but similar action was not contemplated in Britain until 1917, when the importation of Chilean nitrate was threatened by enemy submarines. Proposals were made to establish a plant at Billingham on Tees-side but it was not until 1923 that synthetic sulphate of ammonia was actually produced there. A third plant food to come into general use in the nineteenth century was potash. Potash deposits were found in Germany in 1839 but the exploitation of potash as a fertiliser was delayed until the 1860s when its value was recognised in Yorkshire on Lord Wenlock's estate at Escrick.

Good drainage is an essential preliminary to the successful use of chemical and other fertilising agents. To encourage the undertaking of costly drainage schemes the Government from 1848 made available drainage loans at $6\frac{1}{2}$ per cent. Three years earlier, in 1845, the first step was taken to provide scientific training for agriculturists by the establishment of an Agricultural College at Cirencester.

In addition there was a more widespread use of machinery in farming operations. Mechanisation of farming in Great Britain may be said to date from the late eighteenth century, when improvements in methods of tilling, planting and cultivation were paralleled by the invention of harvesting machinery. A threshing machine worked by a water-wheel was used in Scotland by Menzies as early as 1743. Andrew Meikle (1719–1811) invented the first really useful threshing machine in 1788, James Locke a chaff-cutting machine in 1794, and an Englishman named Boyce a reaping machine in 1799. Such mechanical aids, however, were only used by a handful of wealthy farmers, the majority of cultivators lacking capital and relying as their forefathers had done from time immemorial on rude implements such as spades, pitchforks, hoes, sickles and scythes, made at a blacksmith's forge.

A more widespread use of mechanical farm implements began in the nineteenth century on the mid-Western American plain, where the early pioneers faced an acute labour shortage. William Manning took out a patent for a mowing machine in 1831, and Obed Hussey one for a reaping machine in 1833. In the following year, 1834, a patent was obtained by Cyrus McCormick for an improved reaping machine which came into common use after 1850. The use of agricultural machines was stimulated by their display at a series of exhibitions beginning with the Great Exhibition of 1851 housed in the Crystal Palace.

The early reapers, powered by horses, although they saved manpower in cutting grain, necessitated the employment of many workers in gathering and binding it. The problem was solved in 1878 when the McCormick Company marketed a combined reaper and binder. Steam threshing dates from 1860, and by 1875 combination harvesters and threshers were coming into use. It was not, however, until the twentieth century that mechanical agricultural machines transformed agriculture, teams of horses being widely replaced in the 1930s by tractors. Many other farming activities have also in recent times been revolutionised by the ingenuity of inventors. Modern methods of canning and marketing have widened the markets for fruit growers and vegetable farmers. Incubators, heated by electricty or anthracite, have transformed egg production, and the petrol-driven motor and electricity have ended much of the back-breaking toil associated with food production in past ages.

A science-based innovation of outstanding importance associated with the second industrial revolution was the internal combustion engine. The motor-car and the type of petrol-engine used in it, without which modern civilisation is inconceivable, is a very modern means of transport. The first mechanically-propelled vehicle designed for use on highways, for example, those of the French engineer Cugnot in 1769, and of Trevithick in 1802, were steam carriages. The successful development of steam locomotives naturally encouraged ingenious men to persevere with the design of steam-cars for use on roads instead of horses. But development on these lines was stifled by the opposition of rail and horse-haulage interests, by penal taxation, legislative interference and hostile public opinion. Advances made in the science of thermodynamics, however, suggested a second line of development, the use of internal combustion engines. As in these the fuel was burnt or combusted within the engine, not as in the case of the steam engine outside it, small but powerful engines could be designed to drive motor-cars and later aeroplanes. The explosive mixture could be one of air and a number of fuels. The first road vehicle driven by an internal combustion engine, that of Siegfried Marcus, used a coal tar derivative, benzene. A few years later, in 1885, Gottlieb Daimler designed a powerful light engine which used petrol vapour as a fuel. Simultaneously, as American oil companies needed markets for the "waste" product of their mineral oil, useless for oil lamps and stoves, ample supplies of petrol, the spirit made from refined petroleum, became available.

The piston engine introduced when motoring first began has remained essentially unchanged. Conversely, considerable changes have in recent years taken place in body design and construction. Early motors, designed to suit the wishes of individual owners, could aptly be named "horseless carriages," revolutionary changes in car design being postponed until after 1945. Pneumatic tyres had been introduced by the end of the nineteenth century but fortunate indeed were pre-1914 owners who found them usable for more than 2000 miles. The full potential of the new means of transport was slow in being realised. In 1900 there were only 20,000 motor cars in the whole world. In 1905 the number of motor vehicles of all kinds registered in Great Britain was 74,038, and in 1909, 183,773. Privately-owned cars were possessed only by the well-to-do, the real break-through to popular ownership not taking place until mass-production methods were introduced after the First World War. Great Britain had a small export trade in motor-cars and motor-cycles before 1914 but she was not the leading manufacturer. France was the leading motor manufacturing country in Europe, her output being overtaken in 1906 by that of the U.S.A.

The growth of the motor industry was accompanied by the development of ancillary industries, in particular by a vast expansion of the trade in oil. Petroleum was known to Herodotus, Plutarch and Pliny, but its production on a huge scale is very modern.

World production of crude petroleum, in 1900 a mere 20 million tons, was 249·9 million tons in 1938 and 434 million tons in 1949. Since 1949 production has been massively increased as new sources of supply have been opened up and demand has grown. The consumption of petrol by motorists is only a partial explanation of the tremendous increase in consumption. Before the Second World War the main products obtained from crude petroleum by distillation and other processes, in addition to petrol, were the illuminant, kerosene, diesel oil, lubricating oils, bitumen or asphalt, paraffin and vaseline. Since 1945 it has increasingly taken the place of coal and vegetable products as the raw material for organic chemicals. Derivatives of petroleum include an ever-expanding number of products, among them detergents, synthetic rubber, paints and lacquers, artificial fibres, rayon, nylon, terylene and orlon, plastics, insecticides and fungicides and agricultural fertilisers. The contributions made by industrial chemists and chemical engineers since 1945 towards satisfying the needs of industry and the household have been remarkable. The twentieth century in fact can be described as the age of oil. Without it modern civilisation would grind to a stop.

Chapter XXIII

INDUSTRY AND TRADE

The first half of the nineteenth century was a period of economic gains but also one of falling prices and working-class discontent. Between 1818 and 1855 the annual increase in the rate of industrial output, according to Hoffman's index of industrial production, was between 3 and 4 per cent. Werner Schlotte has calculated that between 1821 and 1851 the annual average increase in the rate of growth of overseas trade was 4·4 per cent. Between 1820 and 1850, according to the price index numbers of Jevons, the general level of prices fell by 25 per cent. The price fall, however, was mainly on raw materials. Food prices, the main item of working-class expenditure, did not fall owing to the pre-1846 policy of agricultural protection. Progress in wellbeing was also impeded by the continuance of low incomes for handicraft workers in those industries in which factory methods of production were gaining ground. Other factors hindering significant rises in living standards were the slowness with which governments discarded *laisser-faire* principles, the failure of workers to unite in efficiently organised trade unions and the rapid growth and increasing urbanisation of the population.

Although the adoption of free trade policies was approved by manufacturing interests only a minority of the contemporaries of Sir Robert Peel lived in an environment dominated by "satanic mills." Agriculture was still very important, providing a livelihood for 21·1 per cent of the working population. The remainder, according to the 1851 census returns, was employed in coalmining (3 per cent), building and contracting (5·5 per cent), manufacturing (33·3 per cent), domestic service (12·9 per cent), commerce—which included offices and shops—(6·8 per cent), transport (3·6 per cent) and other occupations (14 per cent).

In 1851 most industrial workers were to be found working in industries located in their homes or in small workshops in which power was not used or used only to a very limited extent. Typical of such were the framework hosiery knitters of Nottingham, the nailmakers in the Midlands who laboured in little smithies near their homes, and the numerous workers in East London sweat shops. Tailors, glove-makers and shoe-makers were as yet unaffected by machine competition. In rural areas the ancient crafts of wheelwright and blacksmith still flourished. The pottery industry, located in Arnold Bennett's *Five Towns*, Burslem, Stoke, Hanley, Longton and Tunstall, was also one in which mechanical aids were not in use, puddling in the iron industry being also a non-mechanical industrial process. Famous master potters, such as Josiah Wedgwood (1730–95) and the Spode brothers (1733–1827), had introduced technical and artistic improvements, but it was not until after 1870 that automatic aids, such as jiggers and profile tools, were introduced into the industry.

The use of steam power had progressed furthest in the cotton industry, but even in this industry, which in 1851 employed 570,000 workers, hand looms were still to be found. The woollen and worsted trades employed 254,000 workers. Although progressive firms were using steam power, Professor Clapham has reminded us that as late as "1866 the handweavers managed about a quarter of the looms; they still had some importance twenty years later." Nevertheless, although limited in scope, the considerable investment before 1850 in producers' goods, machines and tools, and in improved means of communication, did make possible an increase in the supply of consumers' goods in the second half of the nineteenth century.

After 1850 the tendency towards the industrialisation of the British economy accelerated. Between 1851 and 1901 labour was diverted from agricultural and rural to industrial and urban occupations, the percentage of the working population engaged in agriculture falling to 12·5 in 1881 and to 8·6 in 1901. Industrial expansion brought about an increase in material wellbeing for the middle classes and for those skilled and semi-skilled artisans who were regularly employed. That this prosperity did not permeate into the lowest orders of society can be illustrated by the horrifying, factual descriptions given by Henry Mayhew, the first editor of *Punch*, in *London Labour and London Poor* (1851–64). Much of the poverty, squalor and human degradation Mayhew unveiled was to remain an appalling reality long after his death in 1887.

Despite the admitted grimness of contemporary urban slum life, it still remains true, however, that looked at from the point of view of economic growth, Britain after 1850 was a land in which very considerable economic expansion was taking place. In the third quarter of the century, a period of rising price levels, economic growth was stimulated by various factors. These included free trade, internal stability and freedom from involvement in large-scale warfare. The growth and development of new means of communication, railways and steamships, coupled with the opening of the Suez Canal in 1869, widened the area of international trade by opening up territories hitherto inaccessible. Means of financing this enhanced economic activity became available with the gold discoveries in California (1849), Australia (1851), New Zealand (1861), followed later by those on the Rand in South Africa (1886) and Klondike (1897). The aggregation of capital to finance economic enterprise was assisted by the development of banking and credit facilities, and by the passage of the Limited Liability Acts of 1855 and 1862. But joint stock enterprises only slowly displaced the older forms of business control by owner-managers and small partnerships, first in such industries as mining, engineering, iron and steel, railways and shipping, which called for massive financial investment. Family firms continued to play an important part in business organisation until well into the twentieth century, and are still of major importance in, for example, the building trades and retail shopkeeping.

During the third quarter of the nineteenth century, with the extended use of the recently invented machine tools, and with the increase in the numbers of skilled mechanics or engineers, a greater amount of mechanisation in industry became possible. The coal and iron industries rapidly expanded as there was an increasing demand for iron not only for machinery, but also for railway equipment at home and overseas, and for use in ship construction. In the coalmining industry the number of workers increased from 193,111 in 1851 to 315,398 in 1871, and the average annual output from 66·1 million tons in 1855–59 to 120·7 million tons in 1870–74. This industry was one, however, in which mechanisation took place only to a very limited extent before the twentieth century. Steam pumps, steam winders and colliery locomotives were in common but not universal use. Underground transport with the assistance of pit ponies, and coal extraction, were manual occupations. In 1901 only 1·5 per cent of British coal was machine cut. It was not until the years between the two world wars that any noteworthy mechanisation took place with the installation of mechanical conveyors and loaders underground. In the same period the percentage of British coal cut by machinery increased from 13 per cent in 1920, to 18·76 in 1924 and to 57 in 1937. In this respect Great Britain lagged behind the U.S.A. where two-thirds of the coal mined in 1924 was machine cut.

The average annual production of pig iron increased from 3·5 million tons in the 1855–59 period to 4·9 million tons in 1865–69. John Vaughan's discovery in 1851 of iron-ore deposits in the

Cleveland Hills led to the opening of the Bolchow–Vaughan iron works and the development of Middlesbrough as a major producer and exporter of iron. But by the mid-1870s, when about 20 per cent of British pig iron was being produced on Tees-side, a major technical reorganisation was taking place in the industry. Bessemer may be said, without exaggeration, to have sparked off a new industrial revolution. When Sir Joseph Paxton (1801–65) was building the Crystal Palace to house the Great Exhibition of 1851, he could not have imagined that the new iron age inaugurated by the Darby family and Henry Cort was nearing its end. Yet by the 1870s steel had displaced wrought iron. Ironworks in Staffordshire, South Wales and on the north-east coast had either closed down or been adapted to handle the new processes. As home production could not meet demand, the steel industry came to depend on imported ores. Steel works were therefore sited near the coast, in North East England, South Wales, South Cumberland, North Lancashire and on Clydeside, regions incidentally where coal and iron-ore deposits existed in close proximity.

The steel industry developed most rapidly in the North East and the North West. The speed with which Middlesbrough grew may be cited to illustrate the consequences of the metallurgical innovations. Workers poured into the area, many of them Irish, the population rising from 39,000 in 1871, to over 100,000 by 1907 and to 157,740 in 1966. The 345 inhabitants of Barrow-in-Furness in 1847 had since the early nineteenth century exported iron ore to South Wales and Midland furnaces. Railway construction and the installation of a Bessemer converter by the Barrow Haematite Steel Company in 1866 led to rapid growth, increased as shipbuilding was later added to the industrial activities of the port. In transport steel replaced iron. Steel ships hastened the demise of sailing ships. Where only a lonely farmhouse existed in 1841, the L.N.W.R. built the railway junction of Crewe. In 1864 the L.N.W.R. built a Bessemer plant there, making Crewe a major centre for the manufacture of railway equipment and locomotives.

During the early 1870s there was a boom in the iron and steel industries which was followed by a period of trade depression. The fourth quarter of the century was one in which prices fell, the size of the fall being unprecedented. Between 1874 and 1896 the average retail prices index number fell from 117 to 83. Wages on the other hand did not fall, the average money wages index number for 1874 and 1896 being 156 and 163 respectively. In other words, as the purchasing power of money increased, real wages rose for those in full-time employment. The rise in real wages was considerable, the real wages index number for 1874 being 133 and that for 1896 being 176.

The fall in prices was due to an increase in the demand for gold at a time when gold production was falling, and there was simultaneously taking place a massive expansion in the output of commodities. The increase in the demand for gold has been explained by its increasing use, instead of silver, as the standard of value. Countries like the U.S.A. and Germany were importing gold as backing for their currencies. The increase in the output of commodities was due to improvements in methods of manufacture and transport, and to the opening up of new areas for exploitation. European immigrants into the interiors of North America, Australia, New Zealand, South Africa and the Argentine exported increasing quantities of foodstuffs and raw materials, taking in return manufactures. International commerce was further enlarged by the exploitation of virgin lands in Africa and the Far East with the foundation in the 'eighties of new chartered trading companies. These increasing supplies of food and raw materials were readily marketable in free trade Britain. Imports of cheap food had disastrous consequences for British agricultural producers but beneficial ones for consumers. That there was a notable rise in living standards is shown by the increasing consumption of what had hitherto been luxury products like tea, cocoa, sugar, rice, currants and raisins. Sugar prices fell more than others owing to the competition of European sugar beet (grown with the assistance of bounties and tariffs) with West Indies sugar cane. Tea, which in the 'seventies cost five to ten shillings a pound, had dropped by the 'nineties to a shilling or to one shilling and sixpence, and had therefore become a regular item in working class diet, India and not China being the main source of supply.

It has been estimated that the national income increased from £1133 million in 1874 to £1756 million in 1900 and the income per head of the population from £34·9 to £42·7. But these rises were not continuous, falls in the national income being experienced during the periods of acute trade depressions in the 'seventies and 'eighties. In 1879 11·4 per cent of trade unionists were unemployed and in 1866, 10·2 per cent. Nevertheless, despite these setbacks, the fourth quarter of the century was one in which there were improvements in living standards. The number of men and women gainfully employed rose from 12,117,000 in 1871 to 16,312,000 in 1901. Economic expansion in England and Wales provided a higher standard of living for 32,528,000 people in 1901 than was enjoyed by the 22,712,000 living there in 1871.

The growing prosperity can be illustrated in other ways. The number of travellers on the railways increased from 455·3 million in 1874 to 1014·6 million in 1900, and goods traffic from 185·4 million tons to 419·8 million. Since the repeal of the Navigation Laws the merchant shipping fleet of the United Kingdom had expanded. There were fewer ships on the shipping register in 1900 than in 1874, 19,982 as against 25,497. But the tonnage was greater, 5,979,000 in 1874 and 9,304,000 in 1900, as large steamships had replaced small sailing vessels. Great Britain needed a merchant shipping fleet of greater carrying capacity because the total value of her foreign trade had increased from £668 million in 1874 to £877 million in 1900. Her imports had grown from £370 million in 1874 to £523 million in 1900, and exports and re-exports from £298 million to £354 million. The increase in volume was even greater as the period was one of falling prices. Further, in every year between 1874 and 1900 imports exceeded in value exports and re-exports, the deficiency in the value of payments being partially bridged by shipping earnings which in 1874 were £57·5 million and in 1900 £76·3 million. The growth of industrial power during the last quarter of the century can be illustrated by noting the increase in petroleum imports from 73·9 million gallons in 1885 to 255 million in 1900, and the increase in coal production from 120·7 million tons to 225·2 million between 1870 and 1900. This growing economic activity and investment was reflected in the expansion of bank deposits and bank clearings. Bank deposits increased from £495 million in 1878, £14·4 per head of the population, to £790 million in 1900, £19 per head of the population. Bank clearings increased from £4992 million in 1878 to £8960 million in 1900. It is impossible to estimate what proportion of British commercial and industrial expansion was due to free trade and how much to other factors. But the fact remains that Great Britain under a free trade regime expanded her industrial and commercial power.

Nevertheless, in the closing decades of the nineteenth century there was growing concern about Great Britain's future economic prospects. Lord Randolph Churchill, in a speech at Blackpool in 1884, even went so far as to express the opinion that British trade was stricken with a mortal disease. At this time, when business profits were declining in a period of trade depression, it was only to be expected that business men would take a pessimistic view of the future. The falls in price levels between 1874 and 1896 benefited wage earners and holders of fixed interest-bearing securities, but adversely affected those whose incomes were derived from business profits. Business profits also tended to fall owing to the increase in the supply of capital as a result of the development of joint stock company enterprise and banking. Employers, opposed by the growing power of trade unions, found it harder to keep wage rates low, while social legislation tended to increase rates and taxes. In addition exporters had to face sharper competition from overseas rivals in markets they had formerly monopolised.

Trade returns during the last quarter of the nineteenth century indicated that the British export trade was expanding at a slower rate than in the preceding quarter. The annual average percentage increase in the rate of growth of British exports was 5·3 between 1840 and 1860, 4·4 between 1860 and 1870, 2·1 between 1870 and 1890 and only 0·7 between 1890 and 1900. Between 1850 and 1872 British exports and re-exports increased in value from £71 million to £314·6 million. Expansion was particularly noticeable between 1869, when they were £237 million in value, and 1872, due to the demand for ships and railway equipment which stimulated activity in the iron, steel and coal industries. After 1872 exports decreased in value. Trade expansion is usually associated with periods of prosperity but during the post-1872 era there were three periods of trade depression—1874–79, 1884–86 and 1891–94—during which falls in export values were considerable, totalling only £249 million in 1879. It was not until 1890 when Britain exported commodities valued at £329 million that the 1872 total was exceeded. The values of British exports decreased again in the 'nineties, and it was not until the end of the century that the 1872 total was again exceeded, the relevant figures being £329 million in 1899 and £354 million in 1900. It ought to be borne in mind, however, that as the fourth quarter of the century was a period of falling prices, the volume of exports was greater than might be deduced from figures indicating export values.

The United Kingdom's share of world export trade in manufactured goods declined from 38·1 per cent in 1881–85 to 30·7 per cent in 1896–97. But as world trade had expanded these percentage figures must not be interpreted as indicating a decline in the volume of British trade. Actually it expanded from a total of £226,259,000 in 1881 to £267,905,000 in 1897. A study of British import trade values, on the other hand, shows that the import trade was not subject to the vicissitudes which were a feature of British exports. On the contrary, as Britain was importing increasing quantities of foodstuffs and raw materials, import values rose steadily from £354·7 million in 1872 to £523 million in 1900. Throughout the whole of this period import values exceeded export values, the trade deficit rising from £40·1 million in 1872 to £169 million in 1900.

The persistent adverse trade balance and the fall in the rate of growth of British exports, at a time when some European countries and the U.S.A. were developing their industries, sheltered by tariff walls, inevitably led to the expression of the opinion that British economic supremacy was endangered. An examination of trends in the export trades certainly gave cause for concern. Although cotton exports declined very considerably during the American Civil War (1861–65), when Lancashire was deprived of supplies of raw cotton, there was in all the textile industries a much faster rate of expansion in exports in the 1850–70 period than was achieved between 1870 and 1900. Further, the percentage of the working population employed in the textile industries declined from 15·4 in 1851 to 9·3 in 1881 and to 7·2 in 1901.

In the metallurgical industries, in which before 1870 Britain had led the world, there were also grounds for making pessimistic forecasts. By the closing decades of the century her output was less than that of the U.S.A. and Germany. In the U.S.A., which in the mid-seventies was producing enough steel to satisfy home demands, cut-throat competition led to an increase in the size of business units. Monopolistic combinations, it was claimed, were in the public interest as they reduced production costs, kept prices uniform and ended wasteful competition. Giant industrial trusts came into existence dominated by men of ability and energy who amassed enormous fortunes. Cornelius Vanderbilt became the "Railroad King" of America. John D. Rockefeller, perhaps the richest man of all time, formed the Standard Oil Trust which by 1885 controlled more than 90 per cent of American oil refineries. Contemporaneously the "Steel King," Andrew Carnegie, by ruthless methods eliminated his rivals and formed his Steel Corporation. When Carnegie retired in 1901 J. Pierpont Morgan took over the Carnegie interests, his United States Steel Corporation becoming the largest business unit in the world. Other contemporary American trusts were the American Sugar Refinery Company, the meat packing firms of the Armours and the Swifts, the International Harvesting Corporation, the Duke Tobacco Trust and the coal and copper trusts.

In Germany also during the closing years of the century the formation of industrial combinations known as kartells was a marked feature of the industrial landscape. Industrialisation in Germany was delayed but carried through after 1870 with impressive rapidity. In consequence, unlike Britain earlier, Germany was not competing with countries whose industrial methods were old fashioned. Rather, she had to sell in markets dominated by a long industrialised Britain. To do so successfully she turned to combinations, and as her industrial units were of recent origin they were relatively easily joined together. German kartells were of many forms, some mere price-fixing associations, others controlling output and regulating production. The coal, iron and steel industries were especially suited to combinations as they produced easily standardised commodities, and as their overhead costs were enormous the value of combinations was obvious. In 1893 the Rhenish–Westphalian Coal Syndicate was formed and in 1904 the Steel Works Union with headquarters at Düsseldorf. By 1911, the Union, in which the firm of Krupps was a unit, consisted of some 30 steel works and was the largest steel association in the world outside the U.S.A.

The formation of large business units proceeded much more slowly in Britain. American producers, with access to very large and expanding protected home markets, were better able to cut production costs and control prices than manufacturers were in free trade Britain. British industrial units tended to remain small, producing specialised commodities for sale in numerous markets at home and overseas. Neither were British business men, reared in traditions of *laisser-faire,* easily persuaded to abandon competitive trading. Monopoly in Britain was thought of as harmful to the public interest, a point of view which found expression in such legislation as that abolishing the Bank of England's monopoly of joint stock banking, in the Acts of 1813 and 1833 depriving the East India Company of monopoly trading rights in the Far East, and in railway legislation hindering the formation of a transport monopoly.

In Britain amalgamations long tended to be regarded as harmful to consumer interests. This legal prejudice still has force. By the Monopolies and Restrictive (Inquiry and Control) Act of 1948 a Monopolies Commission was empowered to report on restrictive practices submitted to it by the Board of Trade. Later, in 1956, a Restrictive Practices Court was established with authority to decide on the lawfulness of restrictive arrangements. In contrast, in Germany governments and public opinion encouraged the formation of monopoly associations. Business men there had no inbred dislike of State interference. On the contrary, lacking the advantage British producers enjoyed of access to colonial markets, they welcomed protection for their "infant industries."

The more numerous and smaller British firms found themselves at a disadvantage in competing with the mammoth American and German trusts. Complaints were made that Germany, and to a much less extent the U.S.A., "dumped" pig iron, steel rails and machinery on the free trade British market. That is, they sold goods at low prices, sometimes below the costs of production, recouping themselves by charging higher prices to domestic consumers. Various reasons were put forward to explain the German and

American ability to outpace Britain in iron and steel production. These included the conservatism of British manufacturers, the use of obsolete machinery and methods of production, trade union obstructive policies, and the neglect to provide technical education facilities at a time when production was increasingly being based on the application of scientific principles. In Germany, new industries based on scientific knowledge, the electrical and chemical industries, developed very rapidly, Germany building up a foreign trade in electrical appliances and chemical products no other nation could approach. Above all, it was contended that American and German industrial expansion was due to protectionist policies, which, giving to home producers a monopoly of the domestic market, encouraged the organisation of production by powerful trusts and cartels. The formation of strong business units of a similar pattern was impossible in Britain as long as she adhered to a policy of free trade. It was not until after 1918, when Britain found herself in the same position as Germany had been after 1870, that she began to "rationalise" her industries, seeking to eliminate domestic cut-throat competition, cut out waste and promote greater efficiency by enlarging the size of her industrial units and reducing their numbers.

In the closing decades of the nineteenth century the revival of economic nationalism overseas was adversely affecting Great Britain's staple industries. In the newer industries, those based on scientific research, she was lagging behind. Only one exporting industry, coalmining, could really be described as flourishing. The number of workers employed in the mines increased from 437,000 to 752,000 between 1881 and 1901, and the value of coal exports during the same period from £13,709,000 to £30,622,000. This expansion, however, was thought of as harmful to the long-term interests of the nation. It was considered by some critics to be unwise to export to competitors cheap fuel, the traditional basis of our industrial strength, and short-sighted, as our coal reserves were then estimated to be very limited in extent.

CHAPTER XXIV

AGRICULTURE

In 1850 about two-fifths of British farmers cultivated uneconomic units without the help of hired labour. In subsequent years many gave up the struggle to earn a livelihood, and either emigrated overseas or moved to urban centres, or became farm labourers. Small owner-farmers did not entirely disappear from the countryside, but after 1850 there was an increasing tendency for land to be cultivated in larger units, either by tenant farmers or by bailiffs employed by landowners whose estates were managed by professional land agents. The countryside took on a more prosperous appearance. Farm buildings were improved, on some estates old cottage hovels were replaced by new dwellings, fences were repaired, marshy areas were drained, yields per acre rose and healthy animals grazed in the fields. For those able and willing to take advantage of the new agricultural practices the third quarter of the nineteenth century was a time of prosperity. Disraeli's prophecy that the repeal of the Corn Laws would ruin British agriculture appeared to be false.

That there was agrarian prosperity for a quarter of a century under free trade was due to a fortunate set of circumstances. Railways linked food-producing areas with towns, whose inhabitants at a time of industrial and commercial expansion could afford to buy farm produce at prices which yielded producers a satisfactory profit. The home price for wheat did fall from 58·3s. per quarter during the 1846–48 period to 48·2s. between 1849 and 1854. Between 1862 and 1869, however, it rose to 51·5s. and to 52·6s. between 1869 and 1875. That prices of foodstuffs did not fall was due to the increase in the population of England and Wales from 17,928,000 in 1855 to 22,712,000 in 1871. There was therefore a greater demand for food which at the time could not be satisfied by massive increases in imports. Wheat imports did rise from an annual average of 484,150 metric tons in 1846–48 to 2,057,722 between 1869 and 1875. Imports of other foodstuffs also increased when import duties were reduced. Butter, cheese and eggs, although not then staple foods of the working classes, were imported before 1846. The reduction of duties on these items in 1846 and 1853, and their abolition in 1860, was followed by a sharp increase in imports. A comparison of imports in 1859 with those in 1861 reveals a 138 per cent increase in butter imports, a 76 per cent increase for cheese, and a 37 per cent increase for eggs. Conversely, before the 'seventies very inconsiderable amounts of meat were imported.

The increasing imports of foodstuffs before the 'seventies were due to the inability of British farmers to produce all the food needed by an expanding population enjoying rising living standards. The main areas from which additional supplies could be obtained were in Europe, from which we obtained in the mid-nineteenth century over three-quarters of our corn imports. But increases from Europe sufficient to force down prices to an uneconomic level for home producers were out of the question. The Crimean War (1854–56) closed the Baltic ports. The wars between 1864 and 1871, which Prussia fought with Denmark, Austria and France, restricted trade. The American Civil War (1861–65) prevented wheat exports from the U.S.A. and delayed the opening up of the interior of America. At a time, therefore, when demand was growing in Britain, home producers, blessed with good harvests, experienced a minimum of overseas competition. Rents and profits rose, benefiting landowners and farmers. It ought also to be borne in mind that much farming was financed from borrowed capital. This could be used profitably at a time when prices of farm produce, meat, wool, wheat and dairy produce, offered a fair return on investment.

Unfortunately, the increased income from the land was not shared equitably between all classes of producers. Between 1846 and 1875, a period of rising prices, the standard of living of agricultural labourers did not improve. During the nineteenth century skilled artisans in towns earned twice as much as workers on the land, and unskilled urban labourers about 50 per cent more. According to Professor A. L. Bowley's calculations, the average weekly wages of agricultural and town workers were in 1867 14*s.* and 20*s.* respectively and in 1897, 16*s.* and 25*s.* The differential between the wages of farm workers and industrial employees still exists, despite the facts that farm workers' productivity has risen faster than that of industrial workers and that nowadays their work has become more complex and responsible with the widespread use of agricultural machinery. In February 1967 the Prices and Incomes Board reported that low pay and long hours were the lot of agricultural workers, who had to care for animals and meet the seasonal demands of crop growing and harvesting. Average weekly earnings for farm workers for an average 50·1 hours week were only £14 9s. 4d., the national industrial average being £20 5s. 0d. for 46·4 hours. More than a third of farm workers were reported as earning less than £12 a week, no other industry known to the Board employing so large a proportion of low-paid workers. Justifiably, therefore, the Board recommended an immediate pay increase for the 187,400 regular farm workers in England and Wales, and the negotiation at the earliest possible date of an adequate wage structure for agriculture.

For the nineteenth century, however, reliable conclusions as to the actual standards of living of farm workers cannot be deduced from "average weekly wage" returns, as there were marked regional variations. In the counties north of the Trent, where there was a considerable demand for industrial labour, wages of farm workers were higher than in the south-western counties or in the hill country of Wales, where alternative employment was hard to find. Farm hands in Lancashire and Yorkshire earned twice as much as those in Wiltshire, Dorset, Somerset and Devon. Further, nominal rates of weekly wages must not be multiplied by 52 to determine the annual income of the labourers. In winter and in slack periods actual earnings fell or ceased. Under such circumstances the wages of men had to be supplemented by the meagre earnings of wives and children.

The creation of full-time jobs on the land was impeded by the use of casual labour in some areas, for example the eastern counties. Here farmers contracted with gang masters who provided groups of men, women and children for field work. This gang labour was migratory, housed in barns, ill-fed and very badly paid. The first legislative attempt to get rid of the evils inherent in such a system was the Gangs Act of 1868. But the gang system continued for many years after 1868. Readers of Patrick Macgill's novel, *Children of the Dead End* (1914), will be familiar with the brutal, animal-like existence which was the lot of the Irish men, women, girls and boys recruited by gang masters to harvest potatoes on Scottish farms.

The hours of labour of all farm workers were long, and until the twentieth century, totally unregulated by law. On the estates of a few landowners, for example the Marlborough and Shaftesbury estates, well behaved labourers could supplement their incomes from allotments. A few built new cottages for their employees, but for the majority, housing, much of it in tied cottages, was a disgrace. Agricultural labourers and their families were crowded into damp hovels, made picturesque at least in the eyes of passing strangers by thatched roofs and walls covered by creepers. Rural housing was long neglected by housing reformers and in modern times could still be described as deplorable, lacking water supplies, drainage and conveniences. Agricultural labourers fed the urban masses, but their own diet was meagre, mainly bread, cheese and onions. Very rarely did they eat meat. If they did, despite the game laws and the laws of trespass, it was likely to be poached rabbit or hare. Although Church Schools existed in many parishes, most farm workers in 1870 could neither read nor write. The brave efforts of Joseph Arch between 1872 and 1874 to organise an Agricultural Labourers' Union were defeated by the unrelenting hostility of landowners and farmers, towards whom farm workers had an inbred subservience. Living under such conditions, it is not surprising that young, enterprising villagers left to seek other employment in urban centres. The rural exodus did not begin during the post-1875 period of agricultural depression. It had been gaining in momentum long before the onset of that calamity. In 1851, 2,059,000 workers were employed in agriculture, in 1861, 1,976,000, and in 1871, 1,762,000.

The fourth quarter of the nineteenth century was one of agricultural depression because the factors which had protected British agriculture since the repeal of the Corn Laws ceased to operate. Between 1871 and 1901 the population of England and Wales increased from 22,712,000 to 32,528,000. Population growth of this magnitude would in any case have made essential greater imports of food. No conceivable expansion in the output from British soil would have provided the food requirements of so large an urban population. The people of Great Britain, however, were not threatened by food shortage as new food producing areas were opened up for exploitation overseas. Contemporaneously, improved and cheap transport facilities, railways and steamships, enabled settlers to move into these hitherto empty lands and to market their harvest in Great Britain and Europe.

In the 'seventies two adverse blows, the weather and imports of cheap grain, undermined the prosperity of British landlords and farmers. From 1875 Great Britain experienced unusually wet springs and cold summers, culminating in the catastrophic summer of 1879, the rainiest ever known. Poor harvests, under certain conditions, would have been compensated for by a rise in prices. Instead, prices fell because of a flood of cheap imports, mainly from the U.S.A. Before the American Civil War Britain had imported grain from the eastern states of the U.S.A., but only on a scale which supplemented rather than displaced that of the home producers and the European importer. A new situation was created by the completion of the Union Pacific Railway in 1869. The

Middle West began to fill up, railway companies acting as colonising agents. Settlers poured in from the eastern seaboard of the U.S.A. and from Europe, opening up new grain lands and on the semi-arid lands west of longitude 100 rearing cattle and sheep. By the end of the nineteenth century the U.S.A. was producing a quarter of the world's wheat. Her main problem was to find means of marketing this enormous food surplus in Europe.

Various factors enabled American producers to undersell European farmers. Among the most important was the drastic fall in freight rates after 1870. The use of steel for rails and rolling stock, by making possible larger loads, reduced handling costs and maintenance expenses. As more railways were built than the traffic justified, and as in addition there was competition from water routes, for example the Erie Canal, carriage costs fell still further. On the high seas, owing to the competition of sail with steam, the new steamships completing their voyages more quickly and having greater carrying capacity, there was more ship space than cargoes available to fill it. The construction of elevators along the railway routes facilitated bulk transport. As the elevator companies collected, stored and graded the grain, farmers did not need to erect barns and storage buildings.

Settlers on the prairies, in the early days, had the advantage of cultivating virgin soils which did not need manuring. Settlement was encouraged by the policy adopted by the Federal Government towards the unoccupied lands. The outbreak of the Civil War in 1861 gave to the North the power to decide the principle upon which the settlement of the hinterlands of the original thirteen colonies should take place. Their development became urgently necessary to compensate the North for the loss of the Southern market. The North decided, therefore, against the policy favoured by the South, of parcelling land out in large plantations, in favour of a policy of colonisation on relatively small holdings. By the Free Homestead Act of 1862 settlers could obtain 160 acres, of which they became owners after an actual residence of five years. In 1877, by the Desert Land Act, 640 acres of non-arable land could be obtained. Free land grants created a labour shortage, while as the harvest had to be marketed overseas, involving transport costs, the use of hand labour would have been uneconomic. American farmers, therefore, were compelled to mechanise in order to survive. From the 1850s new ploughs and harrows, and later steam tractors, combined reapers and binders, and steam-driven threshers enabled a handful of men to do the work done in Europe by hundreds of workers using old-fashioned implements. Most of the labour American farmers hired was migratory, seasonally employed in ploughing, harvesting and threshing. In the 1870s a new process of milling spring wheat was introduced. Grown in the northern part of the Middle West where it was exposed to frost, spring wheat was inferior to winter wheat. Its growth, therefore, was a highly speculative business until the new process was introduced making possible extensive settlements in Dakota, Nebraska and Minnesota.

The production of American farms increased enormously, wheat yields rising from 173 million bushels in 1866 to 522 million in 1900. No wonder, as Lord Ernle has explained in *English Farming Past and Present*, British farmers were "confronted with a new problem. How were they to hold their own in a treacherous climate on highly rented land, whose fertility required constant renewal, against produce raised under more genial skies on cheaply rented soils whose virgin richness needed no fertilisers?" Their difficulties were accentuated by two other factors, the opening up of new areas overseas and the inferior quality for bread production of home-grown wheat. By the early 'nineties the Canadian prairies were being settled, following the opening of the Canadian Pacific Railway in 1886, and agricultural products were arriving at the docks from Australia, New Zealand and the Argentine. Other areas of supply were the Hungarian plains and the "black earth" belt of the Ukraine. British wheat came to be primarily used for the manufacture of cakes and biscuits, and for stock and poultry feeding, about 90 per cent of the bread consumed being made from imported grain.

Before the 'sixties expansion of cereal production had kept pace with population increase. The same situation did not exist in the output of meat and dairy products, although improvements in animal husbandry pioneered in the eighteenth century had certainly enabled larger numbers of healthy animals to be reared on manured grasslands. But in the second half of the nineteenth century rising living standards of an urbanised population necessitated the production of more meat than British farmers could hope to supply. The home shortage was made more acute in the mid-sixties as thousands of cattle, stricken by rinderpest disease, had to be slaughtered. The lower cereal prices of the 'seventies induced many farmers to turn part of their arable acreage into grassland, but this proved to be only a temporary solution of their difficulties. Industrial depression in the mid-seventies reduced the purchasing power of town consumers. Contemporaneously, heavy stock losses were suffered owing to an outbreak of foot and mouth disease, and in sheep, of liver rot.

To add to farmers' troubles, the prices of animal products fell. In 1880 the *Strathleven* docked in London with a cargo of frozen mutton from Australia, marking the beginning of a new era in international trade. Meat from North America, Australia, New Zealand and the Argentine was purchased in increasing quantities by British housewives. Britain, after the opening of the Suez Canal and the extension of steamship services, began to rely on overseas producers, not only for beef, mutton and lamb, but also for rabbits from Australia, fresh fruit from the Caribbean, Canada, South Africa and Australia, dairy products from West European countries, Australia and New Zealand, and frozen fish caught by British trawlers in Arctic waters.

In the first half of the nineteenth century British dependence on food imports was insignificant. In the years following the Battle of Waterloo, 75 per cent of British food imports consisted of "luxury foodstuffs," tropical and sub-tropical products such as sugar, coffee, tea and alcoholic beverages. A century later the bulk of British food imports were necessities. In 1854–58 meat imports were 4 per cent of the proportion by value of the net imports of foodstuffs. By 1909–13 the proportion had risen to 23·1. For butter the corresponding percentages were 6·2 and 15·4 and for "luxury foodstuffs," 40·4 and 17·4.

Since the 'sixties there has taken place, firstly, a massive expansion in the volume of overseas foodstuffs marketed in Britain, and secondly, a change in the type of foodstuffs consumed in British homes. The so-called "staff of life," bread, forms a smaller proportion of the food intake than was customary in earlier times. In other words, there has been a revolution in dietary habits. The consumption of "energy" foods, wheat and potatoes, has fallen, while that of "protective" or "health" foods, dairy produce, fruit, vegetables and eggs, has risen. Meat, once a luxury rarely tasted in working-class homes, is nowadays eaten daily. These diet changes were made technically possible by steamships and refrigeration techniques. They were made practically possible because the real wages of those fully employed rose, being, it has been calculated, 70 to 80 per cent higher in 1914 than they were in the mid-nineteenth century.

British farmers since the closing decades of the nineteenth century have been obliged to adjust their methods and techniques to meet the challenges presented by changes in world food supplies and in the dietary preferences of their urban customers. It has been a very painful experience. U.S.A. food surpluses blighted both British and European agriculture. European countries in the 'eighties, in which agrarian interests were politically influential, erected agrarian tariff barriers. In contrast, the United Kingdom until 1932 remained a free trade country. As overseas food was exceptionally cheap, and as a majority of those possessing parliamentary votes lived in towns, she sacrificed her agriculture and concentrated on manufacturing. Exports of manufactures paid for raw materials and the cheap food she needed.

The effects of this decision on the countryside were disastrous. Between 1871-75 and 1894 the average price of wheat fell from 54s. 8d. a quarter to 22s. 11d. The area sown with corn fell from 7,785,000 acres in 1869 to 5,719,000 in 1895 and to 5,582,000 in 1912. Land no longer sown with corn became permanent pasture or was used for forage crops. The total of all the incomes of the agricultural population, it has been estimated, was £42 million less in 1886 than in 1876. In the last quarter of the century rents received by landowners fell by half. In consequence there were landed families, pioneers in agricultural progress since the eighteenth century, which had become too impoverished to develop their estates. Many landowners were absentees, many were more interested in the sporting than in the agricultural potentialities of their land, while others found in business and the City more profitable outlets for investment. As British agriculture was starved of capital, and organisationally was ill-equipped to withstand competition from overseas producers, a marked deterioration became noticeable in the appearance of the farming landscape. Land became derelict, uncultivated fields abounded in crops of weeds, thistles and brambles, hedges, gates, fences and farm buildings fell into a state of disrepair, and costly drainage, installed in the years of prosperity, ceased to function. Competent observers, more than half a century after the onset of the depression in the 'seventies, commented on the state of good farming land in Britain, undermanned, undercultivated and under-stocked. It is not surprising that agriculture was undermanned. The rural exodus quickened, the percentage of the working population employed on the land falling from 12·5 in 1881 to 8·6 in 1901 and to 5·7 in 1931. Whereas in 1881 the census returns listed 1,575,000 workers as employed in agriculture those of 1901 and 1931 listed 1,403,000 and 1,195,000 respectively.

As was only to be expected, it was the more alert and enterprising young men and women who drifted from villages to better their chances in life in towns and overseas. But this flight from the land cannot be wholly attributed to low wages. Actually, in the last quarter of the nineteenth century wage rates rose slightly and in the northern counties became not markedly inferior to those of urban unskilled labourers. There were other influences at work which explain why the drift from the land and the fall in agricultural prices were greater in Britain than in Western European countries. The degree of industrialisation in Britain was much greater than elsewhere, and, therefore, the opportunity of obtaining work in urban areas was greater. Apart from industrial and factory work, for which many country folk had little aptitude or training, there were hosts of other jobs available in expanding urban service occupations, needing skills readily acquired. Further, it was not only wage-paid labourers who found the bright lights of the city more attractive than the quietness and monotony of the countryside. Farmers and their sons also sought greater economic security, in middle class and professional occupations, than the land offered.

The reports of the Richmond (1882) and Eversley (1892) Royal Commissions made plain that the difficulties of the farming community were too deep-seated to be easily and quickly curable. The novelist, Sir Henry Rider Haggard, documented the evils of rural depopulation in *Rural England* (1902) which embodied in two volumes the fruits of a survey of conditions in 27 English counties. Some farmers could make profits, those with large areas of grassland used for stock-rearing, and market gardeners and dairy farmers near urban centres. But by and large farmers showed little disposition to adopt practices of self-help, such as co-operative principles, that proved successful in some European countries, or by cultivating larger units of production, on which labour costs and labour shortages might have been overcome by extended use of machinery. Neither did governments introduce measures well designed to cure agricultural ills. A Department of Agriculture was established in 1889, but with very limited powers. When it enforced compulsory full-time education on children, the Government, farmers considered, was making life difficult for them, as also were the agitations of trade union organisers.

Much of the agricultural legislation of the period was the result of the growing inability of landowners to finance land maintenance and improvements. The State had therefore to assist in filling the gap. As landowners were ceasing to provide the capital to maintain land fertility, tenants who improved the land were given statutory protection against eviction. Instead of being active partners in husbandry landowners tended to become rent receivers only, hence tenants obtained a security of tenure that made them practically irremovable unless they farmed very badly. The Ground Game Act (1880) gave tenants the right to kill rabbits and hares. The Agricultural Holdings Act (1875) enacted that tenants should be paid compensation for improvements. The Agricultural Rates Act (1896) cut by half rates payable by occupiers on land, but not on farm buildings. Landlord rights were still further eroded by Agricultural Holdings Acts in 1906 and 1908 which gave tenants freedom to decide what crops to plant and limited landlord powers to evict tenants.

Radical politicians, led by Jesse Collings, popularised the idea that rural exodus could be checked by establishing peasant proprietors on the land. His proposal in 1886 that labourers should be given the chance of acquiring "three acres and a cow" was followed by the passage of Small Holdings Acts in 1892 and 1907. This legislation had a disappointing outcome, owing to landlord and farmer hostility, county council apathy, and the difficulty experienced in making small holdings economically viable. One policy not implemented, and in the opinion of landowners and farmers the only certain remedy for agricultural distress, was the abandonment of free trade in agricultural products.

After 1907 British agriculture revived owing to a run of good seasons and greater technical efficiency in crop growing and stock rearing. Rising prices increased the purchasing power of home consumers, bringing prosperity to those farmers who produced products enjoying a naturally protected market—milk, vegetables and eggs. Home produced fresh meat was fortunately preferred by many housewives to overseas chilled and frozen meat. Nevertheless it cannot be claimed that British farming in 1914 was in a satisfactory condition. It would remain unsatisfactory as long as the people of Great Britain remained content to live upon the food products of distant lands and failed to exploit the fertility of their own soil.

Chapter XXV

THE TARIFF REFORM MOVEMENT

The decision to become a free trade country was followed by a considerable expansion of Great Britain's industrial and commercial power. Nevertheless from 1880 the wisdom of continuing to permit access to the home market, unhampered by tariff barriers, was questioned. The reaction against free trade may be attributed to a variety of causes. The most potent was the post-1874 depression in agriculture. It could not be expected that landowners and farmers would do other than recall the warnings of Peel's opponents in 1846, that the repeal of the Corn Laws would inevitably lead to a fall in agricultural price levels. A second cause was the failure of other countries to follow the British example. Cobden and the Manchester school of economists had confidently prophesied that other countries would do so, and that the subsequent increase in commercial intercourse would, by increasing international economic interdependence, make war unlikely in the future. Such expectations were built on the belief that the trade patterns of the mid-nineteenth century would persist. Other nations, it was assumed, would be content to remain primarily producers of foodstuffs and raw materials, purchasing from Britain manufactured articles.

Before 1870 there were sound reasons for believing that these optimistic prophecies would be fulfilled. In the U.S.A. the development of manufacturing in New England had led to the adoption of a protective policy in 1816, and the passage in 1828 of the "Tariff of Abominations." But the southern states, primarily interested in cotton exporting, were able to secure the passage in 1846 and 1857 of low tariff Acts. Before the outbreak of the Civil War in 1861, therefore, there was every indication that the U.S.A. would continue to favour liberal trade policies. Liberal trade policies were also followed in Germany. The greater part of the post-1871 German Empire under the guidance of Prussia had by 1851 been economically unified by the formation of the Zollverein. There was free trade between members of the union and, as the Zollverein external tariff was primarily designed to raise revenue, the protective element in it was not large. Finally in France, where protectionist policies were favoured by agrarian, manufacturing and commercial interests, the adoption of free trade principles was delayed until the reign of Napoleon III.

Unfortunately this spread of liberal trade practices was checked after the 'sixties. Instead of enjoying the blessings of peace, Europeans and Americans experienced war, beginning with the Crimean War and continuing with the War of Italian Independence, the American Civil War and the three Prussian wars with Denmark, Austria and France. After 1870 armaments and high tariffs grew together, most European states and the U.S.A. becoming highly protectionist countries. Three main reasons may be cited to explain the collapse of the free trade movement. Firstly, the collapse of prices between 1874 and 1896 caused serious economic depression in Western Europe. Secondly, wars are expensive. In addition to borrowing, the readiest means of paying for them is by indirect taxation, that is by raising customs duties. As behind the shelter of wartime protective barriers industries develop, proposals to return to pre-war fiscal arrangements are resisted. Thirdly, protectionist ideas gained a new lease of life because Britain's trading rivals were not content to remain food and raw material producers. They wished to develop their latent economic potential and to enjoy the greater wealth which manufacturing countries acquire. Foreigners conceded that free trade was a suitable policy for highly industrialised Britain, but not for countries whose economic resources had not been fully exploited.

An intelligent and persuasive argument in support of protectionist policies was that of the German economist, Friedrich List (1789–1846). List differentiated between the needs of individuals, who having a short span of life are interested in immediate gains, and those of the State which can take the long-term view and plan for the future. A country, in the early stages of industrialising its economy, List argued, is justified in giving fiscal protection to its industries in order to prevent them from being destroyed by competition from those of more highly developed competitors. Such a policy may mean losses for a time but in the long run will eventuate in an increase in productive power. When, and only when, industries have become firmly established, free trade policies should be adopted. The effects of List's main book, *The National System of Political Economy* (1841), were considerable, but were not felt immediately. Very gradually, however, a school of thought developed which accepted his argument. Even in Britain the free trade economist John Stuart Mill conceded that protection was justified to foster "infant industries."

In Germany after 1871 List's views gained ready acceptance, as German, unlike British, economists had no inbred antipathy to State intervention. Bismarck's Germany began the retreat from liberal trade policies in 1879. Other British trade competitors, with the notable exceptions of Holland, Denmark and Switzerland, copied Germany's example. France in the 'eighties built up tariff barriers against agrarian imports and in 1892 enacted the Méline tariff which made her highly protectionist. In the U.S.A. the victory of the North in the Civil War, the need for revenue, and pressure from manufacturing interests, led to an increase in the levels of customs duties. With the defeat of the low tariff interests of the South, high protection became accepted national policy, the chief landmarks being the McKinley Tariff of 1890 and the Dingley Tariff of 1897. As a consequence of these fiscal changes, Britain in the closing decades of the nineteenth century found herself following a policy of one-sided free trade.

Opinion on economic affairs was also influenced by the increasing extent of State action to restrict individual liberty. In the closing decades of the nineteenth century it was more and more recognised that individual freedom alone was not enough. To quote from Winston Churchill's *Life of Lord Randolph Churchill*, "Conscience was free, trade was free. But hunger and squalor were also free; and people demanded something more than liberty." The reaction from *laisser-faire* ideals led to the passage of social legislation. Since the intervention of the State was productive of good in the field of social relationships, might it not be advisable to introduce some degree of communal control in the fields of commerce and productive industry. If State action could get rid of disgraceful conditions in factories and uproot squalor from town life, why should it not also intervene, for example, to save the countryside from ruin and the agricultural classes from bankruptcy?

Free trade critics were, as might be expected, most vociferous in times of trade depression. They used various labels for their programmes such as Fair Trade, Colonial Preference and Tariff Reform. In the 'eighties there were demands for "Fair Trade." A leading figure in this movement, Mr Farrar Ecroyd, proposed preferential treatment for Empire products and the imposition of a moderate tariff on foreign manufactures as a bargaining weapon to secure tariff reductions on British exports. A Fair Trade League was formed which was supported by some members of the Tory Party. Upon the President of the Board of Trade, Joseph Chamberlain, fell much of the burden of defending free trade in the House of Commons between 1880 and 1885, principally on the grounds that a protectionist policy would increase food prices, an argument that an urban electorate could be expected to sympathise with. In defence of free trade a former Permanent Secretary to the Board of Trade, Lord Farrer, published a book entitled *Free Trade versus Fair Trade*.

Trade revival in the late 'eighties, coupled with the emergence of Home Rule for Ireland as the dominant political issue, led to a temporary cessation of protectionist agitation. It revived in the closing years of the century under the dynamic leadership of the former free trade spokesman, Joseph Chamberlain. The revival of interest in protectionist policies was linked with a change in the attitude of Great Britain to her overseas dependencies. After 1783 it was generally assumed that sooner or later the colonies, like the U.S.A., would opt for independence. The decision by Great Britain to become a free trade country meant the end of preferential treatment for colonial exports and the abandonment of the ideal of a self-supporting empire. The dismantlement of the old colonial system was a gradual process. With the repeal of the Navigation Laws, trade between Britain and her overseas possessions ceased to be an imperial monopoly. The system of colonial trade preferences and prohibitions was overhauled and finally abandoned. Wheat preferences, never of great practical importance, were abolished in 1846-49, sugar preferences between 1846 and 1854 and lumber preferences in the 'sixties. By the Enabling Act of 1846 the colonies were empowered to abolish preferential duties on imports from Great Britain. In other words, they were given fiscal freedom, but on the assumption that they would follow the example of the Mother Country and adopt free trade policies.

Attempts by the imperial government to insist on free trade policies throughout the empire failed. Having gained fiscal freedom colonial governments insisted on using it to impose protective duties. They were not content to remain producers of primary products only. Instead, being ambitious to become economically more self-sufficient, they erected tariff barriers to protect "infant industries" and to shelter their more highly paid labour from the competition of lower paid British and European workers. Canada was the pioneer in the erection of protective tariffs, her import duties being raised to protective levels by the Cayley Tariff (1858), the Galt Tariff (1859) and by the fiscal legislation of the Macdonald Government in 1879. Victoria, in Australia, followed Canada's example in 1867.

The tariff policies of colonial governments gave support to the opinion that sooner or later imperial links would be severed. After 1815 British governments were reluctant to assume far-reaching overseas responsibilities. New Zealand (1839) and Natal (1843) were annexed, but only to prevent them falling into other hands. The Sand River (1852) and Bloemfontein (1854) Conventions thrust independence upon the two Boer republics north of the Orange River. In 1856 the British Government refused to share in the construction of the Suez Canal, and it was not until the 'seventies that it was persuaded to end the disorderly state of affairs in the Western Pacific by making Fiji a Protectorate (1874) and by appointing a High Commissioner for the area (1875).

Anti-imperialist influences were dominant for several reasons. Overseas possessions were costly to defend and apt to stir up international ill-feeling. As late as 1868 Bismarck recorded, "England is abandoning her colonial policy; she finds it too costly." Anglo-American experience suggested that trade with colonial territories would increase after they had become independent, and that Britain had no need to possess political sovereignty and monopolistic trading rights in order to find markets for textile and iron exports. Free trade, not government regulated commerce, suited her interests better. In any case, markets in the as yet undeveloped, sparsely populated colonial territories were secondary to those in the more highly populated countries of central and western Europe. It is not surprising, therefore, that for two generations after the Napoleonic Wars, dependent, overseas territories were thought of as being more burdensome than profitable.

Contrary to expectation, free co-operation between self-governing countries proved to be a better cement of imperial unity than unimaginative control by the Colonial Office in London. Hence, after 1870, a new climate of opinion about the Empire becomes noticeable. The people of Great Britain became imperially minded, realising with boastful pride during the Royal Jubilees of 1887 and 1897 that Britain was the centre of an empire upon which the sun never set. It was certainly uplifting from 1885 onwards to read the poems and stories of the young journalist from India, Rudyard Kipling, who persuaded his countrymen that they were a chosen people, a conquering race, called to take up the white man's burden and lay down the law to lesser breeds fortunate enough to live within the dominions of their Queen. But the post-1870 overseas expansion was not wholly a British movement. It was a European one. "About 1870," Leonard Woolf has written, "Europe had just become ripe for economic imperialism." Newly industrialised countries needed markets to absorb their exports and sources for supplies of raw materials. These twin economic pressures triggered off a scramble for African and Asiatic territories by Britain, France and Germany, and by Italy and Belgium. The Europeanisation of the greater part of the world was made possible by improved means of communication which annihilated distance and increased the degree of economic inter-dependence between European states and the rest of the globe. Refrigeration made possible the exportation of perishable commodities, while scientific agriculture and tropical medicine enabled tropical lands to contribute their quota to satisfy the food and raw materials needs of industrialised Europe.

Owing to her command of the seas Great Britain acquired more overseas territory than her rivals. As far as she was concerned the new imperial acquisitiveness may be said to have begun with Disraeli's purchase of Suez Canal shares (1875) and the proclamation of Queen Victoria as Empress of India (1877). In the 'eighties and 'nineties annexations took place on an unprecedented and spectacular scale. Egypt and other territories were occupied to safeguard "the highway to India." Claims to vast regions were made by chartered trading companies, the British North Borneo Company (1881), the Royal Niger Company (1882), the British East Africa Company (1888) and the British South African Company (1889) of Cecil Rhodes. As Providence had put "backward peoples" in possession of much land capable of providing the commodities needed by industrialised Europe, it was only common sense to annex their homelands to avoid waste of their economic potential. It would be untrue, however, to attribute British overseas expansion wholly to economic motives. Imperial acquisitiveness was prompted also by military and strategic considerations. As our protectionist-minded rivals monopolised the trade of the lands they annexed Great Britain was more active in the game of imperialist grab than she might have been if free access had been the universal rule. Moral and sentimental motives also played their part, the urge to spread knowledge of Christianity, to introduce the rule of law, to abolish slavery and the slave trade. Hence, missionaries, like Dr Livingstone occupy a prominent place in the roll of nineteenth-century empire builders.

The appointment in 1895 of Joseph Chamberlain (1836–1914) as Secretary of State for the Colonies is a landmark in the history of the relations between Great Britain and the colonies. A Birmingham screw manufacturer, a member of the firm of Nettlefold and Chamberlain, he abandoned business for municipal political life. Chamberlain was a leader of the nonconformists who opposed denominational schools, and as Mayor of Birmingham from 1873 to 1876, championed the cause of municipal reform. Slums were demolished and gas and water undertakings were municipalised. In later life he played a major part in the foundation of the University of Birmingham. When in 1876 he entered Parliament as

M.P. for Birmingham it was as a member of the radical wing of the Liberal Party. But ten years later, disagreeing with Gladstone's Irish policy, he left the party and ultimately joined the Conservatives.

If Chamberlain had continued his association with the radical wing of the Liberal Party his achievements as Colonial Secretary would have been impossible. Unlike many of his former political associates Chamberlain was never "a little Englander." Deeply interested in social reform he saw the Empire as a vast undeveloped heritage, the wise exploitation of which could provide a solution to contemporary social and economic distress. To this end he instituted constructive measures of empire development. The Colonial Loans Act (1899) authorised the Treasury to make loans to Crown colonies for capital expenditure. In 1900 trustee status was given to colonial stocks. Chamberlain played an important part in the institution of imperial penny post and in the foundation of Schools of Tropical Medicine in Liverpool and London. At the third of the Colonial Conferences, that held in 1897, economic policy was a major topic of discussion. His tenure of office was also noteworthy for the beginning of attempts to arrest the declining fortunes of the islands in the West Indies. An enquiry into the causes of their depressed condition was made in 1897 by a Royal Commission, which revealed that their legendary beauty was only a mask hiding the deplorable conditions under which the vast majority of the islanders lived. As a result of its findings the Imperial Department of Agriculture was founded, first in Trinidad, similar departments being subsequently opened in Malaya, West and East Africa and in Egypt.

Chamberlain sought to persuade the peoples of Great Britain that it was sound policy to promote social and economic progress in the undeveloped territories that owed allegiance to the Crown. But before he resigned his post at the Colonial Office he suggested a much more revolutionary scheme, namely, the abandonment of the policy that consumers should always be able to buy at the cheapest possible price. In other words, in order to consolidate empire unity he proposed to abandon free trade and institute a system of preferential tariffs for empire products. Two developments encouraged Chamberlain in recommending this programme, firstly, the assistance given to the Mother Country during the Second Boer War, and secondly, the offer by Canada in 1897, without asking for reciprocal concessions, of preferential treatment to imports from Britain. This amounted to an eighth reduction in duties, raised to one third in 1900. In 1898 Canada also gave preferences to imports from several Crown colonies and from India.

Canadian policy, however, was not the expression of a desire to promote the cause of imperial unity. Rather, it was due to fear of possible economic and political domination by the U.S.A. Eleven times, between 1865 and 1898, Canada offered to sign a trade reciprocity treaty with her giant southern neighbour. The U.S.A. refused, partly because it was absorbed in exploiting its own western hinterlands, and partly because it feared that by lowering duties on imports from Canada it would open a back door through which British manufactures could evade its high tariff walls. Subsequent developments showed that there was no likelihood of Canada becoming an advocate of imperial economic unity. Although from the 'nineties the expanding prairie agricultural communities favoured free trade, the industrial East, politically dominant, supported policies of national development and industrial tariffs.

Chamberlain only got minority support in the Cabinet for his proposals. In 1902, to raise war revenue, the shilling registration duty on corn, abolished in 1866, had been re-imposed. Chamberlain suggested that it should be repealed on empire corn and retained on foreign imports. His colleagues decided to support the Chancellor of the Exchequer and repeal it completely. This led to a split in the Unionist Party. In May 1903, Chamberlain outlined to his constituents in Birmingham proposals for a system of imperial preference designed to promote three objectives, firstly, imperial economic unity, secondly, an increase in revenue to finance measures of social reform, and thirdly, a reduction of unemployment by giving protection to British industries. In July 1903 the Tariff Reform League was formed. In September Chamberlain resigned from the Cabinet, informing the Prime Minister, Arthur Balfour, that he intended to devote himself to the task of converting the electorate. Three eminent economists assisted by publicly criticising "one-sided free trade," Professor W. A. S. Hewins, Archdeacon W. Cunningham, who published *The Rise and Decline of the Free Trade Movement*, and Professor W. Ashley, the author of *The Tariff Problem*. Free traders countered with a manifesto signed by fourteen equally eminent economists. The Prime Minister, primarily concerned to prevent an open breach in the Unionist Party which could be politically disastrous, found himself in a very embarrassing situation. In a memorandum to the Cabinet, made public in September 1903, entitled *Economic Notes on Insular Free Trade,* Balfour pithily summarised the arguments of the warring factions, but without committing himself to supporting either point of view.

Chamberlain opened his campaign in a speech at Glasgow on 6th October 1903, which was followed by speeches in a number of major cities. British manufactures, he told his audiences, had been losing ground since 1872. Those who flocked to hear him at Greenock were told, "Agriculture has been practically destroyed, sugar has gone, silk has gone, iron is threatened, cotton will go. How long are you going to stand it?" The programme he outlined was as follows: no taxes on raw materials; low taxes on food other than colonial, and to offset the slight increase in the cost of living, a reduction in the duties on tea, sugar and other commodities of popular consumption. Home industries were to be protected by an ideal, scientific tariff constructed by a body of experts commissioned by the Tariff Reform League to collect evidence and make recommendations. The free traders met the challenge by organising meetings at which the principal spokesman was the future Prime Minister, Herbert Asquith.

Chamberlain managed to convince a majority of the Unionist Party with the exception of a hard core of free traders. On the other hand his campaign re-united the Liberal Party which had been split by the Home Rule and Boer War controversies. But the country as a whole was not won over, most wage earners preferring the large, cheap, free-trade loaf, to the small, dear, loaf they were told tariff reform policies would bring in their train. The fiscal arguments were in any case too abstruse for comprehension by a Board School educated electorate. It was all too easy for Asquith and other Liberal Party orators to produce statistics contradicting those of the Tariff Reform League.

The early years of the twentieth century were years of depression in which the percentage of trade unionists unemployed rose from 2·5 in 1900 to 6 in 1904. But this period was not one in which the value of British exports and re-exports declined. They did fall from £354 million in 1900 to £348 million in 1901 but rose to £371 million in 1904 and to £461 million in 1906. The actual course of events did not lend credence to the dismal prophecy that British industry was on the verge of ruin. The 1896–1914 period was one of rising prices due in part to the increase in gold production, mainly from the South African Rand. Rising prices meant a boom in trade and industry. The cotton industry showed signs of recovering prosperity, the numbers of workers employed in it rising from 526,000 in 1891, to 548,000 in 1901 and to 620,000 in 1911. Export values, £95,835,000 in 1901, increased to £113,417,006 in 1906. In the woollen and worsted industries the labour force, which had fallen from 275,000 in 1891 to 235,000 in 1900, increased slowly to 261,000 in 1911. Exports fluctuated in value in the early years of the twentieth century, reaching a maximum of £34,818,000 in 1910, roughly equal to the export values in the 'seventies and 'eighties and a little higher than they had tended to be in the 'nineties. It would be erroneous, however, to conclude from the failure of the woollen industries to increase their exports that they were declining ones. World markets for woollens are much less extensive than those for cotton fabrics. Actually between 1900 and 1913 the value of raw wool imports from Australia, New Zealand, South Africa and India rose considerably, the resultant increased production being absorbed by the home market.

In the production of steel the situation was not as unsatisfactory as tariff reform propaganda suggested. It was true that the British share of world production had fallen from one-third in 1880 to less than one-seventh in 1902. On the other hand, British steel workers were producing 1,020,000 tons in 1880 and 4,850,000 tons in 1902. Protectionists made much of the increase in Great Britain's importation of iron and steel goods, mainly from Germany and the U.S.A., between 1897 and 1903, when import values rose from £2,610,000 to £9,582,000. But would it have been in the interests of British industry as a whole to have raised steel prices by imposing a tariff on steel imports? In 1901, out of a total working population of 16,312,000, 1,447,000 were listed in the census returns as engaged in the manufacture of metal goods and vehicles, and in engineering and shipbuilding. Chamberlain's Tariff Commission could not have recommended tariff schedules which would have been equally acceptable to Tees-side smelters and Tyne, Wear and Clydeside shipbuilders. Free traders could counter the criticism of German and American "dumping" of steel by quoting the considerable increases in British exports of steel goods and machinery. Values of exports of iron and steel goods rose from £29,700,000 in 1900 to £38,566,000 in 1905, and those of machinery from £20,755,000 to £24,787,000. By 1913 iron and steel exports had risen to £55,228,000 and machinery exports to £33,670,000.

Tariff reform had no chance of winning majority electoral support at a time when a large proportion of the population could discern no personal advantage in voting for the abandonment of free trade. To the 752,000 miners in 1901, for example, whose labours enabled Great Britain to export 30,622,000 tons of coal, Chamberlain's policies meant higher food prices. Nor was there much support either in Britain or in the overseas territories for Chamberlain's vision of the Empire facing the World as an economic and defence unit. At home agrarian interests regarded Canadian prairie exports as just as harmful as those from the U.S.A., the Ukraine and the Argentine. Nor were the overseas dominions enamoured of suggestions that they should continue to develop primarily as suppliers of food and raw materials to an industrialised Britain. In 1902, except to a very limited extent in Canada, industrialisation within the Empire had hardly begun. The future, however, was to show that the governments of territories in which British and European emigrants had settled would seek to erect tariff barriers to protect their "infant industries."

How unsuccessful Chamberlain had been was made plain in January 1906. The general election of that year saw only 158 Tories successful at the polls, 16 of whom were free traders. In no real sense, however, can these results be interpreted as wholly the result of tariff reform agitation. Other issues had made the Balfour government unpopular—the Education Act of 1902, Chinese labour in the Transvaal, revelations of War Office incompetence during the Boer War and heavy taxation. Shortly afterwards Chamberlain had a paralytic stroke and was therefore politically inactive until his death in July 1914. Two elections took place in 1910 which the Tories failed to win. Then in 1911, Bonar Law, a convinced tariff reformer, succeeded Balfour as Leader of the Opposition, but on the outbreak of the First World War it appeared to most political observers that prospects of Great Britain ceasing to be a free trade country were very remote indeed. Why she did so in 1932 will be discussed in a later chapter.

CHAPTER XXVI

TRADE UNIONISM AFTER 1876 AND THE
RISE OF THE LABOUR PARTY

As explained in a previous chapter, during the third quarter of the nineteenth century, a period of prosperity, skilled workers were able to form stable unions, and to obtain legal recognition of their practices by the passage in 1875 of the Conspiracy and Protection of Property Act and the Employers and Workmen Act. This legislation was naturally accepted with gratification by leading trade unionists. According to one of them, George Odger, the Conspiracy and Protection of Property Act was "the greatest boon ever given to the sons of toil." But such complacency was not shared by the much more numerous "sons of toil," the semi-skilled and unskilled workers. The slumps of 1876–79 and 1884–86 were responsible not only for a fall in business profits but also for widespread destitution, misery and unemployment. Not surprisingly, therefore, a younger generation became critical of the policies of the conservative-minded leaders of skilled craft trade unionism.

Statisticians have shown that during the fourth quarter of the nineteenth century real wages rose. What their figures do not reveal was the existence of countless thousands of derelicts whose existence was made only too evident in 1886 and 1887 when ragged multitudes of starving unemployed rioted in London's West End. It was at this time that the Liverpool shipowner and sociologist, Charles Booth, began his statistical researches into social and economic conditions in London. The results of these, printed in his *Life and Labour of the People in London* (1891–1903), revealed that one-third of London's population lived on the verge of starvation. Evidence of the need for social reform was also provided by the Reports of the Royal Commissions on the Housing of the Poor (1884–89), and on the Aged Poor (1895).

Private philanthropists and social reformers also assisted in making the comfortable classes aware of the existence of deep-seated social evils. The economic historian, Arnold Toynbee (1852–83), who distrusted the study of economics as an armchair, intellectual pursuit, sought by an examination of conditions in

Whitechapel to obtain a better understanding of social and economic problems. His activities as a practical social reformer were commemorated after his death by the foundation in 1884 of a social settlement, Toynbee Hall, the first of the University Settlements designed to improve and uplift the conditions under which the ragged poor lived. It was in Whitechapel also, in 1865, that the Methodist minister, the Rev. William Booth, founded the East London Christian Mission, later called the Salvation Army. The Salvationists' campaigns against the evils of drink and prostitution provoked hooligan brutalities in London and provincial towns that nowadays seem barely credible.

Much thought was given to finding cures for the malady of widespread persistent poverty. One remedy, the taxation of land values, was suggested by the American political economist Henry George (1829–97) in *Progress and Poverty* (1879). Some middle class intellectuals advocated the adoption of socialist policies. Socialist, or to use the word chosen by Marx and Engels, communist ideas, are of great antiquity. Plato in his *Republic* and Sir Thomas More in *Utopia* (1516), for example, describe ideal forms of society organised on communist principles. The organisation of society on a communal basis was a marked feature of life in the Middle Ages. In the first half of the nineteenth century working-class activity was stimulated by ideas derived from the Utopian Socialists, in England Robert Owen, and in France, Saint Simon, Charles Fourier, Etienne Cabet and Louis Blanc. These early socialist writers, however, accomplished nothing towards a practical solution of social ills but they did make public opinion aware of their existence.

The modern socialist movement really dates from the foundation of the Communist League in London in 1847. The objectives of the League were outlined in the Communist Manifesto, drawn up by Marx and Engels, followed in 1867 by "the Bible of Socialism," *Das Kapital* by Karl Marx. It was in London in 1864, where Marx lived and worked, that the first International Working Men's Association was formed. Under the leadership of H. M. Hyndman, a Cambridge graduate who played cricket for Sussex, the Social Democratic Federation was founded (1881). For a few months William Morris, the idealist, poet and craftsman, was associated with the Federation. In the winter of 1883–84 the Fabian Society was formed. The number of members, which included Sidney and Beatrice Webb, Bernard Shaw, Graham Wallas and Annie Besant, was never large, but was distinguished and influential. Their goal was a socialist state to be reached by painstaking research to find the causes of, and cures for, social ills. The principles of collectivism were popularised in a volume of *Fabian Essays,* and in *Fabian*

Tracts which outlined a practical programme of action for reforming politicians elected to serve as Poor Law Guardians, School Board members and local government councillors.

Fabian methods of achieving social reform, by permeation of existing organs of government, were more acceptable to British workers than the recourse to crude violence the intellectuals of the Social Democratic Federation verbally threatened to organise. The unintelligible socialist jargon used by Marxians made their publications difficult to read and impossible to understand. Far more influential in spreading the socialist gospel was the immensely popular *Clarion*, the weekly newspaper of Robert Blatchford, and his books, *Britain for the British* and *Merrie England*.

In the closing decades of the nineteenth century there was never any possibility of a workers' uprising against the bourgeoisie, the class enemy of Marxian analysis. British workmen did not constitute a homogeneous proletariat condemned by Marxian theory to increasing misery. Certainly, the members of skilled craft unions—engineers, textile workers, carpenters, bricklayers and printers—never thought of themselves as members of a starving army of toilers, which could only hope to secure social justice by taking up arms against capitalist oppressors. On the contrary, they enjoyed improving standards of living in a period of falling prices. The more thrifty sought to emulate middle class standards and through building society loans to become owners of their homes. They were members of friendly and co-operative societies and of trade unions which, having built up considerable financial resources, used them to protect their members against the risks of life—sickness, accidents and the impoverishment of old age.

This "labour aristocracy" was not a field of recruitment for a proletarian army dedicated to the use of anarchic violence as the surest means of realising a fanciful socialist utopia. In fact, anxious though they were to influence governments to pass measures of social reform, trade union leaders did not think of themselves as socialists. Many of the most influential of them had been influenced by the Methodist gospel of salvation. They served their chapels as local preachers, and their fellow workers as trade union officials, and sat on co-operative society and friendly societies committees. Two of the most highly respected leaders of the Northumberland miners, for example, the Rt. Hon. Thomas Burt and the Rt. Hon. Charles Fenwick, were local preachers. When they were elected to Parliament it was as working-class members of the Liberal Party, not as socialist M.P.s.

It might plausibly have been forecasted that the non-revolutionary prejudices of the "labour aristocracy" would not be shared by unskilled labourers and by the under-employed denizens of East End slums. Experience has taught otherwise. Many of the underprivileged, enfranchised in 1867 and 1884, so far from using their votes to send socialists to Westminster, did not even support "Lib-Lab" candidates. Disraeli's "Tory democracy" proved to have substance. Widening the franchise strengthened the hold of the Tory Party on the levers of political power.

A younger generation of militant trade unionists, however, did revolt against the conservative complacency of their elders who controlled the craft unions. They found leaders in two engineers, John Burns, the first working man to become a cabinet minister, and Thomas Mann, an agitator with considerable oratorical talents who had joined the Social Democratic Federation. The new militant trade unionism achieved notable successes during the "Great Depression" of the 'eighties. The first was the strike of the Bryant and May match girls, organised by Annie Besant. In 1888 Bryant and May paid their shareholders a 23 per cent dividend. The girls earned four to thirteen shillings a week, less fines for such offences as answering back, dropping matches or having dirty feet. In addition, it was traditional for the firm to deduct one penny in the shilling for no known reason. As the girls ate at benches contaminated with phosphorus, they contracted phossy-jaw, necrosis of the jaw which mouldered. One, only 15 years of age, lost her hair as a result of carrying trays of matches on her head. A public outcry which followed these revelations forced the Company to give way after a strike which lasted from 6th July to 11th July 1888. Deductions and fines ceased and a separate eating room was provided.

The match girls had won a victory which was a landmark in industrial history, demonstrating that militancy offered prospects to unskilled workers which the policies of respectable leaders of craft unionism could not match. The following year, 1889, is memorable for two other notable victories by militant "new unionism." Will Thorne formed the Gas Workers and General Workers Union which demanded and secured an 8-hour day and an increase in pay. Then, led by Ben Tillett, the London dockers struck for a standard wage of 6*d*. an hour, "the dockers' tanner." With the help of Burns and Mann, assisted by the effective mediation of Cardinal Manning and financial help from Australian workers, the dockers won an overwhelming victory.

The New Unionism, drawing its members from the unskilled, badly paid workers, levied low rates of subscriptions to finance aggressive strike action. Many of its leaders supported collectivist policies in contrast to the older generation of craft unionists, who rejected as un-English the Marxian creed with its revolutionary and class warfare undertones. Nevertheless, the thought and practice of the craft union leaders, originally rooted in the doctrines of the classical economists, were modified by support for a programme of social reform through the agency of the Liberal Party. A Labour Representation League was formed in 1869, two miners, Alexander Macdonald and Thomas Burt, becoming M.P.s in 1874. In 1884 the franchise was extended to the rural and mining areas. In many parts of the country local bodies were organised to secure the return of independent Labour M.P.s, a movement led by an Ayrshire miner, James Keir Hardie. Keir Hardie, John Burns and the seamen's leader, Havelock Wilson, became M.P.s in 1892. Ten other Labour M.P.s, five of them miners, were also elected, but under the auspices of the Liberal Party. In the following year, 1893, Keir Hardie founded the Independent Labour Party whose programme of reform included an 8-hour day, a legal minimum wage, full maintenance for the unemployed and the nationalisation of land and basic industries.

The I.L.P., the political wing of the Labour movement, was a socialist party, but in deference to the prejudices of the leaders of the industrial wing of the movement, the trade unions, the word "Socialist" was not included in its name. The men who controlled the trade unions distrusted as too reminiscent of class war the I.L.P. objective, a politically independent group of Labour members in the House of Commons. The leaders of the co-operative movement for their part either favoured political neutrality or were politically attached to Gladstonian Liberalism. The I.L.P., therefore, met considerable opposition in its attempts to organise the working-class voters in one political party, pledged to "secure the collective ownership of all the means of production, distribution and exchange."

Trade unionists attracted to socialist ideas who held key offices in local trade union branches sponsored resolutions at meetings of the Trade Union Congress in favour of co-operation with the I.L.P. Their efforts were assisted by the death of Gladstone in 1898 and by the decline of Liberalism as a political force in the closing decades of the nineteenth century. A resolution in favour of the formation of a Labour Representation Committee was passed at the 1899 Trade Union Congress but its effectiveness was of limited value as trade unions could accept or reject Congress resolutions. The L.R.C. came into existence in 1900, with the future Prime Minister, James Ramsay Macdonald as its secretary. It consisted of representatives from the I.L.P., the Social Democratic Federation, the Fabian Society and a minority of trade unions. But the new organisation was never representative of all shades of opinion within the labour movement. The co-operative societies, traditionally politically neutral, were not represented at the conference convened by the Parliamentary Committee of the T.U.C. at which the L.R.C. was born. Many trade unions, including those of the miners and cotton workers, refused to join an organisation dominated by middle-class socialist theorists. In contrast, the Social Democratic Federation soon defected, as the L.R.C. was committed to a policy of social reform not to one of Marxian socialism. Lastly, Fabians like Sidney and Beatrice Webb, who did not favour the setting up of an independent political party, were a critical influence at L.R.C. meetings.

A factor in weakening trade union resistance to the formation of a separate Labour party was a series of judicial decisions in the closing years of the nineteenth century, which threatened to undermine the legal rights trade unionists thought they had been guaranteed by legislation in the 'seventies. In the cases of Temperton v. Russell (1893) and Trollope and Sons v. The London Building Trades Federation (1896), the courts ruled that a trade union could be sued for damages when loss was suffered by a third party with which it was not involved in a trade dispute. This interpretation of the law was confirmed in the case of Allen v. Flood by the Court of Queen's Bench and the Court of Appeal, but reversed in 1898 by a majority decision in the House of Lords. The legality even of peaceful picketing was challenged by judicial decisions in the cases of Lyons v. Wilkins (1896–98) and Charnock v. Court (1897). Then came the rulings of the House of Lords in the Taff Vale Railway Case (1901), and, two weeks later its decision in the case of Quinn v. Leathem.

In 1900 the employees of the Taff Vale Railway Company went on strike. During the strike there was a certain amount of violence, admittedly not instigated or condoned by the union, the Amalgamated Society of Railway Servants. Nevertheless, when against legal advice the General Manager of the Company, Ammon Beasley, claimed damages, the Company was awarded £23,000 and costs. The second case, Quinn v. Leathem, arose out of the attempt by a Belfast Union of Butchers' Assistants to organise a boycott of the meat of a wholesale butcher named Leathem who employed non-union labour. The House of Lords, in apparent contradiction to its decision in the case of Allen v. Flood, ruled that Leathem was entitled to damages.

To say the least this judge-made law was bitterly resented. It had been promulgated at a time when labour was on the defensive, following the failure of strikes by quarry men in North Wales (1896–98) and by engineers and South Wales miners from 1897 to

1898. If the decisions of the Law Lords were to remain, a resumption of militancy would be a very hazardous undertaking. But not only was this judge-made law damaging to trade union interests, it was also, as Lord Haldane wrote, "in a very muddled condition." Eminent lawyers could not have forecast what judgments in future were likely to be handed down, other than by reasonably assuming that judges could be expected to have an anti-union bias.

Rather short-sightedly, employers did not hesitate to take advantage of the legal situation. Union leaders countered by pressing for legislation reversing the judicial decisions. Unions, which had hitherto held aloof, joined the L.R.C. As the Salisbury and Balfour Tory governments took no action, in the election of 1906, Labour, except in Scotland and a few other areas, co-operated with the Liberals. In all about 54 Labour and "Lib-Lab" candidates were returned, 29 of whom were sponsored by the L.R.C. These latter functioned as a separate party in the House of Commons under the name of the Labour Party.

In 1906 the Trade Disputes Act was passed, its provisions being based on the recommendations of the Royal Commission on Trade Disputes and Combinations. The Act of 1906 legalised peaceful picketing and persuasion. Trade unions were not to be held responsible for Torts, that is civil wrongs for which damages may be claimed. As far as the law was concerned, trade unions, and also employers' associations, had no corporate existence. In industrial disputes the courts were concerned with individuals, employees or employers. These could be and have been prosecuted, but trade union officials enjoy a privileged position, in as much as the Act of 1906 gave them protection against legal proceedings arising out of trade disputes. This fundamental principle of trade union law that unions were not to be treated as responsible agents was breached by the Trade Disputes Act of 1927. By it, in one specific type of strike, the General Strike, participating unions and officials could be held accountable.

In 1909 the Labour Party and trade unions were gravely affected by another judicial decision, the Osborne Judgment. Trade unions had for a very long time spent money on political objects. In their early days such expenditure had been incurred to finance campaigns for an extension of the franchise and amendments to trade union law. Later money was subscribed to promote the election of trade union candidates who voted with whichever party, Liberal or Tory, was currently thought most likely to promote trade union interests. The right of trade unions to use their funds for political purposes remained unquestioned until in the early twentieth century some of them gave financial support to the Labour Party. In fact, the legality of trade union expenditure for political purposes was confirmed by the courts in 1907.

In 1908, the Walthamstow branch secretary of the Amalgamated Society of Railway Engineers, W. E. Osborne, sought a judicial ruling that such a use of trade union funds was *ultra vires*. Osborne lost his case in the Court of King's Bench but this judgment was reversed in the Court of Appeal and by the House of Lords, on the grounds that the legal activities of trade unions, as defined in the trade union legislation of the 'seventies, did not specifically include the support of a political party. The situation was eased by State payment of M.P.s in 1911, but convincing Parliament that it ought to reverse the Osborne Judgment, by passing a law empowering trade unions to coerce members into financially supporting a political party with which they disagreed, was not practical politics. After all, there were strong minorities in trade unions opposed to Labour Party and socialist policies. Legislative action was therefore delayed until the passing of the Trade Union Act of 1913. This recognised the right of trade unions to incur expenditure for political purposes if, by secret ballot, members agreed. A separate political fund had to be established under rules approved by the Registrar of Friendly Societies, and the rights of dissenting minorities were safeguarded by a clause permitting members to "contract out." About 100,000 trade unionists did in fact exercise their right to sign "contracting out" forms in 1925. This procedure remained unchanged until by the Trade Disputes Act of 1927 "contracting in" became the rule. In other words, from 1927 until the Act of 1927 was repealed in 1946, no part of a member's subscription could be used for political purposes without his prior written consent.

The Act of 1913, legalising trade union political activity, was enacted at a time when the prestige of the Labour Party was at a low ebb. The considerable disappointment with the results of reliance upon political activity expressed itself in the industrial militancy which characterised the 1910–14 era. The 1896–1914 period was one in which prices rose. Industrial production increased, markedly so in the boom years from 1910, and British trade expanded. Exports of home products, valued at £240,146,000 in 1896 had risen to £300,711,000 by 1904 and to £525,245,000 by 1913. Imports increased from £571,546,000 in 1896, to £647,327,000 in 1904 and to £768,734,000 in 1913. Profits and interest on invested capital also tended to rise. From income tax returns, it has been calculated, that between 1899 and 1913 there was a 55 per cent increase in gross assessments under Schedule D on profits from a trade, profession and interest payments received.

On the other hand, as the following index numbers show, rises in money wages did not keep pace with increasing living costs.

WAGES AND PRICES IN THE UNITED KINGDOM

1850 = 100

Year	Average money wages	Average retail prices	A real wage index for those in full-time employment
1896	163·0	83	176
1900	179·0	89	183
1904	173·0	93	170
1910	179·5	99	169
1912	184·0	103	168
1914	189·5	102	174

These statistics confirm the contention of contemporary wage earners and their wives that they were not getting a fair share of increasing prosperity. Neither were they certain that work would always be available as there were considerable variations in the level of industrial activity. In boom years the percentage of trade unionists unemployed was low, 2 per cent in 1899 and 2·1 per cent in 1913. In years of depression it was high, 6 per cent in 1904, 7·8 per cent in 1908 and 7·7 per cent in 1909. In addition it should be borne in mind that there were very many non-unionists, the number of whom not regularly employed is unknown. It may of course be argued that wages were only part of the real income of workers who enjoyed considerable benefits from expanding social services which in 1910 absorbed 3·05 per cent of the national income. Such benefits as free education, sickness and unemployment payments, and old age pensions were made possible by an increasing national income. But these were not universally enjoyed, neither did they bulk as prominently in the minds of the workers as the undoubted fact that their real wages had declined.

Militant action was organised and inspired by extremists who advocated strike action to secure the transfer of the ownership and management of industry to organised groups of workers. The name, "Syndicalism," given to this programme, is derived from the French name for trade union, *"syndicat."* Syndicalists opposed both capitalist ownership and state socialism. The latter, in their opinion, meant democratic control not by the workers, but by a soulless bureaucracy. The Syndicalist idea which had been popularised in America by the Marxist, Daniel De Leon, and in France by Georges

Sorel, was introduced from France into Britain about 1910 by Tom Mann, Mann founded an Industrial Syndicalist Education League and published a monthly journal, the *Industrial Syndicalist*.

Syndicalism in Britain was never more than a minority movement, but its advocates had some success in spreading dissatisfaction with reliance on political methods and in organising strikes between 1910 and 1914. In 1911 Havelock Wilson led a successful strike by the National Sailors' and Firemans' Union. Tillett and Mann brought out the dockers in the same year. A two-day strike by employees of the railway companies, the first national railway strike, was ended by the intervention of Lloyd George and the setting up of Conciliation Boards. The numbers of workers affected by strikes and lockouts was even greater in 1912 than it had been in 1911. In March 1912 the Miners' Federation, formed in 1888 and joined by the Durham and Northumberland men in 1908, organised a strike to secure a minimum wage. The miners were, with difficulty, persuaded to return to work when the Government hurriedly passed a law guaranteeing them a minimum wage of five shillings a day. Less successful were the dockers, who, in May, challenged the newly formed Port of London Authority and its tough chairman, Lord Devonport. Despite Ben Tillett's public prayer on Tower Hill to the Almighty, to "strike Lord Devonport dead," the dockers were beaten, although they remained on strike until August. In 1913 the number of workers involved in industrial disputes fell to 516,000, the most noteworthy strike being that of the Irish Transport Workers Union led by Jim Larkin. It ultimately collapsed.

Trade unionism in 1914 differed considerably from that of the 'seventies. Firstly, the numbers of trade unionists was much larger, increasing from 1,928,000 in 1900 to 4,133,000 in 1913. Secondly, although less than a quarter of the working population in 1913 was included in the membership, trade unionism was more comprehensive than it had been in mid-Victorian times, as unions had been founded for unskilled labourers, white-collar workers and women. Thirdly, there was an increasing tendency towards the grouping of unionists in large national unions. This development had become advisable as business units, with the spread of joint stock company enterprise, had increased in size.

As a step towards realising their programme of workers' control, Syndicalists favoured the formation of fewer and larger unions. It was far from easy, however, to negotiate terms for federation, let alone amalgamation. Skilled craftsmen would not become members of industrial unions dominated by unskilled workers. Officials were concerned at the personal loss of status mergers would entail.

Arranging financial terms for uniting unions with varying assets and differing obligations to members was a complex matter of accountancy. The legal obstacles were also considerable, the Trade Union Act of 1876 requiring a two-thirds majority of the whole membership before a change could be made. An Act in 1917, however, simplified the amalgamation procedure, laying down that a 50 per cent poll, with 60 per cent of those voting in favour, should suffice. In spite of these difficulties some notable amalgamations were effected before 1914. In 1910 about 36 unions of waterside transport workers were combined in the National Transport Workers' Federation. A "new model" for subsequent amalgamations was that in 1913 of four unions which brought into existence the National Union of Railwaymen. Significantly, however, the Associated Society of Locomotive Engineers (1880) and the Railway Clerks' Association did not join the N.U.R. A step towards realising the Syndicalists' vision of one workers' union was taken in 1914 by the formation of the "Triple Alliance" joined by the Miners, Railwaymen and the Transport Workers. The threat of a general strike, however, which would have seriously disrupted the economic life of the country, was averted by the outbreak of the First World War.

The leaders of the trade unions refused to join the I.L.P. members of Parliament in opposing the war effort. Instead they co-operated with the Government, some trade union officials accepting ministerial posts. Arthur Henderson became President of the Board of Education in 1915. When Lloyd George became Premier in 1916 Henderson became a member of the War Cabinet, John Hodge, the Steel Smelters' Secretary, Minister of Labour, and George Barnes, a former A.E.U. Secretary, Minister of Pensions. Trade union leaders agreed to suspend many traditional procedures and practices, accepting, for example, arrangements for the employment of unskilled labour, compulsory arbitration and State control of labour. In doing so, they risked being disowned by some of their members, as there was considerable industrial unrest, particularly on the South Wales coalfield and on "Red Clydeside" where militant engineers were organised by shop stewards. This unrest was intensified after the establishment of the Bolshevist regime in Russia. But revolutionary activity was confined to limited localities and was opposed by responsible trade union leaders and the bulk of the rank and file. After all, trade unionists were citizens, many of whom had sons and daughters serving in the armed forces of the Crown.

By co-operating with the Government in the war effort the trade unions gained more than they lost. "The Trade Unions in fact," the

Webbs wrote in their *History of Trade Unionism* (1920), "through shouldering their responsibility in the national cause gained enormously in social and political status." Consultation of the unions by the Government in the preparation and administration of social and industrial legislation had taken place before 1914. This practice was considerably increased during the war years and afterwards. The introduction in 1911 of State schemes for sickness insurance assisted in a rapid increase in union membership as the unions became "approved societies" for the administration of the scheme. During the war membership expanded still further to 6,533,000 in 1918 and to 8,348,000 in 1920.

Trade unions were represented on statutory wage regulating bodies set up under the Trade Boards Acts of 1909 and 1918. By 1922 the wages of about 3 million workers were governed by Trade Boards decisions. The Coal Mines (Minimum Wage) Act was passed in 1912. The first step towards improving the wages of farm workers was taken by the passage of the Corn Production Act (1917), followed in 1924 by the Agricultural Wages (Regulation) Act. This provided for the setting up of county agricultural wages committees on which agricultural workers had representation. The Railways Act of 1921 and the London Passenger Transport Board Act of 1933 provided for union representation on wages boards. By the Coal Mines Act of 1930 disputes on wages and labour conditions could be referred to a Coal Mines National Industrial Board whose seventeen members were appointed by the Board of Trade after consultation with employers, the Miners' Federation and the General Council of the T.U.C. In the road transport industry in 1938 union representatives were appointed members of wages boards and of the industrial court set up to settle disputes.

Before 1914 governments had become aware of the need for the State to concern itself with industrial disputes. The Conciliation Act of 1896 empowered the Board of Trade to investigate the causes of trade disputes and to offer mediation. In 1912 an Industrial Council was set up, with Sir George (later Lord) Askwith as Chief Industrial Commissioner. This did excellent work, mediating in industrial disputes, but arbitration, experience showed, was only acceptable where voluntarily agreed to by both parties. Compulsory arbitration, authorised by the Munitions Act of 1915, proved unenforceable when 200,000 Welsh miners rejected a wage award by Sir George Askwith.

In 1916, as part of the plans for post-war reconstruction, a committee presided over by the Speaker, J. H. Whitley, was instructed to investigate the problem of improving industrial relations. The Whitley Committee reported in 1917 that workers should have "a greater opportunity of participating in the discussions about and adjustments of those parts of industry by which they are most affected." Consultations between both sides were envisaged at national, district and works levels. The Minister of Labour approved the Whitley Committee proposal that joint industrial councils should be established consisting of members of employer associations and trade unions. The Government itself set an example by authorising the formation of Whitley Councils on which its own employees were represented.

The Whitley Report is an important landmark in the history of industrial relations, as it stressed the need to enlist workers' "active and continuous co-operation in the promotion of industry." This was a notable advance on the pre-war situation where a national strike took place in 1911 to secure union recognition by the railway companies. With the help of the Ministry of Labour 73 Whitley Councils came into existence, 58 of which were still functioning in 1923. Councils on the Whitley model were not introduced into the mining, cotton, engineering, shipbuilding and iron and steel industries, in which machinery for settling disputes had long been in existence. But they were formed in industries which hitherto had not possessed machinery to solve disputes without conflict. The Whitley scheme, if not an unqualified success, was a worth-while experiment, a considerable amount of useful co-operation being achieved between both sides of industry. We have not yet learned how to eradicate conflict from industrial relations, hence it would have been unreasonable to have expected the Whitley Joint Industrial Councils to have ended the battle between capital and labour, particularly as British industry after the First World War had to contend with grave economic problems.

PART IX

GREAT BRITAIN DURING THE INTER-WAR YEARS, 1919–39

Chapter XXVII

THE BRITISH ECONOMY AFTER THE FIRST WORLD WAR

Wartime accelerations of tendencies and forces operating before 1914 amounted to a revolution in the social and economic structure of Great Britain. For two generations before 1914, there had been a tendency to discard undiluted *laisser-faire* as a sound theory of the functions of the State. As Sir William Harcourt confessed in the closing decade of the nineteenth century, "We are all Socialists now." But the retreat from *laisser-faire* was not an expression of a conscious application of collectivist theory or an indication that British statesmen were becoming Marxian converts. Rather, it was due to the acceptance of the need for social reform by the Tory Party led by Disraeli, and by the Liberals between 1906 and 1914 —the passage of Factory Acts, Truck Acts, public health, minimum wage, sickness and unemployment insurance legislation, for example, being steps towards the organisation of British life on a collectivist basis.

During the war the need to divert economic resources to feed an insatiable war machine necessitated far-reaching restrictions on individual liberties. The railways, shipping, foreign trade and the mines operated under systems of government controls. With the creation in 1915 of the Ministry of Munitions, under Lloyd George, industry was subjected to a complex system of centralised direction designed to channel productive capacity to war purposes. Measures were taken to hold wages and prices down. The interruption by enemy submarines to the free flow of overseas supplies of food made it imperative to increase the output from British farms, hence trends in land usage since the "Great Depression" were reversed. County Executive Committees were set up in 1916, and by the Corn Production Act (1917) the Board of Agriculture was given compulsory powers to ensure that pasture was brought under the plough and farmers were guaranteed prices for corn. Farm labourers also benefited, as with the setting up of Central and District Wages Boards to regulate hours of work and fix minimum wages, weekly wages of land workers rose from under £1 in 1916 to nearly 50s.

in 1920. Despite these measures, however, reinforced by the employment of soldiers, prisoners of war, school-boys and women on the land, the food shortage was so critical that the Ministry of Food came into existence in 1917, and in 1918 ration cards were issued. One other very important consequence of wartime agricultural conditions ought to be noted, namely, the increase in the number of British farms cultivated by owner occupiers. Heavy taxation and high death duties led to the sale of estates by landlords. Tenant farmers, who had prospered during the war, purchased the land, the percentage of farm land cultivated by owner-occupiers, 10·7 in 1913, becoming 36 by 1927.

The first step towards the abandonment of free trade, to save shipping and to reduce "luxury imports," was taken in 1915 with the impostion of the McKenna duties, a $33\frac{1}{3}$ per cent tariff on motor cars, motor bicycles, watches, musical instruments and films. Even the traditional gold standard was abandoned, as after 6th August 1914, gold coins were replaced as the circulating medium by one pound and ten shilling Treasury notes. The financial costs of the war were immense. Taxation was increased, income tax from ninepence to six shillings in the pound, and Excess Profits Duties were also levied. But as most of the war expenditure was met by borrowing the National Debt rose from £650 million to £7000 million. Interest payments on these war-debts and expenditure on pensions to disabled ex-servicemen, war widows and orphans burdened the economy with heavy financial liabilities. As the Government's financial policy had inflationary consequences, the purchasing power of the pound sterling fell. Both money wages and prices increased, but the real wage index for those in full-time employment decreased from 174 to 161 between 1914 and 1918. The foreign exchange problems of financing overseas purchasing in wartime had been eased, as Great Britain in 1914 had overseas investments nominally valued at £4000 million. But these assets, the income from which helped to bridge Great Britain's excess of imports over exports, had been reduced by 1919 to £3000 million. In addition, the U.S.A., which before 1914 imported capital, during the war became a creditor country, and in 1919 was owed considerable war-debts by both Great Britain and her allies.

The material losses due to the war were also considerable. These included the loss of capital equipment, not built or renewed, while the labour force was otherwise engaged. But as the war was not fought on British soil, apart from slight damage from a few ineffective air raids and brief German warship bombardments, Britain was spared the massive material destruction suffered by other belligerents. Conversely, at sea, although the German High

Seas Fleet rarely ventured out of harbour, U-boats inflicted serious wounds. The United Kingdom gross shipping tonnage fell from 20 million tons to 16·364 million tons between 1914 and 1918

Serious also were both the short- and long-term consequences of wartime interruptions to sea-borne commerce. To Britain, dependent as she was for her security and prosperity upon the peaceful functioning of international commerce, the hazards of war brought dangerous consequences. Her people, engaged in manufacturing the sinews of war, or serving in the armed forces of the Crown, were not available to manufacture export commodities. As a result traditionally British markets were lost to competitors. During the war years there was a massive rise in import values, from £696 million in 1914 to £1316 million in 1918. Exports and re-exports on the other hand were valued at £526 million in 1914 and at £532 million in 1918. In the last year of the war, Great Britain had the largest adverse trade balance hitherto experienced, £784 million, an amount not exceeded until the Second World War, when it was £988 million in 1943 and £1013 million in 1944.

Population Trends

It is impossible to assess statistically the adverse effects of war casualties as it must be borne in mind that it was the flower of British manhood that was prematurely slaughtered. Nearly three-quarters-of-a-million British combatants were killed and about three times that number maimed, many permanently. To this tragic waste must be added countless numbers of unborn children whose potential fathers perished on the battlefields. During the war, the birth rate naturally fell, but this fall was not wholly due to wartime circumstances. As the following statistics show both the birth and death rates had been steadily declining since 1871.

UNITED KINGDOM BIRTH AND DEATH RATES
(PER 1000 OF THE POPULATION)

Year	Birth rate	Death rate	Rate of natural increase
1841–60	33·4	24·0	9·4
1871–75	35·5	22·0	13·5
1911–13	24·0	13·8	10·2
1919	18·5	13·7	4·8
1921	22·4	12·1	10·3
1933	14·9	12·5	2·4
1939	15·2	12·0	3·2

The birth rate reached a record low level in 1933, but as after 1871 yearly birth rates invariably exceeded death rates, the population continued to increase in size, but at a much slower rate than formerly. Contemporary discussions on pre-1939 population problems were very different in character from those at the present day. Demographers wrote explanatory accounts of the menace and consequences of declining populations, it even being predicted that without massive immigration the population of Great Britain within a century would be about 5 million.

Various explanations were suggested to account for these unprecedented demographic trends which were not an exclusive British experience since they were shared by all the industrially-advanced nations. They were certainly not due to adverse social conditions, as the decline in the size of families took place at a time when standards of living of the masses were higher than they had ever been in human history. There may or may not be a connection between increasing prosperity and small families. Those who thought there was argued that manufacturing progress had made available desirable possessions, for example "Baby Austins," which were preferred to the satisfactions derived from having children. Sir Alan Herbert expressed this point of view in 1937:

Five hundred brand-new motor-cars each morning rode the roads,
And flashed about like comets or sat motionless as toads;
Whichever course they took they made the public highway hell,
And to everyone's astonishment the population fell.

Some writers argued that social legislation was a major cause of the decrease in the size of families. Extension of the school-leaving age and restrictions on juvenile employment made children an economic liability instead of a source of income, as in Victorian times, while state aid for the sick and the aged removed an economic incentive for large families. Attention was also drawn to the use of more efficient contraceptives than had hitherto been available. In support of this explanation could be cited the prosecution of Charles Bradlaugh and Annie Besant for publishing an American book on contraceptive methods. Their trial, which took place in 1877, coincided in time with the beginning of the downward curve in the birth rate. But the widespread use of efficient contraceptives, although explaining how conception was avoided, does not account for the preference for small families. In fact, we do not really know why parenthood was avoided during the inter-war years. Perhaps people, like the politicians, were just "playing safe." Certainly the downward demographic trend was not due to an increase in biological sterility, as after the Second World War the confident predictions that the population would decrease in size were not fulfilled. In the 1950s, birth rates, instead of falling, rose, hence discussions nowadays on demographic problems are concerned with the explosive possibilities of too-rapidly expanding populations.

The dislocations in the labour market between the two world wars were in part due to the slowing up of the rate of population expansion. In 1920 when the birth rate was 25·5 per 1000, 957,782 children were born in England and Wales, but in 1937 when the birth rate was 14·9, only 610,557. A government circular in 1937 informed L.E.A.s that in the next 15 years the number of children aged five and over in public elementary schools would be likely to fall by a million. Conversely, with the fall in the death rate, the proportion of the population in the older age groups was increasing. Fewer children meant, a generation later, fewer producers supporting larger numbers of old age pensioners. This in its turn meant changes in demand for consumer goods. Industries catering for the needs of the young were contracting, while those producing goods for older people expanded. Some of the post-1919 unemployment was also due to the slackening demand for capital equipment as population growth decreased. But it would be nearer the truth to judge the slowing up in the rate of population growth as a consequence, rather than as a cause, of the contemporary depression which blighted some industrial areas in Britain.

The Post-war Depression

Thought of at first as likely to be of short duration, until the transition from war to peace conditions had been completed, the slump actually lasted until the outbreak of the Second World War. Unemployment became a way of life for hundreds of thousands, the numbers of unemployed varying from between one-fifth and one-tenth of the insured population. The economic recession was preceded in the immediate post-Armistice period by an inflationary boom. There was an increase in the numbers of unemployed women, discharged to provide work for ex-servicemen, but the numbers of trade unionists unemployed, 2·5 per cent in 1919 and 2·4 per cent in 1920, were well below the pre-war average. The value of United Kingdom exports and re-exports increased from £532 million in 1918 to £1557 million in 1920, the 1920 values not being exceeded until 1948, when they were £1583 million. Boom conditions, however, were of short duration. After November 1920 prices fell. In 1921 export and re-export values declined to £810 million and the percentage of trade unionists unemployed rose to 15·6. But the full impact of the recession on the British economy was postponed, as there was a temporary increase in the demand for British exports owing to the 1922 strike in the U.S.A. coalfields and the general strike in Germany precipitated by the 1923 Franco-Belgian occupation of the Ruhr. British exports and re-exports had risen to £941 million by 1924 and the percentage of trade unionists unemployed had fallen to 9·1.

The lifting of the British recession depended upon two factors, firstly, an increase in total world demand, and secondly, on British exporters obtaining a rising share of this demand. Between 1925 and 1929 world trade did revive, but no significant improvement took place in the British economic situation, the British share in world trade being smaller in 1929 than it had been in 1925. There was a slight increase in the level of industrial activity but the percentage of the insured population unemployed remained high, 10·4 in 1929, while exports and re-exports declined in value from £927 million in 1925 to £839 million by 1929. Then followed the worsening of the world economic situation after the spectacular collapse in 1929 of the American stock market. By the spring of 1931 the slump in Great Britain had been seriously intensified. Export values declined to £416 millions in 1932. The level of industrial activity as measured by the index numbers of Lord Beveridge, 109·1 in 1925, fell to 86·8 in 1931 and to 81·1 in 1932, and the percentage of the insured population out of work rose to 21·3 in 1931 and to 22·1 in 1932.

In subsequent years no significant expansion took place in British exports, hence the numbers of persons unemployed remained high. At the beginning of 1933, when more than one-fifth of the insured population was out of work, the Chancellor of the Exchequer, Neville Chamberlain, confessed that he saw no hope of a reduction in the amount of unemployment "to a comparatively small figure" within the next ten years. The Chancellor proved to be an accurate prophet, the percentage unemployment figures never falling below 10 until the outbreak of the Second World War, when there was a dramatic reduction to 3·1 in 1940. There was a decrease in the numbers of jobless persons in the late 'thirties due in part to the increase in the proportion of the national income spent on armaments, accelerated after the betrayal of the Czechs at Munich in 1938. Nevertheless, despite the increase in the percentage of the national income spent on defence from 2·7 in 1935 to 19 in 1939, 11·1 per cent of the total insured population was out of work when the Second World War began.

Both short- and long-term explanations can be given for the inter-war British recession. There were the difficulties inherent in changing from a war- to a peace-time economy. Firms, used to negotiating government contracts, had to design and make new commodities and to learn the arts of selling them in a competitive market. The absorbing of millions demobilised from the armed forces into gainful employment inevitably meant at least much short-term unemployment. But a permanent high level of industrial activity could only be achieved if the export trades flourished. Unfortunately, there were what at the time were considered to be temporary obstacles to the achievement of a high volume of exports, namely, loss of export markets during the war; impoverishment of peoples living in war-devastated lands; competition from overseas industries sheltered by high tariff barriers; and unprecedented instability of European currencies. The low purchasing power of paper money circulating in Europe made difficult both the purchase of high-priced British exports and the carrying on of any kind of industrial activity. In 1919, for example, 540 German paper marks were needed to purchase commodities costing 20 silver marks in 1913. Inflation became catastrophic in 1921 and 1922, the nominal value of the pound sterling and American dollar becoming thousands of millions of marks. Serious inflationary tendencies were also to be found in other European states, economic recovery in them, therefore, being delayed until measures were taken to create new stabilised currencies.

The contemporary opinion that a revival of world trade would solve the unemployment problem was not based on a sound understanding of the situation. Significantly, the unemployment "black spots" were the areas in which were located the industries Great Britain had pioneered in the first industrial revolution—coal, iron and steel, shipbuilding, textiles and engineering. Both technologically and economically, these staple industries had become obsolescent, while the world trade patterns under which they had flourished no longer existed. As explained in a previous chapter, British predominance in these industries had, before 1900, either been lost or was being challenged. Further difficulties with which these industries had to battle were due less to foreign imports than to changes in customers' tastes, and to technological advances which provided the public with a wide range of consumable commodities unknown to previous generations. Trade revival before 1914 had not reversed these late nineteenth-century trends, but merely postponed their full impact on the British economy. In other words, the post-1920 British recession was not basically due to wartime dislocations of industrial and trade patterns.

Contracting Industries

Among the industries in which Great Britain had been traditionally supreme, shipbuilding was one of the most severely affected. In the days of wooden vessels the Thames had been the chief centre of shipbuilding. With the use of iron and later steel in ship construction and of steam for propulsion, Clydeside became the chief shipbuilding and marine engine making area. Other important centres were the Tyne, Wear and Tees, and Hull, Merseyside, Barrow-in-Furness and Belfast. In the 1890s approximately four-fifths of the world's ships had been launched from British yards.

There was a shipping boom immediately after the war. High freight rates encouraged shipowners to place new orders at inflated prices and to dissipate their reserves by issuing bonus shares and paying high dividends on inflated capital. But by 1921 world trade was insufficient to provide full-time employment for merchant shipping. Freight rates fell and orders were cancelled. Shipowners, so far from signing contracts for new vessels, were laying up their fleets in cheap berths in South Western Peninsula inlets. The shipbuilding industry, with a higher productive capacity than in pre-war days, had also to contend with competition from countries like Germany, Scandinavia and Japan, which in earlier times had purchased ships from Britain. To add to their difficulties, shipbuilding firms had to find capital to modernise the industry to meet demands for bigger ships, new types of motor vessels and for vessels using oil instead of coal. As shipbuilding is an assembly industry, nearly three-quarters of the final costs of most ships representing bought-in materials and components, short time working in the shipyards had naturally far-reaching effects.

Jarrow and other shipbuilding centres were not the only towns to which industrial depression brought mass unemployment and queues at soup-kitchens for halfpenny bowls of soup. The cotton industry also lost the predominance it had possessed in the closing decades of the nineteenth century, when one half of the cotton fabrics exported from Britain were marketed in Eastern Asia, chiefly in India. By 1914 advanced cotton manufacturing techniques were in use in India, China and Japan, the first cotton mill being opened in India in 1838. By 1914 India ranked fourth in the production of cotton fabrics, its output only being exceeded by that of Britain, the U.S.A. and Germany. At first, Asiatic producers were concerned to satisfy domestic demands, but later they became exporters, provoking bitter complaints from Lancashire producers of unfair competition and demands that restrictions should be placed on the flood of cheap cotton goods from overseas.

The value of British cotton exports declined from £124,906,000 in 1913 to £46,773,000 in 1933 and the number of workers employed in the industry from 646,000 in 1911 to only 350,000 in 1938, in which year Lancashire exported 1450 million linear yards, about a fifth of the 1913 export total. That school-leavers were not hopeful of finding employment in Lancashire mills can be illustrated from the statistics of the Union of Lancashire and Cheshire Institutes which record a catastrophic fall in the number of candidates entered for cotton course examinations.

In the woollen and worsted industries, less dependent than cotton on overseas markets, contraction also took place but on a less massive scale. Export values fell from £32,053,000 in 1913 to £14,515,000 in 1933 and the size of the labour force from 261,000 in 1911 to 230,000 in 1938. This decline was due partly to competition in overseas markets from tariff-protected domestic producers, and partly to the development of the British rayon industry, which competed with both woollen and cotton goods in the home market.

Hardship and poverty, still vividly remembered by the older generation, was the lot of those who worked in the coalmining industry. This industry employed in 1921 more men than any other, agriculture excepted, 1,296,000 out of a total working population of 19,369,000. As since the eighteenth century coal had been the foundation upon which British industrial life rested, there had been uninterrupted expansion in both output and exports. Peak production was achieved in 1913, 287 million tons, of which 98 million tons was exported. Before 1914 almost one-tenth of British exports in value, and just over four-fifths in volume, consisted of coal. As imports tended to be in the main bulky commodities such as timber, grain and ores, ships transporting coal from Britain were able to quote lower freight rates for homeward bound cargoes than would have been feasible if they had made the outward journey in ballast.

During the war, as most of the output was needed at home, exports were curtailed, overseas coalfields were therefore developed and encouragement was given to the use of substitutes. By 1920 output had fallen to 229·5 million tons and exports to 43·75 million. Owing to a three months' strike in 1921 output fell to 162·3 million tons, but rose to 249·6 million in 1922 and 276 and 267·1 million in 1923 and 1924 respectively. There was also an increase in coal exports to 81·75 million tons in 1924 owing to increased demand for British coal created by the industrial troubles in America and the Ruhr. In 1925, however, the tide turned, coal exports falling to 68·97 million tons. Neither was the decline in exports compensated for by an increase in home demand. Instead, home demand fell owing to depression in the staple industries.

As more coal was being produced than could be profitably marketed, depressed conditions were experienced in most of the European coalmining areas. This excess of supply over demand was due to impoverishment of pre-war customers, to the cessation of coal exports to Soviet Russia, to widespread trade and industrial depression and to the opening up of new coalfields in Europe and in South Yorkshire and Nottingham. A further factor was the increasing use of substitutes for coal as a source of energy. In some countries advances had taken place in the use of water power for the generation of electricity. In Germany, lignite production was being increased and used for generating electricity for the nitrate and glass industries and for domestic purposes. Oil was being imported instead of coal by the Argentine Railway Companies. A major factor in reducing British coal exports was the substitution of oil for bunker coal. The gross tonnage of vessels fitted to burn oil increased from 1·5 million before 1914 to 2·05 million in 1925. Conversely, bunker coal shipped from British ports for use in external trade fell from 21·03 million in 1913 to 16·2 million tons in 1925.

Expanding Industries

Readers of the preceding paragraphs will doubtless be tempted to conclude that Great Britain during the inter-war years was experiencing a great depression. In parts of North England, Scotland, Wales and Northern Ireland, which had been developing areas during the first industrial revolution, there certainly were to be found grievous pools of poverty and unemployment. But elsewhere the general standard of living improved with increases in general productivity. The explanation of this rather paradoxical state of affairs is that fundamental changes were taking place in the distribution of the working population. The changes were threefold. Firstly, new industries were expanding, secondly, changes were taking place in the location of industry and, thirdly, the organisation of production was changing. The inter-war years can best be described not as a period in which British industry was declining but rather as one in which new industries were taking the place of those upon which British industrial supremacy had previously been based.

The new industries were science-based. The First, as also the Second World War gave a stimulus to scientific researches and their practical applications which the Government encouraged by the foundation in 1916 of the Department of Scientific and Industrial Research. That new industrial techniques based upon scientific investigations were becoming important is shown by the formation in 1918 of the National Union of Scientific Workers. The new industries, which produced commodities associated with rising standards of living, were powered by electricity. Electricity production in the United Kingdom rose from 4275 millions of kilowatt hours in 1920 to 20,409 in 1939, and the number of workers employed in electrical engineering doubled.

Three industries whose expansion was stimulated by war needs were the motor-car, aircraft and chemical industries. Between 1923 and 1938 the number of workers employed in the motor industry more than doubled. Being basically an assembly industry, the expansion of motor-car production in centres such as Coventry and Oxford stimulated industrial activity in other parts of the country. With the introduction of mass-production methods, pioneered by Henry Ford in the U.S.A., a motor-car ceased to be a convenience enjoyed by the wealthy only, while the motor-bus provided a new means of transport that had revolutionary effects on both urban and rural life. Not the least complex of modern problems are those arising from the adaptation of cities and roads to meet the demands of a motoring age.

Advances in aeroplane design during the war prepared the way for the development of civil aviation in the post-war years. The manufacture of chemicals, in which Germany had been pre-eminent before 1914, expanded in Britain during and after the war, the numbers of workers employed rising from· 155,000 in 1911 to 276,000 in 1938. The sending of signals by wireless by Marconi in 1896 and the foundation of the B.B.C. in 1922 were landmarks in the creation of a new medium of communication and brought into existence the radio industry. Television broadcasting, which in Britain began in 1936, owed its practical accomplishment to John Logie Baird, who demonstrated the first transmission of real images to members of the Royal Institution in January 1926. Baird even gave demonstrations of colour television in 1928 at the meeting of the British Association in Glasgow.

One of the most popular forms of entertainment for the masses during the period was a visit to the cinema. Numerous experiments were made in the nineteenth century to find ways of projecting moving pictures on a screen, including those of Thomas Edison, the Lumière brothers in Paris and William Friese-Green, who patented in 1889 a moving-picture machine using celluloid film. The arrival of the cinema as a rival to the stage may be said to have begun in 1914 when D. W. Griffith produced "The Birth of a Nation." The cinema industry grew rapidly after the war, particularly after 1927 when talking films made silent films obsolete. The years between the wars are also noteworthy for the progress in applied science associated with the names of Sir Edward Appleton, Sir Robert A. Watson Watt and members of the research team from the National Physical Laboratory. Their development of radar made it possible to detect the presence of aeroplanes or other objects. Radar, first applied to aircraft location in 1935, gave the

R.A.F. an immense advantage during the Battle of Britain.

Other industries developed to satisfy new needs included the manufacture of bicycles, scientific instruments, rubber, vacuum cleaners, photographic equipment, plastics and electrical apparatus. Refrigerators and washing-machines, although not in common use before 1939, were produced for a minority market. The number of workers in the building and contracting industries increased from 526,000 in 1921 to 1,264,000 in 1938, the large number of new dwellings built stimulating activity in furniture making and carpet manufacturing. The more widespread use of carpets instead of linoleum as floor coverings is a clear indication that standards of living were rising. There also ought to be noted the considerable increase in the percentage of the population employed in transport, distribution and personal services. That a much smaller proportion than formerly was engaged in the production of food and basic necessities, and a much larger proportion in the provision of luxuries, amenities, entertainments and the satisfaction of new desires, is proof that the people of Great Britain in the years between the wars were enjoying higher living standards than their forefathers.

Industrial changes affected Great Britain's ability to wage war. The decline of such basic industries as coal and shipbuilding impeded the mobilisation of its war potential in 1939. On the other hand, the new industries provided the skills and capacities to produce hitherto unknown war aids. Since the days when Archimedes made catapults for the Greeks of Syracuse, men of science have provided fighting men with weapons. But scientific method was applied more consistently and deliberately in the Second World War than in any previous one. The complicated array of apparatus which air crews had at their command in the latter stages of the war bears witness to the immense strides made in operational research. Led by aircraft equipped with a device called Gee, a radar aid to bomber navigation, the first 1000-bomber raid was made on Cologne on 12th May 1942. New equipment was designed to detect submerged submarines and to sink them when found, while successful researches overcame the menace of magnetic and acoustic mines. In short, a major factor in ensuring, firstly, British survival after the fall of France in 1940, and secondly, ultimate victory in 1945, was the good use made of the nation's scientific and engineering resources.

Of all the weapons used in the war the most deadly was the atomic bomb. Modern knowledge of the atom is based on the researches, before and after 1914, of scientists of many nations, including those of Becquerel, Niels Bohr, Einstein, Frederic Joliot and his wife Irene and Professor Soddy. But the most revolutionary contribution to the release of the enormous stores of energy when an atom explodes was given to the world in the years between the wars by Lord Rutherford and his pupils at Cambridge, Chadwick, Cockcroft and Walton. After the outbreak of war, attention was concentrated on the possibility of using atomic energy as a weapon. The gigantic task, however, of designing and building the plant for producing an atomic bomb and releasing atomic energy had to be undertaken, at a cost of £500 million, in the U.S.A.

Chapter XXVIII

THE STATE AND ECONOMIC AFFAIRS, 1919–29

Since the eighteenth century, the re-allocation of population and capital resources in Great Britain had been undertaken by private initiative. The readiness of enterprising individuals to invest risk-capital had resulted in the creation of a highly industrialised, urbanised society. Had Britain remained a thinly-peopled country, inhabited by more or less self-sufficing agricultural communities, State interference in economic affairs could have been kept at a minimum. But a theory of government, based on the premise that it would be harmful for the State to interfere with the freedom of individuals to act in whatever way seemed good to them in economic matters, did not prove to be satisfactory under twentieth-century conditions of life. As explained in previous chapters, it had been found necessary before 1914 to extend the functions of central and local government in order to get rid of glaring social evils. Nevertheless British economic organisation on the eve of the First World War was still substantially one based on freedom of choice, and one controlled, managed and financed by private enterprise.

The extensions of centralised control dictated by wartime pressures were regarded as temporary expedients. It was government policy after the war to restore what were thought of as "normal" economic conditions, those prevailing in 1913. Wartime controls were abandoned, and as we found ourselves in possession of a paper pound which had depreciated in terms of gold, on the recommendations of its financial advisers the Government decided to discontinue the wartime method of increasing the supply of money by printing paper. This policy was inaugurated by a Treasury Minute, issued in December 1919, laying down that the note issue in any future year should not exceed the minimum issue of the preceding year. In 1925, by the Gold Standard Act, the paper currency was made legal tender and convertible into gold. Dual control of the currency between the Bank and the Treasury was abolished by the Currency and Bank Notes Act in 1928.

There were contemporary critics who challenged the wisdom of restricting the amount of currency in circulation and forcing down price levels. The policy benefited creditors, including National Debt stockholders, and the operators of the London money market. But for industry the policy created acute difficulties. Business men who have to make prior commitments find that falling prices threaten losses, hence business activity is reduced and the number of jobless workers increases. Business, it was argued, was sacrificed in the interests of metropolitan finance. In the event, however, the return to the gold standard proved to be a short-lived policy, the National Government elected in the autumn of 1931 taking Britain off the gold standard once again.

But although Conservative governments before 1929 did not want to assume responsibility for economic affairs, they did intervene to a limited extent. Breaches in the wall of free trade were made by the Dyestuffs Industries Act (1920), by the Safeguarding of Industries Act (1921) and by the substantial subsidies given from 1924 onwards to sugar-beet growers. By this last measure it was hoped to make arable farming more profitable, to check the rural exodus, and to ensure that supplies of sugar in wartime would not be placed in jeopardy. Unforeseen technical improvements in the sugar-cane industry, however, which led to a fall in world sugar prices, made the subsidy policy very uneconomic. Home production of sugar rose from 24,000 tons in 1924 to 615,000 tons in 1934, the total sum paid out in subsidies to sugar manufacturers during these years being £40 million. The subsidy policy created a sugar-beet industry capable of meeting one quarter of British sugar requirements, but not surprisingly critics argued that it would have been wiser to have left sugar production unprotected and have given practical help to arable farmers in other ways.

Before 1914 a number of services, which can be classed as public utilities, had been brought under public control. Municipal ownership of water, gas, electricity and tramway undertakings, although not universal, had become common. In 1908 a public corporation, the Port of London Authority, acquired the docks and warehouses from the tidal portion of the Thames from Teddington Lock in Middlesex to an imaginary line drawn from Havengore Creek in Essex to Warden Point in Kent, a distance of 70 miles. After the war, the policy of entrusting the provision of services to public corporations was extended. The British Broadcasting Company, formed in 1922, became a public corporation in 1926. In the same year the generation of electricity was transferred from numerous municipal and private enterprise undertakings to the Central Electricity Board. Two other public corporations set up before the outbreak of the Second World War were the London Passenger Transport Board (1932) and British Overseas Airways Corporation (1939). Lastly, long before nationalisation became politically feasible, Winston Churchill had in 1914 persuaded his Cabinet colleagues to invest £2 million in the Anglo-Persian Oil Company (now B.P.) and to give it a long-term contract to supply fuel for the Navy. This investment, increased by another £3 million in 1919, is nowadays worth about £1,600 m., the value of the British Government's ownership of 51 per cent of British Petroleum Company stock.

Post-war governments took steps to investigate conditions in industries threatened by chronic unemployment. The Balfour Committee on Industry and Trade published seven reports, the last in 1929, dealing with overseas markets, industrial relations and the structure of leading industries. Two Royal Commissions, the Sankey (1919) and the Samuel (1925), investigated the coalmining industry. Still influenced, however, by orthodox economic theory, the Government offered positive measures of help only in the form of a temporary subsidy to the coalmining industry in 1925, the encouragement of amalgamation of coal business units by an Act passed in 1926 and the passage in 1929 of the Derating Act which gave local rate relief to industry and agriculture. It was not until 1938 that it carried out the recommendation of the Samuel Commission to nationalise mineral royalties, thereby retrieving "the error made in times past in allowing the ownership of coal to fall into private hands."

Orthodox economic theory, however, was one thing, but practically there was no escape from government involvement in industrial affairs owing to the intensity of labour unrest. After the war, pre-1914 militant trade unionism revived, many trade unionists taking the view that industrial militancy was a surer weapon than reliance on the weak Parliamentary Labour Party. Such thinking was influenced by the "Red Revolution" in Russia, but actually the British Communist Party never succeeded in winning more than tiny minority support. Militant trade unionism was particularly strong in two industries not immediately decontrolled after the war, the railway and coalmining industries. In January 1919 the Miners' Federation demanded nationalisation of the industry, a 30 per cent wage increase and a 6-hour day. Immediate strike action was averted by the appointment of a Royal Commission whose chairman, Mr Justice Sankey, recommended State acquisition of the mines. In the same year, 1919, an attempt to reduce railwaymen's wages, in a period of rising prices, led to a seven-day stoppage of the railways. It ended on 4th October with a government concession that existing wage rates would be maintained for twelve months.

In 1920, the last year of the post-war boom, as the cost of living continued to rise, industrial troubles multiplied. "The Dockers' K.C.," Ernest Bevin, by resort to arbitration, did succeed in getting an increase in wages for the dock workers. The pre-war Triple Alliance between the Miners', Railwaymen's and Transport Workers' Unions, which had been revived, agreed to support the miners' claim for wage increases. The Government bought time by conceding a temporary increase, which it used to enact an Emergency Powers Act, giving it authority to maintain essential services, and to complete its plans to return to private enterprise the railway and coalmining industries. On 21st March 1921 the mines were decontrolled, and later in the year the railways, by the Railways Act of 1921. As the coal-owners, in what was now a period of falling prices, insisted on the inevitability of wage reductions, the miners looked for support to their partners in the Triple Alliance. The refusal of the Miners' Federation, however, to resume negotiations with the Government led to the cancellation on "Black Friday," 15th April 1921, of the proposed sympathetic strikes. Left unaided, the miners remained on strike until early July, when they were forced to return to the pits and accept wage reductions.

In 1922, the Lloyd George coalition government ended, and in January 1924, Ramsey MacDonald's short-lived first Labour administration was formed. Being a minority government, whose period of office was disturbed by industrial conflicts, it was not capable of solving the problems of unemployment and declining exports. Its fall was followed by a renewal of the conflict between the Miners' Federation, led by Herbert Smith and A. J. Cook, and the Mining Association whose spokesmen were Evan Williams and W. A. Lee. The clash between the owners and the men had been made inevitable by the Gold Standard Act of 1925, which, by raising by some 10 per cent the cost to overseas customers of British exports, had accentuated the export difficulties of the coalmining industry. Foreign demand for British coal was $7\frac{1}{2}$ per cent less in 1924 than it had been in 1909–13. In 1925 it was 22 per cent less. To make the industry remunerative, the only remedy proposed by owners, who held increasing stock piles of coal, was a reduction in wages and a return to the 8-hour day. The answer of the miners, in the words of their firebrand Welsh Secretary, A. J. Cook, was, "Not a penny off the pay, not a second on the day."

The Baldwin government sought to avert trouble in the coalfields, by the grant of a subsidy for the August 1925 to April 1926 period, and by appointing a Royal Commission presided over by

Sir Herbert Samuel. The Samuel Commission advised against nationalisation of the mines, but recommended the acquisition of mineral rights by the State, the reorganisation of the industry under private enterprise, and, as "a disaster is impending over the industry," proposing that working costs should be reduced either by lowering wages or by adding an hour to the working day. Backed by the General Council of the T.U.C., the miners refused to compromise. Negotiations between the Cabinet and the Negotiating Committee of the T.U.C. were suddenly broken off when news was received that the compositors of the *Daily Mail* had refused to permit the printing of the 3rd May edition. Thus began the so-called "General Strike."

Strictly speaking, the strike was not "General." Many unions affiliated to the T.U.C. were not instructed to take part in it. Neither were the leaders politically motivated. The Prime Minister, Stanley Baldwin, and the Chancellor of the Exchequer, Winston Churchill, with other right-wing members of the Cabinet, suspected the existence of a plot to put an alternative government in office. They were encouraged to hold this opinion by the support offered by the Comintern in Moscow, which naïvely saw in local Trades Councils embryonic British Soviets. For their part, trade union leaders bitterly resented accusations that they were inspired by any other motive than support for the miners, the financial aid collected from Russian coalminers being in fact rejected.

The strike had a far lesser impact on the national economy than was thought likely. There was an amazing response to the call for strike action by the railwaymen, transport workers, engineers, electricians, shipbuilders, iron and steel workers and newspaper employees. Apart from a few isolated local incidents, there was a marked absence of disorder, violence and overt actions against blacklegs. Government preparations to ensure the movement of essential supplies, organised by the then civil servant, Sir John Anderson, had been thorough, and volunteers in large numbers, many of them students, aided the armed forces of the Crown and the police in keeping transport moving. Moderate trade union leaders such as J. H. Thomas and Arthur Pugh quickly realised that public opinion did not support the T.U.C., and that the financial burden on trade union funds could become crippling. They therefore agreed after nine days to call off the strike, on the basis of proposals made in a memorandum put forward by Sir Herbert Samuel, which suggested a settlement on the lines of the recommendations made in the Report of his Commission. The miners stood their ground, however, until August when, beaten by starvation, they had to accept an 8-hour day and cuts in wage rates.

The sudden capitulation of the moderate trade union leaders, bitterly denounced by a minority of extremist unionists, brought to an end the period of post-war industrial militancy. The unions were crippled financially, and suffered a drastic loss in membership, from 8,328,000 in 1920 and 5,531,000 in 1924, to less than 5,000,000 by 1927. Although the Prime Minister appealed for no victimisation, the failure of many employers to heed his advice left a legacy of bitterness in the minds of many workers who did not get their jobs back. But in the British labour movement as a whole, opinion swung away from ideas of industrial militancy towards collaboration with employers and co-operation with the Parliamentary Labour Party. This change in the climate of opinion found practical expression in the talks between both sides of industry associated with the names of Sir Alfred Mond, the Chairman of I.C.I., and Ben Turner, the 1928 Chairman of the T.U.C., and in the victories at the polls gained in the 1929 general election, which brought into office the Second Labour Government.

An important consequence of the General Strike was that advantage was taken of the unpopularity of trade unionism to enact in 1927 the Trade Unions and Trade Disputes Act. By it "any strike having any object beyond the furtherance of a trade dispute within a trade or industry in which the strikers are engaged, is an illegal strike, if it is designed to coerce the Government or to intimidate the community or any substantial part of it." Persons taking part in such a strike were liable to imprisonment for up to two years. Intimidation by pickets was made unlawful; civil servants were prohibited from joining unions whose membership included non-government employees; and members of local government staffs were not to be compelled to join a union as a condition of their employment. Lastly, union members who wished to subscribe to the political fund of their union were to "contract in," a change in the arrangements laid down in the Trade Union Act of 1913, by which the positive action required from members had been to "contract out."

This legislation was bitterly resented by trade unionists, partly because its introduction cast a slur on the motives of participants in the 1926 strike, and partly because it allowed the courts of law a wide discretion in its interpretation. This discretion was likely to be used, trade unionists were sure, judging by past experience, to their detriment. So strong and long-lasting was this resentment that one of the first acts of the First Attlee Labour Government in 1946 was the restoration of the legal position laid down in 1906 and 1913 by the repeal of the Act of 1927. The "contracting in" provision of the Act of 1927 did eventuate in a reduction in contributions to the political funds of the unions. But the clauses making illegal sympathetic strikes were never tested in the courts, no Attorney General ever giving an opinion that any particular strike had an objective other than "the furtherance of a trade dispute."

CHAPTER XXIX

THE STATE AND ECONOMIC AFFAIRS, 1929-39

In the late 'twenties a handful of young, progressive-minded Tories, with first-hand experience of the grim conditions of life in "distressed areas," challenged orthodox opinion that sooner or later unaided private enterprise would overcome the obstacles impeding recovery of the export trades. These Young Conservatives, Mr Harold Macmillan recalls in his recently published *Autobiography*, were given the nickname of "Y.M.C.A.," older members of the party very much disliking their advocacy of semi-socialist ideas.

Orthodox economic practice was also challenged by Socialist writers and politicians, by the Lloyd George Liberals in the *Liberal Yellow Book* (1928), and in writings of the brilliant Cambridge economist, John Maynard (later Lord) Keynes (1883–1946). Keynes first became well known to the public when he resigned his appointment as chief Treasury representative at the Versailles Peace Conference to publish *The Economic Consequences of the Peace* (1919). In 1925 appeared *The Economic Consequences of Mr Churchill* in which Keynes correctly forecasted that the restoration of the gold standard would result in the continuance of high levels of unemployment and virtual economic stagnation. In later books, *Treatise on Money* (1930), and *General Theory of Employment, Interest and Money* (1936), Keynes developed his revolutionary economic idea that financial policy should be directed towards stimulating demand. Instead of practising severe economies, and insisting on balanced budgets, governments in periods of depression and unemployment ought to "encourage spending and lavishness."

It was not until after the Second World War, when maintenance of full employment became a government objective, that Keynesian teaching became really influential. Nevertheless, although the impact of the ideas of Keynes on official policy before the war was slight, more extensive State involvement in economic planning could not be avoided. The "Great Divide" was the post-1929 economic blizzard, since when party differences have been about the extent and nature of State assistance rather than conflicts between advocates of undiluted *laisser-faire* and wholesale collectivism. This change in the climate of public opinion became all the more inevitable because in Britain, a country all of whose citizens over 21 years of age possessed a parliamentary vote, politicians had to include remedies for social and economic evils in election programmes.

The post-1929 depression was a world, not an exclusively British experience. According to the 1933 Report of the International Labour Office there was a world total of 30 million registered unemployed. How many unregistered unemployed or underemployed there were it is impossible to estimate. Fundamentally the crisis was a crisis of distribution. Men had learned how to expand enormously the productive capacities of factories and farms, but had not discovered how to guarantee that consumers possessed sufficient purchasing power to equate consumption with production. To expand consumption encouragement was given to the development of the hire-purchase system. But persuading small salary and wage earners by lavish advertising to incur hire-purchase debts did not by itself enable consumption to catch up with potential production. Two other measures were therefore advocated by producing interests. Firstly, they sought to cut costs by forming what were known in Britain and the U.S.A. as trusts and combines, and in Germany as kartells. Modern, labour-saving plant was installed by mammoth business units, securing thereby greater output at lower costs. This, however, did not solve the problems of overproduction as men and women thrown out of work by the mechanisation of industry lacked the purchasing power to buy the flood of commodities. Secondly, pressure was placed on governments to protect domestic markets by erecting higher tariff barriers. In the U.S.A., for example, on the eve of the onset of the slump in 1929, President Hoover was pressurised into signing the iniquitous Smoot–Hawley Tariff Act which raised rates 7 per cent above those of the high tariff legislation of 1922.

These modern capitalist tendencies had progressed further in the U.S.A. than anywhere else. There was a very high level of industrial activity in the 'twenties, but there was also an increase in the numbers of industrial workers thrown out of employment by technological changes. In addition the depressed conditions in agriculture forced many Americans to leave the land in the vain hope of finding alternative employment in towns. In the autumn of 1929, with the sudden collapse of public confidence, the prices of stocks and shares which had spiralled upwards to fantastic, speculative levels suddenly collapsed. President Hoover and his advisers refused to inflate the currency, and failed to check the deepening of

GREAT BRITAIN DURING THE INTER-WAR YEARS

what they believed was a temporary recession. In consequence by 1932 between 15 and 17 millions of Americans were unemployed, banks were failing to honour their obligations, wage rates had more than halved, industrial activity had fallen dramatically, and stockholders had suffered catastrophic losses—a 57 per cent fall in dividends and a reduction of 80 per cent in the capital value of their holdings.

As the U.S.A. had become the world's major creditor country, and one in which policies were determined by domestic considerations, the recession became world wide. During the war the U.S.A. had exported, on credit, munitions of war. After the war she demanded repayment of the debt, approximately £1000 million, and also exported to and invested heavily in Europe. Payment for imports from America, however, was an insoluble problem. Payment in gold was impossible as most of the world's gold stock had crossed the Atlantic, to be buried in the vaults of Fort Knox, and payment in goods was impeded by American tariff barriers. Such a situation could only remain as long as the creditor country behaved like Britain before 1914, keeping in existence large investments overseas. But American bankers who had invested in Europe withdrew their money, the slump becoming in consequence the greatest and most extensive of all slumps.

During the recession producers all over the world attempted to force up prices by reducing the volume of goods for sale. To this end, firstly, governments raised tariff rates, and secondly, at a time when there were millions of people living in poverty, commodities that could not be sold at remunerative prices were wantonly destroyed. Millions of bags of coffee were burned in Brazil, sheep in South America, hogs in the U.S.A., and cattle in Denmark were slaughtered, and in 1934 millions of herrings were thrown back into the sea at Great Yarmouth. In the U.S.A., in order to restrict production to market demand, wheat and cotton farmers were paid by the Federal Government to "plough in" their crops and given a subsidy to restrict production.

For Great Britain, an industrialised country with exportable surpluses, the severe contraction of world commerce inevitably had dire consequences. By the winter of 1932–33 more than a fifth of the working population was unemployed. In South Wales, where unemployment had risen to 36 per cent, half the labour force of Abertillery and about two-thirds that of Merthyr Tydfil had become dependent on national, local or charitable individual sources of aid. Welsh children attended morning school, even grammar schools, poorly fed and badly shod. In the North East more than a quarter of the workers were unemployed, in Jarrow 67 per cent, and in Gateshead about 46 per cent. Workmen employed in the Elswick and Scotswood works of Vickers-Armstrong used to be met at the gates by barefoot children begging for bread. Similarly on Clydeside and in West Cumberland were to be found thousands of men, some fathers of families, who had never learned a trade or known what it was like to be in regular employment. In such areas, euphemistically labelled "Special Areas" in the language of bureaucracy, existed whole families without work or wages, condemned to wear shabby, worn-out garments, and to suffer from malnutrition on a diet of bread and margarine, and soup charitably provided at a cost of one half-penny a bowl. To such unfortunates a plate of fish and chips was a tasty luxury, meat almost unknown, and fresh vegetables only consumed by those of them who cultivated an allotment.

The contemporary need for government intervention in the "Special Areas" coincided in time with a second group of problems, the social and economic consequences of changes in the siting of industries. In deciding where to carry on their activities firms must weigh up the relative importance of such factors as access to raw materials, supply and availability of labour, transport and power costs, and accessibility to markets. As coal is bulky and expensive to move, a pre-1914 industrial location map bears a very close resemblance to a geological map of coal measures locations. The new industries, however, used electric power. Before 1939 coal continued to be the fuel used in the generation of electricity, but as electricity can be transported over long distances, industrial users could give priority to other factors than the need to be near coal supplies in deciding where to site their enterprises.

Coal concentrates but electricity disperses. There were several positive advantages to be gained by avoiding the smoke-laden, industrially derelict landscapes created by the men who pioneered industrialisation upon the twin pillars of coal and iron. The older industrial districts were thought of as possessing climatic disadvantages and as lacking in attractive amenities. Residents in them were burdened with heavy poor law rates levied to maintain unprecedented numbers of destitute persons. But above all, the newer industries primarily catered for the home market, and manufactured commodities which were easily transportable; besides, it was economically desirable to produce them near possible consumers. In consequence they tended to be located in the neighbourhood of the Home Counties, where 8 million consumers lived, and in the Midlands. The working population in south-eastern England therefore, increased more rapidly in the years between the wars than it did in the areas in which the old, staple industries were located.

Even before 1914 significant changes had been taking place in the industrial life of the Midlands, where during the eighteenth century local coal and iron had led to the rise of hardware trades and heavy, structural engineering. From the last quarter of the nineteenth century, with the development of the steel industry in Northern England, coal and iron production declined in the "Black Country," new industries coming into the area. These included electrical and light engineering, the manufacture of motor-cars and cycles, rubber manufacturing which expanded with the growth of the motor industry, and the making of cocoa and chocolate by the firms of Fry and Cadbury. It is not without significance that Joseph Chamberlain, the advocate of protectionist policies, was a Birmingham business man. Whereas in an earlier generation the free traders, Cobden and Bright, had been the spokesmen of Lancashire textile millowners concerned to sell their products overseas, Chamberlain was elected to Parliament by constituents who manufactured commodities, many of which were sold in Britain. Not unnaturally, Birmingham folk responded to proposals to protect the home market against foreign competition.

Reliance on uncontrolled private enterprise to decide where industry should be located had unfortunate consequences. Urban communities in the older industrial districts, possessing all the costly conveniences essential for urban and industrial life, were allowed to decay. Conversely, in what had been predominately agricultural areas, new urban communities were brought into existence, and provided with costly roads and railways, with sewage, gas, electricity and water undertakings, and dwellings, schools, shops and places of recreation and entertainment. As this twentieth-century urban expansion, like that during the first industrial revolution was uncontrolled, there was much urban sprawl and congestion and undesirable ribbon building. Migration into these developing areas was also unplanned. It was the young, ambitious and energetic who deserted the older industrial centres, leaving behind them a population of middle-aged and elderly folk. The more thrifty of the latter, who had taken up mortgages to buy their homes, found themselves marooned in areas where there was little chance of getting work and in possession of assets that were unrealisable.

The National Government led by Ramsay MacDonald, formed on 24th August 1931 from members of all three political parties, had no mandate to create a planned economy. Few people at the time considered that it was the business of government to govern business. Rather, governments were thought of as existing to create the conditions under which private enterprise could function efficiently. The National Government was responsible, however, for two major breaches in British economic tradition, the abandonment of both the gold standard and free trade. It was formed, most of its supporters believed, to restore confidence and defend the gold parity of sterling. Instead it discovered immediately after taking office that this was impossible. Over-valuation of sterling since 1925, while favouring importation at low prices, raised export prices. In these circumstances incurring too large an adverse balance of payments had been avoided by keeping interest rates high, by forcing down export prices, and by submitting to a high level of unemployment.

Before the formation of the National Government two official publications had appeared. The publication on 15th July of the Report of the Committee on Finance and Industry, known as the "Macmillan Report," was immediately followed by the withdrawal of gold to the value of £21 million, mainly to France. The run on the gold reserves of the Bank of England increased in momentum with the publication a fortnight later of the May Committee's Report on National Expenditure, forecasting a large budget deficit. A credit for £25 million granted to the Bank of England by the Federal Reserve Bank of New York and the Bank of France was exhausted within a month. Under these circumstances the National Government on 21st September was compelled to suspend the right of private persons to exchange notes for gold for export purposes.

The pound sterling, no longer linked to gold, fell to about 70 per cent of its former value. Devaluation led to an immediate restoration of British prestige, assisted economic expansion, and cheapened exports, but did not result in sterling ceasing to be a world currency. A number of countries, unable to maintain a gold backing for their note issues, as most of the world's gold stock was in America (and France), and needing an acceptable means of settling international trading debts, used the pound sterling. In conseqence there emerged after 1931 the so-called "Sterling bloc," not to be confused with the "Sterling area" which came into existence after the outbreak of the Second World War. The Sterling bloc included most of the Empire (not Canada), the Middle East, Scandinavia, Portugal, Japan, Brazil and the Argentine, countries for which access to the British market for their exports was of paramount importance. But although it was the most important and biggest of the currency areas which came into existence after 1931, the Sterling bloc was not a consciously created and deliberately organised unit with a permanent membership. Neither was it long-lasting, as it did not survive the outbreak of war in 1939.

The continued use of sterling as an acceptable international currency, instead of gold or the dollar, could not have survived loss of confidence in the stability of the pound. To avoid this, in 1932, the

Government and the Bank of England established the Exchange Equalisation Fund, the gold reserves and foreign currencies (mainly dollars) in it being used to prevent violent fluctuations in exchange rates. At times when Great Britain had a favourable balance of trade the Fund was replenished. In periods of adverse trade balance payments were made out of the Fund. In the late 'thirties, when the pound was under considerable pressure, the gold reserves of the Bank of England were added to the Fund, the whole of the domestic note issue in consequence becoming a fiduciary one. In other words, by 1939 in Great Britain the amount of the note issue (then £460,000,000), was unrelated to gold. Such gold reserves Britain possessed were being used to support the exchange value of the pound.

That the National Government in 1931 had not devised well thought-out policies for dealing with the basic weaknesses of the British economic system, accentuated as they were by the world economic hurricane, is shown by its adoption of both inflationary and deflationary measures. The mildly inflationary effects of the institution of a managed currency were followed by a reduction in Bank Rate to 2 per cent, low interest rates encouraging investment. But these inflationary measures were offset by the deflationary, and according to Keynesian principles, foolish policy of the Treasury. The Chancellor of the Exchequer, Philip Snowden, accepted the recommendations of the May Committee on the need for severe economies in public spending, and sought to achieve a balanced budget at the expense of the teachers, police, judges, members of the armed forces and the unemployed. The inability of members of the Labour Government in 1931 to agree that a cut in payments to the unemployed was necessary, to retain overseas confidence in British financial solvency, had been a major factor in its downfall. Trade union leaders thought that a Keynesian policy of economic expansion made more economic sense. But unlike the sailors at Invergordon, who staged in September 1931 a bloodless mutiny following rumours that it was proposed to cut their pay, the T.U.C. was not prepared to use unconstitutional methods to force the Government to adopt policies designed to increase consumers' purchasing power.

The abandonment of the gold standard and the introduction of foreign exchange controls were not the only major changes made by the National Government in traditional British policies. Opposed by free trade members of the Cabinet, Snowden, Samuel, Maclean and Sinclair, it decided to make Great Britain a protectionist country. By following the example set by other countries in erecting hindrances to the free flow of trade commodities, the National

Government closed what had hitherto been the one great free trade market. By so doing it added greatly to the confusions resulting from the contraction in world trade. It assisted, for example, in strengthening the political power of Hitler's National Socialists in Germany by undermining support for the government of Herr Brüning. The repercussions indeed were widespread, making more difficult a return to general prosperity on which in the long run the prosperity of Great Britain depended.

Joseph Chamberlain and the pre-1914 tariff reformers had contended that tariffs should be imposed to safeguard home industries against unfair foreign competition. A different argument was used by his son, Neville, and the protectionists in the thirties, namely, the urgent need to redress the adverse balance of trade which in 1931 had risen to £104 million. Even many hitherto staunch free traders were convinced that the devaluation of sterling following the departure from the gold standard could not by itself reduce sufficiently the excess of imports. The working classes, who since the repeal of the Corn Laws had favoured free trade as a guarantee of cheap food, were induced to accept protectionist policies by the argument that Great Britain could no longer afford to remain the "dumping ground" for cheap merchandise from selfish rivals who refused to admit British goods into their markets. Other arguments put forward at the time in support of protectionist policies were that, firstly, the massive investment needed to introduce mass-production methods could only be profitable if the home market was protected, and secondly, that as British wage rates were higher than those elsewhere, employers must be assured of higher prices which could only be guaranteed if imports from low-wage countries were restricted.

British protectionist policies had a three-fold aspect, firstly, the imposition of import duties, secondly, an extension of the system of imperial preferences, and thirdly, the limitation by quotas of certain classes of imports. They were inaugurated in November 1931 by the passage of the Abnormal Importations Bill which authorised the Board of Trade to impose duties up to 50 per cent on "dumped imports." This was followed in February 1932 by Neville Chamberlain's Import Duties Bill, authorising a levy of 10 per cent *ad valorem* duties on most imports, and the setting up of an Import Duties Advisory Committee. To this committee was given the responsibility of recommending upon which classes of imports higher rates of duties should be levied. In effect a permanent Tariff Commission, it was created to avoid in Britain the evils of tariff lobbying by vested interests, so prominent a feature of fiscal history in other lands.

Ministers, who claimed that they favoured a low tariff policy, argued that the imposition of protective duties put in their hands a bargaining weapon that could be used to persuade other governments to lower tariff barriers. But instead of taking steps to secure a lowering of the barriers of trade restriction, they actually raised them by agreeing to give preferential treatment to Empire products. In the summer of 1932 Stanley Baldwin led the British delegation at the Ottawa Conference at which discussions took place on means of strengthening commercial ties between the Dominions and the Mother Country. Since 1897, when Canada had offered Britain preferential treatment in the Canadian market, various parts of the Empire had negotiated a network of reciprocal preferences with one another. But before 1914, Great Britain, not being a participant in this network of inter-imperial preferences, could justifiably claim that foreigners had the same commercial opportunities as she herself in imperial territories.

A resolution on the subject of Imperial Preferences was adopted by the 1917 Imperial War Conference, the first step towards giving preferences to goods of Empire origin being taken by Sir Austen Chamberlain in the Budget of 1919. Imports from the Empire were to be charged at only five-sixths of the full rate, and on items on which the McKenna duties were levied duties were reduced by one-third. The Imperial Economic Conference in 1923 passed a resolution supporting the principle of imperial preference, but proposals to extend it failed to get majority support in the House of Commons. A second attempt to give effect to the proposals of the 1923 Conference was made in 1925. Winston Churchill's Finance Act of that year extended existing preferences for ten years, re-imposed the McKenna duties which had been repealed by Snowden in 1924, and gave a one-sixth preference on imports of silk and artificial silk. Subsequent imperial preferences enacted included one on pottery in 1927 and on buttons and enamelled hollow-ware in 1928. Positive action was also taken to stimulate a demand for Empire products in the home market. In 1926 the Empire Marketing Board was created, the Merchandise Marks Act was passed, and, as far as possible, it became established practice for government departments to purchase only United Kingdom or Empire products.

As long as British customs duties were levied on relatively few classes of imports, mainly for revenue purposes, the scope for establishing a system of imperial preference was necessarily limited. This ceased to be the case when Great Britain became a protectionist country in 1931-32. At the Ottawa Conference, therefore, the British delegation agreed to extend for five years existing preferences, to grant additional ones, and to regulate by quotas imports from non-Empire countries of chilled and frozen meat, bacon and ham. This extension of the system of imperial preferences can be criticised as an unwise addition to the existing considerable tangle of tariffs, quotas and exchange controls which were strangling international trade. Giving British producers privileged access to Empire markets was bound to stir up foreign resentments, while at home, British farmers could not be expected to be other than worried about the encouragement given to the importation of agricultural products from the Dominions.

Inter-imperial preferential arrangements were advocated as a cure for the malaise in the export industries. There were even people living at the time who were hopeful that the constituent parts of the Empire could be welded into a economic unit, offering British industry opportunities for substantial growth and providing more than adequate compensation for the loss of markets to foreign competitors. Such hopes were exaggerated and based on very insecure foundations. Empire trade, of course, had long been important. During the 1909–13 period 24·7 per cent of British imports were from the Empire which took in return 35·4 per cent of British exports, proportions not significantly different from those in the mid-nineteenth century. After the First World War, however, the considerable increases in British trade with the Empire justified the Empire Marketing Board in choosing as a title for one of its pamphlets *The Growing Dependence of British Industry upon Empire Markets*. Annual returns of the Commissioners of Customs and Excise reveal that the limited tariff concessions before 1932 had led to increases in the percentages of some imports from Empire countries. Between 1922–23 and 1928–29, for example, the percentage of spirits imported from the Empire increased from 59·7 to 63·6, of wines from 5·7 to 18, of sugar from 22·6 to 38, and of tobacco from 6·2 to 16·7. Still further decline in the proportion of British trade with foreign countries followed the conclusion of the Ottawa agreements, in 1933–35 the Empire supplying 35·4 per cent of British imports and absorbing 43·6 per cent of British exports.

Although after 1932 the increase in British trade with the Empire was striking, the Empire was far from developing into a self-sufficing economic unit. In 1934 it provided 42·3 per cent of British imported foodstuffs, compared with 27 per cent in 1913, but only 31·1 per cent of the industrial raw materials, compared with 28 per cent in 1913. Britain was dependent for most of her supplies of such raw materials as mineral oils, timber, cotton, tobacco and coffee on foreign countries. On the other hand British exports to the Empire consisted mainly of a wide variety of manufactured commodities, but also included spirituous liquors, beer and sugar, and insignificant quantities of coke and coal.

As the Empire in the 'thirties largely consisted of agricultural communities possessing export surpluses, the implementation of a policy which gave preferential treatment to their producers inevitably threatened the well-being of British farmers. The outlook for British agriculture was made even more depressing by contemporary world agricultural over-production and the catastrophic collapse of prices. In consequence farmers all over the world were faced with disaster, their extreme distress and impending bankruptcies forcing governments to come to their assistance. In Britain, since 1846, agricultural policy had been determined by free trade and *laisser-faire* principles. Apart from such measures as the derating of agricultural land and subsidies to sugar beet producers, economic forces had been allowed free play. Farmers had been left unprotected against overseas competition in order to ensure abundant supplies of cheap food for the industrial population.

Consideration of the situation prevailing in rural areas forced the National Government of 1931 to the conclusion that lasting damage would be inflicted on British agriculture, if unregulated competition was allowed to continue. But having decided that it ought to intervene in agricultural affairs, the Government did not find it easy to frame policies which satisfied all the conflicting interests concerned. Agricultural decisions could not be acted upon without due consideration of their likely effects on other parts of the economy. Policies, for example, designed to promote agricultural self-sufficiency might eventuate in less employment for British shipping, and fewer orders in consequence for shipbuilders and steel producing plants. To what extent were British farmers to be given protection against competition from overseas producers, not only in the Dominions but also in such foreign countries as Scandinavia, the U.S.A. and in South America where much British capital was invested? Where also could markets be found for British exports if imports of agricultural products were restricted? Doubtless it was urgently necessary to increase the incomes of farmers and their labourers, but parliamentary candidates were naturally apprehensive that a largely urbanised and industrialised electorate would resent increases in the cost of living. It must also be borne in mind that agriculture is not one but many industries. Under free trade and *laisser-faire* conditions individual farmers had decided what crops to plant and what livestock to rear. The Government now found itself involved in deciding such matters.

It would be untrue to claim that British governments since 1931 have implemented comprehensive, carefully constructed agricultural policies. The measures passed by the National Government after 1931 were designed to prevent irreparable damage to British agricultural life, and included guaranteed prices, import restrictions and quotas, and marketing schemes. Under the provisions of Marketing Acts passed in 1931 and 1933, boards, composed exclusively of producers, were given wide powers to regulate supplies to the market, and to restrict output, a development justifiably criticised on the grounds that consumer interests were insufficiently safeguarded.

By the Wheat Act of 1931 farmers were guaranteed prices, the cost of the subsidy being met from a duty levied on flour paid by millers. Similar assistance was given to growers of oats and barley in 1937. Potato imports were controlled by licences issued by the Board of Trade, and a Potato Marketing Board was empowered to limit output and control distribution through authorised merchants. All hops were sold through a Hop Marketing Board, and, following the collapse of prices in the 1930-31 slump, producers were authorised to set up Milk Marketing Boards for England and Wales and Scotland. Cattle farmers were protected by import restrictions. At the Ottawa Conference it was agreed that Empire chilled beef should be admitted at lower rates of duty than that from the Argentine, and agreements were made with all southern hemisphere producers that shipments from them should be limited. But as the price of beef on the British market did not reach profitable levels for home producers a system of temporary subsidies was introduced in 1934. The subsidy scheme was made permanent in 1937, its administration being entrusted to a Livestock Commission. As far as mutton and lamb were concerned home producers were protected by import agreements with Australia, New Zealand and the Argentine, and by a price insurance scheme introduced in 1939.

Poultry rearing was a rapidly expanding industry during the inter-war years, imports of eggs in shells falling from 63 per cent of our suppliers in 1912 to 36 per cent in 1935-36. Imports were controlled by agreements with foreign countries and by tariffs, and a Poultry Commission was set up to advise on methods of controlling disease. Lastly, pig producers, who were badly affected by the fall in prices during the 1930 slump, were dependent upon imported feeding-stuffs and had to compete with better quality Danish bacon. The Government imposed import restrictions and in 1934 allotted import quotas to foreign countries. But drastic restrictions on imports were impossible to justify as Denmark was a good customer of our exporting industries. A Bacon Development Board was created, its power being increased by the Bacon Industry Act (1938), and producers and curers were assisted by the grant of an annual subsidy of £1 million.

There was also government intervention in the industrial sector of the economy. This took the form of State encouragement of the trend towards combination and concentration. As explained in a previous chapter, during the closing decades of the nineteenth century, the formation of trusts and kartells had been a feature of economic development in the U.S.A. and Germany. At the time, these modern capitalist tendencies, although not unknown, did not manifest themselves to the same extent in Great Britain. Nevertheless in trades where it was possible to standardise methods of production, using specialised power-machinery, some amalgamations took place. In the brewing industry, as railways made possible marketing over wide areas and firms became joint stock companies, there was a very large reduction in the number of brewing firms. Burton-on-Trent became the seat of an enormous brewing trade carried on by some 20 firms including the Bass and Allsopp breweries.

In 1888 an attempt was made to end the competition between salt producers in Cheshire and on Tees-side by the formation of a Salt Union. In the 'nineties some very large industrial combinations came into existence. John Brown and Co. of Sheffield, which owned coal-mines and steel plant, amalgamated with the Clydebank Shipbuilding Company. In 1845 William George Armstrong, a Newcastle solicitor, built a factory in Elswick Village on Tyneside to exploit his invention of an hydraulic crane. At the end of the century the firm took over engineering, locomotive and ordnance works. During the First World War, at Elswick alone was produced one-third of Britain's total production of guns and many millions of shells and cartridges. Other contemporary amalgamations were those which resulted in the formation of the steel firm of Stewarts and Lloyds, and in South Wales and Staffordshire of the firm of Guest, Keen and Nettlefold, which controlled collieries, blast furnaces, and steel plant, and manufactured nuts, bolts and screws.

Amalgamations in the heavy chemical industry prepared the way for the formation of the firm of Brunner, Mond and Co. By amalgamations some very large business units were established in the textile trades, including the sewing-thread combine of J. and P. Coats, the Calico Printers' Association and the Associations of Fine Cotton Spinners, Bleachers, and Bradford Dyers. Worth noting also was the revolution in the manufacture of clothing which followed the introduction of Singer's sewing-machine in 1851. Adapted in the 'fifties for use in the boot and shoe industry, the sewing-machine cheapened production and put within reach of the masses commodities hitherto hand-made and in consequence very expensive. Large establishments for the manufacture of Singer sewing-machines were established at Elizabeth in New Jersey and at Clydebank where thousands of operatives were employed.

These early amalgamations were anticipations of the modern

industrial world in which productive enterprise is dominated by mammoth corporate bodies of employers and employees. But it was not until after the First World War and the collapse of the basic British export trades that the British amalgamation movement really got under way. The modern trend began in 1926 when four leading chemical companies, Brunner Mond, Nobel Industries, the United Alkali Company, and the British Dyestuffs Corporation, amalgamated to form Imperial Chemical Industries Ltd. In the following year, 1927, Vickers, Sons and Co., Sheffield steel-makers, amalgamated with Armstrong Whitworths.

This trend towards the formation of large-scale business units was speeded up with the onset of the post-1931 depression and the imposition of protective tariffs. Government support was given to what was known at the time as the "rationalisation" of British industry. The term "rationalisation," which originated in Germany after the First World War, was used to describe measures of industrial reorganisation. These included the amalgamation and reorganisation of business units, the closing down of unremunerative and inefficient plant, and the concentration of production in industrial units equipped with automatic and semi-automatic machinery. The implementation of such a programme inevitably meant unemployment for workers on the pay rolls of firms forced out of existence. It also brought about what became known at the time as "technological unemployment." In the U.S.A. the existence of "technological employment" had long been a feature of the industrial scene. Great Britain in her turn now had to cope with the social and economic problems created by the substitution of automatic machinery for men, in a wide range of industries producing standardised commodities.

In 1931, however, the massive unemployment in Britain was not "technological" but due to contraction in demand for her staple exports. The remedy suggested by the Balfour Committee on Trade and Industry (1929), and in other official publications, was the closure of inefficient plant. As reliance upon competition to get rid of excess producing capacity would be a slow process, government encouragement was given to the reorganisation of industry by industrialists.

In the rationalising of the shipbuilding industry a prominent part was played by the Clydeside shipbuilder, Sir James Lithgow, who formed in 1929 National Shipbuilders' Security Ltd. Finance was provided by the formation in 1930 of the Bankers' Industrial Development Company whose Chairman was the Governor of the Bank of England, Montagu Norman. Shipyards were purchased, the plant sold as scrap, and the use of the sites for shipbuilding was prohibited for 40 years. In *The Town that was Murdered* (1939) the Labour M.P., Ellen Wilkinson, has vividly portrayed the tragic consequences for the people of Jarrow that followed the closure in 1934 of Palmers' Shipyard. The workmen, skilled craftsmen, not only lost their jobs but also the savings which some of them had invested in the firm. Many of them, still living, participated in 1936 in the march of the Jarrow unemployed to London. Despite this drastic surgery the British shipbuilding industry did not recover its former position of dominance. In 1938, less than one-third of the world tonnage was being built in British yards. British shipowners were even finding it cheaper to order ships from German and Scandinavian firms, a state of affairs which induced the Government in 1938 to pay a subsidy to shipowners ordering new ships to be built in Britain. On condition that the Atlantic fleets of the Cunard and White Star Lines were amalgamated the Government also gave financial assistance towards the building of the *Queen Mary*.

Other methods adopted to stimulate action by private enterprise to cut out excess producing capacity, included taxation concessions in respect of profits used to finance approved schemes, and pressure by the Import Duties Advisory Committee. The imposition of high tariffs, for example, those on iron and steel, was made conditional on rationalisation schemes being implemented. In 1934 government backing was given to the formation of the British Iron and Steel Federation which closed down plants at Coatbridge in Scotland and at Dowlais in South Wales. Following the Report of the Economic Advisory Council on the cotton industry (1930) the Lancashire Cotton Corporation was created, and a Spindles Board, financed by a levy on spinners, was empowered to purchase and scrap redundant spindles. As a further example of government interference with the operation of free competitive enterprise may be cited the restrictions, in the interests of the railways, imposed upon road transport undertakings by the licensing provisions of the Road Traffic Act (1930) and the Road and Rail Traffic Act (1933).

The coalmining industry was dealt with by the passage of the Coal Mines Act of 1930. Price-fixing machinery was established and output was controlled by a system of pit quotas. The Samuel Commission in 1925 had recommended the amalgamation of very small units of production, but the Reorganisation Commission set up under the provisions of the Act of 1930 failed. The British coal industry, located on a relatively large number of scattered producing areas, proved to be less easy to weld into a monopolistic unit, under conditions of private ownership, than did that of Germany, where most of the output was obtained from two large fields, those in the Ruhr and in Silesia. Centralised marketing arrangements, however, were organised in 1936 for each area of coal production.

Government intervention did not arrest the decline of the staple industries. Exports of motor vehicles, rubber tyres, electrical engineering goods, paper and commodities manufactured from imported raw materials, accounted for 7·4 per cent of British exports in 1927-29 and for 9·4 per cent in the slump year, 1932-33. But the increase in such export items did not fully compensate for the decreases in the older export staples. British exports and re-exports, £839 million in 1929, had fallen to £533 million by 1938. In fact in no year between 1929 and 1939 did the total value of British exports rise to the levels achieved in the 'twenties.

The policies of the governments before 1939 did not result in a significant lowering of unemployment levels and their intervention to plan industrial locations and the re-allocation of labour was very limited in scope. The Commissioners appointed under the Special Areas Act of 1934 to revive industrial life in the depressed areas offered firms as inducements to start new industries in North England, Central Scotland and South Wales, relief from local rates, and capital and sites on favourable terms. In the five years preceding the outbreak of war the Commissioners spent £16 million on the development of new industries, on public works schemes, and in promoting local social services. Their efforts were supplemented by those of the Ministry of Labour which, firstly, established labour camps and training centres and, secondly, gave financial aid to assist migration to more prosperous areas. But the Commissioners were not given either the finance or the authority which would have enabled them to fill empty shipyard berths or to re-start unused steel plant and textile machinery. To quote from the report of Sir Malcolm Stewart, Commissioner for England, written in 1935 when the percentage unemployment in the United Kingdom was 15·5: "I see no prospect of any effective reduction of unemployment under existing conditions."

Acting on the suggestion of a Middlesbrough accountant, S. A. Sadler Forster, a trading estate was created in the Team Valley, near Gateshead, Co. Durham, on which light industries were established in factories offered to industrialists at nominal rents. Jewish refugees from Hitler's Germany had by 1939 provided gainful employment there for a mere 5,000 workers. The percentage of unemployment had fallen to 11·1, by 1939 but this was due not to the activities of Jewish refugees and the Special Area Commissioners, but to the rearmament programme which the British Government had initiated in the late 'thirties.

The breaches in the traditional system of free, competitive enterprise made by British governments in the 'thirties have been criticised as unduly favourable to producer interests. The encouragement of redundancy schemes did lead to the cutting out of much excess producing capacity. Industries became more monopolistic in structure but not technically more efficient. Those plants which survived the pruning improved their financial position but on the whole the shortcomings of British industrial organisation were not remedied. When the Second World War began in September 1939 Great Britain was a country with many unsolved social and economic problems, new jobs in the expanding science-based industries not being created fast enough to absorb the many thousands living on the dole or subjected to the humiliations of the means test. The 1938 Anglo-American Treaty providing for slight reciprocal reductions in tariffs was only a minor breach in the massive walls of trade restrictions. The truth was that the economic order inherited from the nineteenth century had vanished beyond recall. Great Britain had not by 1939 learned how to adapt her industrial and agricultural structure to meet the challenges of the new world. Nevertheless precedents had been set. Once the Nazi tyranny had been overcome, public opinion was prepared to accept far-reaching measures of government intervention.

Chapter XXX

THE GENESIS OF THE WELFARE STATE

In June 1941, Arthur Greenwood, the Minister without Portfolio, informed the House of Commons that an "Interdepartmental Committee on Social Insurance and Allied Services" had been instructed to undertake a comprehensive survey of existing schemes of social insurance. The sequel was the publication, in November 1942, of the Beveridge Report, which contained a review of existing schemes of social insurance and a plan for social security. Sir William (later Lord) Beveridge's plan was designed as an attack on "Want." Evidence that, before 1939, very large numbers of people had incomes which did not provide for more than the barest necessities of life, is all too plentiful. In *Poverty, A Study of Town Life* (1901) Seebohm Rowntree estimated than 28 per cent of the inhabitants of York were poverty-sticken. Sociological investigations after the First World War revealed the existence in towns and cities, outside the "depressed areas," of very large numbers of families whose standard of living was "below the poverty line"; in Reading for example, in 1924, 12 per cent, in prosperous Southampton (1931), 20 per cent, and in London (1929–31) over 9 per cent.

Professor A. L. Bowley calculated that at 1935 prices, "a bare subsistence" standard of living would be the lot of a family of five when the weekly wage of the breadwinner was 35*s*. 2½*d*. In his *Human Needs of Labour*, Seebohm Rowntree estimated that the necessities for a healthy life for a similar family could only be provided on a minimum weekly income of 53*s*. in towns and 41*s*. in country areas. As Colin Clark calculated that in 1935 5 per cent of adult workers earned 35*s*. a week or less, 18 per cent between 35*s*. and 45*s*., and 24 per cent between 45*s*. and 55*s*., malnutrition must have been fairly widespread, particularly when it is remembered that very large numbers of wage-earners were working short-time. For the families of the 13·1 per cent of the insured population unemployed in 1936, life must certainly have been grim, as the scales issued by the Unemployment Assistance Board authorised a payment of only 36*s*. to a family of five, three of the children of which fell into the 5 to 14 age-range. The mother of three fatherless children, it may be noted, was only entitled to 27s. Not surprisingly, the death rate was higher in areas of much unemployment than in the country as a whole, and highest in the families of the unemployed. The investigations of the local medical officer, Dr G. E. N. McConigle, for example, revealed that in Stockton-on-Tees the death rate varied from 31 per cent in the poorest households, to 9 per cent in those of the well-to-do.

In any consideration of the distribution of the national income it ought to be borne in mind that the family is the real social unit. In his *Food, Health and Income* (1936), Sir John (later Lord) Boyd Orr concluded that half the population had family incomes of less than 20s. per week, per head. Of this, less than 9s. per head was spent on food. As a way out of this unsatisfactory state of affairs, some contemporaries advocated, firstly, redistributive taxation, and secondly, public ownership of the means of production. Recently, however, it has become increasingly recognised that very high taxation on earned income has a disincentive effect, and that a solution to the problem of raising the standard of living of the lower-paid will have to be sought in a rapid rate of economic growth, greater industrial efficiency and technological advance.

The schemes of social insurance, which the Beveridge Committee surveyed, had grown piecemeal, beginning, the Poor Law excepted, with the passage of the Workmen's Compensation Act in 1897. State intervention in the field of social relationships had been resisted, before and after 1897, by people who considered that it was a man's responsibility to provide for himself and his dependants. To this end working-class people had sought to safeguard themselves by the formation of voluntary associations known as friendly societies. These were mutual insurance societies financed by voluntary subscriptions. Medieval gilds had provided such a form of insurance for their members, the Friendly Movement originating after their suppression in the sixteenth century.

The existence of small and widely-dispersed friendly societies can be traced back to the seventeenth century, but the modern friendly society movement originated in the eighteenth century. In Rose's Act (1793), the first legislative recognition of its existence, they are described as "societies of good fellowship." Following the passage of the Act of 1793, which gave valuable taxation relief, many societies were enrolled, nearly a thousand in Middlesex alone. An Act passed in 1819 stated that the formation of friendly societies was desirable to avoid "the moral deterioration of the people" and "the heavy burthens upon parishes" that resulted from "the habitual reliance of poor persons upon parochial relief." Further legislation followed in 1829: in 1846 the office of Registrar of Friendly Societies was created; and amending and consolidating legislation was enacted in 1850 and 1855. More than 20,000 societies were registered under the Act of 1855 which continued in force until the passage of the Friendly Societies Act in 1875, replaced in 1896 by the Friendly Societies Act and the Collecting and Industrial Assurance Companies Act.

The Act of 1875, which enforced the adoption of sound rules, effective audit and rates of payment sufficient to maintain solvency, was based on the recommendations of a Royal Commission presided over by Sir Stafford Northcote (later Lord Iddesleigh) between 1870 and 1874. The Commission divided registered friendly societies into 13 classes. There were in addition a considerable number of unregistered organisations consisting of affiliated societies such as the Manchester Unity of Oddfellows, the Ancient Order of Foresters, with headquarters in Leeds, the Rechabites and the Druids, who numbered their total membership in many thousands. At the other end of the scale were numerous small "country," "local town" and "village" societies. Among the benefits members received were sick payments, payments upon death and payments on attainment of a certain age.

In the third quarter of the nineteenth century, friendly society activity became a marked feature of skilled craft trade unionism. Profit-seeking private enterprise also entered the field of social insurance, beginning in 1854 with the foundation of the Prudential Assurance Company. Voluntary provision for death and other contingencies through Industrial Life Offices expanded rapidly, in 1939, according to the Beveridge Report, 90 per cent of the business being in the hands of eight large companies, the Prudential, Pearl, Liverpool Victoria, Refuge, Co-operative, Royal London Mutual, Royal Liver and Britannic. Millions of policy holders were protected by the Industrial Insurance Act (1923), which placed industrial assurance companies under the control of the Chief Registrar of Friendly Societies, who was in future to be known as the Industrial Assurance Commissioner.

The system of Industrial Assurance was adversely reported upon by a House of Commons Select Committee in 1889, by the Parmoor Committee in 1919–20 and by the Cohen Committee of 1931–33. According to the Beveridge Report the premium industrial assurance income in 1939 was £74 million, built up from "pennies, sixpences and shillings," collected for the most part week by week from a large proportion of all the households in Britain. That policy holders were receiving an unsatisfactory return is evident from the fact that 37·2 per cent, or 7s. 6d. in every pound of the premium income, was absorbed by management expenses, dividends and taxation.

In modern society there still function a very large number of voluntary societies, financed by subscriptions from private individuals. These include, in addition to many others, St John's Ambulance Association, the Central Council for the Care of Cripples, Dr Barnardo's Homes, the British Legion and Citizens' Advice Bureaux. Assistance in co-ordinating their activities is given by the National Council of Social Services. But that voluntary effort, supplemented by poor law relief and inadequate local government services, would not suffice to protect the bulk of the population against the hazards of old age, sickness and involuntary unemployment became more widely recognised in the early years of the twentieth century.

State intervention in the field of social relationships became unavoidable because, in the form of society created by modern industrialism, the individual has lost control of his economic destiny. The operation of the trade cycle, technological changes, the implementation of schemes of rationalisation, and the tariff and taxation policies of governments have deprived countless thousands of the opportunity of regular employment. The problems of unemployment and destitution in twentieth-century Britain were very different in character from those for which Edwin Chadwick and his contemporaries had sought solutions. Poverty and destitution were no longer confined to Dickensian slums or to the classes impoverished by land enclosures. They now afflicted whole communities inhabiting "depressed areas." This was clearly shown by the report of the Select Committee on Physical Deterioration, which was set up because of the number of sub-standard recruits for the Army during the Boer War. But even before the onset of the post-war slump the need for a new approach to the problems of destitution had been recommended by a Royal Commission on the Poor Laws appointed in 1905. Its reports, the Majority and Minority Reports, published in 1909, criticised the methods used to assist those in want, a disturbing comparison being made with the situation as it was in 1834, "an ever-growing expenditure from public and private funds, which results, on the one hand, in a minimum of prevention and cure, and on the other hand in far-reaching demoralisation of character and the continuance of no small amount of unrelieved destitution."

Destitute persons in England and Wales, known as paupers, were the responsibility of 643 Boards of Guardians. In 1910 they arranged for the education of 48 per cent of pauper children in Public Elementary Schools, a further 35 per cent being taught in "Separate" or "District" Schools. They maintained infirmaries for the sick poor, homes for the aged, asylums for the mentally afflicted and workhouses for vagrants and for those of the indoor poor not housed in specialised institutions. Their efforts were supplemented by those of the local authorities, whose powers were used to prevent the onset of destitution. In 1905 the Unemployed Workmen Act, described by Ramsay MacDonald as "one of the most courageous pieces of statesmanship of our generation," empowered local authorities to establish distress committees to assist in finding work for the unemployed. In 1906 education committees were authorised to feed necessitous children. To a considerable extent the efforts of the poor law authorities and those of local councils overlapped. Yet despite increasing expenditure by both, the numbers of persons unable to support themselves tended to increase rather than to diminish.

Both the Majority and Minority Reports recommended that the forms of assistance given to the poor should be properly systemised and that there should be an old-age pension scheme, school clinics, a State medical service and labour exchanges. Both agreed that the nineteenth-century practice of creating *ad hoc* authorities should be discontinued. Instead the areas of administration for all local government services should in future be those of county and county borough councils. Enlarging the areas of administration would, it was considered, assist in meeting the problems of necessitous areas, cheapen administration and improve the quality of candidates for office.

Both reports recommended the abolition of Boards of Guardians and the General Workhouse, but differed as to the new bodies who were to take responsibility for the care of the poor. The Majority Report, signed by fourteen of the eighteen Commissioners, proposed the transfer of the powers and functions of the elected Boards of Guardians to Public Assistance Authorities, the members of which were to be local authority nominees. They also proposed the setting up in each area of Medical Assistance Committees, consisting of nominated and co-opted members. The Minority Report, however, the work of Mrs Sidney Webb, George Lansbury and two other members, suggested a much more drastic change, namely, the abolition of the distinction hitherto made between paupers and citizens. If their proposals had been adopted, the Poor Law would have ceased to exist, and responsibility for each class of the poor (vagrants and the able-bodied excepted) would have been transferred to appropriate committees of the local authorities. All children of school age, for example, would have been taken care of by the Education Committee, the sick (including expectant mothers) by the Health Committee, the mentally defective by the Asylums Committee and the aged by the Pensions Committee.

After the publication of these reports, John Burns, the President of the Local Government Board, introduced minor administrative reforms but left the fundamental problem untouched. Some of the proposals of the Royal Commission, however, were given legislative effect. In 1908, the year before the reports appeared, the Old Age Pension Act was passed. This provided for the payment of non-contributory maximum pensions of 5s. weekly to persons over 70 in receipt of incomes not exceeding 8s. a week. An Act was passed in 1909, establishing under the Board of Trade Labour Exchanges, known from 1916, when they were transferred to the Ministry of Labour, as Employment Exchanges. By February 1910 the young William Beveridge had brought 61 Exchanges into existence.

Much more controversial, being vigorously opposed by the medical profession, was Part I of the National Insurance Act, introduced by Lloyd George in 1911. This provided for the payment of sickness, disablement and maternity benefits, on a contributory and compulsory basis, to employed persons whose incomes did not exceed £160 a year. The scheme did not cover all these, as members of the armed forces, teachers and public employees were outside its scope. Weekly contributions were collected from employers and employees, in return for which insured persons were entitled to free medical attention and free medicines. The scheme was administered through "approved societies." These included friendly societies and trade unions, contributors being free to select their society and doctor, the latter receiving an annual payment, initially 4s. in respect of each of his panel patients.

Part II of the National Insurance Act, piloted through the Commons by Winston Churchill, initiated a scheme of unemployment insurance. Administered through the Labour Exchanges, the scheme covered approximately 2,250,000 workers in trades in which risks of unemployment were severe, building, engineering, shipbuilding, iron-founding, saw-milling and vehicle construction. Contributions were paid by both employers and employees, unemployment benefit being paid to workers who, unable to find work, had been employed for at least 26 weeks in the preceding five years. The benefit was initially a payment of 7s. weekly, for a maximum of 15 weeks in any one year. This restriction makes plain that the scheme was designed, not to provide "full maintenance," but to tide the recipients over in what were expected to be temporary periods of unemployment.

The pre-1914 pioneering measures of social security included also legislation extending the right to compensation to workers and their dependants for injuries sustained in the course of their employment. The common law provision concerning workmen injured at work was defined and extended by Lord Campbell's Act (1846), the Employers' Liability Act (1880) and the Workmen's Compensation Act of 1897. By the Act of 1880 a new principle was introduced, namely, that employers must pay compensation, but before the enactment of the Act of 1897 workmen had no legal right to compensation, unless they could prove negligence on the part of the employer or of persons to whom he had delegated responsibility. The Act of 1897, described by one Labour M.P., G. W. Barnes, as "one of the best pieces of social legislation which has been placed on the statute book," was limited to certain dangerous employments, but it did make employers liable to pay compensation to workers, or in the case of death to their dependants, whether or not there had been negligence on the part of the employer or anyone in his employ. Further, negligence on the part of the injured workman was not to be a bar to the payment of compensation. Agricultural labourers were brought within the scope of workmen's compensation in 1900. In 1906 these legal provisions were extended to cover all persons working under a contract of service or apprenticeship, non-manual workers earning more than £250 a year (later, £420) being excluded. The Workmen's Compensation Act of 1906 also provided for death or disablement caused by scheduled industrial diseases.

The pre-1914 social security legislation was productive of much administrative confusion. Boards of Guardians continued to function, but as there was growing opposition to the deterrent methods they were legally obliged to use, Parliament had removed large numbers of needy persons from their jurisdiction. In consequence, those in need of communal assistance were being catered for by a variety of central and local government agencies. During the war years, when the percentage of trade unionists unemployed was very low, 1 per cent in 1915 and falling to 0·4, 0·6 and 0·7 per cent in 1916, 1917 and 1918 respectively, the volume of pauperism diminished. Boards of Guardians, therefore, had only to give relief to those of the impotent poor who were not looked after by local authorities or provided for under the provisions of the Old Age Pensions and National Insurance Acts.

In 1917 the Ministry of Reconstruction appointed a Committee to re-investigate the problem of pauperism. Presided over by Sir Donald Maclean, the Committee recommended the abolition of Boards of Guardians, and the transfer of their functions to committees of county and county borough councils and urban districts with more than 50,000 inhabitants. The Government pledged itself to carry out the recommendations of the Maclean Committee, but the Bill it sponsored was rejected by the House of Lords in 1920. Then came the onset of the post-war depression. The Lloyd George unemployment insurance scheme, designed to deal with short-term unemployment, was incapable of dealing with the situation. Hundreds of thousands of unemployed persons, therefore, had no option but to seek relief payments from Boards of Guardians. The Guardians, according to the Minister of Health, had become "the sheet anchor of the nation."

As the following Ministry of Health statistics reveal, the number of persons in England and Wales in receipt of poor relief increased alarmingly, from 632,242 in 1913, to 1,375,982 in 1921, and 1,324,321 in 1925. Of those in receipt of poor relief in 1925, 222,494 were being cared for in institutions and 1,101,820 in their own homes. In addition, in 1925, 119,000 persons, including lunatics in asylums, casuals and persons receiving medical relief only, were a charge on Board of Guardian funds. The total rate-borne expenditure of the Guardians rose from £12,078,000 in 1913 to £31,000,000 in 1925. In Scotland also there was a big increase in the numbers of destitute persons, Scottish poor law expenditure rising from £1,609,538 in 1913–14 to £4,370,609 in 1923–24.

Difficulties were particularly acute in the "necessitous areas," areas in which there was an exceptionally heavy concentration of unemployed persons. In Poplar, one-fifth of the population was dependent on relief, and in 30 Poor Law Unions, one-tenth. In some districts, Guardians had to resort to borrowing, as poor law rate yields were insufficient to enable them to meet their obligations. In face of this situation, government policy tended to be one of masterly inactivity. Parliament did pass the Local Authorities (Financial Provisions) Act in 1921, which relieved the poorer metropolitan districts by providing that the cost of outdoor relief should be met from a Metropolitan Common Fund, but relief payments were not to exceed the "Mond Scales," drawn up in 1922 by the Minister of Health, Sir Alfred Mond.

Conservative governments, unlike the two Labour governments, opposed as too expensive the institution of either "relief" or "public" works as means of reducing unemployment. Nor were steps taken to shift the burden of rescuing the unemployed from starvation off the shoulders of rate-payers to those of tax-payers. But they did give financial assistance to workers moving from "depressed" to more prosperous areas, and did intervene to curb what was considered to be undue generosity by some Boards of Guardians, notably in Poplar. There, socialist members of the Board of Guardians were threatened with surcharges and imprisonment by the District Auditor and the Ministry of Health when they persisted in paying more than the "Mond Scales" permitted. "Poplarism," as such practices were popularly known, was not widespread, the

Government ultimately deciding to deal with defaulting Boards of Guardians by the passage in 1926 of the Boards of Guardians (Default) Act. This empowered the Ministry to suspend Boards and appoint official administrators to take over their duties. This was done at West Ham, Chester-le-Street in Durham and at Bedwellty in North Wales.

By the mid-twenties, however, it had become obvious that Boards of Guardians were unable to cope with mass long-term unemployment. The way for their abolition was prepared by the publication in 1925 of Neville Chamberlain's proposals for Poor Law reform, and by the enactment of a Rating and Valuation Bill. Under this Act, which came into operation on 1st April 1927, the parish ceased to be the assessment area as the rating functions of parish overseers were transferred to town and district councils. This legislation was followed by the Local Government Act of 1929, a major measure of local government reform consisting of eight parts extending over 190 pages of print. For our immediate purpose, Part I is the most important, as by it all existing Poor Law Authorities were abolished, their powers and duties, assets and liabilities being transferred on 1st April 1930 to county and county borough councils.

The Act of 1929 made it obligatory on the councils to appoint Public Assistance Committees, and in the case of the county councils, local committees also. In framing their administrative schemes, the councils were to have regard to the desirability of taking "out of the Poor Law" all the existing services of the Guardians that their own powers enabled them to administer under other statutes. In other words, it was hoped that the stigma of pauperism would be removed from the sick, the mentally afflicted, the blind, and from mothers, infants and children. It would have been possible for reactionary councils to take over the workhouses, infirmaries and other institutions of the Guardians and to continue to administer them as going concerns. On the other hand, the Act of 1929 did offer to progressive councils scope for providing assistance "outside the Poor Law." But no statutory provision was given to treat able-bodied persons other than as paupers. As far as they were concerned, the councils had either to admit them to workhouses or grant outdoor relief "conditional on the performance of 'test work,' however small may be the amount of relief granted." But the fact that councils were legally restricted in dealing with the necessitous able-bodied did not prevent them from providing something more appropriate than poor relief to wives and children.

The pre-1939 trends towards the construction of a Welfare State were strengthened by other legislation. The Ministry of Health, created by statute in 1919, replaced the Local Government Board.

Its activities can be classified under five main heads: (i) the supervision of the public health services provided by local authorities; (ii) the supervision of local government activities and taxation; (iii) housing and town planning; (iv) the supervision of the administration of the Poor Law and Old Age Pensions and Widows' and Orphans' Pensions Acts; and (v) national health insurance services. Local authority maternity and child welfare services date from the passage in 1918 of the Maternity and Child Welfare Act. The Midwives and Maternity Homes Act (1926) provided for the registration and inspection of maternity homes and prohibited unqualified persons from attending women in childbirth. The Nursing Homes Registration Act (1927) gave to local authorities the responsibility of registering and supervising nursing and maternity homes, and by the Midwives Act (1936) local authorities were required to establish services of salaried and trained midwives.

The scope of the pre-1914 Old Age Pensions and National Insurance Acts were also extended. The Old Age Pensions Act (1919) increased non-contributory pensions to 10s. weekly. The Blind Persons Act (1920) fixed 50 (reduced to 40 in 1938) as the non-contributory pension age and empowered local authorities to maintain hostels and homes for blind persons. In 1925, Winston Churchill, the Chancellor of the Exchequer, and Neville Chamberlain, the Minister of Health, introduced the Widows', Orphans' and Old Age Contributory Pensions Act. By it, pensions were payable to insured persons and their wives from the age of 65 and also to widows of insured persons with additional allowances for children. The National Health Insurance Act (1928) enabled new classes of workers to benefit from the health and pension schemes, and also safeguarded the health and pension rights of those who, owing to involuntary unemployment, had accumulated arrears of insurance contributions. The Voluntary Pensions Act (1937) permitted persons of limited means, not in insurable employment, to become voluntary contributors. As a consequence of this legislation, the number of persons under 65 eligible for free medical treatment increased from 13,689,000 in 1914 to 19,706,000 in 1938, while the numbers of persons covered by widows, orphans and old age pension schemes rose from 17,089,000 in 1926 to 20,678,000 in 1938.

Significant changes were also made in the pre-1914 schemes of unemployment insurance. The number of workers covered was increased from 4 million to 12 million by the Unemployment Insurance Act of 1920. Under this Act, as under the Lloyd George Act of 1911, benefits were payable to insured persons for restricted periods, dependent upon the number of contributions paid by applicants into the Unemployment Fund. Owing to widespread distress, however, two modifications were introduced in 1921, firstly, the payment of benefits in respect of dependents, and secondly, payment at the discretion of the Minister of Labour, of "extended benefits." Unemployment payments could now be made for 26 instead of 15 weeks, and longer to those "genuinely seeking work." This "extended" or "uncovenanted benefit" to which the name "dole" was popularly given, was associated with a "means test" which involved taking into consideration the incomes of others members of the household. Unemployed workers whom Ministry of Labour officials ruled were ineligibile for the "dole" were forced to choose between starvation and submission to the traditional destitution tests of the hated poor law.

Unfortunately for the growing army of unemployed persons, British governments were faced with a problem for which they had no solution. In its Election Manifesto, the First Labour Government claimed that it alone "had a positive remedy." Challenged in the House of Commons to produce it, Tom Shaw, the Minister of Labour, plaintively replied, "Does anybody think we can produce schemes like rabbits out of our hats?" Their Tory successors, although they were no more successful in finding jobs for the workless, did enact in 1927 the Unemployment Insurance Act. This, based on the recommendations of the Blanesburgh Committee, appointed in 1927, sought to put unemployment insurance on an approved basis by doing away with the "dole" aspect. Benefits in future were to be a statutory right enjoyed by persons who had paid a required number of contributions within the preceding two years.

The high unemployment levels, however, which reached their peak in the early 'thirties, made unworkable the 1911 notion that relief for the unemployed could be given from an unemployment insurance fund. The Unemployment Fund had become hopelessly insolvent. Although in 1930 the State had assumed responsibility for financing "extended," by that time known as "transitional," benefit, the Fund in 1931 owed the Treasury £110 million. Fears that the "dole" was too great a burden prompted the May Committee on National Expenditure to advise the Second Labour Government to reduce benefit rates and to subject applicants for "transitional" benefits to a stringent means test. The Labour Government did pass the Anomalies Act (1931) which, as administered by its successor, deprived 180,000 married women of benefit, but it was left to the National Government to impose the drastic economies needed to make the Unemployment Fund solvent. Rates of benefit were reduced and strictly limited to 26 weeks, after which the unemployed had to apply for relief, based on a means test, from local authority Public Assistance Committees. But these arrangements were temporary in character, as the Government was awaiting the recommendations of a Royal Commission on Unemployment Insurance.

After the report of the Royal Commission had been received an Unemployment Act was passed in 1934. This measure, firstly, restored the 1931 cuts in unemployment insurance benefit rates, secondly, gave to an Unemployment Insurance Committee the responsibility of ensuring that the Unemployment Fund was administered on a strictly actuarial basis, and thirdly, transferred responsibility for dealing with applicants for "transitional" benefits from local rate-financed Public Assistance Committees to a newly-created statutory body, financed from taxation, the Unemployment Assistance Board. The U.A.B., known after the outbreak of the Second World War as the Assistance Board, made relief payments, pared down to starvation level and based on "a household means test," to unemployed persons who had exhausted or were ineligible for unemployed insurance payments. Relieved of the crippling burden of providing for the able-bodied unemployed, local authority Public Assistance Committees henceforth dealt only with local destitution.

Much had been done by successive governments before 1939 to provide the peoples of Great Britain with social security. The wide range of social services we enjoy today barely existed at the beginning of the twentieth century. In 1880, the greater part of the £15 million spent by the State on social services was poor relief expenditure. A very different state of affairs existed on the eve of the Second World War. Between 1910 and 1938 the percentage of the national income spent on social expenditure rose from 3·05 to 10·1. Social expenditure, the cost of health and education services, national income spent on social expenditure rose from 3·05 to10·1. from £63 million in 1910 to £477 million in 1938. Nevertheless, despite this massive increase, "want" had not been banished from the land. Despite the implementation of pensions legislation, national insurance schemes for health and unemployment, and the disbursal of considerable sums by the U.A.B., poor relief was still being provided by the Public Assistance Committees of the local authorities.

A considerable item in social expenditure in 1939, unknown in 1900, was expenditure under the Housing Acts. Traditionally the provision of dwellings had, for the most part, been left to profit-seeking private enterprise, State enterprise in this field being delayed until after 1918. But even before the war, there had been a serious shortage, one estimate being that in 1911 over 800,000 families in England and Wales lacked houses. Then came the war, which for four years halted further construction. Hence to prevent the operation of the law of supply and demand in a period of acute housing shortage, Rent Restriction Acts were passed in 1915, 1920 and 1923. This policy of protecting low-income tenants has continued to the present day, despite the undoubted fact that it unfairly penalised landlords. During the war, also, the Tudor Walter Committee was appointed to make recommendations on the type of dwelling which should be constructed for working class occupation. It proposed revolutionary changes in standards. Houses were to be built not more than twelve to the acre, each possessing a large living-room, a garden, a bath, an indoor water closet and a larder and coal storage facilities. This standard was accepted by the Government and enforced on local authorities.

When men demobilised from the armed forces returned home after the Armistice, demanding fulfilment of the pledge to provide "homes for heroes," it was obvious that the acute housing shortage could not be overcome by reliance on unaided private enterprise. The discriminatory legislation against landlords militated against private investment in housing, particularly as building costs in the immediate post-war period were abnormally high. Ever since, therefore, political parties have had to place the provision of houses in the forefront of their political programmes. The greatest housing drive this country had hitherto known began in 1919. Approximately 4 million houses were built between 1919 and 1939 by local authorities, usually financially aided by the central government and by private enterprise, both with and without a government subsidy. Labour governments tended to favour action through the local authorities, Conservative governments on the other hand preferring to rely on private enterprise. Actually, the greater contribution was made by unsubsidised private enterprise. Between 1930 and 1939, when Conservative governments were in office, 1,937,000 houses were built by private enterprise and 621,000 by the local authorities.

But in the immediate post-1918 period the situation was such that the Lloyd George Coalition Government had to take the initiative. Under the Addison Scheme, therefore, inaugurated in 1919, lavish subsidies were made available to local authorities, public utility societies and housing trusts. Local authority liability was limited to the product of a penny rate, the residuary costs being borne by the State. Under this scheme, 200,000 houses were built, just over half by local authorities, but at great expense, a charge on the Exchequer of £8 million per annum for 40 years.

The Addison Scheme was discontinued with the collapse of building costs between 1921 and 1923. As private enterprise, however, did not respond to the urgent need for houses suitable for occupation by low-income families, the Conservative Government passed the Chamberlain Housing Act in 1923, and the Labour Government the Wheatley Act in 1924. Under the Chamberlain Scheme a yearly subsidy of £6 for 40 years was offered in respect of each house built by both private builders and local authorities. By 1932, 438,000 houses had been built in England and Wales under these arrangements, most of them being sold at relatively high prices. By the Wheatley Act a subsidy of £9 per annum for 40 years was made available, but only to local authorities, on condition that the houses were "let" and not sold. By March 1935, when building under the Wheatley Scheme ceased, 520,000 houses had been built.

The efforts of successive Ministers of Health between 1919 and 1939 to solve the housing problem had impressive results. The new houses were better planned and situated in healthier suburban environments that those constructed before 1914. But the new dwellings, for the most part, became the homes of those able to pay relatively high rents, or, with the aid of building society loans, of those who could afford to purchase them. A number of local authorities did introduce systems of rent rebates sanctioned by Housing Acts passed in 1934 and 1936. Nevertheless, most low-income families were condemned to continue living in foul evil-smelling slums or in the dreary byelaw-standardised streets built in town centres during the nineteenth century, blackened by smoke from factory chimneys.

Large-scale slum clearance did not begin until after the passage in 1930 of the Greenwood Housing Act. Under this Act, the government subsidy was based on the number of persons re-housed, £2 5s. 0d. for each person for 40 years. A further impetus to slum clearance was given by the Housing Act of 1935, introduced by Sir Hilton Young. Under this Act, special Exchequer subsidies were given, but whereas under the Greenwood Act compensation to landlords had been fixed on a site value basis, under the Hilton Young Act it was determined on the more favourable open market basis. The Act of 1935 also defined overcrowding, making it an offence. It was impossible, however, owing to the chronic housing shortage, to enforce the overcrowding clauses of the Act. Sir Hilton Young planned to demolish and rebuild 300,000 houses under a five-year plan, which unfortunately was denied realisation by the outbreak of the Second World War. In consequence, post-1945 governments have not only had to deal with housing shortages of exceptional difficulty, but have also had to rebuild bombed cities.

PART X

GREAT BRITAIN AFTER THE OUTBREAK OF THE SECOND WORLD WAR, 1939–77

Chapter XXXI

THE WAR YEARS, 1939–45

When in May 1940 the Winston Churchill administration was formed, its members were primarily concerned with national survival. Planning the war effort, unsupported by allies after the fall of France, necessitated an increased readiness by the State to mobilise the full resources of the nation. The list of new government departments established may be cited as some measure of what had to be done; in 1939 the Ministry of Supply, and in 1940 the Ministries of Home Security, Economic Welfare, Information, Aircraft Production, Shipping and Food. Some departments expanded their activities, becoming the Ministries of Labour and National Service, Fuel and Power, and Works and Buildings (later Works and Planning). Towards the end of the war period, when consideration was being given to post-war problems, the Ministries of Civil Aviation, Town and Country Planning, Production, Reconstruction and Education were formed.

Since "guns had to be preferred to butter," the Government, not profit-seeking individuals, controlled investment, that is, decided what uses should be made of labour, key raw materials and existing productive capacity. Government control of citizens had to extend far beyond deciding which of them should serve in the armed forces of the Crown. In May 1940 the Defence Regulations were amended to give the Minister of Labour and National Service authority to direct any person to perform any service "at the rate for the job." These wide powers were used to forbid workers taking advantage of their scarcity value by transferring their services to the highest bidder. The Essential Works Orders restrained workers in "scheduled undertakings" from leaving their employment and employers from dismissing them. The Control of Engagement Orders made it obligatory for such workers to be engaged through a local office of the Ministry of Labour and National Service, and the Control of Employment Order required employers to notify the local office of the same Ministry when employment had been terminated.

As coal, ships, cotton, steel and engineering products were urgently needed the "depressed areas" gained a new lease of life. Full-time work suddenly became available for men who had got rusty in their skills during the long years in which they had been forced to submit to the humiliations of "the means test." The percentage of insured unemployed workers, 11·1 in 1939, fell to 3·1 in 1940, to 1·6 in 1941 and to less than 1 during the 1942–45 period. Additional labour for the war industries was obtained by diverting labour from "less essential" industries. Men (up to 50 years of age) were registered for compulsory direction into civilian jobs. Women took over occupations previously monopolised by men, the age for females compulsorily directed into war work, before the war ended, being raised to 50. "Bevin Boys," as an alternative to service in the armed forces, were drafted into pits.

To house men, women and girls, directed to work away from their homes, hostels were built. With trade union consent, workers who had not served an apprenticeship were allowed to do skilled craftsmen's work, the necessary training being undertaken in workshops and factories, in government training centres and in technical colleges. In some of the colleges night courses were specially arranged. Even housewives, with young children to care for, were given the opportunity to swell production, work being given out to them from factories which they could do in their own homes.

The policies of Ernest Bevin, the Minister of Labour and National Service, like those of Churchill, the Prime Minister and Minister of Defence, were based on the principle that absolute priority had to be given to defeating the Nazis. The degree of success that Bevin achieved in mobilising the man and woman power of the nation was unequalled by any other belligerent country, Hitler's Germany included. Over 20 million served either in the armed forces or in war effort occupations. Yet although Bevin had been given unprecedented powers of compulsion, in the main he relied upon "voluntaryism." Very rarely was the law invoked. Instead, Bevin obtained the willing support of employers, trade unions and the populace for the measures taken to overcome the shortage of labour and its direction into war effort occupations.

Factories were requisitioned and used to produce the sinews of war instead of the luxuries of peacetime—tanks, aeroplanes, guns, ammunition, uniforms, radio valves and magnetos instead of furniture, dwellings, civilian clothing and private motor cars.. Imports were strictly controlled, priority being given to materials vital to the war effort and to the "essential" as distinct from the "luxury" food needs of the population. At the end of the war primary school children had never seen, let alone tasted, oranges and bananas. Prodded by County War Agricultural Committees and by the granting of generous subsidies, farmers concentrated on tillage instead of on animal husbandry. These policies inevitably meant severe shortages for the civilian population. Such conveniences as razor blades, combs, shirts and kitchen utensils were difficult to obtain. Only ankle-length socks for men were on sale, and fortunate indeed were wives and girls given pairs of silk stockings by husbands and boy friends returning home from overseas duties. The coal ration was so meagre that householders could only light one fire during even the coldest weather, and petrol, rationed in 1939, ceased to be obtainable for private pleasure motoring from 1942.

There were fewer opportunities during the Second than during the First World War for the unscrupulous to profit and for the greedy to get more than their fair share of commodities in short supply. Clothing, and with the exception of bread and potatoes, main foodstuffs, were rationed by coupons. For other scarce commodities, such as tinned goods, dried fruits and biscuits a flexible "points" system was introduced which had the merit of giving the housewife a limited freedom of choice.

Effective measures were introduced to keep down the cost of living. Rents were kept from rising by rent restriction legislation. From 1940 food subsidies were introduced which by 1944 were costing the Treasury over £200 millions annually. The health of the post-war generation was safeguarded by supplies of fruit juices, cod liver oil and extra milk and eggs made available to wartime expectant mothers and infants. The rationing problems of housewives, however, were eased by the arrangements for communal feeding in works canteens, local authority British Restaurants, over 2000 of which had been opened by the end of 1943, and by the expansion of the school meals service. An important factor also in keeping down the cost of living was the institution of "utility" standards in clothing and furniture manufactures, prices being strictly controlled at every stage of production.

Inevitably, government expenditure increased enormously during the war, defence expenditure absorbing more than half the national income. As less reliance was placed on borrowing than between 1914 and 1918 taxation was increased to unprecedented levels. Cinema and theatre patrons were taxed, and greatly increased duties were levied on beer, spirits and tobacco. In 1940 the standard rate of income tax was raised to ten shillings and the excess profits tax became 100 per cent. A national savings campaign was vigorously conducted to persuade those who had spare cash to purchase national savings certificates. A major difficulty, however, was the acquisition of sufficient foreign currency, mainly dollars, to pay for essential supplies. Exporters were encouraged by restricting home consumption. But the absorption of a large proportion of the working population in the manufacture of commodities for the armed forces, shortage of shipping space and raw materials, plus the U-boat menace, made it impossible to maintain exports at a sufficiently high level to pay for all imports. These rose from £840 million in 1939 to £1132 million in 1941. Exports and re-exports on the other hand fell during the same period from £486 million to £378 million, and to £276 million in 1942. To bridge the gap Great Britain drew on her gold reserves and sold overseas investments. The nominal value of the latter, £3490 million in 1939, had declined to £2417 million by 1945.

Fortunately the difficulties created by this chronic adverse balance of payments was relieved by President Franklin D. Roosevelt's institution in March 1941 of the system of mutual aid known as Lend–Lease. The United States Government purchased from its own citizens the food, ships, commodities and weapons for use by Great Britain, and also by Russia and China. Britain in return provided goods needed by American forces in Europe. Exports were still used to pay for supplies from neutral countries but those from the U.S.A. henceforth were obtained without drawing on scarce holdings of dollars.

The Second World War had marked effects on the British way of life, but it is far from easy to strike a balance between the good and the bad, and it would be a misreading of the situation to conclude that all the problems of post-1945 Britain flowed from participation in it. The losses sustained could not have been other than considerable. More than 300,000 British combatants died on the battlefields and 30,000 merchant seamen perished at sea. Actually, however, casualties were markedly fewer than those incurred during the struggle with the Kaiser's Germany. Enemy air raids were responsible for widespread material destruction and for about 60,000 civilian deaths, losses incidentally much less than had been pessimistically forecast before 1939. About one-fifth of British homes were destroyed or damaged during the blitz, the replacement of which necessitated a vast post-war building programme. On the other hand it might plausibly be argued that enemy bombers made a welcome contribution to slum clearance by turning into rubble vast acreages of insanitary houses built by nineteenth-century jerry-builders.

The hazards of war also posed threats to the unity of family life. Fathers were absent for long periods serving in the armed forces, or working in new productive centres established for security reasons in areas remote from their homes. Those living at home were, after the work day was over, engaged in compulsory Home Guard or

Civil Defence duties. Many mothers were engaged in the double jobs of running their homes and working in wage-paid occupations. Hundreds of thousands of children were evacuated to safer reception areas, but not all of them remained until the end of the war with foster parents. But against these distressing strains on the family as a unit, must be set the growing sense of national duty, encouraged by wartime perils shared in common and by collectivist tendencies in government. This sense of national unity made more readily acceptable the implementation after the war of policies bringing into communal ownership important sectors of the economy, and the passage of measures designed to create a more egalitarian form of society.

The mood of people "when the lights went on again" was very different from that of their parents in 1919 who wanted the return of what was thought of as the "normal" state of affairs, the world of 1913. In 1945, in contrast, the past was associated in people's minds with economic disasters, perpetual unemployment and the hated household means test. Promises, vigorously insisted upon by Ernest Bevin, that the return of peace would not be accompanied by such hardships, were freely given. As an earnest of its concern for the wellbeing of the citizen the Churchill government established official committees of experts to study post-war reconstruction problems. In addition such private organisations as Nuffield College, Oxford, Political and Economic Planning, and the Fabian Society were also active in the fields of social and economic research.

Even during the darkest days of the war significant improvements were made in the social services. An Old Age Pensions Act (1940) lowered the pensionable age for insured women to sixty and authorised the payment of supplementary pensions to pensioners in need. In 1941 and 1943 the scope and benefits payable under Workmen's Compensation legislation were upgraded. Two Determination of Needs Acts (1941 and 1943) abolished the household means test for pensioners and widows, and the National Health Insurance Contributory Pensions and Workmen's Compensation Act (1941) increased benefit payments and raised the annual income limit for contributors from £350 to £420.

On 21st March 1943, the Prime Minister, Winston Churchill, in a broadcast speech, outlined a Four-Year Plan. This was followed by the publication of a series of White Papers describing his government's post-war reconstruction proposals. The White Paper on Educational Reconstruction was issued in May 1943. In May 1944 the White Paper on Employment Policy stated that one of the primary aims and responsibilities of the Government after the war would be the maintenance of a high and stable level of employment.

Other White Papers were those dealing with a National Health Service (February 1944), Social Insurance (September 1944) and Industrial Injury Insurance. Legislation to implement these proposals included in 1944 the Butler Education Act, the Ministry of National Insurance Act, and in 1945 the Family Allowances Act. The latter provided for a payment of 5s. weekly in respect of each child, the first excepted. Plans to meet the needs for houses in the immediate post-war period were embodied in two Acts passed in 1944, the Housing (Temporary Provisions) Act and the Housing (Temporary Accommodation) Act.

During the war also methods of obtaining more effective controls over industrial locations, town planning and land use were discussed. A Royal Commission on the Distribution of the Industrial Population (the Barlow Commission) reported in 1940 in favour of a central planning authority to influence the location of industry and to check haphazard industrial development. The Uthwatt Report (1942) recommended State purchase of development rights in land required for development and the Scott Report (1942) proposed that planning powers should be used to prevent the taking of good agricultural land for other purposes. Steps towards the implementation of these proposals began with the creation of the Ministry of Town and Country Planning and the issue of a White Paper on the Control of Land Use (June 1944). In 1944 the Town and Country Planning Act was passed, and in 1945 the Distribution of Industry Act, landmarks in government acceptance of the need for State control of economic development. But further measures to carry into effect the Churchill Four-Year Plan were not introduced, as in the summer of 1945 the electorate rejected the Conservative Party. In its place the Attlee Labour Government was given mandates to preside over the transition from war to peace and to plan the post-war Britain.

CHAPTER XXXII

GREAT BRITAIN AND THE POST-WAR WORLD, 1945–67

The two twentieth-century world wars have radically changed Great Britain's standing as a world power and accelerated changes in her economy. She has ceased to dominate the ocean highways, a state of affairs already apparent after the First World War, when the Washington Naval Conference in 1921–22 fixed naval ratios in capital ships, at 5·5, 5·5 and 3 respectively for Britain, America and Japan, and for France and Italy 1·6. When in January 1942 General Wavell told an incredulous Winston Churchill that Japan could not be prevented from capturing Singapore, it was all too evident that, unaided, Great Britain could no longer simultaneously sustain armed forces in Europe, the Middle East and in the Indian and Pacific Oceans. Although Winston Churchill once angrily remarked that he had not become First Minister of the Crown to preside over the dissolution of the British Empire, it has since evolved into a Comwealth of independent nations.

In his recently-published *Autobiography* Mr Harold Macmillan illustrates the effects of "the winds of change" by recalling that 10 Prime Ministers or their representatives attended the 1957 Commonwealth Conference, 16 that of 1962 and no fewer than 21 that of 1965. Nasser's seizure of the Suez Canal on 26th July 1956, and the subsequent humiliating withdrawal of British and French forces from the Canal Zone in November, brought home to the peoples of Great Britain the realisation that the age of gunboat diplomacy had vanished beyond recall. The historian of post-1945 Britain is therefore concerned with recording how, and estimating with what degree of success, the peoples of these islands have adapted themselves to living in a world dominated by two super-powers, the U.S.A. and the U.S.S.R., with a third, Communist China, threatening to emerge in the not too distant future.

In the immediate post-war period the Attlee Labour Government pursued policies aimed at economic growth and the maintenance of full employment. The transition from a war to a peacetime economy was effected with less dislocation and popular unrest than in 1919.

Dr Hugh Dalton, the first Labour Chancellor of the Exchequer, introduced a later, much criticised "cheap money" policy. Interest rates fell as low as 2½ per cent and Bank Rate to 2 per cent. Employment was maintained at a high level, the percentage of the insured population out of work being only 2·2 in 1946. By May 1951, four months before the Churchill Tory Government took over, only 0·91 per cent of the industrial population was registered as unemployed. An increasing number of workers were employed in the building and contracting industries, steps being taken by the Ministry of Education to increase the skilled labour force by encouraging L.E.A.s to establish Junior Building Schools. Electricity production, 26·4 million kilowatt hours in 1939, had risen to 43·98 million kilowatt hours by 1947. The output of coal though lower than in pre-war days (227 million tons in 1938) rose from 184 million in 1945 to 197·4 millions in 1947. Government success in maintaining full employment was assisted not only by the needed expansion of the older basic industries to overcome wartime shortage, but also by the development of the new science-based industries. The number of workers employed in the chemical industries, for example, was 276,000 in 1938, and 376,000 in 1948. There was also an encouraging rise in the value of British exports and re-exports, from £281 million in 1944 to £450 million in 1945 and to £1135 million in 1947.

This Keynesian policy of expansion, however, was not consistently followed owing to the onset of the first of the post-war balance of payments crises. Although export values after the war had risen, by 1946 Great Britain had an adverse balance of payments totalling £344 million, which by 1947 had increased to £545 million. In addition, during the war years, she had persuaded other countries to provide her with commodities in exchange for paper pounds. Confidence in the stability of British currency was such that Great Britain was able to accumulate a vast volume of external indebtedness. In 1946 the sterling balances amounted to £3755 million, two-thirds of this being held by countries in the Sterling area, that is, countries whose currencies were based on sterling. In these circumstances, doubts as to the credit worthiness of sterling were bound to have widespread repercussions.

Unfortunately, this is what has happened with distressing frequency, in 1947, 1949, 1951, 1955, 1957, 1961, 1964 and 1966. As overseas holders of sterling have unloaded their pounds, and the Bank of England has been faced with dangerously lowered reserves when it bought pounds with foreign currency holdings, British governments have had to choose between two alternatives. The first is to devalue, that is, lower the pound's international exchange rate.

In this way they could hope to increase exports by reducing their prices in overseas markets, but at the cost of breaking faith with holders of sterling. At the root of our troubles, at a time when world population and trade are increasing, is the failure of bankers and finance ministers to agree on a new world monetary system. At present the main world currencies are gold, dollars and sterling. There is just not enough gold hewn out of the earth to keep pace with commercial needs, hence the use of dollars and sterling as "reserve currencies." Thus until monetary reforms have been agreed upon, no British government can resort to devaluation as easily, for example, as those of India, Argentina and Chile, whose currencies are used mainly by their own citizens.

The second alternative is to take measures to reduce imports. The methods that can be used include an increase in Bank Rate, higher tariffs, import quotas and reductions in purchasing power by heavier taxation and more onerous hire-purchase regulations. Such policies divert goods into export channels, reduce productive activity, increase the level of unemployment and get rid of what in popular jargon is known as "over-heating" the economy.

As already explained in previous chapters, British governments before 1939 tolerated a high level of unemployment and a slow rate of economic growth in order to maintain the value of sterling. After 1939 they tended to give priority to high levels of investment and government expenditure and to the maintenance of full employment. Such policies eventuated in an increase in imports and an unfavourable balance of trade. When such a situation showed itself, deflationary policies were substituted for inflationary ones. In other words, what in popular jargon is known as "Stop–Go" has become a notable feature of the British economy. To overcome recurrent balance of payments difficulties a long-term expansion of export sales is needed. The need to sell more British goods overseas is due, firstly, to the relative decline in "invisibles" (that is, payments for shipping and financial services, and interest on overseas investments), and secondly, to rises in import costs, the consequence of full employment policies and increased home consumption.

British balance of payment difficulties were intensified by what has become known as "the dollar gap." This was not a new phenomenon, as for many years, even before 1914, Great Britain and Europe had exported less to the U.S.A. than they had imported from them. During the First World War, the European (including the United Kingdom's) excess of imports from the U.S.A. rose, in 1918 to $3538 million, the excess for the United Kingdom alone being $1912 million. During the Second World War the problem of obtaining dollars was dealt with by Lend–Lease arrangements and by a system of exchange controls. Countries in the Sterling area paid their gold and dollar holdings into a Central Reserve, "the dollar pool," from which they drew dollars as needed. In 1945, however, President Truman, without consultation or prior warning, ended the Lend–Lease arrangements. Temporary relief was afforded by the negotiation by Lord Keynes of a $3750 million loan granted on condition that Great Britain by 1947 ended the wartime system of exchange control and discrimination against the dollar, by restoring the full convertibility of sterling. The attempt to do so, following the dreadful winter of 1947 when heavy snowfalls disorganised production, precipitated a very serious financial crisis. The American loan (and also one from Canada), which it was hoped would give Great Britain a three year period of adjustment, was exhausted within one year.

To deal with the siutation created by the rapid dwindling of Central Reserves dollar holdings, an era of austerity was inaugurated by Sir Stafford Cripps. Cripps, who headed the newly created Ministry of Economic Affairs in 1947, in the autumn of that year succeeded Dalton at the Treasury. With his arrival the Treasury for the first time became responsible for guiding the economic affairs of the country instead of concerning itself, as hitherto, only with financial matters. The policies of Cripps were, to say the least, unpalatable. The convertibility of sterling experiment was abandoned and not tried again until 1962. To the list of rationed commodities bread and potatoes were added. A contemporary poster reminded citizens that "We Work or Want." Those with gardens were exhorted, as in wartime, to "Dig for Victory." Even more distasteful was the insistence by Cripps, powerfully supported by the Foreign Secretary, Ernest Bevin, on the need for wage restraint. Exports, it was argued, had to be increased if national recovery was to be achieved. But the "export drive" would flounder if higher labour costs drove up prices.

The initial reaction of trade union leaders to government insistence that money incomes must be kept in line with productivity was one of blazing anger and distrust. Within a few months, however, key members of the T.U.C., notably Arthur Deakin (Bevin's successor as General Secretary of the Transport and General Workers' Union), Tom Williamson (General and Municipal Workers), James Bowman and Will Lawther (Miners), Lincoln Evans (Steel), Mark Hodgson (Boilermakers), Alf Roberts (Cotton) and the General Secretary of the T.U.C., Vincent Tewson, were persuaded to cooperate. Their influence and the voting strength they commanded defeated opposition to wage restraint, nearly three-quarters of the voting strength of the T.U.C. being cast in support of the continuance of the wartime Order 1305 making strikes illegal, and submission of disputes to the National Arbitration Tribunal obligatory.

Trade union officials who supported government policy had to face considerable Communist-inspired opposition. Some unions, the Electrical Trades, Foundry Workers and Fire Brigades, came under Communist control. A Communist, Arthur Horner, was elected Miners' Secretary, and in other unions Communists obtained official posts and seats on union executives. Nevertheless, despite penetration of trade unions by Communist militants, the wage restraint policy achieved a surprising amount of success. Between 1948 and 1950 increases in wage rates were slowed down more than in any other period since 1945. Prices did tend to rise faster, but in 1949 Cripps was successful in persuading a large number of business firms to hold down the level of their dividends. As far as the export drive was concerned, the success achieved was impressive, from £1135 million in 1947 to £1818 million in 1949. Further, as the imports bill rose less steeply, from £1560 million in 1947 to £1971 million in 1949, the adverse trade balance was converted into a £30 million favourable one. In 1949, for the first time since 1935, Great Britain had avoided an adverse balance of payments.

The acute "dollar crisis" during the summer of 1947 also prompted a policy of retrenchment in overseas expenditure. Steps were taken to withdraw from India, Ceylon and Burma and later the Mandate for Palestine was given up. In Europe, the U.S.A. had to take over from Britain major responsibility for resisting Soviet imperialism. Further, recognising that the dollar shortage, cutting off vital supplies of food and raw materials from the New World, was threatening the Western World with economic and social chaos, the U.S.A. financed the European Recovery Programme, popularly known as the Marshall Plan. On 5th June 1947 the American Secretary of State, General George Marshall, in a speech at Harvard University offered dollar gifts to speed recovery in all European countries. The U.S.S.R. and her satellites refused to be ensnared in the trap of what they denounced as "dollar imperialism." But the British Foreign Secretary, Ernest Bevin, accepted the generous offer "with both hands," and co-operated with France in convening the European Conference which founded O.E.E.C., the Organisation for European Economic Recovery.

Between April 1948 and 31st December 1950 Marshall Aid allotments to European countries totalled $10,777 million, 2706 million being the share of the United Kingdom. This help, which the U.S.A. gave from its vast resources, assisted Great Britain and Europe back on the road to prosperity. But in 1949, owing to a fall in U.S.A. prices and costs, Great Britain devalued sterling, the par value of the pound being reduced from $4·03 to $2·80, or its equivalent in gold. The wisdom of the 1949 devaluation has been challenged, but the competitive short-term advantages secured by British exporters assisted in the rise of exports and re-exports to the unprecedented value in 1950 of £2221 million, a favourable trade balance of £229 millions being achieved. This favourable competitive position, however, was short-lived, as members of the Sterling area and other countries in their turn devalued, the Belgian franc, for example, from 175 to 140 to the pound, to prevent British undercutting.

In the autumn of 1950, as the T.U.C. refused to co-operate any longer in holding wage rates down, prices and earnings began to rise. Hopes of avoiding balance of payment difficulties were further jeopardised by the outbreak of the Korean War. This brought about rises in import prices and induced the Attlee Government to embark on a £4700 million rearmament programme. Defence expenditure which by 1949 had been reduced to 6·6 per cent of the national income increased to 10 per cent by 1951. This was the state of affairs which led Aneurin Bevan and the future Prime Minister, Mr Harold Wilson, to resign in 1951. Productive capacity, used to increase armaments, the Bevanites protested, was not in consequence available to manufacture export commodities or expand home investment and social services. As far as the export trades were concerned, the effects were long-lasting, as customers Great Britain was unable to satisfy shopped elsewhere.

In the 1950s Conservative governments were no more successful than their Labour predecessors in finding an acceptable solution to the balance of payments problem. Deflationary measures alternated with inflationary budgets, culminating in the financial crisis of 1961. On this occasion Treasury officials persuaded the Chancellor of the Exchequer, Mr Selwyn Lloyd, to introduce financial restrictions so severe that the level of unemployment was increased to over 800,000, and in addition to impose a pay pause to check wage inflation. In July 1962 Mr Reginald Maudling succeeded Mr Selwyn Lloyd. The new Chancellor introduced measures to stimulate the economy, but by 1964, with a general election imminent, there was once again a serious balance of payments crisis. This was passed on as a legacy to the Harold Wilson Labour administration, whose policies culminated in the drastic deflationary package of July 1966 and the 14·3 per cent devaluation of sterling in November 1967.

Although Marshall Aid has not enabled Great Britain to avoid the disruptions in her economy consequent on recurring balance of payments crises, it has had one very important long-term consequence for Europe. The foundation of O.E.E.C. gave an impetus to the post-war movement in Europe for closer union. The 17 member countries gained experience in the formulation of policies of European rather than of merely national concern. European groupings which subsequently came into existence, involving no pooling of sovereignty, included N.A.T.O. and the Council of Europe. Of these Great Britain became a member. Yet although Ernest Bevin had stated in 1948 that "The free nations of Western Europe must now draw closely together," Great Britain did not join other European state groupings which involved a partial loss of sovereignty.

The first of these supra-national authorities, the European Coal and Steel Community (E.C.S.C.), was created by a treaty signed in April 1951. By it, the six member countries, France, Germany, Italy, Holland, Belgium and Luxembourg agreed to set up a High Authority to control common markets for coal and steel products. In December 1954, Great Britain signed a Treaty of Association with the Community under which a Council of Association was formed, on which Great Britain was represented by the President of the Board of Trade, the Minister of Fuel and Power and the Chairman of the Coal and the Iron and Steel Boards.

The founders of E.C.S.C., notably M. Jean Monnet, the first President of the High Authority, and the French Foreign Minister, M. Robert Schuman, had a political rather than an economic objective in mind. By putting coal and steel, the two most essential war materials, under a supra-national authority, they hoped to make impossible war between France and Germany. The economic benefits, however, that occurred from the creation of a common market, free from trade barriers for coal and steel, proved to be greater than expected. The questions therefore of its extension to other commodities and widening the membership of the Community were discussed in 1955 at the Messina Conference by the Foreign Ministers of the six countries. A committee of experts, the Messina Committee, presided over by the Belgian Foreign Minister, M. Paul-Henri Spaak, drew up in 1956 the Spaak Report. This recommended the creation of a large area throughout which the same economic policies should be applied. The sequel was the signing in 1957 of two treaties by the six member nations of E.C.S.C. The first, the Treaty of Rome, established the European Economic Community (E.E.C.), popularly known as the Common Market. The second created Euratom, the European Atomic Energy Committee, to control and co-ordinate the production of atomic energy in the six countries. As happened when E.C.S.C. was formed, Great Britain was invited to join, but declined. As Mr Harold Macmillan has recalled in his *Autobiography*, the matter was discussed, but the views of the Foreign Office and the Treasury, as well as the Board of Trade, were hostile, largely on technical grounds.

The Treaty of Rome provides also, subject to unanimous agreement, for a political union and the election of a European Parliament. National prejudices have impeded the achievements of political union, but progress has been made in working out details of the economic union, difficult negotiations being carried on to eliminate customs duties, to establish a common external tariff, to remove obstacles impeding the free movement of labour, services and capital, and to inaugurate common transport, agricultural and social welfare policies.

The compilers of the Spaak Report had forecasted that the formation of E.E.C. would, by giving producers access to a market of continental area, enable large-scale production to take root with all the savings this entails. Results have justified their optimism that a rapid rise in living standards would take place. Between 1958, the first year of the Common Market, and 1961 industrial production rose more rapidly in all the six member countries than in Great Britain. A favourable balance of trade was obtained, while between 1958 and 1962 wage rates rose by 33 per cent in Federal Germany, by 27 per cent in France, by 17 per cent in Italy and by 20 per cent in Holland, but by only 16 per cent in Great Britain.

As the 169·1 million peoples of the six E.E.C. countries were in possession of competitive advantages denied to the 52·5 million inhabitants of the United Kingdom the obvious conclusion was that economic nationalism is outdated. This was certainly true in the new high technology industries. Great Britain's domestic market and financial and productive resources were hopelessly too small. This can be illustrated by the decision of the Labour Government in 1964 to abandon TSR-2, the modern aircraft which the Air Ministry had persuaded the previous Conservative Government to sponsor. In the present space, nuclear power and computer age, Great Britain could not hope to provide people with rising standards of living by relying on the production of commodities exported in the age of steam. She was therefore compelled to debate the advisability of seeking closer links with her European neighbours. Failure to do so would have exposed her relatively small producing units to future hazardous competition with tariff-protected mammoth European firms created to match giant American combines.

The Macmillan Government sought to secure the advantages of membership of a trading area of continental size by proposing in the 1950s the creation of an industrial free trade area. As originally conceived the British plan was designed to include both E.E.C. and non-E.E.C. countries. Free trade was to be achieved by 1970 (agriculture excepted), but there was to be no common external tariff and members would not be obliged to submit to the limitations on national sovereignty accepted by the Common Market countries. Led by France, however, the E.E.C. countries refused to co-operate, hence the European Free Trade Association (E.F.T.A.) formed by the 1959 Stockholm Convention consisted only of Great Britain, Austria, Portugal, Switzerland and the three Scandinavian countries. To the Seven, Finland was added in 1961 as an associate member.

The creation of a customs union consisting of seven countries inhabited by over 100 million affluent people was a considerable achievement. On 1st January 1967, three years ahead of the original timetable, free trade in industrial commodities became a reality throughout the area. Nevertheless, membership of E.F.T.A. had come to be regarded by both Great Britain and her E.F.T.A. partners as a second best alternative to joining the Common Market. It was certainly the case that since these European trade groupings came into existence a very considerable measure of success had been achieved by British manufacturers in expanding export sales. Between 1956 and 1965, British exports increased by 41 per cent, a large proportion of which went to advanced industrial countries in Europe and North America. Very significant indeed were the changes in recent years in British trade patterns. Since 1945, despite the 1932 Ottawa Agreement, Great Britain's share of Commonwealth trade had steadily declined. Commonwealth countries had sought markets for their produce elsewhere and reduced the fiscal protection given to imports from Great Britain. Conversely, there had been an increase in British exports to Europe as the European economy had expanded and European living standards were improved. Trade with E.F.T.A. countries had expanded, but less so than with the six E.E.C. members, British exports to the latter rising from £520 million in 1960 to £905 million in 1965. In future years, however, the effects of the Common Market external tariff would have made difficult exports to Europe from a Britain not in the E.E.C.

Political and economic pressure to join the E.E.C. resulted in an application being made for membership in August 1961 by the Macmillan Government. Mr Edward Heath was deputed to head the British team of negotiators, but its efforts proved fruitless as on 14th January 1963 the French President, General de Gaulle, brutally vetoed the application. The second application, that of the Wilson Government in 1967–68, was no more successful.

In opposing the British attempt to enter Europe, de Gaulle demonstrated that he was primarily concerned to strengthen French influence and power. Like British governments in the 1950s he had shown himself to be unsympathetic to the ideals of European unity held by M. Jean Monnet and the other founders of the European Economic Community. It would be an over-simplification, however, to assume that de Gaulle's hostility was the sole barrier to British membership. Many obstacles would have to be surmounted before success was achieved. These included sterling's weakness and its role as an international reserve currency, British links with America, the Commonwealth and E.F.T.A., E.E.C. tariff levels, the economic union provisions of the Treaty of Rome and differing agricultural policies. Negotiations were long and difficult, but with time and patience, they were successfully concluded in 1972.

Failure then to enter the Common Market earlier did not end in economic disaster but it certainly made desirable the strengthening of trading relationships with non-E.E.C. countries. Fears were also expressed that exclusion would result in the British economy contracting rather than expanding. The consequences of going in could only be speculated upon. Economists were not unduly pessimistic about the ability of some of our industries to compete successfully under free trade conditions with those in Europe. In the modern science-based technological industries, collaboration with Britain could be of considerable benefit to Europe in achieving economies of scale in research. Inefficient British units on the other hand found it increasingly difficult to survive. No insuperable difficulties were anticipated in bringing our social services into line with those in Europe or in adjusting ourselves to the implications of the free movement of labour, capital and services throughout the Community area.

We have not found it easy to adjust our agricultural policies to those agreed upon by the members of the European Community. Neither for that matter has France, where in the autumn of 1967, in Brittany, the Massif Central and the South-West, small farmers staged a violent "peasant revolt" against the advance to large scale agriculture, an unavoidable consequence of the E.E.C. agricultural policy. British consumers, long accustomed to purchasing cheap food from overseas or from subsidised home farmers, have experienced a rise in food costs amounting to 3 per cent. Unsubsidised home farmers are now exposed to competition from these in Europe. Solutions have also had to be found to accommodate Commonwealth food imports, such as New Zealand lamb and West Indies sugar. Particularly worrying is the strain on the balance of payments which arose from Great Britain's obligation as a major food importer from cheaper non-E.E.C. food sources, to pay levies into the Common Market agricultural fund. This problem was lessened by granting Britain a transitional period to adopt fully the Common Market agricultural policy. Obviously agriculture will continue to present

British negotiators with difficult problems to handle.

Lastly problems will arise if ever the E.E.C. shows signs of becoming the full political federation its founders intended. These matters, however, are not likely to be negotiated in the immediate future. But as members of the E.E.C., since the Treaty of Rome provides for unanimous agreement, we could not be committed without our own consent to a greater degree of supra-national control. In any case, in the modern world the absoluteness of national sovereignty is a myth. All nations are interdependent now.

CHAPTER XXXIII

ECONOMIC PROBLEMS

The social revolution engendered by the war effort created a climate of opinion favourable to the implementation of the policies of the Labour Party. A generation all too familiar with mass poverty before 1939 became accustomed during the war years to governments deciding on the uses to be made of economic and human resources. It had therefore come to be widely believed that only by State planning and action could the people be assured of reasonable security and a decent standard of living. Hopeful that these objectives were capable of realisation, voters returned 393 Labour candidates and only 213 Conservatives.

The legislative programme of the Attlee Government was designed, firstly, to extend the public sector in the economy, and secondly, to create a "Welfare State." Convinced that private ownership of key resources makes for social inequality and economic inefficiency, socialist spokesmen had during long years advocated communal ownership. Labour ministers now had the opportunity of putting this theory to the test. In 1946 the Bank of England was nationalised and the Cable and Wireless and Civil Aviation Acts were passed. On 1st January 1947, ownership of the coalmining industry was vested in the National Coal Board, and in the same year the British Transport Commission was created to take control of the railways, canals and road haulage. In 1948 the British Electricity Authority and subordinate Area Boards, and in 1949 the British Gas Council and Area Boards, were established. The Welfare State part of the Government's programme was embodied in a National Insurance Act, introduced in 1946 by the Welsh M.P., James Griffith, and in Aneurin Bevan's two Housing Acts (1946 and 1949) and in his Health Act. The final demise of the hated Poor Law came with the institution of a National Assistance Scheme which began to operate on 5th July 1948.

The extensions to the public sector of the economy did not measure up to all the expectations of dedicated socialists. Although leading trade union officials, including Lord Citrine, Sir Joseph

Hallsworth, James Bowman and Ebby Edwards were appointed to key positions on the nationalised boards, those who had imagined that public ownership was synonymous with worker control have complained that it has merely enlarged the area of bureaucratic management. The lack of public accountability of the Boards has also been a cause of dissatisfaction. Nevertheless, as the greater part of the nation's productive capacity still remained after 1951 in non-communal ownership, demands for further measures of nationalisation have continued to be made.

With two exceptions, the nationalisation programme of the Attlee Government was not reversed by its Tory successors. Firstly, some road haulage undertakings were denationalised in 1951. Secondly, as the House of Lords delayed the passage of the 1948 Iron and Steel Nationalisation Bill, the Churchill Government was afforded the opportunity of returning the industry, with the notable exception of Richard Thomas and Baldwin, to private ownership, but under the supervision of an Iron and Steel Board. Nearly 20 years elapsed before the Wilson Labour Government was in a position to restore public ownership, on 28th July 1967. On this occasion there was far less resistance, as the industry agreed to co-operate with the British Steel Corporation, chaired by Lord Melchett. The change of heart was due to recognition that at a time of serious recession and growing competition from foreign steel concerns, there was an urgent need for rationalisation. It is hoped that rationalisation will produce substantial cost savings and economies. But world overproduction and recession in the home market remain as formidable obstacles on the road to prosperity for the industry.

Further de-nationalisation measures by the Churchill administration would not have been politically or economically possible. No undertakings could have been run efficiently with the threat hanging over them of being taken back into communal ownership on the advent to power of another socialist administration. In office, Tory ministers responsible for the socialised sectors of the economy never showed any desire to divest themselves of responsibilities. On the contrary, they tried to run the nationalised industries efficiently.

The nationalised Boards inherited by the Tories were left to function uncontrolled by Parliament or ministries. Vast sums of public money were invested in schemes of modernisation, details of which were unknown either to the ministry concerned or the Treasury. This state of affairs was exposed in 1960 by a Select Committee on Nationalised Industries. Questioned by it about the proposal to spend £75 million on the electrification of the Euston–Manchester main line, the Permanent Secretary to the Ministry of Transport replied, "We took the Commissioners' word that they were satisfied overall they would pay this money back." The sequel was the publication in 1961 of Mr Selwyn Lloyd's White Paper on *The Financial and Economic Obligations of the Nationalised Industries*. This clearly laid down that in future the Government intended to make sure "that the procedure within each organisation for scrutinising and approving capital expenditure was effective."

In *Signposts for the Sixties* the Labour Party laid down that the public sector should be advanced at the growing points of the economy. But the Attlee Government had included in the public sector industries, notably coal and railways, which have continued to contract. In framing policies for these industries, no post-war administration has shown itself to be master of events or capable of curing their deep-seated malaise. On vesting day, the National Coal Board took over an industry with a long history of neglect. Since then, there has come into existence what has been described as "the Affluent Society." Rising standards of living created demands for more energy to manufacture and operate public transport vehicles, private cars, cookers, refrigerators, washing machines, spin driers, radio and television sets, and central-heating. In such circumstances coal consumption, the traditional source of energy, could confidently be expected to rise. This is in fact what at first happened. As before 1956 there was an energy shortage, the Coal Board was encouraged to maximise production. Then came the 1957-58 recession, followed by a sudden and dramatic change in the pattern of energy supply. Markets traditionally monopolised by solid fuel were eroded by competition from oil and later by that from nuclear power and natural gas.

A vigorous effort to stop the rot was made by Lord Robens. Minister of Labour in the Attlee administration, the then Sir Alfred Robens was appointed Chairman of the Coal Board by Mr Macmillan. Calculating that coal could only be kept competitive with an annual output of 200 million tons, Lord Robens started an aggressive sales campaign. Uneconomic pits were closed, output being concentrated in fewer and bigger units, and mining operations and management were revolutionised. The tendency has been towards concentrating output in the East Midland and South Yorkshire coalfields. Conversely, collieries in North and South Wales, West Cumberland, Lancashire, Scotland, Durham and Northumberland have either been closed or classed as having a doubtful future. In Durham, for instance, of the 135 collieries taken over by the Coal Board on 1st January 1947, 41 were closed between 1957 and 1966, manpower being reduced by 46,000.

The results of the £1000 million of capital expenditure since 1947 are impressive. Between 1960 and 1964 production increased by

19·1 per cent and by 4·1 per cent in 1965, consumption in 1965 being 198 million tons. Geological explorations have revealed the existence of huge reserves of workable coal in areas not yet exploited. Revolutionary technical progress has led to a significant increase in output per man shift. The new techniques, by getting rid of the cruel burdens of toil and danger at the coal face, have made mining a more attractive occupation. By 1965 the world's most modern pit, at Bevercotes near Retford, was ready to begin production. Here remotely-controlled and automated techniques were confidently predicted to be capable of making coalmining a highly profitable business. But in its efforts to do so, the Coal Board has been hampered by the difficulty of negotiating a pay settlement in the modernised sector of the industry, and by absenteeism. In 1965, for example, in the North-Western Division, machines at the coal face were working only one-third of the available production time, as absenteeism was running as high as 19 per cent.

Absenteeism has accelerated pit closures. Yet despite the human and social distresses these create, even the Wilson Labour administration, pressurised as it was by the bloc vote of miner-M.P.s, showed extreme reluctance to accept the Coal Board's production target. Since the coal market had shrunk and showed every indication of shrinking further, a White Paper on fuel policy published in October 1965 suggested 175 million tons annually as a target. Two years later, 120 million tons was being proposed by government planners as a more realistic output for 1975.

There are many cogent reasons why the industry must be regarded as a contracting one. There has been a catastrophic fall in exports: of the 200 million tons produced in 1958, only 4 million being sent overseas. Exclusion from the Common Market kept British coal out of Europe, which in any case had coal surpluses of its own. In Federal Germany, for instance, the Government had given assistance to the industry in the form of heavy taxation on oil, and transport concessions and in other ways. But even these measures failed to prevent the accumulation of vast stocks of coal on the ground, pit closures, and a fall in the mining labour force in the Ruhr industrial belt from 520,000 in 1964 to 330,000 in 1965. Clean air legislation in Britain has reduced the volume of coal burnt by householders on open fires but this has been partially offset by the Coal Board's production of new smokeless fuels for use on open fires or in glass-fronted room heaters designed to provide hot water and warm radiators. But even more disturbing to the Coal Board is the determination of the Chairmen of the nationalised electricity, gas and railway Boards to cut drastically their purchases of coal.

The compilers of the 1962 Report of the National Coal Board saw the main threat to the industry in industrial conversion from coal to oil, despite the protection of £60 millions from the fuel oil tax. The Board therefore had been pressurising the Gas Council to use its Lurgi complete gasification process instead of making gas from refinery products. It hoped to persuade the Electricity Generating Board to minimise its dependence on fuels other than coal, and encouraged the use of its solid fuels in public and private central-heating systems. Given time, the authors of the Report were confident that 200 million tons of saleable coal could be produced annually. But unfortunately for the Coal Board, the emergence of two other fuels, nuclear power and natural gas, have made unrealistic the bases of its long-term planning.

Before 1956 nuclear power had been harnessed only for military purposes, but in that year, with the coming into service of the Calder reactor in Cumberland, for the first time in world history it was used to produce electricity on a commercial scale. Even before the Calder reactor went on power, the Government had approved the Electricity Generating Board's programme of nine nuclear power stations. The first two, those at Bradwell in Essex and Berkeley in Gloucestershire, came into service in 1962. The full programme, planned for completion by 1969, was anticipated to provide 5 per cent of the total British consumption of fuel and power.

The British nuclear industry is centred on the government-controlled Atomic Energy Authority, whose Chairmen were successively Lord Plowden (1954–59), Sir Roger Makin (1959–64) and Lord Penney (1964–67). In 1944 Lord Penney had been a member of the British team sent to Los Alamos to assist in developing the first atomic bomb. As Chairman of the Atomic Energy Authority, he shelved the idea of a nuclear ship, both on technical and economic grounds, but played a decisive part in building up Great Britain's technical lead in the commercial exploitation of nuclear power. As a pioneer, Great Britain risked erecting plants which could be outdated by technical progress. This is in fact what happened, the generating costs of the "first generation" of nuclear power plants proving to be higher than those incurred using conventional generating methods.

For the "second generation" of nuclear power stations, planned to come into operation by 1975, it was decided to adopt a British designed gas-cooled reactor, known as A.G.R. The construction of the first of these, Dungeness B, was authorised by the Minister of Power in 1965. With the A.G.R., however, only in the development stage, a "third generation" of reactors was being planned to operate from the late 1970s. These will be what Lord Penney has described as fast reactors, "which can be fuelled with the plutonium contained in the spent fuel of the earlier types of reactor, and at the same time can breed further supplies of plutonium for other fast reactors to use." Confident that the development of cheap nuclear power should be given first priority, Lord Penney authorised the building of a fast reactor prototype at Dounreay; then, without waiting to see if it fulfilled expectations, took the much more difficult decision to start building a full-size fast reactor.

A change over to nuclear energy as the fuel of the future is being vigorously resisted by the Coal Board. In the autumn of 1967 a stormy verbal battle was being waged between the Coal and Electricity Generating Boards, following the request of the latter to the Ministry of Power for permission to build a nuclear power station at Seaton Carew, Hartlepool, on the Durham coalfield. A coal-burning station would safeguard the life of three big collieries and the jobs of 8000 miners for the next 25 years. On the other hand, the Electricity Generating Board estimates that the proposed advanced gas cooled reactor will produce electricity at 0·51 pence per unit compared with 0·69 for coal. As millions of units will be produced there would be an extra cost, annually, of £6 million for a coal-burning station. In October 1967 a contract was signed to build Hunterson B, a nuclear power station in Ayrshire. The South of Scotland Electricity Board estimates that this station will produce electricity at unit costs 0·1 pence cheaper than the Coal Board's newest coal-fired station now being built at Longannet in Fifeshire.

Lord Robens, reasonably complaining that he had never been asked to quote a price for Durham coal, questioned the accuracy of the calculations of the generating boards. On the assumption, however, that they were not faulty, the Minister of Power had a difficult decision to make. He had to choose between retarding the possible arrival of cheap nuclear power and authorising a programme that would accelerate the running down of the coal industry. According to Lord Penney economic considerations should prevail. The short-term interests of miners ought not to be allowed to retard the coming of cheap nuclear power, and the growth and consolidation of a British nuclear engineering industry. After a year-long study by Ministry of Power experts, the Minister announced his decision in the White Paper on fuel policy published in November 1967. It was in favour of cheap energy. Coal, the basic fuel which provided the power for Britain's first industrial revolution, will be replaced by cheaper fuels to assist industry in its competitive struggle against overseas rivals. "Excessive protection for coal," to quote from the White Paper, "would lead to a misapplication of manpower and capital to the detriment of the economy as a whole."

No country has a larger programme than Great Britain for

generating electricity by nuclear methods. According to Lord Penney in 1964, "We have already produced over 15,000 million kilowatt hours of electricity from nuclear fission—more than twice as much, I believe, as the rest of the world put together." But this programme was not the only contemporary threat to the long dominance of coal. A second has been the North Sea gas strikes. Gas explorations there were described in 1965 by the President of the North-West Area of the National Union of Miners as "the North Sea bubble." His hopes that the bubble "could easily burst" have not materialised. Instead, gas has emerged as a serious factor in accelerating the decline of the coal industry. Actually, however, the State-owned gas industry began its metamorphosis before North Sea explorations commenced.

Until the late 1950s the industry was a languishing one, gas in the popular mind being thought of as dangerous, smelly and old-fashioned. But an enterprising management, determined to make gas competitive, changed methods of production and encouraged the manufacture of more efficient appliances. An advertising campaign was mounted, culminating in the 1960s in the "High Speed Gas, Heat that Obeys You" slogan. This aimed at convincing the public that gas was preferable to electricity for heating and cooking, and to oil and solid fuel for central-heating installations. In addition, in the development of new appliances, equipment and techniques for industrial users, help was given by an Industrial Development Centre in Manchester.

The hitherto costly dependence on coal was ended by researches into ways of making gas efficiently from oil and oil feedstuffs. By 1962 a process was in use, developed by I.C.I., for making gas from naphtha, an oil refinery by-product. The discovery of a means of transporting liquid natural gas by ship was, to the dismay of the Coal Board, taken advantage of by the Gas Council. From 1964 frozen and liquefied methane, a highly inflammable hydro-carbon gas, was being regularly imported from Arzew in Algeria to Canvey Island in Essex. From there, a high-pressure grid was constructed through the eastern counties to Leeds. This, as the Gas Council boasted, unlike the pylons and wires of its rival, the Electricity Board, did not spoil the view, as it ran underground, and did not increase road congestion as oil transporters do.

The change in gas production from coal to oil brought about what may fairly be described as a renaissance in the industry. The sales of what had come to be known as "natural gas" mounted steadily, an achievement helped by the fact that it was non-toxic and therefore safer than town gas, manufactured from coal, which contains carbon monoxide. Then came the North Sea bonanza. It began with the discovery in 1959 near Slochteren in North Holland of one of the world's largest natural gas fields. Geological surveys from 1962 revealed that enormous deposits also existed under the North Sea. Licences were allocated by the Government to various companies, the first strike being made 40 miles from the Humber by the British Petroleum Company. Costly plans were forthwith made, firstly, to construct and to lay pipe lines to convey the gas to British homes and factories, and secondly, to convert gas appliances to use it.

Natural gas has emerged as a major fuel, destined to have revolutionary effects not only on the British economy, but on that of other lands also, as enormous deposits are known to exist under land and shallow seas in many parts of the world. This much can be said with certainty, that the gas industry will grow and that the new world it will serve will be cleaner and more attractive than the old, based on coal. For the industry itself the trend will be away from large numbers of manual workers, toiling in dirty surroundings in small gas works, towards a smaller staff of white-coated technicians.

A third nationalised industry that has moved away from dependence on coal is British Rail, which in its turn has suffered a severe loss of freight revenue with the decline in coal traffic. In the British Transport Commission's 1956 *Modernisation and Re-equipment Report,* it was stated that only by a change of power source would it be possible to provide "a reliable and speedy transport service." This involved the replacement of the old, faithful steam engine by diesel and electric traction. Diesel engines have become a familiar sight on the greater part of the railway network, but on the busiest stretch of railway track, that between London and the North West, it was decided that electrification, despite the high initial capital outlay, was the ideal solution. Planning and surveying began in 1957, and in April 1966 the electrified track between London and Manchester came into service.

Despite costly modernisation projects, British railways failed to make a profit—a record deficit, £135 million, being incurred in 1966. To examine the situation and to suggest solutions, in 1961 Mr Ernest Marples, the Minister of Transport, appointed Dr Richard (later Lord) Beeching, of I.C.I., Chairman of British Rail. After painstakingly collecting the basic information Lord Beeching published his "Re-shaping Report." This made plain the extent to which there was duplication of railway provision, an inheritance from the days when, firstly, they were not under single ownership, and secondly, there was no other competing form of transport. Much of the network was shown to be grossly uneconomic. In rural areas of low traffic density, where even bus services are uneconomic, train services' revenue covered only one-third of the cost of providing them.

In urban areas of dense population, where the bulk of the passenger traffic is restricted to "peak periods," railways, it was explained, could not be remunerative unless economic fares were charged.

The failure of British Rail to achieve profitability is also due, in part, to the employment of too large a labour force, wage costs accounting for 65 per cent of working expenses. The number of employees in 1967, 360,000, was 142,000 smaller than it was four years earlier. But even this reduction is less than is economically desirable. As there are no boilers to stoke, diesel and electric trains do not need firemen, while automatic braking systems have out-dated emergency hand brakes. Trade union resistance, however, has impeded full acceptance of the new technical situation which would permit the manning of trains by one or two men instead of three, a driver, a fireman and a guard.

The remedies suggested in the Beeching Report were drastic. They included the closure of uneconomic lines and stations, the withdrawal of railways from the field of local movement and distribution, and reorganisation to attract more of the longer-distance traffic. It was stressed in the Report that what was needed was the rationalisation of transportation as a whole. But when Lord Beeching resigned in 1965 as chairman and surgeon of British Rail, it was obvious that the implementation of his policies was being impeded by the resistance of competing interests. In areas where train services are uneconomic, their cessation was being resisted on the grounds that they should be provided as "a social service." For their part the railway unions, whose members dread redundancy in an industry with a contracting labour force, have been unco-operative in the attempts made by the management, such as the introduction of containerisation techniques, to attract freight to the railways.

Meanwhile, the debate on transport policy continues. The Ministry of Transport published four White Papers which formed the basis of a Transport Bill issued in December 1967. This proposed a drastic revision of the State-owned road and rail undertakings. When first nationalised both were placed under the British Transport Commission, but in 1962, on the recommendation of Lord Beeching, the publicly-owned road services were transferred to a Transport Holding Company. Under the proposed transport reshuffle, on 1st January 1969 a new statutory body, a National Freight Corporation took over British Rail's road vehicles, containers, warehouses and depots, and the Transport Holdings Company's road vehicles. The passenger buses owned by the Transport Holding Company, including the 24,000 recently purchased from British Electric Traction, were handed over to a new National Bus Company. To integrate and develop local bus and rail services about 30 Passenger Transport

Authorities were established, four at first in the Manchester area, Merseyside, the West Midlands and Tyneside. The Passenger Transport Authorities are responsible to local authorities and have been given power to acquire private bus companies and those railway lines which for economic reasons British Rail may wish to close. In other words, for the Beeching method of getting rid of rail deficits by drastic pruning of services, it was proposed to substitute the subsidisation by the new Passenger Transport Authorities of uneconomic rail and bus services. As far as the canal system is concerned it was proposed that parts of it should be retained for recreational purposes.

Since 1945, Great Britain has avoided the large-scale depression and accompanying mass unemployment she experienced before 1939. But one pre-war problem that still awaits solution is the existence of less prosperous areas. These include, firstly, North-west Scotland, West Wales and West Ulster, remote rural areas scantily populated. In these unemployment levels in 1967 were well above the national average, 20 per cent in Londonderry and 27·3 per cent in Stornoway. A second type of depressed area exists in those regions where the contracting industries are located, in addition to coalmining, textiles and shipbuilding.

In recent years many millions of pounds have been spent on modernising the cotton textile industry, and shift working has been widely adopted. Yet, despite these considerable efforts, the pre-1939 trends towards contraction, so far from being arrested, have accelerated. Between 1951 and 1965 United Kingdom imports of raw cotton fell from 451,000 to 205,000 tons, the number of spindles from 27·8 to 4·9 million and of looms from 312,000 to 113,000. In the same period yarn production declined from 865 to 393 million pounds and cotton cloth production from 2202 to 1015 million yards. In 1966 there were 79 mill closures; 50 more mills had closed their door by October 1967, and the labour force in May 1967 was only 108,480, 15 per cent less than in May 1966. During the first quarter of 1967, for the first time in the history of the industry, imports of cloth exceeded home production, but in March 1967 when a deputation of Lancashire mayors and chairmen of urban district councils complained about the harmful effects of imports of cotton fabrics from Hong Kong and Portugal, they left dissatisfied with the only remedy the President of the Board of Trade offered, the appointment of an Imports Commission.

In Durham, for those remaining in mining the last 20 years have brought improved living standards, but the future holds only prospects of further pit closures. In addition shipyards on Tyne and Wear, like those on Clydeside, in Belfast and other shipbuilding centres, are losing orders to foreigners. Great Britain, which used to have the greatest shipbuilding industry in the world, had by 1965 sunk to third place. In that year, according to Lloyds *Register of Shipping* the gross tonnage launched by Japan, 44 per cent of the world total, was 5,363,000, putting her at the top for the tenth successive year. Sweden came second with 1,170,000 gross tons, Great Britain's 1,073,000 just exceeding the 1,023,000 of Federal Germany. But Great Britain still possessed in 1965 the largest merchant fleet, 13·43 per cent of the global aggregate, compared with 26·12 per cent in 1939 and 44·63 per cent in 1901.

Immediately after the Second World War the need to replace wartime losses kept the shipyards busy, but after Suez, orders for new tonnage became difficult to obtain. Basically, shipyard berths were empty because existing world tonnage was in excess of demand. Some yards were forced to close. The North East was particularly badly hit, two yards closing down at Sunderland, one at Hartlepool and one at Blyth. The Conservative Government introduced a shipbuilding credit scheme, but this was a short term measure, not one designed to effect a permanent cure.

Details of a project to improve British productive capacity were made public in May 1965. Thirteen leading shipbuilding firms on the Wear, Mersey and Clyde, and Harland and Wolff at Belfast, combined to design a standard version of an "economy class bulk carrier." This, it was anticipated, could be produced with a reduction of 5 per cent in overall costs and a possible saving of up to 10 per cent in fuel costs. But even this standardised large cargo ship could not be produced at costs and delivery dates matching those of Japanese shipyards. The Geddes Report, published in 1966, stressed the need for rationalisation, that is, the concentration of production in fewer and more efficient units. To save overheads and increase efficiency, the Report recommended the mergers of 27 major firms in four or five groups. Following the passage of the Shipbuilding Industries Act, to encourage rationalisation and modernisation, discussions were begun which aimed at the reorganisation of the industry on Geddes lines. When they were completed the industry still found difficulty in meeting foreign competition, largely because of the effects of world-wide over-capacity and economic nationalism. As far as relationships between labour and management are concerned, the example set at Fairfields, the Clyde yard recently saved from closing down by State, trade union and management co-operation, points the way towards a better understanding between the two parties.

The greater efficiency made possible by the introduction of modernisation techniques, computer-controlled machinery and good labour relations may enable Britain to join the leaders in the intensely competitive shipbuilding field. An indication that this may happen was given by the news announced in the autumn of 1967 by Swan Hunter, the senior partner in the Tyneside group in which Vickers, Hawthorn Leslie and John Redhead are the other partners. This was that the firm had beaten Japanese and continental yards for the contract to build for American owners, the heaviest ship ever to be built in Europe, a 255,000-ton tanker.

Brief reference must be made to the recent revolutionary changes in freight handling brought about by the use of containers. British Rail is trying to meet road haulage competition by introducing freightliner trains loaded with standard-sized containers in which freight is stowed. But the container revolution is not confined to road transport. Ships and aircraft are also being designed to handle such containers, which will be carried from door to door. The adoption of these techniques has brought about equally revolutionary changes in handling methods at the docks and produced a reduction in the time spent by ships at the quayside. Such changes have obvious economic advantages, but as their introduction has reduced the demand for dock labour, solutions have had to be found for human problems of considerable complexity, to enable the revolution to be completed.

Unemployment is wasteful. The continuance of high levels of unemployment in the depressed regions means that even in boom times full use is not being made of the country's productive resources. The situation has been alleviated by the transfer of many thousands to the more prosperous areas in the South and the Midlands. But as the more mobile workers are the most skilled, those who remain behind tending to be the old and relatively unskilled, migration does not bring about any significant decreases in unemployment levels. Long-term strategy, therefore, must be based on expanding the productive capacity of the depressed areas.

As spontaneous growth of new industry is insufficient to absorb all the labour released as the traditional industries decline, State action is unavoidable. During the winter of 1962–63, when North-east England was experiencing a severe economic blizzard, Lord Hailsham made a well-publicised tour of the area. Since then successive governments have introduced measures to promote economic growth in what are now significantly known as "development areas." These include the issue of development certificates, the construction of factories and the payment of investment grants. Further, as "development areas" vary in their needs, it has come to be recognised that local involvement in planning is desirable. Hence in 1965 the Government decided to set up, under the Department of Economic Affairs, Regional Economic Councils, and in 1966 passed an Industrial Development Act introducing new arrangements for assistance with capital expenditure.

The White Paper published after Lord Hailsham's tour initiated development plans for Tees-side and Tyneside, new town construction at Washington and Cramlington, and a road building programme. Much of this programme was implemented, 64,000 new jobs being created between 1962 and 1966, percentage levels of unemployment falling from 7·4 in January 1963 to 2 in July 1966. As the creation of new jobs, however, had failed to keep pace with the decline in the traditional basic industries, Mr Fred Lee, in 1967 appointed liaison minister between the Department of Economic Affairs and the North, was given the duty of working out long-term solutions to the problems of stimulating regional growth.

Reshaping the economic structure in development areas involves far more than inducing firms to site factories in them. There must also be a massive programme to re-train the unemployed in new skills. This will necessitate, the Prime Minister told the 1967 Labour Party Conference, the removal of trade union restrictions on their employment. There were too many cases, he went on, when people trained at government expense had "been frustrated and negatived by a vote from shop stewards." In the Manchester area, for instance, there were no engineering classes, except for welding, because trainees are not recognised by the local branch of the A.E.U. Transport facilities must also be improved, particularly in the remote areas, and the squalid heritage of the age of coal and steam, which is a positive deterrent to immigration by key personnel and their wives, must be removed. Fortunately, albeit tardily, steps are being taken to improve environments littered by industrial waste and smoke-blackened slum housing.

Great Britain cannot hope to remain in the front rank of industrial nations, unless investment is concentrated at the growth points of the economy, instead of being wastefully directed, on social grounds, towards bolstering up declining industries. It might also be reasonably argued that the substitution of natural gas and nuclear power as alternative sources of energy would be welcomed by coal-miners as guaranteeing freedom for their children from exposure during their working lives to the discomforts and perils of toiling underground. For this reason, policies designed to attract new industries into mining areas, and re-training the labour released from coalmining, will be advantageous to the long-term interests both of the mining community and the nation as a whole.

Chapter XXXIV

SOCIAL PROBLEMS

Great Britain in the 1960s was a country wrestling with deep-seated social problems. Among the most pressing are those arising from long-term population trends, the probable consequences of which can only be satisfactorily dealt with by stimulating economic growth in the development areas. Between 1951 and 1961 the population of England and Wales increased by 0·52 per cent annually. In 1964 the Registrar-General forecasted that it would be 54·5 million in 1981 and 66 million by 2001. But population growth is only one aspect of the problem. The others are distribution trends and changes in composition. Distribution trends are revealed in the following table:

POPULATION DISTRIBUTION IN THE UNITED KINGDOM, 1951, 1961 AND 1971

	Percentages of total population		
Region	1951	1961	1971
England	82·0	82·5	82·9
Scotland	10·1	9·8	9·4
Wales	5·2	5·0	4·9
Northern Ireland	2·7	2·7	2·8
	100	100	100
Total population	50·2m	52·7m	55·5m

According to the 1961 census, between 1931 and 1961 only in Greater London and Merseyside did the population decline in size, while the rate of increase on Tyneside, South-east Lancashire and in most of Wales was below the national average. In contrast there was a high annual percentage rate of increase in the Home Counties, Hertford (3·16), Buckingham (2·36), Berkshire (2·25) and West Sussex (2·45). A *laisser-faire* attitude to these trends will increase to intolerable levels in the south-eastern counties pressures on demands for land, housing and other social capital. The drift, particularly if the Channel Tunnel is ever built, towards making South-east England a vast built-up area can only be avoided by exploiting the resources of northern and western parts of the country. Both on social and economic grounds, therefore, the investment of national resources in developing neglected regions will prove to be a sound policy.

Contemporary changes in the composition of the population are also significant. Post-war increases in the birth rate and falls in the death rate have brought about increases in the proportions of the population under 15 and over 65. There has been a population loss due to migration, Australia being the most popular choice, but this has been more than compensated for by immigration from Eire, India, Pakistan and the West Indies.

Immigration into our island is no new phenomenon. After the Angles, Saxons and Jutes, came the Vikings, and soldiers and artisans in the wake of the Norman Conquest. English commercial and industrial development owes much to the Flemings who settled in the country in the fourteenth century and during the reign of Elizabeth I, and in the seventeenth century to Dutch engineers who drained the Fens and to Huguenots fleeing from France after the Revocation of the Edict of Nantes (1685). From the early nineteenth century Irish immigrants settled in Liverpool and other Lancashire towns, or were recruited to the gangs of workmen who built the railways and industrial centres. The post-1880s saw a considerable influx of Jewish migrants from the Empire of the Czars into London's East End, and into Manchester and Leeds, reinforced during the inter-war years by Jewish refugees from Hitler's Germany.

Before 1939 immigration was on a relatively small scale. But that of coloured peoples which took place in the 1950s and 1960s was large-scale immigration, the largest in our history. There have long been settlements of coloured people here. Before 1939 many lived in such ports as Liverpool, Cardiff, Swansea and South Shields or studied in British universities and technical colleges. In 1951 it has been estimated that about 50,000 Asians, Africans and West Indians were resident here. Since then, there has been a mass influx, the numbers in 1964 being estimated to be 800,000. More than half were from the West Indies, 165,000 from India and 100,000 from Pakistan.

These immigrants tend to concentrate in prosperous industrial areas; in some towns they constitute a very considerable section of the population. As was the case with the nineteenth-century Irish and Jews, poor social conditions are characteristic of the areas they occupy, multi-occupancy of houses creating slums. At first the new arrivals were welcomed, as there were acute labour shortages in unskilled manual occupations and in public transport. Large numbers, for instance, settled in Bradford and other West Riding towns, filling vacancies in those sections of the wool textile industry requiring unskilled labour from which white workers had drifted. Racial tensions, however, as their numbers increased, inevitably led to demands for restrictions on entry, culminating in 1962 in the passage of the Commonwealth Immigration Act. This established three categories of immigrants: (i) those with Ministry of Labour permits for specified jobs; (ii) those with special skills; and (iii) those with no special skills. Admission is allowed freely to professionally qualified immigrants such as doctors. Since 1962 unskilled applicants have been refused entry, but as many wives, children and dependants of those settled here are allowed entry, the number of coloured immigrants has increased since 1962. By A.D. 2000 it is estimated that there will be $2\frac{1}{2}$ million coloured inhabitants in these islands.

A second group of problems for which Great Britain in the 'sixties was seeking solutions were those concerned with industrial relations. Daily, newspapers reported strikes, usually "wildcat strikes," leaving thereby in the minds of readers an impression that trade union activities were harmful to the best interests of the nation. Should there be a law, it was being asked, against strikes? Ought contracts between unions and employers to have the force of law? There was no likelihood, however, of any major revision of trade union law until the report was received of the Royal Commission on Trade Unions and Employers' Associations which sat under the chairmanship of Lord Donovan and reported in 1968.

Following complaints that they had behaved unlawfully towards their members, there have in recent years been a number of judicial decisions affecting trade unions. Two cases, those of Lee v. Showmen's Guild (1952) and Bonsor v. Musician's Union (1954), were concerned with allegations of wrongful expulsion of members. Other cases in which damages were awarded against union officials were Huntley v. Thornton (1957) and Rookes v. Barnard and Others. The union concerned in the latter case, the Association of Engineering and Shipbuilding Draughtsmen, had an agreement with B.O.A.C. which barred strikes. Union officials in furtherance of a "closed shop" policy, that is compulsory membership of their union for all employees, threatened strike action unless Mr Rookes rejoined the union. He refused and in 1956 was dismissed in consequence. In court, the defendant union officials Messrs Barnard, Fistal and Silverthorne relied on the section of the Trade Disputes Act of 1906 providing immunity to union officials against an actionable claim. Counsel for the plaintiff argued that by unlawfully threatening to break a contract of employment, the defendants had committed a civil wrong, the tort of intimidation. The High Court found for the plaintiff, a judgment reversed in the Court of Appeal, but in 1964 upheld by the House of Lords.

The decision that Mr Rookes must be paid damages left the precise limits of trade union legal indemnity in a very uncertain position. Attention was drawn to the need for clarification, to avoid "industrial chaos," by a Court of Appeal judge in Stratford v. Lindley (1964). For their part the unions took the view that as the Rookes judgment constituted a serious threat to the right to strike, the "balance of industrial power" should be restored by legislation. The Wilson Labour Government, although not prepared to go as far as the trade unions would have liked, did introduce in 1965 a Trade Disputes Bill. This forbade legal action in three cases: (i) when an employee "threatens" an employer; (ii) when someone "threatens" that a contract of employment, to which he himself is not a party will be broken, as Silverthorne, the district organiser of the union, did in the Rookes v. Barnard case; and (iii) when someone "threatens" to induce another person to break a contract of employment.

As the 1965 Bill only covered threats to break a contract there still remained considerable uncertainty in the law governing trade disputes. In Stratford v. Lindley, the Law Lords ruled that the phrase "trade disputes" does not apply when a union takes strike action against an employer's decision to recognise a rival union. A second circumstance which might result in liability to court proceedings was "blacking action," that is, the imposition of an embargo on goods thereby interfering with a firm's contractual or commercial relations.

Reform of trade union law bristles with difficulties. In origin trade unions were voluntary associations granted exceptional legal privileges to ensure that they enjoyed bargaining powers equal to those of employers. But modern unions are not small groups of workers locked in an unequal struggle with harsh employers. Rather, they are powerful associations capable, firstly, of inflicting immense harm on the community, and secondly, of depriving individuals of common law rights.

Unions which enforce a "closed shop" and exclude government trainees from employment have forfeited the right to be treated as voluntary associations. It has been estimated that half of the British trade unionists work in 100 per cent union shops. In the printing, shipbuilding and steel industries, only those possessing union cards are employed. Boilermakers and printers restrict the number of apprentices, while in the steel industry unions enforce the rule that promotion is based on seniority procedures controlled by local union branches. Inevitably, therefore, it has been suggested that union practices should be controlled by the law. No one questions the right of unions to use their collective power to negotiate with collective associations of employers. But the use of their collective power to the detriment of individuals, it is argued, ought to be brought under legal control.

A major factor in forfeiting a high place for trade unionism in public esteem has been the pertinacity with which they cling to old forms and practices. It is impossible to calculate the cost of restrictive practices, but they are certainly a major factor in holding back the modernisation of British industry. The Luddites met the threat of machinery by smashing it. Their twentieth-century descendants use their formidable collective power to retain obsolete manning standards on newly-invented equipment. Overmanning in the motor industry, the bulk of the workers in which are semiskilled, has been estimated at 40 per cent. A ton of steel, produced by one worker in the U.S.A., needs three in Great Britain. Restrictive practices in the highly-paid printing industry are notorious, the Royal Commission on the Press in 1961-62 revealing that 34 per cent of manpower in excess of needs was employed by the national newspapers. In 1963 output per man in the shipyards was said to be half that in Japanese yards, and in Smithfield Market there are various categories of porters employed to carry meat. "Drawers back" pull the meat from inside lorries to the tailboards; "pitchers" carry the meat to wholesalers' stalls; within the market the meat is moved by "humpers" and inter-stall portering is the monopoly of "bummarees."

Changes in techniques and materials are making obsolete many traditional craft skills and making possible multi-skilled manning of industrial establishments. For instance, the traditional skill of plastering has been eroded by the use of plaster boards. Yet skilled craft unions refuse to concede that many jobs need no longer be monopolised by apprentice-trained labour. In the winter of 1965-66, there was a five-weeks dispute in a Bristol shipyard between boilermakers and shipwrights, members incidentally of the same union, over the issue of who should draw pencil guide lines on plastic templates for a new type of electronic steel cutting machine.

Such disputes can be accounted for by workers' feelings of insecurity and dread of the onset of unemployment. In addition, low basic wage rates, nationally negotiated, explain adhesion to work rules which ensure overtime is available at higher rates. In fact workers have come to rely on overtime to balance their domestic budgets. Since 1945 the basic working week has been shortened. Between 1946 and 1950 the 44-hour week replaced 47- or 48-hour weeks for most manual workers. Between 1960 and 1961 it became

42 hours and since 1962 in many industries a basic working week of 40 hours has been conceded. But the actual week worked has not decreased. In 1938 it was an average one of 47·7 hours. In 1964 men were still working an average of 47·8 hours weekly.

Reliance on high overtime rates of pay can be eliminated by sweeping away restrictive practices and accepting new work methods and automatic machinery. As yet only a handful of individual firms have succeeded in increasing efficiency enough to warrant substantial rises on basic pay. A pioneer effort was that at Esso's Fawley Refinery in July 1960, where maintenance and construction employees worked an average 49 hours weekly for £15. By 1962 they were paid on average £16 for 41 hours and by 1965 a high percentage of craft workers earned £21 for 41 hours work. Another oil firm, Mobil, has eliminated paid overtime at its Coryton Refinery in Essex. The men are guaranteed a weekly salary, instead of hourly rates, for a genuine 40-hour week. Other firms with efficiency plans to reduce the length of the actual working week include British Oxygen. In the electricity supply industry in 1965 a revolutionary agreement was being negotiated to raise the status of manual workers to that of staff employees. Meanwhile, as Mr Ray Gunter, the Minister of Labour, told the House of Commons in April 1965, "We are attempting, on the National Joint Advisory Council, to come to terms with some of the main problems—excessive overtime, shift working, and all the rest of it." Automation and new manufacturing methods are, one can only conclude, making it increasingly urgent to find solutions to these problems on a national basis.

The introduction of labour-saving techniques can in the long run bring greater leisure and higher living standards. But in the transition period unemployment may cease to be an evil associated only with such declining industries as coal, textiles and railways. To compensate a worker for loss of a job Mr Gunter in 1965 introduced the Redundancy Payments Bill. This required employers to pay compensation to workers who became redundant and established a central fund, financed by contributions from the employers, and from which those who make redundancy payments can recover some 60 per cent of the overall cost. The Minister made clear that the Government was committed to payment of both wage-related unemployment benefits and redundancy payments. Redundancy payments are made, irrespective of whether that leads to any unemployment, to compensate for the loss of security, possible loss of earnings and fringe benefits, and the uncertainty and anxiety of change of jobs. Unemployment benefit on the other hand is designed to provide a regular source of income during unemployment.

During the debate on the second reading of the Redundancy

Payments Bill, a Tory M.P., Mr Charles Curran, reminded the House that "in the British working class there is a deadly built-in fear of unemployment." Acceptable solutions, therefore, to the problems of modernising British industry are only likely to emerge if there is full consultation with organised labour. But trade unions can only hope to play an effective part if they, in their turn, modernise their present chaotic structure. Ideally there should be one union for one industry, so that only one organises in a single plant. But in the motor industry, for instance, employing about 250,000, the personnel managers of the Big Five, B.M.C., Ford, Vauxhall, Leyland and Rootes had to negotiate with a score of national unions. The Trade Union Amalgamation Act (1964) made it easier for unions to amalgamate or transfer their engagements, but little advantage has been taken of its provisions. In 1964 the number of trade unions decreased by 11 to 591, their total membership at the end of the year, according to the *Ministry of Labour Gazette*, being 10,065,000, an increase of 138,000 during the year.

Multiplicity is not the only aspect of trade unionism in need of a shake-up. The big national unions tend to be undermanned and under-financed. Power at shop floor levels is all too often exercised not by union officials, but by shop stewards, many of whom have to shoulder responsibilities for which they have been inadequately trained, or by militant individuals. It was the free-lance Jack Dash, not the accredited union representatives, who wielded most influence among London dockers. On 26th October 1967 the General Secretaries of the five Building Unions inserted a full-page advertisement in the national press, informing members that the nearly year-long demonstrations and picketing at the Barbican site in London of the Joint Building Sites Committee were organised by a handful of unrepresentative individuals and had no official union authority. The motor industry suffers more strikes than its overseas rivals, but most are "wildcat" strikes, not union sponsored ones. Not the least intractable, therefore, of the problems trade unions must solve are those concerned with guaranteeing that agreements they negotiate will be honoured by all in whose name they claim to speak. Union members are for the most part loyal, but there is always the possibility that militant minorities will undermine union authority. "Unholy Alliance—Bosses, Union, Government," a slogan on one of the banners carried by militants at the Barbican site, serves to remind us that official trade unionism is, and has long been, a conservative force.

In seeking to raise the living standards of their members, trade unions rely upon wage bargaining with employers. Even during the Second World War, when they surrended the right to strike and accepted to a limited extent government direction of labour, they refused to give up the traditional wage bargaining system. This, however, in recent years has been criticised, as collective bargaining by individual unions can lead to a fundamental conflict of economic interests between the participating parties and the community as a whole. The implementation of State policies directed towards full employment, planned increases in income related to national productivity, stable prices, fast economic growth and a healthy balance of payments, may be jeopardised.

The Wilson Labour administration, which came into power in 1964, pledged to modernise Britain, had therefore insisted that unions could not be excluded from the modernising process and it pursued policies restricting "free" collective bargaining. Faced with a critical balance of payments problem, it imposed, as Mr Selwyn Lloyd did in 1961–62, a wage freeze, established under Mr Aubrey Jones a Prices and Incomes Board, and sought from the T.U.C. and the Confederation of British Industry co-operation in checking increases in wages and prices. Mr George Brown, the First Secretary of State in 1965, did gain verbal support from the T.U.C. and C.B.I. for an incomes plan, despite the vigorous opposition of Mr Frank Cousins and his Transport and General Workers' Union.

Like that of Mr Selwyn Lloyd in 1961–62, the incomes policy of the Wilson Government met with only limited success. Despite the Government's efforts to keep wage increases to within $3-3\frac{1}{2}$ per cent in the first six months of 1965 increases actually averaged 6 per cent. The Government therefore decided that, failing self-discipline, a statute-based wages and prices policy could not be avoided, legal powers being given to the Prices and Incomes Board to suggest increases in line with productivity. The unions for their part are naturally apprehensive of governmental interference with wage bargaining procedures. Collective bargaining processes, as hitherto known, developed in a free market economy. They will doubtless continue, but in an era of State planning and industrial ownership, subject to State intervention in the public interest. In any case it is as well to bear in mind that collective bargaining was never in any real sense "free." The power of trade unions has been, and always will be, effectively limited by economic considerations.

In Great Britain, in the field of industrial relations, reliance on voluntary means has been a characteristic feature. But there has also been a long history of State intervention when labour disputes have been harmful to the public interest. Further, beginning with the pre-1914 Trade Boards legislation, minimum standards have been imposed in selected industries. This tradition was continued in recent years by the instructions to the Prices and Incomes Board that preferential treatment should be given to the applications for wage increases for the lowest-paid workers. These included among others, some 3½ million workers whose terms of employment were regulated by statutory wages councils. It may be that social justice to the lower paid worker will only be obtained when planned incomes become government policy. As yet, however, no British government has included even a statutory minimum wage in its legislative programme.

Those not gainfully employed are catered for by the apparatus of the Welfare State. The percentage of the national income spent on social services, including education and housing subsidies, increased from 10·6 in 1945 to 17·8 in 1954, and the cost during the same period from £886 million to £1989 million. In 1964 Great Britain's annual bill for welfare, not including education and housing subsidies, was £2623 million, spent as follows:

	£ million
National Health Service	1141
Retirement Pensions	807
National Assistance	233
Sickness Benefits	161
Family Allowances	135
Widows' Benefits	84
Welfare Foods	37
Maternity Benefits	25
	£2623

A major landmark on the road towards the construction of the Welfare State was the 1942 Beveridge Report, written on the assumption that widespread poverty and hardship would remain a feature of British life. The Beveridge Plan in truth was designed as a solution to the social problems of the 'thirties, not to the utterly different ones of the 'fifties and 'sixties. Although allowing that efforts on the part of the Government could be expected to secure fuller employment, the Report cautiously anticipated an average of 10 per cent unemployment among insured workers. Neither was the Beveridge Plan designed as a blanket cover for all. Social security was to be achieved by co-operation between the State and the individual. "The State," Beveridge wrote, "in organising security should not stifle incentive, opportunity, responsibility; in establishing a national minimum, it should leave room and encouragement for voluntary action by each individual to provide more than a minimum for himself and his family."

Conceived as an attack on Want, the Plan for Social Security was as Beveridge wrote "a scheme of social insurance against interruption and destruction of earning power and for special expenditure arising at birth, marriage or death." He proposed State insurance covering unemployment, sickness, old age and widowhood and the payment of children's allowances. These insurance schemes in combination with national assistance and voluntary insurance would, it was hoped, "make want under any circumstances unnecessary." The cash payments to beneficiaries, apart from family allowances, which were proposed as a charge on the Exchequer, were to be made, without a means test, from a Social Insurance Fund built up by contributions from insured persons, from employers and from the State.

The Beveridge Report, a real "best seller," fired public imagination to an extent which made legislative action unavoidable. The first Act, the National Insurance Act of 1946, came into full operation on 1st July 1948. By it, a National Insurance Scheme, administered by the newly-created Ministry of National Insurance, replaced the existing Unemployment Insurance, National Health and Contributory Pension Schemes and the Workmen's Compensation Acts. All persons living in Great Britain over school leaving age became insurable, the money to pay benefits coming partly from weekly contributions by insured people and employers and partly from taxation. The benefits contributors could receive were sickness benefit, widows' benefit, unemployment benefit, guardians' allowance, retirement pension, death grant and industrial injury benefits.

In his Report Lord Beveridge made his proposals conditional upon the fulfilment of three assumptions. These were the introduction of children's allowances, the maintenance of employment and the institution of comprehensive Health and Rehabilitation Services. In a White Paper published in 1944, the Churchill Government announced its intention to establish a National Health Service free to all who wished to use it. In the event, however, a free service was provided by the Attlee Government's National Health Service Act (1946) but only after a bitter struggle with the medical profession. The service was controlled by the Ministry of Health, the voluntary hospitals taken over being administered by regional boards.

The edifice of the Attlee Government's Welfare State was completed by the passage of the 1948 National Assistance Act. This empowered the National Assistance Board through regional offices to assist persons without resources and persons whose resources needed supplementing. The local authorities were left with the duties of (i) providing residential accommodation for persons in need of care and attention, for instance, the elderly, infirm, disabled and sub-normal; (ii) providing temporary accommodation for persons in urgent need thereof; (*iii*) providing for the welfare of the blind, deaf or dumb and other substantially handicapped. In carrying out these duties local authorities could employ as their agent any voluntary organisation having as its sole or principal object the welfare of handicapped persons.

Compulsory social insurance, the mechanism by which citizens are required to pay for their security, has not completely abolished Want. The 'fifties and 'sixties saw all but full employment and rising standards of living in the nation as a whole. The National Health Service, State housing policies, benefits given without regard to need, such as family allowances, maternity grants and welfare foods, certainly made life more secure and pleasant for many families. Nevertheless, there still exist many unfortunates inadequately provided for, the disabled, unmarried mothers, deserted wives and the 1,420,000 children in 1967 living, according to the Ministry of Social Security, in overcrowded slum dwellings. There are still living many, who when the Welfare State began were too old to make the necessary qualifying payments. For the aged, sick and widows' contributory benefits, enjoyed as of right, are inadequate. For instance in 1948, retirement pensions were 26*s*. weekly. In 1964, when according to the National Assistance Board the minimum income of a married couple (excluding rent) should be £5 4*s*. 6*d*., the retirement pension was £3 7*s*. 6*d*. The National Assistance Board was empowered to pay supplementary grants, and did so, nearly two-thirds of those applying being old people. How many of the elderly were too proud to plead poverty and submit to the "needs test" of the Board is not known, but they are certainly numbered in many scores of thousands. A further criticism is that the existing system discourages self-help, as the earnings rule penalises pensioners and widows who take up gainful employment.

As listeners to B.B.C. appeals will be well aware, the new social order has not made obsolete voluntary effort. Numerous local charitable trusts and almshouses for "the deserving poor" still function, though doubtless more rational use could be made of some of their resources. Many voluntary organisations, sometimes aided by public money, help the under-privileged. The Ministry of Social Security operates reception centres, but many British vagrants seek shelter in the hostels of the Church Army, the Salvation Army and the Simon Community, which runs centres for methylated spirit drinkers and other drifters. The qualified social workers of the Family Welfare Association assist problem families. Thousands of the invalid elderly poor would be deprived of hot meals but for the Meals on Wheels service of the W.V.S. Lastly, although children in need of care are looked after by the local authorities, there is still a social need for such organisations as Dr Barnardo's Homes, the National Spastics Society and the Save the Children Fund, which runs homes, clubs and play-groups in Britain in addition to its work overseas.

As all areas of social need are not covered, the Beveridge universal formula, on which the Welfare State has been based, is being re-examined by those who think that resources should be concentrated in areas of greatest need. In November 1967 the Labour Minister of Social Security, Mrs Judith Hart, described means-tested family allowances as "an affront to human dignity." For the opposition, Lord Balniel spoke in favour of "a major reconstruction of the health and welfare services, with a concentration of the cash benefits towards helping needy families." In recent years there has been a trend towards relating retirement, sickness and unemployment benefits to individual earnings. The first step in this direction was taken by the Conservative Government in 1961, when it introduced a graduated pensions scheme applying to employees whose firms are not themselves operating financially-sound wage-related pension schemes.

On 6th August 1966 the National Assistance Board was replaced by the Supplementary Section of a new Ministry, the Ministry of Social Security. In making this administrative change the Government hoped to get rid of the idea that payments to those in need are a charity "hand-out," in favour of the concept of payment by right. Meanwhile, the debate will continue as to how far industrial security should be sought for the people of Great Britain by increasing the Social Wage element in personal incomes. That progress in the past along these lines has been hesitant is partly the fault of trade unions whose members have been more interested in pay claims than in the principle of social and industrial security.

In the final analysis, those in need can only be rescued from hardship to the extent that those of working age are willing to surrender claims on consumable resources. In plain terms that means how far they are willing to pay higher taxes. Until the closing years of the eighteenth century, the theory and practice of taxation has been indirect. On occasions direct taxes had been levied, for instance, Danegeld, Ship Money and Land Tax, but they were unpopular and administered inefficiently. During the war period 1793–1815 as indirect taxation did not produce sufficient revenue, the first Income Tax Act was passed (1799) and the office of the Commissioners for the Affairs of Taxes was set up. The rate was 2s. in the £, and by the end of the war, the yield had risen to £16 million.

That the tax was regarded as an unwelcome, unjust and temporary imposition is shown by the provision that all documents and records were to be torn into small pieces and pulped. Fortunately for historians, the law also laid down that copies were to be sent to the King's Remembrancer who preserved them. Against the wishes of the Exchequer, which badly needed the revenue, the tax was abolished in 1816, and not revived until Sir Robert Peel's fiscal reforms made it necessary to find an alternative source of revenue. In his budget speech in March 1842, Peel told the Commons, "I propose that for a time to be limited, the income of the country shall bear a charge not exceeding 7d. in the £."

After 1842 successive Chancellors of the Exchequer continued to regard income tax as an impermanent feature of the fiscal system. Gladstone reluctantly extended its levy to meet the costs of the Crimean War. Hopes for its abolition continued to be expressed, increasing prosperity after 1860 making it possible to drop the rate to 4d., and during the second Disraeli Government to 2d. But total repeal was never achieved as the growing cost of armaments after the 'seventies and the later expansion of the social services led to income tax becoming a complex fiscal machine. Asquith in 1907 introduced the principle of taxing unearned income at a higher rate than earned income, and in 1909 Lloyd George added to income tax supertax (known since 1927 as surtax), an additional but deferred instalment of income tax levied at higher rates. During the Second World War, as millions of weekly wage earners were for the first time liable to pay income tax, the Pay-as-You-Earn method of collecting it was introduced. Lastly in 1963 Schedule A was abolished, a tax levied on owner-occupiers assessed on the income they might be expected to receive if they let their houses. What had in origin been a simple war tax by the twentieth century was being used, firstly, as a means of collecting revenue, and secondly, as a means of controlling the purchasing power of citizens and redistributing wealth.

In 1966 direct taxation yielded £6000 million, from in addition to income tax and surtax, the corporation tax, the capital gains tax, stamp duties, estate duty, the selective employment tax and national insurance contributions. Until 1965 a company paid income tax and profits tax, the latter being a tax introduced as a wartime measure in 1915. The Finance Act of 1965 abolished profits tax and exempted companies from paying income tax. Instead, company profits were charged to corporation tax. The new tax was assessed on the whole of a company's profits, and not as income tax had been on the profits distributed to shareholders. The capital gains tax, as its name implies, is payable on the disposal of a capital asset. First introduced in 1961 its scope was considerably extended by the Finance Act of 1965.

Chapter XXXV

BRITISH ECONOMY AND SOCIETY, 1967–77

The Economy 1967–77

Many of the problems faced by the British economy between 1967 and 1977 were problems of long standing. The most important of these were growth, the balance of payments and inflation.

Most governments and economists place great stress on the importance of economic growth as a measure of the success achieved by the economy. But compared with other members of the Organisation for Economic Co-operation and Development (O.E.C.D.) Britain's performance in this respect was rather poor. The following table illustrates this fact.

ANNUAL PERCENTAGE GROWTH RATES OF OUTPUT, 1960–1976

	1960–1973 average	1974	1975	1976
Real gross domestic product:				
United Kingdom	3·3	−0·1	−1·8	1
O.E.C.D. members	5·5	0·3	−1·2	5

Source: *Midland Bank Review*

Despite this comparatively poor performance it must be remembered that Britain's average growth rate since 1945 was higher than at the time of the industrial revolution. Nevertheless, in spite of this historical insight it was the inter-country comparison which was uppermost in the minds of politicians. Several efforts were instigated in an attempt to break the pattern of poor growth.

In 1962, the Conservative Government set up the National Economic Development Council which, in a report published in 1963, envisaged a growth rate of four per cent per annum for the years 1961–65. The economy was then coming out of a recession and as unused resources came back into use the growth rate suggested by the N.E.D.C. seemed feasible. But the slack in the economy was soon taken up and it became evident that the planned growth rate could not be maintained. Imports began to rise quickly and the understanding was entered into with the trade unions, which came to be known as the "social contract." In July 1975 the government felt sufficiently confident of this understanding to propose that a flat rate maximum increase of £6 per week should be agreed as the norm. In 1976 the norm was reduced to £4 per week. Certainly, the policy had some success. The rate of inflation fell from around 27 per cent in 1975 to about 17 per cent in 1977. This state of affairs clearly left employees with reduced real incomes, so that considerable opposition built up to the proposed third phase of the social contract. A strike of toolroom workers at British Leyland in March 1977 highlighted the problems which the contract had created, especially for skilled workers who had seen their pay differentials severely eroded. Substantial trade union pressure for a return to free collective bargaining developed from the summer of 1977.

Any effort which the government makes to control prices and incomes at home must always be made with a view to Britain's place in the world economy. As a major trading nation, Britain takes a large amount of the exports of other countries. It is therefore in the interests of those countries that Britain should continue to do so. The recurring balance of payments problems encountered had led successive governments to borrow as much as they were entitled from the International Monetary Fund. By late 1976, it was obvious that further sums had to be borrowed to support the payments deficit. Application was duly made to the I.M.F. for a borrowing facility of $3 billion. This was eventually agreed, but only after close scrutiny of the economy and its planned development had been made: very stringent terms were laid down as conditions on the loan.

These conditions were agreed to in a letter of intent from the Chancellor to the Fund dated 15th December 1976. The terms included a reduction in the share of resources required by the public sector and a reduction in public sector borrowing which, it was hoped, would "encourage investment and support sustained growth and ... control ... inflation."

Although the economy and society as a whole was faced with several major problems of a persistent nature between 1967 and 1977, it is by no means true to say that the picture has been one of unrelieved gloom. No sector of the economy has been without its problems, but in some the problems were of a relatively minor nature.

Agriculture
Chapters II and III described the revolution which took place in the agricultural industry in the eighteenth century. That revolution continues to this day. Agriculture is not often the focus of sudden

breakthroughs in technology or know-how. Rather, it displays gradual progress in both these areas. This progress is the result of research and experimentation in universities, research stations, agricultural colleges and on farms.

Today agriculture is very much a science-based industry. It has been the application of scientific knowledge which has enabled farmers, by producing better seed and fertilisers, to increase the yields of wheat and barley by $1\frac{1}{2}$ cwts. to $1\frac{3}{4}$ and $1\frac{1}{2}$ tons per acre respectively since 1965. Similarly, the milk yield of the average dairy cow has increased by 100 gallons to reach 870 gallons per year. Breeding experiments are at present being conducted with Simmental and other cattle from the Continent in an attempt to increase beef production.

The application of scientific methods to agriculture, however, has not been entirely without criticism. Factory farming, where calves and poultry are kept in small areas, in sheds, without ever seeing the light of day, has come under heavy attack. Nevertheless, this has proved to be a relatively efficient method of production.

The result of the application of scientific methods to farming is that agriculture is one of Britain's most efficient industries: it employs just under three per cent of the country's work force and contributes a similar percentage to the gross national product. It produces more food by value than Canada, or than Australia and New Zealand together.

The nature of Britain's agriculture varies widely from region to region and in total about 55 per cent of the nation's food is grown by its farmers. The remainder has to be imported. In 1974 British food imports cost £2000 million which imposed a severe strain on the U.K. economy. But the industry has the capacity to produce more and the Government was determined that it should. To this end a White Paper entitled *Food From Our Own Resources* (Cmnd. 6020) was published in 1975. The major theme of the paper was that there should be a planned expansion of milk, beef, mutton, sugar beet and cereals in order to save £530 million on food imports by 1980. Apart from the technical difficulties of stepping up production one major problem must be faced—the E.E.C.'s common agricultural policy (C.A.P.), in particular the question of price supports.

Between the 1930s and 1973 government support was given to farmers in two ways. Direct grants were available for capital investment in buildings, drainage and machinery. Secondly, prices paid to farmers were guaranteed at an agreed minimum level which was reviewed annually. This price-support system worked by allowing the forces of supply and demand to set a price which farmers received for their produce. If this was below the guaranteed level, then a very rapid decline in coal output, which has been both cause and effect of pit closures. Government economic policy guarantees a future for coal as an electricity-generating fuel, particularly as large reserves have been discovered at Selby and Musselburgh.

There can, however, be no doubting coal's decline as a domestic fuel. Three reasons can be offered for this. The cost of coal to the domestic consumer rose substantially after the Second World War, so that other fuels became cost competitive. Secondly, the other fuels were cleaner, easier to use and more flexible in use than coal. This was particularly important in an age of rising living standards. Thirdly, as part of the plan to improve the environment, large areas of the country were declared to be smokeless zones by the Clean Air Act 1956, so that consumers were forced to switch to alternative sources for heating their homes.

Electricity generation is a very diverse business. Again, the traditional fuel for electricity generation was coal, but during the 1950s and 1960s oil began to be used quite extensively. The recent price increases of oil however caused coal to come into favour once again. Several new coal-burning power stations have been or are being built. Water is used quite extensively by the North of Scotland Hydro-Electric Board to generate electricity, but is relatively insignificant in U.K. terms. The great hope for the future is for the generation of electricity by means of nuclear fission. Nine production units of the Magnox type of generator were built but although quite efficient, the design was thought to have become obsolete by 1971 and a second programme of units based on Advanced Gas Cooled Reactors was begun. Five were ordered at Dungeness, Heysham, Hartlepool, Hinkley Point and Hunterston.

The future of nuclear fuels, however, is very much in the balance. In the mid-1970s there was a very lengthy debate in the United Kingdom on which type of reactor to adopt for the third generation of nuclear power stations. Many engineers and economists favoured the American-designed light-water reactors but others favoured the essentially British alternative—the steam-generating, heavy-water reactors. At the time of writing the debate seems to have been settled by a compromise despite the fact that several of the American reactors already in use in the U.S.A. have developed cracks.

The major question being raised, however, is whether Britain should develop this source of energy at all. Environmentalists object to it on the grounds that the waste products are difficult and dangerous to store. There have already been leaks from the atomic waste storage depot at Windscale in Cumbria. It is also under attack from economists who claim that it is unnecessary, that fuel economies in industry and homes render its development pointless. They point to

the estimates of coal reserves, which indicate that Britain has sufficient workable coal to last for 300 years.

The future of atomic energy will almost certainly be decided on political grounds. As a member of the European Atomic Energy Community (Euratom) Britain is committed to co-ordinating its research and development programme with that of other Community members. As Britain has already committed large resources to the development of this programme, it is unlikely that she will withdraw. Future decisions on energy policy are most likely to be made in Europe.

The fuel which has developed its market share most rapidly is gas. The discovery and exploitation of natural gas in the North Sea produced a dramatic change in energy procurement and consumption. From the late 1960s consumers' appliances began to be converted on a large scale so that they could burn natural gas rather than the old, coal-based, town gas. The capital costs of doing so have been enormous, but the result was to make gas the cheapest domestic fuel—a fact which led to a considerable increase in demand. Between 1969 and 1974 sales of gas rose at a rate of 21 per cent per annum and by 1977 nearly all gas used was natural gas.

Britain's future as an energy consumer seems reasonably assured but other highly developed nations are not so fortunate in their natural resources. The United States and some European countries could face quite severe energy shortages in the next 20 years. Britain could be well placed to supply some of those needs.

Nationalised Industries

The Nationalised Industries are of course very much a political problem. In 1967 the White Paper *Nationalised Industries: A Review of Economic and Financial Objectives* (Cmnd. 3437) outlined pricing and investment rules for government controlled industries. In particular, it recognised the fundamental difference between private and nationalised industries—that the latter, in addition to criteria of economic performance, must also meet criteria of public service.

The nationalised industries include, as well as those energy industries mentioned above, the British Steel Corporation, the Post Office, British Rail, British Airways, other parts of the transport industry, the shipbuilding industry and the aerospace industry. Together they account for 11 per cent of the Gross National Product and their annual gross fixed capital formation is almost as much as the whole of private manufacturing industry. Despite large losses in the early 1970s only British Rail, British Steel and the National Freight Corporation remained loss-makers in 1977.

Government attitudes to the nationalised industries vary with the political complexion of the party in power. The 1970–74 Conservative Government policy was to "hive-off" the profitable parts of nationalised industries and to this end Thomas Cook, the travel agency, was sold to private interests in 1972. But when the Labour Party returned to power in 1974 it was firmly committed to the extension of government control of industry. A White Paper *The Regeneration of British Industry* (Cmnd. 5710) was published in August of that year. The Industry Act 1975 which followed provided for (i) the extension of planning agreements between industry and Government; (ii) further financial assistance to industry; (iii) the extension of public ownership of industry, and (iv) the creation of a National Enterprise Board which was designed to promote efficiency and profitability in industry as well as safeguarding employment.

Many saw the National Enterprise Board as a new version of the Industrial Reorganisation Corporation which assisted in the restructuring of industry between 1966 and 1971, but there were many others who saw it as a major vehicle for expanding nationalisation. The fears of the latter group have been largely eradicated, as the N.E.B. has a budget of only £225 million per annum until 1980. A fund of that magnitude is insufficient to provide for a major extension of government ownership of industry.

The one main area where nationalisation was extended was the shipbuilding industry, which came into public ownership in 1977. The problems facing British Shipbuilders are many. Worldwide, the industry faces over-capacity as high as 40 per cent. Late deliveries from some yards, poor labour relations and high costs in others complete the unhappy picture facing the industry. Britain has about 5 per cent of the world market as against nearly 50 per cent in 1948.

Private Manufacturing Industry

The most striking feature of private manufacturing industry in recent years has been the degree of concentration which has taken place. This has not been a new phenomenon. Indeed the merger process began in the nineteenth century but it has rapidly accelerated since the early 1960s. The major mergers in the period under discussion were A.E.I. and G.E.C.; Unilever and Allied Breweries; Imperial Tobacco and Courage; Schweppes and Cadbury; Rowntree and Mackintosh; B.M.C. and Leyland.

The result of this activity has been to make the economy more dependent for its growth and employment on fewer, but larger, companies. In 1968 the fifty largest companies accounted for 42 per cent of net output and 37·8 per cent of total employment. Small companies, although significant, have less economic importance than the larger companies.

The major reasons behind the mergers were the quest for greater efficiency and the desire to reduce uncertainty. An increase in the size of a business unit may enable it to take advantages of economies of scale, e.g. the sheer size of the Ford Motor Co. works at Dagenham enables it to operate its own steel-making plant, thus cutting out the British Steel Corporation. Having its own capacity enables Ford to obtain cheaper steel and to be more certain about supplies.

Mergers reduce the amount of competition in markets and therefore the degree of uncertainty. The concentration of market power in fewer and fewer hands enables the large firms to be more certain about the markets for their products and therefore to have more confidence about planned output levels.

Market power, however, is open to abuse and governments have been alive to this danger. The 1948 Monopolies Act set up the Monopolies Commission to investigate, report and make recommendations on concentrations of market power where one third or more of the output, or processing or export of a commodity, was under the control of one company or group of companies. In practice, largely because of the way in which it was composed, the Monopolies Commission proved to be a rather ineffective device for the control of monopolistic tendencies.

In 1956, however, government power in this area was extended by the Restrictive Practices Act, which required the registration of all agreements between companies with respect to sales, prices and production. These agreements, once registered, could be put on trial before the Restrictive Practices Court where the defendants had to prove that they were acting in the public interest. This proved to be a more successful control of monopolistic practices than the original Monopolies Commission.

In 1965, the Commission was revised and given new powers by the Monopolies and Mergers Act. Service industries could now be investigated as could mergers, actual or proposed, where the total assets involved were over £5 million. This legislation heralded a period of renewed activity for the Commission. Very often the mere threat of investigation was sufficient to persuade companies to abandon restrictive practices, e.g. all but one of the tariffs in the insurance markets were abandoned between 1967 and 1970, following the threat of investigation of the Fire Offices Committee in 1967.

Although the Government was at pains to control monopolies and restrictive practices where these were against the public interest, it was also keen to encourage merger activity where this would enhance industrial efficiency. To this end the Industrial Re-organisation Corporation was set up in 1966. Its role was to identify areas where mergers would benefit the public and to assist these mergers to go through. The Leyland/B.M.C. and G.E.C./A.E.I. mergers were amongst those in which the I.R.C. played a constructive part. Despite its successes, the Conservative Government disbanded the Corporation in 1971.

The two themes of government policy—efficiency and control—were reiterated and re-inforced by the Fair Trading Act of 1973. This Act established the office of Director-General of Fair Trading, whose duties included bringing agreements before the Restrictive Practices Court. The power of the Monopolies Commission was widened to include reference to market situations where companies or groups enjoyed a quarter (rather than a third) of sales.

When the Conservative Government was returned to power, in 1970, there was a period when policy towards industry was non-interventionist but when Rolls-Royce and Upper Clyde Shipbuilders failed in 1971 there occurred a reversal of this policy. The 1972 Industry Act provided an extensive system of aids and incentives for industry.

The 1974 Labour Government's White Paper *The Regeneration of British Industry* announced the intention to have a system of planning agreements between industry and Government which would harmonise the activities of industry with the requirements of the national economy. A further White Paper in 1975, *An Approach to Industrial Strategy*, envisaged developing a programme for quickening development at the growth points of the economy. In particular this strategy was designed to avoid some of the errors of previous government policy, e.g. by enquiring into what the results of general economic policy were on the individual firm as opposed to the economy as a whole. Only this way can planning the economy have any hope of success.

The question of government policy for industry also has a geographical dimension. Since the 1930s, the prime objective of regional policy has been the reduction of unemployment, which has been habitually higher in some areas than in the Midlands and the South. Although some aspects of regional policy have been politically motivated, much has been done to ensure a better and more effective use of natural and manpower resources.

The history of regional policy since 1945 has been one of continued experimentation. The direction of present policy was laid in 1966 and consists of named development areas. At the time of writing these comprise the whole of Scotland and the Northern Region of England; Wales (except for its eastern fringes); North Yorkshire and Humberside; and North Devon and Cornwall. Areas singled out for special assistance include Clydeside, Merseyside, Tyneside-Wearside and North and South Wales.

Current policy is contained in the 1972 Finance Act and Industry Act which gave effect to the ideas expressed in the White Paper *Industrial and Regional Development* (Cmnd. 4942). There have been two strands to the policy. One is designed to prevent development in non-assisted areas and the other to promote active growth in the development areas.

The first of these consists of the Industrial Development Certificate which is required for factory building or extension. It can, and has been, withheld from proposed developments in non-development areas. In this way companies have been forced to expand in areas of high unemployment, e.g. the Rootes Group (later Chrysler) opened a factory at Linwood near Glasgow, when it really wanted to open one in the Midlands.

Positive inducements to companies to open in the development areas include grants and loans; provision of advance factories for sale or lease at moderate rates; tax allowances on capital investment introduced from 1963 and replaced in 1966 by a system of cash grants and again replaced by tax allowances in 1970. A regional employment premium was introduced in 1967 and doubled in 1974 but it was phased out in 1977. Employers in these areas also benefited from the premium payable under the Selective Employment Tax which was abolished in 1972. In short, the list of incentives to industry in development areas is very extensive.

Since 1945, British economic policy has been geared to maintaining a high level of employment and in this Britain has been more successful than nearly every other industrialised country. But other countries have been pursuing policies of growth rather than employment. Rather belatedly, British politicians have come to realise that a healthy, growing economy will generate its own employment and that prime emphasis should be given to investment and industrial growth rather than the maintenance of employment by various means.

The main trends in manufacturing industry in this period have been a rise in output at a rate higher than that achieved during the Industrial Revolution, but which has been markedly slower than that currently achieved by Britain's main industrial competitors. There has also been a decline in total employment of half a million jobs between 1964 and 1974 and a growth in productivity which, between 1970 and 1975, while comparing well with most industrial countries, was significantly lower than that achieved by Japan and France. This relatively poor industrial performance has been particularly noticeable in the traditional industries such as shipbuilding, but has also been marked in the newer industries such as car manufacturing; British Leyland had to be rescued by the Government in 1975 and Chrysler (formerly Rootes) was bailed out in 1976.

The point has often been made by economists and politicians that Britain's relatively poor industrial performance has been the result of a lower level of investment. To improve this situation, the financial institutions have co-operated with the Government in setting up organisations to provide the required funds e.g. the Industrial and Commercial Finance Corporation, Finance for Industry and the recently formed Equity Bank. It does seem possible, however, that what is lacking is not the finance, but the enterprise to make use of it.

Retailing

The retailing revolution began in the second half of the nineteenth century with the acceleration of the Co-operative movement and the development of multiple chain stores and department stores, notably by Thomas Lipton and the Watson brothers (Maypole Dairies). These organisations operated on small profit margins and depended for their profits on having a very large volume of sales.

Since 1945 this revolution has continued with developments of the original idea. Supermarkets were opened by all the major food groups. The idea of these was, not only to buy cheaply, but also to sell cheaply. This was achieved by cutting costs, e.g. by making the stores "self-service." The success of these paved the way for further economies not only in the food retailing business but also in the electrical goods trade, e.g. the Comet and Trident groups spread discount stores all over the country from the late 1960s. Despite easy access to shops, super-stores and even hyper-markets, the fastest growing method of retailing has been mail-order, principally for clothes, led by the giant Littlewoods group. There are an estimated five million mail order accounts with various groups which suggests that a large number of consumers prefer the comfort of shopping in their own homes.

The people who have suffered most in this have been the small shopkeepers. Many have been forced out of business because of competition from larger and more cost-efficient stores, but many still remain. Small shopkeepers have not been without imaginative responses to the growth of super markets, e.g. some have formed themselves into bulk-buying organisations such as Spar and Vivo, which enables them to buy as cheaply as the supermarkets. Others have taken advantage of the growth of Cash and Carry warehouses which are, essentially, discount stores for retailers. Many small shopkeepers are protected by the fact that their shops are in areas not well served by the supermarkets or discount stores, which tend to be located in densely-populated areas.

Many of the new retailing developments of the past few years were made possible by the ending of resale price maintenance in 1965. Resale price maintenance by manufacturers had imposed uniform selling prices on retailers no matter what kind of store they were running. Numerous attempts had been made to undermine this process in the early 1960s, notably by the Tesco Group, but with little success. By 1964, however, the ending of resale price maintenance had become government policy and to this end the Resale Prices Act was passed in 1964. Even before the Act was passed some producers, e.g. I.C.I. and Distillers had discontinued the practice. The result of this legislation was the developments outlined above.

Also of interest in the area of retailing has been the enormous growth of interest in consumer protection. To some extent this movement has been imported from the United States, where it is led by Ralph Nader. In the U.K., the Consumers' Association via its magazine *Which?* informs its half-million subscribers and other readers of the best buys in a very wide variety of markets.

Pressure from this and other groups resulted in the passing in 1973 of the Supply of Goods (Implied Terms) Act and the Fair Trading Act, both of which were designed to give a greater measure of protection to consumers against malpractices by retailers.

Transport

The transport sector of the economy which includes roads, railways, shipping and airways is a complex mixture of public and private enterprises, e.g. the roads which are built and maintained by central and local government are used by both publicly and privately owned vehicles. It is further complicated in that it caters for two categories of users, i.e. freight and people. Furthermore it is an industry which has undergone considerable change in recent years. The following tables indicate some of the magnitude of this change.

U.K INLAND FREIGHT TRANSPORT 1967 AND 1975
(000M TONNE-KILOMETRES)

Year	Road	Rail	Coastal Shipping	Inland Waterways	Pipelines	Total
1967	74·6	22·3	24·9	0·2	1·6	123·5
1975	88·3	23·5	18·3	0·1	3·3	133·5
% change	18·4	5·4	−26·5	−50	106·2	8·1

U.K. INLAND PASSENGER MILEAGE
(000M PASSENGER-KILOMETRES)

Year	Public Service Vehicles	Private Transport	Rail	Air	Total
1967	61·0	267·0	34·0	1·9	363·9
1975	54·0	357·0	35·1	2·2	448·3
% change	−11·5	33·7	3·2	15·8	23·2

Source: *Annual Abstract of Statistics*

In 1968 the Transport Act reorganised several sections of the industry (see pp. 391–2), but in 1976 the *Consultative Document on Transport Policy* produced by the Department of the Environment spotlighted a number of problems. These included the lack of co-ordinated transport policies for the nation and the regions, the extent of environmental pollution by transport and the extent of government subsidies. The document pointed out that the bulk of transport subsidies go to the railways, but the richest 20 per cent of the households account for 50 per cent of rail travel while the poorest 40 per cent of households account for only 15 per cent of rail travel, so that subsidies are not a very effective way of helping the poor.

At the time of writing the Consultative Document is being widely discussed and may give rise to adjustments of policy in the future.

By far the largest growing mode of transport over the period was road transport both for people and freight. The number of private cars licensed rose from 10·3 million in 1967 to 13·7 million in 1975. There was some check on the use of private cars in 1974 due to the substantial rise in petrol prices. Generally-rising living standards account for most of the increase in car ownership but the changes in the relative costs of car and public transport also encouraged the greater use of the former as public transport became relatively more expensive.

Cost advantages were also responsible for the increasing use of road freighting at the expense of railways. Since the appearance of the 32 ton juggernaut on the roads, it has often been argued that it would be environmentally beneficial if the bigger loads were forced to use the railways, but a Department of the Environment study published in 1976 revealed that even if all bulk-freight journeys over 100 miles were forced to use the railways this would result in a 2–4 per cent reduction in road traffic with only a marginal benefit to the environment. Despite this some success has been made with the Freightliner and similar services, where containers travel on trains for the major part of their journey and are then transferred to lorries for despatch to their destination.

The railways which were taken into public ownership in 1946 have always been a problem area for governments. Even after the Beeching axe (*see* p. 391) the railways have failed to make a profit in almost every year. To a large extent this is because there is still some confusion about whether the railways should be a social service or whether they should aim to make a profit. Even government subsidies do not cover losses on "social service" lines. Further difficulty is, however, caused by manning levels, which are still reckoned to be excessive despite massive reductions in total employment since the Beeching axe.

Notwithstanding the problems of British Rail there has continued to be a high level of capital investment—principally in the electrification process which has, for example, cut the travelling time from Glasgow to London to five hours. The advanced passenger train which recently came into service on some lines will cut even that time by a further hour. This will make the railway very competitive when compared with air transport when journey times and fares are measured from city centre to city centre.

Air transport displayed steady growth over the period under review. There are two main airlines—British Airways, which is government-owned and British Caledonian, plus a number of smaller operators. The two major airlines do not compete with one another to any extent, either in domestic or international traffic, but they compete very actively with the airlines of other countries for their international business. Indeed the key to profitability in this traffic is the lucrative North Atlantic route. In 1977 another airline, Laker Airways, was given permission to begin a cut-price service on this route; this action provoked a price war.

In the late 1960s and throughout the 1970s the British and French aircraft building industries co-operated to build a supersonic passenger aircraft—the Concorde, which made its first commercial flight in 1976. This plane is capable of cutting flying time between London and New York by half but has met with strong opposition from environmentalist groups in the United States, which claim that it is too noisy and that it damages the ozone layer in the atmosphere. American planemakers who had abandoned their attempts to build a supersonic passenger plane several years previously also opposed Concorde for the obvious economic reason that its popularity would undermine their business.

The shipping industry has been perhaps the most profitable of all the means of transport, although it too has had problems. Although much of the British-owned merchant fleet sails under a flag of convenience, the profits which it earns are an important source of foreign earnings to the British economy and of course contribute towards the balance of payments— £2648 million (£12 million net) in 1975.

The sector of the shipping industry which was most troubled in the 1970s was the oil tanker business. Following the oil price increases of 1973–74 the market for oil, and therefore for tankers, declined, with the result that many vessels had to be laid up because there was no work for them to do. The shipbuilding industry was also badly affected. Countries which specialised in this type of vessel, such as Norway, were particularly badly hit, but in Britain where the merchant fleet was more varied and the interests of the shipbuilders more diverse, the oil tanker recession was not quite so badly felt.

The passenger liner business also enjoyed mixed fortunes in the 1970s. The Cunard Line, whose *Queen Elizabeth 2* made a profit of £1 million on a world cruise in 1976, was faced with very little competition—most of the French and American liners had been withdrawn from service before this date.

Finance

The most notable features of the financial world in the 1960s and 1970s were the merger activity amongst banks and the substantial growth of the system.

In 1968 there were 11 English clearing banks and 5 Scottish banks. By 1977 these had been reduced to 6 and 3 respectively. The merger activity began in January 1968 with the junction of the National Provincial Bank and the Westminster Bank. In February 1969 two Scottish banks, the Royal Bank and the National Commercial, announced their intention to merge. The reorganisation caused by this had implications for English banking. Williams Deacon's and Glyn Mills were subsidiaries of the Royal and the National Bank was owned by the National Commercial. The result was a merger of these three clearing banks to form Williams & Glyn's. A proposed merger between Barclays, Lloyds and Martins was vetoed by the Monopolies Commission, but that between Barclays and Martins went ahead. In 1969 there was speculation that an English bank would bid for the Bank of Scotland but, instead, that bank took over the British Linen Bank, a Scottish bank, which had been wholly owned by Barclays.

Despite the reduction in the numbers of traditional banks the base of the banking system grew dramatically from £34,000 million in 1970 to £108,000 million in 1975, a compound growth rate of 26 per cent per annum. In large measure this growth was caused by two related factors: the influx of foreign banks and the government policy document *Competition and Credit Control* which was issued in May 1971.

In the early 1960s there were approximately 80 overseas banks in the City. By 1976 there were about 108. Of these 60 were American and nearly 20 were Japanese. These banks play a major part in the finance of international trade. In particular they operate in the Euro-currency market, i.e. they advance money in currencies other than sterling. Their presence in the money market has helped London regain its place as the world's most important financial centre.

Although these foreign banks have greatly assisted in the development of the City, British financial institutions have also demonstrated dynamic growth, both in terms of numbers and business done. Particularly active in the early 1970s were the merchant banks and finance houses (hire-purchase specialists). There have also been numerous formations of consortium banks.

The major factor which facilitated this growth was the government policy known as "competition and credit control." This was a highly complex piece of legislation designed to control the growth of the money supply, but to increase competition amongst the banks at the same time. It has been more successful in the second of these than in the first. The rate of growth of bank deposits has been quoted above. It has been argued that competition and credit control was one of the main causes of the inflation which became so rampant in the 1970s.

Very many of the banks, particularly the secondary (merchant) banks, used their increased deposit resources to make advances on the security of property, which was then increasing very substantially in value as a result of inflation and speculation. When the economy passed the peak of its cycle, however, and the slump set in, property values declined very quickly, with the result that the security which many banks held for advances was worth far less than the amount of the advances. The result of this was that some banks, e.g. Capital and Counties, failed and others, notably United Dominions Trust, had to be rescued by a "lifeboat" operation staged by the Bank of England and the English and Scottish clearing banks.

These events led the Labour Party Conference in 1976 to renew its call for the nationalisation of the banks on the grounds that they had failed to serve the economy as they should. This is, of course, a highly charged political argument, but even although the resolution was passed by the conference, the Prime Minister, Mr Callaghan, declared his own and his Cabinet's opposition to the proposal. Nevertheless the banks took the threat seriously and joined forces to combat it. Their campaign began seriously in May 1977 with advertisements in newspapers inviting the public to express their views on the proposals.

Another industry in the financial sector threatened with nationalisation (partial) is the insurance business. Despite the facts that over £500 million per annum is earned overseas by this industry and that it greatly assists British industry by the facility for transferring risks and the flow of investment capital which it provides, it too is accused of inefficiency. A campaign was also begun to combat the political threat.

The building societies have remained relatively free from the fear of nationalisation. They too became involved in the increased tempo of economic life in the early 1970s. As interest rates generally rose, the societies were forced to follow suit, so that by Autumn 1976 borrowers were paying $12\frac{1}{4}$ per cent for their mortgages. Some controversy arose in the early months of 1977 when general interest rates began to decline. Society rates proved to be less flexible on the way down than they had been on the way up. The societies argued that they had to attract sufficient deposits for lending, especially on new property, as it was felt that they had some obligation to the house building industry.

Housing

Since 1945, central and local government authorities throughout Britain have been preoccupied with the problem of providing an adequate supply and quality of housing for the populace.

The result of that preoccupation has been a comprehensive policy, ranging from new towns and urban renewal to the Rent Acts and rent rebate schemes. The problem at times seemed intractable, especially in the cities where urban decay and war damage combined to create great areas of decrepit housing. So successful has the policy of slum clearance been that even cities like Glasgow, which was once called "the slum capital of Europe," expect to achieve a position of housing surplus in 1981.

Although there may be an adequate supply of good houses throughout Britain by the 1980s, that is not to say that all the problems associated with housing will have been solved. Over eight million new houses have been built in Britain since 1945, so that two families in five now live in a post-war dwelling. The major problem which remains is one of location. With the exception of the new towns it has not always been possible for jobs to follow housing, so that people who live in the new housing estates on the edge of cities may be faced with substantial distances to travel to work. Also, many of these estates lack social amenities, a situation which has given rise to vandalism caused in part by frustration, so that although the standard of housing may be good, the quality of life on the new estates may be relatively poor.

In 1972 there was published the *General Household Survey*

which was a study of the relationship between social class and housing conditions. The survey showed that 49·2 per cent of households were owner-occupied (a sizeable proportionate increase since the war); 30·9 per cent were rented from a local authority; 14·5 per cent were rented in the private sector (mostly unfurnished) and 5·4 per cent of households obtained accommodation either rent-free, or with their jobs, or from a housing association. Those who lived in houses which they owned had the highest standards of housing, while those who lived in privately-rented houses had the lowest standard. The report also showed, as might be expected, that it was the lower social groups who lived in the poorest housing. There were wide regional variation noted in the report, e.g. in Scotland, the number of owner-occupiers was under 30 per cent.

A government-sponsored study of housing was begun in 1975 by Environment Secretary, Anthony Crosland and a Green Paper was published in June 1977. This paper was a compromise of the many conflicting viewpoints expressed to the Secretary, and the result is that there will be no really major change of policy. Owner-occupiers will continue to receive tax relief on mortgage-interest repayments. Changes proposed included help for first-time buyers in the shape of interest-free loans and a charter of rights for council tenants. It was also suggested that the Government should put pressure on building societies to take account of social factors when awarding mortgages.

Although there will be an adequate numerical supply of houses by the 1980s, Mr Peter Shore, Environment Secretary, in an important speech in 1977, warned that there would always be housing-related problems so long as people moved around the country at short notice, family sizes changed, demand for separate accommodation grew, public expectations altered and there was an imbalance of demand and supply.

Education

Between 1951 and 1974 public expenditure on education, at constant prices, increased two and a half times. This figure was caused in part by an increasing government and public awareness of the advantages to be derived from education and, more generally, from an increase in the number of children of school age. This latter factor was further emphasised in 1973, when the school-leaving age was increased from age 15 to 16 years. By 1974, there were 50 per cent more pupils at school than there had been in 1951. The trend over the years has been for many more children to stay on at school voluntarily and to go on to further or higher education.

The most striking educational development in the past decade has been the changeover to a comprehensive organisation for secondary schools. The new system become government policy in 1965, but when the Conservatives returned to power in 1970, local authorities were given the choice of whether they wished to change the system or not. (This option was never made available to Scottish local authorities.) But when the Labour Party won the 1974 election the system was again forced on local authorities. By 1975, just over 50 per cent of secondary school children in England and Wales were educated in comprehensive schools whereas in Scotland (where a similar educational structure had been long established) the figure was 98 per cent. In 1976 the Tameside authority successfully challenged the law in the courts and at the time of writing the Government has appealed against that ruling.

Obviously, the issue of education arouses highly charged emotions amongst parents and politicians. Comprehensive schools have been widely criticised as being inefficient both as organisations and as educational establishments. Research published in the "Black Paper 1977" shows that "A" Level results achieved in comprehensive schools were poorer than those of selective grammar schools. No one has, as yet, produced a satisfactory analysis of why this is the case. In October 1976 the Prime Minister, Mr Callaghan, initiated a "great debate" on standards in schools.

The numbers of teachers in schools has increased even more quickly than the numbers of pupils. Throughout the 1960s and early 1970s there was a shortage of teachers in most areas and special recruitment schemes were inaugurated to attract people into the profession. New teacher training colleges were established. By 1976, however, it become obvious that the teacher shortage was over and that in fact there was an over-supply of teachers in most subjects. The glut was caused by a shortfall of pupils and was accentuated by the cutbacks in government expenditure announced that year, which were a condition of the loan received from the International Monetary Fund. The results of the cutbacks were that a number of teacher training colleges were closed and many thousands of newly-qualified teachers were unable to find jobs.

The most rapidly expanding sector of education has been the further education colleges. The 1964 Industrial Training Act encouraged the formation of industrial training boards (I.T.B.s) for various industries. Many of those established developed training programmes which involved sending trainees on day or block release to colleges of further education. The result was a vast expansion in the number of colleges and the types of course offered by them. In 1976 however they, too, began to have their resources curtailed.

Universities and polytechnics suffered severe reductions in their financial provisions as a result of the austerity measures.

When the cutbacks came they represented a very severe jolt to the ten-year education programme which had been announced in December 1972. The programme had proposed extensive provision of nursery education, improved staffing ratios in schools, better buildings, more opportunity for the training of teachers and an expansion of higher education. Very few of these items have been achieved in a significant way.

Social Welfare

Despite the steadily increasing standard of living and the widespread provision of social welfare which has grown up since the Liberal reforms of the 1900s and the Beveridge Report of 1942, a substantial amount of poverty persists in the United Kingdom. Defining poverty remains a problem, just as it was in the days of the Booths and Rowntree, but an index of prices and incomes is fairly generally accepted as a measure. "Primary" poverty occurs where a person's (or a family's) income falls below that accepted level: "secondary" poverty occurs where income is above that level but where it is spent in such a way that family members do not receive an adequate level of nutrition, housing or clothing. Secondary poverty is much more prevalent than primary poverty.

There have developed five main ways in which the State assists disadvantaged people. National Insurance Benefits include retirement pensions (to be substantially improved from 1978), unemployment and sickness pay which are earnings related. Supplementary benefits are paid to people whose income falls below the standard, i.e. a means test is involved. These benefits are widely paid to people receiving retirement pensions. Family allowances are paid to couples and single parent families. Family income supplements are paid to low wage earners with large families. Miscellaneous other benefits include rent and rate rebates, free health services and free school meals. This is obviously a very complex system and has been criticised, notably by Roy Jenkins in *What Matters Now*, published in 1972, who pointed out that if someone living on the poverty line earned an extra £1 per week the loss of benefits could be so great that the family could be 81 pence per week worse off.

Despite these extensive benefits, deprivation persists. In a major speech in 1972 Sir Keith Joseph, then Secretary of State for Social Services, suggested that there was a cycle of deprivation in which some families were trapped for generation after generation. In a report entitled *Born to Fail* first published in 1973, the National Childrens' Bureau measured the "dimensions of disadvantage" experienced by some poor children and concluded that families with difficulties should be given support by social workers; that education should be more appropriate to poor children but, most importantly, that there should be a redistribution of incomes so that material inequalities that help to cripple the life chances of disadvantaged children should be eradicated. Both the speech by Sir Keith Joseph and the report by the National Childrens' Bureau sparked off considerable study and debate about the causes of deprivation and the cures for it.

The following table sets out the pattern of public expenditure on social services between 1951 and 1974.

PUBLIC EXPENDITURE ON THE SOCIAL SERVICES, 1951–1974
AT CURRENT PRICES (£ MILLION)

	1951	1961	1971	1974
Social security	707	1628	4309	6845
Health and welfare	564	1088	2785	4778
Education	433	1012	3023	4864
Housing	367	555	1253	3942
As a proportion of gross domestic product	16·4	17·7	23·3	28·1

Source: C.S.O., *National Income and Expenditure*

Industrial Relations

Strike activity is always the most publicised aspect of industrial relations but is by no means the most important feature. Of much more importance is the growing political power of trade unions and the system of collective bargaining. Strikes are only a secondary factor in industrial relations.

In 1964, a Royal Commission under Lord Donovan was set up to examine the role played by trade unions and employers associations. The report was published in 1968 and was highly critical of the unofficial stoppages which plagued some sectors of British industry. Accordingly, legislation was proposed in a White Paper *In Place of Strife: a Policy for Industrial Relations* (Cmnd. 3888). The T.U.C., however, was strongly opposed to the restrictive legislation proposed and which was eventually dropped in favour of a T.U.C. undertaking to attempt to control unofficial action by shop stewards.

When the Conservatives were returned to power in 1970 they were pledged to introduce legislation which would formalise the system of industrial relations. Accordingly an Industrial Relations Act was passed in 1971. This established the National Industrial Relations Court, which was empowered to give judgment where unfair industrial practices were alleged and to call for a full ballot of union members, or a cooling-off period where industrial action was proposed. But this formal control of trade unions, together with the counter-inflationary measures met with stiff opposition from many union members (who constituted in total about 11 million people, about half the total workforce at this time). The miners were the most militant and their strike in the winter of 1973 caused the nation to be put on a three-day working week and precipitated a general election which the Conservatives lost. These developments gave rise to further discussion about the nature and extent of trade union political power.

The Labour Government, which was returned to power in February, 1974, lost little time in repealing most of the 1971 Industrial Relations Act and the 1974 Trade Union and Labour Relations Act sought to improve the machinery of collective bargaining by firmly establishing the independent Advisory, Conciliation and Arbitration Service. Agreement was also made with the unions on the operation of the Social Contract which was discussed at the beginning of this chapter.

The end of 1975 saw the 1970 Equal Pay Act come into force which guaranteed equality of pay for men and women doing the same job. The 1975 Sex Discrimination Act made it compulsory for employers to offer jobs to men *and* women and not to discriminate against either sex when making staff appointments. Both these pieces of legislation reflect the changing role of women in society.

The 1975 Employment Protection Act secured rights to employees against unfair dismissal and discrimination on the grounds of union membership. It also improved the provision for redundancy payments and provided further protection of employment, notably for expectant mothers, who worked six months of their pregnancy and who wished to return to work after the birth of their babies.

Prospect

Views of the future of the British economy are almost as numerous as views of the past and are even more diverse in the opinions which they express. Most of these views, notably those expressed by the Hudson Institute in 1974, offer rather gloomy predictions, but others, including one produced by the E.E.C. in 1977, suggest that the future for the British economy is quite bright.

The British press and television (and most history books for that matter) tend to be problem-oriented. They discuss in great detail the troubles which confront the British people and the response which is made to them. It is, of course, very necessary to be aware that there are problems, but to dwell on them gives the impression that there are no bright spots. In short, the media tend to give a rather one-sided view of the economy and society.

In fact, Britain remains one of the world's leading economies. It is technologically highly advanced and exports technological knowhow throughout the world. Furthermore, Britain is still a net creditor nation. Although much has been made of the necessity to borrow short-term from the I.M.F. and other places, the British Government and people still hold assets overseas which exceed those borrowings in value.

The key to Britain's future lies in North Sea oil. If Britain becomes self-sufficient in oil by 1980, this should have the effect of restoring the balance of payments to a long-term surplus. Public and private revenue derived from oil should provide the necessary funds for investment in other productive areas and thereby lay the basis for the future growth of the economy: but oil will not conquer inflation and may in fact exacerbate the problem by increasing the supply of money in the economy.

Ultimately, the future performance of the economy with all its implications for the quality of life will be determined by political considerations. It is in Parliament, and to a lesser extent in the E.E.C., that the future pattern of development will be planned and the conditions within which industry can operate will be determined.

INDEX OF ACTS

Abnormal Importations (1931), 342
Agriculture
   Agricultural Holdings (1875, 1906, 1908), 289–90
      Rates (1896), 289
      Wages (1924), 203, 313
   Commons Registration (1965), 36
   Corn (1436–1814), 39, 123–4; (1815–49), 39, 123–4
      Production (1917), 315
   Enclosure (1801, 1836, 1845), 35–6
   Gangs (1868), 283
   Ground Game (1880), 289
   Marketing (1931, 1933), 346
      Boards (1931–9), 346
   Merton (1236), 27
   Small Holdings (1892, 1907), 290
   Sutton's, Sir Richard (1773), 26
   Wheat (1931), 346
Artificers and Apprentices (1563), 10, 41, 108–10

Banking and Finance
   Bank (1826, 1833), 169
      Charter (1844), 170–3
      Restriction (1797), 168, 170
   Companies (1879), 170
   Currency and Bank Notes (1928), 172, 328
   Finance, 407–9
   Gold Standard (1925), 172, 328
Beer (1830), 207

Chimney Sweeps (1840, 1875), 201
Clear Air (1956), 416
Colonial Loans (1899), 297
Commonwealth Immigration (1962), 398

Distribution of Industry (1945), 371
Dyestuffs Industries (1920), 260, 329

Education
   Balfour (1902), 228
   Butler (1944), 231–2, 371
   Endowed Schools (1869), 227
   Fisher (1918), 226, 231
   Forster (1870), 225–6
   Grant-in-aid (1833, 1839), 223
   Local Authority Default (1904), 228
   Mundella (1880), 226
   Sandon (1876), 226
   Technical Instruction (1889), 230
   Universities Tests (1871), 218, 227
Emergency Powers (1920), 331
Employment Protection (1975), 433
Enabling (1846), 294
Equal Pay (1970), 433

Factory
   Health and Morals of Apprentices (1802), 193, 222; (1819, 1825, 1831), 194; (1833), 197, 222; (1844), 199; (1847, 1850, 1853), 199–200; (1845–66), 200; (1867), 200; (1874), 200; (1878), 201–2; (1891, 1895, 1901), 202; (1937), 199, 202–3
   Laundries (1895, 1907), 202
   Notice of Accidents (1906), 202
   Offices, Shops and Railway Premises (1963), 203
   Retail Shops (1892, 1911), 202
   Trade Boards (1909, 1918), 202–3, 313
   Truck (1831, 1887), 202
   White Phosphorous Matches Protection (1908), 202
Fair Trading (1973), 420, 423
Finance Act (1972), 421
Friendly Societies
   Friendly Societies (1829, 1850, 1855, 1875, 1896), 257, 354
   Industrial and Provident Societies (1852–93), 243–4
   Rose's (1793), 353

Gloucester (1278), 66

Housing
  Shaftesbury (1851), 214
  Torrens (1868), 214
  Artisans' Dwellings (1875), 214
  Housing of Working Classes (1890), 214
  Small Dwellings Acquisition (1899), 214
  Housing and Town Planning (1909), 215
  Addison (1919), 364
  Chamberlain (1923), 364–5
  Wheatley (1924), 365
  Greenwood (1930), 315
  Hilton Young (1935), 215
  Temporary Accommodation (1944), 371
  Temporary Provision (1944), 371
  Housing (1946, 1949), 383
  Rent Restriction (1915, 1920, 1923), 364
  Town and Country Planning (1944), 371

Import Duties (1932), 342
Industrial Development (1966), 395
Industrial Relations (1971), 432
Industrial Training (1964), 430
Industry (1972, 1975), 418, 420, 421

Local Government
  Local Government (1888), (1894), 74; (1929), 360
  Municipal Corporations (1835), 210–11
  Rating and Valuation (1927), 360
  Derating (1929), 330

Manchester (1735), 93–4
Merchandise Marks (1926), 343
Mines
  Mines (1842), 198; (1850), 198–9
  Coal Mines (Minimum Wage) (1912), 203, 311, 313; (1926, 1930), 313, 330
Molasses (1733), 113
Monopolies and Mergers (1965), 419
Monopolies Restrictive (1948), 279, 419
Munitions (1915), 313

Parliamentary Reform

Parliamentary Reform (1832), 179, 236; (1858), 238; (1867), 179, 180, 239; (1872), 239; (1884–85), 180, 239; (1911), 239, 309; (1918), 239
Plantation Duties (1673), 113
Poor Law
  Tudor, 181–2
  Settlement (1662, 1691), 183
  Workhouse (1723), 182–3
  Gilbert's (1782), 183–4, 185
  Amendment (1834), 181, 186–7, 189, 236
  Local Authorities (Financial Provisions) (1921), 359
  Boards of Guardians (Default) (1926), 360
  National Assistance (1948), 405–6
Prices and Incomes (1966), 410
Public Health
  Baths and Washhouses (1846), 211
  Huddersfield Improvement (1848), 210, 211–12
  Nuisance Removal (1855), 214; (1872), (1875), 212; (1946), 383

Rageman (1276), 66
Railways
  Lord Seymour's (1840), 145; (1842), 145; (1844), 146
  Gauge (1846), 144
  Cardwell's (1854), 146
  Regulation of Railways (1871), 147
  Railway and Canal Traffic (1888, 1894), 147
  Railway Rates and Charges (1893), 147
  Notice of Accidents (1884), 147
  Employment (Prevention of Accidents) (1900), 148; (1921), 148–9, 313, 331
  Railway (Road Transport) (1928), 149
  Road and Rail Traffic (1933), 349
Reciprocity of Duties (1823), 126
Registration of Births and Deaths (1836), 197
Resale Prices (1964), 423
Restrictive Practices (1956), 419
Roads
  Highways (1555), 66; (1562), 66; (1663), 66; (1773), 70; (1835), 73
  Tramways (1870), 264
  Roads and Bridges (1878), 74

INDEX OF ACTS

Road Traffic (1930), 329
London Passenger Transport Board (1933), 313

Safeguarding of Industries (1921), 329
Seditious Meetings (1795), 249
Sex Discrimination (1975), 433
Shipping
  Lloyds (1911), 163
  Merchant Shipping (1854, 1876, 1894), 160–1
  Navigation (1650, 1651, 1660), 93, 112–13, 116; Repeal of, 132–3
  Unseaworthy Ships (1875), 161
Six Acts (1819), 63
Slavery and Slave Trade, abolition of (1807, 1833), 101
Social Services
  Old Age Pensions (1908, 1919, 1937, 1940), 357, 361, 370
  National Insurance (1911, 1928, 1946), 313, 357, 361, 405
  Unemployment Insurance (1911, 1920, 1927, 1934), 357, 361–2, 363
  Maternity and Child Welfare (1918), 361
  Blind Persons (1920), 361
  Widows, Orphans and Old Age Contributory Pensions (1925), 361
  Midwives and Maternity Homes (1926), 361
  Nursing Homes Registration (1927), 361
  Anomalies (1931), 362
  Midwives (1936), 361
  Determination of Needs (1941, 1943), 370
  National Insurance, Ministry of (1944), 371
  Family Allowances (1945), 371
  Redundancy Payments (1965), 401

Social Security, Ministry of (1966), 406
Special Areas (1934), 350
Stamp (1763), 115
Supply of Goods (Implied Terms) (1973), 423

Trade Unions
  Combination (1799, 1800), 60, 249; (1824, 1825), 251–2
  Molestation of Workmen (1859), 256
  Master and Servant (1867), 257
  Protection of Funds (1869), 257; (1871), 257
  Criminal Law Amendment (1871), 257–8
  Conspiracy and Protection of Property (1875), 258, 362
  Employers and Workmen (1875), 258; (1876), 258, 312
  Conciliation (1896), 313
  Trade Disputes (1906), 308; (1913), 309, 333; (1965), 399
  Amalgamations (1917, 1964), 312
  Trade Unions and Trade Disputes (1927), 308, 309, 333; (1946), 333
  Trade Union and Labour Relations (1974), 433
Transport (1968), 424
Treasonable Practices (1795), 249

Unemployed Workmen (1905), 356
Union, with Scotland (1707), 12, 96, 113

Weavers (1555), 18
Winchester (1285), 66
Workmen's Compensation
  Lord Campbell's (1846), 358
  Employers' Liability (1880), 358; (1897, 1906, 1941, 1943), 353, 358, 370

GENERAL INDEX

Académie des Sciences, 6
Adult Education, 221–2
A.E.I., 418, 420
Aerospace Industry, 417
Agriculture, 9, 22–9, 30–42, 265–8, 281–90, 316, 345, 412–14
  American, 10, 284–6
  Board of (1793), 34, 266; (1889), 36, 289, 315
  E.E.C.
    Common Agricultural Policy, 413–14
    Community Farm Fund, 414
    factory farming, 413
    price supports, 413–14
  Fertilisers, 267
  Labourer, 282–4, 315–16
  Machinery, 268
  Marketing Boards, 345–6
Air Transport, 423, 425
Airy, Sir G. B., 154
Alberti, Leon Battista, 5
Allied Breweries, 418
Aluminium, 265
Amalgamated Society of Engineers (A.S.E.) (1851), 54, 255
Ampère, 263
Anderson, Professor John, 221
Anti-Corn Law League, 130–2
Applegarth, Robert, 255–6
Appleton, Sir Edward, 325
Apprentices, 108–9
Advisory, Conciliation and Arbitration Service, 433
Arch, Joseph, 284
Arkwright, Sir Richard, 56, 94, 215
Arnott, Dr, 211
Ashley, Lord (*see* Shaftesbury, Earl of)
Ashtons of Hyde, 191
Askwith, Sir (Lord) George, 313
Asquith, H. H., 299
Atomic Theory, 6, 326–7
Attwood, Thomas, 236–7

Aulnager, 110
Avebury, Lord (*see* Lubbock, Sir John)

Bacon, Anthony, 48
Bacon, Francis, 5
Baird, John Logie, 325
Bakewell, Robert, 31–2
Balance of Payments, 337, 369, 373–5, 376, 410, 411, 426
Balfour, A. J., 228, 298
Balfour Committee on Industry and Trade (1929), 330, 348
Bankes, Sir Joseph, 151
Bank of Scotland, 426
Banking, 164–78, 426–7
  Bank (of England), 166–7, 168, 171–3, 427
  Banks (Country), 167
    (Joint Stock), 169, 174–5
    (Lombard St), 165, 167
    (Merchant), 173, 175–6, 427
    (Nationalisation), 427
    (Scotland), 167, 169
Barclays Bank, 426
Barlow Commission on the Distribution of Population (1940), 371
Barlow, Isaac, 57
Barnes, George, 312, 358
Bastiat, Frederic, 134
Beeching, Dr (Lord), 390–2, 424
Bell, Dr Andrew, 220
Bell, Henry, 154
Bell, Thomas, 58
Bentham, Jeremy, 187
Bentinck, Lord George, 132
Berlin and Milan Decrees, 62, 104, 121
Berthollet, 58
Berzelius, 260
Besant, Annie, 303, 305, 318
Bessemer, Sir Henry, 46, 261, 274
Bevan, Aneurin, 377
Bevan, Madame, 219

GENERAL INDEX

Beveridge Report, 352, 354, 404–5, 431
Beveridge, Sir William (Lord), 357
Bevin, Ernest, 331, 367, 375
Birkbeck, Dr George, 221
Birmingham
    League (1867), 225
    Political Union, 236
Black Death, 8, 208
Black, Professor Joseph, 5, 51
Blackwall Frigates, 151–2
Blanc, Louis, 303
Blandesburgh Committee (1927), 362
Blanket, Thomas, of Bristol, 18
Blatchford, Robert, 304
Blewstone, 44
Booth, Charles, 202, 302, 431
Booth, Rev. William, 303, 431
Boulton, Matthew, 6, 43, 47, 48, 51, 52, 53, 61
Boussingault, 267
Bowley, Professor A. L., 282, 352
Boyd Orr, Sir John (Lord), 353
Boyle, Robert, 48
Bradlaugh, Charles, 318
Bradshaw, George, 143–4
Bramah, Joseph, 53
Brassey, Thomas, 137
Brett, Jacob and John, 263
Bridgewater Canal, 50, 77–8
Bridgewater, Duke of, 77–8
Bright, John, 130, 339
Brindley, James, 77–8
British and Foreign Schools Society (1814), 220
British Airways, 417, 425
British Broadcasting Corporation (B.B.C.), 325, 329
British Caledonian, 425
British Iron and Steel Federation (1934), 349
British Leyland, 412, 418, 420
British Linen Bank, 426
British Motor Corporation, 418, 420
British National Oil Corporation, 415
British Steel Corporation, 417, 418
British Transport Commission, 149
British Waterways Board, 84
Brontë, Charlotte: *Shirley*, 60, 62
Brown, George, 410
Brunel, Isambard Kingdom, 143, 154, 155–6
Brunton, John, 137
Bryce Commission (1894–5), 227–8
Buchez, Phillipe, 245

Building Industry, 373
Building Societies, 216, 428
Bull, Rev. G. S., 195, 196
Bullion Committee (1810), 170
Bunsen, Wilhelm von, 265
Burdett, Sir Francis, 236
Burial Grounds, 205–6
Burns, John, 305, 306, 357
Burt, Thomas, 304, 306

Cabet, Etienne, 303
Cadburys, 418
Caledonian Canal, 71, 76, 78
Callaghan, James, 427, 430
Canals, 75–85
    French, 76
    Royal Commission on (1906), 83–4
Capital and Counties Bank, 427
Carlyle, Thomas, 144, 179, 192
Carnegie, Andrew, 262, 278
Carron Ironworks, 43, 44, 47
Cartwright, Rev. Edmund, 58, 60
Cartwright, Major, 58
Cash and carry stores, 422
Cavendish, Henry, 6, 260
Chadwick, Edwin, 179, 186, 187, 196, 211–12
Chamberlain, Sir Austen, 343
Chamberlain, Joseph, 225, 293–4, 296–301, 339
Chamberlain, Neville, 342, 360
Charity School Movement, 218–19
Chartered Trading Companies, 7, 88–92, 296
Chartists, 130–1, 234–9
Chemical Industry, 325
Chevalier, Michel, 134
Children's Employment, Commissions on, 49, 50, 196, 197–8, 199, 200
Cholera Epidemics, 207, 212
Christian Socialists, 245–6
Chronometer, 150
Chrysler, 421, 422
Churchill, Sir Winston, 330, 332, 343, 357, 367, 370, 372
Clanny, Dr William Reid, 49
Clark, Colin, 352
Clifford, Dr John, 228
Coalbrookdale, 43, 44, 45, 46, 47, 49, 138
Coal Industry, 21–2, 48–50, 107, 273, 280, 323–4, 331, 338, 349–50, 373, 385–7, 415–17

GENERAL INDEX

Cobbett, William, 40, 41, 174, 180, 196, 235
Cobden, Richard, 130, 134, 291, 339
Coke, Sir Edward, 12
Coke, Thomas William, of Holkham (Earl of Leicester), 32
Colling, Charles and Robert, 32
Collings, Jesse, 290
Colwyn Committee (1918), 174
Comet Group, 422
Common Day Schools, 221
Common Market (E.E.C.), 378, 379, 380–1, 386, 413–14, 434
    Common Agricultural Policy (C.A.P.), 413–14
    Community Farm Fund, 414
    price supports, 413–14
Common Open Spaces and Footpaths Preservation Society (1865), 36
Concorde, 425
Conference System (Shipping), 159
Consumers' Association, 423
Cook, A. J., 331
Cook, Captain James, 151
Cooke, Sir William, 263
Co-operative Movement
    Consumers', 236, 239–44
    Producers', 244–7, 422
Copernicus, 118
Copper Mining, 47, 51, 52
Cort, Henry, 45–6
Cotton Industry, 13, 16, 50–1, 55–9, 60, 97, 272, 299, 322–3, 392
Coulson, Edwin, 255
Council for the Preservation of Rural England, 36
Council of Europe, 378
Courage, Brewers, 418
Cranage, Thomas and George, 45
Crawshay, Richard, 47
Crewe, Nehemiah, 23
Crinan Canal, 76
Cripps, Sir Stafford, 375
Crompton, Samuel, 55–7, 58
Crookes, Sir William, 267
Crosland, Anthony, 429
Cross, Richard Assheton, 201, 212
Crowther Report (1959), 230
Cugnot, 138, 269
Culley, George, 32
Cunard Line, 426
Cunard, Samuel, 156
Cyfarthfa Ironworks, 47

Daimler, Gottlieb, 269
Dale, David, 56, 191
Dalton, Dr Hugh, 373, 375
Dalton, John, 6, 260
Dame Schools, 221
Darby Family, 43, 44, 45, 46, 48, 51, 52
Darien Scheme, 89
Davies, Dr David, 41
Davy, Sir Humphry, 49, 264, 266
D.C.L., 423
Defoe, Daniel, 15, 16, 18, 34, 68, 77
De Gaulle, President, 380–1
Department of Economic Affairs, 410
Department of the Environment, 424
De Saussure, 267
Development areas, 420
Dickens, Charles, 48, 73, 188, 190, 201, 205, 206
Diesel, Dr Rudolph, 157
Dilke, Sir Charles, 36
Disraeli, Benjamin, 132, 191, 192, 198, 235, 315, 408
Dobson and Barlow, firm of, 57
Docks, 161–2
Doherty, John, 194, 252
Domestic System, 4, 11, 17–19
Donovan Commission, 432
Dorchester Labourers (see Tolpuddle Martyrs)

East India Company, 89, 90, 91, 94–5, 107, 126, 150–1
Edison, Thomas, 325
Education, 217–33, 429–31
    Board of, 228
    Technical, 229–30
Elder, John, 156
Electricity, 263–4, 324–5, 329, 338, 373, 415–16
Eliot, George, 41, 73
Elkington, Joseph, 34
Ellman, John, 32
Embargo Act (1807), 104
Empire Marketing Board, 343, 344
Enclosures, 27–9, 34–42, 206
Energy, 414–17
Engels, Friedrick, 303
Equity Bank, 422
Ericsson, Captain John, 155
Euro-Currency, 427
European Atomic Energy Committee (Euratom), 378, 417
European Coal and Steel Community (E.C.S.C.), 378

GENERAL INDEX 441

European Economic Community (E.E.C.) (*see* Common Market)
Evelyn, John, 20
Eversley Commission (1892), 289
Eversley, Lord, 36
Excess Profits Tax, 316, 368, 408

Faber du Faur of Wasseralfugen, 44
Fabian Society, 303, 306, 370
Factory Acts Consolidation Commission (1876), 201
Factory Acts Reform Association (1872), 201
Fair Trade League (1880), 293–4
Fair Trading, 420
Faraday, Michael, 198, 263
Farrar, Lord, 294
Fenwick, Charles, 304
Fielden, John, 194, 197, 199, 237
Fiennes, Celia, *Journal* of, 68
Finance, 426–8
Finance for Industry, 422
Fire Offices Committee, 419
Fitch, John, 154
Fitzherbert, Sir Anthony, 23, 28
Flax, 19
Flying Shuttle, 55, 57, 59
Forster, William Edward, 225–6
Ford Motor Co., 419
Fourier, Charles, 303
Fox, Charles James, 41, 101, 235, 237
Francis, John: *A History of the English Railway*, 142
Franklin, Benjamin, 263
Free Trade, achievement of, 125–35
Freightliner, 424
Friendly Societies, 353–4, 357
Friese-Green, William, 325
Frost, John, 238
Fulton, Robert, 154

Galileo, 5
Galvani, 263
Game Laws, 40
Garaz, Blasco de, 154
Garden City Movement, 216
Gas Industry, 48, 205, 389–90, 415–17
Gas, Light and Coke Company, 48, 258
G.E.C., 418, 420
Geographical Revolution, 4, 14, 88
George III ("Ralph Robinson"), 33
George, Henry, 303
Gilbart, James William, 169

Gilbert, Sir Joseph Henry, 267
Gilbert, William, 263
Gladstone, William Ewart, 134–5
Glyn, Mills Bank, 426
Gold, discoveries of, 10, 273
Gold Standard, 168, 172, 173–4, 275, 316, 328–9, 331, 340
Goldsmiths, 164–5
Gott, Benjamin, 61
Gough, Rev. Thomas, 219
Grand National Consolidated Trades Union, 252–3
Grant, Philip, 195
Gray, Thomas, 139
Green, Richard, 152
Greg Family of Styal, 109, 191, 193
Gregory, Charles, 143
Griffith, Mr James, 383
Grime's Graves, 1
Guest, John, 47–8
Guile, Daniel, 255
Gunter, Mr Ray, 401

Hadow Report (1926), 231
Haggard, Sir Henry Rider: *Rural England*, 289
Hailsham, Lord, 394–5
Hall, Charles Martin, 265
Hanse Merchants, 14, 87
Hanway, James, 193, 201
Harcourt, Sir William, 315, 409
Hardenberg, Baron, 14
Hardie, Keir, 306
Harris, Dr J. R., 4, 52
Harrison, Frederic, 256
Harrison, John, 150
Hatfield, Dr, 262
Health, Ministry of, 213, 360–1, 405
Health of Towns, Commission on (1844), 211
Heath, Mr Edward, 380
Henderson, Arthur, 312
Herbert, Sir Alan, 318
Hero of Alexandria, 3
Hertz, Heinrich, 263
Higher Grade Classes, 229
Hill, Misses Octavia and Miranda, 213–14
Hill, Samuel, of Soyland, 16–17
Hodge, John, 312
Hodgson, Rev. John, 198
Holyoake, George Jacob, 241
Homework, Select Committee on (1908), 202

GENERAL INDEX

Hong Kong, 107
Hood, Thomas: "Song of the Shirt," 191
Hooke, Robert, 23, 51
Horrocks, John, 58
Hostmen of Newcastle, 22, 50, 80
Houblon, Sir John, 166
Housing, 207–8, 213–16, 363–5, 428–9
Housing and Local Government, Ministry of, 215
Housing of the Poor, Royal Commission on (1884–9), 302
Housing of the Working Classes, Royal Commission on (1885–90), 214
Howard, Ebenezer, 216
Huddersfield, 17, 18, 61, 73, 210
Hudson Bay Company, 89
Hudson, George, 144–5
Hudson Institute, 433
Hughes, Tom, 245, 256–7
Hume Select Committee on Trade Unions (1824), 251
Hume Committee (1840), 127
Huntsman, Benjamin, 46, 48, 261
Huskisson, William, 126–7, 140
Hutcheson, Professor Francis, 119
Huxley, Professor T. H., 36
Huygens, Christiaan, 5
Hyndman, H. M., 363

I.C.I., 423
Imperial Tobacco, 418
Import Duties Advisory Committee (1932), 342, 349
Income Tax, 126, 309, 316, 368, 407–8
Independent Labour Party, 306
Indigo, 94, 260
Industrial Assurance Companies, 354–5
Industrial and Commercial Finance Corporation, 422
Industrial Development Certificate, 421
Industrial Relations, 432–3
Industrial Reorganisation Corporation, 418, 419–20
Industrial Revolution
 Dates of, 3–4, 11, 271–2
 In Europe, 7, 13–14
 Reasons for, 4–14
Industrial Training, 430
Insurance Industry, 428
Inter-imperial Preferences, 294, 343–4

Internal Combustion Engine, 269
International Co-operative Alliance (1896), 239
International Monetary Fund, 412, 430, 434
International Working Men's Association (1864), 303
Interlopers, 90–1
Ireland in the eighteenth century, 117
Ironbridge, 44
Iron Industry, 20–1, 43–8, 107, 273–4
Ismay, Thomas Henry, 156

Jacquard Loom, 58
Jenkins, Roy, 431
Jenner, Edward, 209
John Brown shipyard, 415
Joint Stock Companies, 137, 273
Jones, Charles Ernest, 238
Jones, Rev. Griffith, 219
Joplin, John, 169
Joseph, Sir Keith, 431–2
Jude, Martin, 252
Judicial Decisions
 Allen v. Flood (1898), 307
 Bradlaugh and Besant Prosecution (1877), 318
 Bonsor v. Musicians Union (1954), 398
 Gas Stokers' Case (1872), 258
 Hornby v. Close (1867), 257
 Huntley v. Thornton (1953), 398
 Lee v. Showmen's Guild (1952), 398
 Lyons v. Wilkins (1896–98), 307
 Cockerton Judgment (1901), 229
 Osborne Judgment (1909), 308–9
 Quinn v. Leathem (1901), 307
 Rookes v. Barnard (1964), 398–9
 Sommersett's Case (1772), 101
 Stratford v. Lindley (1964), 399
 Taff Vale Railway Case (1901), 307
 Temperton v. Russell (1893), 307
 Trollope and Sons v. London Building Trades Federation (1896), 307
Junta, the, 255
Jute, 94–5

Kartells (see Trusts and Kartells)
Kay, Dr James (Sir J. Kay-Shuttleworth), 211, 223
Kay, John, 55, 59
Kelly, William, 56
Kelvin, Lord, 263

GENERAL INDEX 443

Kendal Cloth, 16, 61, 63
Keynes, John Maynard (Lord), 335, 375
Kingsley, Charles, 109, 201
Kipling, Rudyard, 295

Labour and National Service, Ministry of, 366
Labour Commission (1894), 202
Labour (Employment) Exchanges, 357
Labour Representation Committee (1899), 306, 308
Labourers' Rising (1830), 41–2
Lace Industry, 19
Laker Airways, 425
Lancashire Cotton Corporation (1930), 349
Lancaster, Joseph, 220–1
Latimer, Bishop, 22, 28
Lavoisier, Antoine Laurent, 6, 260
Lawes, Sir John Bennett, 267
Lead Mining, 15
Leconfield, Lord, 33
Lee, Mr Fred, 395
Lee, William, 19
Leewenhoek, Anthony von, 23
Leland's *Itinerary*, 80
Lend-Lease, 369, 374–5
Leon, Daniel de, 310
Levant (Turkey) Company, 88–9, 91, 93
Liebig, Baron Justus von, 267
Lifeboats, 162
Lighthouses, 162
Linen Industry, 19
List, Friedrick, 292
Lister, Lord, 209
Lister, Miss, diarist, 61
Lithgow, Sir James, 348
Littlewoods, 422
Liverpool, 57, 81, 139
Lloyd George, David, 228, 311, 312, 315, 335, 357, 408
Lloyd, Samuel James (Lord Overstone), 170–1
Lloyd, Mr Selwyn, 377, 385, 403
Lloyds, 162–3
Local Government Board, 212
Lombe, Sir Thomas, 19, 50
London Merchants' Petition (1820), 126
London Working Men's Association, 236, 237
Lovett, William, 237

Lowe, Robert, 135, 224
Lubbock, Sir John (Lord Avebury), 165
Luddites, 2, 62–3
Ludlow, John Malcolm, 245
Lumière Brothers, 325
Lunar Society, 6
Lyell, Sir Charles, 198

Maassen, Karl George von, 14
Macadam, John Loudon, 71–2
Macarthur, Captain John, 60
Macaulay, Lord, 16, 67, 99
Macaulay, Zachary, 101
Macdonald, Alexander, 306
MacDonald, James Ramsay, 306, 356
Machine Tools, 53–4
Mackintosh, 418
McKenna Duties, 316, 343
Maclean Committee (1917), 358
Macmillan, Mr Harold, 335, 372, 378, 385
Macmillan Committee on Finance and Industry (1931), 340
Magnesium, 265
Maiden Castle, 1
Mail order, 422
Malpighi, Marcelli, 23
Malthus, Rev. Thomas Robert, 8, 266
Manchester Education Aid Society, 225
Manchester Literary and Philosophical Society, 6
Mann, Thomas, 305, 310, 311
Manning, Cardinal, 305
Manson, Sir Patrick, 209
Marathon, 415
Marconi, G., 325
Marcus, Siegfried, 269
Marine Insurance, 162–3
Mariner's Compass, 150
Marples, Mr Ernest, 390
Marshall Plan (*see* Organisation for European Recovery)
Martins Bank, 426
Marx, Karl, 303
Maudling, Mr Reginald, 377
Maudsley, Henry, 53–4
Maurice, Rev. F. P., 245, 246
Maxwell, James Clerk, 263
May Committee on National Expenditure (1931), 340, 341, 362
Mayhew, Henry, 272
Maypole Dairies, 422

GENERAL INDEX

Means Tests, 362
Mechanics Institutes, 221–3
Mercantilism, 110–17
Merchant Adventurers, Company of, 87
Messina Conference (1955), 378
Metcalfe, John (Jack of Knaresborough), 71
Mill, James, 245
Mill, John Stuart, 36, 244–5, 292
Millar, Patrick, 154
Miners' Safety Lamps, 49
Moissan, Henri, 265
Mond, Sir Alfred (Lord Melchett), 333, 359
Monnet, M. Jean, 378
Monopolies Commission, 419, 420, 426
Morant, Sir Robert, 228, 229
More, Hannah and Martha, 219
More, Sir Thomas, 28
Morgan, Pierpont, 160, 278
Morland, Sir Samuel, 51
Morris, William, 303
Morse, Samuel, 263
Motor Industry, 268–70, 325
Motor Taxation (1903), 74
Muscovy (Russian) Company, 88–9
Mushet, Robert, 261
Muslin Wheel, 56

Nader, Ralph, 423
Nasmyth, James, 45, 54
National Assistance Board, 383
National Board for Prices and Incomes, 410–11
National Charter Association, 238
National Children's Bureau, 431–2
National Commercial Bank, 426
National Economic Development Council, 409–10
National Education Union (1869), 225
National Enterprise Board, 418
National Incomes Commission, 410
National Insurance Benefits, 431
National Provincial Bank, 426
National Society for Promoting the Education of the Poor (1811), 220
National Trust, 36
National Union of Railwaymen (N.U.R.), 148, 312
Nationalised Industries, Select Committee on (1960), 384
Natural gas, 417

Neale, Edward Vansittart, 245
Nef, Professor John U.: *War and Human Progress*, 3
Neilson, James, 44, 46
Newcastle Commission (1858–61), 223–4
Newcomen, Thomas, 22, 43, 49, 51, 52, 53
New England Colonies, 97–8
Newport, battle of (1839), 237–8
Newton, Sir Isaac, 5, 118
Newton, William, 255
Noble, James, 60
Nonconformist Schools, 218
Non-Intercourse Act (1809), 62, 104
North, Lord, 120
North Atlantic Treaty Organisation (N.A.T.O.), 378
North of Scotland Hydro-Electricity Board, 416
North Sea Oil, 411, 415, 434
Northern Star (1837), 237
Northern Union, 236, 237
Nuclear Power, 387–9, 416–17

Oastler, Richard, 194–5
O'Connor, Feargus, 237, 238
Odger, George, 255, 302
Oersted, Professor, 263, 265
Ogilby, John: *Britannia*, 68
Old Colonial System, 113–15
Oldknow, Samuel, 109
Onions, Peter, 45
Open Field System, 24–7
Opium, 95
Orders in Council (1807–8), 104
Organisation for Economic Cooperation and Development (O.E.C.D.), 409
Organisation for European Economic Recovery (O.E.E.C.), 376, 377
Organisation of Petroleum Exporting Countries (OPEC), 411, 415
Ottawa Conference (1932), 343–4, 346, 380
Overseas Investments, 177–8, 316
Owen, Robert, 6, 109, 194, 215, 239–41, 252, 254, 303
Owenite Societies, 241–2
Oxfam, 1

Palmer, John, 72
Panama Canal, 161
Paper Duties, repeal of, 135

GENERAL INDEX 445

Papin, Denis, 51
Parnell, Sir Henry, 128
Parsons, Sir Charles, 156
Passive Resistance League (1902), 228
Pasteur, Louis, 209
Paterson, William, 166
Paul, Lewis, 55, 60
Paxton, Sir Joseph, 274
Peabody Trust, 214
Pease, Edward, 139
Peel, Sir Robert (the elder), 193
Penney, Sir William (Lord), 387–8
Penny Post (1840), 130, 297
Pepper, 95
Pepys, Samuel, 20, 165
Percival, Dr, 193
Perkin, Sir William Henry, 260
Peterloo, 63
Peto, Sir Samuel Morton, 137
Petroleum, 269–70, 330, 415
Physiocrats, 121
Pickard, J., 52
Pitt, William (the Younger), 120–1, 179
Place, Francis, 237, 250–1
Plimsoll, Samuel, 160–1
Poor Law, 179–89, 359–60
  Board, 189
  Royal Commission (1832–34), 184–6; (1905–9), 355–6
Population, 7–9, 317–19, 338–9, 396–7
  migration of, 9–10, 16, 397–8
Port of London Authority, 329
Pottery Industry, 75–6, 80, 272
Press, Royal Commission on (1961–62), 400
Price, Dr Richard, 8
Prices, 271, 274–5, 276, 299, 310, 316, 319, 321
Prices and Incomes Board, 403–4
Priestley, Dr Joseph, 6, 260
Public Corporations, 329–30, 383–4
Public Health, 204–13
Public Schools, 227, 232
Pugh, Arthur, 332

Quesnay, François, 121

Radar, 325–6
Radcliffe, William, 58
Railway and Canal Commission (1873), 147
Railways, 136–49, 390–2, 423–5
  Board (1846–51), 146
  British, 417, 425

Overseas, 136–7, 141–2
Reade, Charles, 256
Rebecca Riots, 74
Reede, John, 35
Refrigeration, 158, 286–7
Regional Economic Councils, 395
Restrictive Practices Court, 279, 419, 420
Retailing, 422–3
Revised Code (1862), 224
Ricardo, David, 136, 170, 245, 266
Rice, 47
Richmond Commission (1882), 289
Riquet, Paul, 76
Road Board (1909), 74
Roads, 64–74, 423–5
Road freighting, 423–4
Robens, Sir Alfred (Lord), 385, 388
Roberts, Richard, 54, 56, 58
Roberts, W. P., the Miners' Attorney, 198, 255
Robinson, "Prosperity" (Lord Goderich), 126–7
Rochdale Pioneers, 240, 241–3
Rockefeller, John D., 278
Roebuck, J. A., 222
Roebuck, Dr John, 43, 44–5, 47, 51, 52
Rolls-Royce, 420
Ronalds, Sir Francis, 263
Rootes, 421, 422
Ross, Sir Ronald, 209
Rothamsted Experimental Station, 267
Rowntree, Seebohm, 352, 431
Rowntrees, 418
Royal African Company, 99
Royal Agricultural Society (1838), 266
Royal Bank of Scotland, 426
Royal Society, 5, 21–2, 23, 48
Royal Society, Edinburgh, 6
Russell, Lord John, 132
Russell, Sir John, 267
Russian (see Muscovy) Company

Sadler, Michael, 195
Saint Simon, Duc de, 303
Salt, Sir Titus, 216
Saltaire, 215
Samuel Commission (1925), 330, 331–2, 349
Samuel, Sir Herbert, 332, 341
Sanitary Conditions of the Labouring Population, Chadwick's Report on, 211
Sankey Commission (1919), 330
Savery, Captain Thomas, 22, 49, 51

School Boards, 225–6, 228
Schweppes, 418
Scientific and Industrial Research, Department of, 324
Scott Report, 371
Senior, Nassau, 186
Serfdom, 12–13, 40–1
Sewers, Consolidated Commission of, 210
Shaftesbury, 7th Earl of, 195–6, 199, 201
Sharpe, Granville, 101
Shaw of Bolton, 56
Shaw, George Bernard, 303
Shaxby, John, 143
Shelburne, Earl of (Marquis of Lansdowne), 120
Shipbuilding Industry, 112, 321–2, 348–9, 392–4, 417, 418, 421, 426
Shipping, 150–63, 276, 423–6
  American, 133, 151, 152, 160
Shore, Peter, 429
Shovell, Sir Cloudsley, 150
Siemens, Sir William, 46, 261–2, 264
Silbury Hill, 1
Simpson, Sir James Young, 209
Slavery and Slave Trade, 13, 81, 89, 99–102
Small shopkeepers, 422
Smeaton, John, 43, 50, 51, 52, 53, 162
Smiles, Samuel: *Lives of the Engineers*, 71
Smith, Adam, 10, 116, 118–21
Smith, Andrew, 50
Smith, James of Deanston, 34
Smith, Rev. Sydney, 207
Smithfield Club (1798), 31
Smuggling, 115
Snow, John, 208
Snowden, Philip (Viscount), 341, 343
Social Contract, 433
Social Democratic Federation (1881), 303, 304, 306–7
Social Security, Ministry of, 406, 407
Social welfare, 431–2
Society of Arts (1754), 6, 55, 230
Society for Promoting Christian Knowledge (1698), 218
Soho Works, 48, 53
Sorel, George, 310–11
South Sea Bubble, 89
South Sea Company, 89
Southwood Smith, Dr, 196, 211
Spaak Report (1956), 378, 379

Spa Field Riots, 63
Spar shops, 422
Special Areas, 338, 350, 392, 394–5
Speenhamland System, 41, 184
Spens Report (1939), 231
Spinning Jenny, 55–6, 66
Spode, Josiah, 80, 272
Staple, Merchants of the, 87
Steam Power, 50–4
Steel Industry, 261–3, 274, 300
Stein, Baron von, 14
Stephens, Rev. J. R., 195
Stephenson, George, 49, 50, 53, 138, 139, 140, 144
Stephenson, Robert, 138
Sterling Area, 340
Sterling Bloc, 340
Sterling, devaluation of, 376–7, 411
Stocking Frames, 19
Stocks, Rev. Thomas, 219
Stonehenge, 1
Stones, Henry of Horwich, 56
Strikes
  Times Printers (1819), 250; (1824–25), 60
  Match Girls (1888), 305
  Dockers (1889, 1911, 1912), 305, 311
  Gas Workers (1889), 305
  Quarrymen in North Wales (1896–98), 307
  Engineers (1897–98), 307
  Miners (1897–98, 1912, 1921, 1926), 307, 311, 331, 332
  Seamen (1911), 311
  Railwaymen (1911), 148
  Irish Transport Workers (1913), 311
  General Strike (1926), 331–3
  Sailors at Invergordon (1931), 341
  Bristol Shipyard (1965–66), 400
  Barbican Site (1966–67), 402
Strutt, Josiah, 56, 191
Stumpe, William, 18
Submarine Cables, 158, 263
Suez Canal, 94, 157, 273, 372
Sugar, 13, 99, 101, 329
Sunday Schools, 219–20
Sunderland Society, 198
Supermarkets, 422–3
Sutton, W. R., 214
Swammerdam, Jan, 23
Sweating System, House of Lords Select Committee on (1889), 202
Swift, Dean Jonathan, 117

GENERAL INDEX

Symington, William, 154
Syndicalism, 310–11, 312

Tariff Policies
　Great Britain, 121–4, 329, 342–3
　Overseas, 105, 121, 134, 291–3, 294, 297–8, 301, 336
Tariff Reform Movement, 291–301
Taxation, 407–8, 421
Tea, 95, 152
Team Valley Trading Estate, 350
Telegraph, 143
Television, 325
Telford, Thomas, 48, 71–2, 79, 139
Tesco Group, 423
Thomas, J. H., 332
Thomas Cook, 418
Thomas Lipton, 422
Thomas, Sidney Gilchrist, 262
Thompson, Sir William, 154
Thorne, Will, 305
Tillett, Ben, 305, 311
Tin Mining, 15, 47
Tobacco, 96–7
Tolpuddle Martyrs, 42, 253
Tooke, Horne, 237
Tooke, Thomas, 126, 171, 196
Townshend, Viscount, 30–1
Toynbee, Arnold, 3, 10, 302–3
Trade, 86–102, 103–7, 275–6, 277–8, 309, 317, 319–20, 344, 350, 373, 380
Trade Unions, 248–58, 302–14, 375–6, 398–403, 412
　Overseas, 249, 258
　Trade Union Congress (1868), 255, 306
　New Unionism, 305–6
Transport, 417, 423–6
Transport, Ministry of, 74, 148
Treaties
　Methuen (1703), 111, 120
　Utrecht (1713), 89
　Eden (1787), 120
　Cobden (1860), 134
　Anglo-American Trade (1938), 351
　Rome (1957), 378–9, 382
Treitschke, Heinrich, 14
Tremenheere, H. Seymour, 198
Trésaguet, Pierre, 71
Trevithick, Richard, 139, 269
Trident Group, 422
Trimmer, Mrs, 219

Trinity House, 162
Trusts and Kartells, 278–80, 336, 347–51
Tudor Walter Report (1917), 364
Tull, Jethro, 30
Turgot, Baron, 121
Turkey (*see* Levant) Company
Turnips, 9, 24, 31
Turnpikes, 67, 70–1
Tusser, Thomas, 23, 28
Tyndall, Professor John, 209

Unemployment Assistance Board (U.A.B.), 352–3, 363
Unilever, 418
United Dominions Trust, 427
Universities, 227, 431
　Extension Lectures, 232
Upper Clyde Shipbuilders, 420
Uthwatt Report (1942), 371
Utopia (1516), 28, 303

Vanderbilt, Cornelius, 278
Vaughan, John, 273–4
Venice, Merchants of, 14, 86–7
Vermuyden, Cornelius, 23
Villiers, Charles Pelham, 130
Vincent, Henry, 238
Vinci, Leonardo da, 5
Vivo shops, 422
Volta, A., 263
Voluntary Societies, 355, 406–7

Wade, Field Marshal George, 71
Wages, Councils, 203
Walker, Samuel, 48
Wallas, Graham, 250, 303
Water Frame, 56
Water Power, 15, 50–1, 265
Watt, James, 4, 5, 6, 43, 47, 48, 49, 50, 51–3, 61
Watt, Sir Robert A. Watson, 325
Wealth of Nations (1776), 10, 118–20
Webb, Sidney and Beatrice, 303, 307, 312–13, 356
Wedgwood, Josiah, 6, 51, 75, 78, 80, 120, 272
Welsbach, Baron von, 48
Wesley, John, 75, 219
West Indies, 98–102, 297
Westminster Bank, 426
Weston, Sir Robert, 24
Wheatstone, Sir Charles, 263

White Papers
 Control of Land Use (1944), 371
 Educational Reconstruction (1943), 370
 Employment Policy (1944), 370
 Financial and Economic Obligations of the Nationalised Industries (1961), 305
 Fuel Policy (1965, 1967), 386, 388
 Industrial Injury Insurance (1944), 371
 National Health Service (1944), 371, 405
 Social Insurance (1944), 371
 Transport (1967), 391–2
Whitfield, George, 219
Whitley Councils, 313–14
Whitney, Eli, 57, 97
Whitworth, Joseph, 54
Wilberforce, William, 101
Wilkes, John, 235
Wilkinson, John, 43, 47, 51, 52
Wilkinson, Kitty, 211

Williams, Deacons Bank, 426
Williams, Glyns Bank, 426
Wilson, Mr Harold, 377
Wilson, Havelock, 306, 311
Winchcombe, John (Jack of Newbury), 18
Windmills, 50
Wood, John, 194
Woolf, Leonard, 295
Woollen Industries, 15–19, 59–63, 272, 299–300, 323
Woolman, John, 101
Worcester, Marquis of, 51
Workers' Education Association (W.E.A.), 222
Wyatt, John, 55

Yarranton, Andrew, 76
Young, Arthur, 24, 33–4, 36, 40, 41, 47, 68, 138

Zollverein, 14, 127, 133